Microsoft®
SharePoint 2010
Administrator's Pocket Consultant

Ben Curry with
SharePoint Community Experts

PUBLISHED BY
Microsoft Press
A Division of Microsoft Corporation
One Microsoft Way
Redmond, Washington 98052-6399

Library of Congress Control Number: 2010924443

Printed and bound in the United States of America.

1 2 3 4 5 6 7 8 9 WCE 5 4 3 2 1 0

A CIP catalogue record for this book is available from the British Library.

Microsoft Press books are available through booksellers and distributors worldwide. For further information about international editions, contact your local Microsoft Corporation office or contact Microsoft Press International directly at fax (425) 936-7329. Visit our Web site at www.microsoft.com/mspress. Send comments to mspinput@microsoft.com.

Acquisitions Editor: Martin DelRe
Developmental Editor: Karen Szall
Project Editor: Valerie Woolley
Editorial Production: Waypoint Press, www.waypointpress.com
Technical Reviewer: Bob Hogan; Technical Review services provided by Content Master, a member of CM Group, Ltd.
Cover: Tom Draper Design

Body Part No. X16-88501

For my dedicated and loving wife. She continues to stand by me through the good times and the bad. I love you, Kim.

Contents at a Glance

Acknowledgments   *xix*

Introduction   *xxi*

PART I   **DEPLOYING SHAREPOINT SERVER 2010**

CHAPTER 1	Deploying SharePoint Server 2010	3
CHAPTER 2	Scaling to a MultiServer Farm	51
CHAPTER 3	Configuring Core Operations	81
CHAPTER 4	Building and Managing Web Applications	109
CHAPTER 5	Creating and Managing Site Collections	141
CHAPTER 6	Configuring Service Applications	181

PART II   **CONFIGURING SHAREPOINT SERVER 2010**

CHAPTER 7	Web Parts, Features, and Solutions	205
CHAPTER 8	Configuring the Search Service Application	239
CHAPTER 9	Managing the Search Experience	265
CHAPTER 10	Enterprise Content Types and Metadata	329
CHAPTER 11	Document Management	361
CHAPTER 12	Records Management	385
CHAPTER 13	Portals and Collaboration	405
CHAPTER 14	User Profiles and My Sites	419

PART III   **OPERATING SHAREPOINT SERVER 2010**

CHAPTER 15	Configuring Policies and Security	451
CHAPTER 16	Monitoring, Logging, and Availability	489
CHAPTER 17	Upgrading to SharePoint Server 2010	517
CHAPTER 18	Backup and Restore	539
APPENDIX A	Working with Windows PowerShell and SharePoint 2010	561

Contents

Acknowledgments   *xix*

Introduction   *x*

PART I   DEPLOYING SHAREPOINT SERVER 2010

Chapter 1   Deploying SharePoint Server 2010   3

Preparing for Installation 4

   Hardware and Software Requirements   5

   Considerations   7

   Prerequisites Installer   7

   Service Accounts   8

Farm Topologies 9

Installing the First SharePoint Foundation 2010 Server
   in the Farm 13

   Running the SharePoint Products and
   Technologies Preparation Tool   14

   Installing SharePoint Foundation 2010 Binaries   15

   Running the SharePoint 2010 Products
   Configuration Wizard   17

   Using the SharePoint Foundation 2010 Farm
   Configuration Wizard   23

   Performing a Scripted Deployment Using
   Windows PowerShell   24

   Understanding Databases Created During Installation   26

Installing the First SharePoint Server 2010 Server in
   the Farm 26

   Running the Microsoft SharePoint Products
   and Technologies Preparation Tool   27

   Installing the SharePoint Server 2010 Binaries   28

What do you think of this book? We want to hear from you!

Microsoft is interested in hearing your feedback so we can continually improve our
books and learning resources for you. To participate in a brief online survey, please visit:

microsoft.com/learning/booksurvey

Running the SharePoint Products Configuration Wizard   30

Using the SharePoint Server 2010 Farm Configuration Wizard   32

Performing a Scripted Deployment Using Windows PowerShell   33

Understanding Databases Created During Installation   35

Post-Installation Configuration 36

Configure Farm Administrators Group   36

Configure Outgoing E-mail Settings   37

Create a Web Application to Host Site Collections   37

Configure Usage and Health Data Collection   40

Configure Diagnostic Logging   42

Install and Configure Remote BLOB Storage   43

Assigning IP Addresses to Web Applications   46

Language Packs   47

Upgrading SharePoint Foundation to SharePoint Server 49

Installing SharePoint Server 2010 Binaries   49

Running the SharePoint Products Configuration Wizard   49

Chapter 2   Scaling to a MultiServer Farm   51

Preparing for Scaling Out to a Server Farm 51

Single-Server Farm   52

Two-Tier Farm   52

Two-Tier Small Farm   53

Three-Tier Small Farm Not Optimized for Search   53

Three-Tier Small Farm Optimized for Search   54

Medium Farm   55

Large Farm   56

Scaling Web Applications 57

Adding a Web Server to the Farm   57

Web Parts and Custom Code   64

Internet Information Services   65

Scaling System Services and Service Applications............ 65

Service Application Architecture 66

Scaling SharePoint Server 2010 Search 74

Chapter 3   **Configuring Core Operations**   **81**

Introducing Central Administration 81

Central Administration Architecture 82

Working with the Central Administration Web
Application 84

System Settings.. 86

Servers 86

E-mail and Text Messages 88

Farm Timer Jobs 93

Farm Management 96

Database Management................................... 97

Content Databases 98

Default Database Server 104

Data Retrieval Service 104

Configuring Send To Connections 105

Site Subscription Settings 106

Configuring the Content Organizer in the
Destination Site 106

Send To Connections 106

Allow Manual Submissions 107

Chapter 4   **Building and Managing Web Applications**   **109**

Web Application Architecture 110

Managing a Web Application 110

Application Pools 111

Content Databases 112

Creating and Extending Web Applications 115

Create a Web Application 115

Extending a Web Application 123

Deleting a Web Application 126

Deleting an Extended Zone 127

Managing Web Applications 128

    Configuring Web Applications   128

    SharePoint Designer 2010 Governance   135

Alternate Access Mappings 137

    Configure Alternate Access Mapping   139

Chapter 5   Creating and Managing Site Collections   141

Site Creation Modes.................................... 141

    Determining Which Mode to Use   142

    Enabling Self-Service Site Creation   142

    Site Use Confirmation and Deletion   143

Creating Site Collections................................ 144

    Creating a Site Collection Through Central
Administration   145

    Creating a Site Collection Using the
Self-Service URL   146

Site Settings... 147

    Regional Settings   148

    Creating and Managing Document Libraries   148

    Creating and Managing Lists   154

    Sandboxed Solutions   160

    User Alerts   160

    Discussions   162

    RSS (Really Simple Syndication)   163

    Recycle Bin   164

    Portal Site Connection   166

    Information Management Policies   167

    SharePoint Designer Settings   169

Site Collection Security 171

    Site Collection Administrators and Site Owners   171

    People and Groups   171

    List and Library Security   179

Chapter 6   Configuring Service Applications   181

Service Application Architecture. 181

   Service Application Topologies   182

Deploying and Managing Service Applications 183

   Edit Service Application Connections for a
Web Application   184

   Manage Administrators of a Service Application   185

   Delete a Service Application   185

   Publish a Service Application   185

   Connect to a Service Application on a
Remote Farm   186

Service Applications in SharePoint Server 2010 187

   Access Services   187

   Business Connectivity Services   189

   Excel Services   189

   Managed Metadata Service   194

   PerformancePoint Services   194

   Search Service   196

   Secure Store Service   199

   Security Token Service   199

   State Service   199

   Visio Graphics Service   199

   Usage and Health Data Collection Service   199

   User Profile Service   200

   Web Analytics Service   201

   Word Automation Service   201

PART II   CONFIGURING SHAREPOINT SERVER 2010

Chapter 7   Web Parts, Features, and Solutions   205

Installing and Configuring Web Parts. 205

   Web Part Architecture   206

   Web Parts and Pages   207

   Deleting and Closing Web Parts   210

   Web Part Connections   211

   Web Part Properties and Personalization   212

Installing and Configuring Features 215

    Feature Architecture   215

    Feature Life Cycle   216

Managing Solutions 221

    Full-Trust Solutions   222

    Managing Full-Trust Solutions   223

    Deploying Full-Trust Solutions   225

    Retracting Full-Trust Solutions   228

    Deleting Full-Trust Solutions   230

    Upgrading Full-Trust Solutions   231

    Managing Sandboxed Solutions   232

Chapter 8   **Configuring the Search Service Application**   **239**

Farm-Wide Search Settings 240

Managing Crawler Impact Rules 241

Creating the Search Service Application 243

Examining the Search Administration Page 245

Creating and Managing Content Sources 246

Creating and Managing Crawl Rules 247

    Crawl Rule Paths   249

    Exclude/Include Options   249

    Crawl Rule Authentication   249

Managing Server Name Mappings 250

Managing File Types 250

Managing the Search Application Topology 252

    Crawl Databases   254

    Crawl Component   255

    Property Database   256

    Index Partition and Query Component   257

Managing Host Distribution Rules 258

Troubleshooting Search with Crawl Logs 259

Chapter 9 Managing the Search Experience   265

Configuring the Thesaurus and Noise Word Files 266

    Noise Word Files   266

    Configuring the Thesaurus   267

Defining Authoritative Pages 268

Federated Queries 270

    Federated Location Management   270

Managed Properties 278

Creating and Managing Search Scopes 284

Search Results Removal. 289

Site Collection Search Management. 290

    Configuring the Master Page Query Box Control   290

    Site Collection Search Scope Management   291

Working with Keywords and Best Bets. 293

Creating and Customizing Search Centers 297

    Customizing the Enterprise Search Center   297

    Creating New Search Pages   298

    Creating New Tabs   299

    Configuring Custom Page Access   300

Customizing Search Pages 300

Working with Query Reporting 325

Local Search Configuration Options 325

    Searchable Columns   325

    Site-Level Crawl Rules   326

    Crawl Options for Lists and Libraries   326

    Related Links Scope   327

Chapter 10 Enterprise Content Types and Metadata   329

Understanding Enterprise Content Management 329

Configuring the Managed Metadata Service 331

    Creating the Content Type Syndication Hub
    Web Application   332

    Creating the Content Type Syndication Hub
    Site Collection   333

Activating the Content Type Syndication Hub 335

Creating the Managed Metadata Service Application 336

Modifying the Managed Metadata Service Connection 338

Associating Managed Metadata Service Applications 338

Publishing the Managed Metadata Service Application 340

Starting the Managed Metadata Web Service 341

Administrators for Management Metadata Services 341

Managed Taxonomies, Folksonomies, and Term Sets........342

Enterprise Metadata: The Term Store 342

The Term Store Management Tool 344

Enterprise Content Types 349

Creating Content Types 349

Dealing with Content Type Dependencies 351

Consuming Metadata 351

Working with Site Columns 351

Managed Metadata Site Columns 353

Managed Metadata and the Document Information Panel 356

Metadata Navigation Settings 359

Chapter 11   Document Management   **361**

Managing Documents in SharePoint 2010 361

What Is Document Management? 362

Document Collaboration 363

Document Libraries 363

Document IDs and Sets. 365

Document IDs 365

Document Sets 367

List and Library Relationships. 369

Check In/Check Out 370

Content Types 370

Document Version Control. 372

    Content Approval   372

    Major Versioning   373

    Major and Minor Versioning   373

    Version Pruning   373

    Draft Item Security   373

Workflows 374

    Assigning Workflow Settings   375

Inbound E-mail. 375

    Grouping Submissions   376

    Allowing Contributions from Outside the
Organization   376

Offline Support. 377

The Document Center. 378

    Content Organizer and Send To Functionality   379

    Metadata Navigation and Filtering   382

Chapter 12   Records Management   385

Information Management Policies 385

    Retention   387

    Nonrecords   388

    Records   389

    Auditing   389

    Document Bar Codes   390

    Document Labels   390

In-Place Records Management 392

    Allowing Record Declaration at the List and
Library Level   393

The Records Center 394

    Planning for the Records Center   395

    Managing the Records   401

Chapter 13 Portals and Collaboration   **405**

Publishing Infrastructure. 405

     Enabling the Publishing Infrastructure   406

     Master Pages   407

     Page Layouts   411

     SharePoint Designer 2010 Access   412

     Themes   414

     Large Pages Library   415

     Navigation   415

Chapter 14 User Profiles and My Sites   **419**

Creation and Maintenance Tasks in the User
Profile Service 420

Service Administration. 424

Profile Property Administration. 426

Profile Synchronization 429

Enabling Social Features for Users and Groups 436

Social Tags and Note Boards 437

My Site Settings 440

     Setup of My Sites Web Sites   441

     Adding or Deleting a Trusted My Site Host Location   443

     Personalization Site Links   445

     Links to the Microsoft Office 2010 Client
Applications   446

PART III   OPERATING SHAREPOINT SERVER 2010

Chapter 15 Configuring Policies and Security   **451**

Server Farm Security 451

     Farm Administrators   453

     Password and Account Management   453

     Information Policies   460

Web Application Security 464

     SSL and Assigned IP Addresses   465

     Authentication   470

Web Application User Permissions 475

Secure Store Service 476

Blocked File Types 478

Self-Service Site Creation 479

Antivirus Settings 480

Web Application Policies. 481

Zones 481

Web Application Permission Policies 483

SharePoint Designer 2010 Governance 486

Chapter 16 Monitoring, Logging, and Availability   489

Windows Server 2008 489

Event Viewer 490

Monitoring Tools 491

Windows Task Manager 492

Internet Information Services 494

SharePoint Server 2010. 495

SharePoint Server 2010 Health Analyzer 495

Monitoring 496

Health Analyzer 496

Timer Jobs 498

Reporting 501

Web Analytics 504

Diagnostic Logging 514

SQL 2008 Server 515

Chapter 17 Upgrading to SharePoint Server 2010   517

Planning Tools. 518

Farm Planning 519

Web Enumeration 525

In-Place Upgrade 526

Installing the Prerequisites and Binaries 526

Post In-Place Upgrade Tasks 530

Database Attach Upgrade 533

Upgrading Sites and Site Collections 537

Chapter 18 Backup and Restore   **539**

Server Farm Backup and Recovery 540

  Preparing for Server Farm Backups   540

  Farm Backup and Restores Using Central
Administration   542

  Farm Backup and Restore Using Windows
PowerShell   547

  Farm Backup and Restore Using Stsadm.exe   551

Service and Web Application Backup and Restore 553

Granular Backup and Restore. 555

  Site Collection Backup and Restore   555

  Recovering from an Unattached Content
Database   559

**Appendix A Working with Windows PowerShell and
SharePoint 2010**   **561**

SharePoint 2010 Management Shell. 562

Working with Commands. 562

  Working with Cmdlets   562

  Working with Functions   574

Working with SharePoint Cmdlets 574

  Farms   574

  Servers   575

  Web Applications   576

  Managing Sites   578

  Managing Webs   579

  Assigning Resources   580

SharePoint Cmdlet Listing 582

Index   **599**

What do you think of this book? We want to hear from you!

Microsoft is interested in hearing your feedback so we can continually improve our
books and learning resources for you. To participate in a brief online survey, please visit:

microsoft.com/learning/booksurvey

Acknowledgments

One of the challenges when writing a *Pocket Consultant* is that you don't have the space to fully explain all aspects of a product. This is true with any product, but even more so with a product as large as SharePoint Server 2010. Therefore, I have left out information unessential to administrative tasks and provided a technically dense, daily reference guide. This narrow scope allowed the book to be very detailed in the areas that are poorly documented or poorly understood. I really wanted to provide an accurate reference guide that could also be read cover to cover, and I think it fills that bill.

I first want to thank Bill English, who gave me the opportunity to begin my writing career and has helped me immensely through the years. I consider him a mentor and a friend. Thank you, Bill. I also want to thank Martin DelRe, acquisitions editor, because he believed in this book from the very beginning. Karen Szall was the project editor, and she kept me on track and on schedule throughout. She is a wonderful editor, and I learned a great deal from her. Thanks also to Valerie Woolley who helped get chapters through the editing process. Although it is difficult to write original content, answering the technical edits is sometimes harder! Microsoft Press has the most thorough editing review processes in the business, and though they create more work for the author, they result in a better book for the reader. Bob Hogan was the technical reviewer for this book; his input and assistance were invaluable in creating a relevant and accurate book. He was top notch and made sure things worked as expected.

Because there were so many new features in the product, it was impossible for a single person to write this book. To assist me, I asked several SharePoint Products industry experts to contribute content to the book. Core to the success of this book were the contributing authors, and you can find their full bios in the back of the book. Thank you to Josh Meyer, Jim Curry, Philip Greninger, Daniel Webster (one of the best SharePoint professionals I know), Fred Devoir, Michael Mukalian, and Darrin Bishop. Each of these authors provided a unique contribution in their area of specialty. This allowed me to focus on the core features of the product and still deliver top-notch content throughout.

Because of the late release of the beta versions of the product and the depth of the product stack, it took several people to get this book content written. Thanks to Joy Curry, Lori Gowin, Cathy Dew, Spencer Harbar, Mike Watson, Jenn Parry, and the product team at Microsoft for answering a ton of questions and providing content!

Thank you to all of the staff at Microsoft who helped along the way; there are too many of you to count. I also want to thank my father; he has helped me along my writing career and served as a wonderful role model. If I forgot someone, it was truly an accident!

Introduction

From the beginning of the project, the *SharePoint Server 2010 Administrator's Pocket Consultant* was written to be a concise and accurate guide that you can use when you have questions about SharePoint Server 2010 administration. The purpose of the *Administrator's Pocket Consultants* series is to give you valuable, real-world information in an easily referenced format. A thorough index has been provided to help you quickly find the information you need. This is a guide you will want close by when working with the new versions of SharePoint Products and Technologies.

This book provides administrative procedures, quick answers, tips, and tested design examples. In addition, it covers some of the most difficult tasks, such as scaling out to a server farm and implementing disaster recovery. It also covers many of the new Windows PowerShell commands now needed for building and maintaining SharePoint Server. The text contains illustrative examples of many advanced tasks required to implement a SharePoint Products solution for almost any size of organization.

Who Is This Book For?

SharePoint Server 2010 Administrator's Pocket Consultant covers SharePoint Server 2010 Standard and SharePoint Server 2010 Enterprise editions. This book is designed for the following:

- Administrators migrating from Windows SharePoint Services 3.0 and SharePoint Server 2007
- Administrators who are experienced with Windows Server 2008 and Internet Information Services
- Current SharePoint Foundation 2010 and SharePoint Server 2010 administrators
- Administrators who are new to Microsoft SharePoint 2010 Technologies
- Technology specialists, such as site collection administrators, search administrators, and Web designers

Because this book is limited in size, and I wanted to give you the maximum value, I assumed a basic knowledge of Windows Server 2008, Active Directory, Internet Information Services (IIS), SQL Server, and Web browsers. These technologies are not presented directly, but this book contains material on all of these topics that relate to the administrative tasks of SharePoint Products.

How Is This Book Organized?

SharePoint Server 2010 Administrator's Pocket Consultant is written to be a daily reference for administrative tasks. The ability to quickly find and use information is the hallmark of this book. For this reason, the book is organized into job-related tasks. It has an expanded table of contents and an extensive index for locating relevant answers. In addition, there is an appendix for many of the new SharePoint Sever 2010 Windows PowerShell cmdlets. If you are looking for a comprehensive guide to implementing SharePoint Products, you should consider purchasing the *Microsoft Office SharePoint Server 2010 Administrator's Companion*, since the books in the *Administrator's Pocket Consultant* series are stripped to the bare essentials required to complete a task.

The book is organized into three parts and eighteen chapters: Part I, "Deploying SharePoint Server 2010," introduces you to the new features, functionality, and deployment options of SharePoint Server 2010. Chapter 1 provides instructions for preparing for and installing SharePoint Server 2010, implementing database best practices, and creating the required server farm service applications. Chapter 2 shows you the basics of scaling to a multi-server farm for availability and performance. Chapter 3 covers the management of core server farm operations. Chapter 4 guides you through Web application creation and management, a foundational part of SharePoint Server 2010. Chapter 5 is an administrator's guide to creating and managing site collections. Chapter 6 is an installation guide and design overview of the new SharePoint Server 2010 service application architecture.

Part II, "Configuring SharePoint Server 2010," dives deeper into the product stack and extends the basic functionality configured in Part I. Chapter 7 is a guide to installing and managing Web parts, features, and solutions. Chapter 8 is a step-by-step guide to configuring and scaling the search service application. Chapter 9 provides detailed configuration on managing the search experience for users. Chapter 10 is an introduction to Enterprise Content Management (ECM) and a good start for most SharePoint Server 2010 administrators new to ECM. Chapter 11 shows you the new features of Document Management, such as Document Sets and Document IDs. Chapter 12 is an administrator-focused chapter on Records Management. It is not an exhaustive guide for all things Records related; only the administrative tasks to operate and maintain them. Chapter 13 is a configuration guide for creating portals, most importantly the publishing infrastructure. Chapter 14 covers the new and exciting areas of Social Collaboration and profile management.

Part III, "Operating SharePoint Server 2010," primarily deals with operational tasks having to do with service level agreements and upgrades. Chapter 15 will show you how to configure Web application and site collection security policies, in addition to recommended Permissioning guidelines. Chapter 16 details the areas of SharePoint Server 2010 you should monitor and the available tools to do so. Chapter 17 is a basic SharePoint Server 2007 upgrade installation guide, and covers many of the new upgrade tools available in SharePoint Server 2010. Chapter 18 includes the new backup and restore tools, including granular backups. The book completes with Appendix A, an introduction to Windows PowerShell for SharePoint Server 2010.

Conventions Used in This Book

A variety of elements are used in this book to help you understand what you need to know and to keep it easy to read.

- **Note** A Note points out an easily overlooked detail or design issue.
- **Tip** A Tip provides helpful information or spotlights the command-line option available for an administrative task.
- **Caution** When you see a Caution, you should look out for potential problems. Many Cautions were learned through real-world experience.

In addition, terms that are new are in *italics*.

I really hope you find the *SharePoint Server 2010 Administrator's Pocket Consultant* useful and accurate. I have an open door policy for e-mail at *curry@summit7systems.com*. Because my inbox stays quite full, please be patient; replies sometimes take a week or longer. You may also visit *http://pocketconsultant.mindsharp.com* for updates and discussion boards concerning the latest in SharePoint Products and Technologies news.

Questions and Support

Every effort has been made to ensure the accuracy of this book. Microsoft Press provides corrections for books at *http://mspress.microsoft.com/support/*. If you have questions or comments regarding this book, please send them to Microsoft Press using this e-mail address:

msinput@microsoft.com

Please note that product support is not offered through this address. For support information, visit Microsoft's Web site at *http://support.microsoft.com*.

PART I

Deploying SharePoint Server 2010

CHAPTER 1 Deploying SharePoint Server 2010 **3**

CHAPTER 2 Scaling to a MultiServer Farm **51**

CHAPTER 3 Configuring Core Operations **81**

CHAPTER 4 Building and Managing Web Applications **109**

CHAPTER 5 Creating and Managing Site Collections **141**

CHAPTER 6 Configuring Service Applications **181**

Deploying SharePoint Server 2010

- Preparing for Installation **4**
- Farm Topologies **9**
- Installing the First SharePoint Foundation 2010 Server in the Farm **13**
- Installing the First SharePoint Server 2010 Server in the Farm **26**
- Post-Installation Configuration **36**
- Upgrading SharePoint Foundation to SharePoint Server **49**

B efore inserting the installation media and clicking Next, take the time to understand the different options available to you in the setup wizard. If you make the wrong selection during setup, you might need to perform a complete uninstall and reinstall of the binaries. In addition, making good choices in the beginning will make it considerably easier to scale Microsoft SharePoint products. The following decisions must be made before installing SharePoint products:

- **Choose a SQL Server type** During installation, you will have the option either to install all components (including Microsoft SQL Server Express) on a single computer or to choose a dedicated SQL Server installation for the databases. Choose the SQL Server Express option only when you are sure that you will not scale to a server farm in the future. Although scaling to a server farm is technically possible, migrating SharePoint products from SQL Server 2008 Express to SQL Server 2008 Enterprise or Standard is a tedious task.

- **Use assigned IP addresses** Host headers ease installation and reduce administrative overhead, but also assigning IP addresses strengthens your overall security posture. Assigning an individual IP address for every Web application simplifies your logs, prepares for load-balancing, and allows for separate firewall rules.

- **Process security isolation** Depending on the level of security your organization requires, you can choose to install with one or several accounts for Microsoft Internet Information Services (IIS) application pools and database access. It is much easier to install with separate accounts in the beginning than it is to change and isolate application pools later. Be aware that the more application pools you create the greater the amount of memory that is required.

- **Assign administrators** You must define the administrative roles and separation of duties. If you want to granularly define administrative roles, pay close attention to the details of service accounts and groups. If you are in a small organization, consider using a dedicated farm account for all administrative tasks.

- **Select a site template for the Web application root** When creating your first Web application, it is wise to create a site collection in the root managed path. This site can be modified, but the site template cannot be changed, so give careful consideration to the template used.

This chapter covers Microsoft SharePoint Foundation 2010 and SharePoint Server 2010 deployments, when using IIS host headers alone or with assigned IP addresses. When neither Microsoft SharePoint Foundation 2010 nor SharePoint Server 2010 is specified, the material applies to both software products.

NOTE Although this book is focused on SharePoint Server 2010, many developers and beginning administrators will install SharePoint Foundation 2010 early on in their education with SharePoint 2010 products. Therefore, the installation chapter will cover both products.

Preparing for Installation

At a minimum, before installation, sketch out your design, including IIS configuration, SQL Server databases, accounts, administrators, and any other pertinent data you will need. Microsoft Office Visio is a very helpful tool when designing and maintaining server farms with multiple Web applications, IIS servers, and SQL Server databases. In addition, verify that you have met the minimum hardware requirements and have created all Active Directory accounts, if using Active Directory for authentication, before beginning the installation wizard.

Hardware and Software Requirements

The single biggest change in minimum requirements from SharePoint 2007 is that both SharePoint Foundation 2010 and SharePoint Server 2010 require a 64-bit operating system on all farm servers as well as a recommended 64-bit database server. There is not a SharePoint Products 2010 version for 32-bit hardware, even for testing.

Table 1-1 details the minimum hardware requirements.

TABLE 1-1 Minimum Hardware Requirements

COMPONENT	MINIMUM REQUIREMENT
Processor	64-bit, dual processor, 3 GHz
RAM	4 GB for development/evaluation instance
	8 GB for production server
Hard disk	80 GB free space

One improvement that has been made in the installation process is the addition of the Microsoft SharePoint Products and Technologies Preparation Tool to the installation menu. It can install the software prerequisites for you if you just click the option from the installation start page. An Internet connection is required to use this feature because some of the prerequisites are downloaded from the Internet.

Table 1-2 lists the software requirements.

TABLE 1-2 Software Requirements

ENVIRONMENT	MINIMUM REQUIREMENT
Database server in a farm	SQL Server 2005 x64 with Service Pack 3 (SP3) or SQL Server 2008 x64 with Service Pack 1 (SP1)
Development/ evaluation computer	Microsoft Windows Vista x64 with Service Pack 1 or Windows 7 x64

ENVIRONMENT	MINIMUM REQUIREMENT
Stand-alone server	<ul><li>Windows Server 2008 Standard x64 with SP2 or Windows Server 2008 Standard x64 R2</li><li>Windows Server 2008 update patch for Windows Communication Foundation (WCF) (choose the version corresponding to the version of Windows Server 2008 chosen)</li><li>Web Server (IIS) role</li><li>Application Server role</li><li>Microsoft .NET Framework 3.5 SP1</li><li>SQL Server 2008 Express x64 with SP1</li><li>Windows Identity Foundation</li><li>Microsoft Sync Framework Runtime v1.0 (x64)</li><li>Microsoft Filter Pack 2.0</li><li>Microsoft Chart Controls for the Microsoft .NET Framework 3.5</li><li>Windows PowerShell 2.0</li><li>SQL Server 2008 Native Client</li><li>Microsoft SQL Server 2008 Analysis Services ADOMD.NET</li><li>ADO.NET Data Services Update for .NET Framework 3.5 SP1</li></ul>
Front-end Web/ Application Servers in a farm	<ul><li>Windows Server 2008 Standard x64 with SP2 or Windows Server 2008 Standard x64 R2</li><li>Web Server (IIS) role</li><li>Application Server role</li><li>Microsoft .NET Framework 3.5 SP1</li><li>Windows Identity Framework</li><li>Microsoft Sync Framework Runtime v1.0 (x64)</li><li>Microsoft Filter Pack 2.0</li><li>Microsoft Chart Controls for the Microsoft .NET Framework 3.5</li><li>Windows PowerShell 2.0 CTP3</li><li>SQL Server 2008 Native Client</li><li>Microsoft SQL Server 2008 Analysis Services ADOMD.NET</li><li>ADO.NET Data Services v1.5 CTP2</li></ul>
Client computer	<ul><li>Microsoft Silverlight 3.0</li><li>A supported browser</li></ul>

Considerations

Make sure you understand each of the following considerations when planning your installation:

- When using SQL Server 2005 SP3, you must install cumulative update package 3 for SQL Server 2005 SP3 (*http://go.microsoft.com/fwlink/?LinkId=165748*). For SQL Server 2008 SP1, cumulative update package 2 for SQL Server 2008 SP1 (*http://go.microsoft.com/fwlink/?LinkId=165962*) is required. The SharePoint Products and Technologies Preparation Tool does not check for these updates before setup. The Configuration Wizard does check after installation, but you should make sure these updates are applied before running the installer to prevent installation issues.

- When you are installing on Windows Server 2008 SP1, the Prerequisites installer will install SP2 for you automatically.

- If you are using Windows Server 2008 and Windows PowerShell 1.0 is installed, it must be removed before installing Windows PowerShell 2.0 CTP3.

- If using the phonetic name-matching functionality of SharePoint Search 2010, you must install the Microsoft Server Speech Platform and the corresponding speech-recognition language. Additionally, you must update the [HKEY_LOCAL_MACHINE\SOFTWARE\Microsoft\Speech Server\v10.0\Recognizers\Tokens\SR_MS_<LocalCode>_TELE_10.0\Attributes] registry key for every language that you install. Click Start, and then run *regedit*. Find the registry key, and then update the Vendor value to Microsoft Corporation.

  This registry key change can cause errors with other server applications that use speech recognition, such as Exchange 2010, but it is required for the phonetic matching to work correctly in SharePoint Search 2010.

- If using Access Services, you must install the SQL Server 2008 R2 Reporting Services Add-in for SharePoint Technologies.

Prerequisites Installer

The following prerequisites can be automatically downloaded and installed from the SharePoint Server 2010 Start page:

- Application Server Role, Web Server (IIS) Role
- Microsoft SQL Server 2008 Native Client
- Hotfix for Microsoft Windows (KB976462)
- Windows Identity Foundation (KB974405)
- Microsoft Sync Framework Runtime v1.0 (x64)
- Microsoft Chart Controls for Microsoft .NET Framework 3.5
- Microsoft Filter Pack 2.0
- Microsoft SQL Server 2008 Analysis Services ADOMD.NET
- Microsoft Server Speech Platform Runtime (x64)

- Microsoft Server Speech Recognition Language - TELE(en-US)
- SQL 2008 R2 Reporting Services SharePoint 2010 Add-in

Service Accounts

One of the most important aspects of planning for deployment is to identify the service accounts that will be needed. There are several accounts that must be specified, even for the most basic farm topologies. Other accounts will be required depending on the additional functionality deployed.

NOTE It is a recommended best practice to install SharePoint 2010 using "least-privileged" accounts. This decreases the potential damage in the case where an account is compromised.

Table 1-3 lists the service accounts required for all SharePoint 2010 installations, and Table 1-4 lists other service accounts.

TABLE 1-3 Required Service Accounts

ACCOUNT	PURPOSE	REQUIREMENTS
SQL Server service account	Run SQL Server processes: ■ For the default instance, use MSSQLSERVER and SQLSERVERAGENT ■ For a named instance, use *MSSQL$InstanceName* and *SQLAgent$InstanceName*	Either a local system account or domain account Ensure that this account has access to any external resources used to backup or restore. If using a local system account (Network Service or Local System), grant access to *domain_name*\SQL_hostname$.
Setup user account	Run installation and SharePoint Products and Technologies Configuration Wizard	■ Domain account ■ Member of the Administrators group on each server where setup is run ■ SQL Server login on database server ■ Member of securityadmin and dbcreator server roles ■ If using Windows PowerShell, you must be a member of the dbowner fixed role on the database

ACCOUNT	PURPOSE	REQUIREMENTS
Server farm account/ database access account	■ Configure and manage server farm ■ Application pool identity for Central Administration Web site ■ Run SharePoint Foundation Timer Service	■ Domain account Additional permissions are also granted on Web front-end and application servers because they are added to the farm. This account is also added to the following SQL Server roles on the farm database server: ■ dbcreator fixed server role ■ securityadmin fixed server role ■ db_owner fixed database role on all SharePoint databases for the farm

TABLE 1-4 Other Service Accounts

ACCOUNT	PURPOSE	REQUIREMENTS
Search Service account	Run Search Service	This account will default to the farm administrator account, but you should specify a different account for security purposes.
Content Access account	Used to access content sources for crawling. Defaults to Search Service account.	Domain account with read access to content to be crawled.
Application pool accounts	Used for running IIS Web applications that host SharePoint site collections.	Can be a local system account or domain account.

Farm Topologies

Farm topologies vary widely based on a number of factors, including number of users, redundancy requirements, scalability requirements, and service applications being used. With the change from the old Shared Services Provider model to the new Service Applications model, there is much greater flexibility in topology design. Aside from a database server and one or more Web servers, there can be any number of servers hosting one or more service applications.

The recommendation is to use the concept of "server groups" to group services with similar performance characteristics together onto a single server and then add servers based on the needs of those particular services. For instance, Search is implemented as a service application in SharePoint 2010, and small farms might start out using a single dedicated server. As search usage increases, a server might be added to the search "group" to maintain the required level of performance. Using this model to group servers in your farm into logical collections can be a helpful tool in the planning process. Note that this is simply a planning method—you won't find the term "server group" used in Central Administration.

The following is an overview of some standard topologies for farms of varying sizes:

- **Single-server farm** A single-server farm, as seen in Figure 1-1, is ideal for evaluation or development purposes, or for a very small (less than 100) number of users. This farm consists of a single server performing all roles, including the database role. If SQL Server is not installed prior to running the SharePoint 2010 installer, SQL Server 2008 Express will be installed and used.

 Single server performs all
roles, including SQL Server

FIGURE 1-1 A single-server farm consists of SQL Server Standard or Enterprise and all product binaries.

- **Two-server farm** For a user base between 100 and approximately 10,000 users, a two-server farm might be sufficient. As seen in Figure 1-2, this farm consists of a database server and a single Web server that performs all application server roles. For high-availability requirements in a farm with more than 1,000 users, a second clustered or mirrored database server is recommended.

 All Web/application
server roles    Databases

FIGURE 1-2 A two-server farm offloads the database processing.

- **Two-tier small farm** For an environment with 10,000 to 20,000 users with low service usage, a two-tier small farm is recommended. This farm consists of a database server and two Web servers, with one of the Web servers performing all the application server roles as well. Figure 1-3 shows an example of a two-tier small farm.

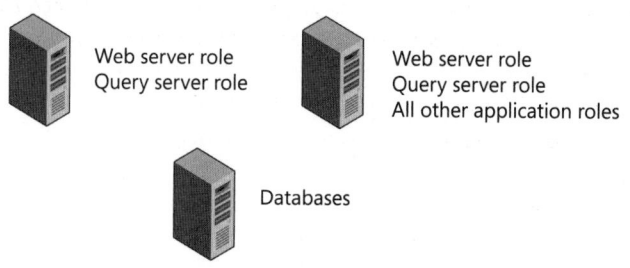

Web server role
Query server role

Web server role
Query server role
All other application roles

Databases

FIGURE 1-3 A two-tier small farm provides additional processing for applications.

- **Three-tier small farm** The three-tier small farm is the same as a two-tier farm, except that a dedicated application server is added between the presentation tier and the data tier to handle moderate service usage. For environments where the search databases are very large (up to 10 million items), the search databases can be moved to a dedicated database server, as seen in Figure 1-4. This will provide the optimum configuration for the Search service application to perform well.

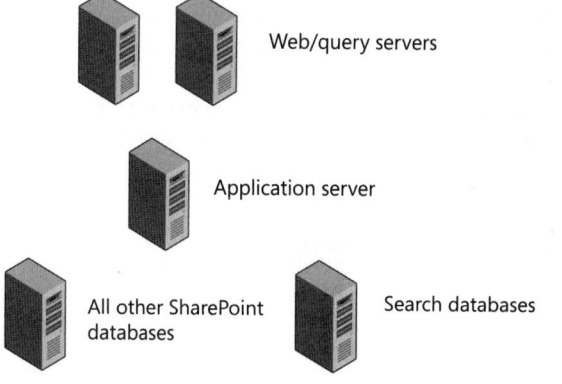

Web/query servers

Application server

All other SharePoint databases

Search databases

FIGURE 1-4 A three-tier small farm allows for great search performance and processing.

- **Medium farm** The medium farm is a three-tier farm. The first tier consists of two or more Web servers. A general rule for planning is 10,000 users per Web server. The middle tier consists of two servers dedicated to crawling content and serving search queries and one or more servers for other service applications. As service applications grow in number or usage, more servers can be added to the middle tier to handle the growth. As seen in Figure 1-5, the third tier uses dedicated servers for the search databases, with one or more servers used for all other SharePoint databases.

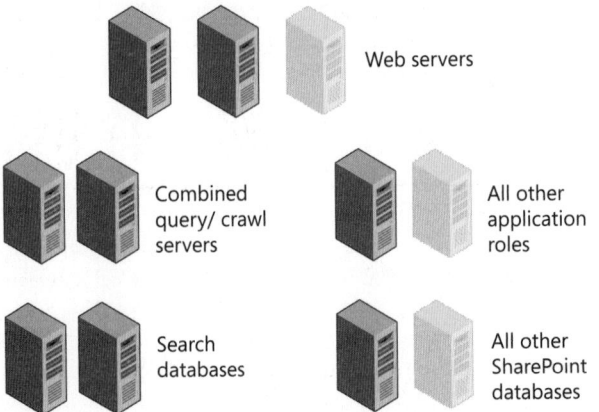

Web servers

Combined query/ crawl servers

All other application roles

Search databases

All other SharePoint databases

FIGURE 1-5 A three-tier medium farm provides substantial processing power for an enterprise.

- **Large farm** The large farm builds on the server group concept used in the medium farm. For example, you can have a dedicated group of servers for handling incoming requests, and one or more separate servers for crawling and administration. Most large farms have at least one dedicated query server, one dedicated crawl server, one or more servers for other service applications, and possibly one or more isolated servers for running sandboxed code. In the data tier, the search databases and content databases will have dedicated servers, with another server handling all other SharePoint databases. Figure 1-6 shows an example of a large farm.

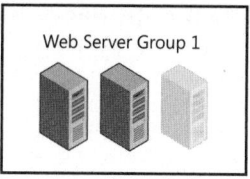

Web Server Group 1

Servers to handle all
incoming requests

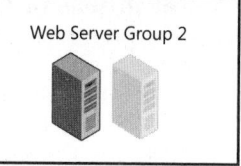

Web Server Group 2

Dedicated to crawling and
administration

Application Server
Group 1

Crawl Servers

Application Server
Group 2

Query Servers

Application Server
Group 3

All other services

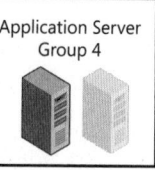

Application Server
Group 4

Servers for executing
sandboxed code

Database Server
Group 1

Search databases

Database Server
Group 2

Content databases

Database Server
Group 3

All other SharePoint
databases

FIGURE 1-6 A large server farm can service thousands of simultaneous requests.

Installing the First SharePoint Foundation 2010 Server in the Farm

After carefully reviewing hardware and software requirements and creating or
obtaining the necessary service accounts, you are ready to begin the installation process for SharePoint Foundation 2010. This chapter covers the installation
of the initial server in the farm. If you are planning a multiserver deployment, see
Chapter 3, "Scaling to a Multiserver Farm," for detailed information regarding
adding servers to the farm.

> **NOTE** When you install SharePoint Server, SharePoint Foundation is installed
> automatically during the installation process. Although it is possible to install
> SharePoint Foundation manually before installing SharePoint Server, you are not
> required to do so.

Running the SharePoint Products and Technologies Preparation Tool

The SharePoint Products and Technologies Preparation Tool helps to ensure that all prerequisites have been installed on your server before you proceed with installation. You must have an Internet connection to automatically install prerequisites; otherwise, prerequisites will have to be installed manually. To run this tool, complete the following steps:

1. If you are using a downloadable installer, double-click SharePoint.exe. If you are using installation media, select Setup.exe from the media.

2. On the SharePoint Foundation 2010 Start page, select Install Software Prerequisites as seen in Figure 1-7.

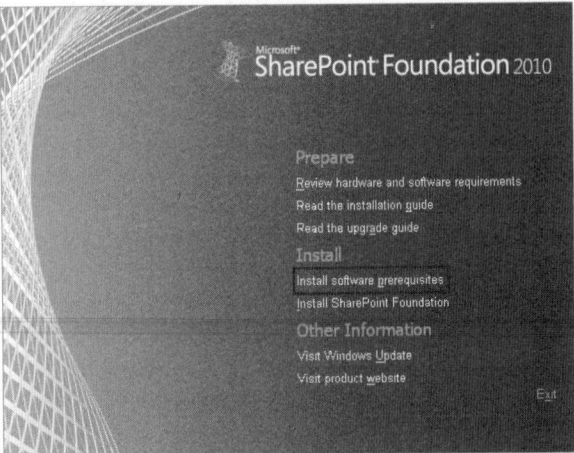

FIGURE 1-7 Install software prerequisites before installing the binaries.

3. On the Welcome To The Microsoft SharePoint Products And Technologies Preparation Tool page, click Next.

4. On the License Terms For Software Products page, review the terms and conditions, select the check box verifying that you agree to the terms and conditions, and click Next.

   NOTE As shown in Figure 1-8, the preparation tool provides feedback as it automatically installs and configures the necessary prerequisite components to ensure a successful installation. It is possible that a reboot might be required. In the event of a required reboot, the installation wizard automatically starts when you log on after the reboot.

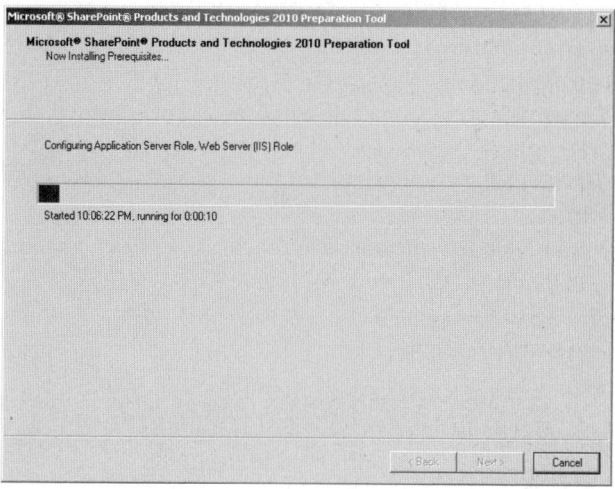

FIGURE 1-8 The preparation tool might take several minutes to complete.

5. On the Installation Complete page, review the components that were automatically installed, configured, or both, and click Finish.

Installing SharePoint Foundation 2010 Binaries

Be sure you've either installed the software prerequisites using the preparation tool, or you've manually installed them. Once the prerequisites have been installed, you can install the SharePoint Foundation 2010 binaries by doing the following:

1. On the SharePoint Foundation 2010 Start page (shown in Figure 1-9), click Install SharePoint Foundation.

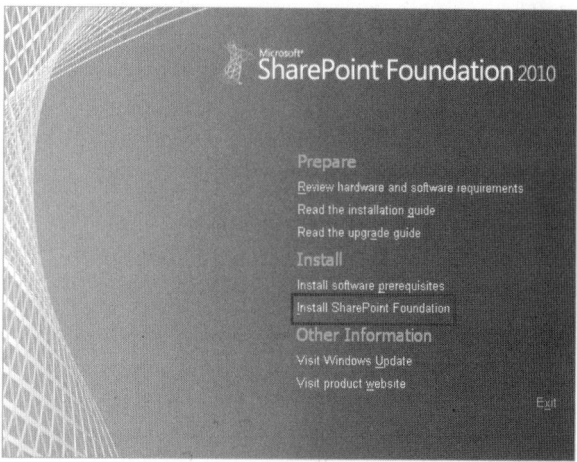

FIGURE 1-9 Install SharePoint Foundation after installing software prerequisites.

2. After clicking Install SharePoint Foundation, review the Read The Microsoft Software License Terms page, select the box verifying that you have read and understand the terms, and then click Continue.

3. On the Choose The Installation You Want page, shown in Figure 1-10, click Server Farm.

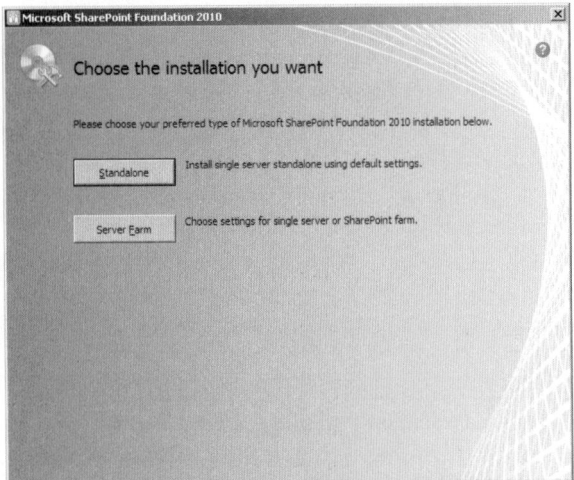

FIGURE 1-10 Click Server Farm when using SQL Server Standard or Enterprise.

4. On the Server Type tab, choose Complete.

5. Verify Complete is selected, as seen in Figure 1-11, when using SQL Server Standard or Enterprise. Click Install Now to perform setup.

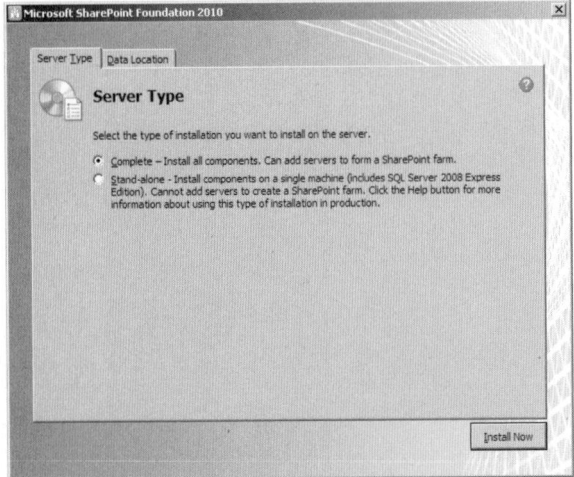

FIGURE 1-11 Choose Complete when installing with SQL Server Standard or Enterprise.

6. When setup completes, leave the Run The SharePoint Products Configuration Wizard Now check box selected, as seen in Figure 1-12, and click Close.

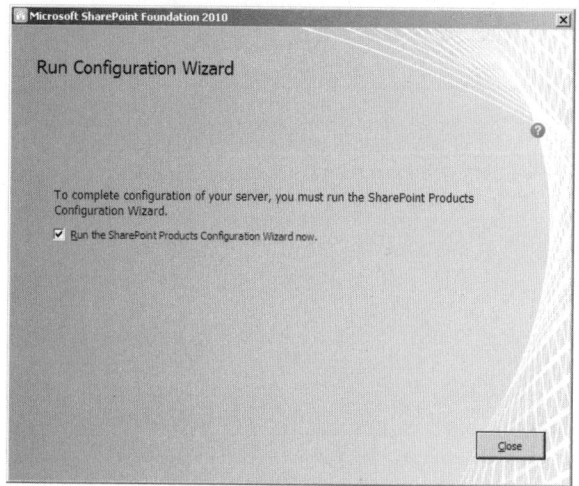

FIGURE 1-12 Select Close to begin the Configuration Wizard.

TIP If setup fails for any reason, you can check the log files in the TEMP folder of the current user. Click the Start menu, and type "%temp%" in the search box. If this resolves to a location ending in "1" or "2", you might have to navigate up one directory to find the log file, which is named Microsoft Windows SharePoint Services 4.0 (<timestamp>).

Running the SharePoint 2010 Products Configuration Wizard

At this point, you've installed the SharePoint Foundation binaries, but you haven't provisioned a server farm. A server farm is defined as a configuration database. The SharePoint Products Configuration Wizard will guide you through the process of provisioning the farm:

1. If the SharePoint 2010 Products Configuration Wizard does not launch automatically, you can find it located at Start, All Programs, Microsoft SharePoint 2010 Products.

2. On the Welcome To SharePoint Products page, click Next.

3. A dialog box, as seen in Figure 1-13, appears stating that some services might need to be restarted during configuration. Click Yes to proceed.

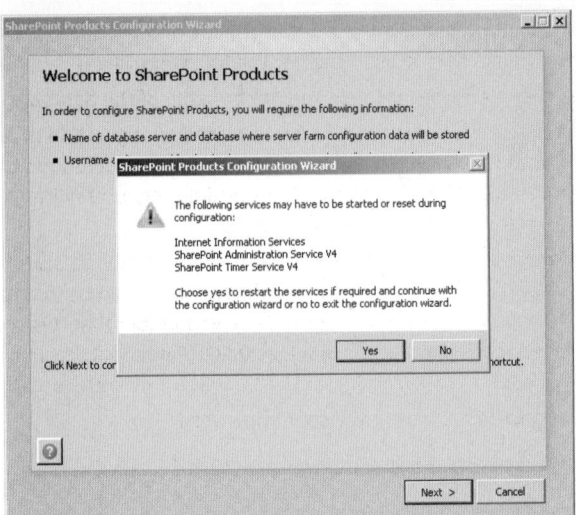

FIGURE 1-13 Click Yes to continue configuration.

4. On the Connect To A Server Farm page, shown in Figure 1-14, choose Create A New Server Farm and then click Next.

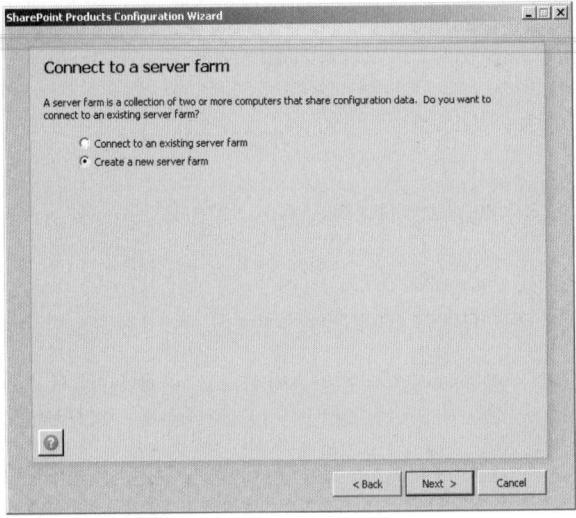

FIGURE 1-14 Select Create A New Server Farm, and click Next.

5. The Specify Configuration Database Settings page allows you to provision a configuration database. You should enter the following values:

- In the Database Server box, type the server name of the database server.
- In the Database Name box, type a name for the configuration database. If the database server is hosting multiple farms, you should type a name that uniquely identifies the farm you are configuring; otherwise, you can keep the default value of *SharePoint_Config*.
- In the Username box, type the server farm administrator account name. If you are using Active Directory, the account name should be in the format *DOMAIN\username*, as seen in Figure 1-15. Remember that this account will be given special access to the relevant SQL Server databases and will be the application pool identity for the Central Administration Web site.
- In the Password box, type the account password.

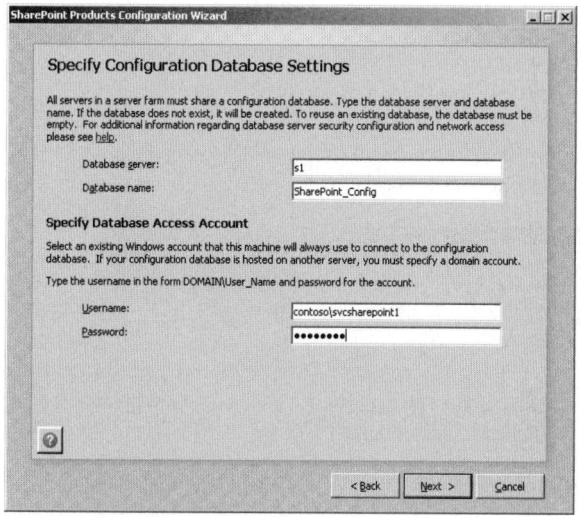

FIGURE 1-15 Verify all information and then click Next.

6. On the Specify Farm Security Settings page, shown in Figure 1-16, type a phrase in the Passphrase box, and click Next. This passphrase should be guarded, and it must be entered any time a server is joined to the farm. It is used to encrypt credentials of SharePoint accounts. This passphrase uses your default domain password security policy. By default, the passphrase must meet the following criteria:

- It should be eight characters in length

- It should contain three of the following four character types:

  English uppercase letters (A through Z)

  English lowercase letters (a through z)

  Numerals (0 through 9)

  Non-alphanumeric characters (such as "!","","#", and so on)*

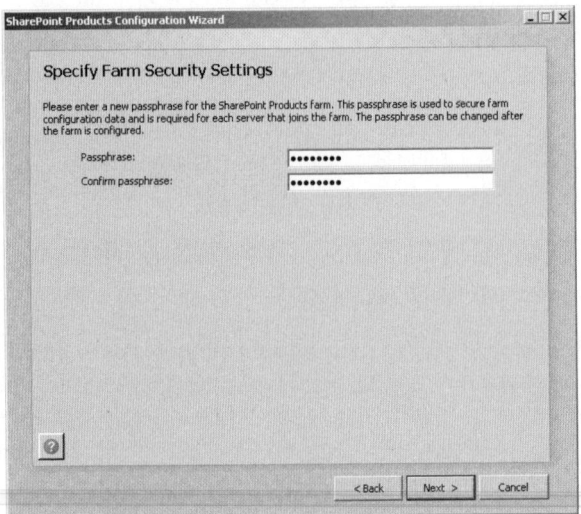

FIGURE 1-16 Be sure to document the farm passphrase.

7. The Configure SharePoint Central Administration Web Application page allows you to specify the settings for the Web site used to perform administrative tasks in SharePoint.

   - Specify a port number for the Central Administration Web site, or use the default as seen in Figure 1-17.
   - Choose the NTLM or Negotiate (Kerberos) option for authentication. Most administrators choose NTLM and change to Kerberos later if required.
   - Click Next.

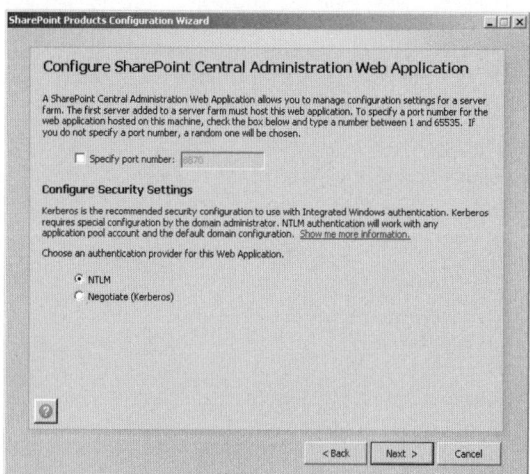

FIGURE 1-17 If unsure, do not specify a port number.

8. Optionally, on the Completing the SharePoint Products Configuration Wizard page, click Advanced Settings and select the check box to enable Active Directory account creation if you want to automatically create unique Active Directory accounts for users. Click OK. Figure 1-18 shows an example of enabling this option.

NOTE Active Directory Account Creation Mode is primarily targeted at Internet service providers that will host multiple customers. It is much more complex to both install and manage and is not recommended for most organizations.

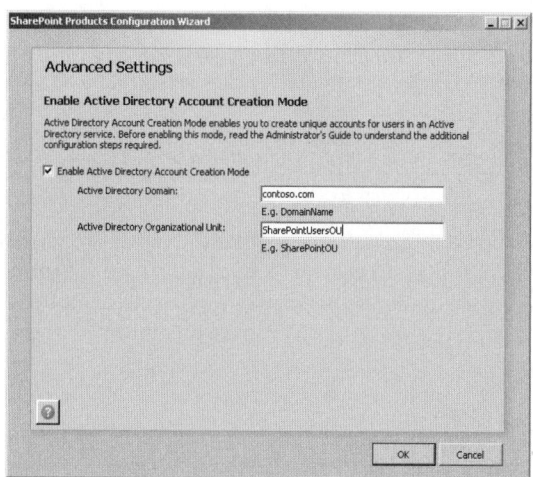

FIGURE 1-18 Enter both the Active Directory Domain and organizational unit (OU).

9. On the Completing the SharePoint Products Configuration Wizard page, review your specified settings and click Next to begin configuration. SharePoint will configure the farm according to your specifications, providing feedback during each step of the process.

10. On the Configuration Successful page, shown in Figure 1-19, be sure to document all settings on the final page of the SharePoint Products Configuration Wizard, and then click Finish.

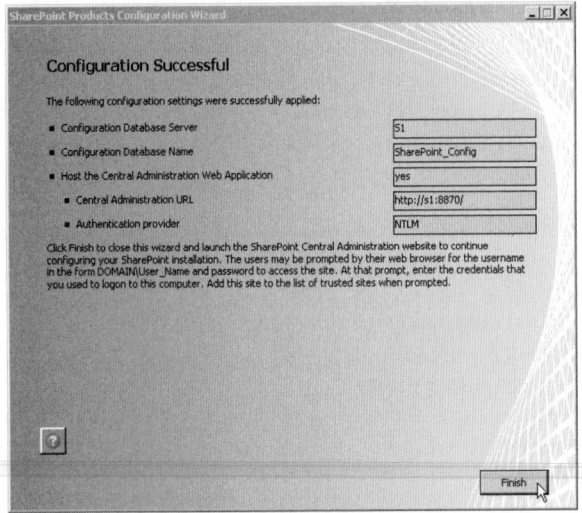

FIGURE 1-19 Be sure to document all settings after a successful configuration.

If the configuration fails, you can check the PSCDiagnostics files located on the drive where SharePoint is installed, in the *%CommonProgramFiles%* \Microsoft Shared\Web Server Extensions\14\Logs folder.

If the configuration is successful, Internet Explorer will be launched and the Central Administration Web site opened. If you are prompted for credentials, you should add the Central Administration URL to your Local Intranet Zone, or alternatively, to your Trusted Sites list and ensure that Internet Explorer is configured to automatically pass user credentials to sites in that list.

If you see a proxy server error message, you need to make sure to configure your browser to bypass the proxy server for local addresses. In Internet Explorer, this setting can be configured on the Tools, Internet Options menu, under the Connections tab. Click LAN Settings to access the proxy server configuration settings.

Using the SharePoint Foundation 2010 Farm Configuration Wizard

If you are an experienced SharePoint products administrator, you probably will not want to use the Farm Configuration Wizard because it limits your installation options. However, using it does make initial farm configuration easier. If you are new to SharePoint Foundation 2010, using the Farm Configuration Wizard is an acceptable method to begin with.

After you run the SharePoint 2010 Products Configuration Wizard, the farm is provisioned, but it must be configured. To use the Farm Configuration Wizard, do the following:

1. Open the Central Administration site (shown in Figure 1-20), and browse to the Configuration Wizards page. To go directly to the page, browse to http://*servername*:28122/default.aspx.

FIGURE 1-20 Click Configuration Wizards to see the available farm product wizards.

2. Choose Launch The Farm Configuration Wizard.

3. Decide whether you'll automatically send information to Microsoft on the Help Make SharePoint Better page. Enter your choice, and then click OK.

4. On the Configure Your SharePoint Farm page, choose Yes, Walk Me Through The Configuration Of My Farm Using This Wizard, and then click Start The Wizard.

5. In the Service Account section, specify the service account you want to use to configure your services, as seen in Figure 1-21. It is recommended that you choose an account other than the farm administrator account for security purposes.

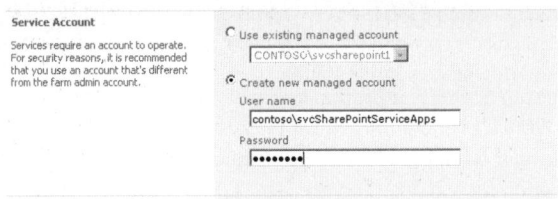

FIGURE 1-21 Verify the account exists in Active Directory before continuing.

6. Decide whether you'll use the two service applications available by default in SharePoint Foundation, as seen in Figure 1-22:

   - **Business Data Connectivity Service**   Enables access to structured data from various line-of-business systems, such as Siebel, SAP, or custom databases

   - **Usage And Health Data Collection**   Collects usage and health data across the farm, and provides reports on the collected data

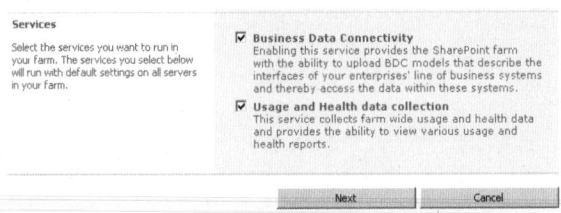

FIGURE 1-22 Choose the appropriate service applications.

7. Click Next.

8. On the Configure Your SharePoint Farm page, select which template you'll use, and then click OK.

9. On the wizard summary page, click Finish to complete the initial configuration.

Performing a Scripted Deployment Using Windows PowerShell

Windows PowerShell is an extremely powerful tool for automating administrative tasks in SharePoint 2010. For deployment, Windows PowerShell can be used to create a repeatable process for performing SharePoint 2010 installations:

1. Download or otherwise obtain the SharePoint Foundation 2010 installation media.

2. Create a folder for install files. This example uses *C:\Install* as the final installation path.

3. If SharePoint Foundation 2010 is downloaded in a single executable, open a command prompt and type the following command, where SharePoint.exe is the name of the downloaded executable:

```
C:\install\SharePoint.exe /extract:c:\install
```

Otherwise, you can copy the contents from the installation media.

4. When you see the Files Extracted Successfully message box, click OK. Open a text editor, add the following example code, and save the file as **spf_install.ps1** in the install location created in step 2.

```
## Settings ##
$SetupPath = "c:\install"
$DBServer = "S1"
$Passphrase = (ConvertTo-SecureString "P@ssw0rd" -AsPlainText -force)
$FarmName = "SP2010"
$CAPort = "12345"
$farm_un = "contoso\svcSharePoint1"
$farm_pw = (ConvertTo-SecureString "P@ssw0rd" -AsPlainText -force)
$FarmCredential = New-Object
ystem.Management.Automation.PsCredential $farm_un,$farm_pw
Write-Host "[1/9] Running prerequisite installer..."
& $SetupPath\PrerequisiteInstaller.exe /unattended | Write-Host
Write-Host "[2/9] Running silent farm binary installation..."
& $SetupPath\setup.exe /config
SetupPath\Files\SetupFarmSilent\config.xml | Write-Host
Add-PSSnapin Microsoft.SharePoint.PowerShell
Write-Host "[3/9] Creating new configuration database..."
New-SPConfigurationDatabase -DatabaseName
"{0}_SharePoint_Configuration_DB" -f $FarmName) -DatabaseServer
DBServer -AdministrationContentDatabaseName ("{0}_AdminContent_DB" -f
$FarmName) -FarmCredentials $FarmCredential -Passphrase $Passphrase
Write-Host "[4/9] Securing SharePoint Resources"
Initialize-SPResourceSecurity
Write-Host "[5/9] Provision Central Administration Site"
New-SPCentralAdministration -Port $CAPort -WindowsAuthProvider "NTLM"
Write-Host "[6/9] Installing Help Files"
Install-SPHelpCollection -All
Write-Host "[7/9] Installing Application Content"
Install-SPApplicationContent
Write-Host "[8/9] Installing Features"
Install-SPFeature -AllExistingFeatures
Write-Host "[9/9] Installing Services"
Install-SPService
Write-Host "Deployment Complete!"
```

5. Close the text editor.

6. Navigate to Start, All Programs, Accessories, Windows PowerShell, right-click Windows PowerShell, and choose Run As Administrator.

7. In the PowerShell command window, change directories to the install directory created in step 2.

8. Type **.\spf_install.ps1**, and press Enter to begin the unattended install.

Understanding Databases Created During Installation

After installation, you will see several databases that are created in SQL Server and will need to be added to your SQL Server maintenance plan:

- **SharePoint Configuration**   The SharePoint configuration database (config DB) holds all of your server farm configuration data and is akin to the Windows Server system registry. Any server that uses this installation's config DB is considered a member of the same server farm.

- **Central Administration content**   Because the Central Administration Web application is a custom site collection in a dedicated Web application, it has a corresponding content database. Rebuilding this Web application is not a simple task and should be avoided by correctly backing up the server for future restoration.

- **Content database**   Each Web application has at least one corresponding content database. If you ran the Farm Configuration Wizard, a Web application was created for you at the URL of your server and it has a corresponding content database.

- **Business Connectivity Services DB**   This database is used by Business Connectivity Services (BCS), and by default it will be named Bdc_Service_DB_<GUID>.

- **SharePoint Foundation Logging**   Used for logging purposes, it is named WSS_Logging by default.

Installing the First SharePoint Server 2010 Server in the Farm

The SharePoint Server 2010 product installation process is similar to the SharePoint Foundation 2010 process. This is understandable because the SharePoint Server product is built on the SharePoint Foundation platform. After reviewing the requirements for hardware and software listed earlier in this chapter and obtaining or creating the necessary service accounts, you can proceed to install SharePoint Server 2010. If you are upgrading from SharePoint Foundation, see the "Upgrading SharePoint Foundation to SharePoint Server" section later in this chapter.

Running the Microsoft SharePoint Products and Technologies Preparation Tool

The SharePoint Products and Technologies Preparation Tool helps to ensure that all prerequisites have been installed on your server before you proceed with installation. You must have an Internet connection to automatically install prerequisites; otherwise, prerequisites will have to be installed manually. Complete the following steps to run the SharePoint Products and Technologies Preparation Tool:

1. Launch the setup executable for SharePoint Server 2010.

2. On the SharePoint Server 2010 Start page, click Install Software Prerequisites as seen in Figure 1-23.

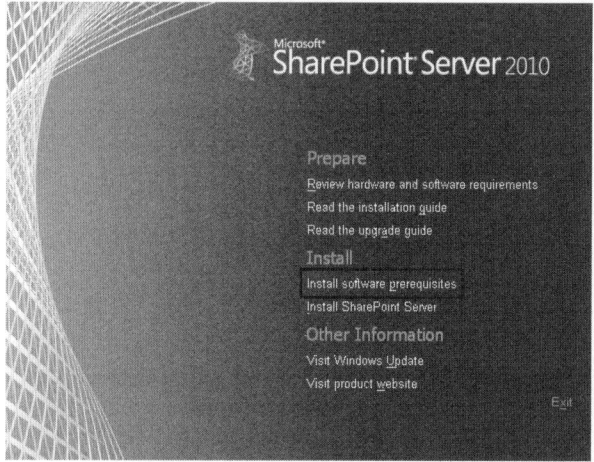

FIGURE 1-23 Install software prerequisites before installing the product binaries.

3. On the Welcome To The Microsoft SharePoint Products Preparation Tool page, click Next.

4. On the License Terms For Software Products page, review the terms and conditions, select the check box verifying that you agree to the terms and conditions, and click Next.

5. On the Installation Complete page, click Finish.

NOTE If you receive the message "Loading this assembly would produce a different grant set from other instances. (Exception from HRESULT: 0x80131401)" upon starting any process or managed application on a server that is also running SharePoint 2010, you should install the hotfix KB963676. This hotfix can be downloaded by browsing to http://support.microsoft.com/kb/963676.

Installing the SharePoint Server 2010 Binaries

Now that all prerequisites have been installed, you can install SharePoint Server 2010 by doing the following:

1. On the SharePoint Server 2010 Start page, click Install SharePoint Server as shown in Figure 1-24.

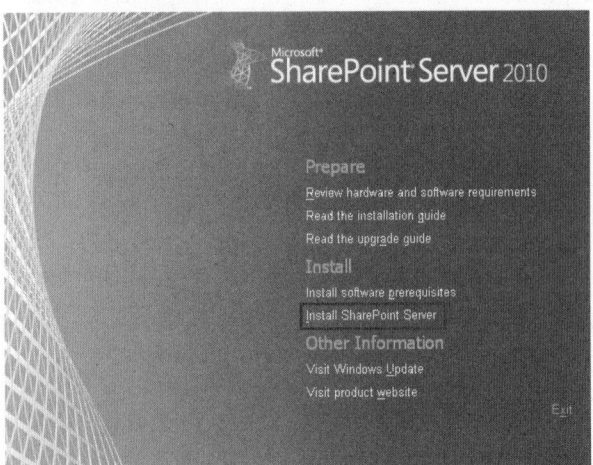

FIGURE 1-24 Install SharePoint Server after you've installed the software prerequisites.

2. On the Enter Your Product Key page, type your product key and click Continue.

3. On the Read The Microsoft Software License Terms page, review the terms and conditions, select the check box verifying that you agree to the terms and conditions, and click Continue.

4. On the Choose A File Location page, enter the installation and search data folder locations, and then click Install Now.

5. On the Choose The Installation You Want page, shown in Figure 1-25, click Server Farm.

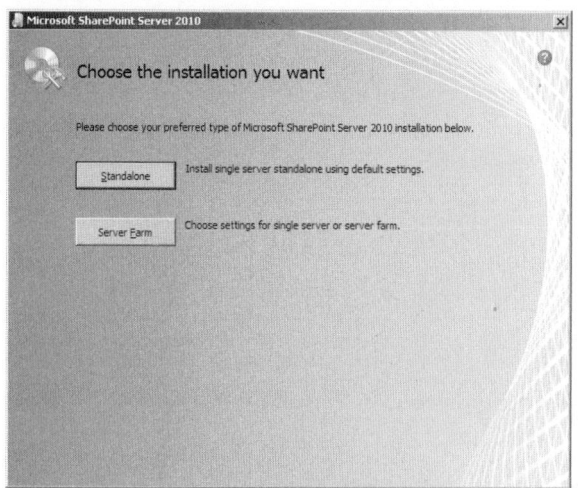

FIGURE 1-25 Click Server Farm when using SQL Server Standard or Enterprise.

6. On the Server Type tab, choose Complete. (See Figure 1-26.)
7. Optionally, you can choose to install SharePoint Server 2010 to a custom location by clicking the File Location tab and entering the location where SharePoint Server 2010 should be installed.
8. Click Install Now to proceed with the installation.

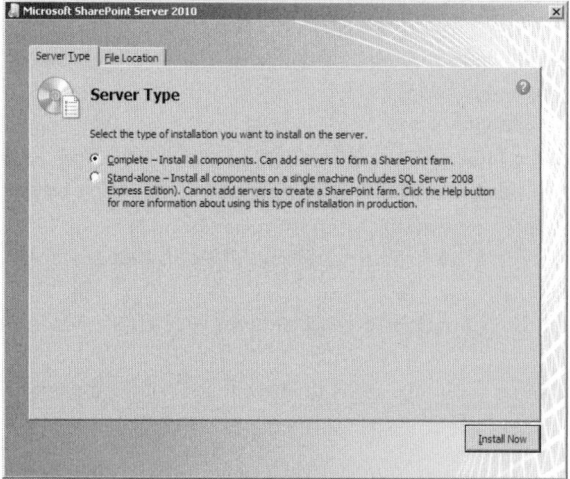

FIGURE 1-26 Select Complete when using SQL Server Standard or Enterprise.

9. When setup completes, leave the Run The SharePoint Products Configuration Wizard Now check box selected and click Close, as seen in Figure 1-27.

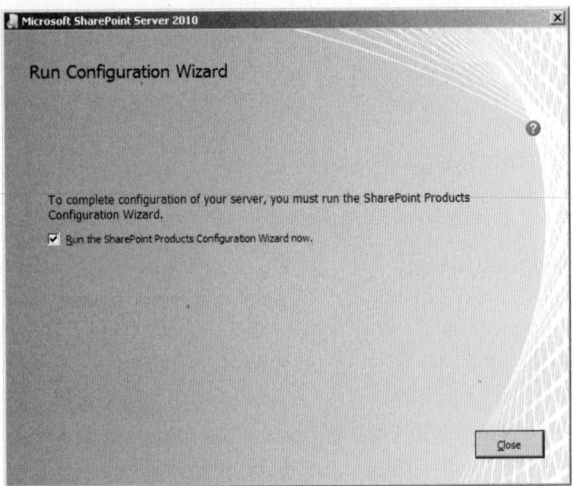

FIGURE 1-27 Click Close to begin the server farm provisioning process.

Running the SharePoint Products Configuration Wizard

At this point, you've installed the SharePoint Server 2010 binaries, but you haven't created a configuration database. It is important to note that a farm is defined by a configuration database. Provisioning a farm is the same as provisioning a new configuration database. The SharePoint 2010 Products Configuration Wizard will guide you through the process of provisioning the farm:

1. If the SharePoint 2010 Products Configuration Wizard does not launch automatically, you can find it located at Start, All Programs. Microsoft SharePoint 2010 Products.

2. On the Welcome To SharePoint Products page, click Next.

3. A dialog box appears stating that some services might need to be restarted during configuration. Click Yes to proceed.

4. On the Connect To A Server Farm page, click Create A New Server Farm, and then click Next.

5. On the Specify Configuration Database Settings page, make the following changes:

   - In the Database Server box, type the server name of the database server.
   - In the Database Name box, type a name for the configuration database. If the database server is hosting multiple farms, you should type a name that uniquely identifies the farm you are configuring; otherwise, you can keep the default value of *SharePoint_Config*.
   - In the Username box, type the server farm administrator account name. If you are using Active Directory, the account name should be in the

format DOMAIN\username. Remember that this account must have SQL permissions of Database Creator and Security Administrator defined before installation of SharePoint Server 2010. This account will also be the application pool identity for the Central Administration Web site, and it will have access to all server farm databases. Thus, be sure to protect this account's credentials.

- In the Password box, type the account password.
- Click Next.

6. On the Specify Farm Security Settings page, type a passphrase and click Next. This passphrase must be entered any time a server is joined to the farm and is used to encrypt credentials of SharePoint accounts. By default, it is constrained by your Active Directory minimum password complexity requirements. If it is the default, the passphrase must meet the following criteria:

- It must be eight characters in length
- It must contain three of the following four character types:

  English uppercase letters (A through Z)

  English lowercase letters (a through z)

  Numerals (0 through 9)

  Non-alphanumeric characters (such as "!","","#", etc.)*

7. The Configure SharePoint Central Administration Web Application page allows you to specify the settings for the Web site used to perform administrative tasks in SharePoint.

- Specify a port number for the Central Administration Web site, or use the default.
- Choose NTLM or Negotiate (Kerberos) for authentication.
- Click Next.

8. On the Completing The SharePoint Products Configuration Wizard page, review your specified settings, and click Next to begin configuration.

9. On the Configuration Successful page, click Finish.

NOTE If the configuration fails, you can check the PSCDiagnostics files located on the drive where SharePoint is installed, in the %CommonProgramFiles%\Microsoft Shared\Web Server Extensions\14\Logs folder.

If the configuration is successful, Internet Explorer is launched and the Central Administration Web site is opened. If you are prompted for credentials, you should add the Central Administration URL to your trusted sites list and ensure that Internet Explorer is configured to automatically pass user credentials to sites in that list.

If you see a proxy server error message, you need to make sure to configure your browser to bypass the proxy server for local addresses. In Internet Explorer, this setting can be configured on the Tools, Internet Options menu, under the Connections tab. Click LAN Settings to access the proxy server configuration settings.

Using the SharePoint Server 2010 Farm Configuration Wizard

If you are an experienced SharePoint Server administrator, you probably will not want to use the Farm Configuration Wizard because it limits your installation options. However, using it does make initial farm configuration easier. If you are new to SharePoint Server 2010, using the Farm Configuration Wizard is an acceptable method to begin with.

NOTE When you are manually configuring the farm, there isn't necessarily one correct way of accomplishing success. But, during the writing of this book, the following order of creating and configuring Web and service applications was followed:

1. Create the primary Web application.
2. Create the My Site Provider (Web application).
3. Create the Content Type Hub Web application (optional).
4. Create and configure the Search Service application.
5. Create and configure the User Profile Service application.
6. Create and configure the Managed Metadata Service application.
7. Create the SPState Service application.
8. Start services on the server for relevant service applications.
9. Verify the association of service applications to Web applications.

If you are using the Configuration Wizard to install SharePoint Server 2010, do the following:

1. Open the Central Administration site (as shown in Figure 1-28), and browse to the Configuration Wizards page. To go directly to the page, browse to http://*servername*:28122/default.aspx.

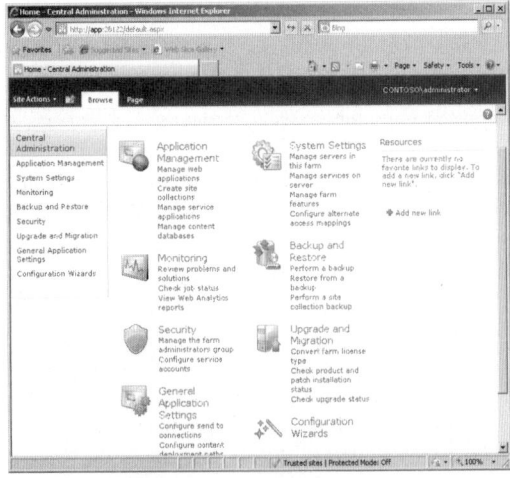

FIGURE 1-28 Click Configuration Wizards to continue.

2. Click Launch The Farm Configuration Wizard.

3. On the Help Make SharePoint Better page, choose one of the options and click OK.

4. On the Configure Your SharePoint Farm page, choose Yes, Walk Me Through The Configuration Of My Farm Using This Wizard, and then click Start The Wizard.

5 In the Service Account section, specify the service account you want to use to configure your services. You should choose an account other than the farm administrator account for security purposes, and it should be in the format *DOMAIN\username*, as seen in Figure 1-29.

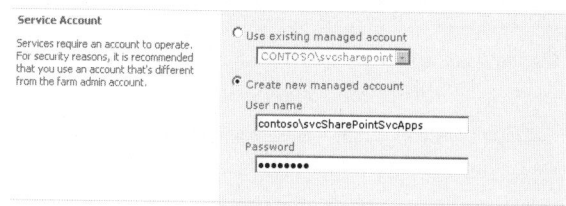

FIGURE 1-29 Enter the account name previously created in Active Directory.

6. There are many more services available by default in SharePoint Server 2010 than in SharePoint Foundation 2010. The decision about which services to use doesn't have to be made at this point. You can re-run the configuration wizard again later and install additional services. Select which services to enable, or just accept the defaults for these services, and click Next.

7. On the Create Site Collection page, click Skip. You can create the first site collection here, but you will probably want to have more control over the initial Web application creation and configuration, so it is best just to skip this step for now. Creating the initial Web application for hosting sites will be covered in the "Post-Install Configuration" section.

8. On the Farm Configuration Wizard summary page, click Finish to complete the initial configuration.

Performing a Scripted Deployment Using Windows PowerShell

Windows PowerShell is an extremely powerful tool for automating administrative tasks in SharePoint Server 2010. For deployment, Windows PowerShell can be used to create a repeatable process for performing SharePoint Server 2010 installations:

1. Download or otherwise obtain the self-extracting executable installer, OfficeServer.exe.

2. Create a folder for install files, such as *C:\Install*.

3. Open a command prompt, type the following command, and press Enter:

```
C:\install\OfficeServer.exe /extract:c:\install
```

4. When you see the Files Extracted Successfully message box, click OK.

5. Navigate to C:\install\Files\SetupFarmSilent, and open the config.xml file in a text editor.

6. Add the line <PIDKEY Value="*ProductKey*"/> within the Configuration tag, where *ProductKey* is your SharePoint Server 2010 product key. Save and close the file.

7. Open a text editor, add the following example code, and save the file as **sp_install.ps1** in the install location you created in step 2:

```
## Settings ##
$SetupPath = "c:\install"
$DBServer = "S1"
$Passphrase = (ConvertTo-SecureString "P@ssw0rd" -AsPlainText -force)
$FarmName = "SP2010"
$CAPort = "12345"
$farm_un = "contoso\svcSharePoint1"
$farm_pw = (ConvertTo-SecureString "P@ssw0rd" -AsPlainText -force)
$FarmCredential = New-Object System.Management.Automation.
PsCredential $farm_un,$farm_pw
Write-Host "[1/9] Running prerequisite installer..."
& $SetupPath\PrerequisiteInstaller.exe /unattended | Write-Host
Write-Host "[2/9] Running silent farm binary installation..."
& $SetupPath\setup.exe /config
SetupPath\Files\SetupFarmSilent\config.xml | Write-Host
Add-PSSnapin Microsoft.SharePoint.PowerShell
Write-Host "[3/9] Creating new configuration database..."
New-SPConfigurationDatabase -DatabaseName
"{0}_SharePoint_Configuration_DB" -f $FarmName) -DatabaseServer
DBServer -AdministrationContentDatabaseName ("{0}_AdminContent_DB" -f
FarmName) -FarmCredentials $FarmCredential -Passphrase $Passphrase
Write-Host "[4/9] Securing SharePoint Resources"
Initialize-SPResourceSecurity
Write-Host "[5/9] Provision Central Administration Site"
New-SPCentralAdministration -Port $CAPort -WindowsAuthProvider "NTLM"
Write-Host "[6/9] Installing Help Files"
Install-SPHelpCollection -All
Write-Host "[7/9] Installing Application Content"
Install-SPApplicationContent
```

```
Write-Host "[8/9] Installing Features"
Install-SPFeature -AllExistingFeatures
Write-Host "[9/9] Installing Services"
Install-SPService
Write-Host "Deployment Complete!"
```

8. Close the text editor.

9. Navigate to Start, All Programs, Accessories, Windows PowerShell, right-click Windows PowerShell, and choose Run As Administrator.

10. In the PowerShell command window, change directories to the install directory created in step 2.

11. Type **.\sp_install.ps1**, and press Enter to begin the unattended install.

Understanding Databases Created During Installation

After installation, you will see several databases that are created in SQL Server and that need to be added to your SQL Server maintenance plan:

- **SharePoint configuration** The SharePoint configuration database holds all your server farm configuration data and is akin to the Windows Server system registry. Any server that uses this installation's configuration database is considered a member of the same server farm.

- **Central Administration content** Because the Central Administration Web application is a custom site collection in a dedicated Web application, it has a corresponding content database.

- **Content database** Each Web application has at least one corresponding content database. If you ran the Farm Configuration Wizard, a Web application was created for you at the URL of your server and it has a corresponding content database. Content databases are where all SharePoint content is stored.

- **Business Connectivity Services DB** This database is used by the Business Connectivity Services (BCS) and by default will be named *Bdc_Service_DB_<GUID>*.

- **SharePoint Server Logging** Used by the Usage and Health Data Collection Service for logging purposes, it is named *WSS_Logging* by default.

- **Secure Store Service DB** Provides storage and mapping of credentials.

- **Search Administration Database** Formerly the SSP database, it hosts the Search application configuration and access control list (ACL) used in crawling content.

- **Search Property Database** Stores crawled properties associated with the crawled data.

- **Crawl Database**   Formerly the Search database in SharePoint Server 2007, it hosts the crawled data and manages the crawling process.
- **Web Analytics Staging Database**   Stores raw, unaggregated Fact data.
- **Web Analytics Reporting Database**   Stores aggregate data for reporting.
- **User Profile Database**   Stores and manages user profile information.
- **Profile Synchronization Database**   Stores configuration and staging data for user-profile synchronization.
- **Social Tagging Database**   Stores social tagging data along with the associated URL.
- **State Database**   Used for storing temporary session state information for SharePoint components.
- **Word Automation Services Database**   Supports Word Automation Services in performing Word-related tasks on the server.
- **Managed Metadata Database**   Stores managed metadata and content types.
- **Application Registry Service Database**   Supports the Application Registry Service.

Post-Installation Configuration

Even though the Farm Configuration Wizard created and configured the basic applications required for your farm, additional configuration steps will probably be required depending on the specific functionality you want to provide to users. Some of the functionality of new Web applications might be missing until the appropriate configuration is performed.

The vast majority of configuration actions performed for a SharePoint farm are performed in the Central Administration Web site. This site should have been installed on at least one of the farm servers when the farm was provisioned and can be used to configure all farmwide and Web application-level settings.

Configure Farm Administrators Group

Farm administrators can be added or removed by going to Central Administration, clicking Manage The Farm Administrators Group under Security, and adding or deleting users. Members of the Farm Administrators group have full access to all settings across the entire farm and can take ownership of any site in the farm. Obviously, this group should be carefully managed and limited to as few individuals as possible.

Configure Outgoing E-mail Settings

Outgoing e-mail must be configured in order for users to receive alerts from SharePoint. The Simple Mail Transport Protocol (SMTP) service must be set up on a server accessible to the SharePoint farm, and it must be configured to allow anonymous messages. You must be a member of the Farm Administrators group to modify these settings.

1. In Central Administration, click System Settings.
2. On the System Settings page, in the E-mail And Text Messages (SMS) section, choose Configure Outgoing E-Mail Settings.
3. In the Mail Settings section of the Outgoing E-Mail Settings page, type the SMTP server name for outgoing e-mail in the Outbound SMTP Server box.
4. Enter the From Address and Reply-To Address to be used. The From address will appear in the From field of any e-mail messages sent by SharePoint. The Reply-to address will be used for replies to any e-mail messages sent by SharePoint.
5. In the Character Set drop-down list, select the appropriate character set.
6. Click OK to save the settings.

Create a Web Application to Host Site Collections

As in previous versions of SharePoint, all SharePoint sites are rendered via Internet Information Services. To create a Web application for hosting site collections, perform the following steps:

1. In Central Administration, click Manage Web Applications in the Application Management section.
2. Click the New button on the left side of the ribbon.
3. Enter the following values for the new Web application:

   - **Authentication** Leave the default choice, Classic Mode Authentication, selected.

   - **IIS Web Site** Choose Create A New IIS Web Site. Give it a descriptive name. Ensure that the Port value is 80 and the host header value uses the FQDN, as seen in Figure 1-30. Leave the default value for Path unless you have specific requirements to do otherwise.

   IMPORTANT If you choose a path other than C:\, be sure that path exists on all current and future members of the farm. Otherwise, the server addition to the farm will fail.

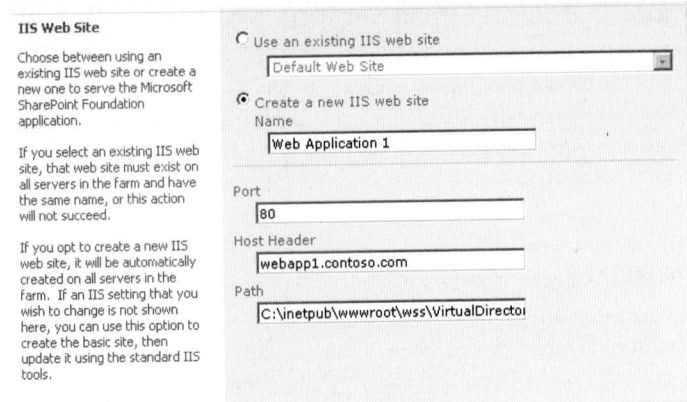

FIGURE 1-30 Use the FQDN for the first Host Header if possible.

- **Security Configuration** Leave the default values selected as seen in Figure 1-31.

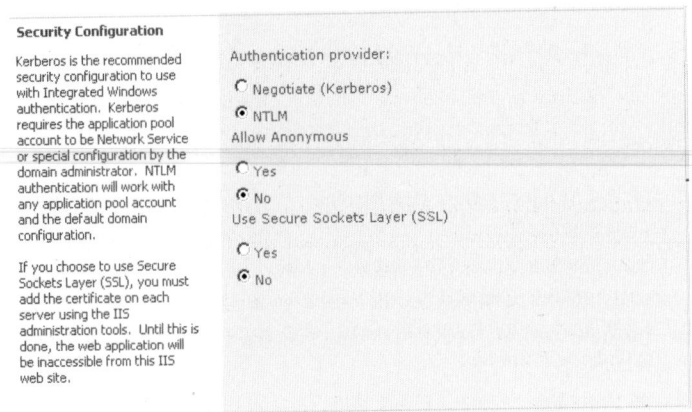

FIGURE 1-31 You can change to Kerberos later if necessary.

- **Public URL** Enter the base URL that will be used to access the Web site, and leave the Zone set to Default. You do not have to include the TCP port number with the URL—for example, *:80*—if on a standard port. Figure 1-32 shows an example of a Web application on TCP port 80.

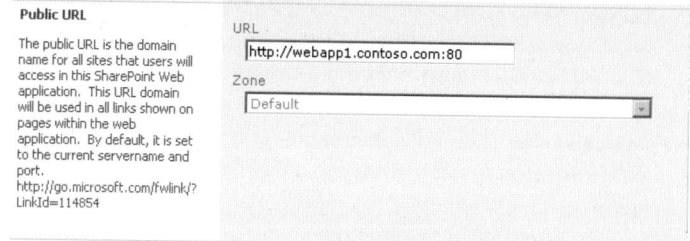

FIGURE 1-32 The default URL should use the FQDN.

- **Application Pool** Select Create New Application Pool, and choose the account to be used to run the application pool, as seen in Figure 1-33.

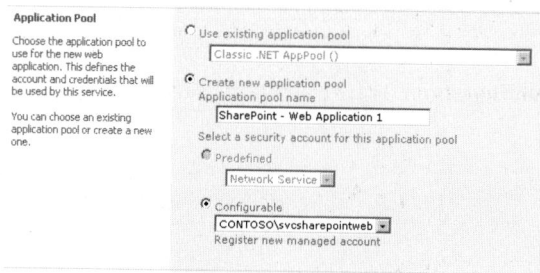

FIGURE 1-33 Create a new application pool for isolation and security.

- **Database Name And Authentication** The database server defaults to the server where the configuration database resides. If needed, you can specify another database server, as seen in Figure 1-34. Choose a database name to distinguish this content database from other databases on the server. Using Windows Authentication to connect to the database is highly recommended.

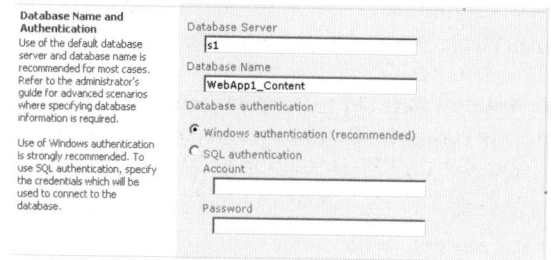

FIGURE 1-34 Enter the database server and database name.

- **Failover Server**   You can specify a failover database server name to be used with SQL Server database mirroring. Note that this only makes SharePoint 2010 Products mirroring aware—you must still configure database mirroring in SQL Server.

- **Search Server**   This value is used only in a SharePoint Foundation 2010–only environment. If you are using SharePoint Server 2010, this option is not applicable.

- **Service Application Connections**   You can accept the default service application settings as seen in Figure 1-35, or you can choose to customize the settings for the new Web application.

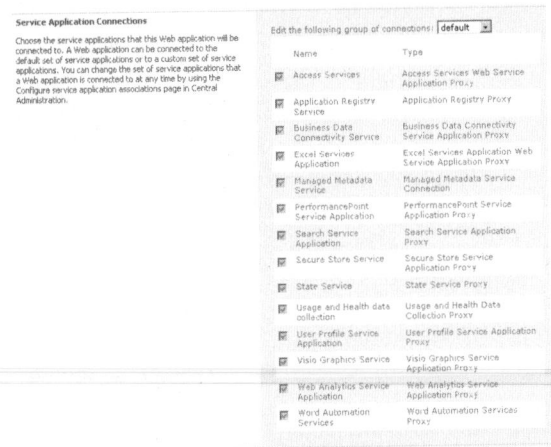

FIGURE 1-35 Select which service applications to associate, or select the default group.

4. Click OK to create the new Web application.

Configure Usage and Health Data Collection

Usage and Health Data collection settings are farm-level settings and cannot be configured for a specific server. The user configuring these settings should be a member of the Farm Administrators group.

1. On the home page of Central Administration, click Monitoring.

2. In the Reporting section of the Monitoring page, click Configure Usage And Health Data Collection.

3. In the Usage Data Collection section of the Configure Usage And Health Data Collection page, enable usage data collection by selecting the Enable Usage Data Collection check box.

4. In the Event Selection list, choose the events to log by clicking the corresponding check boxes as seen in Figure 1-36. Keep in mind that logging uses system resources and can affect performance. Therefore, in a new

installation you might consider setting the event and trace log thresholds to Critical and Unexpected, respectively.

FIGURE 1-36 Select what events you'll log.

5. In the Usage Data Collection Settings section, enter the path where usage and health data should be written in the Log File Location box. This path must exist on all farm servers, and you should ensure that there is sufficient disk space available on the destination drive. The following example, shown in Figure 1-37, uses the C:\ volume. If your log files will be very large, consider using a different volume.

IMPORTANT The Log File Location value must exist on every server in the farm. If a server does not have the specified drive, the server will not successfully be added to the farm.

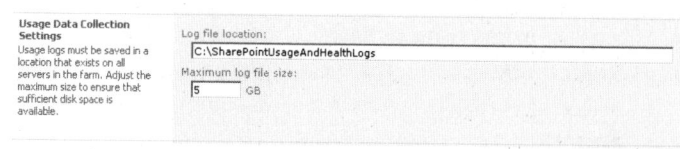

FIGURE 1-37 Verify space exits in the log file location.

6. In the Maximum Log File Size box, enter the maximum disk space allowed for logs, between 1 and 20 gigabytes (GBs).

7. In the Health Data Collection section, select the Enable Health Data Collection check box as seen in Figure 1-38. To change the schedule or disable any health-related timer jobs, click Health Logging Schedule for a list of jobs, and then click the job to change its settings.

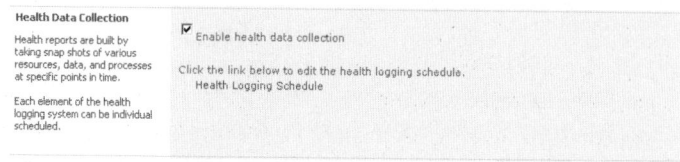

FIGURE 1-38 If needed, enable health data collection.

8. In the Logging Database Server section, select the appropriate authentication mechanism. Windows authentication is recommended. The Logging database server or database name can be changed only with Windows PowerShell.

9. Click OK to save the settings.

Configure Diagnostic Logging

Diagnostic logging for the SharePoint farm is highly configurable and can be performed through Central Administration. You should consider minimizing diagnostic logging in a new installation. You must be a member of the Farm Administrators group to perform these actions.

1. On the Home page of Central Administration, click Monitoring.

2. In the Reporting section of the Monitoring page, click Configure Diagnostic Logging.

3. In the Event Throttling section of the Diagnostic Logging page, you have the following options for configuring Event Throttling:

   a. For all categories:
   - Select the All Categories check box.
   - Select the event log level from the least critical event to report to the event log list.
   - Select the event log level from the least critical event to report to the trace log list.

   b. For one or more categories:
   - Select the check boxes for the categories you want to configure.
   - Select the event log level from the least critical event to report to the event log list.
   - Select the event log level from the least critical event to report to the trace log list.

   c. For one or more subcategories:
   - Click (+) next to the category to expand the subcategories.
   - Select the check box next to the subcategory.
   - Select the event log level from the least critical event to report to the event log list.
   - Select the event log level from the least critical event to report to the trace log list.

   d. To restore the defaults for all categories:
   - Select the All Categories check box.
   - Select Reset To Default from the least critical event to report to the event log list.

- Select Reset To Default from the least critical event to report to the trace log list.

4. In the Event Log Flood Protection section, select the Enable Event Log Flood Protection check box. This prevents the same event from being logged excessively, further degrading performance.

5. In the Trace Log section, enter the path to the folder where the logs should be written in the Path box.

6. Specify the number of days for log files to be kept (from 1 through 366) in the Number Of Days To Store Log Files box, as seen in Figure 1-39.

7. The disk space used by log files can be restricted by selecting the Restrict Trace Log Disk Space Usage check box and entering the maximum number of gigabytes (GB) the log files should be allowed to use. When this limit is reached, older files are automatically deleted.

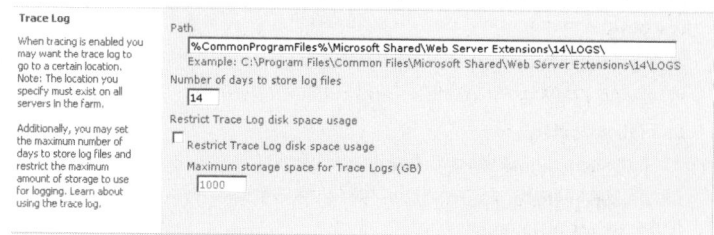

FIGURE 1-39 Restrict trace log disk space usage when using the C:\ volume.

8. Click OK to save the settings.

Install and Configure Remote BLOB Storage

Remote BLOB Storage (RBS) is designed to allow storage of binary large objects (BLOBs) outside of SQL Server with only a reference to the object stored in SQL Server. RBS is an add-on for SQL Server 2008 Express or any of the other SQL Server 2008 editions and consists of auxiliary tables, stored procedures, and an executable.

This is an optional configuration step and should be considered only for testing purposes until you have your full system requirements documented. Although storing large BLOBs outside of SQL will help with large file performance, it can actually decrease performance of smaller files. RBS can also introduce complexities into your backup, restore, and migration strategy. But because it is such an anticipated addition to SharePoint Server 2010, it is included here.

> **IMPORTANT** Before configuring RBS, you must enable FILESTREAM on the SQL Server 2008 computer that hosts the SharePoint databases. Steps for enabling FILESTREAM can be found in the SQL Server 2008 Books Online at *http://technet.microsoft.com/en-us/library/cc645923.aspx*.

Provision a BLOB Data Store

Use the following steps to provision a BLOB data store:

1. Open SQL Server Management Studio, usually located at Start, All Programs, Microsoft SQL Server 2008, SQL Server Management Studio.

2. Expand Databases.

3. Select the content database for which you want to create a BLOB store, and click New Query in the toolbar at the top of the screen.

4. Execute each of the following queries in the order given, replacing [ContentDB] with the name of the content database name and *BlobPath* with the directory path where the BLOB store should be created. If you are using SQL Server 2008 Management Studio, Microsoft IntelliSense will assist you in selecting the correct database.

> **BEST PRACTICES** The recommended best practice is to create the BLOB store on a volume that does not contain the operating system, paging files, database data, transaction log files, or the tempdb file.

```
use [ContentDB]
if not exists (select * from sys.symmetric_keys where name =
'##MS_DatabaseMasterKey##')create master key encryption by password =
N'Admin Key Password !2#4'
```

```
use [ContentDB]
if not exists (select groupname from sysfilegroups where
roupname=N'RBSFilestreamProvider')alter database [ContentDB]
 add filegroup RBSFilestreamProvider contains filestream
```

```
use [ContentDB]
alter database [ContentDB] add file (name = RBSFilestreamFile,
ilename = 'BlobPath') to filegroup RBSFilestreamProvider
```

Install RBS

RBS must be installed on all Web and application servers in the farm.

> **CAUTION** Do not install RBS by double-clicking the RBS_X64.msi file to launch the Install SQL Remote BLOB Storage Wizard. This automatically sets certain default values that are not ideal for SharePoint 2010.

To install RBS on the database server and the first Web server, use the following procedure:

1. On any Web server, go to *http://go.microsoft.com/fwlink/ ?LinkID=165839&clcid=0x409* to download the RBS_X64.msi file.

2. Click Start, Run, type **cmd**, and click OK.

3. Enter the following command into the Command Prompt window. Replace *ContentDB* with the database name, and replace *DBInstanceName* with the SQL Server instance name. This command should be run exactly once with the specific database name and instance name.

```
msiexec /qn /lvx* rbs_install_log.txt /i RBS_X64.msi
TRUSTSERVERCERTIFICATE=true FILEGROUP=PRIMARY DBNAME="ContentDB"
BINSTANCE="DBInstanceName" FILESTREAMFILEGROUP=RBSFilestreamProvider
ILESTREAMSTORENAME=FilestreamProvider_1
```

To install RBS on additional Web and application servers, use the following procedure:

1. Go to *http://go.microsoft.com/fwlink/?LinkID=165839&clcid=0x409* to download the RBS_X64.msi file.

2. Click Start, Run, type **cmd**, and click OK.

3. Enter the following command into the Command Prompt window. Replace *ContentDB* with the database name, and replace *DBInstanceName* with the SQL Server instance name.

```
msiexec /qn /lvx* rbs_install_log.txt /i RBS_X64.msi
BNAME="ContentDB" DBINSTANCE="DBInstanceName" ADDLOCAL="Client, Docs,
Maintainer, ServerScript, FilestreamClient, FilestreamServer"
```

4. Repeat this procedure for all Web and application servers in the farm.

To confirm the RBS installation, use the following procedure:

1. Open the RBS log file, which is located in the same location as RBS_X64.msi, and search within the last 20 lines of the file for the text "Product: SQL Remote BLOB Storage – Installation Completed Successfully".

2. Verify that the RBS tables were created in the content database. There should be several tables with the prefix "mssqlrbs".

Enable and Test RBS

You must enable RBS on one Web server in the SharePoint farm. It does not matter which server it is, as long as RBS was installed using the previous procedure.

To enable RBS, use the following procedure:

1. On the Start menu, click Programs, Microsoft SharePoint 2010 Products, SharePoint 2010 Management Shell.

2. At the Windows PowerShell command prompt, type each of the following commands and press Enter after each one. Replace *http://sitename* with the Web application that is connected to the content database.

```
$cdb = Get-SPContentDatabase -WebApplication http://sitename
$rbss = $cdb.RemoteBlobStorageSettings
$rbss.Installed()
$rbss.Enable()
$rbss.SetActiveProviderName($rbss.GetProviderNames()[0])
$rbss
```

To test the RBS data store, use the following procedure:

1. Connect to a document library on any server in the SharePoint farm.
2. Upload a file that is at least 100 kilobytes (KB) in size to the document library.
3. On the computer where the RBS data store is located, navigate to the store folder.
4. Open the folder that has the most recent modified date, other than $FSLOG, and find the file with the most recent modified date. This should be your file.

Configure RBS for Additional Content Databases

RBS can be configured for additional content databases using the following procedure:

1. Repeat the procedure in the "Provision a BLOB Data Store" section for each additional content database.
2. Type the following command at the command prompt on any Web server in the farm, replacing [ContentDB] with the name of the database and [DBInstanceName] with the name of the SQL Server instance:

```
msiexec /qn /i RBS_X64.msi REMOTEBLOBENABLE=1
ILESTREAMPROVIDERENABLE=1 DBNAME="[ContentDB]"
BINSTANCE="[DBInstanceName]" FILESTREAMSTORENAME=FilestreamProvider_1
ADDLOCAL="EnableRBS,FilestreamRunScript"
```

3. Test RBS using the procedure shown earlier for testing the RBS data store.

Assigning IP Addresses to Web Applications

To assign IP addresses to your Web applications, follow these steps:

1. Add a host (A record) in the DNS Management Console.
2. Add the associated IP address to your Windows Server.
3. After an IIS reset, assign the IP address to the Web application in Web site bindings. Figure 1-40 shows an example of an Internet Information Services configuration.

4. Click the existing binding, and click Edit.
5. If desired, choose the IP address to assign to this Web application from the IP Address drop-down list.
6. Enter the URL from the A record in step 1 in the Host Name box.
7. Click OK to save the binding.

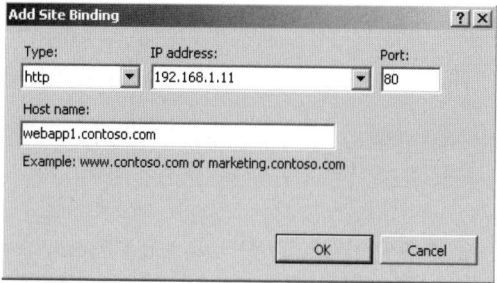

FIGURE 1-40 Enter the host name and port number for the Web application.

8. Open Central Administration and on the Home page, in the System Settings section, click Configure Alternate Access Mappings.
9. Click the name of the Web application, and verify that the URL for the default zone is set correctly. An example can be seen in Figure 1-41.

FIGURE 1-41 Verify the internal URL is defined in DNS.

10. Click OK.

Language Packs

Language packs make it possible to create sites in multiple languages within a single farm without having to install multiple instances of SharePoint. Language packs for available languages can be downloaded from Microsoft.

Prepare the Servers

Before installing any language packs in SharePoint, you must prepare the Web servers by ensuring that all appropriate Windows Server language files are installed on each server. Most language files are installed by default on Windows Server 2008, but certain languages require additional files to work properly. East-Asian languages, languages that use complex script, or languages that are oriented right-to-left require supplemental files, which can be downloaded from Microsoft. You must be a member of the Administrators group on the server to install language files.

To install additional language files, perform the following actions:

1. Navigate to Start, Control Panel, Clock, Language, And Region.
2. In the Region And Language section, click Install Or Uninstall Display Languages.
3. In the Install Or Uninstall Display Languages dialog box, choose Install Display Languages.
4. Click the Browse button, navigate to the folder where you downloaded the language file, and click OK.
5. Choose the languages you want to install, and click Next.
6. Accept the terms, and click Next.
7. Click Install to install the selected language files.

Install a Language Pack

When you install a language pack, the installer runs in the language of the language pack being installed. To install a language pack, complete the following steps:

1. Download the language pack for the language you want to install.
2. Run the setup executable file.
3. Review the software license terms, select the I Accept The Terms Of This Agreement check box, and click Continue.

    The language pack will be installed and progress reported.

4. When the installation is complete, leave the check box selected to automatically run the SharePoint Products And Technologies Configuration Wizard and click Finish.
5. Rerun the SharePoint Products Configuration Wizard, accepting the default settings. This step is necessary for the language pack to be installed correctly.

Re-Run the SharePoint Products Configuration Wizard

After installing the language packs, you need to run the SharePoint 2010 Products Configuration Wizard again. Doing so updates this server's language configuration in the configuration database.

1. Navigate to the configuration wizard, which is located at Start, All Programs, Microsoft SharePoint 2010 Products, SharePoint 2010 Products Configuration Wizard.
2. On the Welcome To SharePoint Products page, click Next.
3. A dialog box appears stating that some services might need to be restarted during configuration. Click Yes to proceed.
4. On the Modify Server Farm Settings page, select Do Not Disconnect From This Server Farm, and click Next.
5. If the Modify Central Administration Web Administration page appears, leave the default settings, and click Next.

6. On the Completing The SharePoint Products Configuration Wizard page, click Next.

7. On the Configuration Successful page, click Finish.

Upgrading SharePoint Foundation to SharePoint Server

The process for upgrading from SharePoint Foundation to SharePoint Server is similar to the process for installing SharePoint Server. Some of the options you are presented with during the SharePoint Server Installation will be skipped when upgrading because they will have been configured during the SharePoint Foundation setup.

Installing SharePoint Server 2010 Binaries

You need to install the SharePoint Server 2010 binaries to enable the additional functionality provided by SharePoint Server 2010:

1. On the SharePoint Server 2010 Start page, click Install SharePoint Server.

2. On the Enter Your Product Key page, type your product key, and click Continue.

3. On the Read The Microsoft Software License Terms page, review the terms and conditions, select the check box verifying that you agree to the terms and conditions, and click Continue.

4. On the Choose A File Location page, enter the installation and search data folder locations, and then click Install Now.

5. When setup completes, leave the Run The SharePoint Products Configuration Wizard Now check box selected, and click Close.

Running the SharePoint Products Configuration Wizard

The SharePoint 2010 Products Configuration Wizard will guide you through the process of upgrading the farm:

1. If the SharePoint 2010 Products Configuration Wizard does not launch automatically, you can find it located at Start, All Programs, Microsoft SharePoint 2010 Products.

2. On the Welcome To SharePoint Products page, click Next.

3. A dialog box appears stating that some services might need to be restarted during configuration. Click Yes to proceed.

4. On the Completing The SharePoint Products Configuration Wizard page, review your specified settings, and click Next to begin configuration.

5. On the Configuration Successful page, click Finish.

CHAPTER 2

Scaling to a MultiServer Farm

- Preparing for Scaling Out to a Server Farm   **51**
- Scaling Web Applications   **57**
- Scaling System Services and Service Applications   **65**

The two primary reasons for scaling out a server farm are to achieve high availability and to improve performance. For example, those looking for high availability need at least two Web servers, two application servers, and a clustered Microsoft SQL Server back end. If top performance is strictly the goal, you might have only a single four-core database server, one very fast Web server, and a single application server. Whatever your goal, be aware that Microsoft SharePoint Server 2010 does not have as many limitations regarding scaling and topology choices as earlier versions. But this increased flexibility in server farm design might make it difficult for some administrators to design an appropriate physical and logical farm topology. If you are not sure how to design your specific server farm architecture, begin with a topology discussed in this chapter and simply change it to meet your needs.

Remember that these topologies are not concrete rules on which to build your specific implementation; they are simply real-world suggestions about where to begin. Most medium-size and larger organizations would do well to begin with an implementation that has at least two Web front-end (WFE) servers, an application server, and a clustered SQL Server back end.

Preparing for Scaling Out to a Server Farm

If you plan to scale out to a farm, be sure to install SharePoint Server 2010 first on the server that is destined to host the Central Administration Web application. This server can also host other services, such as the Microsoft SharePoint Foundation Sandboxed Code service and the Document Conversions Launcher service. In addition to performing server hardware planning, you should also plan your network infrastructure in advance to provide the best level of service possible. A gigabit Ethernet (Gig-E) network infrastructure should be considered the minimum size in most enterprise farm scenarios, but 100 Base-T network speeds are sufficient in smaller farms. In addition, having multiple switches and using Network Interface Card (NIC) teaming, when possible, can add fault tolerance to your solution.

When planning for a farm, be sure to include the SQL Server installation in the planning process because it will be the foundation for your new farm. If you have database administrators (DBAs) on staff, include them in the planning from the beginning. A poorly designed and implemented SQL Server installation can easily become the bottleneck in a SharePoint products server farm.

Single-Server Farm

A single-server farm, shown in Figure 2-1, is configured with every component, including the SQL Server, installed on one server. This configuration is ideal for testing and very small deployments of less than 100 users.

 All roles on one server, including SQL Server

FIGURE 2-1 One-server farm.

Two-Tier Farm

A two-tier farm, shown in Figure 2-2, consists of one server for hosting all SharePoint Server 2010 Web and service applications, while another server is dedicated to hosting the database. If availability is important to your organization, a clustered or mirrored database server is recommended, which will give the database server a higher degree of availability. This solution can handle up to 10,000 users, depending on the hardware, user processes, and user concurrency. Examples of user processes that reduce the effective capacity are SharePoint Workspace 2010 and custom client code.

 All Web and application server roles

 Databases

FIGURE 2-2 Two-tier farm.

Two-Tier Small Farm

With two SharePoint Server 2010 servers hosting a combination of services, both typically host the Web services and have a database server at the back end. Again, SQL Server clustering or mirroring should be leveraged for high availability at the database tier. Be aware that simply adding another WFE server to the farm usually does not increase availability. To increase availability, you must implement load balancing using the Microsoft Windows Server 2008 Network Load Balancing (NLB) service or install a hardware load-balancing solution. A two-tier small farm, shown in Figure 2-3, is not an optimal solution for load balancing because processing is usually not evenly distributed across Web servers. It is a reasonably priced solution to start off with and provides a level of fault tolerance with two Web servers.

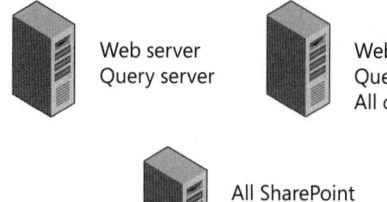

Web server
Query server

Web server
Query server
All other app roles

All SharePoint
databases

FIGURE 2-3 Two-tier small farm.

Three-Tier Small Farm Not Optimized for Search

The standard three-tier small farm configuration, shown in Figure 2-4, consists of two Web servers, one application server, and the database server at the back end. This design is able to handle 10,000 to 20,000 users. This size was considered a medium server farm topology in SharePoint Server 2007. Don't forget to load balance the Web traffic using Windows Server 2008 NLB, or you won't take advantage of having a second server in the farm. A three-tier small farm will likely be the most common farm implemented for SharePoint Server 2010.

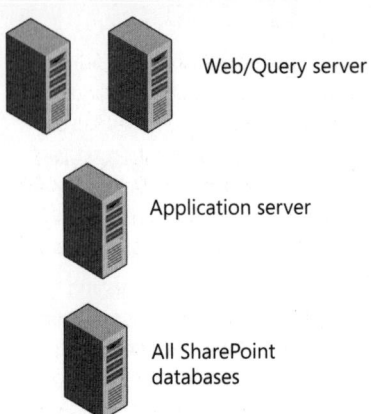

Web/Query server

Application server

All SharePoint
databases

FIGURE 2-4 Three-tier small farm.

Three-Tier Small Farm Optimized for Search

For organizations wanting an optimized search function within its SharePoint
Server 2010 implementation, the standard three-tier configuration (shown in
Figure 2-5) is used, with one notable difference. The database server is configured
to offload search traffic to a dedicated database at the back end. With hardware
dedicated to search databases, this topology is optimized for search to work well in
environments with up to 10 million items in the index.

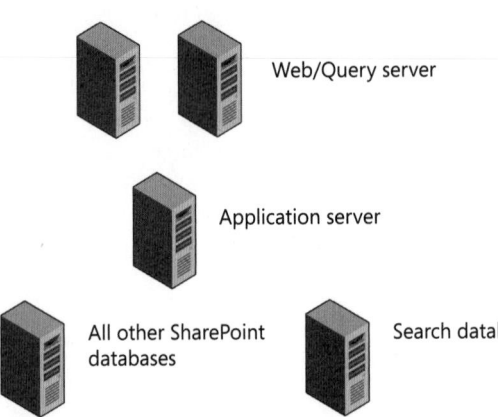

Web/Query server

Application server

All other SharePoint
databases

Search databases

FIGURE 2-5 Three-tier small farm optimized for search.

Medium Farm

A medium farm, shown in Figure 2-6, consists of multiple Web front-end servers, multiple application servers, and a dedicated SQL Server instance. Depending on the hardware and concurrency, the configuration can support up to 50,000 users and scale for search to serve approximately 40 million items. The number of users will affect the requirement for Web servers. A reasonable metric is to factor 10,000 users per Web server as a starting point and reduce the number of users based on how heavily the servers are utilized. If there is heavy use of client services, there will be a corresponding increase in the load on Web servers.

A reasonable starting point is to begin with all application server roles, except search roles, on a single server. From there, based on utilization, consider either adding more servers with all the non-search roles installed, or add more servers to dedicate resources to specific services. For example, if performance data indicates that Excel Services is using a disproportionate amount of resources, offload this service to a dedicated server. Appropriately increase the number of database servers based on the volume of content in the environment and sizing targets for the organization. Monitoring software, such as Systems Center Operations Manager, can create a baseline for performance and give you insight into server farm performance. During the writing of this book, Microsoft Visual Studio 2010 Ultimate Edition was used to create and simulate tests for hundreds and thousands of users.

Web Servers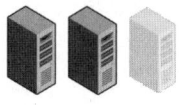

Application Servers

Combined query and crawl server   All other application server roles and services

Database Servers

Search databases   All other SharePoint databases

FIGURE 2-6 Medium farm.

Large Farm

A large farm configuration, shown in Figure 2-7, consists of multiple Web servers and dedicated application servers running various services, as well as multiple SQL Server instances hosting the services data through mirrored SQL Server instances, clustered SQL Server instances, or both. This solution provides the high performance and resiliency necessary for large deployments. The recommended practice for scaling out a large farm is to group services or databases with similar performance characteristics onto dedicated servers and then scale out the servers as a group. The following topology illustrates a practical example of this concept.

Web Servers

 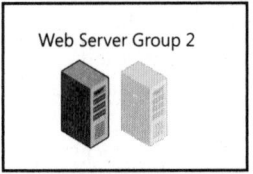

Web servers for all incoming requests

Dedicated Web server(s) for crawling and administration

Application Servers

 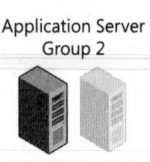  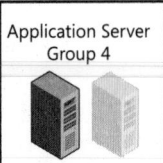

Crawl Servers

Query Servers

All other services (use one of these servers for the Central Admin site)

Servers for executing sandboxed code

Database Servers

Search databases

Content databases

All other SharePoint databases

FIGURE 2-7 Large farm.

Scaling Web Applications

Organizations can begin the process of expanding the scope of an installed SharePoint Server 2010 base by adding servers to the various tiers to produce the scale that is needed. As part of the installation process, it is recommended that the account used to perform the initial SharePoint Server 2010 installation be used when adding servers to the farm. Subsequent servers added to the farm need to be prepared in the same fashion as the first server. The primary installation difference is that you'll connect to an existing farm instead of creating a new farm. As you progress through the next few sections, make design notes on the nuances of each service and how those will affect your design.

A significant portion of data that is being served by SharePoint Server 2010 will be delivered from a SQL Server database. The recommended maximum ratio of Web servers per SQL Server cluster is 8:1. Although you can scale out beyond this point, doing so is not recommended. However, you are not limited to eight WFE servers in a farm because you can have multiple SQL Server installations, each with a set of eight WFE servers. When you require throughput greater than is possible with eight WFE servers, you can add more SQL Server clusters as required. But don't forget: only one SQL Server cluster can host your configuration database. The SQL Server cluster that hosts the configuration database should be monitored constantly for failure.

To add more SQL Server clusters to your server farm, simply select a different SQL Server when creating a new content database. However, include a second SQL Server cluster only when absolutely necessary. Having more than one SQL Server cluster creates complexity in your server farm performance, disaster recovery plan, and troubleshooting efforts.

When creating a Web application, you are actually creating an entry in the configuration database with Internet Information Services (IIS) information, a corresponding IIS Web site, and a content database that will host the site collections within that Web application. However, assigned IP addresses, Secure Sockets Layer (SSL) certificates, and multiple host header entries are not created in the configuration database. In fact, you cannot add multiple host headers from Central Administration.

Adding a Web Server to the Farm

To scale out from a single Web server that already hosts Web applications, you need to install SharePoint Server 2010 on another server in the same Active Directory domain. Preferably, you should scale to a server that is on the same IP subnet and that does not host any other applications. It is also preferable to have the hardware identically configured. To add another WFE server, you must do the following:

1. Install SharePoint Server 2010 using the installation binaries.

2. Run the SharePoint 2010 Products Configuration Wizard to guide you through the process of provisioning additional servers in the farm. If the SharePoint 2010 Products Configuration Wizard does not launch automatically, you can find it located at Start, All Programs, Microsoft SharePoint 2010 Products.

3. On the Welcome To SharePoint Products page, click Next.

4. A dialog box, shown in Figure 2-8, will appear stating that some services might need to be restarted during configuration. Click Yes to proceed.

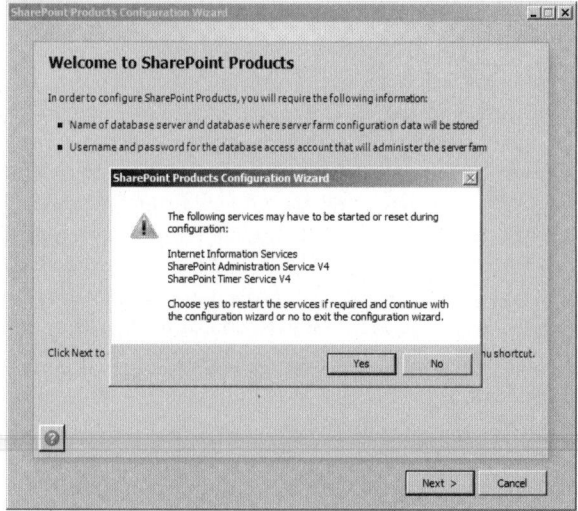

FIGURE 2-8 Click Yes to continue the configuration.

5. On the Connect To A Server Farm page, as seen in Figure 2-9, select Connect To An Existing Server Farm, and then click Next. Remember, a server farm is a configuration database. So connecting to an existing farm means connecting to an existing configuration database.

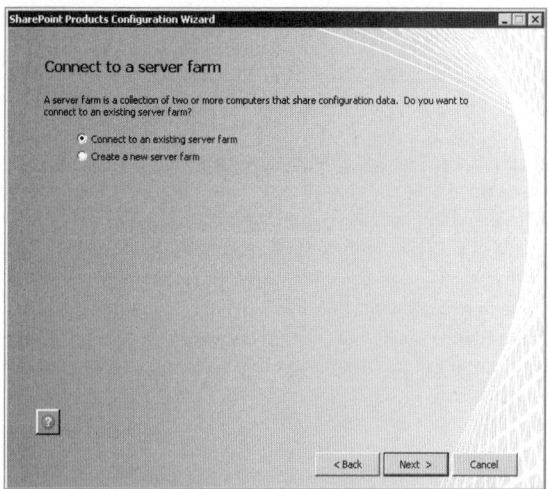

FIGURE 2-9 Select Connect an existing server farm and choose Next.

6. The Specify Configuration Database Settings page allows you to specify a configuration database. You should enter the following values:

   - In the Database Server box (shown in Figure 2-10), type the server name of the database server.

   - Click the Retrieve Database Names button to retrieve the name of the configuration databases hosted on the SQL Server instance. By default, the name of the configuration database will be SharePoint_Config.

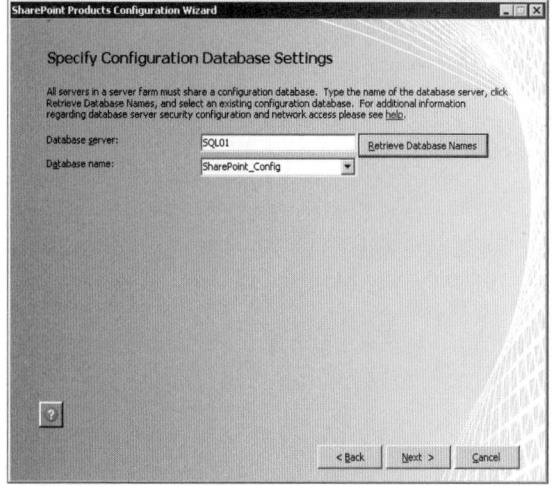

FIGURE 2-10 Verify all information and then click Next.

7. As can be seen in Figure 2-11, the next step is to enter a value in the farm Passphrase text box and click Next. If the passphrase is lost or misplaced, you can, as a last resort, use SharePoint 2010 Management Shell to reset the farm passphrase.

NOTE The Windows PowerShell Set-SPPassPhrase cmdlet sets the passphrase to a new Passphrase value. If the *LocalServerOnly* parameter is *not* used, the farm encryption key is re-encrypted with the new value and attempts to propagate this value to all other servers in the farm. If the *LocalServerOnly* parameter is used, this is updated on the local machine only, and the farm encryption key is not changed. The Passphrase value must be the same on all servers in the farm if the farm is to function correctly. So if the passphrase fails to propagate to all servers, the *LocalServerOnly* parameter can be used to set the remaining servers to the new Passphrase value manually.

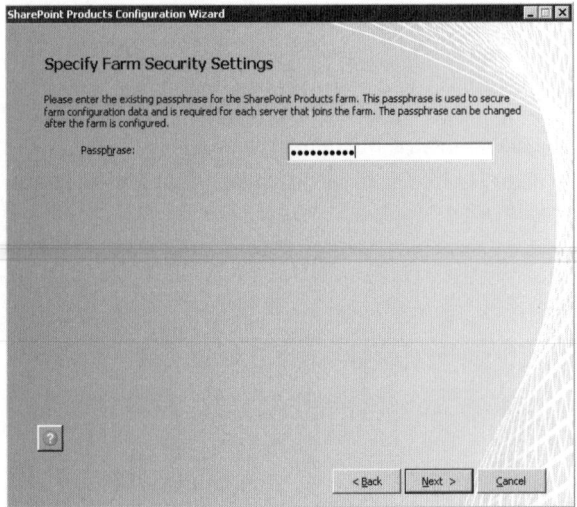

FIGURE 2-11 Enter text in the Passphrase text box, and click Next.

8. The Completing The SharePoint Products Configuration Wizard page, shown in Figure 2-12, allows you to verify the configuration settings that will be applied before you click Next.

   - Confirm the settings are correct, as seen in Figure 2-12.
   - Click Next.

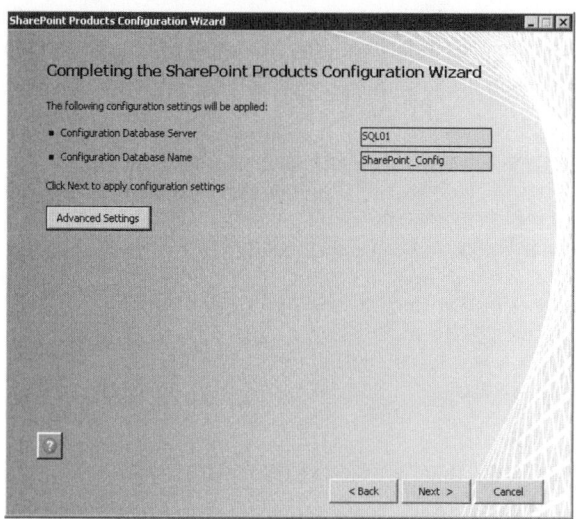

FIGURE 2-12 Confirm the configuration is correct, and click Next.

9. Optionally, on the Completing The SharePoint Products Configuration Wizard page, click the Advanced Settings button to specify whether or not Central Administration will be run from this host, as seen in Figure 2-13.

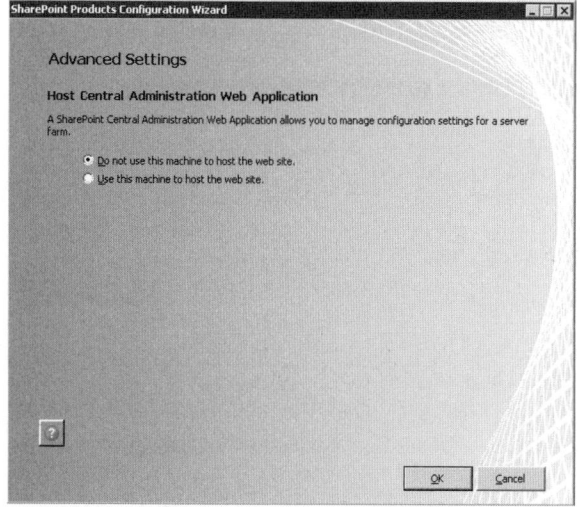

FIGURE 2-13 Select Do Not Use This Machine To Host The Web Site.

10. The SharePoint Products Configuration Wizard will proceed with configuring SharePoint according to the specifications found in the Configuration database, providing feedback during each step of the process as seen in Figure 2-14.

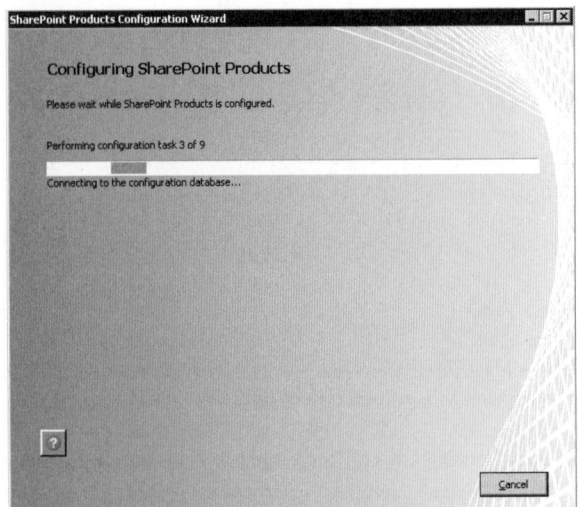

FIGURE 2-14 Configuring SharePoint Products.

11. On the Configuration Successful page (shown in Figure 2-15), click Finish.

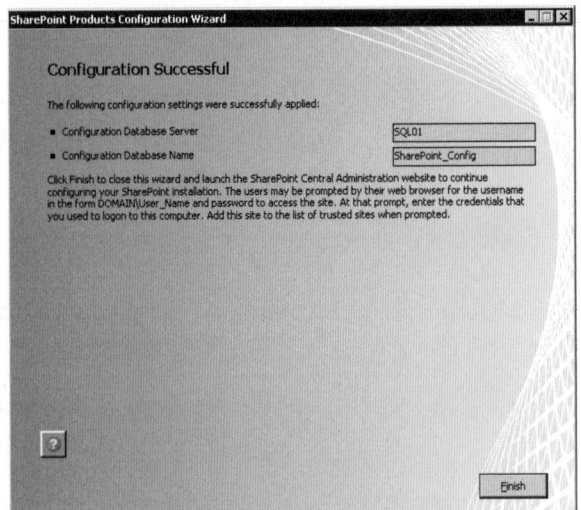

FIGURE 2-15 Update all documentation after a successful configuration.

If the configuration fails, you can check the PSCDiagnostics files located in the %CommonProgramFiles%\Microsoft Shared\Web Server Extensions\14\Logs folder. If the configuration is successful, Internet Explorer will be launched and the Central Administration Web site is opened. If you are prompted for credentials, you should add the Central Administration URL to your Local Intranet Zone, or alternately your Trusted Sites list, and ensure that Internet Explorer is configured to automatically pass user credentials to sites in that list.

TIP If you see a proxy server error message, you need to make sure to configure your browser to bypass the proxy server for local addresses. In Internet Explorer, this setting can be configured in the Tools, Internet Options dialog box, on the Connections tab. Click LAN Settings to access the proxy server configuration settings.

After adding a server to a farm, you'll notice in IIS Manager that all SharePoint-related IIS Web sites are created or are in the process of being created. If all Web applications in this server farm are not immediately present, wait until they have been created before continuing. If you are using host headers, your Web applications are created automatically and can be used independently or added to a load-balancing solution. Remember, until you have made a DNS entry for your new server or added it to a load-balanced solution, the new server will not be used for Web applications. If you did not select a public URL during the initial Web application creation, you must also create an alternate access mapping for your newly created load-balanced URL. If the public URL will not change, you do not need to do the following.

To ready the WFE servers for load balancing, take the following steps:

1. Open Central Administration, System Settings, Configure Alternate Access Mappings in a browser.

2. Select Edit Public URLs.

3. In the Alternate Access Mapping Collection area (existing Web application), choose a collection to which you want to add a URL mapping or edit a URL mapping.

4. Enter the URL, protocol, host, and port for the default zone—for example, **http://portal.contoso.com:80**.

5. Click Save.

Keep in mind that, by default, every Web application exists on every server in the farm. If you want to serve Web applications on isolated hardware, simply exclude the specific Web application you do not want to serve from this server in DNS or load-balancing solutions. For example, if you have three Web applications in a farm named *http://portal, http://mysite* and *http://corporate,* but you want to serve the first two from an internal set of servers and the *http://corporate* site from dedicated, Internet-facing hardware, your solution might look like that shown in Figure 2-16.

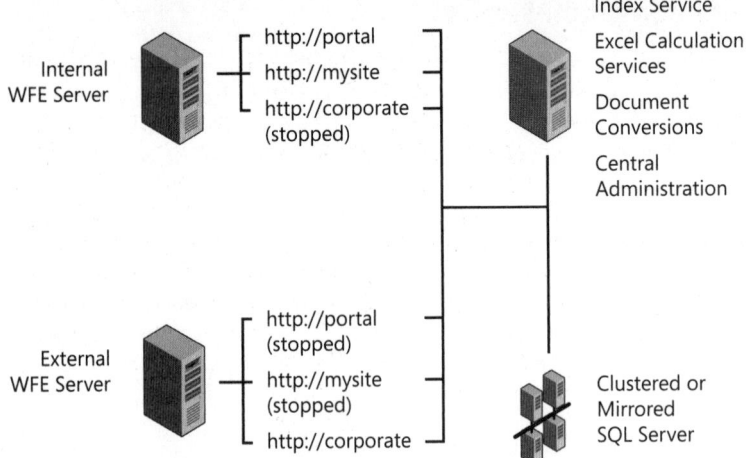

FIGURE 2-16 Simply stop the site in IIS Manager and do not include it in DNS or load-balancing solutions when you do not want to serve specific Web applications on a server.

In the previous example, you stop the unused Web applications in IIS Manager on servers, which reduces the amount of memory used on those servers in addition to verifying IP traffic flow. When using this topology, understand that if this server is restored or if you stop, start, or restart the Windows SharePoint Services Web application service from Central Administration, all servers in the farm will start all Web applications in IIS. This feature must be planned for in case there is a need to modify Web applications from Central Administration.

Web Parts and Custom Code

If you install additional applications, such as antivirus software or custom Web parts, be sure to install them on all the necessary servers in the farm. Forgetting to install a custom Web part on a Web server, for example, can result in an inconsistent user experience in which it works for users on one Web server, but not for the users on another. Here is a short list of items that are often forgotten when adding servers to a server farm:

- Custom features and solutions
- Custom Web parts
- Web.config modifications
- Language packs
- SharePoint-aware antivirus programs
- SSL certificates
- Client certificates for crawling certificate-based SSL content sources, which must exist on all WFE servers in the farm
- Third-party backup and restore software

Internet Information Services

As a general rule, it is best to perform any SharePoint-related IIS maintenance from the Central Administration console when possible. Changes that can be made from Central Administration persist throughout the farm because they are written to the configuration database and are present on all new or replaced servers in the farm. However, there are situations that require direct IIS management, such as installing SSL certificates or implementations requiring load balancing using assigned IP addresses to accomplish IP traffic management. Using assigned IP addresses makes it easier to use hardware load balancing and to use dedicated NICs for Web applications. For example, if you have two Web applications in your Windows SharePoint Services farm, you can assign each Web application a different IP address, with each IP address assigned to a dedicated NIC. Figure 2-17 shows the logical flow of such a setup.

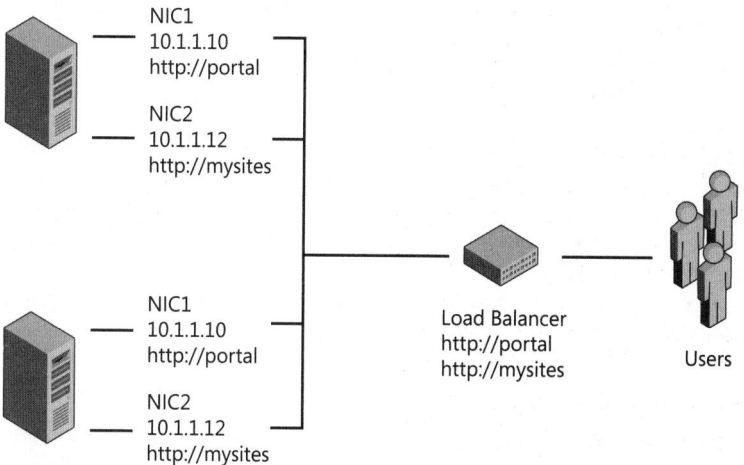

FIGURE 2-17 Assign an IP address to each NIC and the corresponding IP to each Web application in IIS Manager.

Scaling System Services and Service Applications

With the introduction of SharePoint Server 2010, farm architecture is no longer limited by the Shared Services Provider (SSP) architecture. The various components making up the services infrastructure have been moved into SharePoint Foundation 2010 and now include better control over server resources, as seen in Figure 2-18. These components can be configured independently, providing a higher degree of flexibility and more effective management and centralization of services such as Search, My Sites, and Taxonomy.

These service applications can be managed through Central Administration, and they can also be managed and scripted through Windows PowerShell. The new services architecture is extensible, such that third-party companies can build services that can be added to the platform.

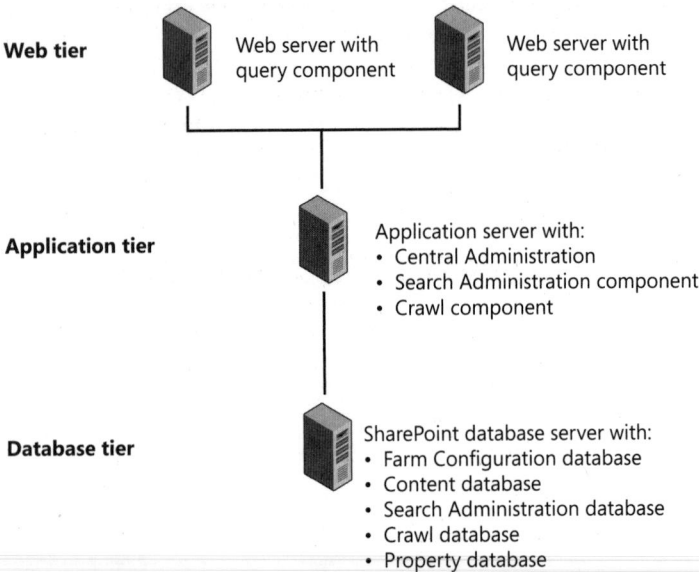

Web tier — Web server with query component; Web server with query component

Application tier — Application server with:
- Central Administration
- Search Administration component
- Crawl component

Database tier — SharePoint database server with:
- Farm Configuration database
- Content database
- Search Administration database
- Crawl database
- Property database

FIGURE 2-18 Server tiers.

Service Application Architecture

Service applications are roughly the equivalent of shared services in SharePoint Server 2007. The primary difference is that each shared service is now a standalone application, called a *service application*. No longer do you need a provider to manage a group of services. Although this is a welcome change for many administrators, it can introduce additional complexity to your design. A basic understanding of how service applications scale is mandatory before you install a multiserver farm.

At the server level, you have SharePoint Foundation 2010 system services. These services are called *system services* and *service application service instances*. Both are accurate, depending on the context in which they are used. Some system services,

such as the Microsoft SharePoint Foundation Sandboxed Code service, are not associated with a service application. Therefore, wherever you have enabled this service
is the only server where processing will occur. To configure system services, you can
browse to Central Administration, System Settings, Manage Services On Server.

NOTE In your server farm documentation, be sure to note the services that are a
service application *instance* and those that are not.

When a Web application is first created, the groupings of service applications
are specified. By default, all service applications are associated with the Web
application. You can modify the service applications that correspond with
a particular Web application at a later time. Figure 2-19 depicts the service
applications that are associated with the default group.

FIGURE 2-19 Default service applications.

Figure 2-20 shows how services on the server interact with service applications.

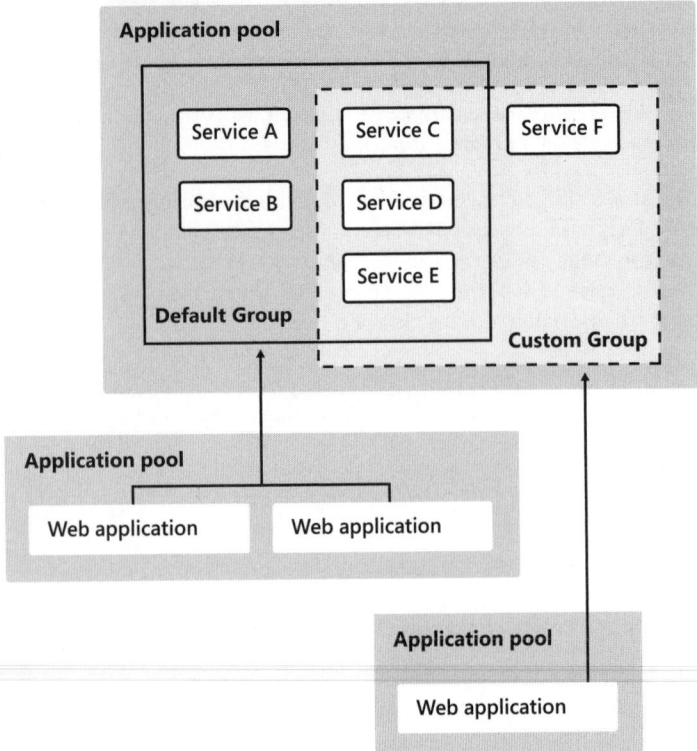

IIS Web site: SharePoint Web Services

FIGURE 2-20 System services can be service application instances.

In Figure 2-20, you can see that a system service can be directly consumed by a Web application, as is the case with the Microsoft SharePoint Foundation Sandboxed Code service. However, system services are often an instance of a service application, as is the case with the User Profile service. The User Profile service is associated with the User Profile service application. The User Profile service application is associated with Web applications.

Additionally, a service application can be published, making it available across multiple server farms. However, as seen in Figure 2-21, this capability does not apply to all service applications.

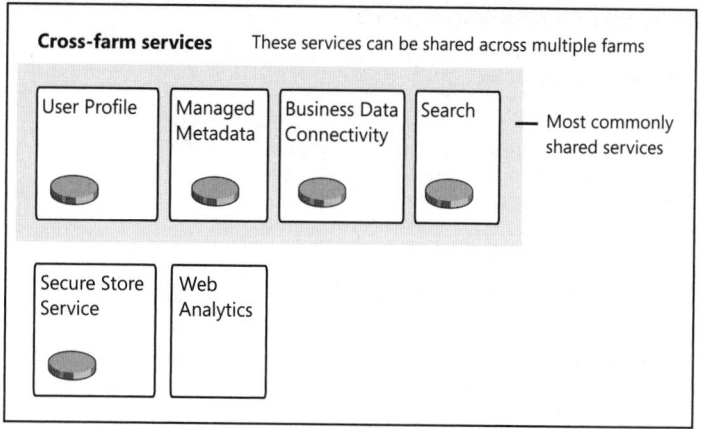

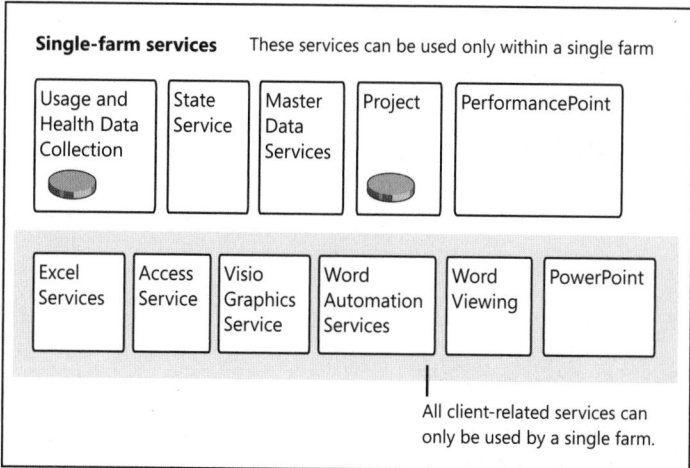

FIGURE 2-21 System services that can be shared and those that cannot.

Some service applications, such as Office Web components and PerformancePoint, can be consumed only within a single server farm. Chapter 6, "Configuring Service Applications," provides detailed information on creating and federating service applications.

Table 2-1 lists some of the services that appear on the Services On Server page in Central Administration. The chart is designed to provide additional topology guidance and recommendations for the placement of services as applicable.

TABLE 2-1 Services on Server

SERVICE	IS THIS SERVICE ASSOCIATED WITH A SERVICE APPLICATION?	SERVER RECOMMENDATION	ADDITIONAL INFORMATION
Access Database Services	Yes	Application server	
Application Registry Service	No	Application server	Backward-compatibility version of the Business Data Catalog service.
Business Data Connectivity	Yes	Application server	
Central Administration	No	Application server	This service runs the Central Administration site.
Document Conversions Launcher Service	No	Application server	Schedules and initiates the document conversions on a server.
Document Conversions Load Balancer Service	No	Application server	Balances document conversion requests from across the server farm. Each Web application can have only one load balancer registered with it at a time.
Excel Calculation Services	Yes	Application server	
Lotus Notes Connector	Yes (Search)	Application server; start this service on the index server	This service is required to crawl content from Lotus Notes Domino servers.

SERVICE	IS THIS SERVICE ASSOCIATED WITH A SERVICE APPLICATION?	SERVER RECOMMENDATION	ADDITIONAL INFORMATION
Managed Metadata Web Service	Yes	Application server	
Microsoft SharePoint Foundation Incoming E-mail	No	Web server or application erver	Typically, this service runs on a Web server. If you need to isolate this service, you can start it on an application server.
Microsoft SharePoint Foundation Subscription Settings Service	Yes Note: This service application is deployed only by using Windows PowerShell.	Web server or application server; in hosting environments, this service is typically started on one or more application servers.	Start this service if you have deployed service applications in multitenant mode or if the farm includes sites using site subscriptions. This service stores settings and configuration data for tenants in a multitenant environment. After it is started, Web applications consume this service automatically.
Microsoft SharePoint Foundation User Code Service	No	Web server or application server; Start this service on computers in the farm that run sandboxed code. This can include Web servers and application servers.	This service runs code deployed as part of a sandboxed solution in a remote, rights-restricted process, and it measures the server resources used during execution against a site collection-scoped, daily quota.

SERVICE	IS THIS SERVICE ASSOCIATED WITH A SERVICE APPLICATION?	SERVER RECOMMENDATION	ADDITIONAL INFORMATION
Microsoft SharePoint Foundation Web Application	No	Web server; ensure that this service is started on all Web servers in a farm. Stop this service on application servers.	This service provides Web server functionality. It is started by default on Web servers.
Microsoft SharePoint Foundation Workflow Timer Service	No	Web server	This service is automatically configured to run on all Web servers in a farm.
PerformancePoint Service	Yes	Application server	
Search Query and Site Settings Service	Yes (Search)	Application server; start this service on all query servers in a farm. However, if it becomes memory intensive, consider moving this service to a dedicated computer to free up memory for query processing.	Load balances queries across query servers. Also detects farm-level changes to the search service and puts these in the Search Admin database.
Secure Store Service	Yes	Application server	
SharePoint Foundation Search	No	In a SharePoint Foundation farm, start this service on the search server. In a SharePoint Server farm, this service is needed only to search online Help. Start the service on any server in the farm.	This service provides search functionality in a SharePoint Foundation farm. For SharePoint Server farms, this service is used only to search online Help. Start this service only on one computer.

SERVICE	IS THIS SERVICE ASSOCIATED WITH A SERVICE APPLICATION?	SERVER RECOMMENDATION	ADDITIONAL INFORMATION
SharePoint Server Search	Yes (Search)	Automatically configured to run on the appropriate computers.	This service cannot be stopped or started from the Services On Server page.
User Profile Service	Yes	Application server	
User Profile Synchronization Service	Yes	Application server	
Visio Graphics Service	Yes	Application server	
Web Analytics Data Processing Service	Yes (Web Analytics)	Application server	
Web Analytics Web Service	Yes (Web Analytics)	Application server	
Word Automation Services	Yes	Application server	Performs automated bulk document conversions. When actively converting, this service will fully utilize one CPU for each worker process (configured in Central Administration). If the service is started on multiple servers, a job will be shared across all the servers.

NOTE The Search Service application components are deployed to servers by using the Search Administration page, not the Services On Server page. Topology changes to search can take several minutes to commit and affect server farm performance during the change. It is best to make all topology changes during maintenance windows.

Scaling SharePoint Server 2010 Search

The most common service application that needs to be distributed is the Search Service application. Although it is similar to the one in SharePoint Server 2007, you'll quickly notice that the index has been merged with the query role.

SEE ALSO For more information on how to configure specific roles in SharePoint Server 2010 Search, see Chapter 8, "Configuring the Search Service Application."

Index Partition and Query Component

An index partition represents a portion of the entire index, and therefore the index is the aggregation of all index partitions. Partitioning the index allows different portions of the index to be spread across multiple query servers. Administrators decide on the number and configuration of each of the partitions. At least one server in a farm must host the query role, and more query servers can be added to increase performance.

Two or more query servers provide redundancy based on the configuration of index partitions. For example, a farm with three query servers can be configured so that each query server has an index partition that represents one-third of the index. Redundancy for the query servers can be achieved by creating a second instance of each index partition on another query server. Deploying index partitions across query servers can help balance the query-processing load, provide redundancy, and increase query performance.

Adding or Moving the Query Component to a Web Server

Note that certain items, such as the Search Administration component, cannot be moved to another server after it has been configured. To move the query component, you must do the following:

1. Browse to Central Administration, Application Management, Manage Service Applications.
2. Click Search Service Application, as seen in Figure 2-22.

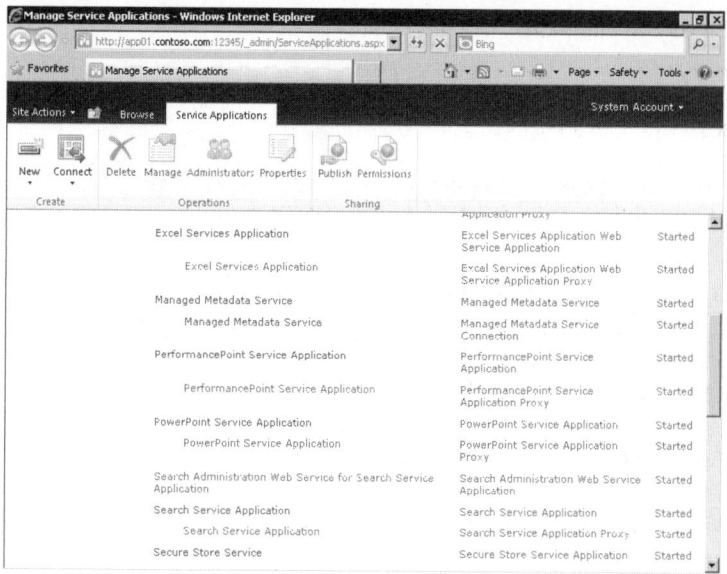

FIGURE 2-22 Click Search Service Application.

3. On the Search Administration page, click the Modify button in the Search Application Topology Web part, as seen in Figure 2-23.

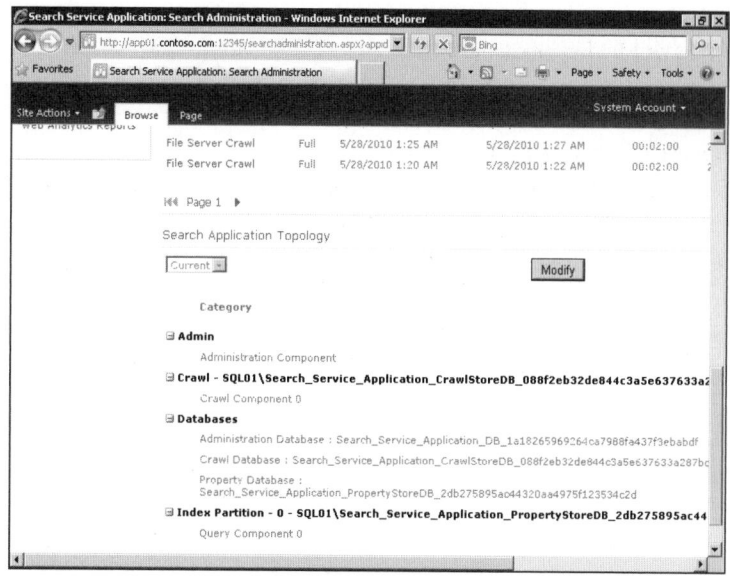

FIGURE 2-23 Click Modify in the Search Application Topology section.

4. Point to the query component you want to change, and select Edit Properties from the drop-down menu, as seen in Figure 2-24.

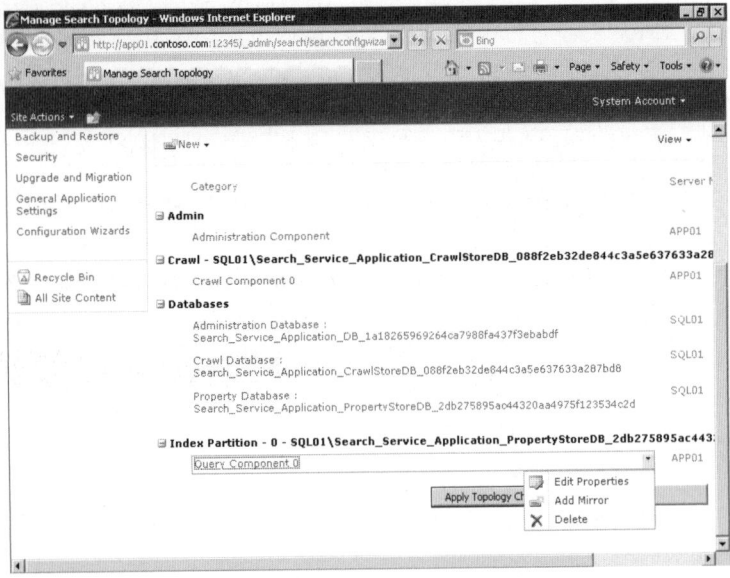

FIGURE 2-24 Click Query Component 0, and then click Edit Properties.

5. As seen in Figure 2-25, on the Edit Query Component page, select a front-end Web server from the Server drop-down list, and then click OK.

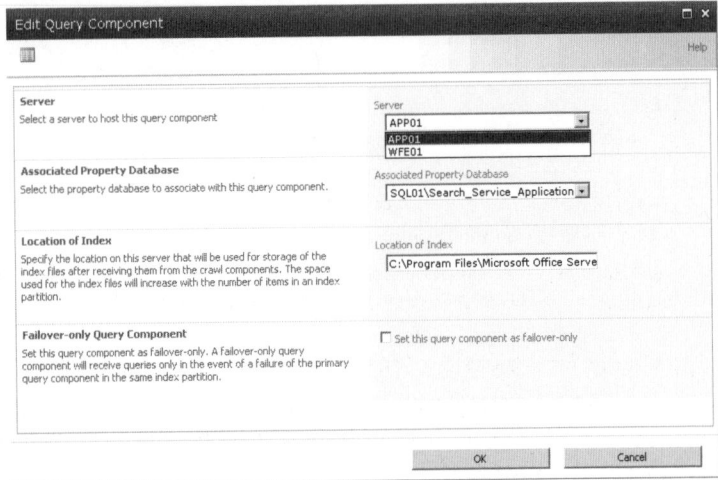

FIGURE 2-25 Select the server that will host the query component.

6. Click the Apply Topology Changes button, and SharePoint will begin the process of moving the query role.

After the operation is completed, a message will be displayed stating that the configuration changes have been applied successfully. If you receive an error, check the diagnostic log files. To add a query component mirror, which is a replica of the index partition, do the following:

1. On the Search Administration page, click the Modify button in the Search Application Topology Web part.

2. Select the query component to modify, and then choose Add Mirror from the drop-down menu, as seen in Figure 2-26.

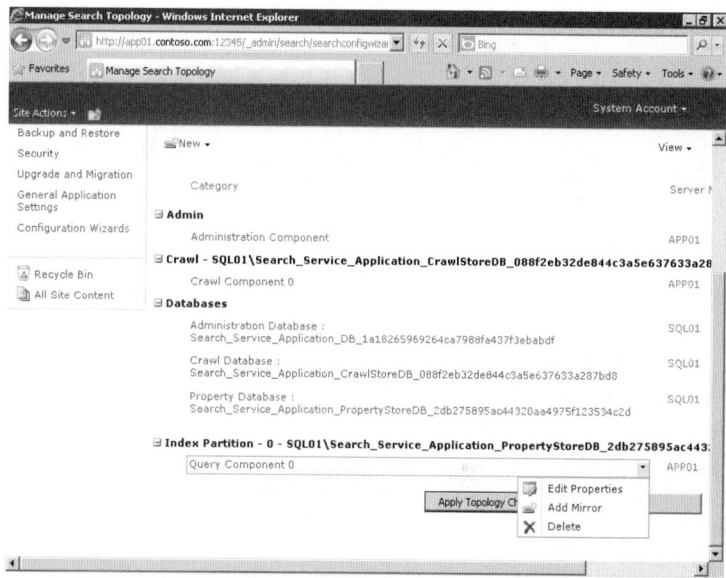

FIGURE 2-26 Click Add Mirror.

3. Select the server that will host the mirror.
4. Optionally, change the location of the Index.
5. Optionally, set the component as failover-only. If this option is selected, the partition is used only if the primary query component fails.

Decision Points for Scaling Out Search

Many times an administrator is tasked with improving different aspects of the overall search process. One of the goals of search in SharePoint 2010 is to return queries at sub-second latency even in environments with 100 million documents. Microsoft has designed the search architecture in a modular fashion so that it can be transformed to accommodate performance, resilience, or both. The number of items will have an impact on farm sizing and growth. Table 2-2 depicts the numeric segmentation of items and the steps that are necessary to achieve the desired outcome.

TABLE 2-2 Scaling Search

NUMBER OF ITEMS	ACTION
0–1 million	All search roles can coexist on one or two servers.
1–10 million	Move the crawl server role to another server while the query server role remains on the Web servers.
10–20 million	Add a crawl server. Each crawl server has one crawler. Create another index partition with query components, and distribute these across query servers.
20–40 million	Add query servers and index partitions, with distributed query components. Add another crawl database associated with a new crawler on each crawl server. Also, add another property database to the second database server, and mirror both property databases.
40–100 million	Isolate each topology layer into *server groups*, in which each role is deployed to its own servers. Each server group can then be scaled out to meet specific requirements for the components in that role.

Performance Metrics

Similarly, to improve the SharePoint 2010 Search experience, various factors have an impact on performance metrics. Table 2-3 details the key performance characteristics and how to decide when scaling of specific search components is appropriate.

TABLE 2-3 Performance Metrics

TO IMPROVE THIS...	DO THE FOLLOWING
Crawl times and index freshness	If the server performing the indexer function is constrained, add more indexers, crawl components, or both.

Because the crawl database can contain content from various sources, add more crawl databases on the same server to distribute the load.

If there are several content sources, multiple crawlers and associated crawl databases will allow the content to be crawled concurrently. |

TO IMPROVE THIS...	DO THE FOLLOWING
Query responsiveness and results	An effective way to reduce query response time is to add query servers and index partitions. It is recommended that index partitions contain about 10 million items. Guidelines for improving performance include adding query components with mirrored index partitions when query throughput is low. Add more SQL Server instances with additional crawl databases when the SQL Server instance is memory or CPU constrained.
Query availability	Deploy redundant query servers and multiple query components for each index partition, and use clustered or mirrored database servers to host crawl and property databases.
Availability of content crawling and indexing functionality	For the purposes of availability and general load distribution, make use of multiple crawlers on redundant crawl server. Add crawl databases as necessary.

Redundancy and Availability

Within the components of search, a number of factors provide improved performance and add fault tolerance. By monitoring the various search functions, administrators can systematically adjust certain components to achieve the desired results. Table 2-4 details which search components are redundant and how the redundancy or failover mechanism works.

TABLE 2-4 Search Service Component Distribution for Redundancy and Availability

COMPONENT	CAN BE DEPLOYED TO MULTIPLE SERVERS?	HOW REDUNDANCY OR FAILOVER WORKS
Index partition	Yes	An index partition can hold up to 10 million items and represents a subset of the corpus (the collection of documents). Using a query partition can be an effective way to mirror each index partition. A general guideline is to add a query server for each index partition that is added.

COMPONENT	CAN BE DEPLOYED TO MULTIPLE SERVERS?	HOW REDUNDANCY OR FAILOVER WORKS
Query components	Yes	Generally speaking, adding a mirrored copy of the query component and deploying it to another server should satisfy performance and redundancy requirements.
Search Administration component	No	There is only one Search Administration component required in a farm.
Crawler	Yes	Crawlers are limited to the resources that are available on any given crawl server. It is recommended that each crawler be associated with a specific crawl database.
Property database	Yes	Metadata for all crawled content is stored in the property database. Consider adding another property database when the content grows in excess of 25 million items. To provide redundancy, databases can be mirrored or a clustered SQL Server solution can be implemented.
Crawl database	Yes	For optimal performance, it is recommended that the crawl database content be stored on different physical hard disk spindles than the property database. An effective way to mitigate I/O contention is to deploy a crawl database to a separate database server. To provide redundancy, databases can be mirrored or a clustered SQL Server solution can be implemented.
Search administration database	No	Search administration resides in only one database per search service application. The only way to add redundancy is through a mirrored or clustered SQL Server implementation.

CHAPTER 3

Configuring Core Operations

■ Introducing Central Administration   **81**

■ System Settings   **86**

■ Database Management   **97**

■ Configuring Send To Connections   **105**

*C*ore operations refers to farm-level settings and applications such as Central Administration, server services settings, and e-mail configuration. There are items—such as Service Applications, Search, and Web Applications—that are such large and important topics that they have dedicated chapters. This chapter will cover the core farm operations not covered elsewhere in the book. Much of this chapter will show you how to set up farm operations that are configured only once, such as Short Messaging Service (SMS) mobile services. Although the interaction with other Microsoft SharePoint Server functional areas will be discussed, please reference the chapter for each of those functional areas for detailed information.

Introducing Central Administration

At the heart of every server farm is the configuration database. This database stores the majority of your core server farm configuration. The association of Service Applications, configuration of Web Applications and content databases, e-mail settings, server services architecture, farm solutions, and farm features are stored in this database. To manage all of this configuration data, you need a tool to do so. Central Administration is the primary administrative tool available to you. The Central Administration interface can be started by clicking Start, All Programs, Microsoft SharePoint Server 2010 Products, SharePoint Server 2010 Central Administration. Figure 3-1 shows Central Administration as installed out of the box.

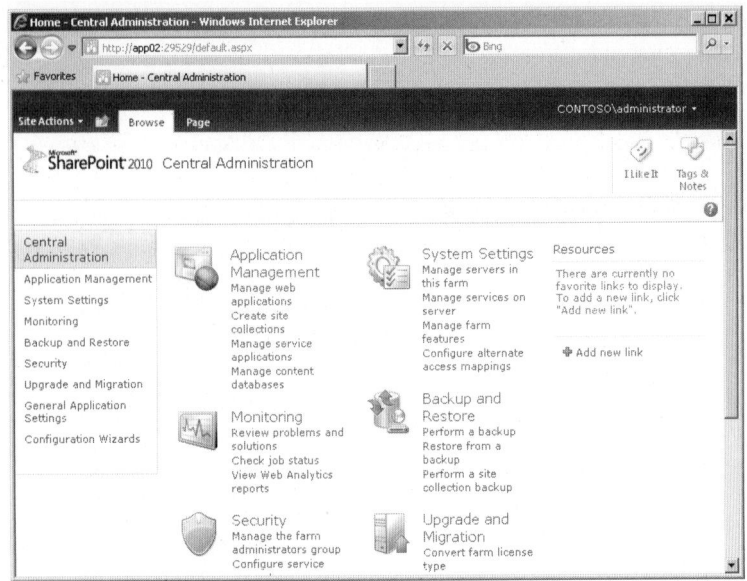

FIGURE 3-1 Central Administration is the primary administrative interface for SharePoint Server 2010.

As you can read in the Appendix, Microsoft Windows PowerShell can also be used to manage your farm configuration in addition to Central Administration. The Windows PowerShell console can be started by clicking Start, All Programs, Microsoft SharePoint Server 2010 Products, SharePoint Server 2010 Management Shell. Additionally, *stsadm.exe* is an administrative tool that can be used for basic farm administration tasks. Note that *stsadm.exe* is slated for removal in the next version of SharePoint Server. Therefore, it is wise to begin transitioning from *stsadm.exe* to Windows PowerShell.

> **TIP** You can find stsadm.exe in C:\Program Files\Common Files\Microsoft Shared\
> Web Server Extensions\14\bin. You can either include this directory in your system
> path or create a shell script to navigate to the directory to make it easier to execute.
> It can also be executed from the SharePoint Server Management Shell.

Central Administration Architecture

It's important to understand that Central Administration is a site collection contained in a dedicated Web application. As such, it has an associated content database for the Web application. If you use the SharePoint 2010 Products Configuration Wizard, the content database will be named *SharePoint_AdminContent_<GUID>*, as can be seen in Figure 3-2. Note that this database is not easily changed after the fact. Therefore, if you want a different name for your Central Administration content database, you need to use Windows PowerShell to create your server farm.

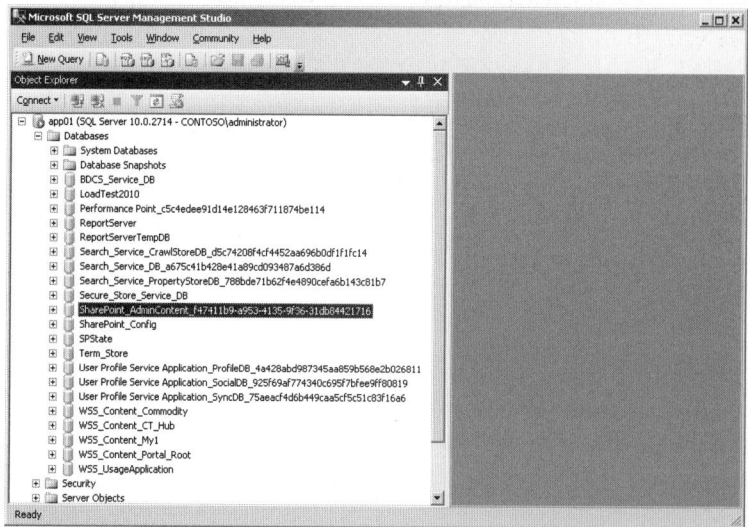

FIGURE 3-2 You can view your Central Administration content database using Microsoft SQL Server Management Studio.

Because Central Administration requires write access to your server farm configuration database, you should never use this Web application or associated application pool for collaborative Web applications. Doing so could provide a hacker with potential write access through another Web application. Central Administration was created automatically when you ran the SharePoint 2010 Products Configuration Wizard and should not be modified. Although Central Administration is technically just another site collection and can be modified as such, a best practice is to leave it in the default state. Only administrators access the site collection, so branding and customization shouldn't be an issue.

As seen in Figure 3-1, Central Administration has eight primary areas:

- **Application Management**   Hosts administrative links to Web applications, site collections, service applications, and databases. Chapter 4, "Building and Managing Web Applications," explains this section and associated tasks in depth.

- **System Settings**   Contains your server and server service management, e-mail and text messaging, and other farm management settings. Most of the functionality discussed in this chapter can be found in System Settings.

- **Monitoring** Has been greatly expanded in SharePoint Server 2010 and includes Reporting, Analytics, Timer Jobs, Health Analyzer, and Usage information. Chapter 16, "Monitoring, Logging, and Availability," covers Reporting and the Health Analyzer in detail. Only the server farm timer jobs are discussed in this chapter.

- **Backup And Restore** Location where both farm and granular backups and restores are performed. Chapter 18, "Backup and Restore," provides more information.

- **Security** Includes links to manage the farm administrators group, configure farm accounts, manage passwords for those accounts, define blocked file types, configure antivirus settings, manage Web Part security, and control Information Management Policies global settings. Chapter 15, "Configuring Policies and Security," instructs you how to align SharePoint Server 2010 security settings with your environment.

- **Upgrade And Migration** Upgrade-specific information can be found in Chapter 17, "Upgrading to SharePoint Server 2010."

- **General Application Settings** Includes external service connections, document conversions, InfoPath forms services, site directory, SharePoint Designer, farm-scoped search settings, and content deployment.

- **Configuration Wizards** Contains configuration wizards for your installation. Depending on additionally installed products, this screen can present multiple options for the automated configuration of your farm.

As you manage a SharePoint Server 2010 farm, there will be administrative tasks you perform on a regular basis. Remember that Central Administration is a Web-based interface, so you can create favorites in your Web browser to save time. Additionally, you will see multiple locations to manage the same item, such as Web application general settings, within Central Administration.

Working with the Central Administration Web Application

Although Central Administration is a SharePoint Server Web application, it differs from others because you don't create and deploy the Web application. Because the deployment of other Web applications is done *from* Central Administration, the provisioning of Central Administration itself is performed at either the command line or via the SharePoint 2010 Products Configuration Wizard. To deploy Central Administration to a server other than the one on which you first installed SharePoint Server, you must install the SharePoint Server binaries and run the SharePoint 2010 Products Configuration Wizard. You can run this wizard at any time by clicking Start, All Programs, Microsoft SharePoint Server 2010 Products, SharePoint Server 2010 Products Configuration Wizard. Be *very careful* not to disconnect from the server farm, which can be specified with the option shown in Figure 3-3.

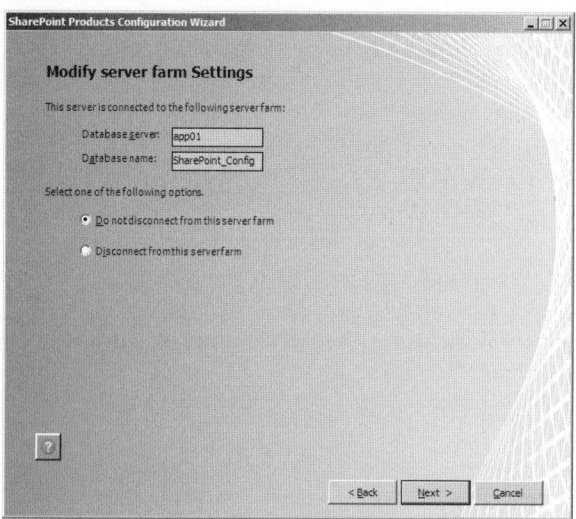

FIGURE 3-3 If provisioning Central Administration, be sure to *not* disconnect from the server farm.

After you click Next twice, select Advanced Settings to provision Central Administration. Select Use This Machine To Host The Web Site as seen in Figure 3-4.

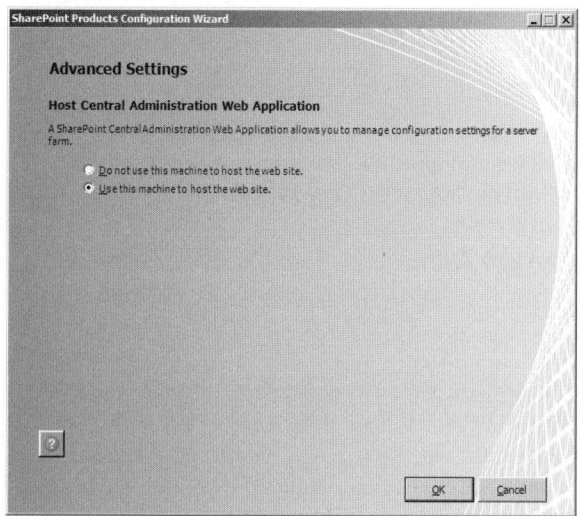

FIGURE 3-4 Select Use This Machine To Host The Web Site, and click OK.

You must wait for the farm timer job to complete and the Web application to provision before use. Upon completion, the wizard will take you to Central Administration.

You can also use the SharePoint 2010 Products Configuration Wizard to repair a broken Central Administration, assuming it is an Internet Information Services (IIS) configuration error causing the fault. To unprovision Central Administration, simply choose Yes, I Want To Remove The Web Site From This Machine. You should wait a few minutes to allow the farm configuration to update and also to allow time for the local IIS configuration to update. When the Web application is no longer visible from IIS, you can re-run the SharePoint 2010 Products Configuration Wizard to reprovision the Central Administration on that server.

> **NOTE** A Web application problem with Central Administration might require you to make a technical support call. The actual content of Central Administration is contained in the associated content database, and farm configuration is contained in the configuration database.

System Settings

The System Settings area of Central Administration contains crucial settings that you need to plan and carefully control modification of. Most of the system settings affect all Web applications and associated users in your server farm. System Settings is divided into three sections:

- Servers
- E-Mail And Text Messages (SMS)
- Farm Management

Servers

The Servers section of System Settings gives you, at a glance, visibility into your server farm topology, including your application services topology. It also provides the SharePoint Foundation 2010 configuration database version and SQL Server name. Much of the same information is contained in both the Manage Servers In This Farm and Manage Services On Server areas.

Servers In Farm

From the Manage Servers In This Farm link, you can see all the servers in your farm, as contained in the configuration database. You'll see five headings beneath the configuration database information:

- **Server** Lists all servers in your server farm. You can click on the Server text itself to sort the list alphabetically.
- **SharePoint Products Installed** Displays the relevant SKU information about that server.
- **Services Running** Is a valuable tool when discovering and troubleshooting a SharePoint Server server farm. You are able to quickly see where specific application services are provisioned. If you were troubleshooting the User

Profile Service as an example, you could find what server or servers were processing that data. You can then go to the relevant server and begin troubleshooting. Figure 3-5 shows an example of a multiserver farm and the Services Running column.

Farm Information

Configuration database version: 14.0.4536.1000
Configuration database server: app01
Configuration database name: SharePoint_Config

Server↑	SharePoint Products Installed	Services Running	Status	Remove Server
APP01		Microsoft SharePoint Foundation Database	No Action Required	Remove Server
APP02	Microsoft SharePoint Server 2010	Central Administration Managed Metadata Web Service Microsoft SharePoint Foundation Incoming E-Mail Microsoft SharePoint Foundation User Code Service Microsoft SharePoint Foundation Web Application Microsoft SharePoint Foundation Workflow Timer Service Search Query and Site Settings Service SharePoint Server Search User Profile Service Web Analytics Data Processing Service Web Analytics Web Service	No Action Required	Remove Server
FE01	Microsoft SharePoint Server 2010	Microsoft SharePoint Foundation Incoming E-Mail Microsoft SharePoint Foundation Web Application Microsoft SharePoint Foundation Workflow Timer Service	No Action Required	Remove Server
FE02	Microsoft SharePoint Server 2010	Microsoft SharePoint Foundation Incoming E-Mail Microsoft SharePoint Foundation Web Application Microsoft SharePoint Foundation Workflow Timer Service	No Action Required	Remove Server

FIGURE 3-5 Services on servers can be seen quickly from the Servers In Farm page.

NOTE Figure 3-5 shows the services provisioned on a server and not necessarily the current status. It's possible that a service is nonfunctional and still shows as running on this screen. It's also possible that a server is completely offline, because that status is not displayed.

- **Status** Displays whether a server action is required or is being performed. Examples of this are service packs, language packs, and platform additions such as Office Web Server.

- **Remove Server** Use this option if you want to remove a server's entry in the configuration database. Use this option with caution because it is irreversible. You should need to remove a server using Central Administration only if that server is no longer operational. The best way to remove a server from a farm is using the SharePoint 2010 Products Configuration Wizard on the server you want to remove, and then selecting to disconnect it from server farm.

Manage Services On Server

The Manage Services On Server page is used to stop and start farm server services. These services are not Windows Server services. Although turning one of these services on or off in the configuration database might result in a Windows Service being turned on or off, the consequences of mistakenly stopping a SharePoint service are much worse than stopping a Windows Server service. For example, turning off the SharePoint Server Search service will update the configuration database and remove all entries related to that search server. Therefore, all relevant search content, such as the index, will be deleted and the associated Windows Server service will be stopped. Basically, everything you start or stop in this screen is making configuration database changes. The timer job will subsequently pick up those changes from the database and modify application services accordingly.

The Manage Services On Server page also controls where processing of information is performed in your server farm. For example, you could have multiple servers in your farm performing the task of Managed Metadata Services, with each one processing a different Managed Metadata Services Term Store. This allows for scalability of processing. Each server in the farm can process different server farm services. To stop or start services, you can select the Start or Stop hyperlink. If configuration is required to start, you will be automatically taken to the configuration screen. Don't confuse these services with *service applications*. Although service applications might use a service on a server, service applications apply across a server farm and exist a level above services on the server. *Always* verify you are modifying the correct server, as shown in Figure 3-6.

FIGURE 3-6 Verify you are configuring the correct farm server before starting or stopping services.

E-mail and Text Messages

SharePoint Server 2010 provides many ways to communicate via e-mail and mobile text messaging. Pay close attention to the configuration of both incoming e-mail messages and text messages (SMS). There are possible cost and security issues associated with external, automated farm communications.

Outgoing E-mail Settings

Outgoing e-mail is primarily used for system alerts. Alerts allow users to be updated when an object changes, such as a list or document. Depending on the users' choice, they can be alerted immediately, daily, or weekly. Additionally, the system generates messages for workflows and other system content that leverages outgoing e-mail. To configure outgoing e-mail, you need to specify an outbound SMTP server, as seen in Figure 3-7.

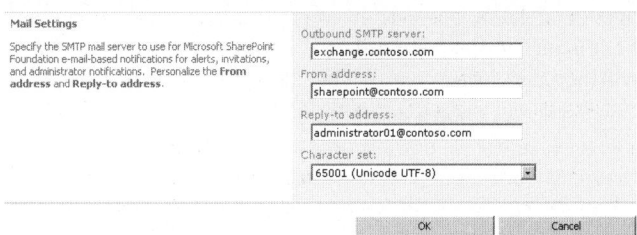

FIGURE 3-7 The From Address and Reply-to Address values can be different.

Although the From and Reply-to addresses can be different, they usually are not. Allowing a different From address might help you with current UCE (Unsolicited Commercial E-Mail) white lists, as an example. You can also change the character set if needed for a different language. Be sure both the SharePoint Foundation 2010 and SharePoint Server 2010 language packs are loaded for the selected language.

NOTE SharePoint Server 2010 cannot send credentials for outbound SMTP. Therefore, you must allow relaying on your SMTP server from SharePoint Server 2010 servers that will send mail. Always confirm that the required TCP ports and DNS entries are correct before troubleshooting a problem with SharePoint Server 2010 outgoing e-mail.

Incoming E-mail Settings

Configuring incoming e-mail is more complex than configuring outgoing e-mail and requires changes to both your Windows servers and Active Directory configuration. First, you must have an SMTP server loaded on the servers that will accept incoming e-mail. SharePoint Server 2010 does not include an SMTP service, but the default Windows Server SMTP server should work quite well. In Windows Server 2008, you add the SMTP server from Server Manager, Features.

You also need to configure Active Directory if you want to use the Directory Management Service. An Active Directory organizational unit (OU) should be created to store SharePoint Server 2010 contacts and distribution lists. The server farm account defined in the setup should be delegated the Create, Delete, And Manage User Accounts permission in this OU. To delegate permissions to the OU, do the following:

1. On your Active Directory controller, open Active Directory Users and Computers from Administrative Tools.

2. Right-click the Organizational Unit you want to integrate with SharePoint Server 2010; and choose Delegate Control.

3. Choose Next in the wizard, click Add, and select your SharePoint Server 2010 farm account. If you aren't sure what account this is, check the application pool identity for Central Administration.

4. Under Delegate The Following Common Tasks, select Create, Delete, And Manage User Accounts.

5. Click Next and then click Finish.

After you have created and delegated permissions in Active Directory, you can proceed with configuring Central Administration Incoming E-Mail settings. If you have enabled the Directory Management Service, distribution lists can be created automatically when enabled for SharePoint Server sites. Creating distribution lists automatically creates a distribution list in Active Directory and keeps it synchronized from SharePoint Server to Active Directory. Doing so allows users to easily send e-mail to SharePoint Server groups when needed.

NOTE The Directory Management Service is a one-way service. In other words, users are added to the Active Directory distribution list when they are added to a SharePoint group, but users are not added to the SharePoint group when they are added directly to the Active Directory distribution list.

An additional function of the Directory Management Service is that it automatically creates an Active Directory contact when e-mail–enabling a list or library. Although it is not required or always desired, you can have the e-mail address available in the Global Address List (GAL) after e-mail enabling a list. If you have not enabled the Directory Management Service, you must manually, or through a custom process, create an entry for each mail-enabled document library and list you want to receive e-mail.

To configure incoming e-mail, select Configure Incoming E-mail Settings in the System Settings area. You must then fill out the configuration page as follows:

1. Select Yes to enable sites on this server to receive e-mail.

2. Select Automatic unless you are using an SMTP server other than the native Windows Server SMTP Service. If you are using a third-party SMTP server, be sure to define the e-mail drop folder at the bottom of the page. Be aware that many third-party SMTP servers will not integrate with SharePoint Server 2010.

3. Select Yes to create a distribution group or contact, or select Use Remote if you already have an existing Directory Management Service. Note that if you do not have Microsoft Exchange Server installed in this Active Directory, you need to extend the schema with both the *ms-Exch-mail-Nickname* and *ms-Exch-RequireAuthToSendTo* attributes. You can add these by using the Exchange Server installation media. For more information on extending the Active Directory schema, please reference *http://technet.microsoft.com/exchange*. Note that you do not have to install Exchange Server binaries to enable Directory Management Services integration; you need only to extend the schema.

4. This step requires you to have previously configured the OU in Active Directory. In this example, we are using OU=SharePointDMS, DC=contoso,

DC=com. SharePointDMS is the OU in Active Directory. Figure 3-8 shows an example of the OU and SMTP server settings. Observe that you might not be able to view the entire container path and you might need to scroll to the right with the mouse.

Directory Management Service

The Microsoft SharePoint Directory Management Service connects SharePoint sites to your organization's user directory in order to provide enhanced e-mail features. This service provides support for the creation and management of e-mail distribution groups from SharePoint sites. This service also creates contacts in your organization's user directory allowing people to find e-mail enabled SharePoint lists in their address book.

To use the Directory Management Service you need to provide the SharePoint Central Administration application pool account with write access to the container you specify in the Active Directory. Alternatively you can configure this server farm to use a remote SharePoint Directory Management Web Service.

Use the SharePoint Directory Management Service to create distribution groups and contacts?

- No
- Yes
- Use remote

Active Directory container where new distribution groups and contacts will be created:

`OU=SharePointDMS, DC=contoso, DC=`

For example, OU=ContainerName, DC=domain, DC=com

SMTP mail server for incoming mail:

`app02.contoso.com`

For example, server.sharepoint.example.com

FIGURE 3-8 Carefully type the full path to the container specified for the Directory Management Service.

5. Next, type the name of the SMTP server where you will accept incoming e-mail. This server must be a member of the server farm. The Microsoft SharePoint Foundation Timer on this SMTP server will monitor the default e-mail drop folder. When it discovers an e-mail with a corresponding incoming e-mail address in SharePoint Server 2010, it will route the e-mail constrained by the list or library settings.

6. You must decide whether to accept messages from authenticated users or all users. If you decide to accept messages from authenticated users, a Send-to e-mail address must match that of a user with write access on the destination list or library.

7. Next, select whether or not to allow the creation of distribution lists. You can configure SharePoint Server 2010 to create contacts in Active Directory without creating distribution lists for synchronization with SharePoint Groups. If you decide to create distribution lists, you also need to decide what level of scrutiny the list names will have. You have four options when managing the creation and modification of distribution groups:

- Create New Distribution Group
- Change Distribution Group E-mail Address
- Change Distribution Group Title And Description
- Delete Distribution Group

Note that there is no approval option when creating contacts. Approval settings exist only for distribution groups.

TIP Consider carefully whether to select any of the change options, because selecting them causes any previous e-mail messages sent on the distributions list to bounce when replied to.

8. You can also define the incoming e-mail server display address. Figure 3-9 shows an example of setting the value. Be aware that only defining the display address will not route e-mail correctly. In this example, the server name is app02.contoso.com, but the display address is contoso.com. Care must be taken to correctly route the e-mail from the SMTP server servicing the contoso.com domain.

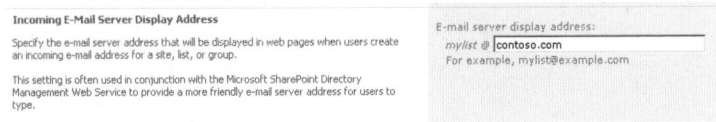

FIGURE 3-9 Verify you first have a routing rule on the SMTP server when configuring the incoming e-mail display address.

9. Ensure that DNS has the correct records for routing e-mail. SMTP and SharePoint Server 2010 both need to have the correct DNS configuration before incoming e-mail will function correctly.

10. If you will be accepting e-mail from external sources, it is wise to configure the Safe E-Mail Servers setting. This setting can force incoming e-mail to route through your safe mail servers that perform antivirus and antispam scanning. It can also reduce the surface area for Internet-based attacks. To specify a safe server, enter the IP address—for example, 10.1.1.200. Entering the fully qualified domain name (FQDN) of the mail server will not work.

11. Last, you can now enable lists and libraries for incoming e-mail. Figure 3-10 shows an example of configuring incoming e-mail for a document library contained in a team site collection. You can edit the library settings from *Document Library*, List Settings, Incoming E-Mail Settings.

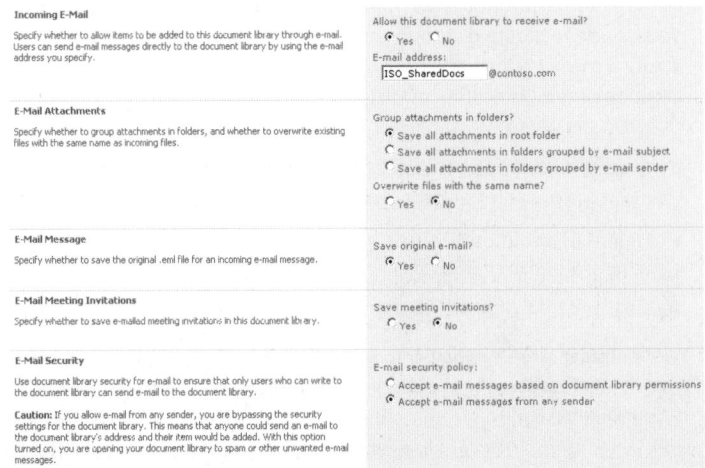

FIGURE 3-10 To enable a list or library for incoming e-mail, configure the Incoming E-Mail settings.

Mobile Account

The Mobile Alert feature allows users to subscribe to alerts with their mobile phones. The idea behind the functionality is many professionals prefer to get important alerts via mobile text (SMS) rather than via e-mail. Not all users have smart phones or smart phones that are compatible with their corporate e-mail system. Configuring mobile alerts allows notification to almost any cellular telephone. The feature does come with some drawbacks, however. First of all, you must have a subscription with a third-party SMS provider. The SMS provider acts as a "man in the middle" to relay mobile messages to cellular providers. This comes at a cost. Although the future of this space is widely unknown, current prices range from $.02 USD to $.06 USD. You can find a list of SharePoint Server 2010–compatible providers at *http://messaging.office.microsoft.com/HostingProviders.aspx?src=O14&lc=1033*. There is a constantly changing list, and your costs will vary based on your geographic location and volume of prepaid SMS alerts.

> **NOTE** There is no method to throttle alerts at the Web-application level. If you have a user who subscribes to hundreds of alerts or you have a system error, you could quickly increase the costs associated with your third-party provider. Most administrators will want to configure throttling with the third-party provider to mitigate these risks.

To configure the text message (SMS) service, do the following:

1. Subscribe to an online SMS provider, and note the URL and user name and password given by the provider.
2. Browse to Central Administration, System Settings, Configure Mobile Account.
3. Enter the URL provided by the SMS provider.
4. Enter the user name and password given to you by the SMS provider.
5. Test account settings.

Farm Timer Jobs

The Microsoft SharePoint Foundation Timer service runs on each server in the farm and is the master process for all timer jobs. It is not configurable—that is, it cannot be started and stopped from within Central Administration. It can, however, be restarted if you suspect a problem from Windows Server services from Start, All Programs, Administrative Tools, Services. It is listed as SharePoint 2010 Timer. You should not directly modify the logon account or other settings directly from Windows Server. You should restart only if necessary.

Timer jobs are created and deleted by SharePoint Server 2010 features or by developers via custom code. If your developers will deploy timer jobs to support custom code, be sure to test on an environment other than your production servers, and test for 24 hours or longer. Many timer jobs do not immediately display errors.

Only time will show if the custom timer job has a problem. Third-party products that create timer jobs should be tested to the same level as customer code. Be sure to test any custom timer jobs before a major service pack or SharePoint Server 2010 version change.

To see the currently defined timer jobs, browse to Central Administration, Monitoring, Review Timer Jobs, and look at the job definitions. When opening the Service Job Definitions page, you'll notice approximately 180 timer job definitions in a fully configured SharePoint Server 2010 server farm. This number will vary depending on the number of Web applications, configured service applications, and the configuration of core operations. Figure 3-11 shows a portion of the timer jobs in the Server Job Definitions page.

Immediate Alerts	Content Type Hub	Minutes
Immediate Alerts	Contoso Portal	Minutes
Immediate Alerts	My Site Provider	Minutes
Indexing Schedule Manager on APP02		Minutes
InfoPath Forms Services Maintenance		Daily
Information management policy	Content Type Hub	Weekly
Information management policy	Contoso Portal	Weekly
Information management policy	My Site Provider	Weekly
Licensing Synchronizer Job		Hourly
Microsoft SharePoint Foundation Diagnostics Service Configuration		One-time
Microsoft SharePoint Foundation Diagnostics Service Configuration		One-time
Microsoft SharePoint Foundation Diagnostics Service Configuration		One-time
Microsoft SharePoint Foundation Get Incoming E-Mail Configuration		One-time
Microsoft SharePoint Foundation Incoming E-Mail		Minutes
Microsoft SharePoint Foundation Site Inventory Usage Collection	Content Type Hub	Daily
Microsoft SharePoint Foundation Site Inventory Usage Collection	Contoso Portal	Daily
Microsoft SharePoint Foundation Site Inventory Usage Collection	My Site Provider	Daily

FIGURE 3-11 Every Web application you create will instantiate several timer jobs.

Some of these timer job definitions will be minutes, while others are hourly, daily, weekly, or monthly. New in this version of SharePoint Server is the ability to easily change the timer job's schedule from the user interface. Caution should be used when modifying the default schedule because it can affect server farm and application functionality. For the most part, you should leave the timer jobs in the default state. For some timer job definitions, such as the Content Type Hub and Content Type Subscriber, you will be very tempted to increase the frequency of the timer job. Although this action will make enterprise content types more available and give the subscribing site collections more frequent updates, it comes with a compromise in performance. Timer jobs take both processor power and memory, so you need to weigh the benefits with the performance penalty. Figure 3-12 shows an example of changing the Content Type Hub frequency. Also notice that you can always click Run Now. This option often negates the need for increasing the frequency of a timer job because you can force an update manually.

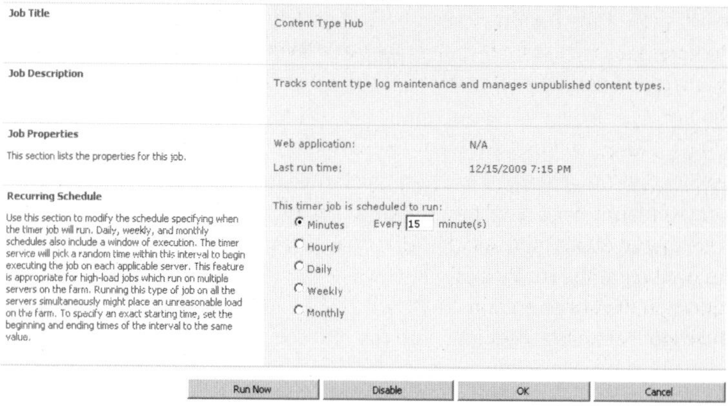

Job Title	
	Content Type Hub

Job Description	
	Tracks content type log maintenance and manages unpublished content types.

Job Properties		
This section lists the properties for this job.	Web application:	N/A
	Last run time:	12/15/2009 7:15 PM

Recurring Schedule	
Use this section to modify the schedule specifying when the timer job will run. Daily, weekly, and monthly schedules also include a window of execution. The timer service will pick a random time within this interval to begin executing the job on each applicable server. This feature is appropriate for high-load jobs which run on multiple servers on the farm. Running this type of job on all the servers simultaneously might place an unreasonable load on the farm. To specify an exact starting time, set the beginning and ending times of the interval to the same value.	This timer job is scheduled to run: ● Minutes Every 15 minute(s) ○ Hourly ○ Daily ○ Weekly ○ Monthly

[Run Now]   [Disable]   [OK]   [Cancel]

FIGURE 3-12 Click Run Now to manually start a timer job.

> **BEST PRACTICE**   Be careful when creating multiple Web applications. Although it is often necessary to create multiple Web applications for requirements such as My Sites and the Content Type Hub, keeping your Web applications to a minimum will increase system performance. Every Web application you create will automatically gener-ate many timer jobs that consume system resources. So in addition to the memory space used by the application pool and associated management overhead, you now also have more timer jobs and potential issues with the SharePoint Foundation Timer service.

Although timer jobs run on every server in the farm by default, you can select a preferred server to execute timer jobs on per-content-database basis. Workflows were one of the driving factors to include this functionality. Using this example of workflows will help you understand why server timer job affinity is important.

SharePoint Server 2010 executes workflow actions on the Web server that the client was connected to when started. If this workflow must wait to con-tinue because of a scheduled time delay or inaction by the user, the SharePoint 2010 Timer service will handle the workflow execution. In a multiple Web server configuration, you can set the preferred server for executing the workflow via the content database that hosts the site collection in question. To set the preferred server for timer jobs, do the following:

1. Browse to Central Administration, Application Management, Databases, Manage Content Databases.

2. Select the database you want to modify.

3. Select the physical server you want to associate as the preferred server. See Figure 3-13 for an example of setting affinity.

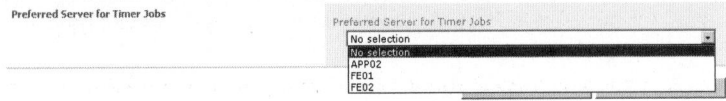

Preferred Server for Timer Jobs

FIGURE 3-13 You can select any server farm member to be the preferred server for a content database.

NOTE If the preferred server is unavailable, another will be selected automatically until the preferred server is back online.

In addition to managing timer jobs, you can also check the job status from Central Administration, Monitoring, Timer Jobs, Check Job Status. (See Figure 3-14.)

FIGURE 3-14 The Timer Job Status page.

The Timer Job Status page allows you to view the status of scheduled jobs, see running jobs, and view timer job history. You'll find this page useful when trouble-shooting problems within your farm. Hung processes, such as workflows or backup and restore, can be deleted to allow for future instances. It is recommended that you not delete timer jobs when you are not sure of the consequences of that action. The product team has removed the option for you to delete platform-level jobs that would have dire consequences. Instead, they have replaced the delete option with a disable option. Always document your action for future reference if you delete or disable a timer job.

Farm Management

The Farm Management area, located under System Settings, is essentially a bucket for items that are associated with the configuration database or didn't fit neatly elsewhere. The Farm Management functional areas are as follows:

- **Alternate Access Mappings** Details about this configuration option can be found in Chapter 4.
- **Manage Farm Features, Manage Farm Solutions, and Manage User Solutions** Details on these options are presented in Chapter 7, "Web Parts, Features, and Solutions."

- **Configure Cross-Firewall Access Zone**   This option is discussed in Chapter 15.
- **Configure Privacy Options**   This configuration option allows you to decide whether your server farm will automatically connect to Microsoft for the Customer Experience Improvement Program (CEIP), error reporting, and external Web-based help. Be careful when turning these on if you are in a secure environment. Many times, servers in a secure environment will not have outbound HTTP enabled. If that is the case, Web-based help will not function.

Database Management

The bulk of SharePoint Server 2010 content is almost entirely contained in SQL Server. As such, a properly designed and managed SQL Server infrastructure is critical to a well-running SharePoint Server environment. Because SQL Server has many books dedicated to the product, you'll be introduced only to the topics every SharePoint Server administrator should know in this section. Database management is contained in the Application Management section of Central Administration. The majority of Application Management deals with Web applications, service applications, and site collections. Although databases are used with all three of these, there is a dedicated section for database management, as seen in Figure 3-15.

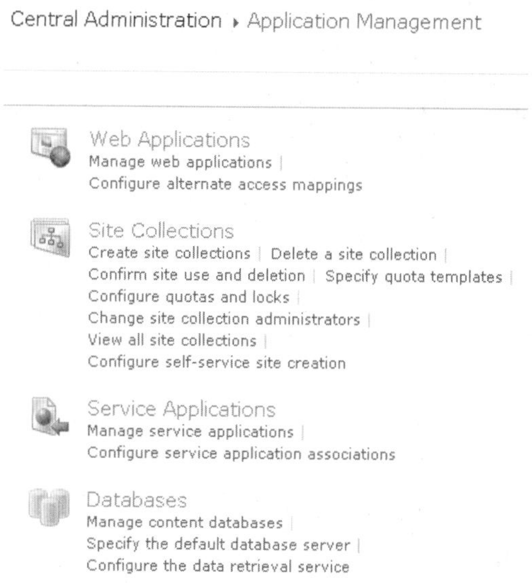

Central Administration ▸ Application Management

 Web Applications
Manage web applications |
Configure alternate access mappings

 Site Collections
Create site collections | Delete a site collection |
Confirm site use and deletion | Specify quota templates |
Configure quotas and locks |
Change site collection administrators |
View all site collections |
Configure self-service site creation

 Service Applications
Manage service applications |
Configure service application associations

 Databases
Manage content databases |
Specify the default database server |
Configure the data retrieval service

FIGURE 3-15 Databases are contained in the Application Management grouping.

Content Databases

There are many farm-level settings and configuration options you should be aware of with content databases. While the first content database is created during the Web application creation, it is created with several default options. The following configuration options should be taken into consideration when managing content databases:

- Size of the content database
- Number of site collections per content database
- Status of content databases
- Read-only content databases
- Location on SQL Server physical disk

Controlling Database Sizes

SharePoint Server 2010 does not provide direct functionality to limit the content database size. Although SQL Server can provide this option, it is generally recommended that you control the content database sizes with SharePoint Server 2010 site quotas. First, you need to know that site quotas are *actually* site collection quotas. There is no native method to limit site quotas. Second, you can limit the number of site collections in a database, but you cannot limit the number of sites. Once again, the Central Administration interface is ambiguous on sites vs. site collections. When we're discussing items within Central Administration, the word "sites" always references site collections. To limit the size of a content database using SharePoint Server options, you need to combine the following three SharePoint Server 2010 settings:

- **Maximum Number Of Sites That Can Be Created In This Database** This setting is found in Central Administration, Application Management, Manage Content Databases, after selecting a content database:

Database Capacity Settings
Specify capacity settings for this database.

Number of sites before a warning event is generated
9000
Maximum number of sites that can be created in this database
15000

- **Quotas of the sites (site collections) contained in the database** These settings can be found in Central Administration, Application Management, Configure Quotas And Locks:

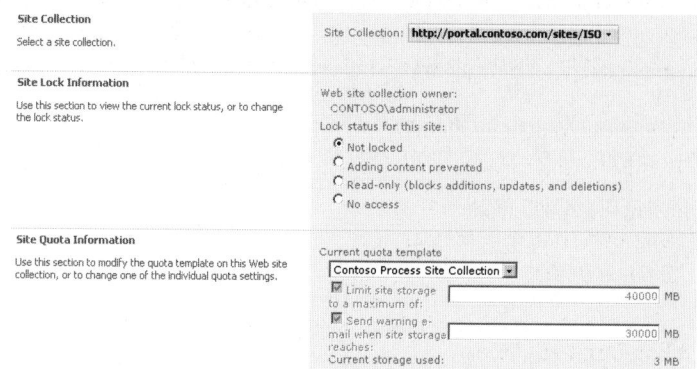

- **Percent of site (site collection) used for the second-stage Recycle Bin** These settings are located in Central Administration, Manage Web Applications, and General Settings on the Web Applications tab.

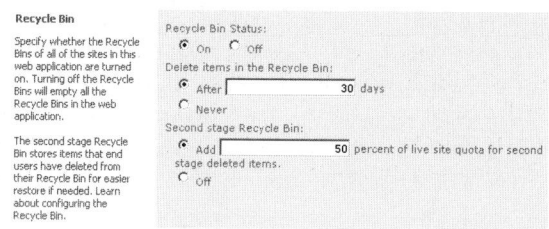

Using the settings just shown, you define the maximum database size by using the following formula:

(Maximum number of sites) x (site quota) x (1 + % of live site quota for second stage)

Number of Site Collections per Content Database

The default number of sites (site collections) per content database should almost assuredly be changed. The default settings of 9000 sites before a warning and 15,000 sites as the maximum is entirely a fail-safe mechanism in the product. Using the formula previously mentioned, here is the result for a 15,000-site maximum:

15,000 sites x 10-GB site quota x 1(.50 second stage) = possible database size of 219 terabytes

A more likely scenario is this:

20 sites x 10-GB site quota x 1(.20 second stage) = possible database size of 250 GB

The maximum database size recommended is somewhere between 200 GB and 300 GB. Your databases can be much larger in theory, but the practical daily management becomes difficult beyond the recommended limit.

> **TIP** You should be very careful with maximum site collection sizes (the site quota settings). Large, busy site collections are likely to have SQL locking/blocking errors. A rule of thumb is to have large site collections and a few users, or small site collections with a large user population.

If you must have large content databases, try to isolate very busy site collections in a dedicated content database. This gives you the flexibility of managing the disk I/O of the site collection at the SQL level. Note that this does not scale, however. It is recommended that you have no more than 100 content databases per Web application.

Content Database Status

The Content Database Status can be set to either Ready or Offline. The status of Offline is a bit confusing because the real purpose of taking a content database offline is to not allow more site collections to be created therein. In fact, site collections contained in an offline content database can still be seen and written to. However, there were unexpected problems with this in SharePoint Server 2007 and there might be again in SharePoint Server 2010. The safest way to limit the number of site collections in a content database is by following these steps:

1. Turn off warning events by setting the threshold to zero.
2. Set the maximum number of site collections to the current number listed in the user interface. Be sure to create a new content database before creating a site collection; otherwise, the creation will fail.

Read-Only Content Databases

SharePoint Server 2010 now supports read-only SQL Server content databases. When you set a content database to Read-Only, the permissions in all site collections will automatically be reflected in the users' Web browser. For example, Figure 3-16 shows an example of a document library contained in a read/write content database, and Figure 3-17 is the same document library after setting the content database to Read-Only.

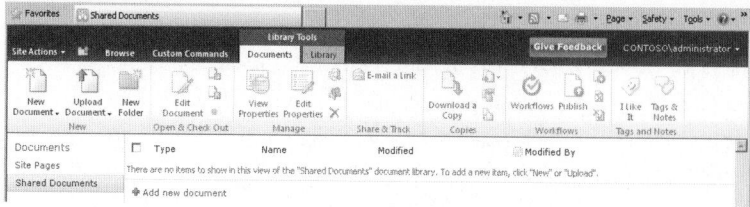

FIGURE 3-16 This is an example of a document library contained in a Read/Write content database.

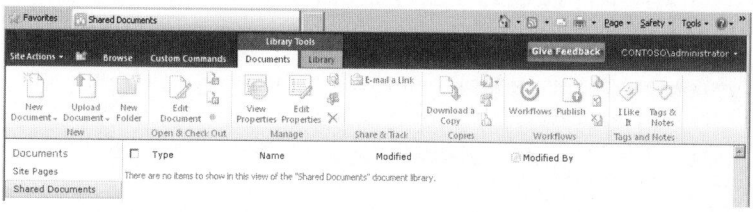

FIGURE 3-17 When the hosting database is set to Read-Only, no editing commands are available.

You can see the current state of a content database by browsing to Central Administration, Application Management, Manage Content Databases, and selecting the relevant database. SharePoint Server 2010 displays only the status, however, and cannot be used to set the database state. To set a database to Read-Only, you must do so from SQL Server Management Studio. To configure a database to be Read-Only, do the following on the SQL Server console:

1. Open SQL Server Management Studio. (Its location will vary based on your version and edition of SQL Server.)

2. Locate the SQL Server database you want to modify, right-click, and select Properties.

3. Select the Options page, and under Other Options scroll down until you see the State options.

4. Locate Database Read-Only, and click False, as seen in Figure 3-18.

5. Change the status from False to True, and click OK.

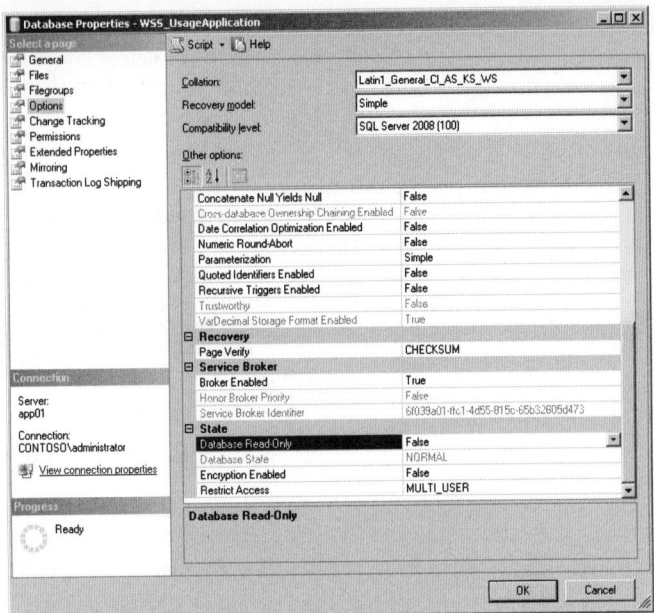

FIGURE 3-18 Select the down arrow to the right of False to change the status.

Database Location on SQL Server Physical Disk

Although SharePoint Server 2010 can create databases and perform a minimal SQL Server database setup, you still want to do basic configuration of the databases on the SQL Server physical disks. Maintenance plans and recovery models can be quite extensive and are not covered in this section. It is recommended that you leave the recovery model as it is set by the SharePoint Server configuration wizard, unless you have advanced SQL Server experience and can verify that you'll be in a supported configuration.

> **MORE INFORMATION** For detailed information on SQL Server maintenance plans and system configuration, see *http://technet.microsoft.com/sqlserver*.

If your SQL Server content will need to be highly available, service a significant number of requests, or both, you should separate the transaction log files and data files. Content is always written to the transaction log first, regardless of the recovery model. This allows the database to be brought back into a consistent state if you need to recover the database using SQL Server restore tools. Next, a SQL Server checkpoint process runs at regular intervals and writes the transactions to the *data file*.

> **NOTE** In the Full recovery model, transaction log records are retained until you back up the database and truncate the transaction log.

When users are viewing your Web applications, they are almost always consuming the data file on SQL Server. By contrast, write actions are processed in the transaction log. Therefore, it is safe to assume that in a read-only server farm the data file physical disk will be the most utilized. Because of the nature of SharePoint Server transactions, the transaction log and data file are usually equally used in a collaborative environment.

By default, SQL Server places both the data files and transaction logs on the same volume on SQL Server. You can change this default behavior by modifying the default SQL Server settings. To change the default location for new databases, do the following on your SQL Server console:

1. Open SQL Server Management Studio.
2. Right-click the server name and select Properties.
3. Select Database Settings.
4. In the Database Default Locations settings, choose a previously created volume.

Note that if multiple volumes share the same physical disks you will not see a performance increase. If possible, you should separate the transaction logs and the data files on separate physical disks and not on the system volume. Figure 3-19 shows an example of changing the data file location to the D: volume and the transaction logs to the L: volume.

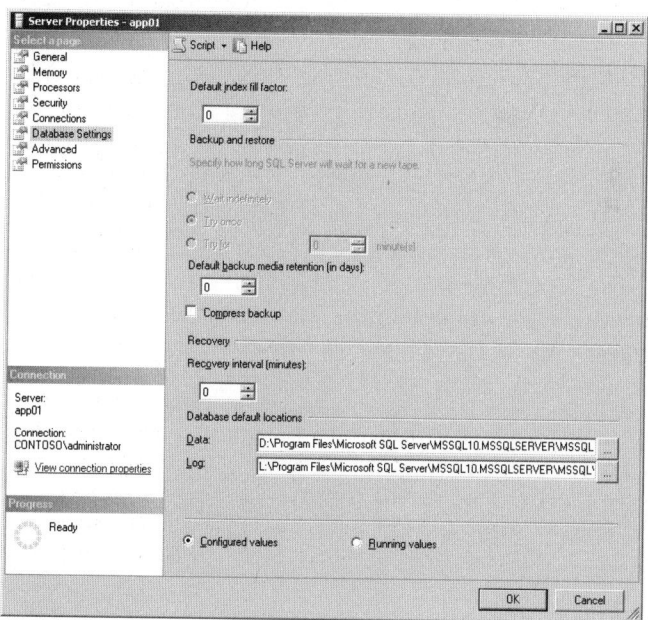

FIGURE 3-19 You can change the database default locations in SQL Server Properties.

MORE INFORMATION For information on testing the SQL Server I/O subsystem, browse to *http://technet.microsoft.com/en-us/library/cc966412.aspx*. Specifically, you can find more information here about using the SQLIO.exe tool.

Default Database Server

When you installed SharePoint Server 2010, you selected a database server for the configuration database. The SQL Server you selected became the default content database server. You can change this default at any time from Central Administration, Application Management, Specify The Default Database Server. Unless you are in a specialized environment, do not use SQL Server authentication. Windows authentication is almost always the correct choice. Do not fill in the Database Username and Password fields when using Windows authentication. SharePoint Server 2010 automatically configures the SQL Server permissions when using Windows authentication.

Data Retrieval Service

The Data Retrieval Service was first introduced in Windows SharePoint Services 2.0 and allowed for a connection to internal or external data sources via Web services. SharePoint Server 2010 continues to build on the service, and it can be configured for the entire server farm or on a per–Web application basis. For the most part, you leave this configuration set to default unless you are requested to change it by a designer or developer. For example, you might need to change it when requiring access to stored procedures on a non–SharePoint Server database, external content source (OLEDB), or XML and SOAP Web services from within SharePoint Server 2010.

To configure the Data Retrieval Service, browse to Central Administration, Application Management, Configure The Data Retrieval Service. There are seven configuration options:

- **Web Application** Be sure you are selecting the correct Web application before continuing. Note that the user interface refers to Global Settings— those are also selected in the Web application drop-down menu, as seen in Figure 3-20.

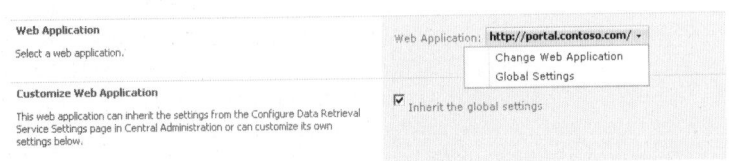

FIGURE 3-20 Select Change Web Application or Global Settings using the drop-down menu.

- **Customize Web Application**   If you want to use Web-application scoped settings, clear this option. If you want to override prior Web-application changes, you can also select this box to reapply the global settings. This is useful if you made a mistake configuring a specific Web application.

- **Enable Data Retrieval Services**   Be careful when deciding whether to turn off this option. Both SharePoint Designer 2010 and Visual Studio 2010 might leverage these services via Web parts and custom code. Check with your development team before disabling these services.

- **Limit Response Size**   Unless directed by your development team, the default OLEDB response size should be selected. You should monitor your server's memory utilization if you increase the defaults, and you should do so over a period of several days. Large OLEDB queries can quickly use server memory.

- **Update Support**   This option is disabled by default, but many developers will want to enable this option. A common reason for doing so is that custom code might call a stored procedure in a non–SharePoint Server 2010 database. This is often more efficient than bringing the data into .NET for processing.

- **Data Source Time-Out**   Unless you are calling data sources over a wide area network (WAN), the default time-outs should be sufficient.

- **Enable Data Source Controls**   Data Source Controls allow controls to bind to other controls, without the need f~   ~. This option is usually enabled.

strator's ability to
you worked with
l for connections,
it was scoped to the
many site collec-
bed to Web applica-
connections are
ill walk you through
entral Adminis-
f publishing a

llection, you must first
~~~~~~~. rne connection is valid for an entire
~~~~ application, but you must configure an entry to each site collection you want to connect to. In the following example, the destination site collection is *http://portal.contoso.com/sites/ISO*.

To begin configuration, browse to Central Administration, General Application Settings, External Service Connections, Configure Send To Connections. Always verify you are configuring the correct Web application before continuing.

Site Subscription Settings

SharePoint Server 2010 allows for multitenancy and was primarily targeted at SharePoint Server hosting providers. This allows for isolation of hosted site collections, as well as the ability to consume service applications at the site collection level. This segmentation is known as a *site subscription*. Although most readers will not have their implementation configured in such a fashion because of the complexity involved, you can limit the ability of these tenants to create connections beyond their environment. If you do not have multitenancy configured, this option can be left as the default. If you do have multitenancy enabled, you must decide whether to allow connections between tenants. This decision is a business, process, and security decision.

Configuring the Content Organizer in the Destination Site

Before you can configure Central Administration for Send To connections, you must first enable the Content Organizer feature in the destination site. The Content Organizer feature allows settings and rules to route inbound files to the site. Based on the defined settings and rules, the destination site will sort and route files to the appropriate library, or even to other site collections. To enable the Content Organizer in the destination site, do the following:

1. Browse to the site where you want files to be routed to.
2. From the Site Actions menu, select Site Settings.
3. Under the Site Actions grouping, select Manage Site Features.
4. Locate the Content Organizer feature, and click Activate.
5. From Site Actions, Site Settings, configure Content Organizer Settings And Rules.

MORE INFORMATION For more details on configuring the Content Organizer, see Chapter 12, "Records Management."

Send To Connections

You can configure multiple Send To connections and even create multiple connections to the same site using different rules. If this is your first connection, just continue completing the form. If this is a subsequent connection, either choose New Connection or select one for editing. Note that you can select the Add Connection control if you'll configure multiple Send To connections. This prevents the configuration screen from closing and allows you to immediately add another connection.

Figure 3-21 shows an example of the Send To Connections configuration page while adding the *http://portal.contoso.com/sites/ISO* connection.

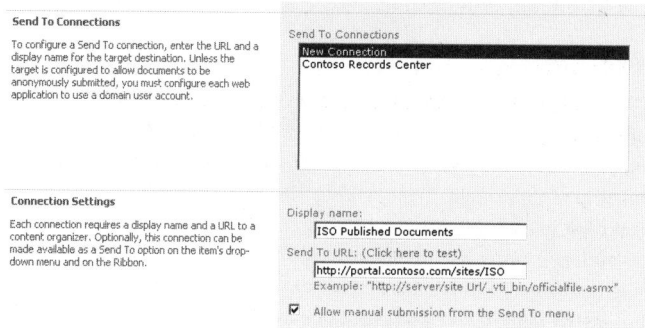

FIGURE 3-21 Highlight New Connection when creating a new Send To connection.

NOTE Before you can add a new Send To connection, you must first activate the Content Organizer feature in the destination site.

Allow Manual Submissions

A commonly configured option is to Allow manual submissions from the Send To menu, as seen in Figure 3-21. Selecting this option allows users to manually send to the destination site from the user menu in a library. If you do not select this option, you'll have to use another mechanism, such as custom code or SharePoint Designer 2010, to enable the file transfer. If you select to allow manual submissions, the user experience is similar to that shown in Figure 3-22.

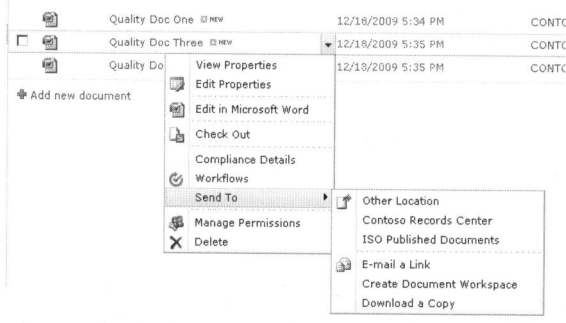

FIGURE 3-22 Select the external connection defined in Central Administration to test.

CHAPTER 4

Building and Managing Web Applications

- Web Application Architecture **110**

- Creating and Extending Web Applications **115**

- Managing Web Applications **128**

- Alternate Access Mappings **137**

Web applications are the top of the hierarchy at the farm level and are foundational to any Microsoft SharePoint Server 2010 implementation. SharePoint Server 2010 Web applications differ from most Web sites in that content exists in a database, not on the Web server file system. Only the minimal content required to connect an Internet Information Services (IIS) server to the databases exists on a SharePoint server. The logical structure of a Web application exists entirely in Microsoft SQL Server databases. The configuration of a Web application configuration is stored in the configuration database. The user content of a Web application is stored in one or many content databases.

From a physical architecture perspective, Web applications represent a specific IIS Web site and application scope, providing the ability for end users to interact with content via a Uniform Resource Locator (URL). The end user does not have a visual representation of the Web application. It is completely managed at the farm level with Central Administration or by using Microsoft Windows PowerShell. The stsadm.exe administrative tool can still be used for basic farm administration tasks, but it is slated for removal in the next version of SharePoint. It would be wise to begin transitioning to Windows PowerShell.

Web Application Architecture

A Web application can be created from Central Administration and will associate an IIS Web site with at least one content database created on your SQL Server implementation. Remember, a new Web application is an empty shell and contains no site collections by default. If you try to navigate to a Web application before a site collection has been created, you will see a 404 Page Not Found error.

> **NOTE** IIS creates a Web site for each Web application created in SharePoint. SharePoint creates site collections within SharePoint Web applications.

If you use the Farm Configuration Wizard, the wizard will guide you through the steps to create the first Web application as well as its first site collection. Figure 4-1 shows the relationship among site collections, Web applications, and content databases.

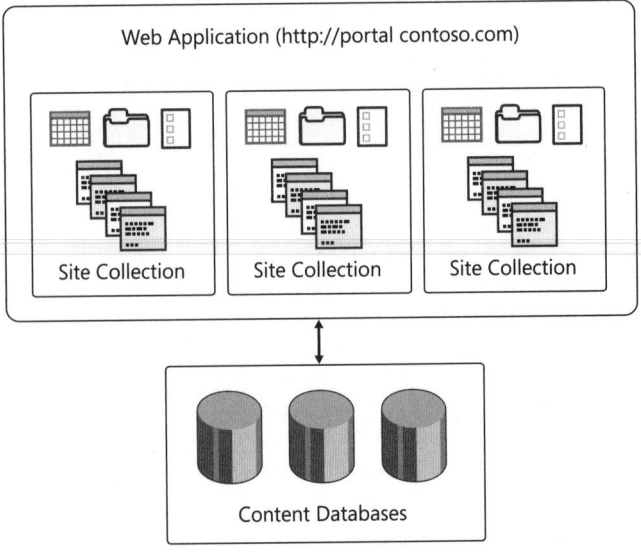

FIGURE 4-1 The relationship between Web applications, site collections, and content databases.

Managing a Web Application

Web applications can be managed using Central Administration. There are two links to the Manage Web Applications page. The first is located on the Central Administration home page listed under the Application Management section as seen in Figure 4-2.

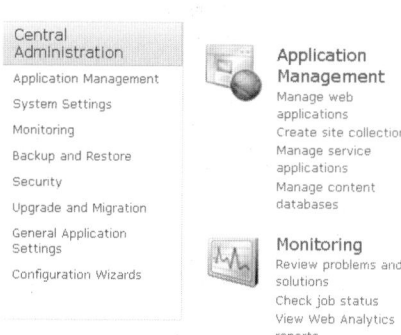

FIGURE 4-2 The Manage Web Applications link is located on the Central Administration home page.

The Manage Web applications link can also be found in Central Administration under the Application Management section. Listed in the Application Management page is the Web Applications grouping, as seen in Figure 4-3.

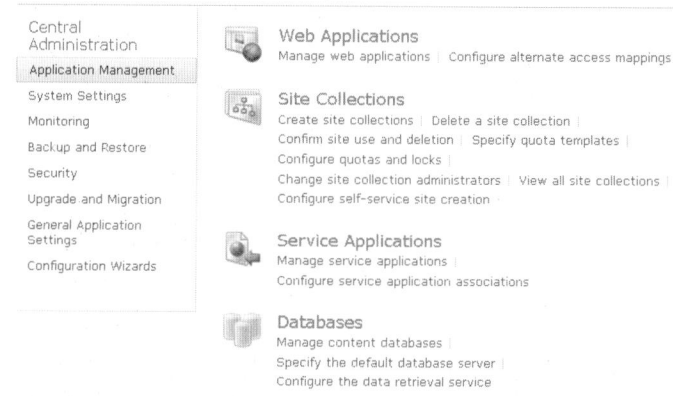

FIGURE 4-3 The Manage Web Applications link is also located in the Application Management section.

Application Pools

An IIS application pool is an isolated memory space that is routed to one or more worker processes within the security context of a user. A worker process (w3wp.exe) runs Web applications and handles requests sent to a server for a specific application pool. A Web application with its own application pool will not be affected by problems with other applications in separate application pools. In Figure 4-4, two Web applications (*https://extranet.contoso.com* and *http://portal.contoso.com*) are using the same application pool. Sharing an application pool in this fashion reduces the memory footprint, but it introduces the risk of both Web applications crashing in the event one of them crashes from poorly written code or a compromised server.

http://extranet.contoso.com

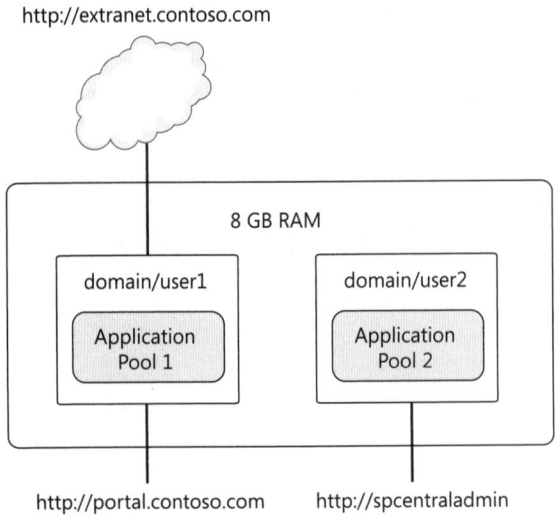

FIGURE 4-4 Application pools hosting Web applications in memory.

Implementing a different application pool and user name (identity) for each Web application strengthens your overall security stance, but every additional application pool requires more memory. If possible, you should use a separate Web application pool for isolation, even if the two pools will use the same identity.

The decision of whether or not to use multiple application pool identities depends on the level of security your organization requires. Generally, Web applications with the same level of security share an application pool identity. Otherwise, you can choose to install with one or several accounts for IIS application pools and database access. It is much easier to install with separate accounts in the beginning than it is to change and isolate application pools later.

Content Databases

Content databases contain all site collection content, including most customization performed in the browser or SharePoint Designer. By default, a single content database is created per Web application. You should create additional content databases to limit the size of your content databases or for isolation on the SQL Server physical disk. For example, if your site collection quota is 10 GB and you want to limit your content database size to 100 GB, you need to create a content database for every ten site collections in the associated Web application.

TIP A content database completely contains a site collection. A content database associated with Web Application1 can be removed and associated with Web Application2. All site collections in this content dataset will then be available in Web Application2 under its original managed path. The exception is when the URL is already in use, such as the root managed path.

To manage content databases, browse to Central Administration, Application Management, Databases, Manage Content Databases, as shown in Figure 4-5.

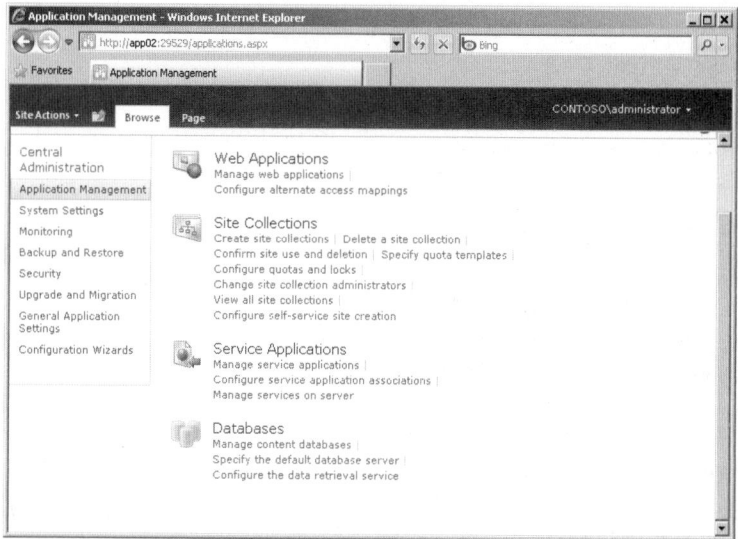

FIGURE 4-5 Location of the Manage Content Databases link in Central Administration.

You add more databases via the Manage Content Databases interface. From here, you can add or manage content databases, as well as view information about a content database, as shown in Figure 4-6.

Add a content database					Web Application: **http://corp-sp2010/** ▾	
Database Name	Database Status	Database Read-Only	Current Number of Site Collections	Site Collection Level Warning	Maximum Number of Site Collections	Preferred
WSS_Content	Started	No	2	9000	15000	

FIGURE 4-6 The Manage Content Databases interface.

There are seven primary properties for each content database:

- **Database information** The database information section shows the database server name, database name, and status. Changing the status to Offline prevents new site collections from being created in that content database. It also shows the type of authentication that was defined during the associated Web application creation when it is the first content database, or during content database creation for subsequent databases.

IMPORTANT To prevent site collections from being created in a database, set the maximum number of sites to the current number in the database. Offline databases have had issues in previous versions of SharePoint Server and might in 2010 as well. Note that this interface refers to site collections, not subsites.

- **Database Versioning and Upgrade** New for SharePoint Server 2010, this property is helpful when upgrading databases to a new version of SharePoint. It will display the current patch version as well as the SharePoint Server version. Regardless of whether you upgraded from SharePoint Server 2007 or not, the page displays databases and their relevant information to service packs and updates.

- **Failover Server** This is a new feature in SharePoint Server 2010 to support SQL database mirroring. Configuring this setting does not configure database mirroring, it only makes SharePoint Server 2010 mirroring-aware. To successfully finish the configuration, you must configure database mirroring in SQL Server Management Studio.

- **Database Capacity Settings** You should make an educated decision about what values to use for the Number Of Sites Before A Warning Event Is Generated and Maximum Number Of Sites That Can Be Created In This Database settings. For example, if you do not want your content databases to be larger than 100 GB and your site quotas are set to 1 GB, you need to change the maximum number of sites to 100. The default settings are almost always too high and should be changed. Note that this screen refers to site collections, not subsites.

- **Search Server** If you are using SharePoint Server 2010, you can safely ignore the setting for Search Server. It is used only in a SharePoint Foundation 2010 installation where SharePoint Server 2010 Search is not available.

- **Remove Content Database** Removing a content database disassociates the database with a Web application, it does not delete it from SQL Server. There is almost never a reason to remove a content database without removing the entire Web application. But you might do so when taking sensitive data offline immediately, without losing the data, or re-associating a content database with a new Web application. When removing a content database, all data remains in the database and can be attached to another Web application for access. Re-associating content databases to another Web application should be performed only after thorough testing in a lab.

- **Preferred Server For Timer Jobs** A new option in SharePoint Server 2010, this supports the separation of services on different servers. The SharePoint 2010 Timer service, for example, executes workflow steps when they are continued from a delay tier or an event received elsewhere.

Creating and Extending Web Applications

Creating Web applications is one of the most basic and fundamental aspects of administering SharePoint products. A Web application provides the interface that users interact with from their browsers. Web applications are a combination of IIS virtual servers, associated content databases, and entries for both in the configuration database.

Create a Web Application

Before creating a Web application, verify that the initial configuration is correct. Many settings, such as those for the host header, cannot be changed after Web application creation. Although you can modify the settings in IIS, it is not possible to change the settings in the configuration database. All settings entered in Central Administration are written to the configuration database and will be used whenever you add new servers to the farm. If the configuration is incorrect, you must remember to manually update any new servers to the farm and update existing servers if you restart the Microsoft SharePoint Foundation Web Application service.

To create a new Web application, do the following:

1. Browse to Central Administration, Application Management, Web Applications, Manage Web Applications, and then click New on the Ribbon as shown in Figure 4-7.

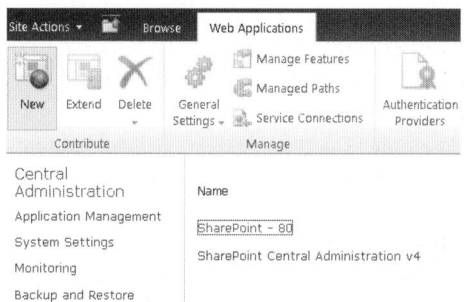

FIGURE 4-7 The New button on the Ribbon is used to create a new Web application.

2. Next, select the authentication type for this Web application. Unless your organization is leveraging Claims Based Authentication, select Classic Mode Authentication as seen in Figure 4-8. Changing the selection of authentication type refreshes the dialog and presents different options in the Create New Web Application dialog window.

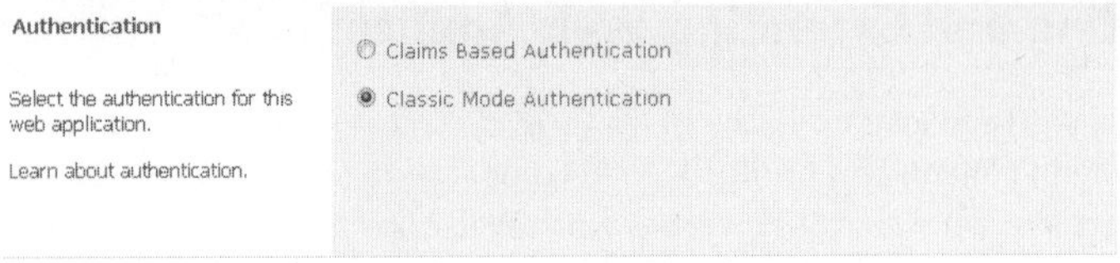

Authentication

Select the authentication for this web application.

Learn about authentication.

○ Claims Based Authentication

● Classic Mode Authentication

FIGURE 4-8 The Authentication options for a new Web application.

- **Claims Based Authentication** This is a new feature in SharePoint Server 2010 that is built on the Windows Identity Foundation (WIF). It uses the identity of the user as well as other details, which can originate within the user's organization, other organizations, or the Internet. It enables authentication across Windows-based systems and systems that are not Windows based. Claims Based Authentication is a flexible framework based on standard Security Assertion Markup Language (SAML) tokens, but it is not the actual means of authentication.

  TIP If you are upgrading from SharePoint Server 2007 and used Forms-based authentication or Web single sign-on (SSO) authentication, you must convert to Claims Based authentication before SharePoint Server 2007 Web applications can be used in SharePoint Server 2010.

- **Classic Mode Authentication** This mode essentially uses IIS authentication for SharePoint Server 2010 Web applications. If you simply want to use Kerberos or NTLM, select Classic Mode Authentication. Note that Basic authentication can be configured after the creation of a Web application, but not during the creation. Always use Secure Sockets Layer (SSL) when leveraging Basic authentication.

3. Next, you need to create a new IIS Web site. If you select Use An Existing IIS Web Site, the Web application will read the IIS configuration of the server running Central Administration. This setting is rarely used; it's usually used to fix a broken Web application. For this example, select Create A New IIS Web Site. Choose a name that is easily identified in IIS Manager. The IIS Web Site, Port, Host Header, and Path options are shown in Figure 4-9.

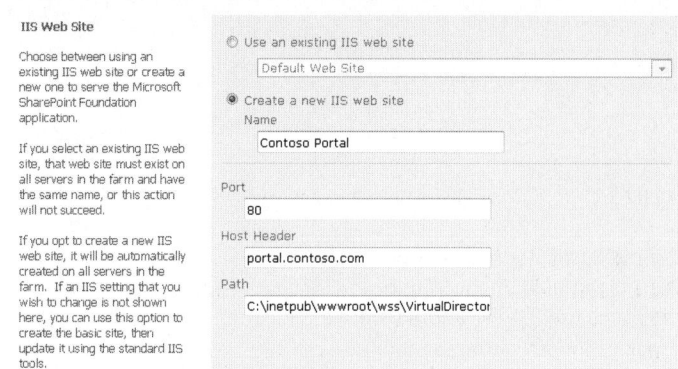

FIGURE 4-9 The IIS Web Site configuration default settings.

4. After defining the IIS Web site name, you need to define the port number. This is usually port 80 for HTTP or port 443 for HTTPS.

5. Next, define the host header for the Web application. This should usually be the fully qualified domain name (FQDN) for the Web application. Although this can be changed later in IIS on every server in the farm, it cannot be changed in the configuration database. You need to correctly configure the host header during Web application creation.

IMPORTANT Only one host header can be defined during Web application creation. If you require multiple host headers, such as http://portal.contoso.com and http://portal, you must add the latter in IIS on every server in the farm.

6. Define the path for the Web site. Unless you are directed to use settings other than the defaults, the default settings should work well. If you must change the path, verify the drive letter exists on every Web server in the farm. Otherwise, the creation of the Web application will fail on servers that do not have the drive letter.

7. Depending on whether you selected Claims Based Authentication or Classic Mode Authentication, you'll be presented with one of the following options for configuring security:

Selecting the Classic Mode Authentication security configuration option displays the settings shown in Figure 4-10.

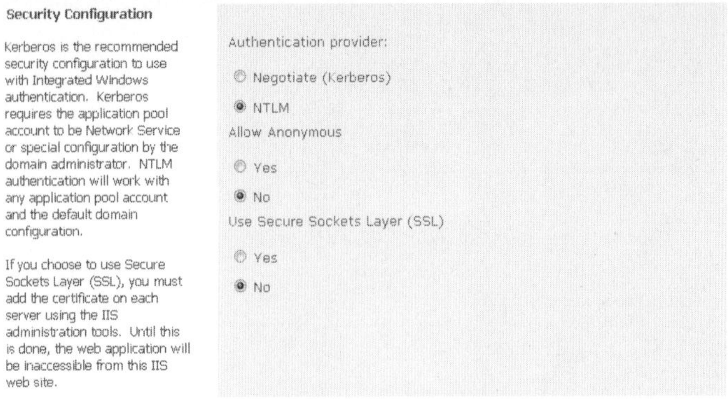

Security Configuration

Kerberos is the recommended security configuration to use with Integrated Windows authentication. Kerberos requires the application pool account to be Network Service or special configuration by the domain administrator. NTLM authentication will work with any application pool account and the default domain configuration.

If you choose to use Secure Sockets Layer (SSL), you must add the certificate on each server using the IIS administration tools. Until this is done, the web application will be inaccessible from this IIS web site.

Authentication provider:

○ Negotiate (Kerberos)

◉ NTLM

Allow Anonymous

○ Yes

◉ No

Use Secure Sockets Layer (SSL)

○ Yes

◉ No

FIGURE 4-10 The security configuration default settings for Classic Mode authentication.

- **Authentication Provider**   If you are creating an intranet Web application, strongly consider using Kerberos for user authentication. Kerberos is more secure and offers better performance than NTLM. If you have multiple subnets, you are separated by firewalls, or the Web application is Internet facing, you should use NTLM (default) for authentication. If users cannot see your Kerberos Distribution Center (KDC) or the time is out of synchronization, Kerberos will fail. Remember to set service principal names (SPNs) when selecting Kerberos. See Chapter 15, "Configuring Policies and Security," for information on using and configuring Kerberos.

- **Allow Anonymous**   Unless you are serving content for public consumption, you should not allow anonymous access. Although enabling anonymous access is allowed for collaborative site collections via its Web application, it is generally a bad practice to enable it. Keep in mind that enabling anonymous access for a Web application doesn't allow anonymous access by itself. A site collection administrator must also enable anonymous access at the site level.

- **Use Secure Sockets Layer (SSL)**   If your organization plans to collaborate via an Internet-facing Web application, enabling SSL is recommended for security. You must still add an SSL certificate in IIS Manager if choosing SSL. Selecting SSL here only changes the Web application scheme (https://) in the configuration database, it does not bind a certificate to the Web site.

Selecting the Claims Based Authentication security configuration option displays the settings shown in Figure 4-11. An identity provider handles requests for trusted identity claims as an Identity Provider Security Token Service (IP-STS). An IP-STS stores and manages identities and their associated attributes. The identity store can be an SQL database table, or it can use a more complex identity store such as Active Directory Domain Services (AD DS) or Active Directory Lightweight Directory Services (AD LDS).

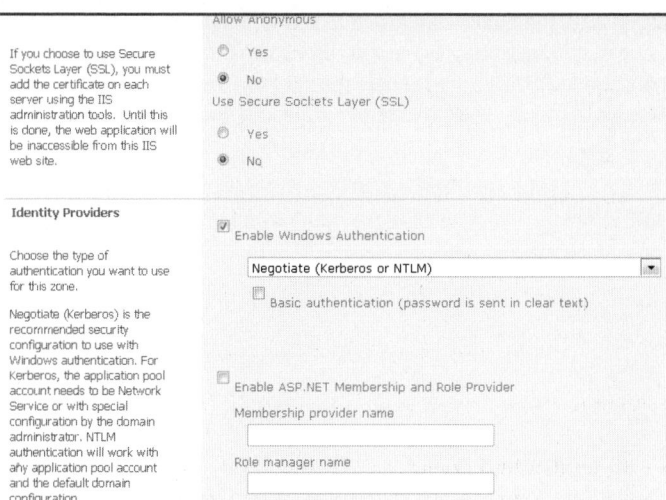

FIGURE 4-11 Configuring Identity Providers settings.

- **Enable Windows Authentication**   Selecting Kerberos or NTLM with Claims Based Authentication is not the same as selecting it for Classic Mode Authentication. You must have previously configured the Security Token Service (STS). If you want to use only Kerberos, Basic, or NTLM, use Classic Mode Authentication. If selecting Basic, you need to modify the authentication provider after the Web application has been created.

- **Enable ASP.NET Membership And Role Provider**   Type a membership provider name and a role manager name. This is usually provided by your development team.

- **Federated Identity Provider**   If using Federated Claims authentication, enter the appropriate information in the Trusted Identity Provider text box. This information is usually provided by your development team.

- **Sign In Page URL**   The Sign In Page URL section shown in Figure 4-12 is available only when Claims Based Authentication has been selected.

FIGURE 4-12 The Sign In Page URL configuration settings.

- The sign-in page URL is required when configuring Forms-based authentication. It defines the page displayed for collecting the logon credentials. The form will be deployed by your designers or developers.

8. Next, enter the public URL. The public URL should be the one most likely to be visited by your users, usually an FQDN. Unless you are selecting a nonstandard HTTP port, remove the *:80* from the URL, as seen in Figure 4-13. Be sure to modify your DNS server to include the new Web application.

Sign In Page URL

When Claims Based Identity authentication methods are enabled, a URL for redirecting the user to the Sign In page is required.

Learn about Sign In page redirection URL.

◉ Default Sign In Page

○ Custom Sign In Page

Public URL

The public URL is the domain name for all sites that users will access in this SharePoint Web application. This URL domain will be used in all links shown on pages within the web application. By default, it is set to the current servername and port.
http://go.microsoft.com/fwlink/?
LinkId=114854

URL
http://portal.contoso.com

Zone
Default

FIGURE 4-13 The Public URL configuration settings.

> **NOTE** SharePoint Server 2010 gives users the ability to differentiate incoming traffic based on zones. Zones can help sort incoming traffic to different extended Web applications with matching URLs. The URL entered in the user's browser is mapped to the correlating zone, allowing greater flexibility in isolating and directing incoming traffic. All Web applications must be created initially on the Default zone. Refer to Chapter 15 for detailed information on creating and leveraging zones.

9. Decide if you'll use an existing application pool or create a new application pool. If security and process isolation is important to your organization, you must create an application pool for each Web application. Creating an application pool requires additional resources such as memory and administrative time. In the 64-bit environment mandated by SharePoint Server 2010, multiple application pools are more appealing because you do not have the 32-bit memory restrictions. To create a new application pool, provide an easily identifiable name, as shown in Figure 4-14.

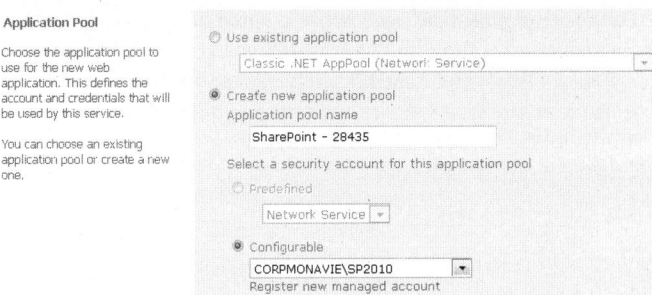

FIGURE 4-14 Configuring Application Pool settings.

10. Select the managed account for the application pool identity, or register a new managed account. Note that you'll have to re-enter all previous information on the page when creating a new managed account.

11. Next, enter the database server and database name, as seen in Figure 4-15.

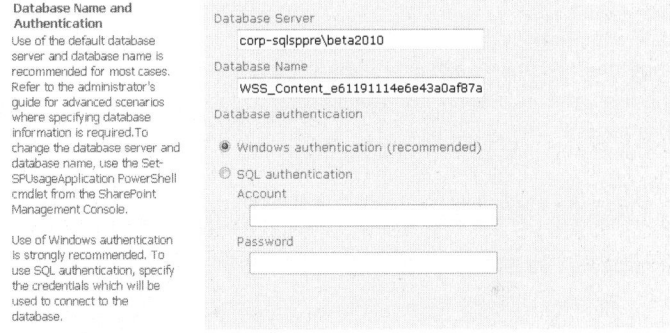

FIGURE 4-15 Configuring Database Name and Database Authentication settings.

- **Database Server** For most installations, use the default SQL server that was specified during the configuration of the farm. You might select a different SQL server (instance) if you have several large Web applications that require dedicated, isolated content databases. If you are using multiple instances, use this format: <SERVERNAME\instance>.

- **Database Name** Always change the default database name to correlate to the Web application name. For example, if the Web application is *http://sales.contoso.com*, use WSS_Content_Sales for the database name. Intelligent naming of Web applications, application pools, and databases greatly eases the management of medium to large SharePoint Server 2010 implementations.

- **Database Authentication** The recommended authentication type is Windows authentication. Use SQL authentication only when working in a workgroup environment and when you have selected SQL authentication for all database connections, including the configuration database. The user logged on to Central Administration must also have the ability to create SQL Server databases.

12. Optionally, define a failover database server. This is a new feature in SharePoint Server 2010 to support SQL database mirroring. SQL database mirroring allows a database to fail over from one server to another or to another instance. The principle server is the original instance, and when it fails, SharePoint automatically retries the connection with the failover server every 15 seconds (the default setting). The SharePoint content database will need to be configured in SQL Server mirroring to have a backup database on the failover server. Setting the name of the failover server in SharePoint does not configure the SQL backup. See Figure 4-16 for a view of the Failover Server configuration section.

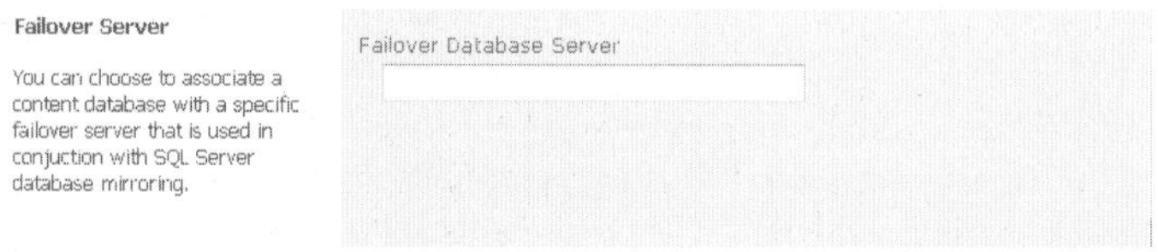

Failover Server

You can choose to associate a content database with a specific failover server that is used in conjuction with SQL Server database mirroring.

Failover Database Server

FIGURE 4-16 The Failover Database Server setting.

13. Optionally, define the SharePoint Foundation 2010 search server. Associate a search server running SharePoint Foundation 2010 Search service with the content database for the new Web application. This setting is for the SharePoint Foundation 2010 search server, not the SharePoint Server 2010 search server. It is ignored if SharePoint Server 2010 is installed in the farm.

14. Optionally, change the default Service Application Connections settings. Most implementations will not require a change. If you have custom service application proxy groups, you need to configure the service applications for this Web application.

> **MORE INFO** See Chapter 6, "Configuring Service Applications," for more information on service application proxy groups.

In SharePoint 2007, services such as Search were managed by a Shared Services Provider. In SharePoint 2010, each service is a standalone service and can be associated individually, rather than as an association with a provider. A proxy group is similar to a Shared Services Provider in that you can associate it with the entire group. In the drop-down menu, the default is set, which automatically configures the services selection. From the drop-down menu, select Custom to configure the server application connections for the Web application. The configuration area is shown in Figure 4-17.

Service Application
Connections

Choose the service applications
that this Web application will be
connected to. A Web application
can be connected to the default
set of service applications or to
a custom set of service
applications. You can change
the set of service applications
that a Web application is
connected to at any time by
using the Configure service
application associations page in
Central Administration.

Edit the following group of connections: [default ▼]

Name	Type
☑ Access Services	Access Services Web Service Application Proxy
☑ Application Registry Service	Application Registry Proxy
☑ Business Data Connectivity	Business Data Connectivity Proxy
☑ Excel Services	Excel Services Web Service Application Proxy
☑ Managed Metadata Service	Managed Metadata Service Connection
☑ PerformancePoint Service Application	PerformancePoint Service Application Proxy
☑ Search Service Application	Search Service Application Proxy
☑ Secure Store Service	Secure Store Service Application Proxy
☑ State Service	State Service Proxy
☑ Usage and Health data collection	Usage and Health Data Collection Proxy
☐ User Profile Service	User Profile Service Application

FIGURE 4-17 Configuring Service Application Connection settings.

15. Last, Select Yes or No to participate in Microsoft's Customer Experience Improvement Program. The overhead of this feature is minimal, but it still has an impact.

16. Click OK.

Extending a Web Application

Extending Web applications allows the same content databases to serve content via multiple IIS virtual servers via *zones*. An example of this is an organization that needs to serve content internally via *http://portal* using Windows Integrated authentication but also serve the same content externally via *https://portal.contoso.com* using Forms authentication over SSL for security.

> **TIP** If the URL needs to be accessed both internally and externally, consider using the most available URL as the default URL. This approach allows system-generated e-mail messages using the default URL to be available, whether they are internal or external. Using the previous example, the default URL is https://portal.contoso.com.

To extend a Web application, do the following:

1. Browse to Central Administration, Application Management, Web Applications, Manage Web Applications, and select the Web application to extend.

2. Click Extend on the Ribbon as shown in Figure 4-18.

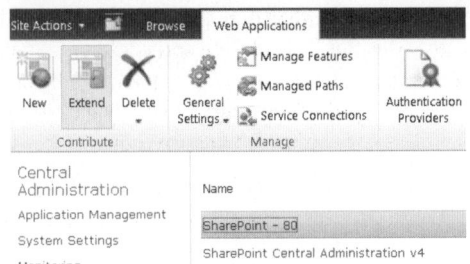

FIGURE 4-18 The Extend button on the Web Applications tab on the Ribbon.

3. Select Create A New IIS Web Site. Enter a name that is easily recognizable in IIS Manager.

4. Define the port number. If you are using HTTP, this is usually port 80. As with Web application creation, this information is written to the configuration database but can be changed manually in IIS Manager on every Web server in the farm. It is best to correctly define it when creating the zone.

5. Enter the host header. The host header is usually the FQDN of the zone, such as *extranet.contoso.com* as seen in Figure 4-19. You should type information in the Host Header text box even if you'll assign IP addresses in Internet Information Services Manager.

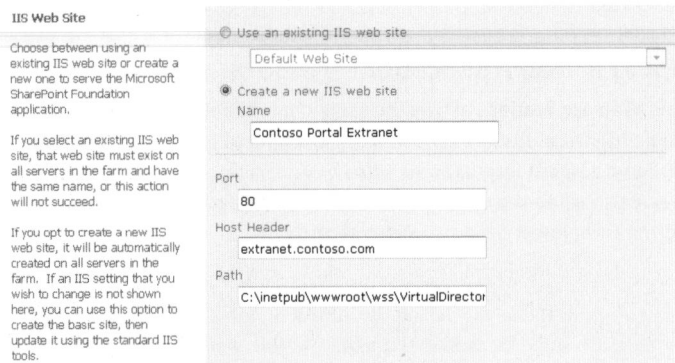

FIGURE 4-19 Always use intelligent names for IIS Web sites.

NOTE If you are using host headers, the description changes automatically to the host header plus the TCP port number.

TIP If you plan to assign IP addresses to Web applications, you should enter the host header information at this point and change the port to 80. You can always add more host headers as required in IIS Manager. This simplifies the process of adding more Web front-end (WFE) servers to the farm.

6. Next, you decide if you'll use NTLM, Kerberos, or Basic authentication. If you need to use Basic authentication, select NTLM and configure authentication providers after you finish extending the Web application. If you use Kerberos, don't forget to register the SPN for the Default zone's Web application pool identity. Security configuration options are shown in Figure 4-20.

MORE INFO For more information on configuring the Kerberos service principal name for the domain user account, refer to Chapter 15, "Configuring Policies and Security."

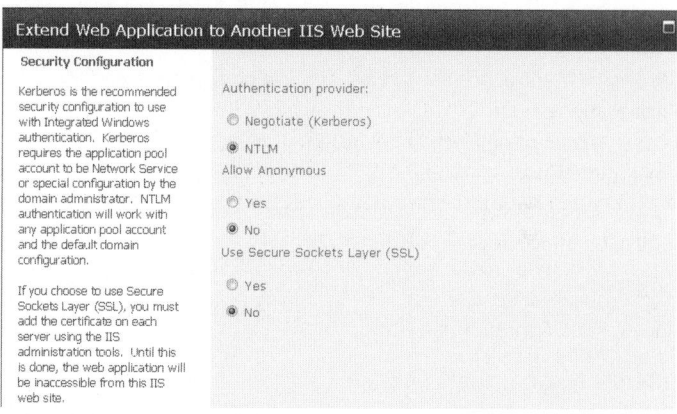

FIGURE 4-20 Extending the Web application security configuration.

CAUTION You are not given the option to create another Web application pool. Doing so would break the functionality of the Web application extension. Therefore, never change the application pool of an extended site in IIS Manager.

7. If you are extending the configuration to leverage the security of SSL, be sure to select that option here. Although this setting can be changed later, it is easier to do it now. Note that you must configure a certificate for this site in IIS Manager after creation before it can successfully serve content via SSL. SharePoint Server 2010 does not bind the certificate to the IIS Web site.

NOTE SSL certificates and assigned IP addresses are not stored in the configuration database. If you must restore a Web server for any reason, you will need to reconfigure the Web applications using SSL or assigned IPs. Alternately, you can restore IIS from the last backup.

8. Next, define the public URL. The URL can be set to a previously defined Domain Name System (DNS) host name for this Web application, or it can be set to a DNS host name for a Network Load Balancing (NLB) IP address. In SharePoint 2007, this was named the Load Balanced URL.

9. Select the zone.

10. Click OK.

Deleting a Web Application

Caution should be exercised when deleting a Web application. Before deleting a Web application, always have a verified farm backup. To delete a Web application, do the following:

1. Browse to Central Administration, Application Management, Manage Web Applications.

2. Select the Web application you want to delete, and click Delete on the Ribbon.

3. If you want to delete the content databases, select Yes. Otherwise, leave the default settings as seen in Figure 4-21.

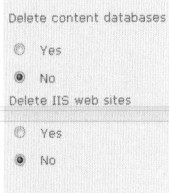

FIGURE 4-21 The options available when deleting a Web application.

4. To delete the IIS Web site, select Yes. It is possible to delete the definition of the Web application in the configuration database while leaving both the content database or databases and the IIS Web site.

5. Click Delete.

To remove an extended Web Application from IIS, follow these steps:

1. Open Central Administration, Application Management, Web Applications, Manage Web Applications.

2. Select the Web application you want to delete.

3. On the Ribbon click the down arrow to display the drop-down menu for Delete, and select Delete Web Application. (See Figure 4-7 for the Ribbon location.)

4. If you want to delete the content databases, select Yes.

5. Select Yes to delete all the IIS Web sites created for and used by the Web application.

6. Click Delete.

Deleting an Extended Zone

Deleting an extended zone is much like deleting a Web application, with the exception that you can select the IIS Web site associated with the zone, but not the content database. When you choose to remove SharePoint from an existing IIS Web site, be very careful when selecting the option from the Ribbon. Do *not* click the Delete button, which is the primary option to delete—you need to click the down arrow on the Delete button to select the Remove SharePoint From IIS Web Site option, as seen in Figure 4-22.

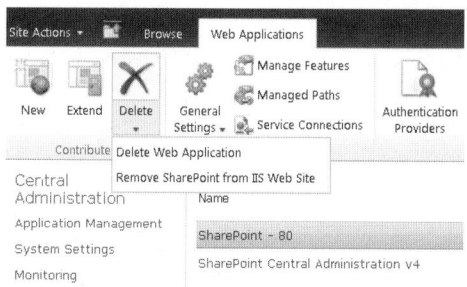

FIGURE 4-22 Delete a Web application, or remove it from IIS.

To delete an extended zone, do the following:

1. Browse to Central Administration, Application Management, Manage Web Applications.

2. Select the Web application with the associated zone that you want to delete. Figure 4-18 shows an example of the Web application selection.

3. On the Ribbon, click the down arrow to display the drop-down menu for Delete, and select Remove SharePoint From IIS Web Site.

4. Click the down arrow to display the drop-down menu under Select IIS Web Site And Zone To Remove.

5. Select Yes, and click OK.

IMPORTANT Exercise caution when deleting or removing SharePoint from an IIS Web site. The default zone will be displayed and will break all zones if deleted.

Managing Web Applications

SharePoint Server 2010 has a new Ribbon interface for all the settings related to managing applications. The majority of common tasks can be found in the management Ribbon from Central Administration, Application Management, Manage Web Applications. When a Web application is selected, the Ribbon changes to display relevant configuration options. The Ribbon interface is divided into the following areas:

- Contribute
- Manage
- Security
- Policy

Additionally, you need to manage the alternate access mappings (AAMs), which can be found in Central Administration, Application Management, Configure Alternate Access Mappings. These are the same AAM settings found in Central Administration, Security.

Configuring Web Applications

After creating a Web application, many other tasks need to be completed. The process of creating a Web application accomplishes only the minimum requirements for defining a Web application in the configuration database, which include configuring IIS and creating the first associated content database.

To manage a content database, you need to set the focus of the Ribbon to a Web application. In the example shown in Figure 4-23, SharePoint – 80 has been selected as the Web application to configure.

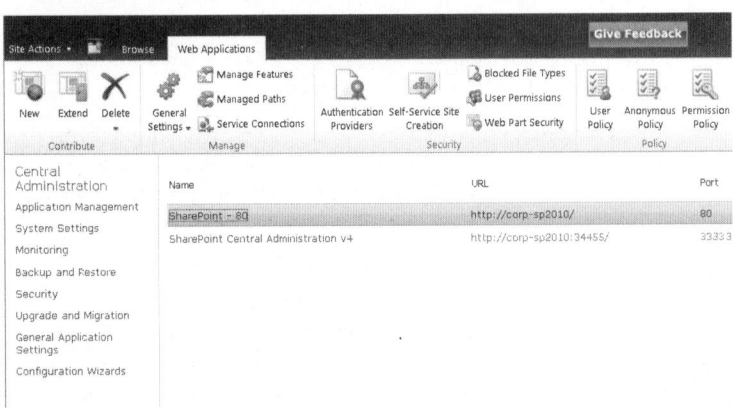

FIGURE 4-23 The Web Applications Management page in Central Administration.

Each Web application has individual settings that affect all sites and site collections hosted in that Web application. Figure 4-24 shows the extended General

Settings menu, which includes different options than those contained in the primary General Settings tab.

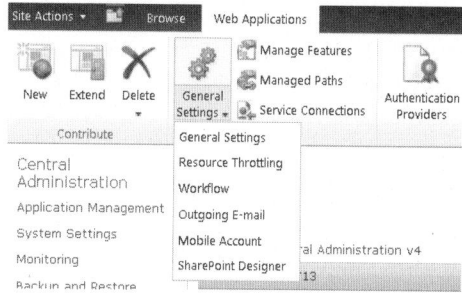

FIGURE 4-24 The General Settings drop-down menu in the Web Application Management page.

General Settings

The General Settings page contains the most common Web application settings. Although it's not mandatory to do so, most administrators will change one or many of the following items:

- **Default Time Zone** By default, each Web server uses the time zone of the operating system. If you need to set the Web application to another time zone, configure it here. It is generally a good idea to manually set the time zone here to prevent inconsistencies in a load-balanced server farm.

- **Default Quota Template** Each Web application can have a suggested quota template for site collections created therein. New site collections will display this template by default, but the quota can be changed by the administrator creating the site collection. You must have previously created a quota template from Central Administration, Application Management, Specify Quota Templates.

  NOTE If you have existing site collections in this Web application, changing the quota template will not affect those site collections. Site (site collection) quotas are used only when creating site collections. If you want to change a site collection quota after creation, you must set an individual quota. Individual quotas are configured in Central Administration, Application Management, Configure Quotas And Locks.

- **Person Name Smart Tag And Presence Settings** Presence settings are used to configure whether you'll allow the display of the online status for Office Communicator Server (OCS) users in SharePoint Server 2010. The presence status is displayed next to a user's name wherever the user's display name appears. When this option is disabled, presence information will no longer appear for users of the site. By default, it is enabled for all Web applications.

- **Alerts**   Users are allowed to create alerts on all sites they have access to in a given Web application if this setting is enabled. The default limit is 500, which is a reasonable limit for most organizations. However, you might need to increase or decrease this number based on your requirements. Be careful not to raise the limit too high, because a user might subscribe to thousands of alerts and the resulting effect would be both SharePoint Server 2010 and Exchange Server performance degradation.

- **RSS Settings**   Really Simple Syndication (RSS) feeds allow users to subscribe to lists and libraries for sites with a compatible RSS reader, such as Microsoft Outlook 2010. By default, this is enabled for the Web application and is available to many Web parts. Note that it must be manually enabled for many lists and libraries.

- **Blog API Settings**   This is enabled by default and allows user names and passwords to be sent via the Blog API. One of the most common uses of the blog API is using Microsoft Office Word 2010 to compose blogs and then publish directly to a SharePoint Server 2010 blog site.

- **Browser File Handling**   When users upload files to SharePoint Server 2010 or you have custom code in lists, libraries, or the SharePoint Root, you can define how those files are executed. Unless you have a controlled environment, you should leave the default setting of Strict. This prevents attacks, such as cross-site scripting, from compromising the integrity of your server farm. The Strict setting forces the code to be executed on the client browser, not on the physical SharePoint Server 2010 Web server.

- **Web Page Security Validation**   This property will automatically cease a session for sites in the Web application if the session has been idle for a specific amount of time. By default, the time setting is 30 minutes. If users attempt to access a page in a site after being idle for more than the set amount of time, the page will have to be refreshed or the connection will have to be re-established. This is most useful when a Web application is using Forms-based authentication. If a client logs on from a public computer, the session is authenticated for only 30 minutes. This minimizes the risk of a SharePoint Server 2010 session browser being used for an indefinite period of time. If you are using Windows authentication with Internet Explorer's automatic logon with current user name and password, the revalidation of security will happen transparently to the user.

- **Send User Name And Password In E-mail**   This functionality is used only when SharePoint Server 2010 is installed in Active Directory account creation mode. This mode is for Internet Service Providers and is rarely used for organizational SharePoint Server 2010 server farms. If you did not select the advanced installation option of Active Directory account creation mode, this setting has no effect on your Web application, regardless of the setting.

TIP Although this setting probably doesn't affect your Web application for better or worse, many administrators will set this to No to reduce concerns from the Information Assurance auditor.

- **Master Page Setting For Application _Layouts Pages** If you do not enable this setting, all _layouts pages for this Web application will use the application.master page in the SharePoint Root directory. This is usually unacceptable because pages, such as the Site Settings page, will use a different master page than the rest of the site. Figure 4-25 shows the Site Settings page. Note the URL in the address bar of *http://portal.contoso.com/ hr/_layouts/settings.aspx.*

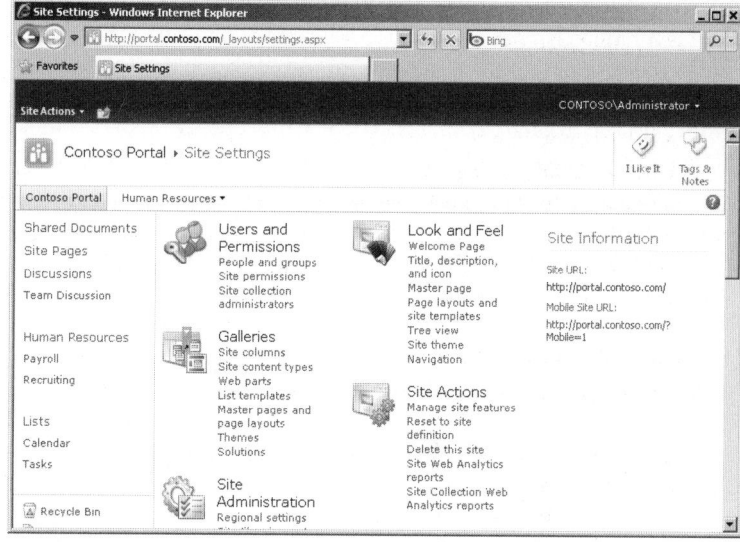

FIGURE 4-25 Site Settings is an example of a page using _layouts.

- **Recycle Bin** First, turning off the Recycle Bin on an active Web application will empty both the first and second stages on all Recycle Bins, and that action is not easily reversed. Second, the time-based expiration setting is a global setting. Therefore, items do not expire from the first stage to the second stage. When the time-based limit is reached, the item is expunged. Think of it this way: if the time-based setting was 90 days and a user emptied her Recycle Bin 60 days after initially deleting an item, the item will remain in the second stage for 30 days. Third, if you turn off time-based expiration and do not use site quotas, the second stage will have no limit. Because the second stage is based on the site quota, site collections without quota will essentially have no second stage storage limit. As you can see, the Recycle Bin should be carefully thought out.

- **Maximum Upload Size**   The maximum upload size limits the size of single files or the aggregate size of multiple files in a single upload action. The latter option is often misunderstood or unknown to administrators. The default setting is 50 MB. For most network infrastructures, 200 to 300 MB is the upper limitation unless there will be no Internet access or wide area network (WAN) access by users. If you begin to get timeouts on uploads you might need to decrease the maximum upload size setting.
- **Customer Experience Improvement Program**   The overhead of this feature is minimal, but it still has an impact. It is not recommended for Internet-facing sites.

Resource Throttling

Resource throttling is a new feature in SharePoint Server 2010, with options for throttling server resources and large lists for each Web application. Throttling is a performance control designed to limit users' ability to negatively affect server performance and to control resource utilization during peak usage. Server resources monitored by default are CPU, Memory, Requests in Queue, and Wait Time.

SharePoint Server 2010 checks resources every 5 seconds and a throttling period will begin after 3 unsuccessful checks. This throttling period will end with a successful check. During a throttle period, HTTP GET requests and Search Robot requests will generate a 503 error and will be logged in the event viewer. No new timer jobs will start during a throttling period.

To enable resource throttling, do the following:

1. On the General Settings Ribbon, select Resource Throttling.
2. Enter values for the List View Threshold option. This option limit queries within a list to guard against performance degradation with too many list items. In SharePoint Server 2010, a list can support up to 50 million items. If a list contains a large number of items, queries with too many results will be very slow. If a user tries an action that would hit a throttle limit, a message will appear listing alternative methods that will not affect farm performance. Two thousand items in a view is the accepted performance limit in SharePoint Server 2010. Increasing the limit beyond 2000 items can have negative performance implications for your Web servers and database servers. The default setting is 50000.
3. Allow or disallow object model override. This allows users with the correct permissions to programmatically override the List View Threshold setting for specific queries. Custom code will most often communicate directly with the object model.
4. Set the list view threshold for auditors and administrators.
5. Define the List View Lookup Threshold. The default of 8 generally works in new implementations. List view lookups can often go beyond six fields. In this event, you need to increase the limit. Queries that have many lookup fields can significantly decrease database performance.

6. Define the List Unique Permission Threshold. This option is rarely changed.

7. Turn Backward-Compatible Event Handlers on or off. By default, this is off. If you have a large amount of development work in SharePoint Server 2007 that leveraged event handlers for lists or libraries, you will want to turn this on. Check with your developers if you are upgrading from SharePoint Server 2007.

8. Configure HTTP Request Monitoring And Throttling. This changes the setting in IIS for all Web servers in the farm, for this Web application.

9. Define the Change Log constraints. Be careful not to reduce this too much because it will negatively affect servers that rely on history information for sites contained in the Web application.

10. Click OK.

Workflow

From the General Settings drop-down menu, select Workflow. Workflows are enabled by default for all Web applications. You can modify the global workflow settings from the Workflow Settings option in Central Administration. In the Web application Workflow Settings management interface, you can enable or disable workflows for a Web application and modify task notifications. Here are the options in that interface:

- **Enable User-Defined Workflows** When set to Yes, this option allows users to create and deploy SharePoint Server 2010 declarative workflows. Users will need at least the design permission level on the site in a particular Web application. These are not code-centric workflows deployed to the server as compiled code.

- **Alert Internal Users Who Do Not Have Access** You can decide whether to alert internal users who do not have site success yet have been defined as a workflow participant. This notification is enabled by default. Upon selecting the embedded hyperlink e-mailed to them, users can request permission to access the site. Selecting No allows workflow tasks to be assigned only to users who have prior permission on the target item of the workflow.

- **Allow External Users To Participate In Workflow** You can enable documents to be e-mailed to external participants in a workflow. This feature is disabled by default, and if security is paramount in your organization it should be left disabled.

Outgoing E-mail

At a minimum, you should select outgoing mail settings, or alerting will not function. The SMTP Relay Server, From Address, and Reply To Address settings must be defined for outgoing e-mail to work.

> **SEE ALSO** Details on Incoming E-mail settings are detailed in Chapter 3, "Configuring Core Operations."

To configure Outgoing E-mail settings, do the following:

1. From the General Settings drop-down menu, select Outgoing E-mail.

2. Define the outgoing SMTP server. This can be any SMTP-compliant server that SharePoint can connect to using TCP port 25.

3. Define the from address. This address will appear as the sender of the e-mail message.

4. Define the reply-to address. This does not need to be the same as the from e-mail, which allows the e-mail to be sent to a different address.

5. Select the character set. This will be the character set of the e-mail being sent. The default is UTF-8, which is most commonly used for e-mail, and allows for characters being used in all languages Unicode supports.

> **IMPORTANT** The SMTP server specified in SharePoint Foundation 2010 and SharePoint Server for outgoing e-mail must allow relaying by IP address. SharePoint products do not authenticate outbound e-mail. You must use another method for high availability, because neither SharePoint Foundation 2010 nor SharePoint Server allows for multiple SMTP server addresses.

Mobile Account

The mobile alert feature allows users to subscribe to alerts with their mobile phones. The idea behind the functionality is many professionals prefer to get important alerts via mobile text (SMS) rather than via e-mail. Not all users have smart phones, or smart phones that are compatible with their corporate e-mail system. Configuring mobile alerts allows notification to almost any cellular telephone.

The feature does come with some drawbacks, however. First of all, you must have a subscription with a third-party SMS provider. The SMS provider acts as a "man in the middle" to relay mobile messages to cellular providers. This comes at a cost. Although the future of this space is widely unknown, current prices range from $.02 USD to $.06 USD. You can find a list of SharePoint Server 2010 compatible providers at *http://messaging.office.microsoft.com/HostingProviders.aspx?src=O14&lc=1033*. There is a constantly changing list, and your costs will vary based on your geographic location and volume of prepaid SMS alerts.

> **NOTE** There is no method to throttle alerts at the Web application level. If you have a user who subscribes to hundreds of alerts or you have a system error, you could quickly increase the costs associated with your third-party provider. Most administrators will want to configure throttling with the third-party provider to mitigate these risks.

To configure the Text Message (SMS) service, do the following:

1. Subscribe to an online SMS provider, and note the URL and user name/password given by the provider.

2. Browse to Central Administration, System Settings, Configure Mobile Account.

3. Enter the URL provided by the SMS provider.
4. Enter the user name and password given to you by the SMS provider.
5. Test account settings.

SharePoint Designer 2010 Governance

New in SharePoint Server 2010 is the ability to govern SharePoint Designer 2010 users. To manage SharePoint Designer 2010 policies, browse to Central Administration, Application Management, Manage Web Applications, and select the Web application to configure. Select SharePoint Designer from the General Settings drop-down menu in the management Ribbon, as seen in Figure 4-26.

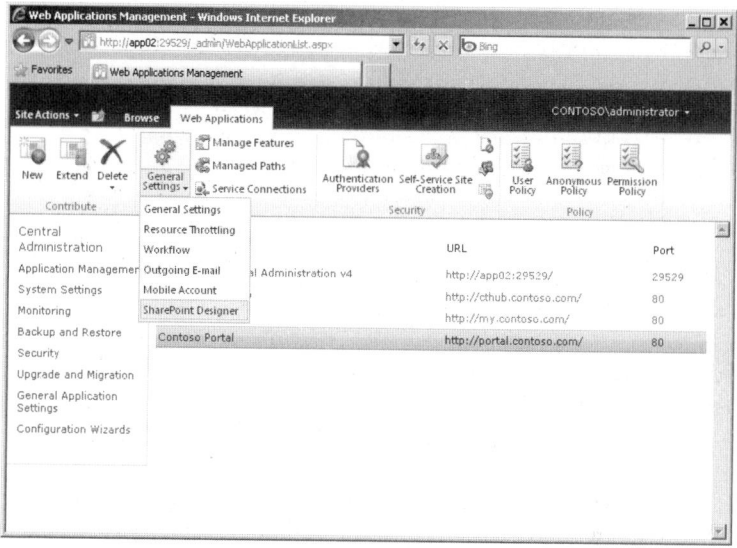

FIGURE 4-26 Select SharePoint Designer from the General Settings menu.

The following options are available to control SharePoint Designer 2010 users:

- Allow SharePoint Designer To Be Used In This Web Application
- Allow Site Collection Administrators To Detach Pages From The Site Template
- Allow Site Collection Administrators To Customize Master Pages And Layout Pages
- Allow Site Collection Administrators To See The URL Structure Of The Web Site

Site collection administrators can further delegate SharePoint Designer permission to site owners. To delegate permissions to site owners, browse to a site collection. From Site Actions, Site Settings, select SharePoint Designer Settings in the Site Collection Administration grouping. Site collection administrators can then control the same options seen in Central Administration.

Manage Features

In a SharePoint Server 2010 farm, there are different levels where features can be installed: farm, Web application, site collection, and site. In Central Administration, Application Management, you can deactivate and activate installed features that are scoped to the Web application. To activate or deactivate features, click Manage Features on the Ribbon. Be sure you select the correct Web applications before modifying, as seen in Figure 4-27.

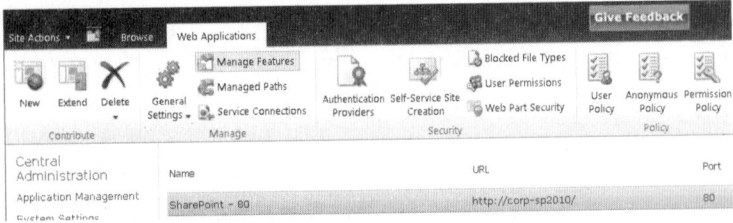

FIGURE 4-27 The Manage Features option on the Web application Ribbon.

Managed Paths

From the Manage area of the Ribbon on the Web Applications tab, click Managed Paths, as seen in Figure 4-28.

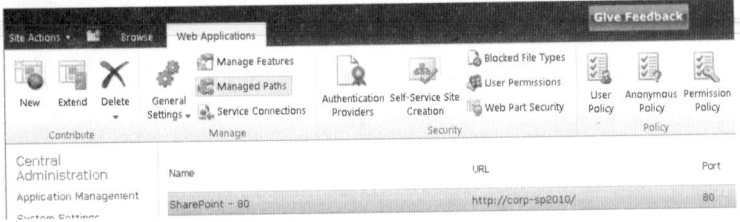

FIGURE 4-28 The Manage Paths option on the Web application Ribbon.

If you have a medium-scale or larger implementation, give serious consideration to extending the default set of managed paths. A managed path is defined as the path in the Uniform Resource Identifier (URI) that is managed by SharePoint products. As an example, *sites* is the managed path in *http://portal.contoso.com/sites/madison*. Managed paths cannot be limited for use by specific security groups, nor can they be targeted directly with audiences. They are simply a way to organize a large quantity of site collections. When using managed paths, you can have two site collections with the same name. For example, *http://portal.contoso.com/HR/Meetings* and *http://portal.contoso.com/Sales/Meetings*.

When adding a new path, you have the option either to include only that path (explicit inclusion) or to specify that path and all subordinate paths (wildcard inclusion). If the path *http://portal.contoso.com/sites* was specified as an explicit inclusion, content can still be served from the WFE file system at *http://portal.contoso.com/sites/path*. When creating an explicit-inclusion managed path, you can then create a single site collection in the root of that path. If *http://portal.contoso.com/sites* was specified as a wildcard inclusion, multiple named site collections can be created under that path.

SEE ALSO For more information on service connections, see Chapter 6.

Alternate Access Mappings

Alternate Access Mappings is the second option in the Web Application area of Application Management in Central Administration. (See Figure 4-29.)

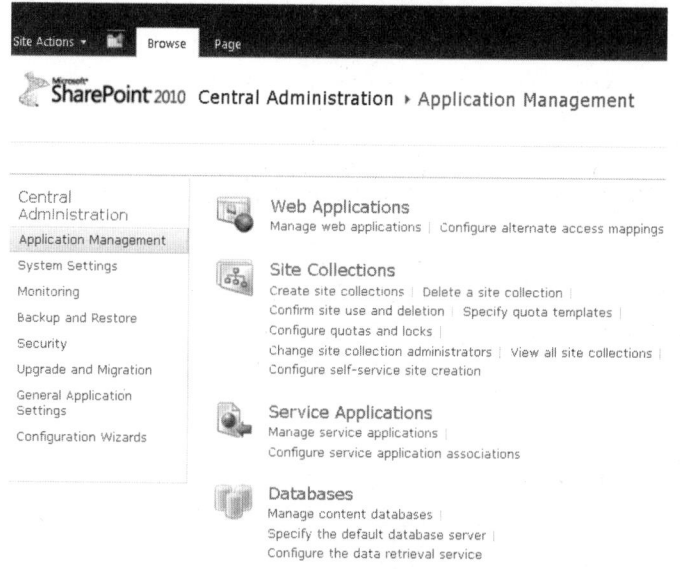

FIGURE 4-29 The Web Applications section of Application Management in Central Administration.

To access alternate access mappings, follow these steps:

1. The account logged into Central Administration must be a member of the farm Administrator's group.

2. From Central Administration, select Application Management.

3. Under Web Applications, you will find two links: Manage Web Applications and Configure Alternate Access Mappings. Select the second link, Configure Alternate Access Mappings. Figure 4-30 shows the Alternate Access Mappings configuration page.

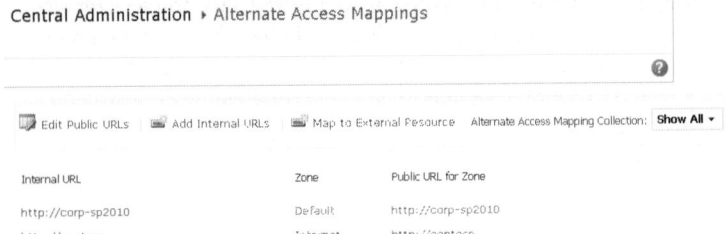

Internal URL	Zone	Public URL for Zone
http://corp-sp2010	Default	http://corp-sp2010
http://contoso	Internet	http://contoso

FIGURE 4-30 The Alternate Access Mappings page.

Alternate access mappings (AAMs) provide a way to change your Web application URLs, configure Network Load Balancing Web applications, and add URLs for alternative access. For example, if you served content from a single Web application via multiple host headers for security, you would need to map the additional host headers with alternate access mapping URLs. Figure 4-31 shows an example of the Web application *http://portal.contoso.com* being served securely and externally as *https://external.contoso.com*.

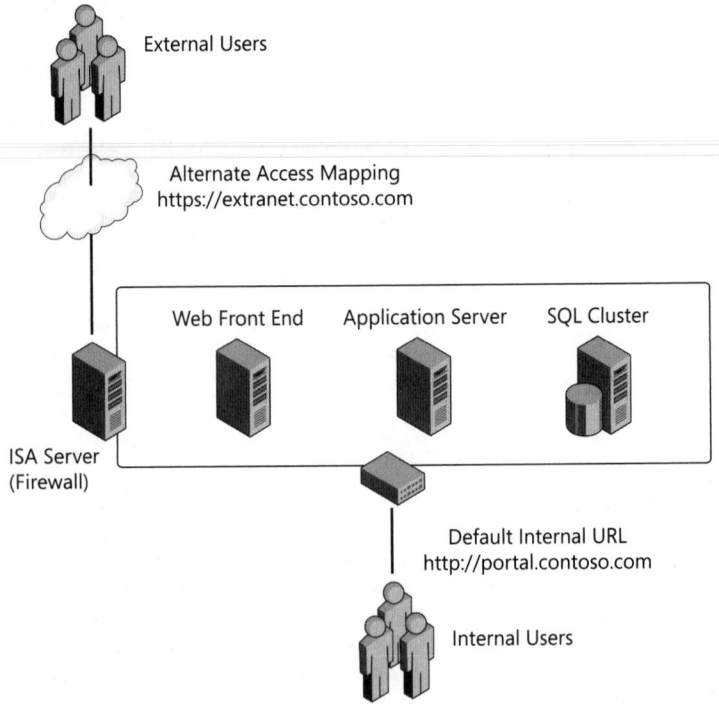

FIGURE 4-31 You must add an alternate access mapping for each additional URL that you configure for a Web application.

In this example, the internal URL already exists, but you must add an alternate access mapping for the external URL. If you do not add the alternate access mapping URL, the host field returned in an external user's browser will be incorrect. Therefore, an external user would be returned *http://portal.contoso.com*, when in fact the user should be returned *https://external.contoso.com*. In addition, the embedded URLs in alert e-mails would be sent incorrectly.

> **CAUTION** Absolute URLs (URLs that are hard-coded on a Web page or document) cannot be mapped.

Configure Alternate Access Mapping

You can edit the public URLs from the Configure Alternate Access settings under Web Applications found in the Application Management section of Central Administration.

There are three choices when modifying AAMs: Edit Public URLs, Edit Default Internal URL/Add Internal URL, and Map To External Resources.

Edit Public URLs

You can edit public URLs from the Alternate Access Mappings page shown in Figure 4-30. By default, there is no AAM collection selected; this feature is for your protection.

After selecting a collection, you have several options for defining the public URLs. Public URLs fill in the URI and authority to correspond with the originating URL from the browser. For example, if a user types **http://portal.contoso.com**, that will be the return address in the browser. Conversely, if a user types **https://external.contoso.com** in the browser, he will be directed to that URL. If the user types a URL that does not exist as an alternate access mapping, the request will fail. For example, if you are using two different IIS virtual servers to publish the same content database or databases and your default internal URL is *http://portal* and your extranet URL is *https://external.contoso.com*, you configure alternate access URLs as follows:

- The default internal URL is *http://portal.contoso.com*.
- Either the Internet, Extranet, or Custom URL setting should be *https://portal.contoso.com*.

When users visit *http://portal*, they are assumed to be on the internal network and will be returned content to *http://portal.contoso.com*. Conversely, if they visit *https://portal.contoso.com*, it is assumed that they are coming from an external network and are returned to https://portal.contoso.com as the correct address. This being the case, your security should not rely on AAM and zones because they merely supplement your firewall and router policies.

Edit Default Internal URL/Add Internal URL

To edit the default URL, select Add Internal URL, select the AAM collection, and change the URL protocol, host, and port; however, do not change the zone. Alternately, you can simply select the hyperlink of the Web application to reach the same interface.

Map To External Resources

In addition to mapping server farm URLs, you can also map URLs to external resources. Most installations do not use this feature, but it can be enabled to allow access, through SharePoint, to other IIS Web applications.

CHAPTER 5

Creating and Managing Site Collections

- Site Creation Modes **141**
- Creating Site Collections **144**
- Site Settings **147**
- Site Collection Security **171**

Creating site collections is one of the basic functions performed by SharePoint administrators, and sometimes, users. Part of the success of Microsoft SharePoint is the ease with which new sites can be provisioned, which is a major advantage over building a Web site from scratch. This chapter will explore the ins and outs of site collections, particularly the different ways they can be created and their management after creation.

Site Creation Modes

One critical decision that must be made by a SharePoint Server 2010 administrator in the process of planning a medium or large-scale deployment is how, and by whom, new sites will be created. Without adequate thought given to this issue, a SharePoint Server 2010 farm can quickly become unmanageable. The ease with which a new site collection can be provisioned necessitates a well thought-out strategy to prevent an explosion of sites with no real organizational hierarchy or that are unmanageable. There are two natively supported site creation modes: administratively controlled site creation and self-service site creation. This section clarifies the differences between the two and provides some guidance in choosing a site collection creation strategy.

Determining Which Mode to Use

The decision of which site creation mode to use is dependent on many factors relating to your farm architecture and the level of a typical user's SharePoint Server 2010 education. With administratively controlled site creation, only farm administrators can create new site collections and only through Central Administration. In an environment where site collection creation must be tightly controlled, limiting this ability to farm administrators is preferred. Power users (or anyone with Full-Control or Hierarchy Manager permissions) can still create subsites directly from parent sites without needing access to Central Administration. If certain users need the ability to create site collections, possibly for informal or "throw-away" type use for temporary projects or other collaborative needs, you can enable self-service site creation. This functionality allows specified users to create their own site collections in the Sites directory.

One other consideration in determining how sites should be created is the handling of permissions. Site collection permissions must be specified individually, whereas subsites can inherit permissions from a parent. In a situation where many users need access to many different site collections, permissions can be difficult to manage with self-service site creation because of the need to specify permissions for each site collection individually.

Enabling Self-Service Site Creation

To enable self-service site creation for a particular Web application, there must be a site already created at the root of the Web application. Otherwise, you will receive an error when attempting to enable self-service site creation. To enable self-service site creation, do the following:

1. Open the Central Administration Web site.

2. In the Application Management section, click the Manage Web Applications link.

3. On the Web Applications Management tab, select a Web application by clicking on it.

4. In the Security section of the management Ribbon, click the Self-Service Site Creation button, as seen in Figure 5-1.

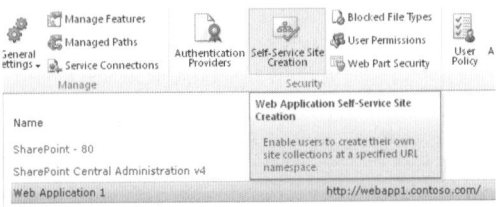

FIGURE 5-1 Self-Service Site Creation button on the Ribbon.

5. In the Self-Service Site Collection Management dialog box, select the On option to enable self-service site creation.

6. Optionally, select the Require Secondary Contact check box to require that a secondary contact name be supplied when users create sites using self-service site creation, as seen in Figure 5-2. If you'll use automatic site deletion, requiring a secondary contact is recommended.

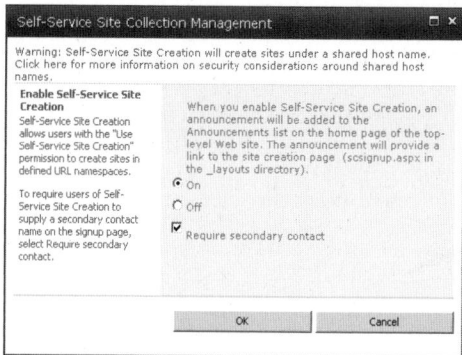

FIGURE 5-2 Self-Service Site Collection Management page.

7. Click OK to save the settings.

Site Use Confirmation and Deletion

Site use confirmation and deletion provides a method of cleaning up the content database by deleting sites within a Web application that are unused or no longer needed. When notifications are turned on, site owners automatically receive e-mail messages regarding sites that have been unused for a specified number of days. They can then confirm that their site collection is still in use or allow it to be deleted if automatic deletion is enabled.

IMPORTANT Outgoing e-mail must be configured for the farm in order for notifications about sites to be sent to site contacts.

The following steps can be used to enable site use confirmation and deletion:

1. Open the Central Administration Web site.

2. On the Home page, click the Application Management heading.

3. On the Application Management page, in the Site Collections section, click the Confirm Site Use And Deletion link.

NOTE Although the Confirm Site Use And Deletion link is found under the Site Collections heading, this setting is configured at the Web-application level. This setting cannot be configured on a site-collection basis.

4. On the Site Use Confirmation And Deletion page, in the Web Application section, choose a Web application, as seen in Figure 5-3.

Web Application
Select a web application.

Web Application: **http://webapp1.contoso.com/** ▾

FIGURE 5-3 Web Application section of the Site Use Confirmation And Deletion page.

5. In the Confirmation And Automatic Deletion Settings section (shown in Figure 5-4), select the Send Email Notifications To Owners Of Unused Site Collections check box.

6. Type the number of days to wait after site creation or confirmation before sending e-mail notifications in the text box.

7. Select the frequency and time of day to check for unused site collections and send notifications.

8. Optionally, select the Automatically Delete Site Collections If Use Is Not Confirmed check box, and in the text box type the number of notices that should be sent before deleting. Be sure to thoroughly test this functionality in your implementation before enabling it. It is possible that all site collection administrators could be notified to keep or delete a site collection.

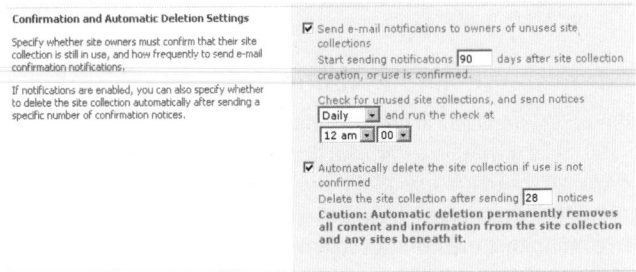

FIGURE 5-4 Confirmation And Automatic Deletion Settings section of New Site Collection page.

9. Click OK to save the settings.

Creating Site Collections

A *site collection* is a grouping of sites that includes a top-level site and all subsites. Subsites are created from the top-level site through the Site Actions menu and are generally related to the top-level site as well as each other. Subsites can inherit their security settings and navigational scheme from their parent, or they can define their own.

Creating a Site Collection Through Central Administration

Site collections are created from the Central Administration Web site. To create a site collection, perform the following steps:

1. Open the Central Administration Web site.

2. In the Application Management section, click the Create Site Collections link.

3. On the Create Site Collection page, in the Web Application section, choose the Web application where the site collection should be created.

4. In the Title And Description section, type a title for the site in the Title text box and (optionally) type a description for the site in the Description text box.

5. In the Web Site Address section (shown in Figure 5-5), choose a managed path for the site and type the URL where the site should be created.

   NOTE Only the wildcard managed paths that have already been defined will be available in the drop-down menu. See Chapter 4, "Building and Managing Web Applications," for information on creating managed paths. The *sites* managed path is created automatically when a Web application is provisioned.

FIGURE 5-5 Web Site Address section of the New Site Collection page.

6. In the Template Selection section (shown in Figure 5-6), choose a site template to use to create the top-level site in your site collection.

   NOTE The templates that are available will vary based on a number of factors, including which version of SharePoint Products is installed and whether there are any custom site templates installed.

   If you have multiple language packs installed, you will also need to select a language for the site.

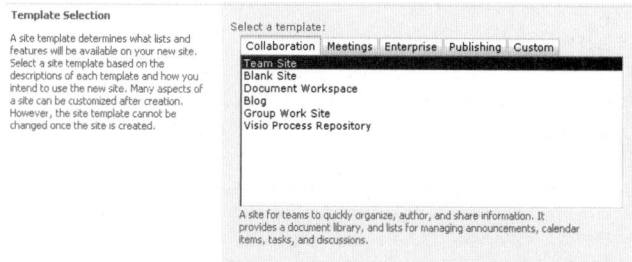

FIGURE 5-6 Template Selection section of the Create Site Collection page.

7. In the Primary Site Collection Administrator section, type the name of the user who will perform the site collection administrator duties for the site collection.

8. Optionally, in the Secondary Site Collection Administrator section, type the name of a secondary site collection administrator.

9. Click OK to create the site collection. When the site collection has been created, you will be directed to the Top-level Site Successfully Created page, where there will be a link to the newly created site collection.

Creating a Site Collection Using the Self-Service URL

When an administrator enables self-service site creation, an announcement is added to the top-level site in the site collection with a link to the self-service URL. This URL can be provided to users for creating sites as needed. To create a site collection, do the following:

1. Navigate to the top-level site in the site collection and find the self-service site creation announcement in the Announcements list.

   NOTE The Announcements list is not automatically shown on the Home page of the Team Site template as it was in SharePoint 2007. Either you have to add the list view Web part to the home page manually or users will have to click the View All Site Content link and then click the Announcements link under Lists.

2. Open the announcement.

3. In the body of the announcement, click the link provided, as shown in Figure 5-7.

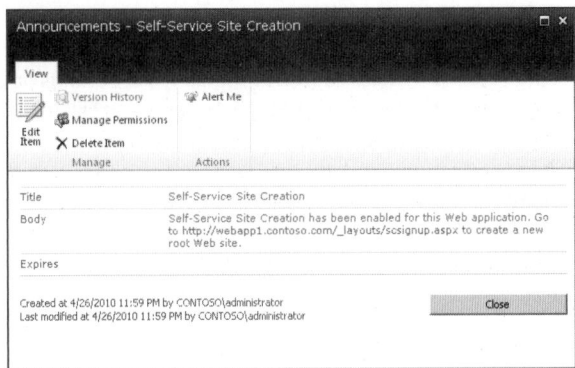

FIGURE 5-7 Self-service site creation announcement.

4. In the Title And Description section, type a title for the site in the Title text box and (optionally) type a description for the site in the Description text box.

5. In the Web Site Address section, type the URL where the site should be created. Only wildcard managed paths are available outside of Central Administration.

6. In the Template Selection section, choose a site template to use to create the top-level site in your site collection.

7. Click Create to create the site collection.

8. You will be sent to the Set Up Groups For This Site page, where you can create the groups to be used for the Visitors, Members, and Owners roles on the site.

9. In the Visitors To This Site section, leave Create New Group selected and leave the default name in the Name text box. You can add users to this group directly from this page by adding them using the People Picker below the membership list text box, as demonstrated in Figure 5-8.

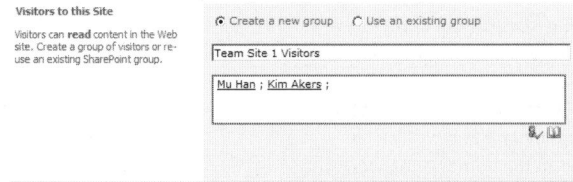

FIGURE 5-8 Site Visitors group membership section of the New Site Collection page.

10. Add users to the Members and Owners groups as needed.

11. Click OK to save the group settings.

Site Settings

Top-level sites, as well as subsites, are managed through the Site Settings page. In a site collection, each subsite has its own Site Settings page, and the top-level site has a Site Settings page that applies to the site collection itself. To access the Site Settings page for any site, simply click the Site Settings link on the Site Actions menu. From the Site Settings page of a subsite or workspace, the site collection settings page can be accessed from the Site Collection Settings section, where there is a link to the top-level Site Settings page. The settings shown on the Site Settings page are filtered based on the user's role within the site collection.

> **TIP** To manage the site collection settings, you must be a site collection administrator. To manage site settings (for the top-level site and subsites), you must be a site owner. If you see site settings only in the top-level site, and not the site collection settings, you are not a site collection administrator.

Regional Settings

Regional settings control how a site behaves, including how lists are sorted and how values such as dates are displayed. Regional settings for a site are based on standards for a particular region of the world. For example, some parts of the world use a 24-hour clock, and others, such as the United States, use a 12-hour clock as a general rule. Also, some regions of the world use the Gregorian calendar and other regions use different calendars. Here are the regional settings available to a site:

- **Locale**   The world region that settings should be based on.
- **Sort Order**   The method used for sorting.
- **Time Zone**   The standard time zone.
- **Calendar**   The type of calendar used, such as Gregorian or Buddhist.
- **Secondary Calendar**   An additional calendar to provide extra information about the calendar features.
- **Work Week**   The standard working days of the week for the region. This includes other settings, such as first day of the week and first week of the year, as well as workday start and end times.
- **Time Format**   Defines either the 12-hour or 24-hour clock.

Regional settings for a site can be managed through the Regional Settings link on the Site Settings page of the site.

Creating and Managing Document Libraries

Document libraries provide a central location for storing and managing documents. They can be organized into folder hierarchies as in the traditional network file share model, but with much better management capabilities, such as document check-in and check-out, automatic versioning, and integrated workflow.

Create a Document Library

To create a document library, follow these steps:

1. From the Site Actions menu, click New Document Library.
2. Type a name and description for the document library.
3. Specify whether to display the new document library on the Quick Launch toolbar.
4. Specify whether to turn on versioning for the document library.
5. Choose a document template to be used when creating new documents in this library.
5. Click Create to create the document library.

Configuring Document Library Versioning Settings

One of the most powerful document management features of SharePoint Server 2010 is versioning. Versioning tracks changes to a document throughout its life cycle and provides the ability to go back and look at the document as it existed at any previous point where a version was saved. SharePoint provides the ability to track major and minor versions of a document.

Document libraries can be configured to require documents to be checked out before they can be edited. Checking out the document locks it for editing to prevent multiple users from interfering with one another while trying to edit the file. If check-out is required, a user must check in a document before another user can check it out for editing. To configure versioning and check-out requirements for a document library, do the following:

1. From the document library default page, click the Library tab in the management Ribbon.

2. In the Library Ribbon, in the Settings section, click Library Settings.

3. On the Document Library Settings page, click Versioning Settings.

4. On the Versioning Settings page, in the Content Approval section, select Yes to turn on content approval for the document library. This will cause new items and changes to existing items to remain in a draft state until they are approved.

5. In the Document Version History section, choose whether to implement major versions, major and minor versions, or no versioning. You can also specify how many major versions to keep and how many of those major versions to keep drafts for.

6. In the Draft Item Security section, choose who should be able to view drafts of documents in the library.

7. In the Require Check-Out section, choose whether to require documents to be checked out before editing.

8. Click OK to save the settings. An example of the Versioning Settings page can be seen in Figure 5-9.

Content Approval	
Specify whether new items or changes to existing items should remain in a draft state until they have been approved. Learn about requiring approval.	Require content approval for submitted items? ○ Yes ● No
Document Version History	

Specify whether a version is created each time you edit a file in this document library. Learn about versions.	Create a version each time you edit a file in this document library?
	○ No versioning
	○ Create major versions
	   Example: 1, 2, 3, 4
	● Create major and minor (draft) versions
	   Example: 1.0, 1.1, 1.2, 2.0
	Optionally limit the number of versions to retain:
	☑ Keep the following number of major versions:
	   [5]
	☑ Keep drafts for the following number of major versions:
	   [3]

Draft Item Security	
Drafts are minor versions or items which have not been approved. Specify which users should be able to view drafts in this document library. Learn about specifying who can view and edit drafts.	Who should see draft items in this document library? ● Any user who can read items ○ Only users who can edit items ○ Only users who can approve items (and the author of the item)
Require Check Out	
Specify whether users must check out documents before making changes in this document library. Learn about requiring check out.	Require documents to be checked out before they can be edited? ○ Yes ● No

FIGURE 5-9 Document library Versioning Settings page.

Configuring Document Library Advanced Settings

The document library Advanced Settings page provides a catch-all for miscellaneous settings related to document libraries. The following list describes the settings available on the Advanced Settings page:

- **Content Types**   Specifies whether to allow the management of content types on this document library. Each content type will appear on the new button and can have a unique set of columns, workflows, and other behaviors.

- **Document Template**   Specifies the URL to the template to be used for new documents. If multiple content types are enabled, this setting is managed per content type.

- **Opening Documents In The Browser**   Specifies the behavior that should be used when opening a document, whether to open the document in the client application or the browser. If the client application is unavailable, the browser will always be used.

- **Custom Send To Destination**   Specifies the name and URL of a destination that should appear in the Send To context menu option of documents in the library.

- **Folders**   Specifies whether the New Folder menu item is available in the toolbar.
- **Search**   Specifies whether documents in the library should be included in search results.
- **Offline Client Availability**   Specifies whether the document library should be available to offline clients.
- **Site Assets Library**   Specifies whether this library should be presented as the default location for storing images or other files that users upload to their wiki pages.
- **Datasheet**   Specifies whether datasheet mode is available for bulk editing of this document library.
- **Dialogs**   If dialog boxes are available, specify whether to launch the new, edit, and display forms in a dialog box. Selecting No causes these actions to navigate to the full page.

Configuring Other General Settings

There are many other settings that can be configured for document libraries. The following list describes the most common ones:

- **Validation settings**   New for SharePoint 2010, you can now enter validation formulas to be evaluated when documents are added to a document library.
- **Column default value settings**   Administrators can specify default column values for documents added to the library.
- **Rating settings**   You can enable ratings for documents in a document library, which will add ratings fields to the content types used by the library and to the default view.
- **Audience targeting settings**   Enabling audience targeting creates a targeting column for the library, which can be used to filter the view of the library by audience.
- **Metadata navigation settings**   This page can be used to configure metadata navigation hierarchies and key filter input controls. You can also enable the automatic creation of indices on the library to enhance query performance.
- **Per-location view settings**   This page allows for the management of views available for the library. Views can be specified explicitly here or configured to be inherited from a parent.

Managing Acceptable Document Types and Sizes

SharePoint 2010 provides the ability to specify the document types that are allowed to be stored and created in document libraries through the use of the Blocked File Types list. This list is managed through the Central Administration Web site.

Blocked file types are specified on a per–Web application basis. To add a file to the Blocked File Types list, do the following:

1. Open SharePoint 2010 Central Administration, and click the Security link in the left navigation pane.

2. Select Define Blocked File Types in the General Security section.

3. Choose the Web application to define blocked file types for.

4. Add the file extension of the file type to be blocked on a new line in the list, as seen in Figure 5-10.

5. Click OK to save the changes.

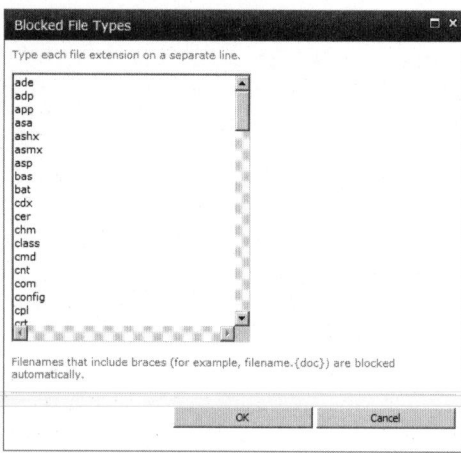

FIGURE 5-10 The Blocked File Types list.

Setting Size Limitations on Documents

You cannot limit the size of documents from within the Site settings or Document Library settings. You can only limit the size of files uploaded to a Web application. This setting is available from the SharePoint 2010 Central Administration Web site and can be modified in the following way:

1. Open Central Administration, and click Manage Web Applications in the Application Management section.

2. Click the Web application whose upload size limit you want to modify.

3. In the Manage section of the management Ribbon, click the General Settings drop-down menu and choose General Settings.

4. On the Web Application General Settings page, scroll down to the Maximum Upload Size section near the bottom of the page.

5. In the Maximum Upload Size text box, type the maximum allowed size for uploads.

6. Click OK to save the settings.

NOTE The Maximum Upload Size setting applies to any single upload, whether it's a single file or a group of files. Therefore, even if the individual files are below the maximum, if the combined size of a group of uploaded files exceeds the maximum you will receive an error upon attempting the upload.

Using Content Types in Document Libraries

Content types were introduced in SharePoint 2007 to provide a means of encapsulating settings and metadata for a particular type of content. A single document library can host one or more content types simultaneously. When a new document library is created, a content type called Document is provisioned with a document template based on the default document type of the document library. For example, if the default document type is set to be Microsoft Excel, the document template for the default Document content type will be template.xls.

By default, content types cannot be managed for a document library. To perform actions such as adding a content type or modifying the default content type, you must first allow management of content types in the Advanced Settings menu of the document library settings. To add a content type to a document library, perform the following steps:

1. From the document library default page, click the Library tab in the management Ribbon.

2. In the Library Ribbon, in the Settings section, click Library Settings.

3. On the Document Library Settings page, click Advanced Settings.

4. On the Advanced Settings page, in the Content Types section, choose Yes to allow management of content types.

5. Click OK to save the settings.

6. In the Document Library Settings page, a new section is available called Content Type. Click the Add From Existing Site Content Types link.

7. On the Add Content Types page, choose Document Content Types from the Select Site Content Types From drop-down list because you are adding a content type to a document library. Figure 5-11 shows the Add Content Types page with the Form content type being added to a document library.

8. Choose the new content type to add from the Available Site Content Types list, and click the Add button to add it to the document library.

9. Click OK to finish adding the new content type to the document library.

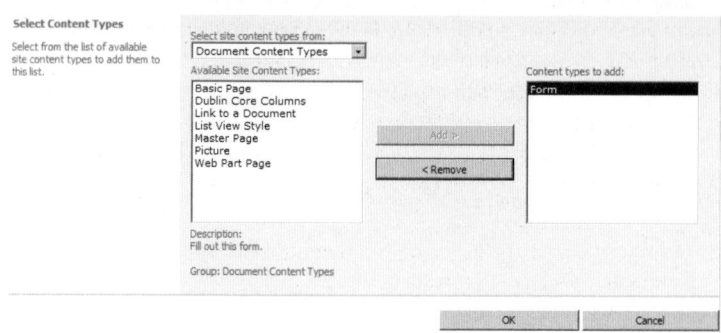

FIGURE 5-11 The Add Content Types page.

Creating and Managing Lists

Lists provide the basic building blocks of SharePoint 2010 products. They allow data to be organized logically and manipulated easily. List creation and management is a fundamental concept to understanding SharePoint 2010 Products. To create a list, follow these steps:

1. From the site where the list is to be created, click the Site Actions menu and choose More Options.

2. Choose the type of list to create. For this example, you will create a new Announcements list, so click Announcements.

3. On the Create page, type a name for the list and (optionally) give it a description, by clicking More Options.

4. Specify whether to display a link to the list on the Quick Launch toolbar.

5. Click Create to create the list.

NOTE The various library types, such as document and picture, as well as discussion boards and surveys are all specialized types of lists.

Site Columns (Field Definitions)

Shared list columns, also called *site columns*, provide a column definition that can be reused among lists without the need to redefine the column in each list. The site column is defined once at the site level and saved as a template from which lists and content types can reference it. When a site column is added to a list, a local copy of the column is created as a list column. Any changes made to that column from the list are local changes, applying only to the list column.

There were a few problematic points in site columns in SharePoint Server 2007 that have been resolved in SharePoint Server 2010. In SharePoint Server 2007, there was no out-of-the-box way to specify that a site column should be unique. Also, there was no easy way to provide validation on data entered into a column. These problems were solvable using custom development, and there were certainly some creative solutions developed by the community, but most IT professionals did not have the time or expertise to delve into the world of custom development. Furthermore, these were features that just seemed like they should be available and require minimal effort to implement. In SharePoint 2010, these features are available out of the box, as can be seen when creating a new site column. To create a new site column, do the following:

1. From the site where the column should be created, click the Site Actions menu and choose Site Settings.

2. In the Galleries section of the Site Settings page, choose Site columns.

3. On the Site Columns page, click Create.

4. In the Name And Type section, type a name in the Column Name box.

5. Choose a type for the column in the type list, as seen in Figure 5-12. You will choose Single Line Of Text for this example.

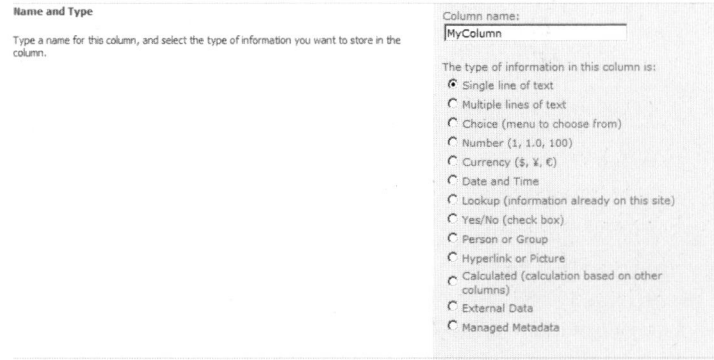

FIGURE 5-12 Available column types provided by default.

6. Choose a group for the new column. Groups are simply a means of organizing site columns to make them easier to browse.

7. In the Additional Column Settings section, (optionally) type a description for the column.

8. Choose whether to make the column required by default.

9. Choose whether the column values should be unique.

10. Because you chose Single Line Of Text, you are asked to specify the maximum number of characters for the column. The default is 255.

11. You can also provide a default value, either text or some calculated value. If this setting is left blank, no default value will be used.

12. Optionally, in the Column Validation section, enter a formula to be used to validate data in the column. This formula must evaluate to True for the validation to pass.

If you are providing a validation function for the site column, you should also type a user message to explain to those entering data in the column what is considered valid data.

13. Click OK to save the new site column.

After you have created a new site column, you can now add it to a list. To add a site column to a list, do the following:

1. From the list where the site column should be added, click the List tab in the List Tools area of the management Ribbon.

2. In the Settings section on the List Ribbon, and choose List Settings.

3. In the Columns section of the List Settings page, click Add From Existing Site Columns.

4. Leave the Select Site Columns From drop-down list set to All Groups, and find the column you want to add in the Available Site Columns list.

5. Click on the column you want to add, and then click the Add button to add it to the Columns To Add list.

6. In the Options section, choose whether to add the column to the default view of the list.

7. Click OK to finish adding the column to the list.

Content Types

As in SharePoint Server 2007, content types are one of the building blocks of lists in SharePoint Server 2010. As stated previously, content types provide a means of encapsulating settings and metadata for a particular type of content in a template that can be reused and is independent of any particular list or library. Content types can include one or more of the following:

- Content metadata, represented by columns that will be added to the list or library upon addition of the content type
- Custom forms, used for New, Edit, and Display functions
- Workflows that can be designed to start automatically based on some event or condition or manually started by a user
- The document template on which to base the documents created from this type (for document content types only)
- Custom information stored as XML files

Just like site columns, content types are scoped at both the site and list levels. Content types are created at the site level and then are available to the containing site and any subsites beneath it. When a content type is added to a list or document library, a local copy of the content type is created. This is known as a list content type, and any changes made to it directly apply only to the list where it resides. To create a new content type, do the following:

1. From the Site Actions menu, choose Site Settings.

2. In the Galleries section, click Site Content Types.

3. On the Site Content Types page, click Create.

4. On the New Site Content Type page, type a name for the new content type in the Name box and (optionally) type a description.

5. Choose the type of parent content type the new content type will be created from, and choose the parent content type. All new content types must be created from a parent content type, as seen in Figure 5-13.

6. In the Group section, specify the group for the new content type. You can either choose an existing group or specify a new group.

7. Click OK to save the new content type.

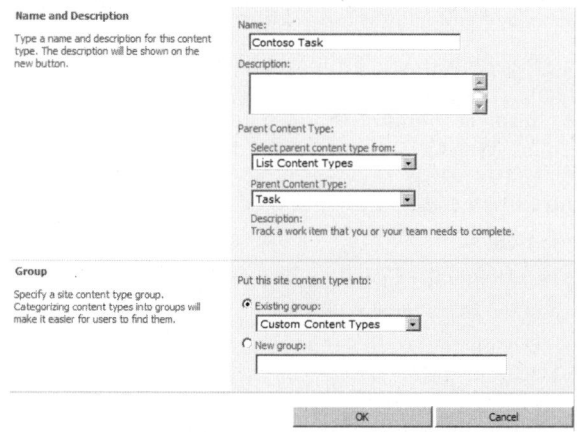

FIGURE 5-13 New Site Content Type page.

Adding the content type to a list can be accomplished the same way as adding a content type to a document library. After a content type has been added, the content type will be available on the New Item menu when creating new list items. Figure 5-14 shows the New Item menu of the Task list with a custom content type called Contoso Task added.

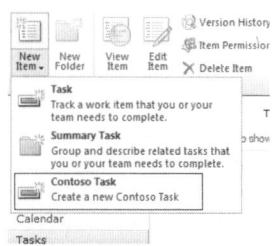

FIGURE 5-14 New Item menu of the Tasks list with the Contoso Task content type added.

List Forms

One of the great features of SharePoint going back to the very beginning has been the ability to perform Create, Read, Update, and Delete (CRUD) functions on lists through the user interface (UI) without having to actually build the UI forms. When a list is created, the pages for performing these actions are automatically provisioned. This works great if you want your users to be able to edit all of the columns in the list when a new item is inserted or updated. But what if you want only certain columns to be available through the UI, and you want other columns to be updated through an event handler on the list? In previous versions of SharePoint, this required some creativity. By default, all columns were available on insert and update and there was no easy way to modify the forms for an individual list.

This problem has been addressed in SharePoint Server 2010 with the ability to modify the forms for each individual list in Microsoft InfoPath Designer 2010. InfoPath can be used to add and remove fields and to add pictures, validation, formatted text, and more. When a list is created, the default forms are provisioned as in SharePoint 2007, but an administrator can build customized forms to be used instead using InfoPath 2010. To modify a task form using InfoPath Designer 2010, perform the following steps:

1. From the list where the site column should be added, click the List tab in the List Tools area of the management Ribbon.
2. In the Settings section on the List Ribbon, and choose List Settings.
3. In the General Settings section of the List Settings page, click Form Settings.
4. On the Form Settings page, click OK to customize the default Tasks form using InfoPath 2010.
5. In the Design view for the form, right-click inside the Predecessors row and choose Delete and then Rows.
6. Do the same for the Priority row.
7. Click the File tab, and choose Publish to publish the changes to SharePoint.
8. On the Publish page, choose SharePoint List.
9. When you receive the message that the form has been published successfully, click OK.

Figure 5-15 shows the default form for the Tasks list, and Figure 5-16 shows the edited form with the Predecessors and Priority rows removed.

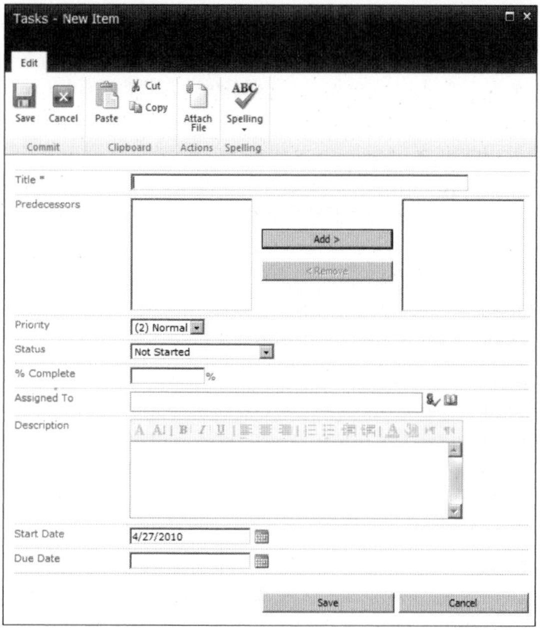

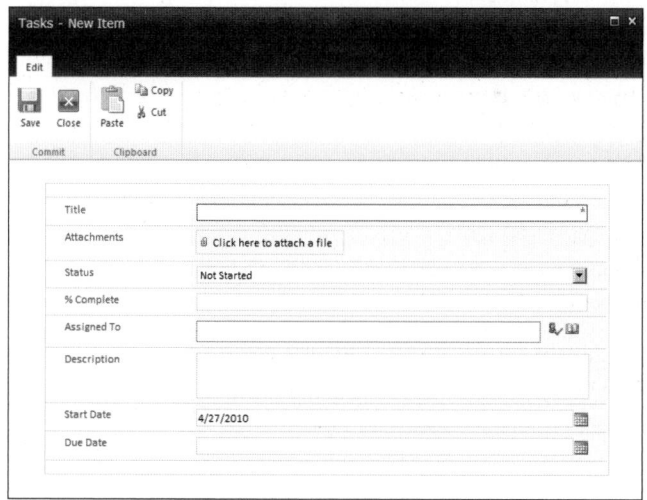

FIGURE 5-15 Default Tasks form.

FIGURE 5-16 Customized Tasks form with Predecessors and Priority fields removed.

Sandboxed Solutions

SharePoint Server 2007 introduced solutions as a way to package functionality for deployment to a server farm. When functionality is deployed using a solution, SharePoint automatically manages the deployment of the functionality on servers that are added to the farm. In SharePoint Server 2007, however, solutions could only be deployed at the farm level by a farm administrator. Microsoft has addressed this limitation by providing a new feature called *sandboxed solutions*.

> **TIP** Many places in the UI refer to sandboxed solutions as *user solutions*. They are one and the same.

Sandboxed solutions are solutions that can be deployed to a specific site collection and are limited in scope to that site collection. This means that the solution is effectively placed within a "sandbox" and can affect only the site collection where it is deployed. Sandboxed solutions can also be limited in the amount of resources they can consume and be automatically disabled if resource consumption crosses the defined threshold. To deploy a sandboxed solution, do the following:

1. From the site collection where the solution will be deployed, click the Site Actions menu and choose Site Settings.

2. On the Site Settings page, in the Galleries section, click Solutions.

3. In the Solutions Library, click the Solutions tab in the management Ribbon and choose Upload Solution.

4. In the Upload Document window, click the Browse button, find the solution file to be uploaded, and then click Open.

5. Click OK to upload the solution.

6. On the Solutions tab, click Activate.

User Alerts

As the number of sites, and presumably the number of lists and libraries, in your SharePoint farm grows, it will become a much more difficult task to keep up with the changes to lists and libraries across various sites and Web applications. This is where alerts come in. Alerts provide the ability to be notified by e-mail when a particular type of change happens in a list or library, so they can be created and then essentially forgotten until an event occurs on the list that triggers the associated alert action. To create an alert, perform the following steps:

1. From the site containing the list for which you want to be alerted, click the personalization context menu in the top right corner of the screen, as demonstrated in Figure 5-17.

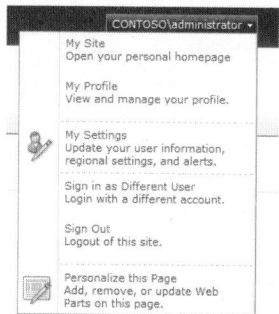

FIGURE 5-17 Personalization context menu.

2. Choose My Settings.

3. On the User Information page, click My Alerts.

4. Click Add Alert.

5. Choose a list or document library to get alerts for, and click Next.

6. On the New Alert page, in the Alert Title section, type a descriptive title for the alert.

7. In the Send Alerts To section, ensure that your user name is listed. Additionally, add the user names of any other users who should receive the same alert.

8. In the Delivery Method section, choose a delivery method for the alert.

   NOTE For alerts to be sent by e-mail, outgoing e-mail settings must be configured for the farm. For alerts to be sent via text message (SMS), the SMS settings must be configured for the farm. All of these settings can be configured in Central Administration in the Email And Text Messages (SMS) section of the System Settings page.

9. In the Change Type section, choose the types of changes that you want to be alerted to. Choosing All Changes will cause alerts to be sent for any additions, modifications, or deletions that occur.

10. In the Send Alerts For These Changes section, choose whether to filter alerts based on specific criteria, such as who made the changes, who created the original item, and whether there is an expiration date associated with the item.

11. In the When To Send Alerts section, choose the frequency with which alerts should be sent. Notifications can be sent immediately or on a daily or weekly schedule.

12. Click OK to save the alert.

Alerts for a user can be managed through the My Alerts page, which is accessed by following steps 1 through 3 in the procedure just shown.

Discussions

A discussion list is a specialized list that uses the Thread and Message content types to provide functionality similar to a Web newsgroup or discussion board. A new thread is created in the discussion list with a subject and body, and then replies can be added. The topics are displayed by subject, but when a user clicks on a topic, the replies can be viewed in a flat or threaded view. An example of the flat view is shown in Figure 5-18.

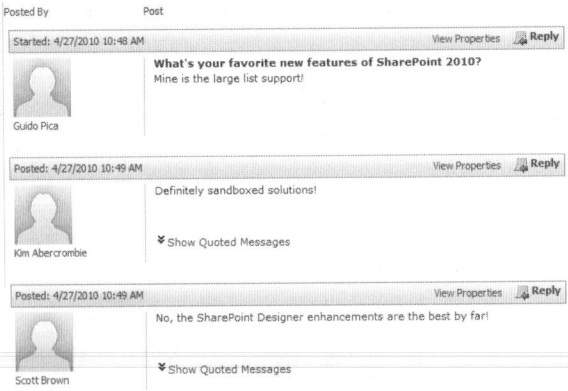

FIGURE 5-18 The flat view of a discussion topic.

The same topic is shown in Figure 5-19 using the threaded view.

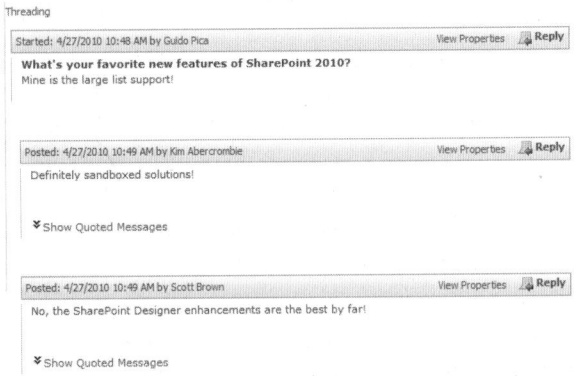

FIGURE 5-19 The threaded view of a discussion topic.

To create a new discussion list, do the following:

1. From the Site Actions menu, click More Options.
2. On the Create page, choose Discussion Board from the Communication category.
3. On the New page, give the discussion board a name and (optionally) a description, by clicking More Options.
4. In the Navigation section, specify whether to show the new discussion board on the Quick Launch toolbar.
5. Click Create to create the new discussion board.

To create a new discussion topic, do the following:

1. Navigate to the discussion board where you want to post a new topic.
2. Click Add New Discussion.
3. Enter a subject and body for the discussion.
4. Click Save to save the new discussion topic.

To post a reply to a discussion topic, follow these steps:

1. From the discussion board where the topic resides, click the topic link.
2. Choose the message to reply to—either the original message or an existing reply—and click Reply from that message.

> **NOTE** Notice that the Subject field is missing from the Reply form. You cannot change the subject of a message when you reply to it. You can only enter text for the body of your reply, which will be appended to the other replies.

3. Click Save to post the reply.

RSS (Really Simple Syndication)

The dynamic nature of SharePoint content makes it a perfect candidate for RSS. RSS provides the ability to monitor changes to SharePoint content in a simple and straightforward way, with the latest changes being automatically downloaded and bubbled to the top of your chosen RSS feed reader, such as Internet Explorer 7 or Outlook 2007. Just as in SharePoint 2007, RSS feed creation in SharePoint 2010 is accomplished automatically for every list created. To view a list using RSS, do the following:

1. Navigate to the list you want to view using RSS.
2. Click the List tab in the List Tools area of the management Ribbon.
3. In the Share and Track section of the Ribbon, choose RSS Feed.

> **NOTE** The content of the list will automatically be rendered using RSS, and the output will be formatted via XSLT for most browsers. If you are using Internet Explorer 8, or any other modern browser, you can subscribe to the feed directly from this page.

4. If you are using Internet Explorer 8, you can simply click Subscribe To This Feed to set up a subscription to the feed.

Managing RSS Settings for a List

The RSS settings for a list can be modified from the List Settings page by clicking the RSS Settings link in the Communications section. Table 5-1 shows the available settings.

TABLE 5-1 RSS Settings for a List.

SETTING	DESCRIPTION
Allow RSS for this list?	Yes or No
Truncate multi-line text fields to 256 characters?	Yes or No
Title	Title channel element of RSS feed definition
Description	Description channel element of RSS feed
Image URL	Image URL channel element of RSS feed
Columns	List columns to be included in RSS feed
Maximum items to include	Integer representing the maximum number of items to be included in the RSS feed
Maximum days to include	Maximum number of previous days to include in RSS feed

Recycle Bin

The Recycle Bin was introduced in SharePoint 2007 and has proven to be a very useful tool in recovering from the accidental deletion of objects in SharePoint. The Recycle Bin provides similar functionality to that of the Windows Recycle Bin, allowing deleted documents or list items to be preserved for a period of time before being permanently destroyed. At any time while a document or list item resides in the Recycle Bin, it can be restored to its original location.

End User Recycle Bin

The Recycle Bin in SharePoint 2010 actually exists on two levels. The first of these levels is the end user Recycle Bin. When a user deletes an item from a list or library, the item gets sent to the end user Recycle Bin where it remains until it is purged by either the user or automatically based on administrative settings.

Site Collection Recycle Bin

When an item is purged from the end user Recycle Bin, it is moved into the site collection Recycle Bin. All objects purged by users in all subsites as well as the top-level site are moved here. This second layer of recoverability allows the administrator to restore files that have been deleted by users and even purged from their Recycle Bins. To restore an item from the end user Recycle Bin, do the following:

1. From the home page of the site, click the Recycle Bin link in the left navigation pane.
2. Select the box next to the item to be restored.
3. Click Restore Selection as demonstrated in Figure 5-20.

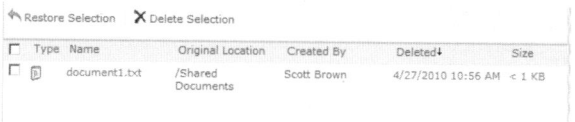

FIGURE 5-20 End user Recycle Bin.

Managing the Site Collection Recycle Bin

The site collection Recycle Bin can be managed from the top-level site settings page. There are two views available for this Recycle Bin: one for viewing items located in end users' Recycle Bins throughout the site collection, and the other for managing items that have been purged from users' Recycle Bins and are now located in the administrative Recycle Bin, with the former being the default.

From the site users' view, you can see all the items deleted by users within the site collection. From here, you can delete individual items, sending them to the administrative Recycle Bin, or you can empty the users' Recycle Bins all at once by clicking Empty Recycle Bin. Using either method, the deleted items end up in the administrative Recycle Bin. From here, they can be permanently deleted or restored to their original locations.

Recycle Bin Settings

The Recycle Bin functionality can be managed on a Web-application basis through Central Administration. Use the following steps to manage the Recycle Bin for a Web application:

1. Open Central Administration, and click Manage Web Applications in the Application Management section of the home page.
2. Click on the Web applications you want to manage Recycle Bin settings for.
3. In the Manage section of the management Ribbon, click the General Settings drop-down menu and choose General Settings.

4. On the General Settings page, scroll down to the Recycle Bin section near the bottom of the page.

Table 5-2 shows the available settings for the Recycle Bin.

TABLE 5-2 Recycle Bin Settings

SETTING	DESCRIPTION
Recycle Bin Status	Turns user-level Recycle Bin on or off
Delete items in the Recycle Bin	Specifies the retention period; default is 30 days
Second-stage Recycle Bin	Specifies amount of storage to add to the quota or whether to disable altogether

Portal Site Connection

A portal provides the ability to aggregate and organize site collections in an organization. It generally provides the ability to browse and search for sites by specified criteria. Any site collection can be linked to from the portal, typically using the Sites Directory, but sites by default don't have a clear path back to the portal. This is the purpose of the portal site connection—it provides a navigational breadcrumb link back to the portal site. The following steps demonstrate how to configure the portal site connection for a site collection:

1. From the Site Actions menu of the site collection, choose Site Settings.

2. In the Site Collection Administration Section, choose the Portal Site Connection link.

3. Select the option to connect to the portal site.

4. Type the Web address of the portal.

5. Type a friendly name for the portal. This will be the name displayed in the breadcrumb link on all pages in the site collection.

6. Click OK.

Figure 5-21 shows the breadcrumb link back to the main portal site, which can be accessed by clicking the folder icon just to the right of the Site Actions menu.

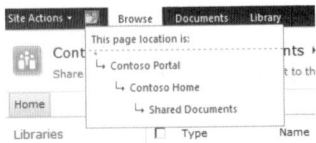

FIGURE 5-21 The portal navigation breadcrumb.

Information Management Policies

An Information Management Policy is a container for a set of rules that can be applied to a type of content. Rules within a policy are called *policy features*. Information management policies allow you to control access to information within your organization and to specify how long it should be retained, what to do when the retention period expires, and so on. Policies can be implemented to enable organizational compliance with legally mandated requirements, such as the Sarbanes-Oxley Act in the US, or internal requirements within an organization.

Policy features are enabled by a farm administrator and, once enabled, can be used by site collection administrators to create and implement policies. Some available policy features include the following:

- **Expiration**   Allows for the disposal or processing of content based on time, such as a specific date, a date based on columns associated with the content, or a length of time relative to some action involving the content.

- **Auditing**   Allows for logging of actions or events related to content, such as editing or viewing of a document, check-in or check-out of a document, changing permissions of a document, or deleting a document.

- **Labeling**   Enables labels to be formatted and for searchable text areas to be automatically associated with a document or list item.

- **Barcode**   Allows tracking of physical copies of documents using a barcode representation of a unique identifier for the document. By default, barcodes are compliant with the Code 39 standard, but custom barcode providers can be plugged in using the policies object model.

CREATING INFORMATION MANAGEMENT POLICIES

These are the default policy features available out of the box, but custom features can be developed or purchased from third-party vendors. To create an information management policy, do the following:

1. Click the Site Actions menu, and choose Site Settings from the site collection where you want to associate an information management policy.
2. In the Site Collection Administration section, click Site Collection Policies.
3. On the Site Collection Policies page, click Create.
4. On the Edit Policy page, type a name and administrative description. This information will be seen by list managers when associating a policy with a list or content type.
5. In the Policy Statement section, type a policy statement to be shown to users any time they open an item governed by this policy.
6. In the Retention section, select the Enable Retention check box.
7. Click Add A Retention Stage.
8. In the Stage Properties dialog, box in the Event section, choose This Stage Is Based Off A Date Property On The Item.

9. Choose Last Modified + 1 Years for the time period.
10. In the Action section, choose Move To Recycle Bin.
11. Click OK. The completed Stage Properties dialog box is shown in Figure 5-22.

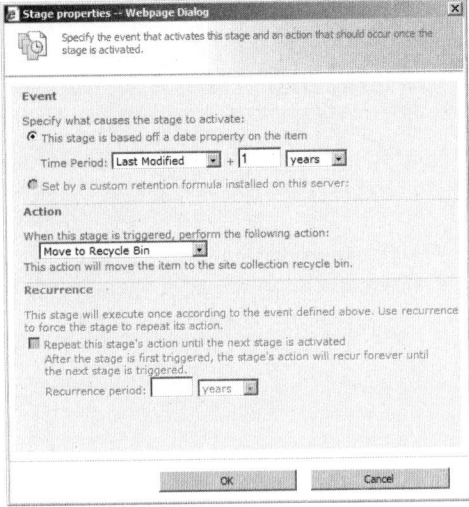

FIGURE 5-22 The Stage Properties dialog box.

12. In the Auditing section, select the Enable Auditing check box and select all of the events to audit.
13. Leave the Enable Barcodes and Enable Labels check boxes cleared.
14. Click OK to save the new information management policy.

Associate an Information Management Policy with a Document Library

After creating a policy, you can then associate it with either a content type or a document library. To associate an information management policy with a document library, perform the following steps:

1. From the document library where the policy will be associated, click the Library tab in the Library Tools area of the management Ribbon.
2. In the Settings section of the Ribbon, click Library Settings.
3. In the Permissions And Management section of the Document Library Settings page, choose Information Management Policy Settings.
4. Leave the Source Of Retention for this library set to Content Types, and click the Document content type.
5. In the Specify The Policy section, choose Use A Site Collection Policy.
6. Choose the site collection policy just created from the drop-down list, as shown in Figure 5-23.

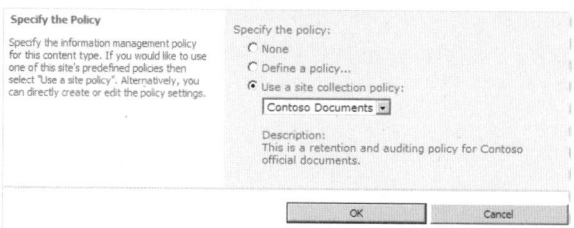

FIGURE 5-23 Policy Settings page for a document content type.

7. Click OK to accept the policy association.

SharePoint Designer Settings

SharePoint Designer is a useful tool for designing and managing SharePoint sites. However, an inexperienced or malicious user could do a lot of damage using SharePoint Designer, so its use should be carefully controlled. The following SharePoint Designer–related settings are available for a site collection:

- **Enable SharePoint Designer**   Controls whether SharePoint Designer can be used by anyone other than a site collection administrator. If this setting is enabled, site owners and designers are allowed to use SharePoint Designer.

- **Enable Detaching Pages From The Site Definition**   Controls whether site owners and designers can detach (formerly referred to as *unghosting*) pages from the site definition.

- **Enable Customizing Master Pages And Page Layouts**   Controls whether site owners and designers can customize master pages and layout pages for a site collection.

- **Enable Managing Of Web Site URL Structure**   Controls whether site owners and designers can view and manage the hidden URL structure of a site collection.

Configure SharePoint Designer Settings for a Site Collection

To configure SharePoint Designer settings for a site collection, follow these steps:

1. From any site within the site collection, click the Site Actions menu and choose Site Settings.

2. On the Site Settings page, in the Site Collection Administration section, choose SharePoint Designer Settings.

3. On the SharePoint Designer Settings page, enable the SharePoint Designer features by selecting the corresponding check box.

4. Click OK to save the settings. The SharePoint Designer Settings page is shown in Figure 5-24.

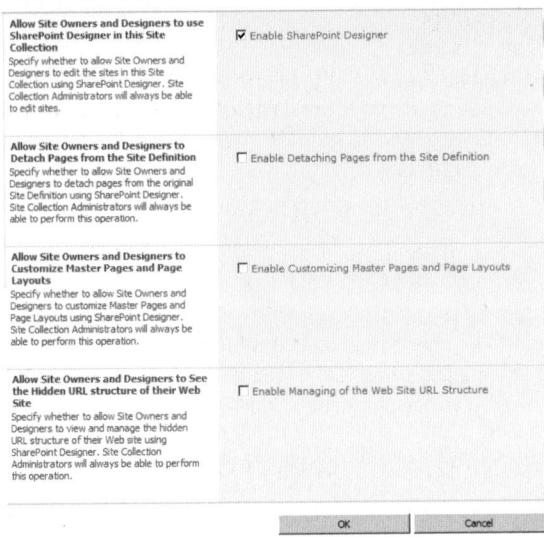

FIGURE 5-24 The SharePoint Designer Settings page.

Site collection administrators will always be able to perform all of these actions unless prohibited at the Web-application level by a farm administrator. If SharePoint Designer is blocked for the Web application, the user will see a message similar to the one shown in Figure 5-25.

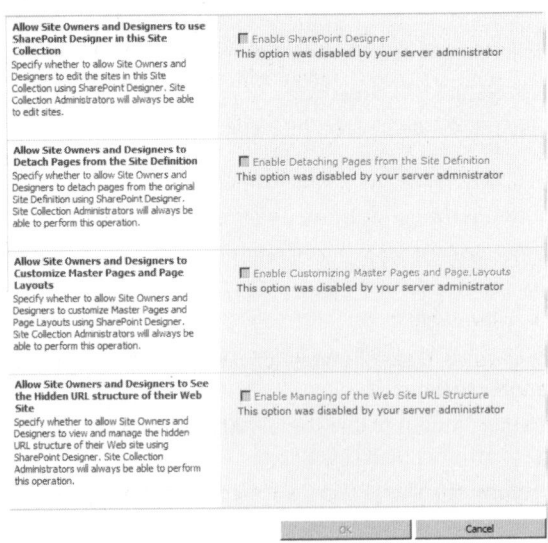

FIGURE 5-25 SharePoint Designer Settings page when it's disabled at Web-application level.

Site Collection Security

Site collection users are managed in much the same way as they were in SharePoint 2007. Site groups are still used to manage groups of users with similar privileges. As in the previous version, security trimming prevents users from being presented with links to content they don't have access to.

There are two ways to control access to objects in SharePoint 2010:

- Permissions can be specified for a group, and then users can be given those permissions by being added to the group.
- Objects can have their own permissions collections, which can be managed independently. For example, the permissions for a list can be managed independently of the permissions for the site in which it is contained. This allows for more granular management of objects.

Site Collection Administrators and Site Owners

Site collection administrators are assigned when a site collection is created. There must always be at least one site collection administrator, and this account cannot be an Active Directory group. For reasons such as dealing with unused site confirmations and enabling administration in the event that the administrator leaves, it is always best to define at least two site collection administrators. Site collection administrators can be managed from two distinct locations: the Site Settings page of a site collection or the Application Management page in Central Administration.

People and Groups

Groups are collections of individual users that are given the same permissions on a particular site. SharePoint Server 2010 sites are created with three basic security groups by default:

- **Owners**   Full control
- **Members**   Can contribute to existing lists and libraries
- **Visitors**   Read only

Create a Custom Site Group

To create a custom site group, follow these steps:

1. From the site where you want to create a new group, click the Site Actions menu and choose Site Settings.

2. In the Users And Permissions section of the Site Settings page, click the Site Permissions link.

3. On the Site Permissions page, on the management Ribbon, choose Create Group.

4. On the Create Group page, in the Name And About Me Description section, type a name for the group and (optionally) a description of the purpose for the group.

5. In the Owner section, specify the group owner.

6. In the Group Settings section, specify who can view and edit group membership.

7. In the Membership Requests section, specify whether to allow requests to join or leave the group.

8. Also specify whether to auto-accept requests.

WARNING If you specify that requests should be auto-accepted, users will be automatically added to the group and granted the permissions specified for the group.

9. Optionally, if requests are allowed, specify an e-mail address where requests should be sent.

10. Click Create to create the new group. The New Site Group page is shown in Figure 5-26.

View Group Permissions

Sometimes it is necessary to determine what permissions a specific group has across the entire site collection. This can be achieved in the following way:

1. From the Site Actions menu, choose Site Permissions.

2. Click on the name of the group for which you want to view permissions.

3. Click the Settings drop-down menu, and choose View Group Permissions.

4. Review the permissions of the group for various sites in the site collection. The View Group Permissions dialog box is shown in Figure 5-27.

NOTE This page will show only the site collection root and any sites that *do not* inherit permissions. This could be misleading if you assume that every site the group has access to, whether permissions are inherited or not, will be listed.

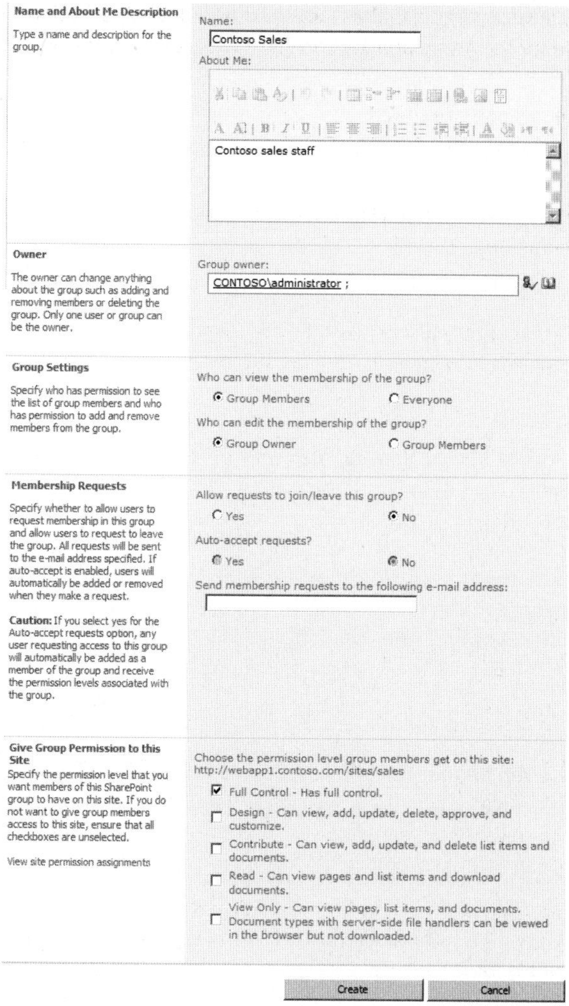

Name and About Me Description

Type a name and description for the group.

Name:

Contoso Sales

About Me:

Contoso sales staff

Owner

The owner can change anything about the group such as adding and removing members or deleting the group. Only one user or group can be the owner.

Group owner:

CONTOSO\administrator ;

Group Settings

Specify who has permission to see the list of group members and who has permission to add and remove members from the group.

Who can view the membership of the group?
- ⦿ Group Members   ◯ Everyone

Who can edit the membership of the group?
- ⦿ Group Owner   ◯ Group Members

Membership Requests

Specify whether to allow users to request membership in this group and allow users to request to leave the group. All requests will be sent to the e-mail address specified. If auto-accept is enabled, users will automatically be added or removed when they make a request.

Caution: If you select yes for the Auto-accept requests option, any user requesting access to this group will automatically be added as a member of the group and receive the permission levels associated with the group.

Allow requests to join/leave this group?
- ◯ Yes   ⦿ No

Auto-accept requests?
- ◯ Yes   ⦿ No

Send membership requests to the following e-mail address:

Give Group Permission to this Site

Specify the permission level that you want members of this SharePoint group to have on this site. If you do not want to give group members access to this site, ensure that all checkboxes are unselected.

View site permission assignments

Choose the permission level group members get on this site: http://webapp1.contoso.com/sites/sales

- ☑ Full Control - Has full control.
- ☐ Design - Can view, add, update, delete, approve, and customize.
- ☐ Contribute - Can view, add, update, and delete list items and documents.
- ☐ Read - Can view pages and list items and download documents.
- ☐ View Only - Can view pages, list items, and documents. Document types with server-side file handlers can be viewed in the browser but not downloaded.

[Create]   [Cancel]

FIGURE 5-26 New Site Group page.

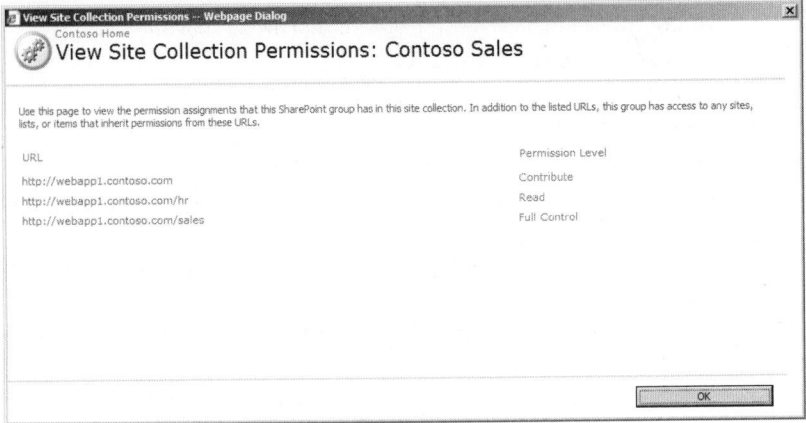

FIGURE 5-27 The View Site Collection Permissions dialog box.

Nesting Active Directory Groups in SharePoint Groups

Although you can add users directly to almost any object, this process becomes very difficult to manage and can make it nearly impossible to manage security in a site. Use the following guidelines when granting rights, and only assign permissions directly to single users if required, such as for online presence:

1. Create an Active Directory group (when using Active Directory for authentication).
2. Create a matching permission level (if custom permission levels are required).
3. Create a matching new site group, and grant it the previously created permission level.
4. Grant the new site group access to an object, such as a document, list, or Web page.

Default Permission Levels

Just as site groups are a collection of users, permission levels are a collection of rights that can be assigned to groups or individual users. Permission levels should always be named the same across multiple sites, and you should *never* modify an existing permission level. Modifying an existing permission level can cause a document, list, or page owner to accidentally grant access to unauthorized users. Always create a new permission level, create a correlating group with the same name, and populate that group with users. Doing this assures you of an easy-to-use permission level and group environment. There are four default permission levels:

- **Full Control**   Can perform any action in the site
- **Design**   Can view, add, update, delete, approve, and customize content

- **Contribute**   Can view, add, update, and delete content
- **Read**   Can view content only

Create a Custom Permission Level

To create a custom permission level, follow these steps:

1. From the site where you want to create a new permission level, click the Site Actions menu and choose Site Settings.
2. In the Users And Permissions section of the Site Settings page, click the Site Permissions link.
3. On the Site Permissions page, in the Manage section of the management Ribbon, click Permission Levels.
4. On the Permission Levels page, click Add A Permission Level.
5. On the Add A Permission Level page, in the Name And Description section, type a name for the permission level and (optionally) type a description.
6. In the Permissions section, select the permissions to include in the new permission level.
7. Click Create to create the new permission level.

The available permissions are enumerated in Table 5-3.

TABLE 5-3 Available Permissions

PERMISSION	DESCRIPTION	CATEGORY
Manage Lists	Create and delete lists, add or remove columns in a list, and add or remove public views of a list	List Permissions
Override Check Out	Discard or check in a document that is checked out to another user	List Permissions
Add Items	Add items to lists, add documents to document libraries, and add Web discussion comments	List Permissions
Edit Items	Edit items in lists, edit documents in document libraries, edit Web discussion comments in documents, and customize Web part pages in document libraries	List Permissions
Delete Items	Delete items from a list, documents from a document library, and Web discussion comments in documents	List Permissions

PERMISSION	DESCRIPTION	CATEGORY
View Items	View items in lists, documents in document libraries, and Web discussion comments	List Permissions
Approve Items	Approve a minor version of a list item or document	List Permissions
Open Items	View the source of documents with server-side file handlers	List Permissions
View Versions	View past versions of a list item or document	List Permissions
Delete Versions	Delete past versions of a list item or document	List Permissions
Create Alerts	Create e-mail alerts	List Permissions
View Application Pages	View forms, views, and application pages; enumerate lists	List Permissions
Manage Permissions	Create and change permission levels on the Web site, and assign permissions to users and groups	Site Permissions
View Web Analytics Data	View reports on Web site usage	Site Permissions
Create Subsites	Create subsites such as team sites, Meeting Workspace sites, and Document Workspace sites	Site Permissions
Manage Web Site	Grants the ability to perform all administration tasks for the Web site as well as manage content and permissions	Site Permissions
Add and Customize Pages	Add, change, or delete HTML pages or Web part Pages, and edit the Web site using a Windows SharePoint Services–compatible editor	Site Permissions
Apply Themes and Borders	Apply a theme or borders to the entire Web site	Site Permissions

PERMISSION	DESCRIPTION	CATEGORY
Apply Style Sheets	Apply a style sheet (cascading style sheets, or .CSS, file) to the Web site	Site Permissions
Create Groups	Create a group of users that can be used anywhere within the site collection	Site Permissions
Browse Directories	Enumerate files and folders in a Web site using SharePoint Designer and Web DAV interfaces	Site Permissions
Use Self-Service Site Creation	Create a Web site using Self-Service Site Creation	Site Permissions
View Pages	View pages in a Web site	Site Permissions
Enumerate Permissions	Enumerate permissions on the Web site, list, folder, document, or list item	Site Permissions
Browse User Information	View information about users of the Web site	Site Permissions
Manage Alerts	Manage alerts for all users of the Web site	Site Permissions
Use Remote Interfaces	Use Simple Object Access Protocol (SOAP), Web DAV, or SharePoint Designer interfaces to access the Web site	Site Permissions
Use Client Integration Features	Use features that launch client applications; without this permission, users will have to work on documents locally and upload their changes	Site Permissions
Open	Allow users to open a Web site, list, or folder to access items inside that container	Site Permissions
Edit Personal User Information	Allow a user to change his or her own user information, such as adding a picture	Site Permissions

PERMISSION	DESCRIPTION	CATEGORY
Manage Personal Views	Create, change, and delete personal views of lists	Personal Permissions
Add/Remove Personal Web Parts	Add or remove private Web parts on a Web part Page	Personal Permissions
Update Personal Web Parts	Update Web parts to display personalized information	Personal Permissions

Add a User to a Site

Follow these steps to add a user to a site:

1. From the Site Actions menu, click Site Settings.
2. Select People And Groups from the Users And Permissions section.
3. From the People And Groups page, individual users can be added to the site or new groups created. To add a user to a site group or assign permissions to the user directly, click the New drop-down menu and choose Add Users.
4. Type the user names, group names, or e-mail addresses of users to be added.
5. Choose a group to add the user to, or choose the permissions to assign directly.
6. Click OK.

Modify User Properties and Permissions

Follow these steps to modify user properties and permissions:

1. From the Site Actions menu, choose Site Settings.
2. Select Site Permissions from the Users And Permissions section.
3. Select the check box next to the user you want to edit permissions for.
4. In the Modify section of the management Ribbon, click Edit User Permissions. Figure 5-28 shows the Edit Permissions window.

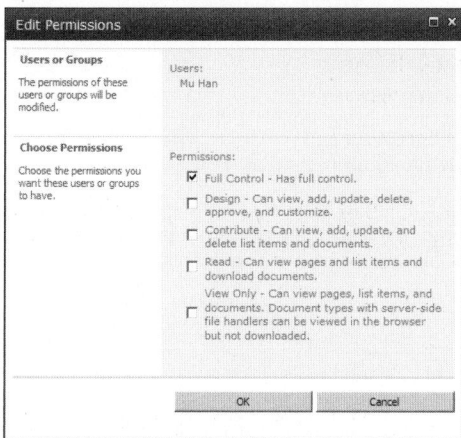

FIGURE 5-28 Edit Permissions page for a user.

5. Modify the permissions of the user.

6. Click OK to save the changes.

List and Library Security

Lists and libraries, like sites, have permissions that can be inherited from the parent site or explicitly defined. When a new list or library is created, it inherits the permission settings of its parent site by default. Use the following steps to break the permission inheritance of a list:

1. From the list where you want to break security, click the List tab in the List Tools section of the management Ribbon.

2. In the Settings section of the Ribbon, click List Permissions.

3. On the List Permissions page, in the Inheritance section of the Ribbon, click Stop Inheriting Permissions, as demonstrated in Figure 5-29.

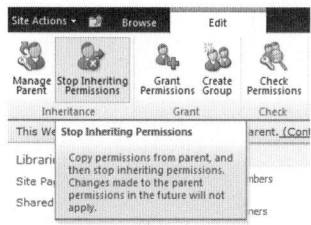

FIGURE 5-29 Breaking permission inheritance on a list.

Check Permissions

Use the following steps to check permissions:

1. From the list where you want to break security, click the List tab in the List Tools section of the management Ribbon.

2. In the Settings section of the Ribbon, click List Permissions.

3. In the Check section of the Ribbon, click Check Permissions.

4. In the Check Permissions dialog box, type the name of a user or group to check permissions for.

5. Click Check Now to check permissions for the specified user or group.

6. Review the permissions for the specified user or group. The Check Permissions dialog box is shown in Figure 5-30.

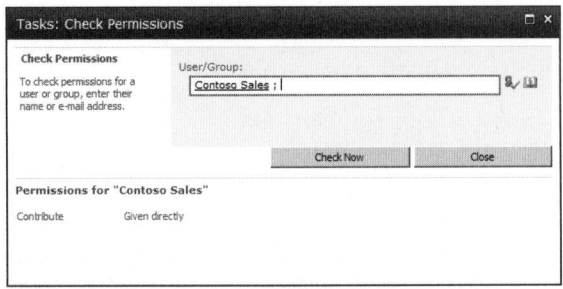

FIGURE 5-30 The Check Permissions dialog box.

CHAPTER 6

Configuring Service Applications

- Service Application Architecture **181**

- Deploying and Managing Service Applications **183**

- Service Applications in SharePoint Server 2010 **187**

Service applications represent the evolution of shared service providers (SSPs) from previous versions of SharePoint. Shared service providers were collections of services, such as Search, Profiles, InfoPath Forms Services, and Excel Services. In SharePoint 2007, it was difficult to configure a Web application to consume services from multiple SSPs. Web applications were really designed to consume all services from a single SSP, and this lack of flexibility was a major drawback. Service applications in SharePoint 2010 solve this problem by providing an extensible, pluggable model that allows Web applications to consume individual services as needed. The services that were formerly provided by an SSP have been broken up and implemented as service applications, and many new service applications are also provided. This complete redesign provides much greater flexibility as well as scalability going forward.

Service Application Architecture

Service applications are just that—distinct applications providing some specific service, such as Search or Profiles. They are deployed to an application server in a SharePoint 2010 server farm, and then accessed through a Web server connection. The Web server might or might not be the same physical server as the application server.

Service applications consist of some or all of the following components:

- Application bits—one or more processes with associated Windows Communication Foundation (WCF) services
- Administration Interface—one or more Web pages to administer the service application
- A database or databases
- An application pool or application pools—if you're using Microsoft Internet Information Services/Windows Activation Service (IIS/WAS) for WCF services

Service Application Topologies

The service application framework has been designed with the greatest flexibility and scalability in mind. The service instance runs on an application server, and you can have instances of the same service running on multiple application servers for redundancy. The service application is the logical representation of the collection of service instances, whether there is one on a single application server or multiple instances on separate application servers. The service application proxy provides an interface between the Web application and the service application, and it resides on the Web front end (WFE).

The simplest service application topology is, of course, a single server deployment. In this case, all service applications and service application proxies exist on the same physical server. Figure 6-1 shows this topology.

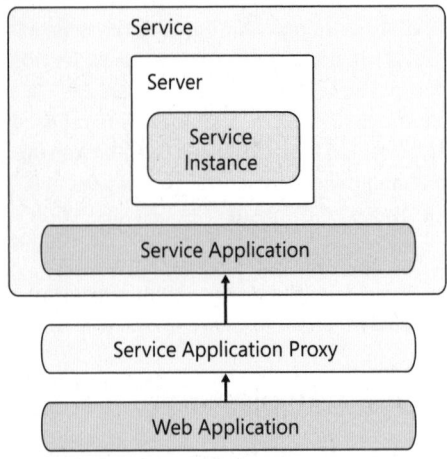

FIGURE 6-1 Single-server topology

This configuration is easy to set up and convenient to manage, but it doesn't provide any redundancy. If you are using a single application server and that server goes down, the service application is unavailable. This approach might be acceptable in some simple cases, but it's not acceptable in most enterprise environments.

As mentioned earlier, a single logical service application can consist of multiple service instances running on different application servers. This arrangement provides some redundancy and can support more users than the single-service approach. Figure 6-2 shows a topology with multiple service instances for a single logical service application, with one of the services installed but not running on the application server.

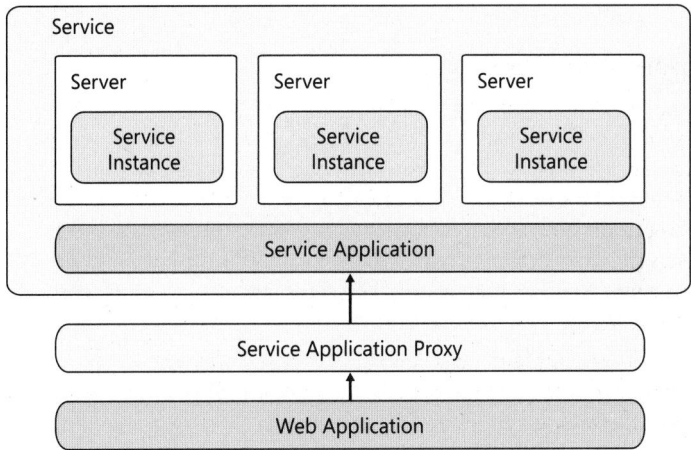

FIGURE 6-2 The service application topology with multiple service instances.

There are countless variations of these topologies that can be used in practice. The same service application could be exposed as multiple endpoints to provide isolation between groups, such as providing the finance department a separate search service from the rest of the company. These diagrams represent only a single service application, but of course a single application server could host many service applications. Also, service applications can be federated, or shared, across multiple farms. This approach allows expensive and maintenance-intensive services to be hosted in a central location, thus providing access to the service without incurring the overhead of maintaining the service for each farm that wants to consume it.

Deploying and Managing Service Applications

Service applications can be deployed automatically using the Farm Configuration Wizard or manually using the Manage Service Applications page of Central Administration. After a service application is deployed, a connection to it can be added for a Web application.

Edit Service Application Connections for a Web Application

Web applications connect to service applications through membership in a service application connection group, also called an application proxy group. To manage application connection groups, you must be a member of the Farm Administrators group.

Edit an Application Connection Group

The following steps should be performed to edit an application connection group:

1. On the Central Administration home page, click Application Management.

2. On the Application Management page, in the Service Applications section, click Configure Service Application Associations.

3. On the Service Applications Associations page, select Web Applications from the View drop-down list.

4. In the list of Web applications, in the Application Proxy Group column, click the name of the service application connection group that you want to change.

5. In the Configure Service Application Associations dialog box, shown in Figure 6-3, use the check boxes to add or remove service application proxies from the application proxy group.

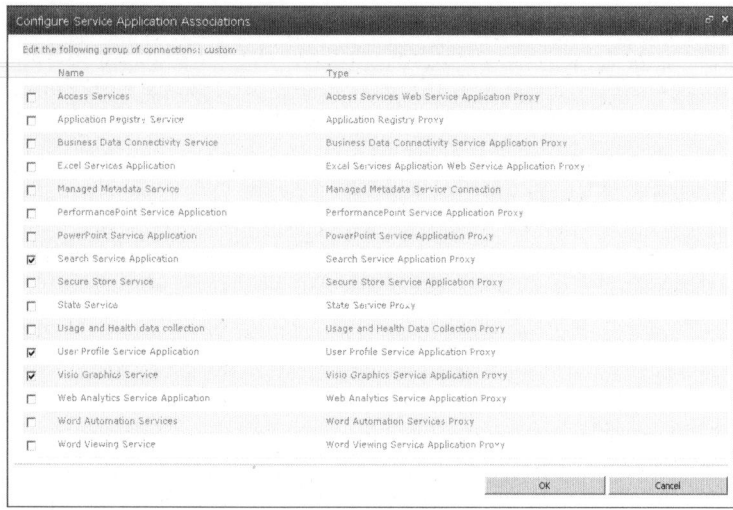

FIGURE 6-3 The Configure Service Application Associations dialog box.

6. Click OK to save the application proxy group settings.

Manage Administrators of a Service Application

You must be a member of the Farm Administrators group to manage service application administrators.

1. On the Central Administration home page, in the Application Management section, click Manage Service Applications.
2. On the Manage Service Applications page, click the row of the service application for which you want to manage administrators.
3. On the management Ribbon, in the Operations section, click Administrators.
4. In the Administrators dialog box, add or remove users or groups.
5. For users or groups you add, use the check boxes to configure permissions.
6. Click OK to save the settings.

Delete a Service Application

You must be a member of the Farm Administrators group to delete a service application.

1. On the Central Administration home page, in the Application Management section, click Manage Service Applications.
2. On the Manage Service Applications page, click the row of the service application you want to delete.
3. On the management Ribbon, in the Operations section, click Delete.
4. In the confirmation dialog box, click the Delete Data Associated With The Service Applications check box if you want to delete the associated database.
5. Click OK to delete the service application.

Publish a Service Application

A service application must be published for it to be accessible by Web applications outside the farm where it is running. To publish a service application, you must be a member of the Farm Administrators group.

1. On the Central Administration home page, in the Application Management section, click Manage Service Applications.
2. Click the row of the service application you want to publish.
3. In the management Ribbon, in the Sharing section, click Publish.
4. In the Publish Service Application dialog box, in the Connection Type section, choose the connection type for the published service to use.
5. In the Publish To Other Farms section, select the check box to publish the service and make it available to other farms.
6. In the Trusted Farms section, you can go ahead and add a trust relationship to another farm, or you can do this at a later time.

7. Make note of the URL in the Published URL section. This will be the URL that other farms use to connect to your service application.

8. Optionally, provide a description and a URL that administrators can use to find out more about the service application or to contact you.

9. Click OK to publish the service application.

Connect to a Service Application on a Remote Farm

You must be a member of the Farm Administrators group to connect to a service application on a remote farm, and you will need the URL to the service application.

1. On the Central Administration home page, in the Application Management section, click Manage Service Applications.

2. On the management Ribbon, in the Create section, click Connect.

3. In the Connect To A Remote Service Application dialog box, type the URL for the publishing service application.

4. Click OK to connect.

   You will see a list of published service applications at the URL you specified, similar to Figure 6-4.

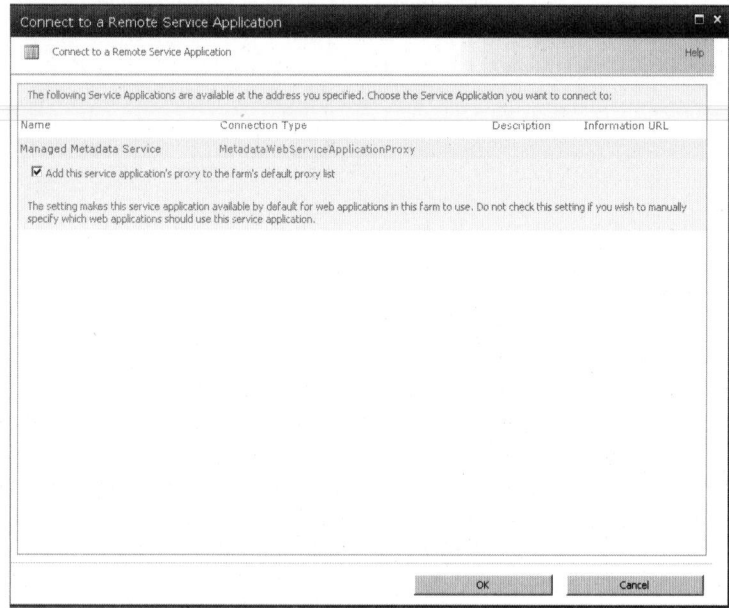

FIGURE 6-4 The Connect To A Remote Service Application dialog box.

5. Click the row of the service application you want to connect to.

6. Select the Add This Service Application's Proxy To The Farm's Default Proxy List check box to add the proxy to the farm's proxy list.

7. Click OK.

8. Give the connection a name, and click OK.

9. In the Success dialog box, click OK.

Service Applications in SharePoint Server 2010

In addition to providing the service application framework, both SharePoint Foundation and SharePoint Server provide some default service application implementations out of the box. SharePoint Foundation provides some basic service applications, such as Business Connectivity Services and Usage And Health Data Collection Service. SharePoint Server adds many more, such as the following:

- Access Services
- Application Registry Service
- Excel Services
- Lotus Notes Connector
- Managed Metadata Service
- PerformancePoint Services
- Search Service
- Secure Store Service
- State Service
- User Profiles Service
- Visio Graphics Service
- Web Analytics Service
- Word Automation Service

Access Services

Microsoft Access provides a quick and easy tool for building small, data-driven applications used by just a few people. Even if it has only a small number of users, however, an Access application placed on a file share can cause all kinds of problems—lack of change management, file locking, and so forth. Access services solves this problem by allowing an Access database to be imported into SharePoint and then accessed through the Web browser or through the client application. There might not be any justification for an Access application used by only a few people to be converted to something more robust, such as ASP.NET and Microsoft SQL Server. Now power users can take advantage of the rapid application development (RAD) capabilities of Access and the centralization and change-management benefits of a Web application without maintaining two different code bases.

Configuring Access Services

Perform the following steps to configure access services:

1. From the Central Administration home page, in the Application Management section, click Manage Service Applications, shown in Figure 6-5.

FIGURE 6-5 The Application Management section of the Central Administration home page.

2. On the Manage Service Applications page, click the Access Services link for the service application (not the service application proxy). See Figure 6-6.

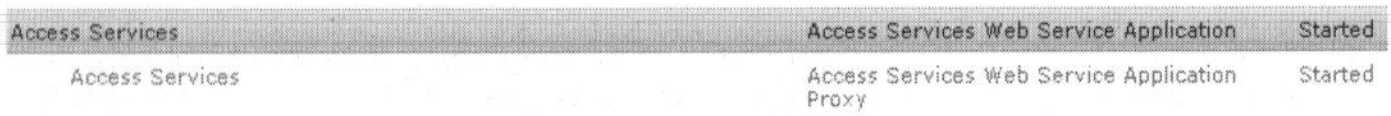

Access Services	Access Services Web Service Application	Started
Access Services	Access Services Web Service Application Proxy	Started

FIGURE 6-6 The Access Services item on the Manage Service Applications page.

3. On the Access Server Settings page, in the Lists And Queries section, configure the following values:

   - **Maximum Columns Per Query** Enter the maximum number of columns that might be referenced in a query. The default is 32.

   - **Maximum Rows Per Query** Enter the maximum number of rows a query should be allowed to return. The default is 50,000.

   - **Maximum Sources Per Query** Enter the maximum number of lists that should be allowed to be used as inputs to a query. The default is 8.

   - **Maximum Calculate Columns Per Query** Enter the maximum allowed number of calculated columns that can be used by a query or subquery. The default is 10.

   - **Maximum Order By Clauses Per Query** Enter the maximum allowed number of order by clauses that can be used in a query.

   - **Allow Outer Joins** Specify whether to allow left and right outer joins in a query. Inner joins are always allowed.

- **Allow Non Remotable Queries** Specify whether to allow queries that cannot be remoted to the database tier to run.
- **Maximum Records Per Table** Enter the maximum allowed number of items that a table in an application can have.

4. In the Application Objects section, enter the maximum number of records for an Access Services Application log list. The default is 3000.
5. In the Session Management section, configure the following values:
   - **Maximum Request Duration** Enter the maximum allowed duration (in seconds) for a request from an application. The default is 30.
   - **Maximum Sessions Per User** Enter the maximum allowed sessions for a single user. The default is 10.
   - **Maximum Sessions Per Anonymous User** Enter the maximum allowed sessions for an anonymous user. The default is 25.
   - **Cache Timeout** Enter the maximum time (in seconds) that a data cache can remain available.
   - **Maximum Session Memory** Enter the maximum amount of memory (in MBs) that a session can use.
6. In the Memory Utilization section, enter the maximum number of private bytes (in MBs) allocated by the Access Services process. The default is –1, which means the limit should be 50 percent of the amount of physical memory on the machine.
7. In the Templates section, enter the maximum allowed size (in MBs) for Access Templates (ACCDT). The default is 30.
8. Click OK to save the settings.

Business Connectivity Services

Business Connectivity Services (BCS) represents the next version of the Business Data Catalog (BDC). BCS has been baked into the platform (SharePoint Foundation) for this release, as opposed to being available only in the server product like before. It provides an extensive framework for interacting with external data, and SharePoint Server has additional Web parts for surfacing that data in your portal. In addition, SharePoint Designer makes it easy to create external content types and lists without having to deal with the messy XML configuration files. It's all done for you behind the scenes.

Excel Services

Excel Services was introduced in SharePoint 2007 as a way to secure and share Excel documents in the browser while maintaining full fidelity with Excel 2007. In SharePoint 2010, the symmetry with Excel 2010 is continued and improved, as is the SharePoint integration.

Configuring Excel Services

Perform the following steps to configure Excel Services:

1. On the Central Administration home page, in the Application Management section, click Manage Service Applications.

2. On the Manage Service Applications page, click the Excel Services Application link.

3. On the Manage Excel Services Application page, click Global Settings.

4. In the Security section of the Excel Services Application Settings page, choose a file access method, either Impersonation or Process Account. Impersonation will use the credentials of the current user to access non-trusted file locations, and Process Account will use the same account for all requests.

5. Choose whether encryption is required between clients and Excel Services.

6. To allow cross domain access, select the Allow Cross Domain Access check box.

7. In the Load Balancing section, choose a load-balancing scheme.

8. In the Session Management section, specify the maximum number of sessions allowed for a single user. The default is 25. When the maximum is exceeded, the oldest session will be closed. Enter −1 for unlimited.

9. In the Memory Utilization section, configure the following settings:

   - **Maximum Private Bytes**   The maximum amount (in MBs) of memory allocated for the Excel Calculations Services process. The limit is 50 percent of the physical memory on the machine.

   - **Memory Cache Threshold**   The percentage of the Maximum Private Bytes value that can be allocated to inactive objects. When the threshold is exceeded, cached objects that are not currently in use are released. A value of 0 (zero) prevents caching altogether.

   - **Maximum Unused Object Age** The maximum time (in minutes) that inactive objects remain in the cache. Valid values can range from −1 unlimited) to 34,560 (24 days).

10. In the Workbook Cache section, specify the location where the workbook cache should be stored. If this setting is left blank, the workbook cache will be stored in the system temp directory.

11. Specify the maximum size of the workbook cache in MBs. The default is 40,960 (40 GB).

12. To allow caching of unused files, select the Caching Enabled check box under the Caching Of Unused Files heading.

13. In the External Data section, specify the connection lifetime, which is the maximum amount of time (in seconds) a connection can remain active. Expired connections are automatically recycled. You can specify −1 to never recycle connections, but this is not recommended.

14. Optionally, specify the unattended service account to be used when credentials are set to None or non-Windows credentials are used. This must be an application ID that exists in the registered Secure Store Service application.

15. Click OK to save the settings.

Adding a Trusted File Location

Perform the following steps to add a trusted file location:

1. On the Central Administration home page, in the Application Management section, click Manage Service Applications.

2. On the Manage Service Applications page, click the Excel Services Application link.

3. On the Manage Excel Services Application page, click Trusted File Locations.

4. On the Trusted File Locations page, click Add Trusted File Location.

5. On the Add Trusted File Location page, in the Location section, enter the trusted file location. This can be a SharePoint Foundation location, network file share, or Web folder.

6. Choose the storage type for the location.

7. To extend trust to child libraries or directories, select the Children Trusted check box.

8. Optionally, add a description of the trusted location and its purpose.

9. In the Session Management section, configure the following settings:

   - **Session Timeout**   The maximum amount of time (in seconds) that an Excel Calculation Services session can remain active. Valid values range from −1 (unlimited) to 2,073,600 (24 days).

   - **Short Session Timeout**   The maximum amount of time (in seconds) that an Excel Services Application session can remain active. Valid values range from − 1 (disabled) to 2,073,600 (24 days).

   - **New Workbook Session Timeout**   The maximum amount of time (in seconds) that an Excel Calculation Services session for a new workbook can remain active. Valid values range from − 1 (unlimited) to 2,073,600 (24 days).

   - **Maximum Request Duration**   The maximum duration (in seconds) of a single request in a session.

   - **Maximum Chart Render Duration**   The maximum time (in seconds) spent rendering any single chart.

10. In the Workbook Properties section, specify the maximum size (in MBs) for workbooks and charts or images in the corresponding boxes.

11. In the Calculation Behavior section, enter a value (in seconds) for the Volatile Function Cache Lifetime box. This is the maximum amount of time that a computed value for a volatile function is cached for automatic recalculations. The valid values are – 1 (calculated once on load), 0 (always calculated) and any integer from 1 to 2,073,600 (24 days).

12. Choose the workbook calculation mode for workbooks from this location. If File is chosen, the calculation mode for individual files is used.

13. In the External Data section, configure the following settings:

   - **Allow External Data**   Specifies whether to allow external connections to trusted data connections, allow connections to trusted and embedded data connections, or disable external data completely.

   - **Warn On Refresh**   Specifies whether to display a warning before refreshing data from external sources.

   - **Display Granular External Data Errors**   Specifies whether to display granular error messages for failures that occur in files within this location.

   - **Stop When Refresh On Open Fails**   Determines whether to stop the open operation on a file that has a Refresh On Open data connection and cannot be refreshed while it's opening and the user does not have Open Item permissions on the workbook.

   - **External Data Cache Lifetime**   The maximum time (in seconds) that data from an external query can be used without refreshing. Values must be specified for Automatic Refresh and Manual Refresh.

   - **Maximum Concurrent Queries Per Session**   The maximum number of queries that can execute concurrently per session.

   - **Allow External Data Using REST**   Allow requests from the REST API to refresh external data connections.

14. In the User-Defined Functions section, specify whether to allow user-defined functions to be executed in workbooks within this location.

15. Click OK to save the trusted file location.

Add a Trusted Data Connection Library

Perform the following steps to add a trusted data connection library:

1. On the Central Administration home page, in the Application Management section, click Manage Service Applications.

2. On the Manage Service Applications page, click the Excel Services Application link.

3. On the Manage Excel Services Application page, click Trusted Data Connection Libraries.

4. Click Add Trusted Data Connection Library.

5. On the Add Trusted Data Connection Library page, enter the address of the data connection library and (optionally) enter a description for the newly trusted library, as seen in Figure 6-7.

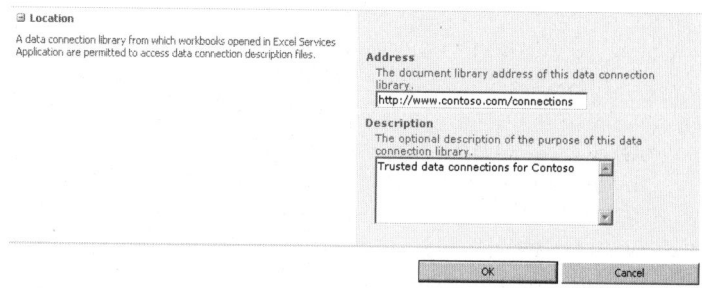

FIGURE 6-7 The Add Trusted Data Connection Library page.

6. Click OK to save the trusted data connection library.

Register a User-Defined Function Assembly

User-defined functions can be defined in assemblies (dynamic-link libraries, or DLLs) that can then be referenced from Excel Services. All such assemblies must be registered with the Excel Services application to let SharePoint know that the assembly is safe.

1. On the Central Administration home page, in the Application Management section, click Manage Service Applications.

2. On the Manage Service Applications page, click the Excel Services Application link.

3. On the Manage Excel Services Application page, click User-Defined Function Assemblies.

4. On the User-Defined Functions page, click Add User-Defined Function Assembly.

5. On the Add User-Defined Assembly page, enter the strong name or full path for the assembly containing user-defined functions. If you are referencing an assembly in the global assembly cache (GAC), you should specify the strong name. If you are referencing an assembly on the file system, you should specify the full path to the file.

6. Select the Assembly Location of the assembly.

7. Select the Assembly Enabled check box to allow the assembly to be called from Excel Services.

8. Optionally, enter a description for the assembly.

9. Click OK to register the assembly with the Excel Services application.

The Add User-Defined Function Assembly page is shown in Figure 6-8.

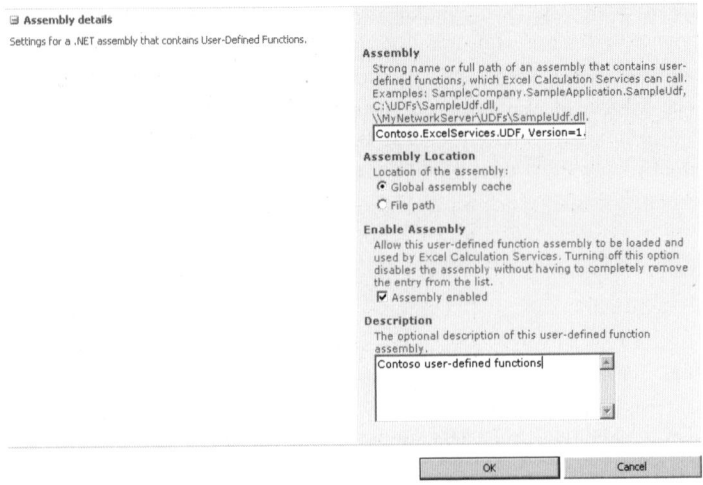

FIGURE 6-8 The Add User-Defined Function Assembly page.

Managed Metadata Service

Managed metadata in SharePoint 2010 refers to a hierarchical collection of terms used to describe various types of items, such as documents and list items. The terms can be managed using the Term Store Management Tool and then exposed, along with content types, via the Managed Metadata Service. This allows multiple site collections, Web applications, and even farms to share terms and content types.

The Managed Metadata Service application will be discussed in more detail in Chapter 10, "Enterprise Content Types and Metadata."

PerformancePoint Services

PerformancePoint Services provide tools to manage and analyze performance in an organization, such as dashboards, key performance indicators (KPIs), and other business intelligence functionality. Previously, PerformancePoint was a standalone product built on IIS, but in SharePoint 2010 it is integrated into the product in the form of a service application, providing all the benefits described earlier in the chapter.

Manage the PerformancePoint Services Application

Perform the following steps to manage the PerformancePoint Services application:

1. On the Central Administration home page, in the Application Management section, click Manage Service Applications.

2. On the Manage Service Applications page, click the PerformancePoint Services Application link.

3. On the Manage PerformancePoint Services Application page, click PerformancePoint Services Application Settings.

4. On the PerformancePoint Services Application Settings page, in the Secure Store And Unattended Service Account section, specify the secure store service to use and the unattended service account to be stored for the PerformancePoint service application.

5. In the Comments section, select the Enable Comments check box if you want comments to be enabled on scorecard cells.

6. Specify the maximum number of annotated cells allowed per scorecard.

7. In the Cache section, specify the cache expiration threshold.

8. In the Data Sources section, specify the timeout (in seconds) for data source queries.

9. In the Filters section, enter the amount of time to remember user filter selections and the maximum members to load in the filter tree.

10. In the Select Measure Control section, specify the maximum number of measures to load in a dashboard Select Measure control.

11. In the Show Details section, specify the initial retrieval limit when a user clicks Show Details. You can also specify the maximum retrieval limit, or select the radio button to allow the limit to be controlled by Analysis Services.

12. In the Decomposition Tree section, specify the maximum number of individual items (per level) returned to the decomposition tree visualization.

13. Click OK to save the settings.

Configure Trusted Content Locations

By default, all content locations within SharePoint are trusted. To specify that only certain locations be trusted, use the following steps:

1. On the Central Administration home page, in the Application Management section, click Manage Service Applications.

2. On the Manage Service Applications page, click the PerformancePoint Services Application link.

3. On the Manage PerformancePoint Services Application page, click Trusted Content Locations.

4. On the Trusted Content Locations page, under the Trust Content In heading, choose Only Specific Locations.

5. Click Apply.

Add a Trusted Content Location

Perform the following steps to add a trusted content location:

1. On the Central Administration home page, in the Application Management section, click Manage Service Applications.
2. On the Manage Service Applications page, click the PerformancePoint Services Application link.
3. On the Manage PerformancePoint Services Application page, click Trusted Content Locations.
4. Verify that Only Specific Locations is selected.
5. Click Add Trusted Content Location.
6. In the Edit Trusted Content Location dialog box, enter the address to the trusted content location.
7. Choose the location type. This might or might not be selectable, depending on the URL specified.
8. Optionally, enter a description for the new trusted content location.
9. Click OK to save the trusted content location.

Search Service

Search was provided as part of an SSP in SharePoint 2007, but like other former SSP services it has been implemented as a separate service application in SharePoint 2010. Some of the settings for search, such as proxy server and timeout settings, are managed through the General Application Settings section of Central Administration, but most are managed at the search service application level.

Add a Content Source

You must be a service application administrator for the search service application to add a content source.

1. On the Central Administration home page, in the Application Management section, click Manage Service Applications.
2. On the Manage Service Applications page, click the Search Service Application.
3. On the Search Administration page, in the Crawling section in the left pane, click Content Sources.
4. On the Manage Content Sources page, click New Content Source.
5. On the Add Content Source page, in the Name section, type a name for the content source in the Name text box.

6. In the Content Source Type section, choose the type of content to be crawled.

7. In the Start Addresses section, type the URLs from which the crawler should begin crawling in the Type Start Addresses Below (One Per Line) box.

8. In the Crawl Settings section, select the desired crawling behavior.

9. In the Crawl Schedules section, select or define a schedule for full crawls and incremental crawls. Full crawls crawl all content defined by the content source, whereas incremental crawls only crawl content that has changed since the last crawl.

10. In the Content Source Priority section, select the priority for the content source.

11. In the Start Full Crawl section, select the Start Full Crawl Of This Content Source box if you want to go ahead and start a full crawl.

12. Click OK to save the content source.

Add a Crawl Rule

You must be a service application administrator for the search service application to add a crawl rule.

1. On the Central Administration home page, in the Application Management section, click Manage Service Applications.

2. On the Manage Service Applications page, click Search Service Application.

3. On the Search Administration page, in the Crawling section in the left pane, click Crawl Rules.

4. Click New Crawl Rule.

5. On the Add Crawl Rule page, in the Path section, type the path to which the crawl rule will apply.

6. To use regular expressions instead of wildcard characters in the path, select the Use Regular Expression Syntax For Matching This Rule check box.

7. If you want to match the capitalization when matching the rule, select the Match Case check box.

8. In the Crawl Configuration section, choose between the following:

   - Choose Exclude All Items In This Path to exclude items in the path from crawls. Choose the Exclude Complex URLs (URLs That Contain Question Marks (?)) option if you want to exclude URLs that have parameters that use the question mark notation.

- Choose Include All Items In This Path to include items in the path in crawls.
  - Choose the Follow Links On The URL Without Crawling The URL Itself option to omit the starting URL from crawls.
  - Choose the Crawl Complex URLs (URLs That Contain Question Marks (?)) option to include URLs that have parameters that use the question mark notation in crawls.
  - Choose the Crawl SharePoint Content As HTTP Pages option to use the HTTP protocol to crawl SharePoint content rather than using the special protocol normally used. If you choose this option, item permissions for crawled content will not be stored.

9. In the Specify Authentication section (if available), choose the authentication mechanism. You have the following choices:
   - Use The Default Content Access Account
   - Specify A Different Content Access Account
   - Specify Client Certificate
   - Specify Form Credentials
   - Use Cookies For Crawling

10. Click OK to save crawl rule.

Start a Full Crawl

Perform the following steps to start a full crawl of a content source:

1. On the Central Administration home page, in the Application Management section, click Manage Service Applications.

2. On the Manage Service Applications page, click Search Service Application.

3. On the Search Administration page, in the Crawling section in the left pane, click Content Sources.

4. On the Manage Content Sources page, point to the content source you want, click the arrow that appears, and then choose Start Full Crawl.

You can start an incremental crawl, pause a crawl, resume a crawl, or stop a crawl by following the preceding steps and choosing the appropriate option from the content source context menu.

Secure Store Service

The Secure Store Service represents the evolution of the Single Sign-on service in SharePoint 2007. This service provides a secure database for storing credentials and mapping them to application IDs, which represent specific applications that users can access. This allows for seamless access to SharePoint and other applications without users having to log on to each application separately. This also allows groups of credentials to be mapped to a single application ID, therefore not requiring each individual to have an account in the application.

Security Token Service

The security token service is an identity management service used to support Claims-Based authentication in SharePoint 2010. This service will be covered in more detail in Chapter 15, "Configuring Policies and Security."

State Service

The State Service is used by SharePoint 2010 to save state information across related HTTP requests within a SQL Server database. This service is required by many components of SharePoint Server 2010, including InfoPath Forms Services and the Chart Web part. The State Service is configured using the Farm Configuration Wizard or Windows PowerShell. Using the Farm Configuration Wizard, the State Service can be configured by simply selecting the corresponding check box—the wizard will perform the configuration automatically.

Visio Graphics Service

The Visio Graphics Service is a new service application that allows for sharing and viewing of Microsoft Visio diagrams through the Web browser. In addition to being viewed, diagrams can be bound to data and updated as the underlying data sources are updated. This is especially useful for visualizing workflows running within SharePoint 2010.

Usage and Health Data Collection Service

The Usage And Health Data Collection Service collects and logs usage and health status data for reporting and analysis. This service collects data from a wide variety of sources, such as performance counters, event logs, search usage data, site collection and site usage data, and so forth, and compiles it for creating various types of usage and health status reports.

A new addition for SharePoint 2010 is the SharePoint Health Analyzer, which runs a set of predefined rules to determine the health of various parts of the SharePoint farm. When the Health Analyzer is run and a rule check fails, a message is written to the Health Reports list and the Windows Event Log. Also, an alert is created in the Health Analyzer Reports list on the Review Problems And Solutions page in Central Administration. Rules can be scheduled, or they can be run manually by an administrator.

SharePoint has a standard set of health and status reports, and custom reports can be created.

User Profile Service

The User Profile Service application provides a centralized store for user information. Table 6-1 describes the functions of the User Profile Service in more detail.

TABLE 6-1 User Profile Service Application

FEATURE	DESCRIPTION
User Profiles	Used to store information about users and to import and synchronize from various sources. It is highly customizable and searchable.
Organization Profiles	Used to store information about an organization.
Audiences	Used to target content to users based on user profile information.
My Sites	Personal sites where users can store data such as documents and links, connect with colleagues, and update profile information.
Social Tags and Notes	Allows users to add tags to items in SharePoint or to external items such as Web pages, blog posts, and so forth. Notes can also be posted to any type of SharePoint page. Administrators have the ability to remove tags and notes for a user or to disable them altogether.

The User Profile Service application is highly configurable and will be discussed in more detail in Chapter 14, "User Profiles and My Sites."

Web Analytics Service

The Web Analytics Service compiles some basic analytics information for SharePoint sites—such as page hits, search terms, browser information, and so forth—that can give insight into usage patterns for the site and help improve site design and search configuration.

Word Automation Service

The Word Automation Service is a new service application in SharePoint 2010 that provides unattended, server-side conversion of documents into formats that are supported by the Microsoft Office Word client application. Tasks that used to require the Word client can now be automated on the server without having to install the client at all. The Word Automation Service supports the following file formats:

- Open File Format (.docx, .docm, .dotx, .dotm)
- Word 97-2003 files (.doc, .dot)
- Rich Text files (.rtf)
- Single-file Web pages (.mht, .mhtml)
- Word 2003 XML documents (.xml)
- Word XML documents (.xml)

The Word Automation Service can save files in all of the formats listed, as well as Portable Document Format (.pdf) and XML Paper Specification (.xps) formats.

Configuring the Word Automation Service

You must be a member of the Farm Administrators group to configure the Word Automation Service.

1. On the Central Administration home page, in the Application Management section, click Manage Service Applications.

2. On the Manage Service Applications page, click the Word Automation Services link.

3. On the Word Automation Services page, in the Supported File Formats section, choose which file formats should be supported by selecting the check box next to the format.

4. In the Embedded Font Support section, specify whether to disable embedded fonts.

5. In the Maximum Memory Usage section, specify the percentage of available memory that should be used by the Word Automation Service.

6. In the Recycle Threshold section, specify the number of documents that should be converted by a conversion process before it is recycled.

7. In the Word 97-2003 Document Scanning section, specify whether to disable Word 97-2003 document scanning. This provides added security for Word 97-2003 documents, but it does incur some overhead cost. This feature should be disabled only if all documents loaded by the service can be trusted.

8. In the Conversion Processes section, specify the number of conversion processes created on each server used by the service application. A different conversion process must be used for each conversion that is performed simultaneously.

9. In the Conversion Throughput section, specify the frequency (in minutes) with which groups of conversions are started, and the number of conversions performed in each group.

10. In the Job Monitoring section, specify the length of time (in minutes) before conversion status is monitored and, if necessary, restarted.

11. In the Maximum Conversion Attempts section, specify the maximum number of times a conversion is attempted before its status is set to Failed.

12. Click OK to save the settings.

PART II

Configuring SharePoint Server 2010

CHAPTER 7   Web Parts, Features, and Solutions   **205**

CHAPTER 8   Configuring the Search Service Application   **239**

CHAPTER 9   Managing the Search Experience   **265**

CHAPTER 10   Enterprise Content Types and Metadata   **329**

CHAPTER 11   Document Management   **361**

CHAPTER 12   Records Management   **385**

CHAPTER 13   Portals and Collaboration   **405**

CHAPTER 14   User Profiles and My Sites   **419**

CHAPTER 7

Web Parts, Features, and Solutions

- Installing and Configuring Web Parts   **205**
- Installing and Configuring Features   **215**
- Managing Solutions   **221**

This chapter will cover the interrelated topics of Web parts, features, and solutions. *Web parts* are one of the principal ways of customizing Microsoft SharePoint Server 2010. Web parts are reusable controls that allow users to create pages to solve business problems using only the browser. *Features* are SharePoint Server 2010–specific programming artifacts that work as the control panel for a host of functions. Features configure SharePoint Server 2010 and copy and provision lists and libraries. They are critical for controlling the deployment and the functionality of SharePoint Server 2010. *Solutions* are the only supported method for deploying developer artifacts consistently to multiple servers in a farm. Solutions, combined with features, provide a mechanism for extending SharePoint Server 2010 functionality to meet changing requirements.

Installing and Configuring Web Parts

Web parts are modular, reusable pieces of code that allow users to modify their appearance, content, and behavior. For example, users might modify the appearance of a Web part by adjusting its height and width. Content might be modified for a Web part that displays a table of data by selecting which columns are displayed and in what order. As an example of modifying behavior, a Web part could display either a summary or details of certain information. The Web part might switch between listing every invoice for every sales person invoiced for the past 90 days or simply listing a total dollar amount for each sales person. Web parts are the building blocks for SharePoint Server 2010 Web user interface interactions.

Web parts are broadly scoped; they serve as windows in SharePoint Server 2010 to the broader world of IT. They are windows into external data sources such as Microsoft SQL Server or Oracle databases. Additionally, they allow a glimpse into Web services or they can integrate with business applications. Predictably, they serve as windows into SharePoint Server 2010 by allowing interaction with information stored in lists and libraries. Finally, Web parts are windows into the users of SharePoint Server 2010. They provide a mechanism for interacting with and empowering users to solve business problems.

Web Part Architecture

There are two types of files associated with Web parts: an assembly and an XML file. All Web parts require a binary assembly, a dynamic-link library (DLL), which contains the code that the Web part executes. The XML file registers the assembly, telling SharePoint Server 2010 that the Web part exists and indicating what assembly it uses, and it sets the properties that control how the Web part behaves. Web parts have to be deployed using either full-trust or sandboxed solutions.

SharePoint Server 2010 ships with many useful Web parts that can be configured to accomplish any number of tasks. Custom Web parts, either ones that are purchased or Web parts created in house, will be deployed via solution packages. Deployment does not add the Web parts to any pages—it simply puts the Web parts' required resources in place on the farm servers so that they can be added to pages.

For a Web part to appear as an option to be added to a page, its XML file must be located in either a Web application's WPCATALOG folder or the Web part gallery of a site collection. Web parts deployed to WPCATALOG are scoped at the Web-application level and are available to all site collections contained in the Web application. Web parts added to a Web part gallery are scoped to the site collection that contains the gallery. A site collection's Web part gallery can be viewed by navigating to Site Actions, Site Settings, Galleries, Web Parts. The Web part gallery is a document library configured to contain Web part XML files. As with any document library, items can be created, uploaded, and deleted from the gallery.

> **NOTE** Although Web parts added to WPCATALOG are immediately available for use, site collection–scoped Web parts require a feature to be activated in order to add the copy of the Web part XML file to the Web part gallery. The default location for WPCATALOG is C:\INETPUB\WWWROOT\WSS\Virtual Directories\{WebAppName} {PortNumber}.

Because of the specific nature of the Web part gallery, the function of the New button has been customized. The Web part gallery New Web Parts page provides a list of Web part assemblies that can be used in the site collection. To be included in the New Web Parts list, a Web part must be a public assembly that inherits from one of the Web part base classes and it must be marked as safe, in a Safe Control entry, in the Web application's *Web.config* file. The following is a sample Safe Control entry:

Safe Control

```
<SafeControl Assembly="System.Web, Version=1.0.5000.0, Culture=neutral,
PublicKeyToken=b03f5f7f11d50a3a" Namespace="System.Web.UI.WebControls"
TypeName="*" Safe="True"/>
```

Safe Control entries function as gate keepers that limit the assemblies that can run in a site collection to only those that have been explicitly marked as safe. Any control that is not marked as safe is considered unsafe and will not be allowed to run.

In addition to marking controls as safe to run, safe controls can be useful for denying a specific control from running. Suppose the assembly *TwoParts* contains two Web parts named *GoodPart* and *BadPart*. The following two safe control entries allow *GoodPart* to run but explicitly prevent *BadPart* from doing so:

```
<SafeControl Assembly="TwoParts, Version=1.0.0.0, Culture=neutral,
PublicKeyToken=1234567810111213" Namespace="TwoPartsNS" TypeName="*"
Safe="True"/>
```

```
<SafeControl Assembly="TwoParts, Version=1.0.0.0, Culture=neutral,
PublicKeyToken=1234567810111213" Namespace="TwoPartsNS" TypeName="BadPart"
Safe="False"/>
```

The first entry marks all Web parts in the namespace *TwoPartsNS* in the assembly *TwoParts* as safe. The second safe control entry overrides the first entry and explicitly registers *BadPart* as not safe, thus preventing it from running. A Web part not marked as safe cannot be added to a page, and a Web part already added to a page will cease running if its safe control status is changed.

Web Parts and Pages

Pages enable related content to be consolidated into a unique page that is optimized for a specific purpose. For instance, you can consolidate related information into a single page to provide an overview. Pages collect and organize Web parts to create a customized layout and customized functionality.

Creating a Content Page and Adding Web Parts

In previous versions of SharePoint Server, Web parts were largely restricted to being placed in predefined Web part zones. SharePoint Server 2010 allows Web parts to be placed into content areas and positioned using standard markup. Freeing Web parts from Web part zones allows users greater flexibility in creating and customizing presentations. For the many instances when simple predefined regions are sufficient for organizing Web parts, the more structured Web part pages are still available. Although the predefined zones of Web part pages are less flexible, they also require less effort to organize the presentation.

There are several ways to create the various pages. The most readily available approach is to select New Page from the Site Actions drop-down menu. The New Page option from the Site Actions drop-down menu creates a page that uses the *Body Only* page layout. The Body Only page layout has a single large content area that can contain Web parts and other markup. To create a Body Only page and add Web parts to it, do the following:

1. Open the site where you want to add the page.
2. From the Site Actions menu, select New Page.
3. Enter a name for the new page, and click Create.
4. Click the Insert tab on the Ribbon as seen in Figure 7-1.

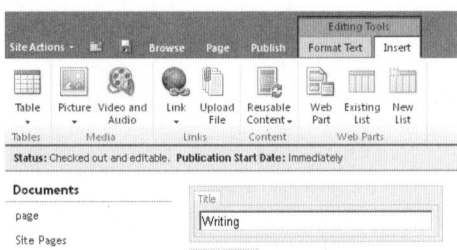

FIGURE 7-1 Selecting the Insert tab on the Ribbon.

5. Click the Web Part button.
6. Select a category.
7. Select a Web part.
8. Select where to add the Web part.
9. Click the Add button.

After the Web part is added to the rich content area, you can customize its layout by directly editing the markup of the content area. You can edit the content area's markup by clicking on the Format Text tab on the Ribbon and selecting Edit HTML Source from the HTML drop-down menu.

Creating Web Part Pages and Adding Web Parts

In many instances, the flexibility of adding Web parts directly to the content area is not necessary. Web part pages come with predefined Web part zones to provide a default organization for Web parts. With some creativity, these Web part pages can be adapted to a variety of layout requirements. The first thing to know about Web part pages with a predefined layout is that after the layout is chosen, it cannot be easily altered. Therefore, the more flexible the layout you choose, the better off you will be.

The second thing to know is that an empty Web part zone renders as nothing. If a Web part page with three columns is chosen and only two are used, the page renders as two columns. The third, unused column does not use up valuable screen real estate. Therefore, it is best to use a Web part page layout with as many Web part zones as possible. The unused zones are ignored, taking up no page space, but they are still available for future use. Figure 7-2 shows the page in edit mode and demonstrates the absence of a Web part in Row 1. Figure 7-3 shows the same page as users would see it.

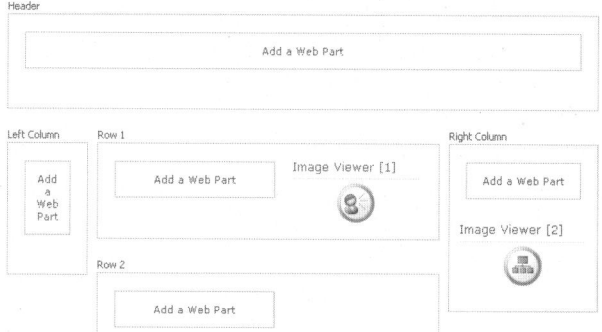

FIGURE 7-2 Web part zones are seen in edit mode when they are empty.

FIGURE 7-3 Users will not see the empty Web part zone.

Experience has shown that the Header-Footer-4-Columns page, Left-Column-Header-Footer page, and Right-Column-Header-Footer page are the most useful Web part pages because they provide the greatest number of possible combinations. To create a Web part page, do the following:

1. Open the site where you want to add the page.
2. From the Site Actions drop-down menu, select View All Site Content.
3. Click the Create hyperlink at the top of the All Site Content page.
4. Choose Page from the Filter By menu.
5. Click the Web Part Page icon.
6. Click the Create button.
7. Name the Web part page.
8. Choose a layout template.
9. Select the document library to save the page in.
10. Click the Create button.

When the Web part page is created, it will automatically be in edit mode. Because the page is in edit mode, all the Web part zones on the page are displayed. After the page is published, only the zones that contain Web parts are actually rendered. Any empty zones are ignored. The process for adding Web parts to the Web part page is somewhat different from the process for content pages. To add a Web part, do the following:

1. Click the Add A Web Part button in the zone where you want to add the Web part.
2. Select a category .
3. Select a Web part.
4. Optionally, select a different zone from the Add Web Part To drop-down menu.
5. Click the Add button.

Deleting and Closing Web Parts

There are two options for removing Web parts from a page: close and delete. Although the two have similar effects, they are different enough that you need to understand how to use them appropriately. Deleting a Web part deletes the Web part from the page permanently. Although the same Web part can be added to the page again, all customization or configuration of the deleted Web part is lost. There is no Recycle Bin capability for Web part customizations. To delete a Web part, do the following:

1. Open the page where the Web part is located.
2. Select Edit Page from the Site Actions drop-down menu.
3. Click the Web part to be deleted.
4. Click the Web Part Tools tab on the Ribbon.
5. Click the Delete Button, and then click OK in the warning dialog.

Closing a Web part preserves the Web part's configuration and customization by moving the Web part to the Closed Web Parts gallery. The Web part can be returned to the page from the Closed Web Parts gallery with all of its configuration and customizations intact.

> **TIP** A major improvement in SharePoint Server 2010 is that closed Web parts no longer consume the same system resources as open Web parts.

As an alternative, many Web parts can be exported, thus preserving their customizations without requiring them to be maintained in the gallery. To close a Web part, do the following:

1. Open the page where the Web part is located.
2. Click the Web part.
3. Select Close from the Web part's shortcut menu, as seen in Figure 7-4.

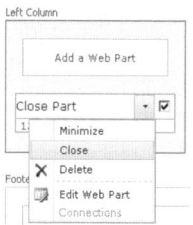

FIGURE 7-4 Select Close to preserve the Web part's customization.

Closed Web parts can be returned to the page by going through the process to add a Web part, and then selecting a Web part from the Closed Web Parts category. A quick way to see a list of all closed Web parts on the page is to use the Web Parts Maintenance page. The Web Parts Maintenance page can be opened by appending *?contents=1* to any page that contains Web parts.

For example, *http://portal.contoso.com/Pages/default.aspx?contents=1* would open the Web Parts Page Maintenance for the Contoso Portal home page. From the Web Parts Page Maintenance, Web parts can be closed, deleted, and reset. The Web Parts Maintenance page can also be a useful tool for removing Web parts that keep the page from loading.

Web Part Connections

Web parts support a connectivity model that allows them to interoperate. Connected Web parts can be used to do tasks such as filtering result sets or providing related parent and details views of data. Not all Web parts support connections, and some Web parts can be connected only to certain types of Web parts, depending on how the Web part was developed. Although the Web part framework has been greatly improved to ensure *type safe* Web part connections, you can still connect Web parts in meaningless, but technically valid, ways—for example, supplying a Social Security number in the place of a telephone number. Therefore, always test to verify that Web part connections behave in the way they are intended. To connect to Web parts, do the following:

1. Open the page that contains the Web parts.
2. Select Edit Page from the Site Actions menu.
3. Click Connection in the Web part's shortcut menu.
4. Select the type of connection.
5. Select the target Web part.
6. Optionally, provide required connection information.

The behavior of connected Web parts vary depending on the types of Web parts involved. Some Web parts allow unlimited connections, while others allow only one connection at a time. Web parts can support multiple types of connections, but many Web parts implement only a single connection type. There are some guidelines provided when developing Web parts in Microsoft Visual Studio, but a developer can choose to override them.

In general, Web parts do not support bidirectional connections. Information can be passed from one Web part to another, but not back and forth. Web parts typically provide an unlimited number of connections to other Web parts but allow only a single consuming connection. As an example, image Web parts can be connected to libraries that contain images. A library can provide a connection to multiple image Web parts, but an image Web part consumes images from only one library at a time.

Although bidirectional Web part connections are not supported, a Web part can be both a consumer and provider. To do so, it must provide a connection to one Web part and consume a connection from a different Web part. After Web part connections have been established, they can be terminated easily. To break a Web part connection, do the following:

1. Open the page that contains the Web parts.
2. Select Edit Page from the Site Actions menu.
3. Select Connections in the Web part's shortcut menu, as seen in Figure 7-5.

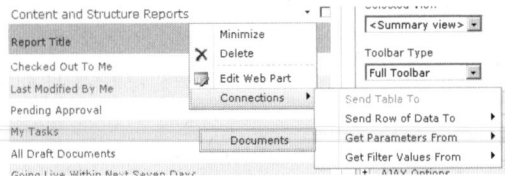

FIGURE 7-5 Select Connections in the drop-down menu.

4. Select the connection that is to be terminated.
5. Click the connection to be terminated.

Web Part Properties and Personalization

Web parts are configured and customized by modifying Web part properties. Although Web parts have different properties, almost all Web parts share certain common properties. To modify a Web part's properties, select Edit Web Part from the Web part's shortcut menu, as shown in Figure 7-6. Table 7-1 shows the common Web part properties that most Web parts possess.

FIGURE 7-6 Editing the Web part.

TABLE 7-1 Common Web Part Properties

PROPERTIES	DESCRIPTIONS
Title	Changes the title of the Web part on the page.
Height	Either fits the Web part to the page or sets a fixed height.
Width	Either fits the Web part to the page or sets a fixed width.
Chrome State	Choosing minimized displays only the Web part's title and adds a Restore option to its menu.
Chrome Type	A control displaying the title and border.
Hidden	Specifies that the Web part will not be displayed but will still execute.
Zone	Changes the Web part's zone.
Zone Index	Changes the order of the Web part in its zone.
Allow Minimize	A control that sets the chrome state to minimized.
Allow Close	A control that allows the Web part to be closed.
Allow Hide	A control that allows the Web part to be hidden.
Allow Zone Change	A control that allows the Web part to be moved between zones.
Allow Connections	A control that allows Web part connections.

Web part properties have three possible states:

- **Shared** These properties are the default values shared by all users. They are the values the Web part begins with before it is personalized.

- **Personalized** These properties are created when a user personalizes a page. When a user personalizes a page, the shared value becomes the user's new personalized value. Personalization allows users to reorder Web parts on a page and customize the behavior of the Web parts on a per-user basis. To personalize a page, click on the Welcome User control (where your user name is displayed) and select Personalize This Page, as seen in Figure 7-7.

FIGURE 7-7 Click Personalize This Page on the Welcome User control.

- **Private** These properties are analogous to Personalized properties, except they apply to private Web parts that only you can see.

NOTE To view the shared view of the page, repeat the process but click Show Shared View instead of Personalize This Page. There is a quirk that requires you to exit edit mode to allow you to switch to the shared view of a page.

When editing a personalized page, users should see a message that they are editing a personal version of the page. After users personalize a page, they can configure Web parts for their individual needs. For example, users can make Web parts they frequently work with large, while minimizing Web parts that are of less interest to them.

Problems can arise with users inadvertently personalizing Web parts with values that need to be shared. A common issue is that users personalize Web parts with connection strings. If a Web part that shares a connection string is personalized, the Web part continues to work normally until the value of the connection string changes. If that happens, the Web part continues to work for everyone but the user who personalized the Web part. Proper coding techniques will prevent this problem from occurring. Unfortunately, proper coding techniques are not always followed. If a single user has problems with Web parts that no one else has, check to make sure that the user does not have problems with a personalized page. If personalization issues are the problem, use the Web Parts Maintenance page to view the personalized copy of the page and reset the Web parts on the personalized copy.

In addition to personalizing Web parts already on a page, users can add Web parts to a personalized page. These Web parts are private to the user and have only personalized properties. Private Web parts can be helpful in allowing users to integrate information of value to them into the shared version of a page.

Installing and Configuring Features

Features are SharePoint Server 2010–specific declarative (XML) programming elements. Whereas Web parts do things *in* SharePoint Server 2010, features do things *to* SharePoint Server 2010. Features configure, associate, define, create, and copy. Features are most commonly used for the following:

- To define the columns that make up list types and the fields that the columns are based on
- To copy Web parts and master pages to their respective galleries
- To associate Visual Studio workflows with a list or site
- To modify and extend the configuration of the SharePoint Server 2010 user interface
- To serve as a control panel that allows code and configuration changes to be turned on and off in the browser

NOTE Features can affect four different scopes: farm, Web application, site collection, and site. Site-scoped and site collection–scoped features can be controlled by information workers, which allows farm administrators to delegate responsibility for them.

Feature Architecture

Features are XML files and must be contained in a folder in C:\Programs Files\ Common Files\Microsoft Shared\Web Server Extensions\ 14\TEMPLATE\FEATURES.

Feature files not deployed to a subfolder in TEMPLATE\FEATURES will not be recognized as features and will not work. Features are generally composed of two types of files: a feature header file and one or more element files. Because the feature files are simply XML and because they are located in TEMPLATE\FEATURES, they can be easily inspected by browsing to the appropriate folder and examining the contents of the files. Feature header files are generally named *Feature.xml*. The following is an example of a feature.xml file:

Feature.xml (Feature Header File)

```
<Feature xmlns="http://schemas.microsoft.com/sharepoint/"
Id="9965A8BB-3F03-448c-A4F1-57C66B13F7A2" Title="FlyOutMaster"
Description="Custom Master Page" Scope="Web" Hidden="TRUE"
ReceiverAssembly="FeaturesTalk, Version=1.0.0.0, Culture=neutral,
            PublicKeyToken=580b0c2207433027"
ReceiverClass="FeaturesTalk.FlyOutMasterFeatureReceiver">
<ElementManifests>
   <ElementManifest Location="Elements.xml"/>
   </ElementManifests>
</Feature>
```

The header file specifies the ID, title, description, scope, and whether or not the feature is hidden. If a feature is hidden, it will not be seen in the browser but can be activated with Stsadm.exe, with Windows PowerShell, or programmatically in Visual Studio.

A feature receiver, or its dependent features, behave differently depending on the scope of the features involved. If a feature has a dependency on a higher scoped feature, the higher scoped feature must be activated before the feature with the dependency can be activated. For example, the site-scoped SharePoint Server Publishing feature requires that the site collection–scoped SharePoint Server Publishing Infrastructure feature be activated first.

If a feature has a dependency on a feature of the same scope, the dependent feature is automatically activated. Higher scoped dependencies are generally used to guarantee that required resources are available to the dependent feature. Similarly scoped dependencies are generally used to synchronize the activation and deactivation of a number of interrelated and interdependent features. In the case of similarly scoped dependencies, the dependent features are typically hidden, thereby preventing their accidental activation or deactivation.

Feature Life Cycle

There is a four-stage feature life cycle. Features are installed, activated, deactivated, and uninstalled. Features can be manipulated with Stsadm.exe, Central Administration, and Windows PowerShell. Features are deployed using solution packages with either full-trust or sandboxed deployment mechanisms. They form an essential part of solution deployment.

NOTE Solution packages bundle and deploy SharePoint Server 2010 artifacts and use features to control activation, configuration, and replication of those artifacts.

Installing Features

Features are deployed with solution packages and should be automatically installed when deployed. Although it is uncommon to have to manually install features, you should know what the installation process does to install features.

To install a feature, the necessary feature files must already be deployed to the TEMPLATE\FEATURES directory on all servers in the farm. Installing a feature simply makes it available to be activated. Any installed feature that does not have the property *Hidden=True* can be seen and activated through the SharePoint Server 2010 user interface.

NOTE Feature installation does not cause the feature to do anything. It simply makes the features available for activation and visible in the browser.

There is no mechanism for installing features using Central Administration— Central Administration is used only to manage previously installed features. Features must be installed using either Stsadm.exe or Windows PowerShell. Stsadm.exe is located in C:\Program Files\Common Files\Microsoft Shared\Web Server Extensions\14\BIN. To install a feature using Stsadm.exe, use the following command:

```
stsadm.exe -o installfeature
{-filename <relative path to Feature.xml from system feature directory> |
-name <feature folder>} [-force]
```

The *Name* parameter refers to the name of the folder in TEMPLATE\FEATURES that the feature resides in. Only features that use the naming convention of *Feature.xml* for their feature header file can be referred to by their folder name. If a feature does not follow the Feature.xml naming convention, the file name parameter must be used with a relative path to the header file in TEMPLATE\FEATURES. To install a feature using Windows PowerShell, use the following command:

```
Install-SPFeature -Path <String> [-AssignmentCollection
<SPAssignmentCollection>] [-Confirm [<SwitchParameter>]]
[-Force <SwitchParameter>] [-WhatIf [<SwitchParameter>]]
[<CommonParameters>]
```

The *Path* parameter can be either the name of the feature's folder in TEMPLATE\FEATURES or a relative path to the feature's header file. The *Confirm* parameter asks for confirmation before executing a command. Use the *Force* parameter to force the reinstallation of an already installed feature.

Activating and Deactivating Features

A feature must be activated for it to take effect. Farm-scoped features deployed with full-trust solutions and site collection–scoped features deployed with sandboxed solutions are automatically activated when they are deployed. Deactivation does not necessarily reverse the results of activation. For example, if activating a feature provisioned a custom list, deactivating the feature probably will not delete the list. This behavior is intentional and follows a general philosophy of SharePoint Server 2010 to do no harm. As a general principle, SharePoint Server 2010 will not destroy or delete information unless explicitly instructed to do so.

> **TIP** Be aware that when you deactivate features they might not clean up after themselves and you might need to do the cleanup manually.

After deactivating any feature with which you are unfamiliar, check the result of the deactivation.

MANAGING FEATURES FROM CENTRAL ADMINISTRATION

Unlike installation, features can be activated and deactivated through the Central Administration interface in addition to using Stsadm.exe and Windows PowerShell. The location for activating and deactivating features is different for each feature scope. To activate or deactivate a farm-scoped feature using Central Administration, do the following:

1. Browse to Central Administration, System Settings, Manage Farm Features.
2. Click either the feature's Activate or Deactivate button.
3. To deactivate a feature, confirm the deactivation.

Activating Web application–scoped features in Central Administration has changed considerably and is now accomplished using the new management Ribbon. To activate a Web application–scoped feature, do the following:

1. Browse to Central Administration, Application Management, Manage Web Applications.
2. Click the row that contains the Web application that the feature should be activated on.
3. Click the Web Application tab in the management Ribbon.
4. Click the Manage Features button in the management Ribbon, as seen in Figure 7-8.

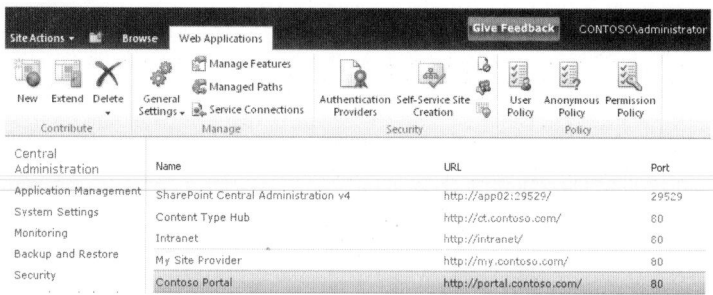

FIGURE 7-8 Select the row of the Web application, and then Manage Features.

5. Click either the feature's Activate or Deactivate button.
6. To deactivate the feature, confirm the deactivation.

ACTIVATING AND DEACTIVATING FEATURES IN A SITE COLLECTION

If a feature has been installed to the farm and scoped to a site collection, a site collection administrator can then either activate or deactivate the feature. To activate or deactivate a site collection–scoped feature, do the following:

1. Open the appropriate site collection in the browser.
2. From the Site Actions drop-down menu, click Site Settings.
3. Click the Site Collection Features hyperlink in the Site Collection Administration group, as seen in Figure 7-9. If the Site Collection Administration group contains a Go To Top Level Site Settings hyperlink, click on it to go to the top-level site, and then click the Site Collection Features hyperlink.

4. Click the Activate or Deactivate button.

5. To deactivate a feature, confirm the deactivation.

ACTIVATING AND DEACTIVATING FEATURES IN A SITE

If a feature has been installed to the farm and scoped to a site, a site owner can activate and deactivate the feature. To activate or deactivate a site-scoped feature, do the following:

1. Open the site in the browser.

2. From the Site Actions drop-down menu, click Site Settings.

3. Click the Manage Site Features hyperlink in the Site Actions group, as seen in Figure 7-9.

FIGURE 7-9 Choose to manage features in the relevant scope.

4. Click the Activate or Deactivate button.

5. Confirm the deactivation.

ACTIVATING AND DEACTIVATING FEATURES USING STSADM.EXE

Features can also be activated and deactivated from the command line using Stsadm.exe. Activate or deactivate features using the appropriate stsadm.exe command:

```
stsadm.exe -o activatefeature
{-filename <relative path to Feature.xml> | -name <feature folder> |
-id <feature Id>} [-url <url>] [-force]
```

Or

```
stsadm.exe -o deactivatefeature
{-filename <relative path to Feature.xml> | -name <feature folder> |
-id <feature Id>} [-url <url>] [-force]
```

The *Name* parameter refers to the name of the folder in which the feature resides in TEMPLATE\FEATURES. If the feature does not use a feature header file named Feature.xml, the *Filename* parameter must be used and relative path to the header file must be specified. In addition to being referred to by name or file name, features can be referred to by *ID*. With the *ID* parameter, you can specify the feature's GUID in place of the name and file name parameters. If the feature is scoped at the Web application, site collection, or site scopes, the *URL* of the Web application, site collection, or site must be specified. When you are activating a feature, the *Force* parameter forces any custom code associated with the feature to rerun.

ACTIVATING AND DEACTIVATING FEATURES USING WINDOWS POWERSHELL

Windows PowerShell uses a slightly different naming system than Stsadm.exe and the user interface. Instead of using the *activate* and *deactivate* parameters, Windows PowerShell use the verbs *Enable* and *Disable*. To activate (enable) or deactivate (disable) features with Windows PowerShell, use the appropriate cmdlet:

```
Enable-SPFeature -Identity <SPFeatureDefinitionPipeBind>
[-AssignmentCollection <SPAssignmentCollection>]
[-Confirm [<SwitchParameter>]]
[-Force <SwitchParameter>] [-PassThru <SwitchParameter>] [-Url <String>]
[-WhatIf [<SwitchParameter>]] [<CommonParameters>]
```

Or

```
Disable-SPFeature -Identity <SPFeatureDefinitionPipeBind>
[-AssignmentCollection <SPAssignmentCollection>]
[-Confirm [<SwitchParameter>]]
[-Force <SwitchParameter>] [-Url <String>] [-WhatIf [<SwitchParameter>]]
[<CommonParameters>]
```

When you are enabling or disabling a feature, the *Identity* parameter must refer to either the name of the folder in which the feature resides in TEMPLATE\FEATURES or the feature's unique ID. The *Force* parameter forces the reactivation of an already activated feature, therefore causing any custom code associated with the feature to be rerun. If the feature is scoped at the Web application, site collection, or site scopes, the *URL* of the Web application, site collection, or site must be provided.

Uninstalling Features

When a feature is uninstalled, its feature files are not deleted. Uninstalling a feature causes SharePoint Server 2010 only to ignore the feature files deployed to TEMPLATE\FEATURES. An uninstalled feature will not be displayed in the user interface, and it cannot be activated with Stsadm.exe or Windows PowerShell without first being reinstalled. This behavior allows you to uninstall a problem feature to keep it from affecting farm performance and stability.

> **NOTE** Because features are deployed using solution packages, it is not a good idea to manually delete the feature files. If a feature needs to be permanently and completely removed from the farm, the appropriate steps are to retract and delete the solution package that deployed the feature. If other assets from the solution package are still required, a new version of the solution package must be created and redeployed.

Just as with installation, features cannot be uninstalled through the user interface. To uninstall a feature, use either Stsadm.exe or Windows PowerShell. The appropriate Stsadm.exe command to uninstall a feature is as follows:

```
stsadm.exe -o uninstallfeature {-filename <relative path to Feature.xml> |
-name <feature folder> | -id <feature Id>} [-force]
```

The *Name* parameter is the name of the folder in TEMPLATE\FEATURES that the feature is located in. If the feature does not use a feature header file named Feature.xml, either the *Filename* or *ID* parameter must be used instead. Use the *Filename* parameter to refer to the feature by specifying a relative path to the feature's header file. The *ID* parameter references the feature by its unique ID. Using the *Force* parameter causes the feature to be uninstalled even if it is still activated.

UNINSTALLING VIA WINDOWS POWERSHELL

Because Windows PowerShell is replacing stsadm.exe, it's a good idea to begin administrative tasks using Windows PowerShell. To uninstall a feature via Windows PowerShell, use the following cmdlet:

```
Uninstall-SPFeature -Identity <SPFeatureDefinitionPipeBind>
[-AssignmentCollection <SPAssignmentCollection>]
[-Confirm [<SwitchParameter>]] [-Force <SwitchParameter>] [-WhatIf
[<SwitchParameter>]] [<CommonParameters>]
```

The *Identity* parameter must specify either the name of the folder in TEMPLATE\FEATURES where the feature is located or the feature's unique ID. The *Force* switch causes the feature to be uninstalled even if it's currently activated.

Managing Solutions

SharePoint Server 2010 is both a powerful product and a flexible and extensible platform. Some organizations will be able to accomplish their goals using SharePoint Server 2010 as their only product. When the native functionality of SharePoint Server 2010 is no longer sufficient to fulfill an organization's requirements, SharePoint Server 2010 can be extended and enhanced using custom code. Because of SharePoint Server 2010's multiserver architecture and its ability to delegate administrative tasks to information workers, it has some specific methods for deploying custom developer artifacts. SharePoint Server 2010 has two related technologies for packaging and managing developer artifacts, full-trust and sandboxed solutions. Sandboxed solutions are new to SharePoint Server 2010 and provide a mechanism for allowing information workers to manage extending the native platform while control of the process is maintained by farm administrators. Full-trust solutions are directly managed by farm administrators and principally used to deploy and retract developer artifacts on multiple servers.

Full-Trust Solutions

The flexible and scalable nature of SharePoint Server 2010 provides some unique deployment challenges. Multiple artifact types—such as Web parts, master pages, and features—need to be deployed to multiple locations on multiple servers. As the number of items deployed increases, the number of locations deployed to increases, and as the number of servers in the farm grows, manual deployment rapidly ceases to be an option. It is therefore critical to understand full-trust solutions and how to use them.

Full-trust solutions provide a method for consistently deploying artifacts to all the servers in a SharePoint farm. Full-trust solutions are cabinet (.CAB) files that contain a group of artifacts to be deployed and an XML file named Manifest.xml, and these files have .WSP added as a suffix. The Manifest.xml file defines the deployment locations and other properties of the artifacts contained in the full-trust solution. Full-trust solutions can deploy artifacts to the following locations:

- Global assembly cache (GAC), located at C:\Windows\Assembly
- SharePoint Root Folder, located at C:\Program Files\Common Files\ Microsoft Shared\Web Server Extensions\14
- Inetpub, located at C:\Inetpub\WWWRoot\WSS\VirtualDirectories\ [WebAppName][Port Number]

The contents of a full-trust solution can be inspected using the following process:

1. Copy the full-trust solution .WSP file.
2. Change the file extension to .CAB.
3. Open the renamed file to view the contents.
4. Extract the Manifest.xml file to determine where and how the contents of the full-trust solution will be deployed.

Adding a full-trust solution to the store does not deploy, activate, or implement any of the solution package's components. The full-trust solution is simply made available to be deployed across all servers in the farm in a consistent manner. After the full-trust solution is added to the store, it can be deployed immediately or at a scheduled time, or it simply can be left in the store for future use.

When a full-trust solution is deployed, it is deployed on all servers throughout the farm. Items are copied to each of the servers in the farm, but they still might not be functional. They must be activated either via custom code or manually in site and site collection settings. Deployment simply guarantees that items are copied to their appropriate locations. In addition to providing a mechanism for consistently deploying items, full-trust solutions also coordinate the removal of items that have reached the end of their life cycle. Full-trust solutions pass through the following life-cycle process:

1. Adding a solution to the solution store
2. Deploying the solution's content

3. Upgrading the solution
4. Retracting the content deployed by the solution
5. Deleting the solution from the solution store

Managing Full-Trust Solutions

Central Administration, Stsadm.exe, and Windows PowerShell can all be used to manage full-trust solutions, but only Stsadm.exe and Windows PowerShell can add a solution to the configuration store.

Adding and Inspecting Full-Trust Solutions Using STSADM

To add a solution to the solution store using Stsadm.exe, execute the following command:

```
stsadm.exe.exe -o AddSolution -filename <Solution Filename> [-LCID
<Language>]
```

In practice, full-trust solutions are often in locations that require extremely long paths, which are prone to typographical errors. Experience has shown that the most convenient way to add a full-trust solution to the store when using Stsadm.exe is to drag the file from Windows Explorer into the command prompt window. To add a solution without manually typing the path, do the following:

1. Open a command prompt.
2. Type the command **stsadm.exe.exe -o AddSolution –filename**, making sure to place a [space] after the *filename* flag.
3. Open the location of the full-trust solution in Windows Explorer.
4. Drag and drop the .WSP full-trust solution file from Windows Explorer into the command line. This will paste the full path of the WSP file into the command line.
5. Press the Enter key to execute the command.

Adding and Inspecting Full-Trust Solutions Using Windows PowerShell

Although it is not possible to add a full-trust solution to the solution store using Central Administration, it is possible to add a solution to the solution store using Windows PowerShell. To add a full-trust solution to the solution store using Windows PowerShell, do the following:

1. Open the SharePoint 2010 Management Shell located at Start, All Programs, Microsoft SharePoint 2010Products.
2. Type the following command: **Add-SPSolution <FilePath>**. Dragging the file from Windows Explorer into the Windows PowerShell console will copy the path to the Windows PowerShell command line.

You can examine the contents of the solution store from the command line using Stsadm.exe. To see a list of the solutions in the solution store, execute the following command:

```
stsadm.exe.exe -o EnumSolutions
```

You can also display the contents of the solution store using Windows PowerShell. To display the contents of the solution store using Windows PowerShell, execute the following from the SharePoint 2010 Management Shell:

```
Get-SPSolution
```

The output of Stsadm.exe *EnumSolutions* is useful for understanding solution deployment and the issues surrounding it:

Output from stsadm.exe.exe -o EnumSolutions

```
<Solutions Count="1">
  <Solution Name="apcsolution.wsp">
    <Id>5dg00777-defb-bb2f-aaaa-1234848eabc</Id>
    <File>apcsolution.wsp</File>
    <Deployed>FALSE</Deployed>
    <WebApplicationSpecific>TRUE</WebApplicationSpecific>
    <ContainsGlobalAssembly>TRUE</ContainsGlobalAssembly>
    <ContainsCodeAccessSecurityPolicy>
      FALSE
    </ContainsCodeAccessSecurityPolicy>
  </Solution>
</Solutions>
```

Here is a summary of the key elements:

- **Id**   Every full-trust solution must have a unique ID.

- **File**   The name of the solution will be the same as the file name and will include the .wsp file extension. The file names are converted to lower case when added to the solution store, making them case insensitive.

  NOTE Unfortunately, there is no description text for full-trust solutions. The only natural language text that is provided is the file name. Therefore, meaningful file names are helpful for determining what a solution does. For solutions that do not have meaningful file names, you should keep a record of what solution name deploys what artifacts.

- **Deployed**   Solution resources can be deployed either globally or to specific Web applications. The *Deployed* element returned by *EnumSolutions* lists all the Web applications where the solution is deployed or FALSE if isn't deployed anywhere.

- **WebApplicationSpecific**   Any solution that is Web application–specific contains resources that will be deployed to the Inetpub directory of a Web application, such as the BIN and WPCATALOG directories.

- **ContainsGlobalAssembly**   Full-trust solutions marked *True* deploy assemblies to the global assembly cache. The global assembly cache is located at C:\Windows\Assembly, and all solutions deployed to the GAC execute with full trust.
- **ContainsCodeAccessSecurityPolicy**   Code Access Security (CAS) policies are intended to "right size" the trust level of assemblies. When properly implemented, CAS policies enhance security by providing enhanced trust that is greater than a Web application's default value but less than the full trust enjoyed by using assemblies in the GAC.

Deploying Full-Trust Solutions

Full-trust solutions can be deployed using Stsadm.exe, Windows PowerShell, and Central Administration. When a solution is deployed, the solution's Manifest.xml file is inspected, which determines what items will be deployed and where they will be deployed. When the full-trust solution is deployed, it copies files consistently to every server in the farm. The following deployment locations are possible for full-trust solution deployment:

- SharePoint Root Folder, C:\Program File\...\Web Server Extensions\14
- Web Application Directories, default C:\Inetpub\WSS\Virtual Directories\
- Global assembly cache, C:\Windows\Assembly

Deploying Solutions Using stsadm.exe

To deploy full trust solutions from the command line, type the command **stsadm.exe.exe -o DeploySolution**, which has the following options:

```
stsadm.exe -o deploysolution -name <Solution name> [-url <virtual server
url>]
  [-allcontenturls] [-time <time to deploy at>] [-immediate] [-local]
  [-allowgacdeployment] [-allowcaspolicies] [-lcid <language>] [-force]
```

The *Name* parameter refers to the name of the solution in the solution store. If a solution contains items scoped for a Web application, either a *URL* or the *AllContentURLs* flag must be specified. Assuming Web applications are created at the default location, Web application–scoped items will be deployed beneath C:\Inetpub\WWWRoot\WSS\Virtual Directories\[WebAppName]. Examples of items that are deployed in the Web-application scope are assemblies (.DLLs), which are placed in the *bin* directory, and Web part XML files, which are placed in a folder named *wpcatalog*.

If a *URL* is specified, the solution is deployed to the appropriate IIS Web application directory. If the *AllContentURLs* flag is specified, the solution's contents are deployed to all nonadministrative Web applications in the farm.

There are three options for scheduling deployment: *Time, Immediate, and Local*. The *Time* flag deploys the solution at the appropriate time, and *Immediate* causes the solution to be deployed immediately. The *Local* flag deploys the solution immediately, but only on the server where the command is being run. The *Local* flag is useful for developers testing solution deployment on a single machine but is not of practical, real-world use. Because of the potential security concerns associated with deployment to the global assembly cache or when deploying code access security policies, you must explicitly allow the deployment of both. If a full-trust solution contains either CAS policies or GAC-deployed assemblies and the appropriate *AllowGACDeployment* and *AllowCASPolicies* flags have not been set, a message will be returned informing you of the required flag. Specifying a value for the *LCID* flag causes the assembly to be deployed for a particular language pack—for instance, 1033 United States English. If no value is specified, the *LCID* value is assumed to be 0 and the solution will be deployed language agnostically. The *Force* option causes the solution to overwrite files deployed by a solution with a different unique ID.

Deploying Full-Trust Solutions Using Central Administration

Full-trust solutions can also be deployed using Central Administration. To manage full-trust solutions, do the following:

1. Open Central Administration.
2. Click the Systems Settings hyperlink.
3. Click the Manage Farm Solutions link in the Farm Management group.

The Solution Management interface displays a list of all full-trust solutions in the solution store. If a solution isn't displayed, it needs to be added to the solution store from the command line. The summary includes the deployment status of the solution and some of the locations where the solution is deployed. For more information about the solution, click on its name to open a details page that lists its deployment status, where it is deployed, the results of the last operation performed on the solution, and whether the solution contains GAC-deployed assemblies, CAS policies, or Web application–scoped resources. (See Figure 7-10.) From the details page, you can also retract and deploy solutions. Open Central Administration.

Deploy Solution   Remove Solution   Back to Solutions

Name:	apcsolution.wsp
Type:	Core Solution
Contains Web Application Resource:	Yes
Contains Global Assembly:	Yes
Contains Code Access Security Policy:	No
Deployment Server Type:	Front-end Web server
Deployment Status:	Not Deployed
Deployed To:	None
Last Operation Result:	The solution was successfully retracted.
Last Operation Details:	APP02 : http://ct.contoso.com/ : The solution was successfully retracted. APP02 : http://portal.contoso.com/ : The solution was successfully retracted. APP02 : http://my.contoso.com/ : The solution was successfully retracted.
Last Operation Time:	12/18/2009 11:15 AM

FIGURE 7-10 The solution details page controls deployment and provides deployment information.

To deploy a solution using Central Administration, do the following:

1. Click the Systems Settings hyperlink.
2. Click the Manage Farm Solutions hyperlink.
3. Click the name of the full-trust solution to be deployed.
4. Click the Deploy Solution hyperlink, seen in Figure 7-10.
5. Set a date and time for the deployment, or choose Now.
6. Choose the deployment target, either All Content URLs or a Web application to deploy to.
7. Note any, warnings listed in red, about the full-trust solution deploying items to either the global assembly cache or deploying code access security policies.
8. Click OK.

The deployment process is done via timer jobs and might not execute instantaneously, even for immediate deployments. Also, it might be necessary to perform IIS resets on all the servers in the farm to ensure that the solution takes effect immediately. If it is not necessary for the solution to take effect immediately, the Web application will refresh after 15 to 20 minutes by default. Remember, all the servers must be handled in the same manner; otherwise, errors will occur when servers begin behaving differently. The full-trust solution deployment interface is shown in Figure 7-11.

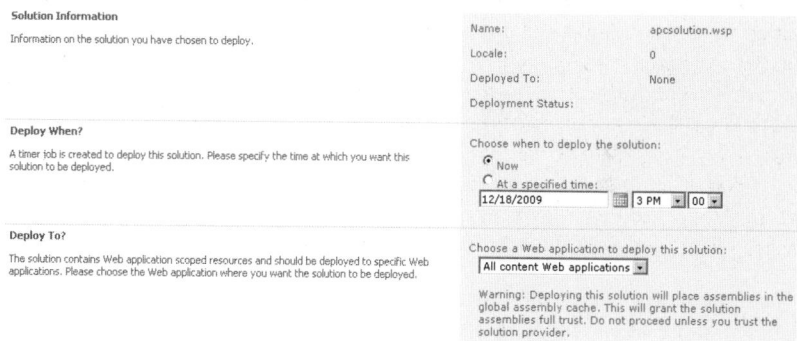

FIGURE 7-11 Schedule deployment in the solution deployment interface.

Deploying Full-Trust Solutions Using Windows PowerShell

Full-trust solutions can also be deployed using Windows PowerShell. Not all of the life-cycle names in Windows PowerShell match the names in either Stsadm.exe or Central Administration. When using Windows PowerShell, the verb *install* replaces the term *deploy*. To deploy a full-trust solution using Windows PowerShell, use the following cmdlet:

```
Install-SPSolution -Identity <SPSolutionPipeBind>
[-AllWebApplications <SwitchParameter>]
[-AssignmentCollection <SPAssignmentCollection>]
[-CASPolicies <SwitchParameter>] [-Confirm [<SwitchParameter>]]
[-Force <SwitchParameter>] [-GACDeployment <SwitchParameter>]
[-Local <SwitchParameter>] [-Time <String>]
[-WebApplication <SPWebApplicationPipeBind>]
[-WhatIf [<SwitchParameter>]] [<CommonParameters>]
```

The *identity* parameter is the name of the full-trust solution in the solution store, including the .wsp file extension. If the full-trust solution contains Web application–scoped artifacts, you must specify either *AllWebApplications or WebApplication* and a *URL*. To schedule a deployment, specify a value for the *Time* parameter; otherwise, the deployment will occur immediately. If the *Local* flag is specified, the full-trust solution will be deployed on only the server where the command is being run. The *Force* parameter overwrites items installed by other solutions. To deploy assemblies to the global assembly cache or using code access security policies, you must use the *GACDeployment* or *CASPolicies* flags. If the *Confirm* flag is specified, you will be prompted to confirm the command before it executes. Although this is not very useful when used directly from the command line, it can be useful when scripting.

Retracting Full-Trust Solutions

Over the course of time, resources deployed with full-trust solutions need to be updated and removed. Artifacts deployed via full-trust solution can be retracted from one or all Web applications where they are deployed in a manner similar to deploying them. Retracting a full-trust solution removes the deployed artifacts from the servers in the farm, but it does not delete the full-trust solution from the solution store. If a full-trust solution is retracted from some, but not all, Web applications where it is deployed, only the Web applications being retracted are affected by retracting the solution.

For example, consider a full-trust solution that contains an assembly deployed to the Web application *bin* directory and a feature that is deployed to SharePoint Root\TEMPLATE\FEATURES. For instance, consider a solution that deploys two assemblies one to the Web application *bin* directory and one to the GAC. When the solution is deployed, the GAC assembly is copied to the global assembly cache and the *bin* assembly is copied to the *bin* directory of every Web application that it is deployed to. If the full-trust solution is retracted from a single Web application, only one copy of the *bin* assembly is deleted from the Web application that solution is being retracted from. The copy of the assemblies deployed to the other

Web applications and to the GAC are unaffected. It is acceptable and safe to retract a solution from one Web application but not another.

Retracting Solutions Using stsadm.exe

To retract a solution using Stsadm.exe, execute the following:

```
stsadm.exe -o retractsolution -name <Solution name> [-url <virtual server
url>]
    [-allcontenturls] [-time <time to remove at>] [-immediate] [-local]
    [-lcid <language>]
```

The *name* parameter is the name of the solution in the solution store, including the .wsp file extension. If the solution deploys resources to one or more Web applications, you must specify either a single Web application using the *URL* parameter or *AllContentURLs*. This retracts the full-trust solution from all Web applications where it was deployed. Use the *Time* flag to delay retracting the solution, or specify *Immediate* to retract the solution immediately. The *Local* parameter causes the solution to be retracted immediately, but only on the server where the Stsadm.exe command is being run. To retract the solution for a given locality, specify an *LCID* value, such as 1033 for United States English.

Retracting Solutions Using Central Administration

Solutions can also be retracted using Central Administration. To retract a solution using Central Administration, do the following:

1. Open Central Administration.
2. Click the Systems Settings hyperlink.
3. Click the Manage Farm Solutions hyperlink.
4. Click the name of the full-trust solution to be retracted.
5. Click the Retract Solution hyperlink.
6. Set when to retract the full-trust solution, or choose Now.
7. Choose which Web application to retract the full-trust solution from, either All Content URLs or a single Web application.
8. Click OK.

TIP Because a timer job is used to retract the full-trust solution, it is likely that the status of the solution will be shown as Retracting for several minutes.

Retracting Solutions Using Windows PowerShell

You can also retract full-trust solutions using Windows PowerShell. Unlike Central Administration and Stsadm.exe, Windows PowerShell uses the verb *uninstall* in the place of the term *retract*. To retract a solution using Windows PowerShell, execute the following cmdlet:

```
Uninstall-SPSolution -Identity <SPSolutionPipeBind> -AllWebApplications
-WebApplication <SPWeb ApplicationPipeBind>
<SwitchParameter> [-AssignmentCollection <SPAssignmentCollection>]
[-Confirm [<SwitchParameter>]] [-Language <UInt32>] [-Local
<SwitchParameter>] [-Time <String>] [-WhatIf [<SwitchParameter>]]
[<CommonParameters>]
```

The *Identity* parameter specifies the name of the full-trust solution in the solution store, including the .wsp file extension. If the full-trust solution contains artifacts scoped at the Web-application level, you must use either the *AllWebApplications* flag or the *WebApplication* parameter specifying the URL of a Web application. To schedule a retraction, use the *Time* parameter; if no time is specified, the retraction occurs immediately.

Deleting Full-Trust Solutions

When full-trust solutions are retracted, they are not actually removed from the solution store. Full-trust solutions can be deleted using Stsadm.exe, Central Administration, and Windows PowerShell.

Deleting Full-Trust Solutions Using stsadm.exe

To permanently remove a solution from the solution store using Stsadm.exe, execute the following command:

```
stsadm.exe -o deletesolution n-name <Solution name> [-override]
    [-lcid <language>]
```

The *Name* parameter is the name of the full-trust solution in the solution store, including the .wsp file extension. The *Override* flag removes the full-trust solution from the solution store even though it is currently deployed. If the *Override* option is used, you cannot retract the solution after it is deleted from the solution store. For this reason, it is best to avoid using the *Override* option. If a value is specified for the *LCID* option, the full-trust solution will be deleted for the given locale.

Deleting Full-Trust Solutions Using Central Administration

Although you cannot add full-trust solutions using Central Administration, you can delete them. To delete a full-trust solution using Central Administration, do the following:

1. Browse to Central Administration, System Settings, Manage Farm Solutions.
2. Click the name of the full trust solution to be deleted.

3. Click the Remove Solution hyperlink.

4. Set when to retract the full-trust solution, or choose Now.

5. Confirm that you want to delete the full-trust solution by clicking OK.

Deleting Full-Trust Solutions Using Windows PowerShell

To delete a full-trust solution using Windows PowerShell, use the following command:

```
Remove-SPSolution -Identity <SPSolutionPipeBind> [-AssignmentCollection
<SPAssignmentCollection>] [-Confirm [<SwitchParameter>]] [-Force
<SwitchParameter>] [-Language <UInt32>] [-WhatIf [<SwitchParameter>]]
[<CommonParameters>]
```

The *Identity* parameter specifies the name of the full-trust solution in the solution store. The *Force* parameter deletes the full-trust solution from the solution store even though artifacts from it are still deployed. If the *Force* parameter is used, you will not be able to retract (uninstall) the full-trust solution,

Upgrading Full-Trust Solutions

You can also upgrade solutions using Stsadm.exe. Upgrading the solution replaces the full-trust solution in the solution store with a new version and deploys the contents of the new full-trust solution. Full-trust solutions can be upgraded using Stsadm.exe and Windows PowerShell.

Upgrading Full-Trust Solutions Using stsadm.exe

To upgrade a solution using Stsadm.exe, use the following command:

```
stsadm.exe -o upgradesolution -name <Solution name>
    [-filename <upgrade filename>] [-time <time to upgrade at>]
    [-immediate] [-local] [-allowgacdeployment] [-allowcaspolicies]
    [-lcid <language>]
```

The *Name* parameter is the name of the full-trust solution in the solution store, and the *Filename* parameter is the name of the new full-trust solution that replaces the previous version in the solution store. Specify a time to schedule the deployment or use the *Immediate* flag to run the upgrade immediately.

> **IMPORTANT** The *Local* flag runs the upgrade immediately on only the server where the Stsadm.exe command is being executed. Because this would break the synchronization of the servers in the farm, the *Local* flag is intended only for single-server development environments.

When upgrading a solution, you must explicitly permit the deployment of assemblies to the global assembly cache or code access security policies by specifying *AllowGACDeployment* or *AllowCASPolicies*, respectively. If the *LCID* parameter is specified, the solution will be upgraded for a specific local machine.

Just as with deploying artifacts, you must run an IISRESET on every server in the farm for the upgrade to take immediate effect. Unfortunately, there is not an option for upgrading solutions from Central Administration. This means that the process cannot be accomplished using a graphical user interface.

Upgrading Full-Trust Solutions Using Windows PowerShell

To upgrade a full-trust solution using Windows PowerShell, execute the following cmdlet:

```
Update-SPSolution -Identity <SPSolutionPipeBind> -LiteralPath <String>
[-AssignmentCollection <SPAssignmentCollection>]
[-CASPolicies <SwitchParameter>] [-Confirm [<SwitchParameter>]]
[-Force <SwitchParameter>] [-GACDeployment <SwitchParameter>]
[-Local <SwitchParameter>] [-Time <String>]
[-WhatIf [<SwitchParameter>]] [<CommonParameters>]
```

The *Identify* parameter specifies the name of the full-trust solution in the solution store and should include the .wsp file extension. The *LiteralPath* parameter is the path to the new full-trust solution package file that will be used for upgrade. To allow either code access security policies to be deployed or assemblies to be deployed to the global assembly cache, you must use the *GACDeployment* or *CASPolicies* flag. To schedule an update at a later time, use the *Time* parameter. If no value for the *Time* parameter is specified, the update is processed immediately. Including the *Local* flag causes the update to occur on only the server where the command is being run. The *Local* flag is intended for use by developers in a single-server environment.

Managing Sandboxed Solutions

Sandboxed full-trust solutions are new to SharePoint Server 2010 and were created to provide new levels of flexibility and control when deploying SharePoint Server 2010 artifacts. Instead of deploying items farmwide, sandboxed solutions are contained within a single site collection. Instead of being stored in the solution store, sandboxed solutions are stored in the site collection gallery like Web parts and list templates. One advantage of scoping sandboxed solutions at the site-collection level is that it allows site collection administrators, instead of farm-level administrators, to manage solutions packages.

Although allowing information workers to deploy code might seem risky at first glance, sandboxed solutions actually provide a security enhancement compared to full-trust solutions. Sandboxed solutions are run using a restrictive set of code access security policies and are limited to a specific subset of the SharePoint Server 2010 object model. In addition to running with limited trust, sandboxed solutions are monitored to ensure that they do not affect server performance by consuming too many system resources. Furthermore, because sandboxed solutions are limited to operation within a single site collection, problems are limited to only that site collection.

Sandboxed solutions can also be set to execute on a single dedicated server. If the security enhancements present in sandboxed solutions are not adequate for your environment, they can be disabled entirely by farm administrators. When used properly, they provide a more elegant trust solution than code access security because they are monitored, controlled, and adaptable to different requirements using different quotas for each site collection. Additionally, the responsibility for sandboxed solutions can be delegated to information workers.

Sandboxed solutions present a new standard for deploying SharePoint Server 2010 artifacts. Unfortunately, sandboxed solutions cannot do certain things and therefore are not a complete replacement for full-trust solutions. Table 7-2 shows the allowed and disallowed functions when using sandboxed solutions:

TABLE 7-2 Allowed and Disallowed Items and Actions in a Sandboxed Solution

ALLOWED ITEMS AND ACTIONS	DISALLOWED ITEMS AND ACTIONS
Custom list templates	Farm-scoped features
Creating lists	Web application–scoped features
Extending the user interface	Hiding and grouping items in the UI
Copy files to lists, libraries, and galleries	Content type bindings
Web parts not requiring full trust	Web parts that contain user controls
InfoPath Forms not requiring full trust	Running with elevated privileges
Silverlight controls and JavaScript	Accessing external data
Workflow	Interacting with other site collections
List, item and site event receivers	Timer jobs

Sandboxed solutions have the same basic structure as full-trust solutions. They are cabinet files with the .wsp suffix instead of .cab. They contain an XML file named Manifest.xml that describes the contents of the solution and how to deploy them. As with full-trust solutions, you can inspect the contents of a sandboxed solution by changing the file extension to .cab, as discussed previously in this chapter.

NOTE You can upload a full-trust solution to a solution gallery, but if the solution is activated and attempts to violate the partial-trust policy, an error will occur.

For sandboxed solutions to run properly, the Microsoft SharePoint Foundation Sandboxed Code service must be started. The service does not have to be started on every server, only on the servers that will run sandboxed solutions. The recommended configuration is for the service to be started on one, or perhaps more, application servers. Doing so insulates Web front-end servers from the performance requirements of running sandboxed solutions. To start the Microsoft SharePoint Foundation User Code service, do the following:

1. Browse to Central Administration, Systems Settings, Manage Services On Server.
2. Select a server to run the Microsoft SharePoint Foundation Sandboxed Code service.
3. Click the Start hyperlink for Microsoft SharePoint Foundation Sandboxed Code service.
4. Repeat steps 3 and 4 if additional servers will be used to run the Sandboxed Code service.

Not surprisingly, sandboxed solutions have a different life cycle than full-trust solutions. Instead of being added, deployed, retracted, and deleted, sandboxed solutions are uploaded, activated, deactivated, and deleted. There is also an upgrade option similar to the one provided for full-trust solutions.

Uploading, Activating, and Renaming Sandboxed Solutions

To upload a sandboxed solution, do the following:

1. Open the site collection where the solution is to be added.
2. Select Site Settings from the Site Actions menu.
3. Click the Solutions hyperlink in the Galleries group. If Solutions isn't present in the Galleries group, click the Go To Top-Level Site Settings hyperlink in the Site Collection Administration group.
4. Click the Solutions tab on the Ribbon as shown in Figure 7-12.

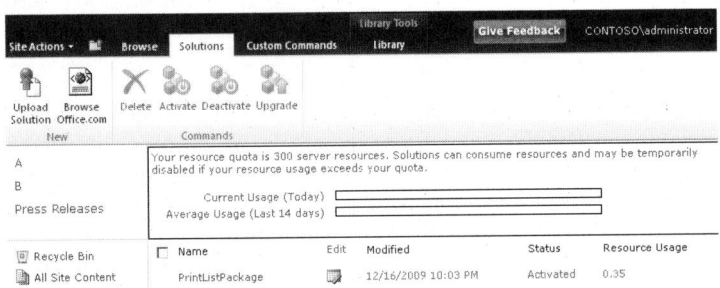

FIGURE 7-12 Managing sandboxed solutions using the Ribbon.

5. Click the Upload Solution button on the Ribbon.
6. Browse to the location of the solution file.
7. Click OK.

To download a sandboxed solution, click on the solution's name. To change the name of a solution, click on the edit icon. Upon being uploaded to the gallery, a sandboxed solution does not automatically do anything; it is simply available to be activated. When a sandboxed solution is activated, it automatically activates any site collection–scoped features that it contains. Site-scoped features must be manually activated for every site where they are to run. To activate a sandboxed solution, do the following:

1. Open the site collection where the solution is to be added.
2. Select Site Settings from the Site Actions menu.
3. Click the Solutions hyperlink in the Galleries group.
4. If Solutions isn't present in the Galleries group, click the Go To Top-Level Site Settings hyperlink in the Site Collection Administration group.
5. Click the row that contains the full-trust solution, causing it to be highlighted.
6. Click the Activate button on the Ribbon, as shown in Figure 7-13.
7. Click the Activate button in the window that opens
8. Wait for the sandboxed solution to activate and the window to close.

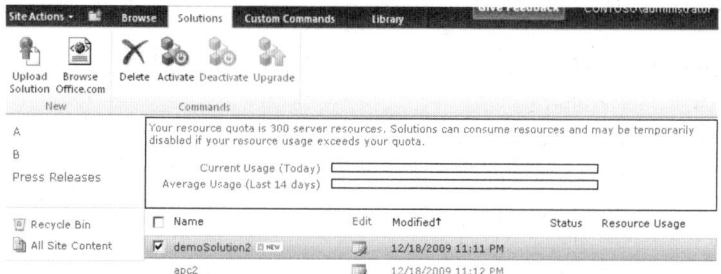

FIGURE 7-13 Activating a sandboxed Solution using the management Ribbon.

Sandboxed Solution Monitoring

One of the biggest advantages to sandboxed solutions is the ability to monitor them and terminate execution if they consume excessive system resources. Previously, the only way to gauge the impact of deployed solutions was by monitoring overall system performance and making comparisons between when solutions were and were not deployed. As the number of solutions deployed in the farm grew and the baseline comparisons became more outdated, pinpointing the source of performance problems became more and more difficult. It was not uncommon to know something was not performing well without the ability to easily pinpoint what the problem was.

To address these problems, sandboxed solutions have been moved entirely out of the standard Internet Information Services (IIS) worker processes and are instead run in a separate process named *SPUCWorkerProcess*. Usage quotas can be set for each site collection, and sandboxed solutions that exceed the quota for a site collection will not be allowed to run. Because the quotas are per site collection, you can assign different values for different site collections based on their intended use. This approach effectively allows for a balance of different sandboxed solution service agreements for different site collections in your organization. To manage sandboxed solution quotas, do the following:

1. Browse to Central Administration, Application Management, Configure Quotas And Locks.

2. Select the site collection to be configured from the Site Collection drop-down menu as shown in Figure 7-14.

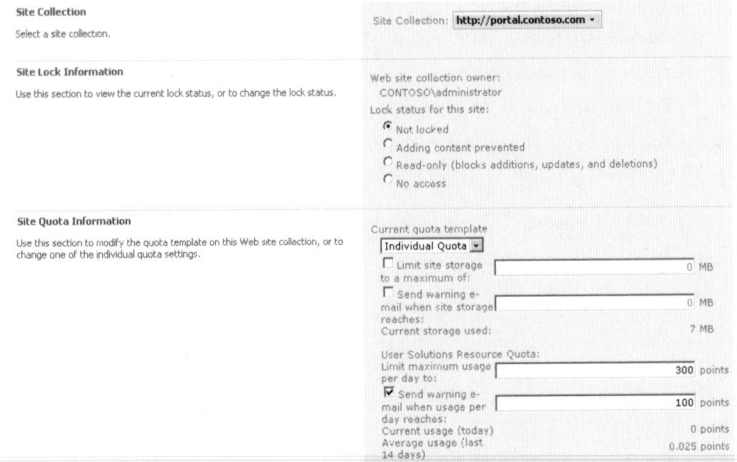

FIGURE 7-14 The sandboxed solution quota management interface.

3. Click OK.

The Sandboxed Solutions Resource Quota value specifies a maximum resource utilization for sandboxed solutions for the selected site collection. The value is specified in resource points. Resource points are an abstract concept and not directly related to any specific measure of server performance. Instead, the resource components are themselves based on a set of 14 metrics that measure specific conditions. These 14 metrics, listed in Table 7-3, are then weighted to balance their overall influence on the resource point scale. There is no way to view the actual metrics and their point values within Central Administration. You can use the following short Windows PowerShell script to display the list of metrics and their current weighting:

```
Add-PSSnapin Microsoft.SharePoint.Powershell
[System.Reflection.Assembly]::Load("Microsoft.SharePoint, Version=12.0.0.0,
    Culture=neutral, PublicKeyToken=71e9bce111e9429c")
$s=[Microsoft.SharePoint.Administration.SPUserCodeService]::Local
$s.ResourceMeasures | Select-Object Name,ResourcesPerPoint
```

TABLE 7-3 Resource Point Metrics and Weighting

NAME	RESOURCES/ POINT	ABSOLUTE LIMIT	UNITS
AbnormalProcessTerminationCount	1	1	Count
CPUExecutionTime	3600	60	Seconds
CriticalExceptionCount	10	3	Events
InvocationCount	100	100	Events
PercentProcessorTime	85	100	%
ProcessCPUCycles	100000000000	100000000000	Cycles
ProcessHandleCount	10000	1000	Items
ProcessIOBytes	10000000	100000000	Items
ProcessThreadCount	10000	200	Instances
ProcessVirtualBytes	100000000	1000000000	Bytes
SharePointDatabaseQueryCount	20	100	Instances
SharePointDatabaseQueryTime	120	60	Seconds
UnhandledExceptionCount	50	3	Instances
UnresponsiveprocessCount	2	1	Instances

Essentially, the process works like this: each metric, also referred to as *resource measures*, has a *resources per point value*. When a sandboxed solution's resource utilization exceeds one of the resource per point values for a resource measure, one resource point is deducted from the daily quota.

For example, every time an Abnormal Process Termination occurs, it consumes a resource point from the daily quota. Likewise, if the sandboxed solution uses 3600 seconds of CPU time, 1 point from the daily quota is used. The daily quota is cumulative for all sandboxed solutions in the site collection. That is to say, when the quota is exceeded by one or more solutions, no sandboxed solutions can run in that site collection for the remainder of the day. To keep one really badly behaving sandboxed solution from stopping execution of all sandboxed solutions, there is an absolute limit that controls execution of the single offending sandboxed solution. If a single sandboxed solution consumes more than 85 percent of processor time or if it encounters more than three unhandled exceptions, it is locked. The absolute limit provides fault tolerance in the event a single solution seriously malfunctions.

You can create predefined quotas that can be used repeatedly instead of setting values for each site collection. To create a predefined quota, do the following:

1. Browse to Central Administration, Application Management.
2. Click the Specify Quota Templates hyperlink in the Site Collections group.

3. Select the Create A New Quota Template radio button.
4. Select a template to base the new template on.
5. Give the template a meaningful name.
6. Specify a storage limit for the site collection and e-mail warning level. An e-mail message will be sent when either value is reached.
7. In the Sandboxed Solutions With Code Limits section, set the maximum daily usage and e-mail warning levels.

Sandboxed Solution Load Balancing

By default, sandboxed solutions run only on servers that have the Microsoft SharePoint Foundation Sandboxed Code Service running. This allows sandboxed solution execution to be offloaded from individual Web front-end servers and isolated on one or more servers. You can also have sandboxed solutions execute directly on the Web front-end servers. To change the sandboxed solution load-balancing scheme, do the following:

1. Open Central Administration.
2. Click the Systems Settings hyperlink.
3. Click the Manage User Solutions hyperlink.
4. Select either All Sandboxed Code Runs On The Same Machine As The Request or Requests To Run Sandboxed Code Are Routed By Solution Affinity.
5. Click OK.

Blocking Sandboxed Solutions

To prevent a truly pernicious sandboxed solution from executing, you can implement a list of blocked solutions. Blocked solutions are prevented from executing. To block a sandboxed solution, do the following:

1. Browse to Central Administration, System Settings, Manage User Solutions.
2. Under Add New Solution To Block, click the Browse button, and select the solution.
3. Provide a message that users will see when attempting to use the blocked sandboxed solution.
4. Click the Block button.

CHAPTER 8

Configuring the Search Service Application

- Farm-Wide Search Settings   **240**

- Managing Crawler Impact Rules   **241**

- Creating the Search Service Application   **243**

- Examining the Search Administration Page   **245**

- Creating and Managing Content Sources   **246**

- Creating and Managing Crawl Rules   **247**

- Managing Server Name Mappings   **250**

- Managing File Types   **250**

- Managing the Search Application Topology   **252**

- Managing Host Distribution Rules   **258**

- Troubleshooting Search with Crawl Logs   **259**

Aggregated search and indexing is one of the most important features of Microsoft SharePoint Server 2010. This chapter shows you how to create a search service application and configure the crawl process. Configuring and customizing the query process will be covered in the following chapter.

At the heart of the search engine is the crawler. The crawler goes out and gathers from the content source the content that needs to be placed in the index. After the index is built, users execute a query against the index to receive a result set. The crawler does only what it is instructed to do. Therefore, when it crawls content, it crawls only the content that you have instructed it to crawl, and the crawl actions occur within the security rule and timing rules that you create manually.

The crawler works by connecting to the content source and downloading all files listed to be crawled. The crawler will also load various file-type iFilters (index filters)—such as Word, Excel, and text—so that, once connected, the crawler can open the files and read their content. The iFilter instructs the crawler what portion of documents is text and what portion is formatting. Some SharePoint 2010 indexing connectors use the protocol handler method, and some use the new connector framework.

After the crawler has connected to the content source and has cracked open the documents, it streams the content from the content source to the index process. The indexer chunks the stream into 64-KB chunks, performs word breaking and stemming on the words, removes the noise words (words that you have specified not to appear in the index), and then sends the content to the index (the content store) and the metadata and security access control lists to the SQL search databases for the search service.

Under the SharePoint 2010 service architecture, there is no longer a Shared Services Provider. Each SharePoint 2010 service is managed separately, including search. Although some services must first be started in the Services On Server Central Administration page, the search service must be started as part of creating a search service application and is managed within the Search Service Application topology.

With the new service architecture, a single SharePoint 2010 farm can provide multiple instances of search services and applications, and different applications can be associated with one or more of these services. One of the goals of SharePoint search in SharePoint Server 2010 is to provide sub-second query latency even when scaled to 100 million documents.

Toward this goal, Microsoft has componentized the system so that bottlenecks can be indentified and removed. Although the planning and scaling of these components is beyond the scope of this book, it is important to note the configuration options.

> **NOTE** Because crawl components do not use noise-word files in SharePoint 2010, they will be discussed in Chapter 11 with the search results customizations.

Farm-Wide Search Settings

Although most configurations are unique to the search service instance, the farm-wide settings are followed by all crawlers. Some settings that are identified as farm settings are just default settings that can be overwritten by local services settings. The settings page shown in Figure 8-1 can be accessed from the Central Administration page by clicking General Application Settings, and then Farm Search Administration under the Search section.

Farm-Level Search Settings

Proxy server	None
Time-out (seconds)	60, 60
Ignore SSL warnings	No

Search Service Applications

Name	Modify Topology
Search Service Application	Modify Topology

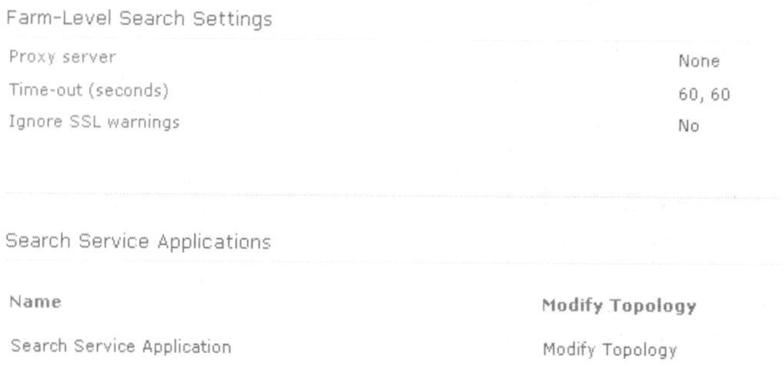

FIGURE 8-1 Farm-Wide Search Settings page.

Because the crawler for Web sites is essentially a browser, the proxy settings are the same as for Internet Explorer with the exception of an option that directs federated queries to use the same settings.

The default connection timeouts of 60 seconds are for connection to content sources and for waiting for request acknowledgments.

The Boolean Ignore SSL Warnings choice controls whether the browser will treat sites as legitimate even if their certificate name does not exactly match. If this setting is not selected, a site with a faulty certificate will not be crawled.

The link to Modify Topology opens the same page as the link provided on the Search Service administration page. Because the topology is "per service," it will be discussed in service administration.

Managing Crawler Impact Rules

Crawler impact rules are an optional mechanism to control the rate at which the crawler indexes a source. The crawler impact rule site-configuration settings are for a particular crawler target regardless of which search service, content source, or crawler instance is addressing the target. The Crawler Impact Rules management page can be accessed from the Central Administration page by clicking General Application Settings, and then Crawler Impact Rules, under the Search section. It can also be opened from Search Administration for any search service, but the configurations are always farmwide. On this page, click Add Rule to open the Add Crawler Impact Rule page, shown in Figure 8-2, or select an existing rule to edit.

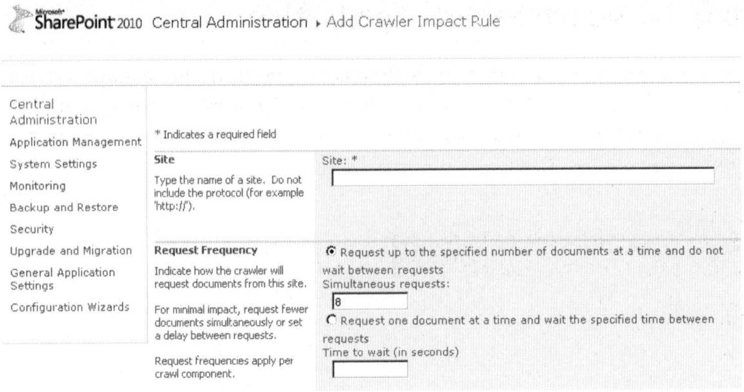

SharePoint 2010 Central Administration ▸ Add Crawler Impact Rule
Central Administration
Application Management
System Settings
Monitoring
Backup and Restore
Security
Upgrade and Migration
General Application Settings
Configuration Wizards
* Indicates a required field
Site
Type the name of a site. Do not include the protocol (for example 'http://').
Site: *
Request Frequency
Indicate how the crawler will request documents from this site.
For minimal impact, request fewer documents simultaneously or set a delay between requests.
Request frequencies apply per crawl component.
Request up to the specified number of documents at a time and do not wait between requests
Simultaneous requests:
8
Request one document at a time and wait the specified time between requests
Time to wait (in seconds)

FIGURE 8-2 Add Crawler Impact Rule page.

Valid crawl rules do not define the protocol (http://, https://, or file://) because the rule applies without regard to the connector used in the crawl or the content source containing the target. Here are some examples:

- Site name: 'www.contoso.com'
- All inclusive: '*'
- Partial: '*.contoso.com'
- Machine name: 'WFE01'

If you want to limit the number of simultaneous requests, you can change the default of 8 to 1, 2, 4, 16, 32, or 64. A useful example is when you must first build the index. You can create a rule for * and throttle the requests to 1.

You can also configure the crawler to request one document at a time and send the requests to the queue. There is a large difference between 1 simultaneous request and a 1-second delay. Rarely will you need to set the delay greater than 1 second.

> ***NOTE*** **Reducing the crawl rate can extend the crawl time so much that the crawl does not complete before it's time to start again.**

Creating the Search Service Application

Like all service applications, a search application is created from the Manage Service Applications page, which can be accessed from the Service Applications section of the Application Management page of Central Administration. From the New menu, click Search Service Application as shown in Figure 8-3.

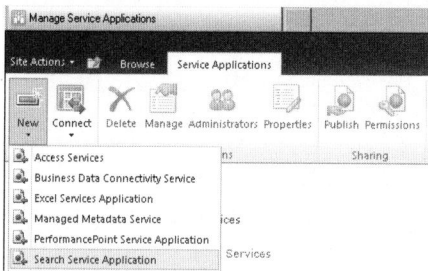

FIGURE 8-3 Option to create a new search service application.

Once created, the service application has three distinct pages where you will specify the properties. These settings can be changed by selecting the application and using the properties button in the Manage Service Applications page shown in Figure 8-3.

The initial topology with your new search service application will have all components on one application server and all databases on one database server. This topology can be changed later using the Modify Topology link located on the Farm-Wide Search Administration page or from the Search Service management page.

In the first section of the New Search Service Application page shown in Figure 8-4, name the service according to your naming convention for services. For SharePoint search services, leave the FAST Service Application option set to None.

You must specify the search service account. This account must be a managed service account, and it will be the same for all search services in the farm. Like other managed service accounts, it can be changed from the Configure Service Accounts page under the General Security section of the Security page in Central Administration.

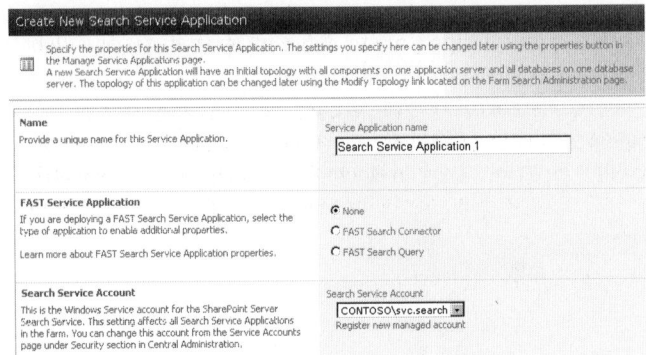

FIGURE 8-4 First section of the New Search Service Application page.

In the next section, shown in Figure 8-5, configure the application pool to be used by the first of two Web services required for the search application, the Search Admin Web Service. This application pool, as well as its identity, can be shared with other applications or they can be unique. The security account used as its identity must be a managed account.

FIGURE 8-5 Configuration section for Search Admin Web Service.

Finally, in the third section, which is shown in Figure 8-6, you configure the application pool and credentials for the Search Query And Site Settings Web Service for this search application. Again, these can be unique or shared with other services and require a managed account.

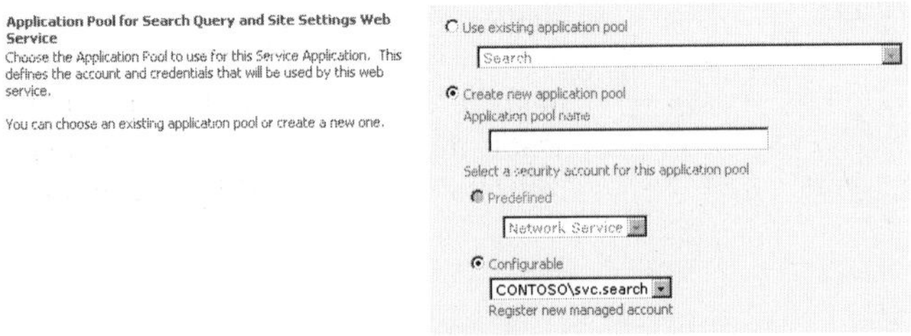

FIGURE 8-6 Search Query And Site Settings Web Service configuration section.

After completing the required information on the New Search Service Application page, click OK at the bottom and the appropriate databases and Web services will be created and configured.

If you will have search administrators who are not farm administrators, you need to give them permission to manage the search service application. From the Manage Service Applications page shown in Figure 8-3, highlight your new search service and click the Administrators button in the management Ribbon to open the page shown in Figure 8-7.

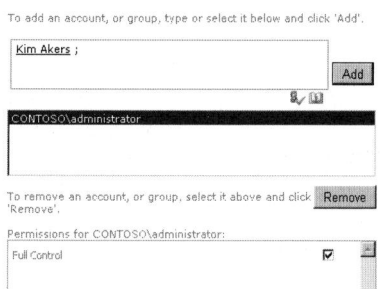

FIGURE 8-7 Configure search service administrators.

You can add individual accounts or Active Directory groups on this page. For the Search Service, Full Control is the only permission option. Individuals added here will be granted access to Central Administration but will have links only to pages to manage this service.

Examining the Search Administration Page

From the Manage Service Applications page shown in Figure 8-3, highlight your new search service and click the Manage button in the management Ribbon to open the Search Administration page. This page presents dashboards for System Status, Crawl History, and Search Application Topology. This design of including dashboards continues throughout many of the search management pages.

The Quick Launch area has links to search management pages organized as Administration, Crawling, Queries And Results, and Reports, as shown in Figure 8-8. The Search Application Topology dashboard in the lower portion of the page is not shown in Figure 8-8 and will be discussed later in this chapter. Administration pages organized under Queries and Results and Reports will be discussed in Chapter 11.

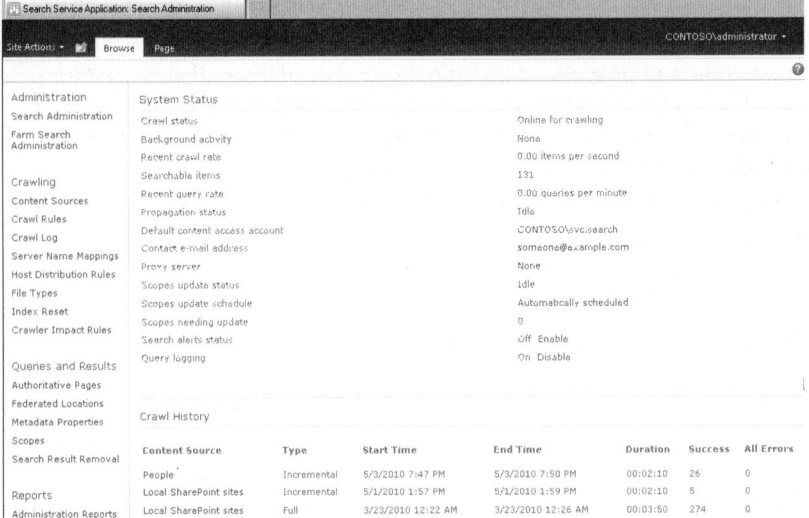

FIGURE 8-8 Search Administration page.

Several configuration links in the System Status dashboard are presented as links that open dialog boxes or as toggles:

- The Default Content Access Account sets or changes the account used for authentication by the crawler for this search application.

- The Contact E-mail Address applies to all search applications on this farm.

- The Proxy Server configuration is a farm-wide setting, as discussed previously.

- The Scopes Update Schedule option can be set to Automatically Scheduled or On Demand Updates Only, and it applies to this search application only. By default, the scope update timer job runs every 12 minutes.

- The Search Alerts Status can be toggled, and it should be disabled when resetting the index so that users do not receive alerts on saved searches as existing content is re-crawled.

- The Query Logging option can be toggled as needed. Query logging is necessary for all query reports.

Use the Crawl History dashboard to review recent crawl performance, and use the hyperlinked numbers for quick access to filtered logs for successes and errors.

Creating and Managing Content Sources

Creating content sources is the first administrative task in building an aggregated search and indexing topology. This work is accomplished inside the Search Service interface. To manage content sources, open the administration page for your search service, and click on the Content Sources link in the Quick Launch area as shown in Figure 8-8.

Essentially, a, content source is a collection of start addresses that are accessed with the same type connection and collectively managed. A start address is the URL location where the crawler starts the process. The crawl settings define the depth and, potentially, the width for the crawl process.

The content source types include the following:

- SharePoint sites
- Web sites
- File shares
- Exchange public folders
- Line of business data
- Custom repositories defined by custom connectors

The crawl setting terminology varies so that the settings that appear are appropriate for the selected content source type. To create a new content source, click the New Content Source link to open the Add Content Source page and then follow these steps:

1. Enter a name for the content source.
2. Select the content source type.
3. Enter the start address or addresses. All of them must match the content source type.
4. Select the crawl settings.
5. Select the crawl schedule or schedules.
6. Select the High or Normal priority for the content source processing.
7. Optionally, select Start Full Crawl Of This Content Source.
8. Click OK.

Creating and Managing Crawl Rules

Crawl rules allow you to configure include/exclude rules, specific security contexts for crawling that are different from the default content access account, and the actual path to which you want the rule to apply.

Crawl rules are global to the search service and are relative to the target site, not a content source. For example, you can have two content sources: one each for http://WSS01/sites/IT and http://WSS01/sites/HR. Both can be covered by one crawl rule with a path of http://WSS01. Likewise, you can also specify a crawl rule for a subset of a content source, such as http://WSS01/sites/legal, if http://WSS01/ was the listing in the content source.

To manage existing crawl rules or create new ones, click the Crawl Rules link in the Quick Launch area as shown in Figure 8-8, which opens the Manage Crawl Rules page shown in Figure 8-9.

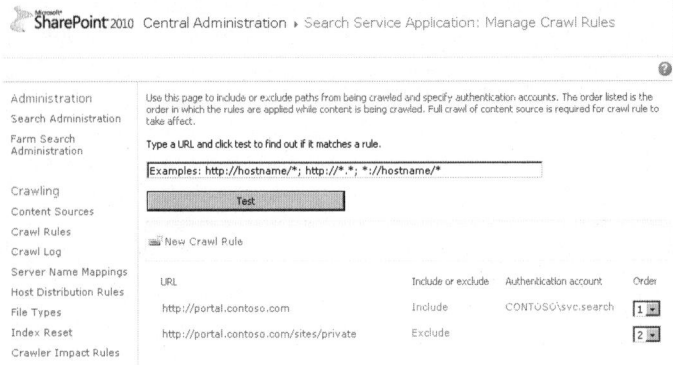

FIGURE 8-9 Manage Crawl Rules page.

If your search service has several crawl rules defined, use the Test button to locate any existing rules that might impact crawls of the site where you intend to create a new rule.

Crawl rules are applied in the order listed on the Manage Crawl Rules page. In Figure 8-9, the Exclude rule overrides some content addressed by the Include rule that is applied first. To create a new crawl rule from the Manage Crawl Rules page, click the New Crawl Rule link, which opens the Add Crawl Rule page shown in Figure 8-10.

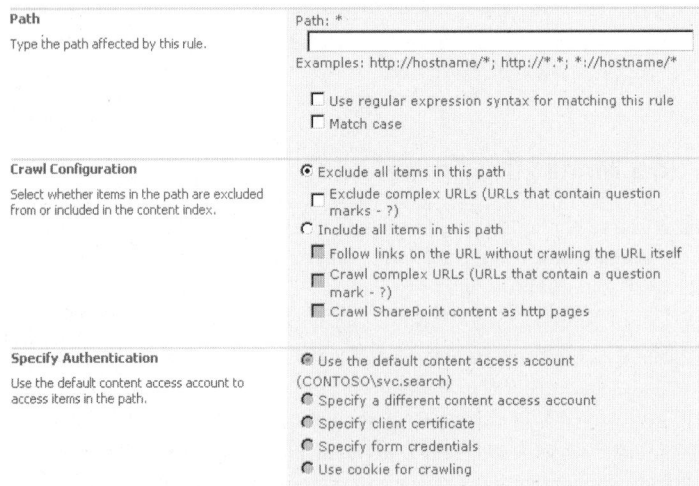

FIGURE 8-10 The Add Crawl Rules interface.

Crawl Rule Paths

Enter a URL path in the Path input box in the following form:

- Web application: http://www.contoso.com
- Web application path: http://www.contoso.com/path
- All inclusive: http://*
- Scheme independent: *://www.contoso.com
- Domain: http://*.contoso.com

Crawl rule paths in SharePoint 2010 can also include regular expressions (REGEX) and be case sensitive if required.

Exclude/Include Options

You can also set the crawl information to exclude all items in the path or to include all items in the path. If you select Include All Items In This Path, you also have the following options:

- **Follow Links On The URL Without Crawling The URL Itself**   This is useful when the starting point of a crawl is a menu.
- **Crawl Complex URLs**   If you want to crawl content where there is content beyond a '?', select this option. Complex URLs are common with SharePoint and also often point to information contained in databases.
- **Crawl SharePoint Content As HTTP Pages**   If you want the crawler to ignore SharePoint content such as security and versions, you can select this. It is often desirable to crawl external SharePoint Server content as HTTP pages when the audience is the Internet. This prevents accidental surfacing of private information regarding security and minor versions, among other things.

Crawl Rule Authentication

You can specify unique authentication via a crawl rule. The indexer uses the default content access account unless you create a crawl rule to change this behavior. Simply enter the user name and password to access the resource. You can also restrict Basic authentication. The unique account specified here is not included in managed accounts, and the password must be manually changed. Changing this account triggered a full crawl in the previous version.

You can specify a client certificate to access a content source. This certificate must first exist in the index server's Personal Certificate Store for the local computer before it will show up in the selection list.

> **NOTE**   For Information Rights Management (IRM) files stored in SharePoint, the crawler will be able to index the files. However, for IRM files in other storage, the certificate for the crawler account must have read permission on the files.

Crawl rules also support Forms-Based authentication (FBA) and cookie-based authentication. Crawler rules do not support FBA with complex authentication pages that change content without refreshing the page or require entries or selection based on content appearing on the page.

NOTE Be careful setting these one-off content source passwords of nonmanaged accounts using crawl rules. Remember that this password must be manually changed whenever the account's password changes. This should be a documented process in your search-and-indexing maintenance plan, as well as in your disaster recovery plan.

Managing Server Name Mappings

There might be situations where content needs to be crawled using an address other than one of the Alternate Access Mapping URIs defined for user access to SharePoint content. Create server name mappings to override how URLs are shown in search results and correct the name displayed to users. The Server Name Mapping management page is accessed by clicking Server Name Mapping in the Crawling section of the Search Service management page of the Quick Launch navigation area shown in Figure 8-9. Click the New Mapping link to open the Add Server Name Mapping page shown in Figure 8-11.

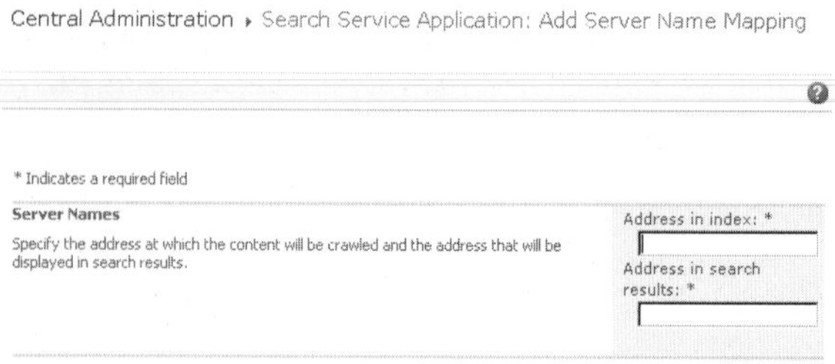

Central Administration ▸ Search Service Application: Add Server Name Mapping

* Indicates a required field

Server Names
Specify the address at which the content will be crawled and the address that will be displayed in search results.

Address in index: *

Address in search results: *

FIGURE 8-11 Add Server Name Mapping page.

Instances where this might be required include the following:

- The need to crawl content using HTTP when users will access it using HTTPS.
- It is necessary to crawl with Windows authentication when the normal authentication method is not supported for the crawler, such as smart-card authentication.

Managing File Types

For each search service application, you can instruct the crawler as to what type of files should be crawled by using the Manage File Types page shown in Figure 8-12. The crawler requests only the file types that appear on the Manage File Types screen from content sources.

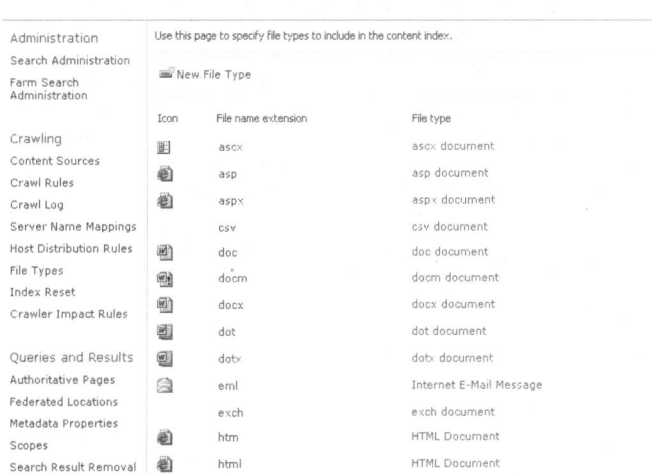

Administration

Search Administration

Farm Search Administration

Crawling

Content Sources

Crawl Rules

Crawl Log

Server Name Mappings

Host Distribution Rules

File Types

Index Reset

Crawler Impact Rules

Queries and Results

Authoritative Pages

Federated Locations

Metadata Properties

Scopes

Search Result Removal

Use this page to specify file types to include in the content index.

New File Type

Icon	File name extension	File type
	ascx	ascx document
	asp	asp document
	aspx	aspx document
	csv	csv document
	doc	doc document
	docm	docm document
	docx	docx document
	dot	dot document
	dotx	dotx document
	eml	Internet E-Mail Message
	exch	exch document
	htm	HTML Document
	html	HTML Document

FIGURE 8-12 Manage File Types page.

To add a new file type, follow these steps:

1. Click on the File Types link in the Quick Launch area of the Search Service Management page as shown in Figure 8-12 to open the Manage File Types page.

2. Click the New File Type link. The Add File Type page appears, as seen in Figure 8-13.

3. Enter the file's extension in the File Extension input box.

4. Click OK.

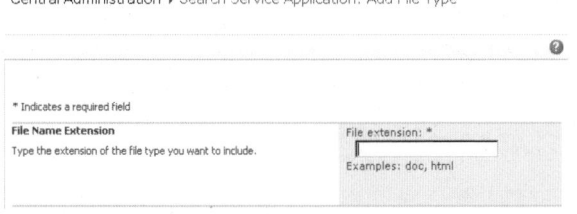

Central Administration ▸ Search Service Application: Add File Type

* Indicates a required field

File Name Extension
Type the extension of the file type you want to include.

File extension: *

Examples: doc, html

FIGURE 8-13 Add File Type page.

At this point, the crawler requests all files with this extension. However, if you have not installed an iFilter for that file type on your SharePoint server or servers, it can crawl only the properties of the files. Because iFilters are used by various search engines, they are installed on the operating system and configured for the search product. SharePoint does not provide an interface to indicate which iFilters have been installed on your servers or a tool for installing iFilters. You must follow the setup instructions from the iFilter's manufacturer to install and use the iFilter. These instructions should also include configuring the icon for the file type.

You must also rely on your deployment documentation to inform you whether the correct iFilter for that file type has already been installed.

REAL WORLD In the SharePoint 2010 beta, there were three third-party iFilters available for pdf files, with varying costs and performance. FAST Search for SharePoint installs with a pdf iFilter by default.

To remove a file type for a search service application, click Delete on the context menu of the file type listing on the Manage File Types page, as shown in Figure 8-14.

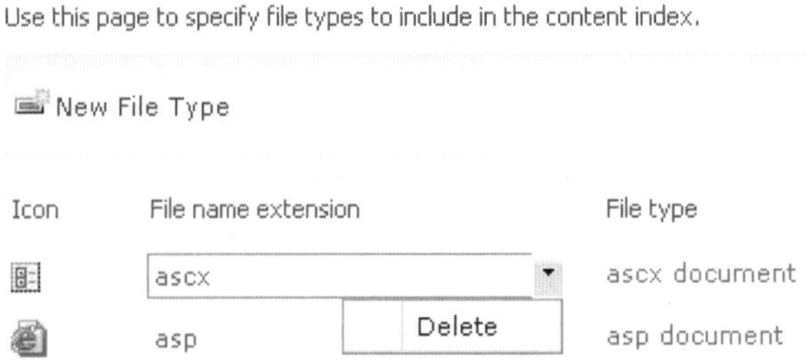

Use this page to specify file types to include in the content index.

🖭 New File Type

Icon	File name extension		File type
🗒	ascx	▾	ascx document
🗒	asp	Delete	asp document

FIGURE 8-14 Delete the file name extension listing.

Managing the Search Application Topology

The change in services architecture in SharePoint 2010 introduces a new area of management concern, the search application topology. A single SharePoint 2010 farm can provide multiple instances of a search service application. Microsoft has componentized the system so that each service instance can support multiple component instances designed for performance, for resiliency, or to isolate information.

SEE ALSO For more information on planning and design, see the "SharePoint Server 2010 Administrator's Companion" (Microsoft Press, 2010).

The initial topology of a new search service application will have all components on one application server and all databases on one database server. This topology can be changed using the Modify Topology link located on the Farm-Wide Search Administration page or from the Search Service Administration page. The SharePoint Search topology cannot be changed in standalone installations.

The Search Application Topology dashboard presents the current topology in the lower portion of the Search Administration page, shown in Figure 8-15, which displays an expanded topology.

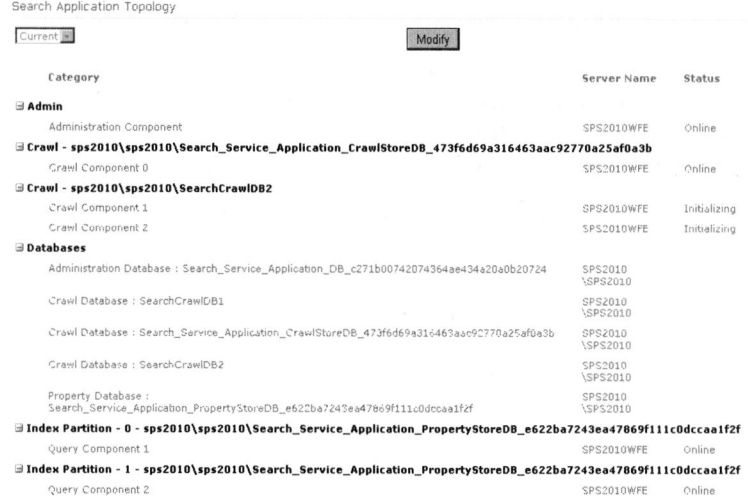

FIGURE 8-15 Search Application Topology page.

To make any change to the topology, click the Modify button at the top of the page to open the topology management page. Figure 8-16 shows this page with the default topology for a new search service application.

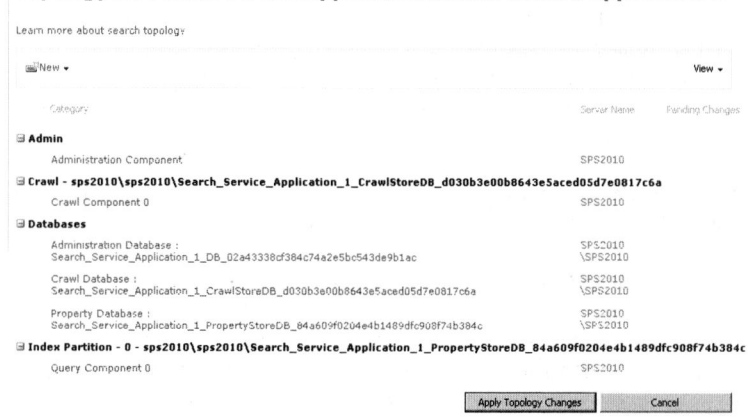

FIGURE 8-16 Manage Search Application Topology page.

Changes to the topology are defined in the appropriate dialog boxes: New, Properties, or Delete. However, changes are not implemented until the Apply Topology Changes button is clicked. Clicking this button starts the SharePoint timer job, which accomplishes the actions required. You can make multiple changes to the search topology and then apply them all at once by clicking the Apply Topology Changes button. Because many changes can impact performance during their application, you might want to choose to define the changes in the relevant search management pages but use Windows PowerShell scripts to schedule their implementation.

To create a new component, click the New link in the top, left corner of the page and select the appropriate component from the drop-down list shown in Figure 8-17.

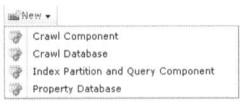

FIGURE 8-17 Select New context menu.

To delete a topology component, select Delete from the context menu of the component as shown in Figure 8-18.

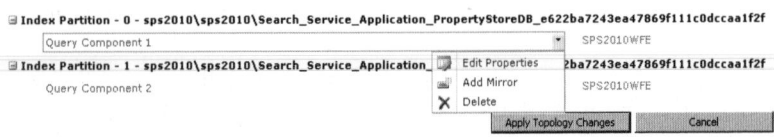

FIGURE 8-18 Topology Component context menu.

Crawl Databases

Crawl databases contain configurations and instructions required by the crawler component, tables used during crawls to queue items to be crawled, and log information used in crawl logs. You might need to create a new crawl database for performance to be used with a new crawl component or for resiliency to be mirrored by SQL as a failover database.

Select Crawl Database from the New menu in Figure 8-17 to open the Add Crawl Database page shown in Figure 8-19.

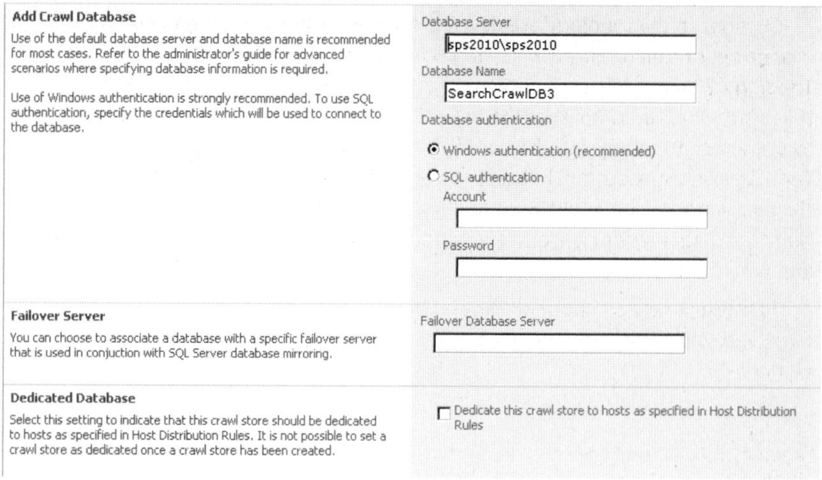

FIGURE 8-19 Add Crawl Database page.

Configure the following settings for the new crawl database:

- The database server can be the default server for the farm or a separate SQL Server instance for performance purposes.

- Name the database according to your naming conventions to indicate its usage.

- Choose the authentication required. In most instances, the default Windows authentication will be used.

- If this database will be mirrored for resiliency, associate the database with the failover database server.

- The Dedicated Database default option will use the auto host distribution rules. If you select the box, only the hosts specified in the Host Distribution Rules area will be controlled by this crawl database.

- Click OK to save the topology configuration changes.

Crawl Component

Additional crawl components can be added for performance or resiliency purposes, depending on the crawl database association configuration. Select Crawl Component from the New context menu in Figure 8-17 to open the Add Crawl Component page shown in Figure 8-20.

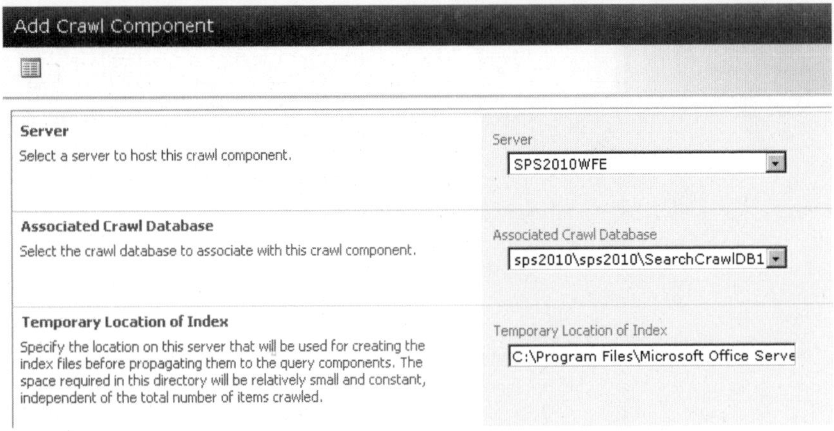

Server Select a server to host this crawl component.	Server `SPS2010WFE` ▾
Associated Crawl Database Select the crawl database to associate with this crawl component.	Associated Crawl Database `sps2010\sps2010\SearchCrawlDB1` ▾
Temporary Location of Index Specify the location on this server that will be used for creating the index files before propagating them to the query components. The space required in this directory will be relatively small and constant, independent of the total number of items crawled.	Temporary Location of Index `C:\Program Files\Microsoft Office Serve`

FIGURE 8-20 Add Crawl Component dialog box.

Configure the following settings for the new crawl component:

- Select the farm member server to host the crawl component.
- Associate the component with a crawl database. If multiple crawl components are associated with the same database, all of them share the duties defined in the database.
- Choose the location for the temporary index files. A share will be created for this location because query servers pull index files with SharePoint 2010 instead of using the push process of previous products.
- Click OK to save the topology configuration changes.

Property Database

Property databases contain metadata associated with crawled content. They can be distributed across multiple SQL Server instances to reduce query bottlenecks. Property databases are associated with index partitions, and they return any metadata associated with content in query results from those indexes. We discuss index partitions later.

To add a property database from the Manage Search Topology page, click New, and then select Property Database to open the Add Property Database dialog box shown in Figure 8-21.

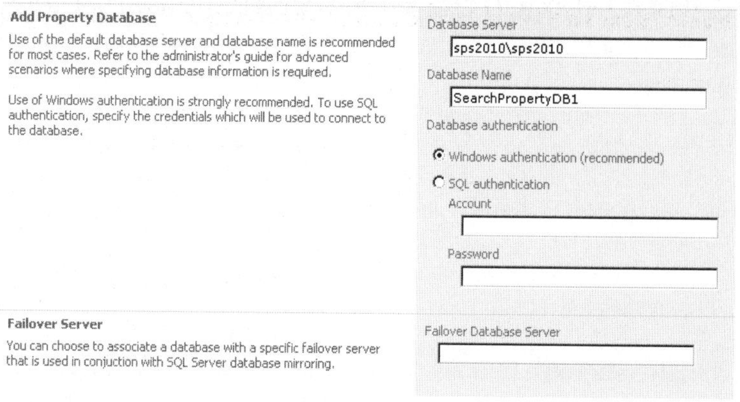

Database Server

`sps2010\sps2010`

Database Name

`SearchPropertyDB1`

Database authentication

- ⦿ Windows authentication (recommended)
- ○ SQL authentication

  Account

  Password

Failover Database Server

FIGURE 8-21 Add Property Database dialog box.

Configure the following settings for the new property database:

- Select the database server to host the property database. This can be the default farm SQL Server instance or a separate server for performance.
- Name the database according to your naming conventions.
- Configure the required authentication.
- If this database will be mirrored for resiliency, associate the database with the failover database server. Do not enter a server name into this field unless SQL Server database mirroring is currently configured and operational.
- Click OK to save the topology configuration changes.

Index Partition and Query Component

SharePoint Server 2010 Search supports dividing the full text index into subsets called *index partitions*. In this configuration, a group of query components receives the query and returns search results from the group's portion of the total index to the query originator. Each index partition must be associated with a specific property database containing metadata associated with a specific set of crawled content. This index partitioning reduces the query response time by distributing the load of query servicing across different farm members.

To create a new index on the Manage Search Topology page, follow these steps:

1. Select Index Partition And Query Component from the New menu, which opens the Add Query Component dialog box shown in Figure 8-22.
2. From the Server drop-down list, select the farm server to which you want to add the first query component of the new index partition.
3. In the Associated Property Database drop-down list, click the property database with which you want to associate the new index partition.

4. You can optionally change the default location on the server that will be used for storage of the index files after retrieving them from the crawl components.

5. Select the Set This Query Component As Failover-Only check box if you want the query component to receive queries only in the event of a failure of the primary query component in the same index partition. Add a failover-only query component to the index partition only after creating the first query component.

6. Click OK to add the configuration to the job queue. Adding the first query component also creates the new index partition.

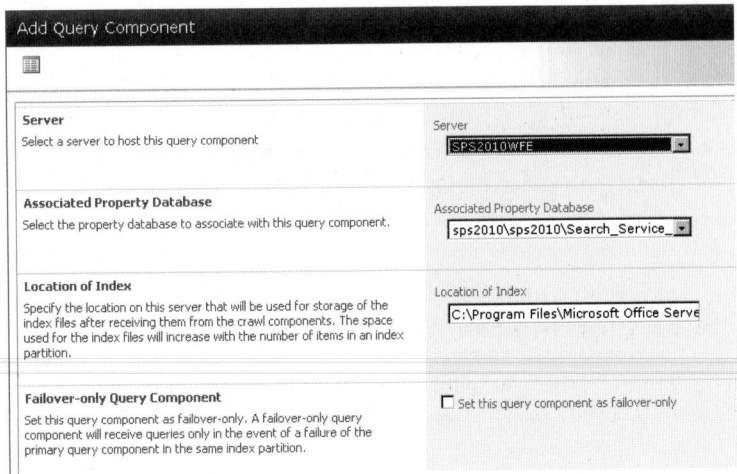

FIGURE 8-22 Add Query Component dialog box.

Multiple query components can also support the same index partition to balance the load of servicing queries or to act as failover servers for resiliency.

A search service application must always have at least one index partition. If you remove all the query components from an index partition, the index partition will be removed from the farm completely but all the data from the partition will be copied and distributed into the remaining partitions. This operation can take a long time and can affect farm performance.

Managing Host Distribution Rules

As you have seen, SharePoint Server 2010 supports multiple crawl databases for performance and resiliency. Host distribution rules are used to manually assign specific content to a crawl database that has been dedicated to accept these assignments. You cannot even open the page to create a Host Distribution list until at least one dedicated database has been created.

The Host Distribution Rules management page is accessed from the Quick Launch menu of the search service application management page. In the Add Host Rule page shown in Figure 8-23, enter the host name without the protocol, select the appropriate database and click OK. All content from that host will be placed in the database regardless of what protocol was used when crawling the content.

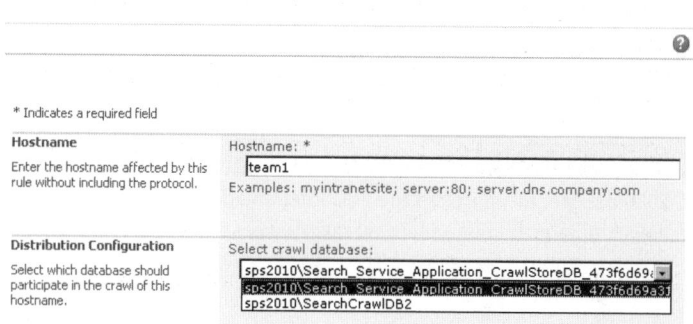

Central Administration ▸ Search Service Application: Add Host Rule

* Indicates a required field

Hostname
Enter the hostname affected by this rule without including the protocol.

Hostname: *

team1

Examples: myintranetsite; server:80; server.dns.company.com

Distribution Configuration
Select which database should participate in the crawl of this hostname.

Select crawl database:

sps2010\Search_Service_Application_CrawlStoreDB_473f6d69...
sps2010\Search_Service_Application_CrawlStoreDB_473f6d69a3f
sps2010\SearchCrawlDB2

FIGURE 8-23 Add Host Rule page.

Troubleshooting Search with Crawl Logs

The crawl logs present the results of the crawl efforts, including successes, warnings, and errors. On the search service management page, the crawl history page shown in Figure 8-24 gives you a quick overview of recent crawls, including performance data, successes, and errors by content source.

Crawl History

Content Source	Type	Start Time	End Time	Duration	Success	All Errors
People	Incremental	5/3/2010 7:47 PM	5/3/2010 7:50 PM	00:02:10	26	0
Local SharePoint sites	Incremental	5/1/2010 1:57 PM	5/1/2010 1:59 PM	00:02:10	5	0
Local SharePoint sites	Full	3/23/2010 12:22 AM	3/23/2010 12:26 AM	00:03:50	274	0
Local SharePoint sites	Incremental	3/20/2010 6:27 PM	3/20/2010 6:29 PM	00:02:30	5	0

FIGURE 8-24 Crawl History page.

To access the Crawl Logs page, from the Search Service Application management page, click Crawl Log in the Crawling group of links in the Quick Launch toolbar to open the page shown in Figure 8-25. From here, you can click the Crawl History link.

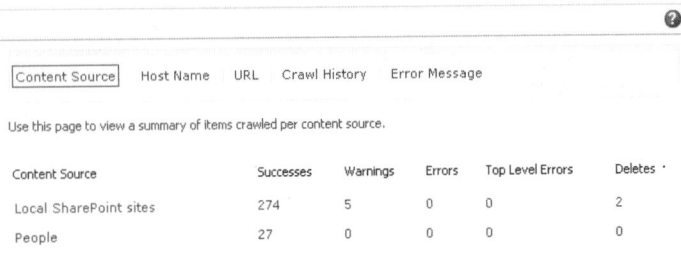

Content Source	Successes	Warnings	Errors	Top Level Errors	Deletes ·
Local SharePoint sites	274	5	0	0	2
People	27	0	0	0	0

FIGURE 8-25 Crawl Log page, Content Source view.

SharePoint 2010 has greatly improved the presentation and analysis of crawling activities. The crawl log page enables you to do quick reviews and drill downs from five links that give you various perspectives. The first view, shown in Figure 8-24, gives statistics by content sources.

The Host Name view shown in Figure 8-26 presents the crawl results for each host name or SharePoint application grouped by crawl databases. This view also offers a tool to filter by crawl database and a search tool to drill down into different levels of an application.

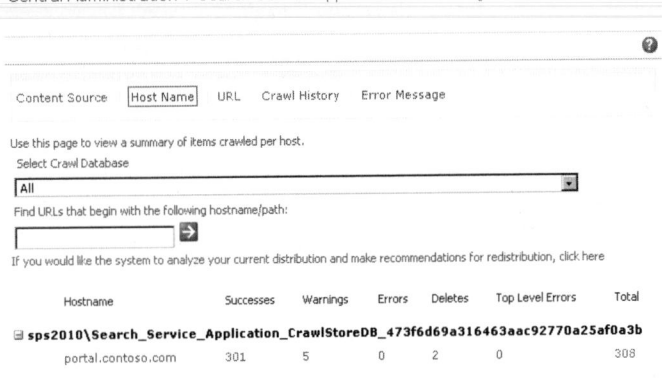

Hostname	Successes	Warnings	Errors	Deletes	Top Level Errors	Total
sps2010\Search_Service_Application_CrawlStoreDB_473f6d69a316463aac92770a25af0a3b						
portal.contoso.com	301	5	0	2	0	308

FIGURE 8-26 Host Name view of the crawl log analysis.

This page also presents a link to open the Auto Host Distribution page. This new tool analyzes the balance of content across crawl components, recommends redistribution to improve performance, and can automate the redistribution as shown in Figure 8-27.

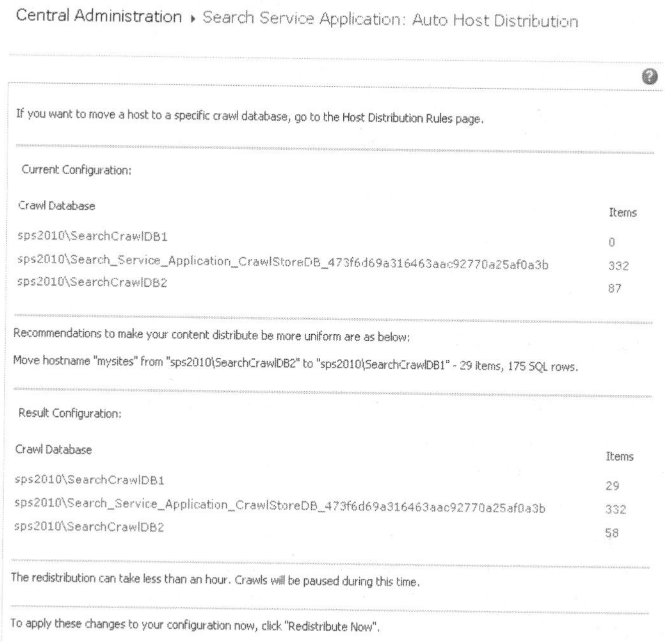
Central Administration ▸ Search Service Application: Auto Host Distribution
If you want to move a host to a specific crawl database, go to the Host Distribution Rules page.
Current Configuration:
Crawl Database
Items
sps2010\SearchCrawlDB1
0
sps2010\Search_Service_Application_CrawlStoreDB_473f6d69a316463aac92770a25af0a3b
332
sps2010\SearchCrawlDB2
87
Recommendations to make your content distribute be more uniform are as below:
Move hostname "mysites" from "sps2010\SearchCrawlDB2" to "sps2010\SearchCrawlDB1" - 29 items, 175 SQL rows.
Result Configuration:
Crawl Database
Items
sps2010\SearchCrawlDB1
29
sps2010\Search_Service_Application_CrawlStoreDB_473f6d69a316463aac92770a25af0a3b
332
sps2010\SearchCrawlDB2
58
The redistribution can take less than an hour. Crawls will be paused during this time.
To apply these changes to your configuration now, click "Redistribute Now".

FIGURE 8-27 Auto Host Distribution page.

At the top of the Auto Host Distribution page is a link to the host distribution rules page, where you can manually control the crawling activity as discussed earlier in this chapter.

Returning to the crawl log analysis page, the URL page shown in Figure 8-28 presents a detailed list of crawl database items, the actions performed, and status of the items. This page also introduces tools to filter this list by content source or URL, and it can be further refined by the *crawl database* used during the crawl. Additional filters permit refining the list according to status, error message, and time frame.

The small icons to the left of list items in Figure 8-28 visually indicate the status:

- The square black with a yellow center is a deletion.
- The green circle is a success.
- The yellow triangle marks a warning that an item could not be loaded.
- The red diamond indicates an error in crawling.

These reports are significant for more than just crawling. Remember that the crawler account is given access permission via an application's security rules. If this account cannot open an item to crawl it because of a lack of permissions, file type, URL length, corruption, or any other reason, it is reasonable to assume that users cannot read or download the items either.

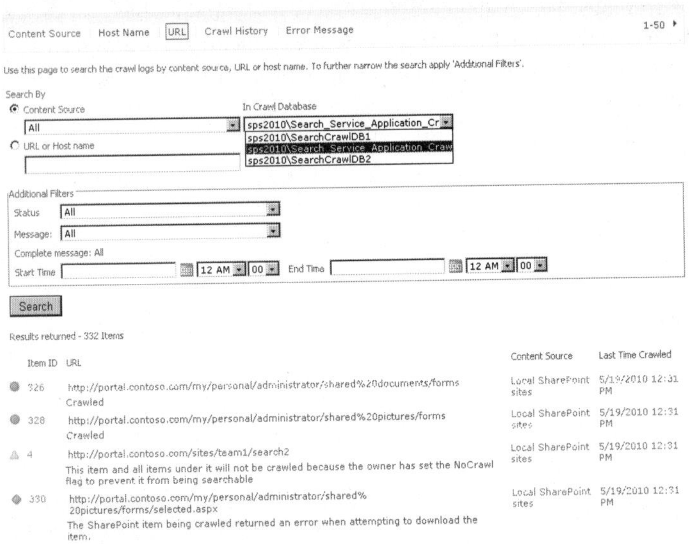

FIGURE 8-28 Crawl Log - URL page.

Figure 8-29 shows a filtered list along with the item context menu, which offers actions that can be taken on individual items during the next crawl.

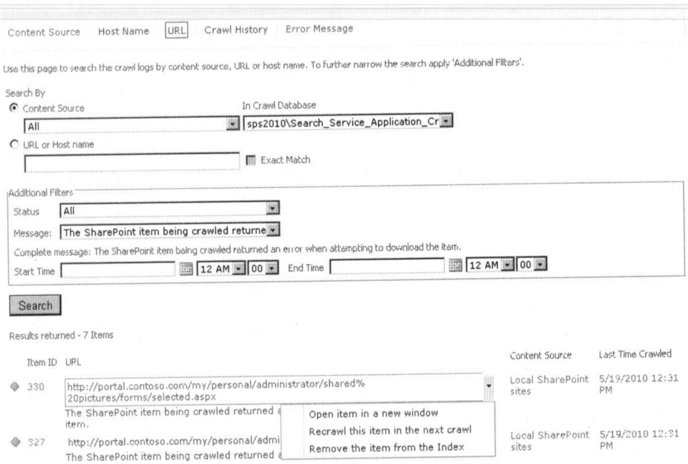

FIGURE 8-29 Context menu of a crawl database item.

The Crawl History view of the crawl logs shown in Figure 8-30 gives a summary of activities useful in determining not only the length of time required for each crawl, but also the changes within the corpus (all crawled content) between crawls.

The numbers presented here might differ from other presentations because a single item could be registered more than once in logs as a warning, an error, and an eventual success. Information given in this presentation can be used to adjust the crawl types and schedules.

FIGURE 8-30 Crawl History view of crawl activity logs.

The Error Message view shown in Figure 8-31 presents statistics on the various errors encountered and filter tools for content sources and host names.

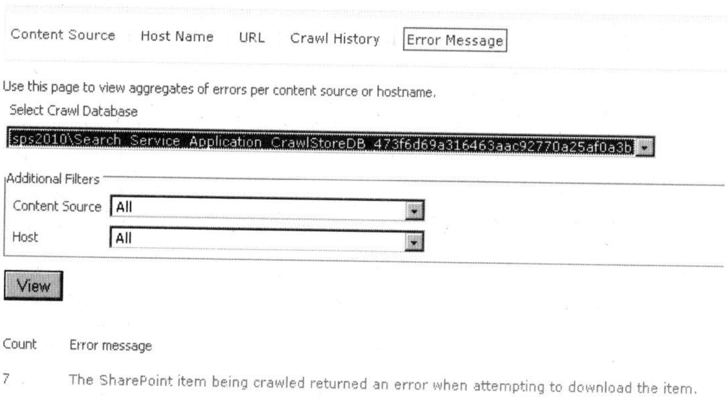

Content Source   Host Name   URL   Crawl History   Error Message

Use this page to view aggregates of errors per content source or hostname.

Select Crawl Database

sps2010\Search_Service_Application_CrawlStoreDB_473f6d69a316463aac92770a25af0a3b

Additional Filters

Content Source   All

Host   All

View

Count	Error message
7	The SharePoint item being crawled returned an error when attempting to download the item.

FIGURE 8-31 Error Message view of a crawl log.

CHAPTER 9

Managing the Search Experience

■ Configuring the Thesaurus and Noise Word Files **266**

■ Defining Authoritative Pages **268**

■ Federated Queries **270**

■ Managed Properties **278**

■ Creating and Managing Search Scopes **284**

■ Search Results Removal **289**

■ Site Collection Search Management **290**

■ Working with Keywords and Best Bets **293**

■ Creating and Customizing Search Centers **297**

■ Customizing Search Pages **300**

■ Working with Query Reporting **325**

■ Local Search Configuration Options **325**

When a user executes a search query, the goal is quite simple—to get a results set that includes everything relevant to the search and nothing else. Achieving this goal is not so simple, but this chapter will show how to configure search so that users can easily define and refine both the query and the results. The chapter is organized according to the scope of the configurations: starting with the file systems and then moving on to the search services application, the site collection, and the search centers.

Configuring the Thesaurus and Noise Word Files

Microsoft SharePoint 2010 continues to provide thesaurus and noise word files to manipulate the search process, but the scope of their usage has been changed in this product. In this section, we discuss the more common ways to configure these elements.

Crawl components no longer use the files to eliminate words from the index. However, query components use both the noise word files to remove words from query terms and thesaurus files to modify queries.

Noise Word Files

A *noise word file* is a text file that contains all the words that have little or no refinement value in a search query in your environment. Such words often include your organization's name, product names, registered names, and so on. Noise words apply only to text content, not metadata.

SharePoint Server 2010 provides noise word and thesaurus files in 54 languages. They are located in a number of directories named *Config*. The hierarchy of these directories is significant because the installation and implementation of SharePoint Server determine which set of files is used during a query.

Files located in the %ProgramFiles%\Microsoft Office Servers\14.0\Data\Config folder are for SharePoint Foundation Server installations. This folder is not used in SharePoint Server 2010.

For a SharePoint Server 2010 standalone server farm or Microsoft Search Server 2010, the files under %ProgramFiles%\Microsoft Office Servers\14.0\Data\Office Server\config are copied to the Microsoft Office Servers\14.0\Data\Office Server\ Applications\(serviceGUID)\Config folder to be used at query time.

When you are setting up a complete server farm, whether it contains one server or more, files under %ProgramFiles%\Microsoft Office Servers\14.0\Data\Office Server\config are copied to all %ProgramFiles%\Microsoft Office Servers\14.0\Data\ Office Server\Applications\(service and service component GUID)\Config folders. However, only files under query component GUIDs are used at query time.

For consistent query responses, all files under all query components on all servers should be identical. If noise word and thesaurus file modifications are known before you create search service applications, the set of files in the %ProgramFiles%\ Microsoft Office Servers\14.0\Data\Office Server\config folder can be modified prior to the copy process. These files must be identical on all members of the farm because any member can host the search service components.

To configure a noise word file, perform the following steps:

1. Go to the appropriate noise word file, and open it using a text editor such as Notepad.

2. Enter the words you do not want used in queries, one word per line. Maintaining the list in alphabetical order makes reviewing terms easier.

3. Save the file.

IMPORTANT A noise word file must have at least one entry in it, even if the entry is only a period (.) character.

Configuring the Thesaurus

The thesaurus provides a mechanism to assist users in constructing a query by expanding or replacing query terms as the query is executed against the index. It differs from search suggestions in that the changes are transparent to the user and are not optional for the user. You can create expansion or replacement sets, as well as weight or stem the terms within the expansion or replacement sets.

You can use thesaurus file entries to correct commonly misspelled query terms, add synonyms to queries, or replace query terms. Because modifying these files requires access to the file system of all Web front ends, you probably will find the new functionality of search suggestions easier to maintain.

The thesaurus is configured via an XML file, which has the format of TS<*XXX*>.XML, where *XXX* is the standard three-letter code for a specific language. For English, the file name is Tsenu.xml.

The default code for the file is as follows:

```
<XML ID="Microsoft Search Thesaurus">
<!-- Commented out
    <thesaurus xmlns="x-schema:tsSchema.xml">
    <diacritics_sensitive>0</diacritics_sensitive>
        <expansion>
            <sub>Internet Explorer</sub>
            <sub>IE</sub>
            <sub>IE5</sub>
        </expansion>
        <replacement>
            <pat>NT5</pat>
            <pat>W2K</pat>
            <sub>Windows 2000</sub>
        </replacement>
        <expansion>
            <sub>run</sub>
            <sub>jog</sub>
        </expansion>
    </thesaurus>
-->
</XML>
```

To create new expansion sets, perform the following steps:

1. Open Windows Explorer, and go to the location of the thesaurus XML file.

2. Open the XML file using Notepad or some other text editor.

3. Enter your expansion terms within the tags using well-formed XML, as illustrated here:

```
<expansion>
    <sub>term1</sub>
    <sub>term2</sub>
    <sub>term3</sub>
</expansion>
```

4. Save the file.
5. Restart the Mssearch.exe service.

To create new replacement sets, perform the following steps:

1. Open My Computer, and go to the location of the thesaurus XML file.
2. Open the XML file using Notepad or some other text editor.
3. Enter your replacement terms within the tags using well-formed XML. Note that the terms being replaced are in the *<sub>* extensions, and the term to replace them is in the *<pat>* extension. This is illustrated here:

```
<replacement>
    <sub>term1</sub>
    <sub>term2</sub>
    <pat>term3</pat>
</replacement>
```

4. Save the file.
5. Restart the SharePoint Server Search 14 service (**Net stop/start osearch14**).

Defining Authoritative Pages

Search results relevance settings can be managed through the authoritative pages in the search service. The relationship of individual documents or content items to authoritative pages is defined in terms of *click distance*. Click distance is not based on URL depth. If all other ranking elements are equal, the more clicks that are required to traverse from the authoritative page to the content item, the less relevant that item is for a given query. Placing a link to an object on an authoritative page elevates that object in search results, with no regard to the actual location of the object.

Your farm will have some locations that contain official, approved content for your organization. These locations are the URLs you should enter into the Authoritative Web Pages input boxes, which are shown in Figure 9-1.

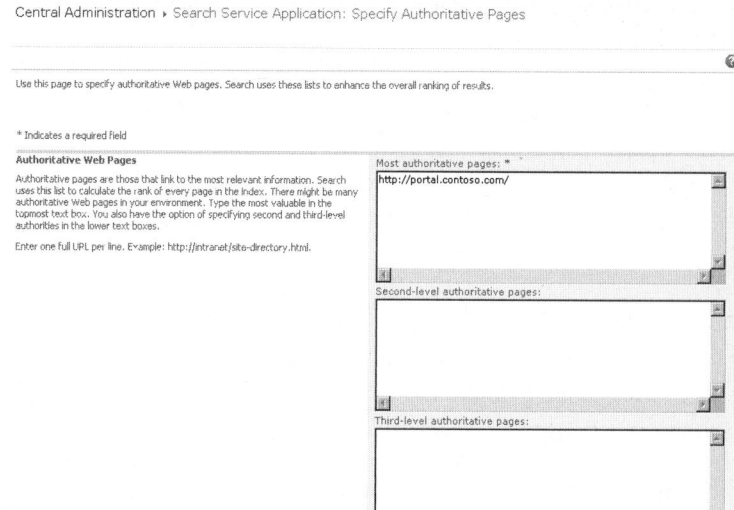

Use this page to specify authoritative Web pages. Search uses these lists to enhance the overall ranking of results.

* Indicates a required field

Authoritative Web Pages

Authoritative pages are those that link to the most relevant information. Search uses this list to calculate the rank of every page in the index. There might be many authoritative Web pages in your environment. Type the most valuable in the topmost text box. You also have the option of specifying second and third-level authorities in the lower text boxes.

Enter one full URL per line. Example: http://intranet/site-directory.html.

Most authoritative pages: *

http://portal.contoso.com/

Second-level authoritative pages:

Third-level authoritative pages:

FIGURE 9-1 The Authoritative Web Pages input boxes.

You can achieve levels of granularity by entering primary, secondary, and tertiary URLs, thereby formulating an overall hierarchical relevance topology for your search application. URLs within the same input box are grouped equally, meaning that there is no hierarchical order implied by the URL list. In addition, wildcards, such as *http:foo/**, are not accepted in these boxes.

You can also insert file shares as authoritative page sources. Use the *file://* protocol scheme when defining file systems. For example, file://fileserver1/archive specifies the archive file share as an authoritative location.

You can also set some sites to be the lowest on the relevance scale by placing their URLs in the Sites To Demote input box, which is shown in Figure 9-2. You should consider the resource implications of recalculating the ranking of your indexes immediately rather than recalculating them during normal schedules.

Non-authoritative Sites

You can specify that all content from certain sites be ranked lower than that of all other sites. Type the URLs of those sites here, one per line.

URLs typed in this section are treated as prefix matches. Example: entering http://archive/ will demote the rank of all URLs that begin with http://archive/.

Sites to demote:

Refresh Now?

Ranking re-calculation will start as soon as you click OK. If unchecked, ranking calculations will occur later according to a predetermined schedule.

☑ Refresh now

FIGURE 9-2 The Non-authoritative Sites input boxes.

To set relevance settings, perform the following steps:

1. Open the Administration page for your search service.

2. In the Quick Launch area, click the Specify Authoritative Pages link under the Queries And Results heading.

3. Input the URLs in the appropriate boxes as required to configure relevance settings for your environment.

4. Select the Refresh Now check box if you want to have the relevance settings recomputed immediately.

5. Click OK.

Federated Queries

Federated queries permit end users to search for and retrieve content from an OpenSearch 1.1–compliant search server. These content sources can be enterprise content repositories, other search engines (including remote SharePoint search), or your SharePoint Server 2010 search services. With a federated query, the server sends the queries to the federated locations, retrieves the results from the location feed, and then formats and renders the results to your users on the same page as results from your crawled content. With SharePoint Server 2010, all queries (including those to the local search service applications) are federated.

Federated Location Management

To access the management page for the federated locations shown in Figure 9-3, click Federated Locations on the Search Service Application page. This discussion will focus primarily on actions available from the Manage Federated Locations page:

- Add a federated location by using the provided New Location UI or by importing existing definition files.
- Edit a federated location using the UI.
- Copy a federated location to use as the basis for another location.
- Delete a federated location.
- Export a federated location into a portable file.

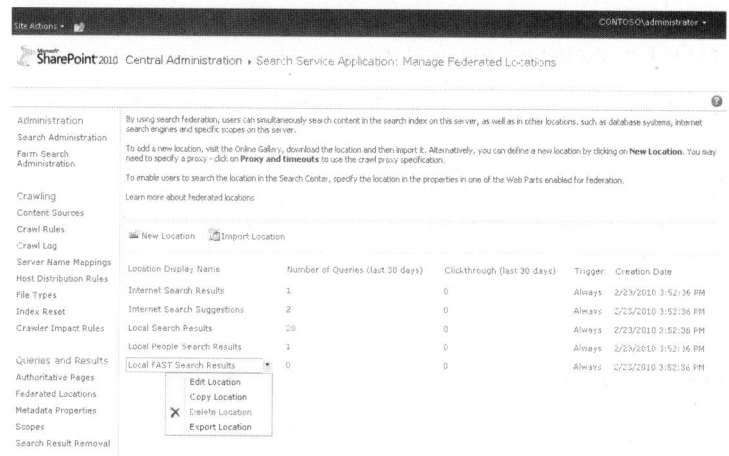

FIGURE 9-3 The Manage Federated Locations page.

Add New Location or Edit a Location

To add and configure a new location in the UI, click the New Location link on the Manage Federated Locations page as shown in Figure 9-3. This opens the Add Federated Location page, where the properties of the location will be configured. Editing an existing location opens essentially the same page except that the location name cannot be changed. Most, but not all, information entered on this page will be included in the Federated Location Definition (FLD) file itself. The configuration entries are grouped under headings that can be expanded or collapsed.

GENERAL INFORMATION

The first three items shown in Figure 9-4 are required information.

The Location Name text box is used to identify this location, and the name chosen must be unique within your organization. It cannot be modified after the FLD has been created. This name is used only by service administrators and developers. More than one FLD can connect to the same search server with different parameters as long as each one has a unique name. This name cannot contain spaces or any punctuation.

The name entered in the Display Name text box for this location should also be unique. Site collection administrators will be the primary users of this name, but they can choose to display this name to end users in federated-enabled Web parts.

The description entered in the Description text box will be visible to service administrators, site administrators, and developers. It should include all information defining how the queries will be run, such as the source (and any limitation or refinements), who can access this location, and what triggers or macros are provided.

Use this page to edit a federated location. On this page, you can enter general information about the location and specify how search results should be obtained and formatted.

* Indicates a required field

	OK	Cancel

General Information

Location Name

Type a unique name to identify this location within your organization. This name will be visible to service administrators and developers, and it cannot be modified once it has been created.

Location Name: *

Display Name

Type a display name for this location. This name will identify the location to service and site administrators. Site administrators can choose to display this name to end-users in federated-enabled Web Parts.

Display Name: *

Description

Type a description for this location. The description will be visible to service administrators, site administrators, and developers.

We recommend that the description include a list of the federation stores, sites, and items against which queries will be run. You can also include information about who can access this federation store, and what triggers are provided.

Description: *

FIGURE 9-4 New location general information.

The next two items, the Author and Version text boxes, are shown in Figure 9-5. Providing this information is optional.

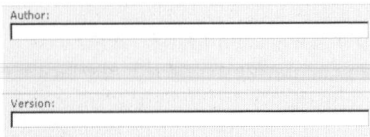

Author:

Version:

FIGURE 9-5 New Location optional information.

The author information you provide depends on whether the location is shared externally or only internally. It is simply a text field in which you can enter your company name, an individual's name, an e-mail address, and so on. This entry does not assign any ownership or permissions.

Information entered in the Version text box is purely optional information. If you choose to enter a value, it must contain at least one period (.). This information is included in the file and simply provides a way to track change history, because there is no way to upgrade a location based on its version.

The Trigger configuration shown in Figure 9-6 is very much functional information and controls whether the location is used in a query and how much of the query term is forwarded to the search server. The location Web part will be displayed on the results page only if results are returned from the query.

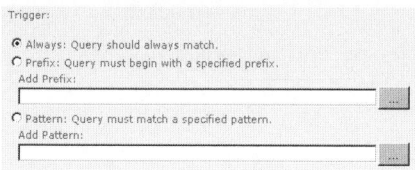

FIGURE 9-6 Trigger configuration.

The default setting, Always, sends all queries to this location. Bandwidth utilization of the traffic generated by all queries being forwarded externally and the latency of results sets being returned should be considered before using this option.

If you choose to use the Prefix trigger, an exact match of a term listed as a prefix is required. Use of prefixes requires users to be trained. The first consideration is that the word used as a prefix *will not be* forwarded to the federated location search engine but *will* be used in searching your local content. If users are properly trained, however, the use of prefixes will enable the selective use of federated locations controlled by users' query constructions.

For example, a prefix trigger for "medicine" will match "medicine Benadryl." In this case, only "Benadryl" will be sent to the location as a search term, because the prefix is not included in *{searchTerms}*. If you want to send both "medicine" and "Benadryl" to the location, you need to use a pattern trigger instead.

A pattern query will probably be transparent to your users. Patterns are defined as .NET regular expressions (REGEX). If the query or part of the query matches the pattern defined, the entire query is forwarded to the location. This pattern-matching of regular expressions quickly parses text to find specific character patterns, which *triggers* the use of the federated location. It can also add the extracted strings to a capture group or collection, which will store it in a named variable for later use in the query template.

For example, the pattern *(^([\w-\.]+)@([\w-]+\.)+([a-zA-Z]{2,4})$)* searches the location for e-mail queries such as *email@contoso.com*. For more information on .NET Framework regular expressions, see *http://go.microsoft.com/fwlink/?LinkId=100710*.

If the pattern were *medicine(?<drug>.*)* and the user query was *medicine Benadryl*, the pattern would match *medicine* and store *Benadryl* in the capture group (or variable) *<drug>*. You could then configure the FDL to send only this capture group to the location by replacing *{searchTerms}* with *{drug}* in the query template. This example behaves just like a prefix trigger in that it does not forward *medicine* from the original query in the federated query.

MSDN has a forum on regular expressions at *http://social.msdn.microsoft.com/Forums/en-US/regexp/threads*.

LOCATION INFORMATION

The next section of configuration settings for the location is grouped under Location Information, as shown in Figure 9-7.

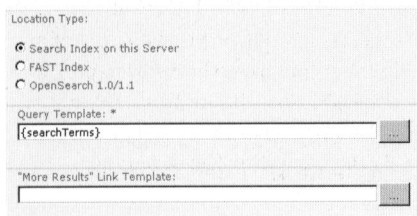

FIGURE 9-7 Location Information settings.

The location type determines the protocol used to connect to this location, and several configuration options change depending on your choice:

- **Search Index On This Server**   Used to run a standard query to get results from the local index. Selecting this option will display results from a pre-defined scope or a managed property with all the specified parameters, including triggers and query templates.
- **FAST Index**   Used to query a FAST server.
- **OpenSearch 1.0/1.1**   Used to display results from another search engine that can receive a query by using a URL and return results as structured XML, including remote search indexes on other SharePoint farms.

A search query is sent to a federated location as URL parameters in a format called a *query template*. This is called the *URL template* in the OpenSearch specification, and the query template syntax is based on the URL template syntax. When using the local index as a federated location, no query template is required because the protocol uses the object model to execute the query.

The default query template simply includes the case-sensitive *{searchTerms}* capture group as a variable, which represents the keywords entered into the search box by users. As we discussed in pattern triggers, you can replace *{searchTerms}* with capture groups created by your pattern. You can include other parameters in the template to specify additional query restrictions. These parameters are managed properties of the index that are probably not known to your users. If a parameter is optional, include a question mark character (?) after the parameter name. Common parameters are the following:

- **scope:<*name of scope*>**   Limits the search to a particular scope. Multiple entries are permitted to combine more than one scope.
- **type:.doc type.docx type.docm**   Returns Microsoft Office Word document results for the keywords entered into the Search box. Other content types can be added to further refine the results—for example, to include only contracts.

Parameters that you specify in the URL template must be URL-encoded. For example, a space must be represented by *%20*.

An example of an OpenSearch template is *http://www.bing.com/search?q={searchTerms}&go=&form=QBLH&qs=n&format=rss*.

The More Results Link Template option specifies the URL of the Web page that displays results for a search query. When this link is configured in the Web part, a More Results link displays beneath the search results from this location. This link opens a page that presents the full list of results from the location, not just the number specified in the results Web part. An example is *http://www.bing.com/search?q={searchTerms}*.

Display Information

The configurations in this grouping control how the results will be displayed within the Web part.

Microsoft federated queries require that federated locations return results in structured XML, which must then be transformed into HTML by XSL before it can be displayed in the Federated Results Web part. The Top Federated Search Results Display Metadata section presents the options to use the default XSL or to edit it for a customized display of results, text, and images as shown in Figure 9-8.

Properties determine the metadata returned with the search results. If you modify the default list of metadata in the list of returned properties, you must also update the XSL to display the new properties.

Sample data is included so that a visual preview is available when editing the Federated Results Web part.

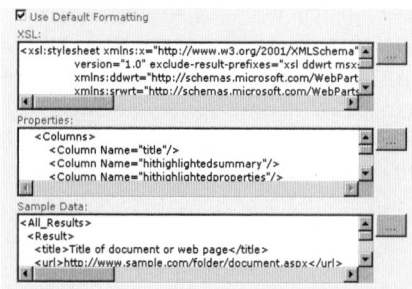

FIGURE 9-8 Federated Search Results Display Metadata.

The Core Search Results Display Metadata and Top Federated Results Display Metadata sections present the same options as the Federated Search Results Display Metadata section shown in Figure 9-8 except that these settings apply when different Web parts present results from the location.

RESTRICTIONS AND CREDENTIALS INFORMATION

The final section controls the usage of the location and what type of authentication is required by the location.

As shown in Figure 9-9, the Restrict Usage section permits the search administrator to control whether all site collections can use an individual federated location or whether the location is restricted to a list of one or more site collections. The default is No Restriction, which permits site administrators from any site to use this location.

Selecting Use Restriction activates the box for listing by URL the specific site collections that can use this location. With this option, you can do the following:

- Restrict access to confidential data
- Limit the number of people who can access the location
- Provide access to the same search server configured differently as unique federated locations for different site collections within your enterprise

A semicolon must be used to separate the start addresses of URLs in the Allowed Sites list. For example, the list *http://team1;http://team2* ensures that the location can be used only in sites starting with *http://team1* or *http://team2*.

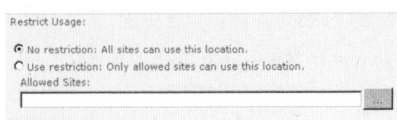

FIGURE 9-9 Restrictions options.

In some instances, authentication might be required. Most Internet search engines do not require credentials. If Search Index On This Server is selected as the Location Type for the federated location, no additional authentication information is required. Results from this federated location will be security trimmed based on user credentials after they have been returned to the Web front-end server. However, if the location type selected is FAST Index or OpenSearch 1.0/1.1, you must specify the authentication method and provide security credentials as shown in Figure 9-10.

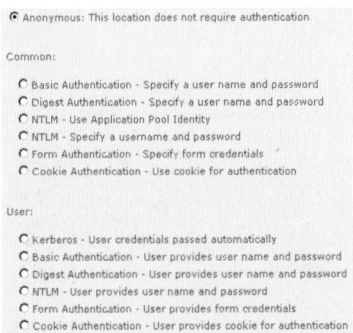

FIGURE 9-10 Authentication settings for FAST or OpenSearch locations.

These authentication options are grouped as follows:

- **Anonymous Access**   Indicates that the location does not require authentication.
- **Common Authentication**   Provides a single user name and password to the location. If you enable this option, you must select the authentication method required by the search server and provide the credentials to be used. Each authentication method, as selected, presents the appropriate dialog boxes for entering the credentials to be used. These dialog boxes are not illustrated here.
- **User-Level Authentication**   Passes individual user credentials to the location using the method that you select.

Download and Import an FDL file

You can download federated search connectors from the Search Connectors Gallery at *http://go.microsoft.com/fwlink/?LinkID=95798*, or you can use custom connectors that you have built and exported to your file system to quickly import a preconfigured connector into your Search Server configuration. The Import Location link on the Manage Federated Locations page opens a page where you can browse to a local file system and select the appropriate .fld file. After importing a location that requires authentication, you must edit the location and re-enter the credentials that were not saved during an export operation.

Copy a Federated Location

The Copy Location option shown in Figure 9-3 copies all the settings of the location except the name, which needs to be unique. This is the easiest way to change the name. It is also useful when you want the same location available with modified parameters for different site collections.

Delete a Federated Location

When you select Delete Location from the context menu shown in Figure 9-3, you will be given one warning. If you click OK, all information about the location is deleted. You might want to export the location before deleting it so that it will be available if you need to restore it later.

Export a Federated Location

Exporting a location from the context menu shown in Figure 9-3 gives you a portable configuration file with an .fld extension, which can be used to restore the location locally or imported onto another search server. However, when you export a federated location to a definition file, your security credentials or settings are not included with the file.

Managed Properties

Although a search query across the full text of a document might be useful, the power of an enterprise search query comes from its ability to query attributes or properties of objects, whether it can crawl the actual content or not. The Search schema contains two types of properties:

- Crawled properties are automatically extracted from crawled content, and the metadata field is added to the search schema. The text values of crawled properties that are included in the index are treated the same as text content unless they are mapped to a managed property.

- Managed properties are created to group common properties with dissimilar names under standardized names and expose this grouping to search tools. Users can perform specific queries over managed properties.

Crawled properties can be columns on a list or document library, metadata for a content type, or properties within the properties of a document created in a Microsoft Office application. If your users use custom names in these scenarios, mapping crawled properties to a managed property will be more difficult than if they used existing properties or columns. Determining which custom properties should be grouped into a managed property is frequently a time-consuming research job, particularly if there is no naming convention established.

The value in mapping crawled properties to managed properties is that it groups metadata into usable units. The metadata (crawled properties) are grouped into a logical, single unit (managed properties). Multiple crawled properties can be mapped to a single managed property, or a single crawled property can be mapped to multiple managed properties. Managed properties can then be used to create search scopes and enable your users to focus their search to a limited portion of the corpus. Managed properties can also be included in the Advanced Search Web part interface to narrow a query to specific properties and in the Refinement Web part for focusing on specific search results. We will discuss these uses later in this chapter.

REAL WORLD Grouping crawled properties into managed properties is essential for many search functionalities. For example, suppose you have three document types: document type A, which lists the author in the Author metadata field; document type B, which lists the author in the Creator metadata field; and document type C, which lists the author in the Originator metadata field. In this scenario, you have (essentially) the same metadata for three different document types residing in three different metadata fields. When these documents are crawled, each metadata field is entered into the property store as separate crawled properties. However, you can group these three crawled properties into a single managed property so that you can use them as a single unit when querying for author names across these three different document types.

To administer metadata properties, navigate to the Metadata Property Mappings page shown in Figure 9-11 by clicking the Metadata Properties link under the Queries And Results heading of the Search Service Application page.

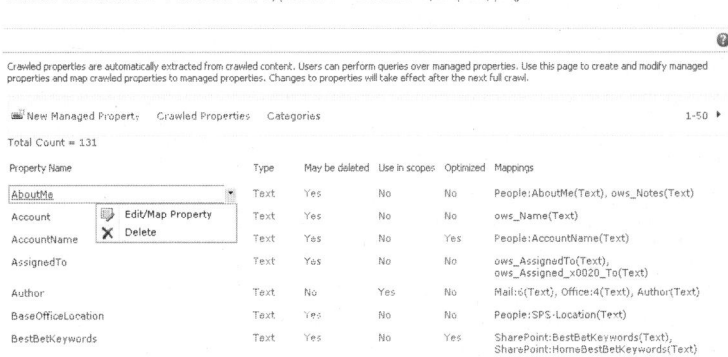

Central Administration ▸ Search Service Application: Metadata Property Mappings

Crawled properties are automatically extracted from crawled content. Users can perform queries over managed properties. Use this page to create and modify managed properties and map crawled properties to managed properties. Changes to properties will take effect after the next full crawl.

New Managed Property   Crawled Properties   Categories   1–50 ▸

Total Count = 131

Property Name		Type	May be deleted	Use in scopes	Optimized	Mappings
AboutMe	▾	Text	Yes	No	No	People:AboutMe(Text), ows_Notes(Text)
Account	☐ Edit/Map Property	Text	Yes	No	No	ows_Name(Text)
AccountName	✕ Delete	Text	Yes	No	Yes	People:AccountName(Text)
AssignedTo		Text	Yes	No	No	ows_AssignedTo(Text), ows_Assigned_x0020_To(Text)
Author		Text	No	Yes	No	Mail:6(Text), Office:4(Text), Author(Text)
BaseOfficeLocation		Text	Yes	No	No	People:SPS-Location(Text)
BestBetKeywords		Text	Yes	No	Yes	SharePoint:BestBetKeywords(Text), SharePoint:HomeBestBetKeywords(Text)

FIGURE 9-11 Metadata Property Mappings page.

Use this page to create and modify managed properties and map crawled properties to managed properties. Changes to properties of existing content take effect after the next full crawl, but they are applied to new content during incremental crawls.

On this page, several properties of each managed property are displayed, including a linked name and linked crawled properties mapped to the managed property. If you need to configure a new managed property, click the New Managed Property link to open the property page shown in Figure 9-12. Editing from the context menu opens essentially the same page. There are several sections to configure:

- **Name And Type**   The name must be unique and should follow a naming convention that is meaningful and easy to remember. The data type must match that of the crawled properties that will be mapped to this managed property. Your choices are Text, Integer, Decimal, Date And Time, or Yes/No. There is also a Has Multiple Values check box you can select to indicate that the property has multiple values.

- **Mappings To Crawled Properties**   This is the collection of crawled properties that will be represented by this managed property. This configuration section also includes the option of including values from all mapped crawled properties or including values from a single crawled property determined by the order in which the mapped properties are listed.

- **Use In Scopes**   This Boolean choice determines whether the managed property will be available in the drop-down list when defining search scopes.

- **Optimize Managed Property Storage** The first of two choices here determines whether the text properties are automatically treated as a hash, which reduces the size but limits comparisons to equal or not equal instead of less than, greater than, order by, and so on. The next choice determines if the managed property will be added to the restricted set of managed properties that are shown in custom search results pages.

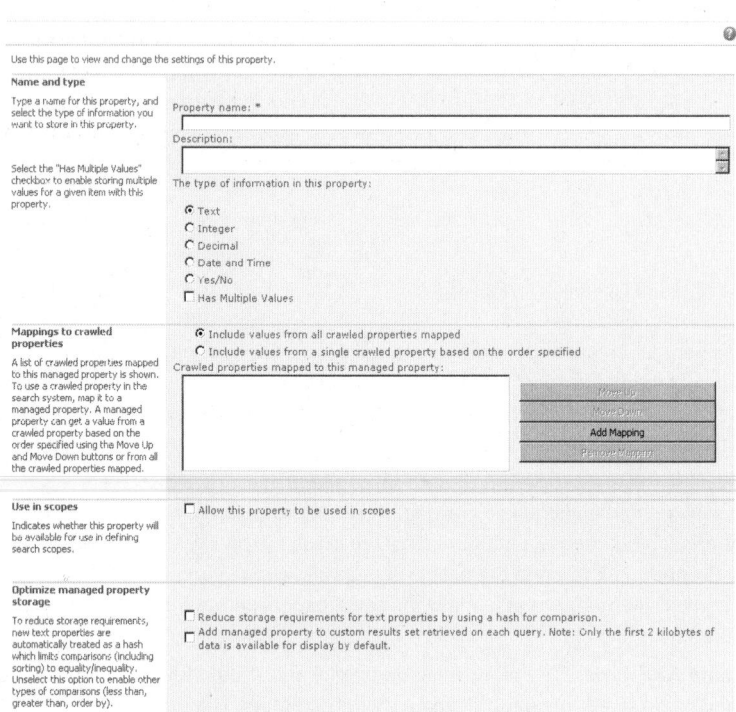

FIGURE 9-12 New (Edit) Managed Property page.

Other settings for managed properties can be configured programmatically using the *Microsoft.Office.Server.Search.Administration.ManagedProperty* class or the Windows PowerShell cmdlets for *SPEnterpriseSearchMetadataManagedProperty*:

- **MappingDisallowed** Indicates whether a crawled property can be mapped to this managed property.

- **Retrievable** Affects whether the property can be displayed, sorted, or used with operators. The two settings under Optimize Managed Property Storage also influence this setting.

- **FullTextQueriable** Governs whether this managed property is stored in the index and can be used in a CONTAINS or FREETEXT clause so that the property is specified through a query.
- **NoWordBreaker** Controls whether the values for this managed property go through a word breaker.
- **RemoveDuplicates** Determines whether the managed property receives multiple values, if there are duplicates.
- **Weight** Adjusts the relevance configuration.

To see all the crawled properties, from the Metadata Property Mappings page click the Crawled Properties link to open the page shown in Figure 9-13. This page presents a view of crawled properties in alphabetical order by name and displays the type, managed property mappings, whether a particular property is included in the index, and whether a particular property is multivalued.

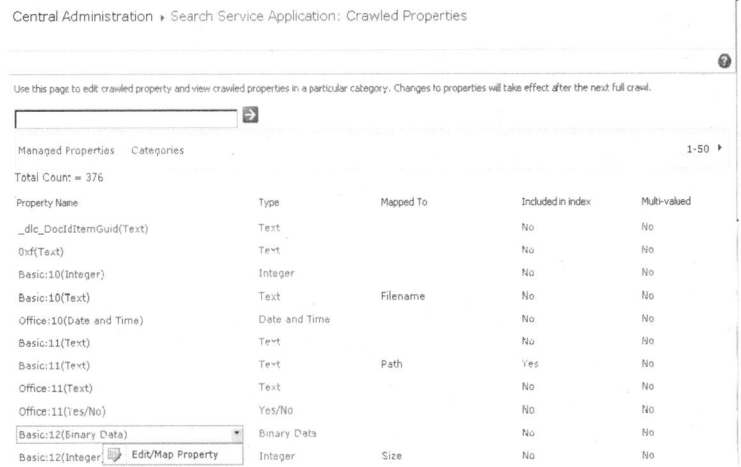

FIGURE 9-13 Crawled Properties page.

To edit a crawled property, select Edit/Map Property from the context menu, which opens the page shown in Figure 9-14.

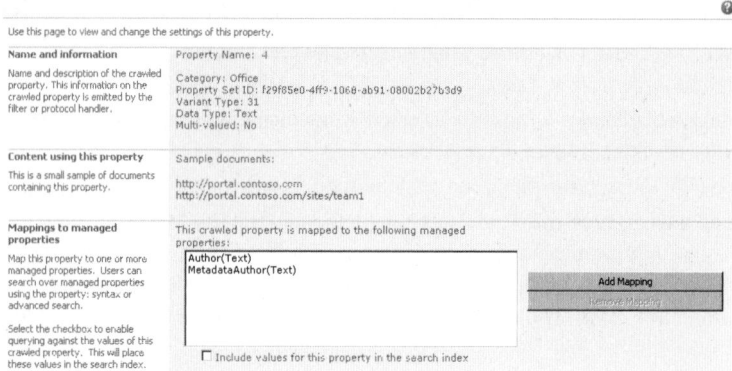

Use this page to view and change the settings of this property.

Name and information	Property Name: 4
Name and description of the crawled property. This information on the crawled property is emitted by the filter or protocol handler.	Category: Office Property Set ID: f29f85e0-4ff9-1068-ab91-08002b27b3d9 Variant Type: 31 Data Type: Text Multi-valued: No

Content using this property	Sample documents:
This is a small sample of documents containing this property.	http://portal.contoso.com http://portal.contoso.com/sites/team1

Mappings to managed properties	This crawled property is mapped to the following managed properties:
Map this property to one or more managed properties. Users can search over managed properties using the property: syntax or advanced search.	Author(Text) MetadataAuthor(Text) [Add Mapping] [Remove Mapping]
Select the checkbox to enable querying against the values of this crawled property. This will place these values in the search index.	☐ Include values for this property in the search index

FIGURE 9-14 Edit Crawled Property page.

Within this page, you can manage the mappings of the crawled property to one or more managed properties. The Include Values For This Property In The Search Index option controls whether the property values is included in queries if the crawled property is not mapped to a managed property. Not including the values reduces the size of the index and the query efficiency but impacts the relevance ranking.

For instance, if this option is not selected and the crawled property is *author*, simple queries such as *Smith* return documents containing the word *Smith* in the body but do not return items whose author property is *Smith*. However, a query against the managed property with the keyword filter *author:Smith* returns the documents. The existence of *Smith* in a property is more relevant than a single instance within the body of a document.

> **NOTE** A change in metadata does not trigger a crawl of an item. Existing items must be recrawled for changes to take effect, while new items are affected with their initial crawl. A full crawl will provide consistent search results.

Crawled properties are organized into categories. The Categories link opens a page of hyperlinked categories, which are shown in Figure 9-15:

- **Basic** Contains metadata associated with the gatherer, search, core, and storage property sets. In my environment, there are 10 different GUIDs (property sets) in the Basic Crawled Property Category.

- **Business Data** Contains metadata associated with content in the Business Data Catalog.

- **Internal** Contains metadata internal to SharePoint.

- **Mail**   Contains metadata associated with Microsoft Exchange Server.
- **Notes**   Contains metadata associated with Lotus Notes.
- **Office**   Contains metadata contained in Microsoft Office documents such as those created with Word, Excel, PowerPoint, and so on.
- **People**   Contains metadata associated with the people profiles in SharePoint. The majority of this metadata is also mapped to various managed properties from Active Directory and SharePoint information.
- **SharePoint**   Contains metadata that is part of the Microsoft Office schema available out of the box.
- **Tiff**   Contains metadata associated mainly with documents that have been scanned or faxed, along with word-processing and Optical Character Recognition (OCR) information.
- **Web**   Contains HTML metadata associated with Web pages.
- **XML**   Contains metadata associated with the XML filter.

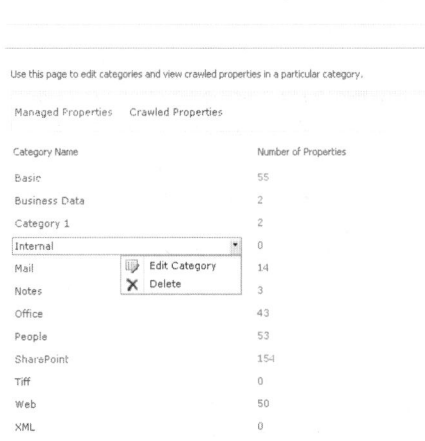

Central Administration ▸ Search Service Application: Categories

Use this page to edit categories and view crawled properties in a particular category.

Managed Properties   Crawled Properties

Category Name	Number of Properties
Basic	55
Business Data	2
Category 1	2
Internal	0
Mail	14
Notes	3
Office	43
People	53
SharePoint	154
Tiff	0
Web	50
XML	0

FIGURE 9-15 Categories page.

Each category can be opened to expose just the crawled properties within that group. You can open the page to edit the properties of each category from its context menu.

Bulk actions on all properties within the category can be taken on the category's property page, shown in Figure 9-16.

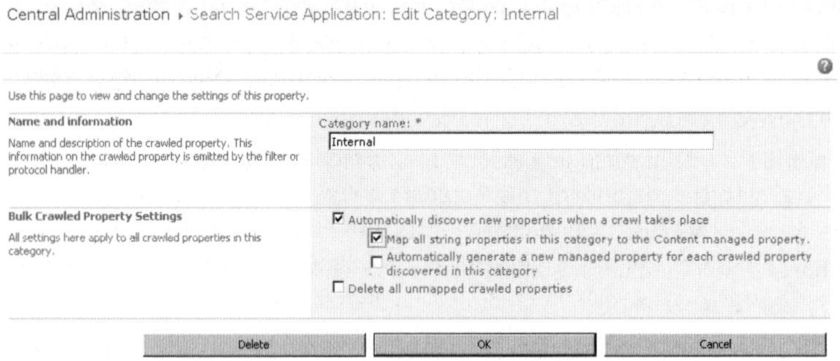

Use this page to view and change the settings of this property.

Name and Information	Category name: *
Name and description of the crawled property. This information on the crawled property is emitted by the filter or protocol handler.	Internal

Bulk Crawled Property Settings

All settings here apply to all crawled properties in this category.

☑ Automatically discover new properties when a crawl takes place

  ☑ Map all string properties in this category to the Content managed property.

  ☐ Automatically generate a new managed property for each crawled property discovered in this category

☐ Delete all unmapped crawled properties

Delete   OK   Cancel

FIGURE 9-16 Edit Category page.

Enabling all these options not only ensures that crawled properties for this category will be discovered, but also that managed properties are automatically created when new SharePoint columns are created.

Your solution can use these new managed properties to present to the user. Unfortunately, the name of the automatically generated managed property is not user friendly. Because SharePoint crawled properties are prefixed with *ows_*, the auto-generated managed property is also prefixed with *ows*.

For example, if a user creates a new column in a document library called CostCenter, the crawled property will be *ows_CostCenter* and the managed property will be *owsCostCenter*. If the column name includes a space, as in *Cost Center*, the crawled property will be *ows_Cost_x0020_Center* and the managed property will be *owsCostx0020Center*.

The programming effort to correct the naming scheme can exceed the cost of manual administration of managed properties.

From the context menu or from the Edit Category page, you can delete an empty category. New categories can be created only programmatically or with the Windows PowerShell SPEnterpriseSearchMetadataCategory cmdlets.

Creating and Managing Search Scopes

A search scope provides a mechanism to group items logically within the index based on common elements. They are used to target a query to only a precompiled portion or *slice* of the corpus to provide a more efficient query and more relevant results.

Essentially, there are two types of scopes. *Authored scopes* are created by search or site collection administrators. *Contextual scopes* are created automatically and presented as This Site or This List. The This And Related Sites scope available in team sites is just a collection of contextual scopes.

To begin to manage search scopes at the search application level, click the Scopes link in the Queries And Results group of the Quick Launch area of the Search Administration page for your search application. This opens the View Scopes page as shown in Figure 9-17.

The People and All Sites scopes were created automatically, but they are authored scopes and can be managed. Because contextual scopes cannot be managed, they are not displayed on the View Scopes page. However, all scopes authored at the service application level or at associated site collections are stored in the search service database and are displayed on this page.

Scopes created at the service application level are known as *shared* scopes and are available for use in any site collection subscribing to the search service application. Scopes created at a site collection are available for use only in that site collection unless they are copied as a shared scope at the service application level. In Figure 9-17, the Team One scope, which was created at the team1 site collection, presents the same context menu as scopes created at the search service application level. However, that scope can be copied only as a shared scope at this level and must be managed at the original site collection location.

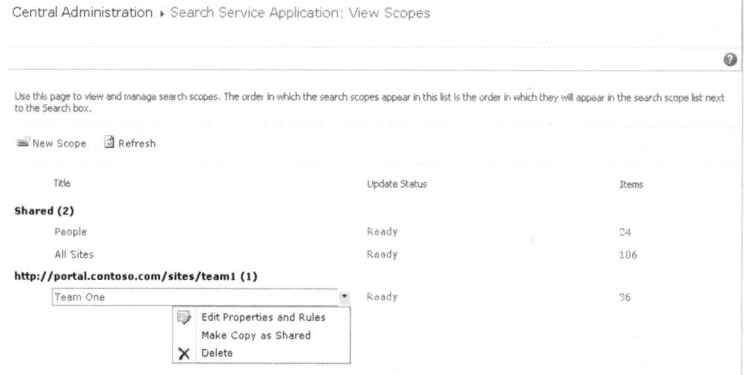

FIGURE 9-17 The View Scopes page.

To create a new scope, click the New Scope link, which is shown in Figure 9-17. The Create Scope page, as illustrated in Figure 9-18, presents the same options as the Edit Scope page. Complete the following steps before clicking OK:

1. Enter a name, in the Title field, that is unique across your enterprise and that clearly defines the content for users. In Figure 9-18, we used Contracts.

2. Enter a description that defines the usage for search administrators. This field is blank by default.

3. Ignore the Last Modified By field, which cannot be edited.

4. Change the Target Results Page settings if you have a custom results page for this scope.

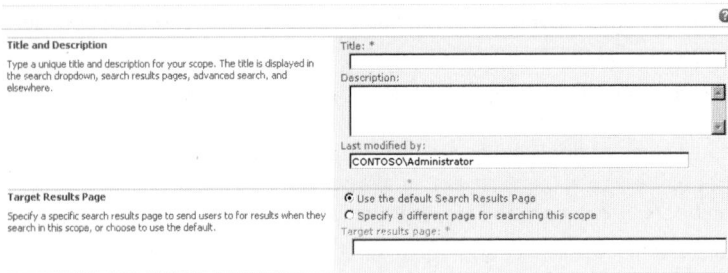

FIGURE 9-18 The Create Scope page.

Because the new scope has no rules applied, it appears on the View Scopes page with a status of Empty – Add Rules, as shown in Figure 9-19. A scope is not functional until you add rules to define the common elements that delineate the boundaries of the scope. The Add Rules link shown in Figure 9-19 is available only for adding the first rule.

Shared (3)

People	Ready	24
All Sites	Ready	106
Contracts	Empty - Add rules	empty

FIGURE 9-19 The View Scopes page with the new scope added.

When you click the Add Rules link, the Add Scope Rule page opens, as shown in Figure 9-20.

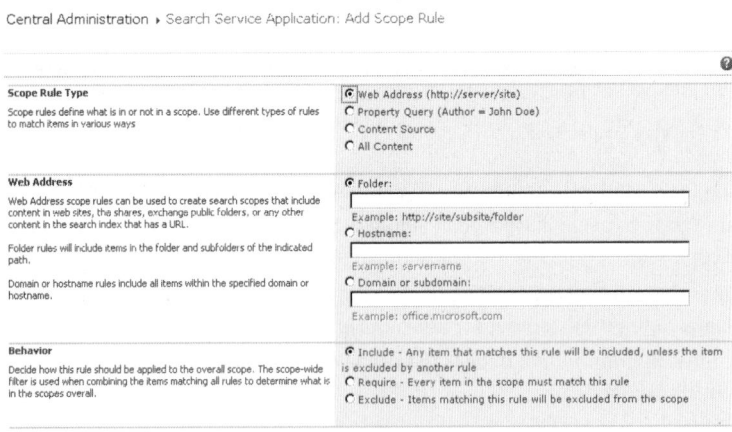

FIGURE 9-20 Add Scope Rule page for the Web Address type.

A scope rule comprises a rule type and any definition of the rule type required, plus the behavior of the rule.

Available rule types are these:

- **Web Address** This type can be any location addressable with a URL in a browser, including Web sites, file shares, public folders, and so on. These addresses can be defined as specific locations called *folders*, any locations on a specific host, or even all locations in a specific domain.

- **Property Query** This type can be any managed property enabled for use in a search scope. The definition section of the Add Scope Rule page changes to that shown in Figure 9-21 for property query rules. Select the managed property from the drop-down list, and enter the value for that property that will be used in the rule. In Figure 9-21, we chose ContentType, which by default is not enabled for use in scopes, and then entered Contract as the value.

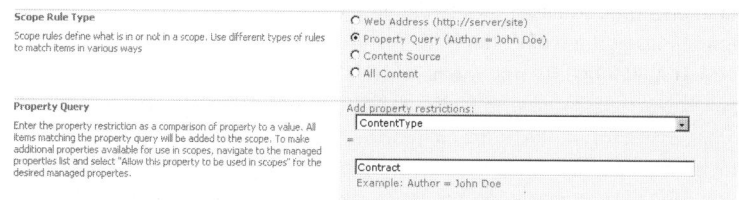

FIGURE 9-21 The Add Scope Rule page with the Property Query option selected.

- **Content Source** This rule type presents a drop-down list of content sources for the search application. Be careful when choosing this option because changes to the content source could be made without regard to their impact on the scope rules.

- **All Content** This type has no additional configuration options.

Scopes can have multiple rules. The Behavior configuration of the rule shown in Figure 9-20 defines how this rule will be applied in compiling the scope. The definitions are straightforward. Both the Include and Require options include content meeting the rule definition, but if the scope has multiple rules all items included must meet the condition of the Require behavior rules.

REAL WORLD Scopes can be quickly created to exclude specific content. First create a rule and choose the All Content option. Then add a rule using other rule types to exclude the content not desired. This approach is sometimes much easier than using a long list of Include rules. The order of rule creation or appearance is irrelevant in scope compilation.

After creating the first rule, you must click the scope name in the View Scopes page to open the Scope Properties And Rules page shown in Figure 9-22. From this page, you can manage the scope rules and edit the scope properties.

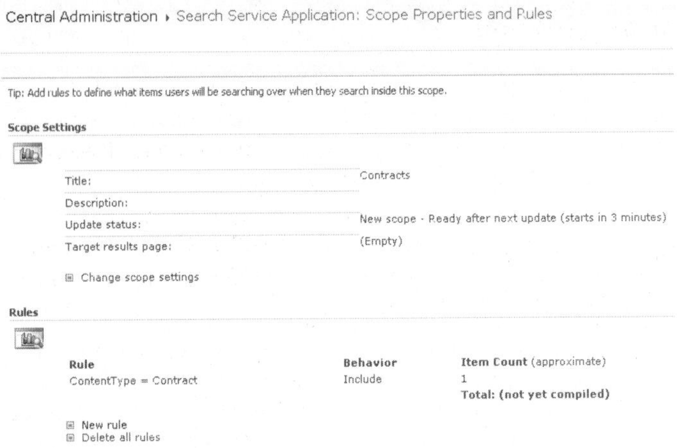

Tip: Add rules to define what items users will be searching over when they search inside this scope.

Scope Settings

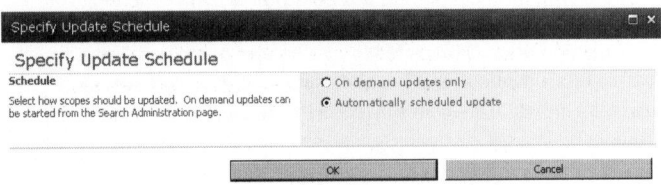

Title:	Contracts
Description:	
Update status:	New scope · Ready after next update (starts in 3 minutes)
Target results page:	(Empty)

☒ Change scope settings

Rules

Rule	Behavior	Item Count (approximate)
ContentType = Contract	Include	1
		Total: (not yet compiled)

☒ New rule
☒ Delete all rules

FIGURE 9-22 Scope Properties And Rules page.

Note in Figure 9-22 that the new scope Update Status is New Scope - Ready After Next Update (Starts In 9 Minutes) and the Item Count Total shows "(not yet compiled)." Items in the index are matched to their scope with a compilation process that is separate from the crawl and indexing process. This process is a scheduled timer job that runs every 15 minutes by default, but it can be initiated manually from the search service application management page when scopes need updating, as shown in Figure 9-23.

Scopes update status	Idle
Scopes update schedule	Automatically scheduled
Scopes needing update	1 Start update now

FIGURE 9-23 Scope update information from the Search Management page.

This process can also be changed to manual by clicking the Automatically Scheduled link to open the Specify Update Schedule dialog box shown in Figure 9-24 and then selecting the On Demand Updates Only option. The timer job schedule cannot be managed from Central Administration.

Specify Update Schedule   □ ✕

Specify Update Schedule

Schedule	
Select how scopes should be updated. On demand updates can be started from the Search Administration page.	○ On demand updates only
	◉ Automatically scheduled update

OK   Cancel

FIGURE 9-24 Specify Update Schedule dialog box for the scope compilation process.

Search Results Removal

If content will be crawled by your search engine that should not be presented in search results, you need to immediately remove it from search results. Remember that search results are derived from the index, so removal of the content itself is not sufficient. The information must be removed from the index.

To remove content from search results, open the Remove URLs From Search Results page shown in Figure 9-25 by clicking the Search Result Removal link in the Queries And Results group of the Quick Launch area of the Search Administration page for your search application.

Enter the URLs of the content to be removed in the URLs, one per line, and click Remove Now. The URLs will be added to a file in the index that will remove them from search results until a crawl can update the index. In addition, crawl rules will be created to prevent the content from being indexed in subsequent crawls.

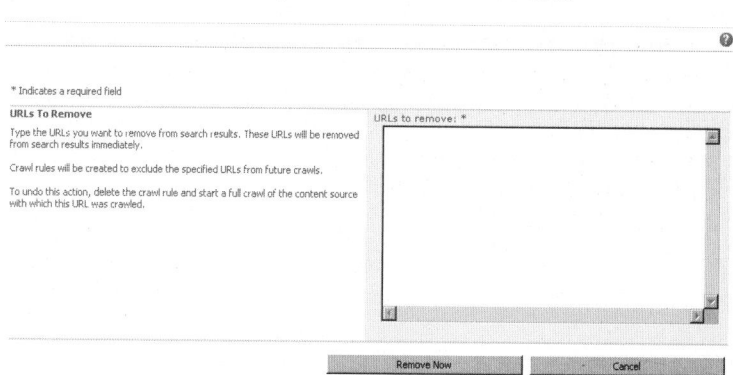

FIGURE 9-25 Remove URLs From Search Results page.

> **REAL WORLD** Sometimes only the permissions were wrong on content that was crawled. If the error has been corrected on the content but it has not been recrawled, search results might still expose inappropriate information to users even if they cannot access the complete documents. In this case, remove the content from the index using the search results removal tool and delete the crawl rule after the permissions have been corrected. Because changes to permissions trigger a recrawl even on file share content in SharePoint Server 2010, the next incremental crawl will update the index.

Site Collection Search Management

Most of the customization with which users interact is created and managed at the site collection level. Even sites, lists, and libraries present settings that control and affect search results. This section will begin a series of discussions on customizations controlled by local administrators and users.

Configuring the Master Page Query Box Control

The first decision for the site collection administrator is whether to use the default context scopes only, such as Windows SharePoint Foundation, or to use custom scopes with a search center in the search query box that appears on all pages. To change from the default settings, open the Search Settings page shown in Figure 9-26 from the Site Collection Administration group in Site Settings.

This page is required because the search query box that appears on each page is a control presented by the master pages. The same configurations are directly available in all Search Query Web parts.

The default configuration, Do Not Use Custom Scopes, executes queries for This Site, including subsites, and presents no scope options. Your design can include leaving the default settings for this query box and creating a search center site for enterprise content searches.

The results are displayed on the results pages defined in the Site Collection Search Results Page section at the bottom of the page. The default location of the page is a generic page in the _layouts directory that is common across all site collections. You can create a custom search results page for local searches and direct queries to it in this section.

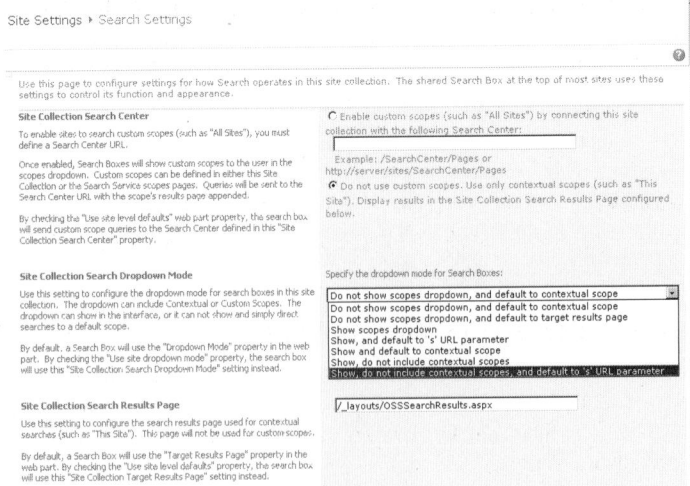

FIGURE 9-26 Site Collection Search Settings page.

If you choose to use custom scopes, you must direct the queries to a search center. The example in Figure 9-26 assumes a search center with tabs, which is a publishing site and has all search pages in a pages library. You can also point to a simple search site. The entry in this dialog box normally is a path relative to the application name such as /Search or /SearchCenter/pages, but it can also be a full path such as http://portal.contoso.com/Search Center/pages. You do not need to include the page because the query will be directed to the appropriate results page.

The default setting is to not display a scope drop-down box and to use the contextual scope. The other choices are as follows:

- **Do Not Show Scopes Dropdown, And Default To Target Results Page**   Does not display a scope drop-down list, and sends the query to the results page with no scope selected. Normally, this will be a custom results page with Web parts configured to use one or more scopes.
- **Show Scopes Dropdown**   Displays the scopes defined in the search drop-down display group and the contextual scopes in the scopes list. This option is shown in Figure 9-27.
- **Show, And Default To 'S' URL Parameter**   Displays the scopes defined in the search drop-down display group and the contextual scopes in the scopes list. The selected scope will be added to the query passed to the results page using the 's' parameter.
- **Show, And Default To Contextual Scope**   Displays the search drop-down list, and automatically selects the This Site or This List scope as the default. Contextual scopes cannot be managed in the search drop-down list.
- **Show, Do Not Include Contextual Scopes**   Displays only the scopes in the search drop-down list that do not include This Site and This List contextual scopes.
- **Show, Do Not Include Contextual Scopes, And Default To 'S' URL Parameter**   Displays only the scopes defined in the search drop-down display group in the scopes list. The selected scope will be added to the query passed to the results page using the 's' parameter.

FIGURE 9-27 Search box control configured with the Show Scopes Dropdown option.

Site Collection Search Scope Management

Search scopes that you create at the service level are considered shared scopes. These scopes are available across all the Web application's site collections that are associated with the service. Site collection owners then have the option to use the scopes within their site collection.

Site collection scopes are managed from the View Scopes page, shown in Figure 9-28. To open this page, from the Site Collection Administration menu in Site Settings, click the Search Scopes link. Notice the Unused Scopes section at the bottom of the page.

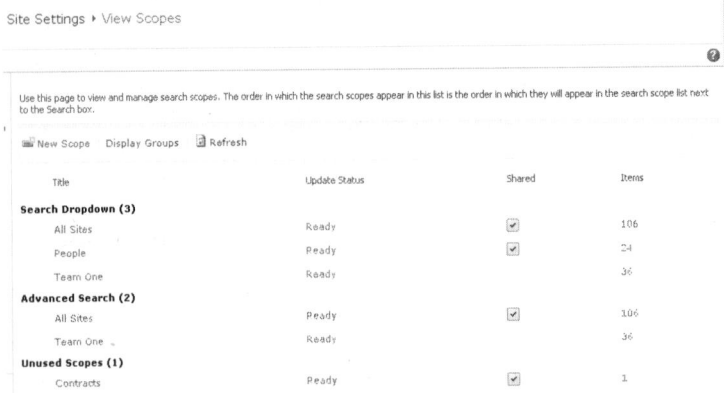

FIGURE 9-28 The Site Collection View Scopes page.

New local scopes are created from the View Scopes page by clicking the New Scope link and following the same steps as creating a shared scope at the search service level. The only differences between a local scope and a shared scope is that a local scope cannot contain a rule using a content source and that it can be used only in the local site collection.

To select how both local and shared scopes are displayed in the site collection, follow these steps:

1. Click the Display Groups link to open the page shown in Figure 9-29.

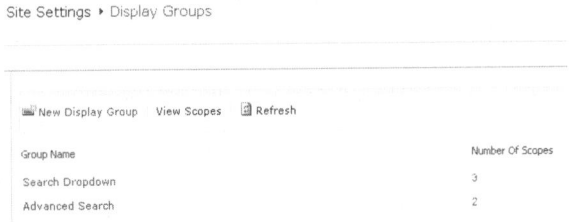

FIGURE 9-29 The Display Groups page.

2. Click the display group that you want to modify. You are then presented with the Edit Scope Display Group page, shown in Figure 9-30.

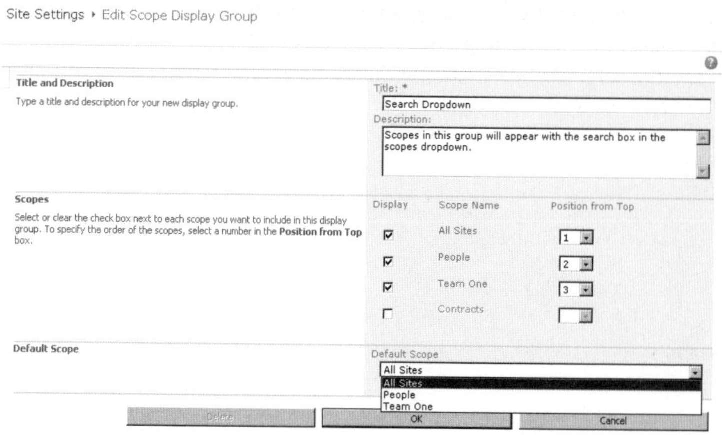

FIGURE 9-30 The Edit Scope Display Group page.

3. Now you can add unused scopes by selecting their check box in the Display column, change the order in which the scopes are listed, and choose the default scope.

4. Click OK.

Now your scope display group will appear correctly when selected for query controls or Web parts.

NOTE Create additional scope display groups by clicking the New Display Group link, shown in Figure 9-29, and completing steps 3 and 4. When configuring Web parts to use the display group, you have to type in the exact display group name because it will not appear in the drop-down list choices.

Working with Keywords and Best Bets

Keywords are terms identified and managed by site collection (search) administrators. When terms have more than one meaning within an organization, keywords can be used to clarify their usage and meaning. More commonly, they are used to display search results so that the results recommend the most appropriate source of information related to the term. These recommended results are known as *Best Bet* locations.

When a keyword is used in a query term, both the keyword definition and the Best Bet location appear in the Best Bet Web part on the search results page. Keywords and Best Bets are configured at the site collection level by the site collection administrator. They are not configured as part of the search service, nor are they transferable between site collections.

To open the Manage Keywords page, shown in Figure 9-31, from the Site Actions menu at the root of a site collection, select Site Settings. The Search keywords link in the Site Collection Administration group will open the page.

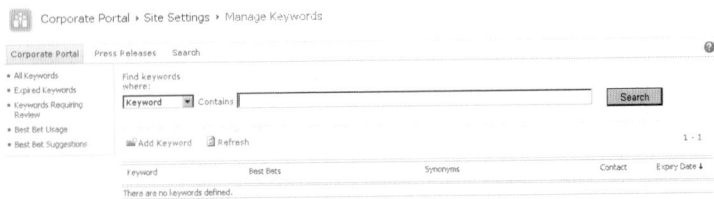

FIGURE 9-31 Manage Keywords page.

In the Quick Launch area are links to three views: All Keywords (the default), Expired Keywords, and Keywords Requiring Review. Two links to usage reports are Best Bet Usage and Best Bet Suggestions. These will be covered later as part of the usage reports discussion.

Because the number of keywords can be quite large, these filter views are useful, as is the keyword search tool shown in Figure 9-32. Using this tool, you can locate keywords by choosing either Keyword, Synonyms, Best Bet Title, Best Bet URL, or Contact.

FIGURE 9-32 Keyword search tool.

Click the Add Keyword link to open the Add Keyword page. The first section of the page, as seen in Figure 9-33, manages the keyword phrase and any synonyms. Any phrase entered in either box will return the keyword results when used as a search term. Synonyms should be separated by semi-colons.

NOTE The Edit Keyword page uses the same.aspx page as the Add Keyword page.

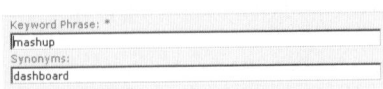

FIGURE 9-33 Keyword Phrase and Synonyms text boxes.

The next section of the page, shown in Figure 9-34, manages the keyword definition, which is the optional editorial text that will appear in the keyword result. Use this rich text editor control to enter a keyword definition that will help explain the keyword result in the result set. The text can include hyperlinks.

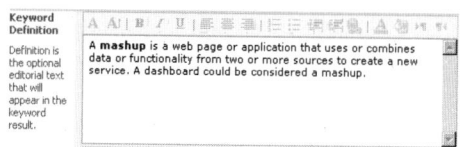

FIGURE 9-34 Keyword Definition rich text editor.

The display of a keyword definition in a search results page when the keyword has no associated Best Bet configured is shown in Figure 9-35. This definition is presented on the results page even though there are no search results to display.

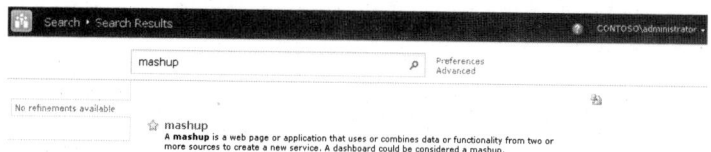

FIGURE 9-35 Presentation of a keyword definition only.

The next section of the page, shown in Figure 9-36, manages Best Bets. A keyword can have multiple associated Best Bets. They will appear in the order specified in this section up to the limits determined by the Best Bets Web part on the results page.

NOTE This screen shot was created from a prerelease version of the product. The blue letters "Remo" next to the Order number selection box will be replaced with two hyperlinks, Remove and Edit, in the released product.

FIGURE 9-36 Best Bet management section of Manage Keyword page.

Clicking the Add Best Bet or Edit links opens the Best Bet management dialog box shown in Figure 9-37. The URL and Title fields are required, while the description is optional. For Best Bets, the description is a text-only entry.

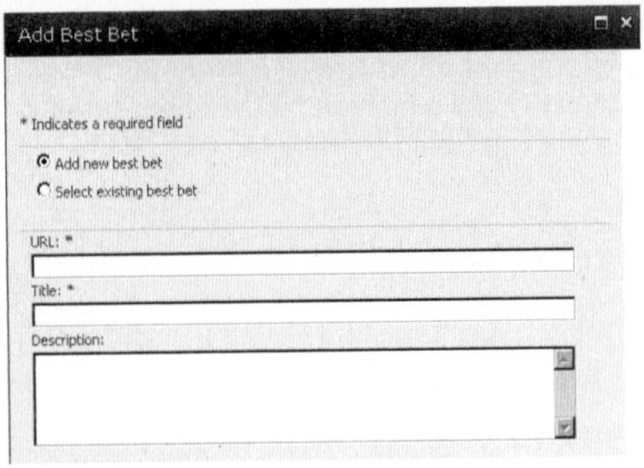

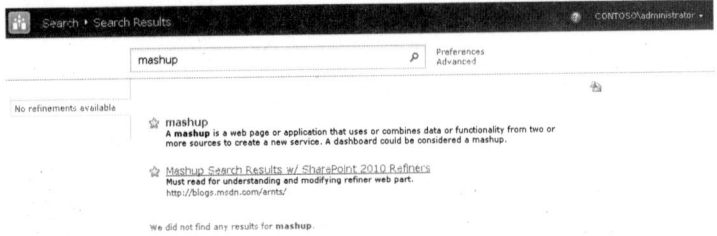

FIGURE 9-37 The Add Best Bet dialog box.

The next section, displayed in Figure 9-38, is management information for the keyword. Enter information for the person to be contacted on the review date. You must schedule a publishing date, but the review and expiration dates are optional.

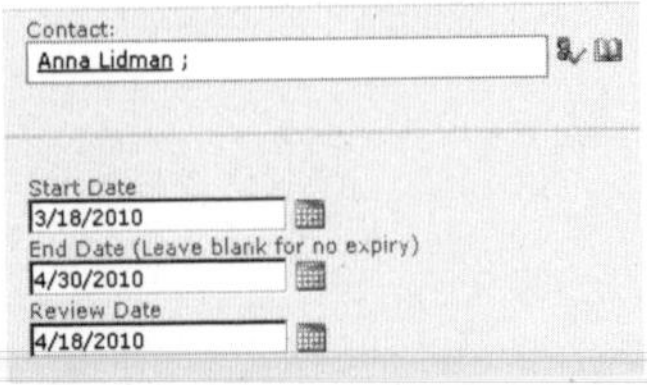

FIGURE 9-38 Keyword contact and publishing information.

After configuring a keyword, you must run a full crawl of all your content indexes so that the new keyword entry is properly associated with content.

The keyword definition and Best Bet will be displayed in search results, as shown in Figure 9-39, even if no other results are located for your search term. The keyword definition and Best Bet display will be the same whether the search term was the keyword phrase or a synonym but, of course, the search results would differ.

FIGURE 9-39 Keyword Definition and Best Bet illustration.

Creating and Customizing Search Centers

The location and number of search centers to use are major decisions in your enterprise search design. You might choose to centralize all searches at a single location, or an organization might choose to customize and control search with local search centers. With either scenario, these customizations will be managed at the site collection level using the resources provided by at the application level.

REAL WORLD In a centralized search environment, you can establish a team dedicated to managing search without giving them control over other content by creating a search center at the root of a separate site collection. Place the site collection in the desired URL location using an explicit managed path.

SharePoint Server 2010 offers three search center site templates in the Enterprise tab, as shown in Figure 9-40:

- **Enterprise Search Center** This was named Search Center With Tabs in the previous version. This publishing site requires the Publishing Infrastructure feature to be activated for the site collection, but it does not require that its parent be a publishing site.

- **Basic Search Center** This template is appropriately named because it offers only three basic search pages and is more difficult to use if you want to add search pages.

- **FAST Search Center** This template is available even without FAST for SharePoint installed, but it requires a FAST search server for functionality. We will not cover this search center or its Web parts in this book.

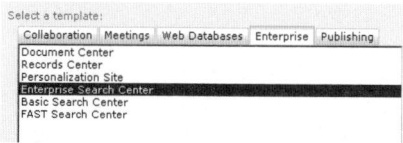

FIGURE 9-40 Search Center template selections.

Customizing the Enterprise Search Center

As a publishing site, the Enterprise Search Center is designed for customization for three significant reasons:

- All three search pages templates provided within the UI are page layout templates for the publishing process that are based on the Welcome page content type.

- All pages are stored in a publishing Pages library with full publishing processes, approvals, and workflows available.

- Within the page layouts of the search and results pages is a special field control, which organizes links to other search pages within customizable tabs. Advanced Search pages do not have a tab field control. The link information used by the tabs field control is stored in one of two link lists:
  - Tabs in Search Pages
  - Tabs in Search Results Pages

The three search pages of the Basic Search Center (default, advanced, and results) are Web part pages designed like the publishing templates, but there is no provision for creating additional pages based on that design.

Creating New Search Pages

From any page of the Enterprise Search Center, you can create a new search page from the Site Actions menu. However, do not select New Page because this creates a new page without presenting options to select a template. Follow these steps:

1. Select More Options, which opens the Create page. The presentation of this page varies greatly depending on whether you have Microsoft SilverLight installed.

2. Select Publishing Page to open the Create Page page shown in Figure 9-41.

3. Enter the appropriate information in the Title, Description, and URL Name text boxes.

4. Select the appropriate page template.

5. Click the Create button.

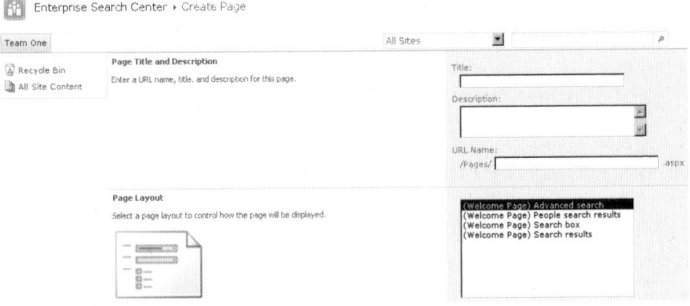

FIGURE 9-41 The Create Page page.

Plan your pages carefully. You will not always need a set of three pages for each customization. For instance, a single Search Box (query) page can contain multiple search boxes, each pointing to a unique Search Results page or People search results page. All search box Web parts do not need to have a corresponding Advanced Search page.

Creating New Tabs

In the edit page mode, the Tabs field control exposes links to management pages for adding new tab links or editing existing tab links, as shown in Figure 9-42. In this example, a custom tab has been added for a search page that returns only contracts in the result set.

FIGURE 9-42 Tab field control.

Clicking Edit Tabs opens the Tabs In Search Pages list shown in Figure 9-43, from which the control builds the tabs. The results pages also have a tab control that uses another list, named Tabs In Search Results. These lists can also be accessed from View All Site Content.

FIGURE 9-43 Tabs In Search Pages list page.

Clicking the Add New Item link or Add New Tab from the control on the page opens the page shown in Figure 9-44.

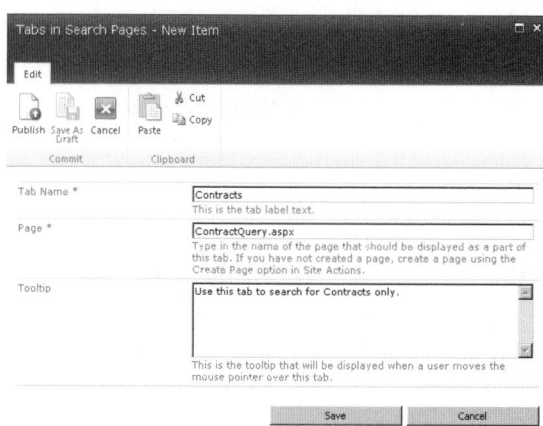

FIGURE 9-44 New Item page for the Tabs In Search Pages list.

The Tab Name field should be self-explanatory to users. The Page field can point to an existing or future custom page. The Tooltip field should briefly explain the purpose of the custom page.

After the custom set of search pages and tabs are created, the new query page can be accessed from its custom tab. The query Web part can then point to the appropriate custom results page, and the Advanced query link can point to the appropriate custom advanced query page.

When a query opens one results page, it will be automatically passed to the results page opened by another tab on the results page.

This combination of UI tools for creating custom search pages plus the control that presents a series of tabs within the pages presents a search center that can be quickly and easily customized for multiple search business needs.

Configuring Custom Page Access

Although we have not yet discussed them all, here are some of the ways that these custom pages can be accessed:

- Site collections can be configured to use a custom set of search pages, even those located elsewhere.
- Scopes, both local and shared, can be configured for a specific results page.
- Query Web parts can be configured to use a specific results page.
- More Results links can point to custom results pages.
- Advanced Search links can point to custom advanced search pages.
- Links placed anywhere within your pages or link lists can point to custom query pages.
- Favorite links in Internet Explorer can be prepopulated with links to custom query pages using Active Directory group policies.
- Internet Explorer and Desktop Search can be configured to use custom query pages.
- Office applications can be configured to use search pages by URL.

Customizing Search Pages

Because the basic three search pages are essentially the same in the Basic and Enterprise search centers, we will first discuss customizing each of these pages and their corresponding Web parts and then discuss the extended customizations available in the Enterprise search center.

Search Web Parts in SharePoint 2010 are based on the federation object model (OM) and are used by both SharePoint Search and FAST Search. The Web parts on a page communicate through a shared query manager identified in the Web parts as the Cross Web Part Query ID. To add new Web parts that interact with existing Web parts, the new Web parts simply need to use the same query ID. Because the out-of-the-box Web parts are no longer sealed, your developers can extend their functionality instead of writing a new one from scratch.

Query Pages

The welcome page of all search centers is a basic query page named default.aspx. Although this page seems rather simple, as shown in Figure 9-45, it supports a number of customization options, even in the basic search center site.

FIGURE 9-45 Portion of the basic query page in edit mode.

The page has two Web part zones but only a single Search Box Web part. You can choose to add other Web parts, such as a content editor where instructions on how to search more effectively can be presented. Because Web parts might be targeted by audience, you can add multiple instances of the same Search Box Web part on the same page customized for different groups of users.

The appearance of the Preferences link is controlled by the Search Box configuration and opens the page shown in Figure 9-46, where users can configure personal preferences for the configuration of the Web part.

Users can choose to prevent the search suggestions from being displayed as they type in query terms. These suggestions are retrieved from the history of queries executed by previous searches. Users can also choose to override the default behavior of searching in the language of the browser and instead choose up to five languages to include in the search results. From that list, they can choose the default language, which is given a higher relevance ranking in the results list.

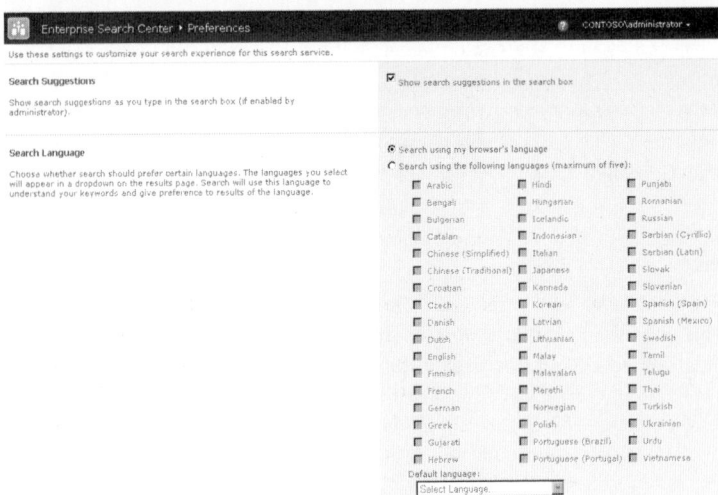

FIGURE 9-46 Edit User Preferences page for the Search Box Web part.

Search Box Web Part

The search Web parts have many configuration sections in common with other Web parts. Because these are discussed in another chapter of this book, we will not cover those sections. The Search Box Web part is used in both search and results pages and has the same functionality as the search box control on the master pages.

To configure the properties of a Web part on the Search page, perform the following steps:

1. From the Site Actions menu or the Page ribbon of the page, select Edit Page.

2. In the Web Part zone, click the small down arrow for the Web part to expose the context menu and select Modify Shared Web Part.

3. Expand the appropriate sections to configure properties as needed.

4. Click OK.

5. For publishing pages, you need to save, check in, and publish the page. For standard pages, the action is simply Stop Editing.

The Scopes Dropdown section of the Search Box Web part is shown in Figure 9-47. The Dropdown mode options are the same as those of the Site Settings Search Settings page discussed earlier. Normally, you do not need to enter text in the Dropdown Label box or modify the default automatic Fixed Dropdown Width setting (0).

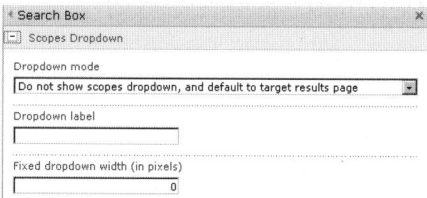

FIGURE 9-47 Scopes Dropdown section of the Search Box Web part properties.

The Query Text Box Label and Query Text Box Label Width text boxes, shown in Figure 9-48, are straightforward. Additional query terms can be added to the user-entered query. This text box is usually empty. The entered text shown in Figure 9-48 limits the results to documents. Any keyword query can be placed here, including scope definitions. Because these terms modify the query transparently to the user, appropriately labeling the query box will inform the user of its functionality. The prompt string will appear in the query box unless the focus is set there automatically or the cursor is placed there manually. The Append Additional Terms To Query check box is critical because the terms entered in this section are not used unless it is selected.

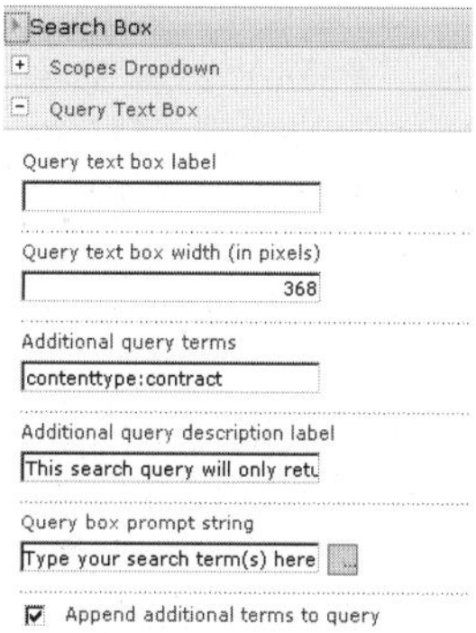

FIGURE 9-48 Query Text Box section of the Search Box Web part properties.

The search query box, shown in Figure 9-49, displays the configurations set in Figure 9-48.

FIGURE 9-49 Customized search query box.

The Query Suggestions section, shown in Figure 9-50, offers global control over the suggestions process, where the preferences page let users specify individual preferences. This section offers more granular control of the search parameters. The

Minimum Prefix Length setting determines how many characters must be typed before suggestions are offered. The Suggestion Delay setting controls the response time, and the Number Of Suggestions To Display setting controls the maximum number of suggestions.

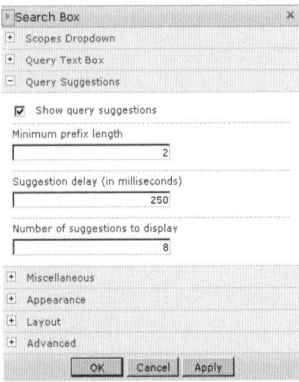

FIGURE 9-50 Query Suggestions section of the Search Box Web part properties.

Despite the name, the Miscellaneous section shown in Figure 9-51 is probably the most often used in customizing search. The first two switches, Use Site Dropdown Mode and Use Site Level Defaults, override the settings in the Scope Dropdown section. Use these options to establish centralized control of multiple Web parts from the Search Settings of the site collection.

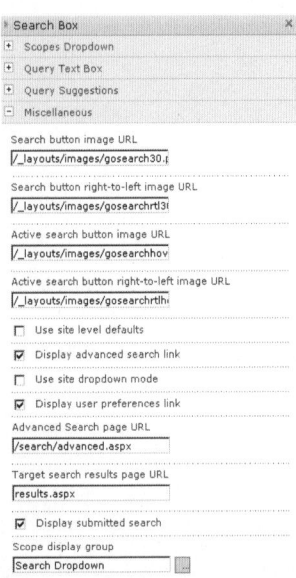

FIGURE 9-51 Miscellaneous section of Search box Web part properties.

The next two switches control the links at the end of the query box. You might choose not to offer an advanced search page for some searches, such as the People Query page in the Enterprise Search Center. Obviously, if you did not select the Show Query Suggestions check box in the previous section, you also might choose to remove the user preferences link. Remember that user preferences also control query languages.

The next four entries control the Search button images. Although customization of the query Web part does permit appending terms to the query, it does not offer the sophistication of an advanced query Web part, nor can it modify the presentation of results as the various search results Web parts do. We will cover those customizations later in this chapter.

In the Advanced Search Page URL box, you can direct the advanced search link to the appropriate custom page. This text box is active even if the Display Advanced Search Link check box is not selected. The text displayed in this box in Figure 9-51 shows a relative path for a page in a Basic Search Center.

The Target Search Results Page URL setting configures the target page for the query from this search query. Because the actual work of the search query is accomplished by the results page, you might configure custom query pages or custom query Web parts where the only customization is the target results page.

The Display Submitted Search check box affects only query Web parts placed on the results page. If these Web parts display the query submitted to the page, the user can easily modify the query without retyping it in its entirety.

If you need to change the scope display group, you must type the name exactly as it appears in the site collection scope management page.

The Appearance, Layout, and Advanced sections are standard for SharePoint Web parts. If you need to target to audiences, you can find the Audiences configuration in the Advanced section. By having multiple Search Box Web parts targeted to different audiences on the same page, you can have a single query page customized to the user opening it.

Advanced Search Pages

The Advanced Search page of the Basic Search Center has only a single Web part zone, although the advanced search pages of the Enterprise Search Center have two additional zones at the top of the page. In both instances, the pages contain the single advanced search Web part shown in its default configuration in Figure 9-52.

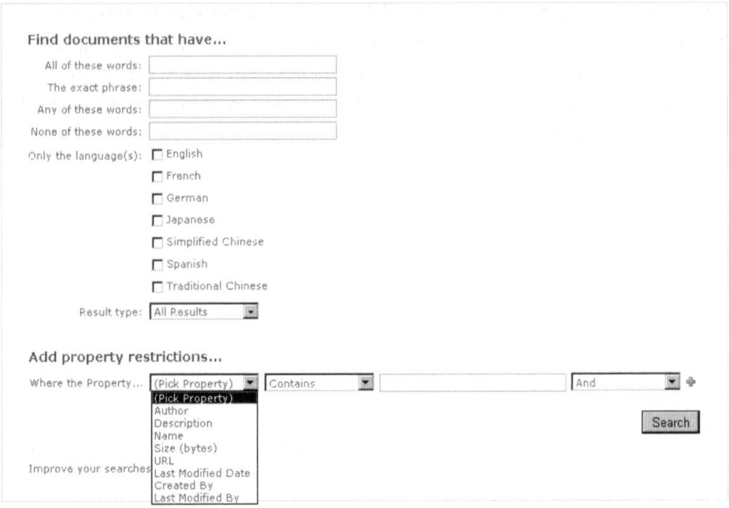

FIGURE 9-52 Default Advanced Search Web part.

Although much of the Web part can be customized easily in the property UI, three critical portions require modifying XML. We will walk through the properties as they appear. To edit the Web part, first place the page in Edit mode from either the Site Actions menu or the Page ribbon. Then to the upper right of the Web part, from the drop-down arrow menu choose Edit Web Part.

The first section of the Advanced Search Web part is shown in Figure 9-53. These Search Box settings affect the query terms. All of these query terms can be entered directly in the basic query box if the user knows how to construct the query. Each option includes a text label box and a selection to enable it.

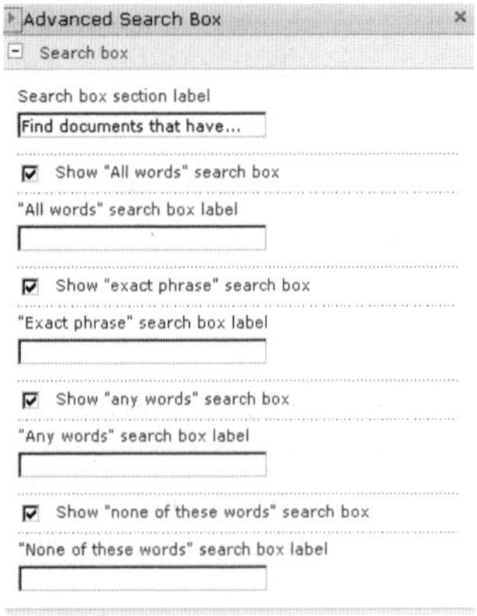

FIGURE 9-53 Advanced Search Web part properties Search Box section.

The next section, displayed in Figure 9-54, is named Scopes and controls a series of query filters. Again, options are presented for labels with enabling selections. Although the Display Group used by the scope picker is configured within this section, both the Language and Result Type pickers are controlled by an XML section that will be discussed later.

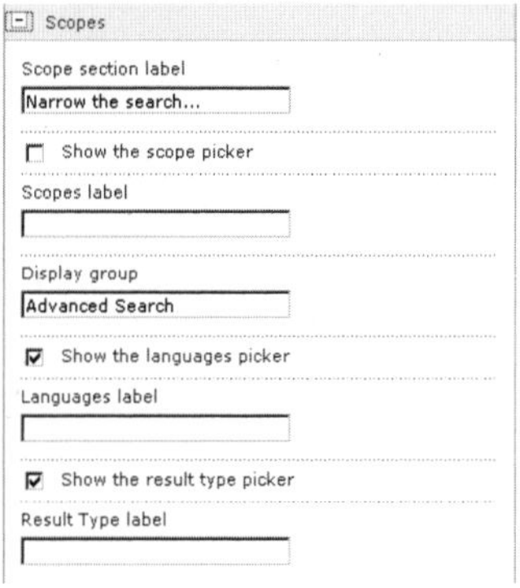

FIGURE 9-54 Advanced Search Web part properties Scopes section.

The Properties section, shown in Figure 9-55, continues to manage query filters using managed properties. An XML string contained in the Properties text box controls the managed properties available for use here, as well as the languages exposed in the language picker and the file types defined in the result type picker.

To edit this code, place the cursor in the text box to expose the blue builder text editor button to the right of the text box. Because the file is a single line in this editor, you might want to copy the entire text to your favorite XML editor, make the changes, and paste the modified text back into the builder for saving to the Properties settings.

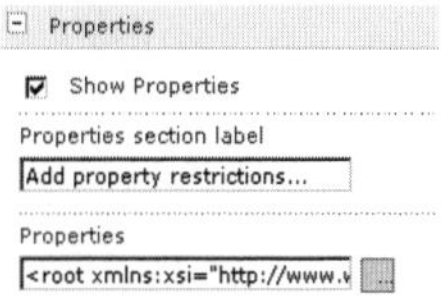

FIGURE 9-55 Advanced Search Web part Properties section.

We will examine the portions of this file in the order of appearance. The first section defines the languages supported by search. For each language definition (LangDef), the display name is given in quotes, and the assigned language ID is given in quotes. You do not need to modify this portion. A small portion of the code follows.

```
<root xmlns:xsi="http://www.w3.org/2001/XMLSchema-instance">
<LangDefs>
  <LangDef DisplayName="Simplified Chinese" LangID="zh-cn" />
  <LangDef DisplayName="Traditional Chinese" LangID="zh-tw" />
  <LangDef DisplayName="English" LangID="en" />
  <LangDef DisplayName="Finnish" LangID="fi" />
  <LangDef DisplayName="French" LangID="fr" />
  <LangDef DisplayName="German" LangID="de" />
  <LangDef DisplayName="Italian" LangID="it" />
  <LangDef DisplayName="Japanese" LangID="ja" />
  <LangDef DisplayName="Spanish" LangID="es" />
</LangDefs>
```

The next section of the code specifies the languages by LangID to be displayed in
the language picker, as shown in the following code sample. To change the languages displayed, simply add or remove lines from these default settings and save
the code back to the Properties text box.

```
<Languages>
  <Language LangRef="en" />
  <Language LangRef="fr" />
  <Language LangRef="de" />
  <Language LangRef="ja" />
  <Language LangRef="zh-cn" />
  <Language LangRef="es" />
  <Language LangRef="zh-tw" />
</Languages>
```

The next portion of the XML string is the Property Definition section, as shown in
the following code block. These properties must be managed properties. Additional
property entries must include the real managed property name, the data type, and
the name to display in the Web part.

```
<PropertyDefs>
  <PropertyDef Name="Path" DataType="text" DisplayName="URL" />
  <PropertyDef Name="Size" DataType="integer" DisplayName="Size (bytes)" />
  <PropertyDef Name="Write" DataType="datetime" DisplayName="Last Modified
Date" />
  <PropertyDef Name="FileName" DataType="text" DisplayName="Name" />
  <PropertyDef Name="Description" DataType="text" DisplayName="Description"
/>
  <PropertyDef Name="Title" DataType="text" DisplayName="Title" />
  <PropertyDef Name="Author" DataType="text" DisplayName="Author" />
  <PropertyDef Name="DocSubject" DataType="text" DisplayName="Subject" />
  <PropertyDef Name="DocKeywords" DataType="text" DisplayName="Keywords" />
  <PropertyDef Name="DocComments" DataType="text" DisplayName="Comments" />
  <PropertyDef Name="CreatedBy" DataType="text" DisplayName="Created By" />
  <PropertyDef Name="ModifiedBy" DataType="text" DisplayName="Last Modified
By" />
  </PropertyDefs>
```

You can add other managed properties to these definitions. Managed properties do not have to be designated for use in a scope to be used in the Advanced Search Web part. After they are defined, these properties can then be used in the result types filter definitions and in the managed properties filters:

```
<ResultType DisplayName="Word Documents" Name="worddocuments">
  <KeywordQuery>FileExtension="doc" OR FileExtension="docx" OR
FileExtension="dot" OR FileExtension="docm" OR
ileExtension="odt"</KeywordQuery>
  <PropertyRef Name="Author" />
  <PropertyRef Name="DocComments" />
  <PropertyRef Name="Description" />
  <PropertyRef Name="DocKeywords" />
  <PropertyRef Name="FileName" />
  <PropertyRef Name="Size" />
  <PropertyRef Name="DocSubject" />
  <PropertyRef Name="Path" />
  <PropertyRef Name="Write" />
  <PropertyRef Name="CreatedBy" />
  <PropertyRef Name="ModifiedBy" />
  <PropertyRef Name="Title" />
</ResultType>
```

There are result types for the following categories:

- Default
- Documents
- Word Documents
- Excel Documents
- Presentations

You can enter new managed properties as property definitions, and then create new result types or modify existing ones in this file. After you edit the string, save it back into the Property text box

The Miscellaneous section contains a single, but very important, setting for the target results URL, as shown in Figure 9-56. In particular, a custom Advanced Query Web part might need to point to a custom results page where the presentation of the results Web parts has been customized to meet business needs. This custom results page can also contain non-search Web parts that connect to the search Web parts.

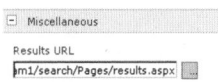

FIGURE 9-56 Advanced Search Web part Miscellaneous section.

A sample search query constructed by the advanced search Web part can be passed as the following:

```
ALL(searchterm) (DetectedLanguage="en") (IsDocument="True")
Write>=02/01/2010
```

A knowledgeable user can enter the search in a basic query box as the following and achieve the same results:

```
searchterm DetectedLanguage="en" IsDocument="True" Write>=02/01/2010
```

However, most users will find the UI of the advanced search easier to use.

Results Pages

The results pages are the most complex of the three default search pages, with a total of eight Web part zones and up to 12 Web parts, depending on the results page type. Each of these Web parts is responsible for a different view of the results or information about the results. Figure 9-57 displays the default results page from the Enterprise Search Center.

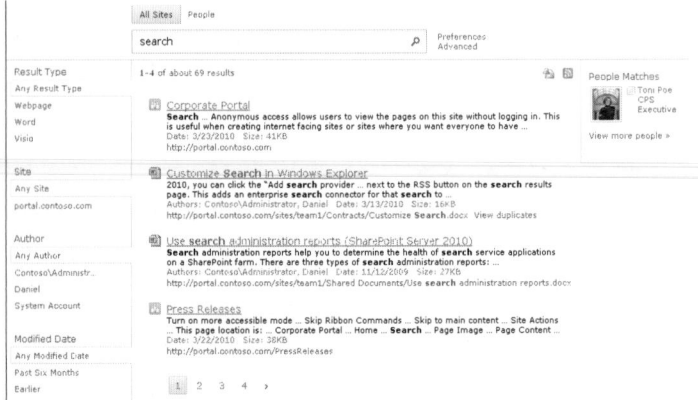

FIGURE 9-57 Results page from Enterprise Search Center.

The People Search Results page, shown in Figure 9-58, shares six of the same Web parts, but with different configurations.

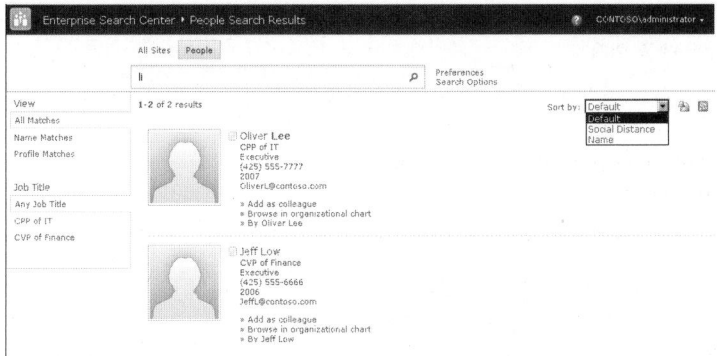

FIGURE 9-58 People Search Results page.

Two Web parts are not displaying on the People Search Results page. The Summary Web part displays only to suggest search terms when the query contains a term that is only close to those contained in the index, such as misspelled words. Despite its name, the results appear prefaced with "Did you mean," as shown in Figure 9-59.

FIGURE 9-59 Summary Web part.

The People Search Results page does not need this Web part because the fuzzy logic and phonetic searches in people searches make the corrections for the user. In Figure 9-58, the search term "li" retrieved people named "Lee" and "Low."

The Related Queries Web part is located in the zone on the right of the results page, and it suggests other search terms that have been used and contains terms within the current query.

> **MORE INFORMATION** For more information on adding and configuring Web parts, see Chapter 7, "Web Parts, Features, and Solutions."

Results Pages Functionality

Core Results Web parts and their derivatives instantiate an object called the Query Manager and send their query requirements to their Query Manager. These Web parts all have a Cross-Web Part Query ID property that identifies the Query Manager that they share.

The Query Manager object executes the query for local results, receives the search results as XML data, and passes the appropriate results to the different search Web parts on the results page. The content and format of the XML data that is passed depends on the Web part that is receiving the data based upon the parameters originally sent to the Query Manager. Each Web part then displays the XML data, formatted according to the XSL Transform specified for that Web part's XSL property.

Federated Results Web parts using OpenSearch 1.1 pass the query to the target search engine directly and format the results according to the XSL configured for the Web part. Because these Web parts are not participating with the Query Manager, they can load asynchronously.

Search Web Parts Configurations

Search Web parts have many configurations that are common to all SharePoint Web parts. Because those were covered in Chapter 7, we will not include those in this discussion. Our focus will be the configurations that are unique to each Web part or that affect the functionality of the Web part. Because FAST Search for SharePoint uses the same Web parts, there seem to be some options that have functionality only with that product.

SEARCH CORE RESULTS

This same Web part with different configurations is used in multiple locations on results pages. We will show only the properties of the Core Search Results from the Results.aspx and indicate the variations between that and the People Core Results and Search Action Links uses.

- **Location Properties** Because SharePoint Server 2010 search uses the Federated Search object model, the first section is Location Properties, which is shown in Figure 9-60. For Core Results, the location is Local Search Results as defined in Federated Search Locations. For both People Search Results and Search Action Links, the location is None.

   The Description box is populated from the location selected. Enter the name in the Scope box if you want to filter the results to a particular scope. You need to type the exact scope name because there is no drop-down list.

FIGURE 9-60 Location Properties.

The next list of check boxes appears only if Show Action Links is selected in the Miscellaneous section. By default, these options are used in the Search Action Links Web part but not in others. Figure 9-61 shows the results of all options selected in both Web parts. Two options, Display "Search From Windows" Link and Allow Users To Display Language Picker, seem to have no functionality in Beta code and might work only with FAST Search for SharePoint.

FIGURE 9-61 All action links enabled.

- **Display Properties** The first six configurations of this section, shown in Figure 9-62, are straightforward. The setting of 4 in the Results Per Page box is not the default; instead, it is a modification made to produce smaller pages for the screen shots in this chapter.

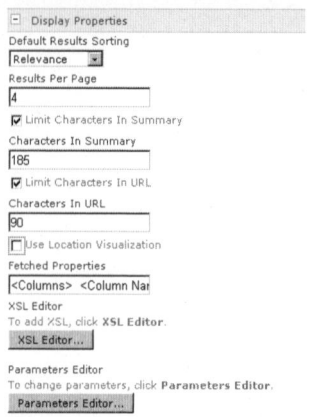

FIGURE 9-62 Display Properties section.

The Use Location Visualization check box must be cleared if you need to customize the Web part from the default settings defined in Federated Locations. It is the XML string contained in the Fetched Properties text box that defines much of the functionality of the Web part. These managed properties are sent to the Query Manager as managed properties to be retrieved for each search result in the result set.

The code in the Core Results and Search Action Links Web parts follows:

```xml
<Columns>
  <Column Name="WorkId" />
  <Column Name="Rank" />
  <Column Name="Title" />
  <Column Name="Author" />
  <Column Name="Size" />
  <Column Name="Path" />
  <Column Name="Description" />
  <Column Name="Write" />
  <Column Name="SiteName" />
  <Column Name="CollapsingStatus" />
  <Column Name="HitHighlightedSummary" />
  <Column Name="HitHighlightedProperties" />
  <Column Name="ContentClass" />
  <Column Name="IsDocument" />
  <Column Name="PictureThumbnailURL" />
  <Column Name="PopularSocialTags" />
  <Column Name="PictureWidth" />
  <Column Name="PictureHeight" />
```

```
<Column Name="DatePictureTaken" />
<Column Name="ServerRedirectedURL" />
</Columns>
```

The code for the People Core Results Web part code follows:

```
<Columns>
    <Column Name="WorkId" />
    <Column Name="UserProfile_GUID" />
    <Column Name="AccountName" />
    <Column Name="PreferredName" HitHighLight="true" />
    <Column Name="YomiDisplayName" HitHighLight="true" />
    <Column Name="JobTitle" HitHighLight="true" />
    <Column Name="Department" HitHighLight="true" />
    <Column Name="WorkPhone" HitHighLight="true" />
    <Column Name="OfficeNumber" HitHighLight="true" />
    <Column Name="PictureURL" />
    <Column Name="HierarchyUrl" />
    <Column Name="WorkEmail" HitHighLight="true" />
    <Column Name="Path" />
    <Column Name="HitHighlightedSummary" />
    <Column Name="HitHighlightedProperties" />
    <Column Name="Responsibility" HitHighLight="true" />
    <Column Name="Skills" HitHighLight="true" />
    <Column Name="SipAddress" HitHighLight="true" />
    <Column Name="Schools" HitHighLight="true" />
    <Column Name="PastProjects" HitHighLight="true" />
    <Column Name="Interests" HitHighLight="true" />
    <Column Name="OrgNames" HitHighLight="true" />
    <Column Name="OrgUrls" />
    <Column Name="OrgParentNames" HitHighLight="true" />
    <Column Name="OrgParentUrls" />
    <Column Name="Memberships" HitHighLight="true" />
    <Column Name="AboutMe" HitHighLight="true" />
    <Column Name="BaseOfficeLocation" HitHighLight="true" />
    <Column Name="ServiceApplicationID" />
    <Column Name="SocialDistance" />
</Columns>
```

If you add managed properties to these lists, you must also modify the XSL to specify how the property is to be displayed. There are two options for modifying the style sheet for the Web part. In this section, you can click the XSL Editor button to expose the XSL code within the Web part. You will probably find it easier to copy the code into your favorite editor for modification and then paste the modified code back into the editor to save it. In the Miscellaneous section, you can enter the URL for an external style sheet used by one or more Web parts.

Finally, the Parameters Editor permits the addition of parameters to the Web part.

- **Results Query Options**   The Query Language picker shown in Figure 9-63 appears only if the Show Action Links is check box is not selected in the Miscellaneous section. The default setting, Browser Locale, probably should read "Default" because using the language of the browser locale configuration can be overwritten by a user preference in the search box.

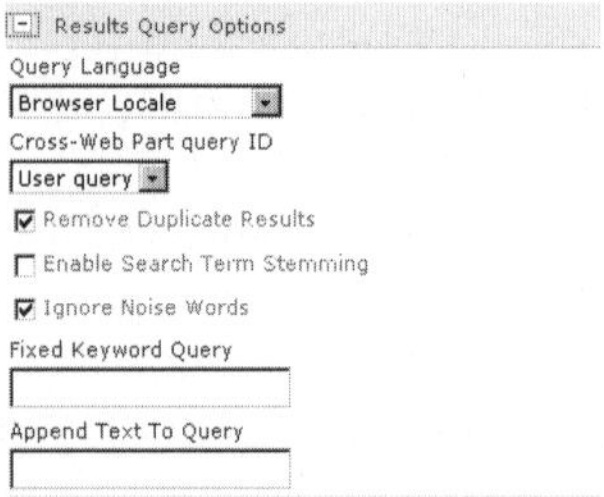

FIGURE 9-63 Results Query Options section.

The Cross-Web Part Query ID picker options are User Query, Query 2, Query 3, Query 4, and Query 5. As discussed earlier in Results Pages Functionality, this ID is used by results Web parts to identify the Query Manager that they share. Web parts with the User Query option selected share the query sent to the results page. Those with Query IDs 2 through 5 share a Fixed Keyword Query and can be placed on any page where they process the query when the page loads.

Remove Duplicate Results causes "duplicate" results to be merged. "Duplicate" in this case does not mean exact matches, particularly in the case of large files, because the crawler indexes only the first 16 megabytes (MB) of a file. Sometimes, if the content is the same, even a variation in file name does not disqualify a file as a duplicate.

You can select Enable Search Term Stemming to link word forms to their base form. For example, variations of "run" include "running," "ran," and "runs." Stemmers are not available for all languages.

When the Ignore Noise Words check box is selected, any words listed in the noise word file for the query language are eliminated from queries. In SharePoint 2010, noise words are indexed and can be used for searches if this option is not selected.

The Fixed Keyword Query text box can specify that the query contain any search term, including filters such as managed properties and scopes. Do not enter anything in this box if using the User Query Cross-Web Part query

ID as the entry will cause the Web part to reject the user query. Core Results Web parts become powerful tools to roll up and display information from across boundaries that restrict other Web parts. For example, a simple entry of "announcements:1" in the Fixed Keyword Query box would cause the Web part to display links to all announcements in the search application index that the user had permissions to see. When placing multiple results Web parts with Fixed Keyword Query entries, they must all use a unique Cross-Web Part query ID.

The value entered in the Append Text To Query text box differs from a value entered in the Fixed Keyword Query box in that it adds the terms and filters to the query entered by the user. Unlike the Additional Query Terms setting of the Search Box Web part, this entry is transparent to the user because it is added on the results page, not passed to the results page as part of the query.

The More Results List Options section (not shown) is irrelevant to Results Web parts on a results page because the page uses the Paging Web part to expose other results. However, if it's used independently on a separate page, you might want to enter a link to a full results page to receive the query and present a full results list.

The Appearance, Advanced, and AJAX Options sections are common to all Web parts and were discussed in Chapter 7. Remember that if you need to target a Web part to an audience, that configuration is found in the Advanced section.

- **Miscellaneous** Appropriately named, the Miscellaneous section, shown in Figure 9-64, contains some vital configurations for this Web part. First, the default 1000 count for the Highest Result Page setting is the count for pages, not items in the result list. Given the default 10 results per page, 10,000 items in a result list is probably more than any user will examine even with the new Refinement Web part filtering capability. Lowering this number when permissible will improve performance.

Discovered definitions appear in the lower portion of the results Web part as "What people are saying about *<term>*". These results are automatically extracted by the linguistic processing built into the indexing process. The process is seeking any phrase that infers a meaning. The smaller your index, the less likely you are to get a discovered definition.

If you deselect the Show Search Results check box and configure the action links, you now have an Action Links Web part. The Search Actions Links Web part does not have this option.

As discussed previously, selecting Show Action Links exposes the action links options in the Location Properties section and hides the Query Language picker in the Results Query Options section.

The Show Messages setting enables the Web part to display error messages if an error occurs. This setting is useful when troubleshooting;otherwise, the Web part might not display at all when it has no results.

The Sample Data setting is present only for testing the XSL presentation, but the XSL Link setting permits centralizing style sheets to control the presentation of multiple Web parts of the same type.

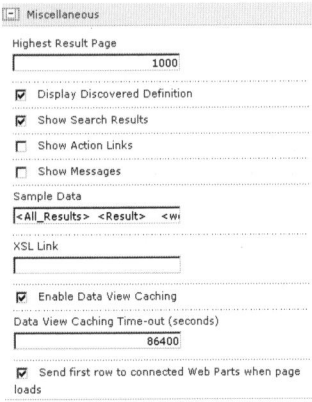

FIGURE 9-64 Miscellaneous

Consider changing the Data View Caching Time-Out setting in a dynamic environment. Although a 24-hour cache improves performance on common queries, it might not present accurate results with frequent crawls.

Search Web parts using the same Cross-Web part Query ID communicate with the Query Manager and not through connections. Although the Send First Row To Connected Web Parts When Page Loads option is selected, it is not required unless you have another Web part to connect to this one. Deselect this option to improve the performance of the Web part.

Federated Result

This Web part is similar to the Core Results Web part, so we will discuss only the differences. It is also used as people matches when using the Local People Search Federated location. First, it is not interacting with the Query Manager for local results but directly sending the query to another OpenSearch 1.1–compliant search engine. Any configurations relevant to manipulating local results are missing.

In Figure 9-60, all configurations in the Location Properties below Description are removed. In Figure 9-62, the Default Results Sorting setting is no longer controlled by the Web part because the results are received already sorted by the search engine. New options, shown in Figure 9-65, are added.

Selected by default, Retrieve Results Asynchronously permits the page to load without waiting for this Web part to receive and display its results. Show Loading Image is not selected by default but will display the animated gif specified in Loading Image URL while the Web part is waiting for a response from the remote search engine. If you want to change this image, place the replacement in the same location as the default.

FIGURE 9-65 Federated Result Web part Display Properties addition.

In Figure 9-63, the only options left in the Results Query Options list are Fixed Keyword Query and Append Text to Query, which operate the same as in the Core Results Web part. For the Miscellaneous section, shown in Figure 9-64, only the configuration options below Show Messages are available.

Top Federated Result

As shown in Figure 9-66, you can configure multiple federated locations for this Web part. However, it displays only the results from the first federated location to return search results. Otherwise, it is a Federated Results Web part.

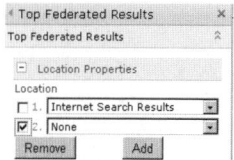

FIGURE 9-66 Top Federated Results location properties.

Search Best Bets

The Best Bets Web part does interact with the Query Manager object, but most of the configurations are substantially different from the Core Results Web part, as shown in Figure 9-67.

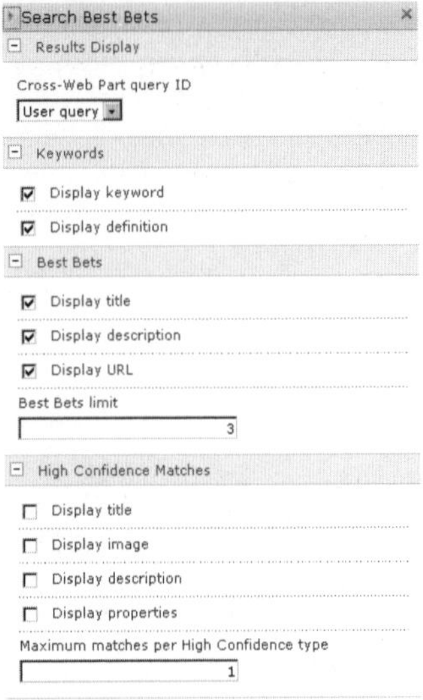

FIGURE 9-67 Best Bets Web part.

The Results Display section has a configuration only for the query ID. This Web part has no configuration for a fixed query, but it will use the fixed query from a results Web part on the page that uses the same query ID even if it is hidden or has no results to display.

For Keywords, choose whether to display the keyword, keyword definitions, or both. For Best Bets, you can modify the display without changing the style sheet. Your options are Display Title, Display Description, Display URL, and Best Bets Limit. Displaying only the description does not give the user a hyperlink to access the Best Bet object.

This Web part was called the High Confidence Results Web part in previous versions of SharePoint Search. This section is configured to display an exact match in a people search. Much of this functionality has been replaced and enhanced by the Local People Search Federated Location, which is used by a Federation Results Web part.

Search Paging

For a search results page, this Web part extends the capabilities of a simple More Results link to a new page by providing a series of paging links before and after the current page of results within the Core Results Web part. Although the Results Web part controls the number of results in each page, the Paging Web part presents a common interface for scrolling through the results set. The properties, shown in Figure 9-68, are straightforward and easy to understand. Labels for the Previous and Next links are probably not necessary, and if you choose to change the images, be sure to place your images in the same location to avoid permissions issues. The only configuration that seems out of place is the Cross-Web part query ID, which is in the Miscellaneous section. This Web part must share the query ID of the Results Web part.

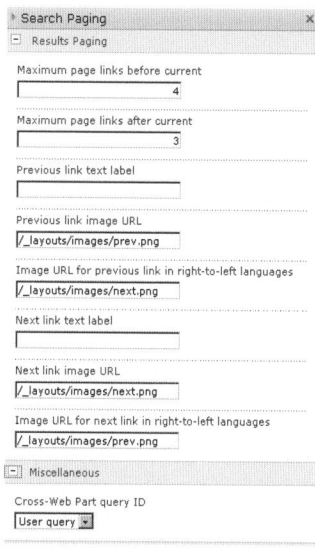

FIGURE 9-68 Search Paging properties.

Search Statistics

The Search Statistics Web part is also easy to understand and configure as shown in Figure 9-69. The display mode options are One Line or Two Lines. Selecting Display Total Number Of Results produces a disturbing "of about ## results."

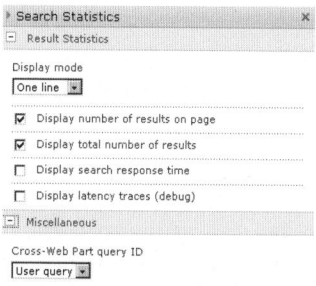

FIGURE 9-69 Search Statistics properties.

This number changes if the user re-sorts the results or scrolls through pages of results. Security trimming of the results list is performed on the results page. With the default potential results list being 10,000 items, the overhead of security trimming the entire list prior to displaying 10 items would be tremendous. So the trimming is done as the items are prepared to be displayed. Because the Statistics Web part total number of results will include items that might be trimmed due to security, the count cannot be accurate until all items are viewed.

If your server response time is really good, you can choose Display Search Response Time. Again, this Web part must share the query ID of the Results Web part.

Related Queries

This Web part displays user queries that contain the term that the current query contains. The more search is used, the more valuable this Query Suggestions tool becomes. The configuration options are very limited, as shown in Figure 9-70. Probably the only change that you might make will be the Results Per Page setting.

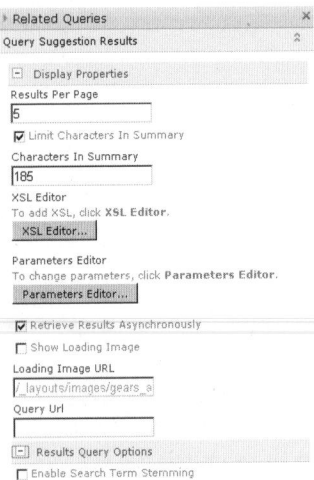

FIGURE 9-70 Related Queries properties.

Search Summary

The simplest Web part to configure is Search Summary, shown in Figure 9-71. Other than the standard Appearance, Layout, and Advanced sections, there is only a Show Messages check box and the Cross-Web Part query ID section. Deceptively named, this Web part is located just below the Search Query Web part and presents terms from the index that are similar to the query term passed to the results page. It is probably most useful for correcting misspelled query terms.

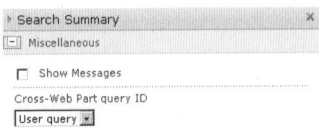

FIGURE 9-71 Search Summary properties.

Refinement Panel

Although the Related Queries Web part presents a tool to expand your query on the right side of the results page, the Refinement Panel on the left side presents dynamic options to refine or drill down into the search results without initiating a new query.

Configuration of this "faceted search" Web part has both simple and complex components. The simple, properties piece is shown in Figure 9-72. For the term Category, think Manage Property.

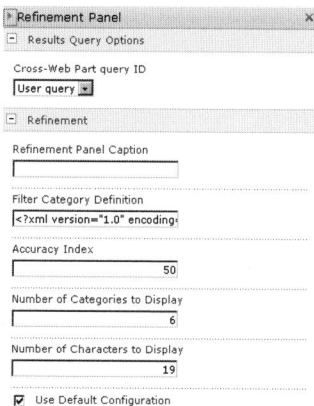

FIGURE 9-72 Refinement Panel properties.

This Web part must share the query ID with the core results Web part. If you prefer to use another name, type it in the Refinement Panel Caption box. We will address the Filter Category Definition setting later. The Accuracy Index setting determines how far down the results list the Web part will collect metadata to use in "faceting" its results. The Number Of Categories To Display setting is straightforward, and the Number Of Characters To Display setting refers to each line in the display. The character count is not exact as the ellipses at the end of an incomplete word counts as two characters.

Editing the Filter Category Definition setting is the more complex part. Before beginning to edit the XML string, clear the Use Default Configuration check box or the Web part will not save your changes.

Place your cursor in the Filter Category Definition text box to activate the Builder text editor blue button. Click the button to open the editor. It will be easier to copy the entire contents and use your favorite XML editor to make changes, and then paste the modified string back into the Builder text editor to save the changes.

The first portion of the code that specifies a category based on file extensions follows:

```xml
<?xml version="1.0" encoding="utf-8" ?>
<FilterCategories>
<Category Title="Result Type" Description="The file extension of the item"
Type="Microsoft.Office.Server.Search.WebControls.ManagedPropertyFilterGener
ator"MetadataThreshold="5" NumberOfFiltersToDisplay="4"
MaxNumberOfFilters="0"SortBy="Frequency" SortDirection="Descending"
SortByForMoreFilters="Name"SortDirectionForMoreFilters="Ascending"
ShowMoreLink="True"MappedProperty="FileExtension" MoreLinkText="show more"
LessLinkText="show fewer">
<CustomFilters MappingType="ValueMapping" DataType="String"
ValueReference="Absolute" ShowAllInMore="False">
  <CustomFilter CustomValue="Word">
  <OriginalValue>doc</OriginalValue>
  <OriginalValue>docm</OriginalValue>
  <OriginalValue>docx</OriginalValue>
  <OriginalValue>dot</OriginalValue>
  <OriginalValue>nws</OriginalValue>
  </CustomFilter>
```

If you have additional file types that are not included in the XML, you can add them by carefully following the structure given, where *CustomValue* is the display name of the application and the multiple entries of *OriginalValue* are all the possible file extensions for this application.

The following string identifies a specific managed property to be used as a facet for filtering search results. This construct can be used to add any custom managed property. Text managed properties must not be stored as a hash to be used in the Refinement Web part. The managed property must also have the Add Managed Property To Custom Results Set Retrieved On Each Query option selected.

```xml
<Category Title="Author" Description="Use this filter to restrict results
authored by a specific author"
Type="Microsoft.Office.Server.Search.WebControls.ManagedProperty
FilterGenerator"MetadataThreshold="5"NumberOfFiltersToDisplay="4"
MaxNumberOfFilters="20"SortBy="Frequency" SortByForMoreFilters="Name"
SortDirection="Descending"SortDirectionForMoreFilters="Ascending"
ShowMoreLink="True"MappedProperty="Author" MoreLinkText="show more"
LessLinkText="show fewer" />
```

Following the examples in the default XML string, even nonprogrammers can easily modify the metadata used to refine the search results if it exists for the objects in the results list.

Use the XSL Editor to customize the style sheet where needed.

Working with Query Reporting

Within the search service and at the site collection level, you can view query activities to help you understand the words and phrases used in search queries and the usage within the results. These reports also assist in determining what sites and keywords to configure as Best Bets. In addition, you might be able to discover how to better train your users in using the search features by learning about their past behavior.

At the site-collection level, Search Web Analytics reports include the following:

- Number of Queries
- Top Queries
- Failed Queries
- Best Bet Usage
- Best Bet Suggestions
- Best Bet Suggestions Action History
- Search Keywords

MORE INFORMATION For more information on Query Reports, see Chapter 14 in SharePoint Server 2010 Administrator's Companion (Microsoft Press, 2010).

Local Search Configuration Options

Site owners and list or library owners have configuration options that have an impact on search results.

Searchable Columns

At the site level, any column created within the site can be excluded from search results. For the root site of a site collection, this means all columns can be managed except those created at a subsite level. At the subsite level, only columns created at that level can be managed.

There is no granularity for this setting. The metadata contained in the column for any object within the site will be affected. To configure these settings, from the Site Actions menu, select Site Settings. On the Site Settings page, under Site Administration, select Searchable Columns to open the page shown in Figure 9-73. Locate the appropriate column, and select the box beside it.

Excluded Columns from Search Indexing	Excluded	Column Name	Group Name
Select columns that will be excluded from search indexing. Values in these columns will not be processed by the search service when items are indexed.	☐	% Complete	Core Task and Issue Columns
	☐	Active	Document and Record Management Columns
	☐	Actual Work	Core Task and Issue Columns
	☐	Address	Core Contact and Calendar Columns
	☐	Aliases	Document and Record Management Columns
	☐	Anniversary	Core Contact and Calendar Columns
	☐	Append-Only Comments	Base Columns
	☐	Article Date	Publishing Columns

FIGURE 9-73 Portion of the Searchable Columns page.

Site-Level Crawl Rules

At the site level, a site owner can set "do not crawl" rules for the entire site and set rules for crawling ASPX pages. To configure these settings, open Site Settings for the site and under the Site Administration heading, click Search And Offline Availability.

In the page shown in Figure 9-74, configure the appropriate indexing settings for the site in the Indexing Site Content section. Although not explicitly stated in the page documentation, the reason that the content does not appear in search results is that it is no longer crawled.

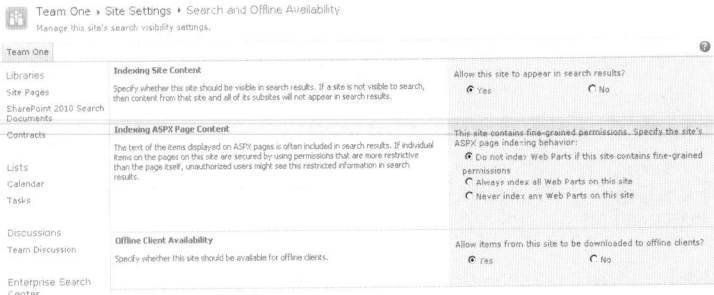

FIGURE 9-74 Search And Offline Availability page.

Frequently, the Web parts on pages expose content from other locations that all users do not have permissions to see. This content can also be crawled from the default location where everyone who can access the page can see all content. To prevent crawling the same content more than once, site owners can configure indexing options for Web parts within the site in the Indexing ASPX Page Content section of this page.

Crawl Options for Lists and Libraries

Each list and library can be configured with crawl rules by users who can manage the list or library. For the list or library, open the settings page and select Advanced settings. The fourth section down is the Search section, shown in Figure 9-75. Selecting No in the Allow Items From This Document Library (List) To Appear In Search Results will set do not crawl rules for the library or list.

FIGURE 9-75 List and library crawl setting.

Related Links Scope

At each site level, site owners can create a collection of contextual scopes that can be used as a single contextual scope at that site level only. Like all scopes, this configuration is stored at the search application level and requires the scope update to run before it is usable.

To open the Manage Search Scope For Related Links page shown in Figure 9-76, open Site Settings for the site and select Related Links Scope Settings under the Site Administration heading.

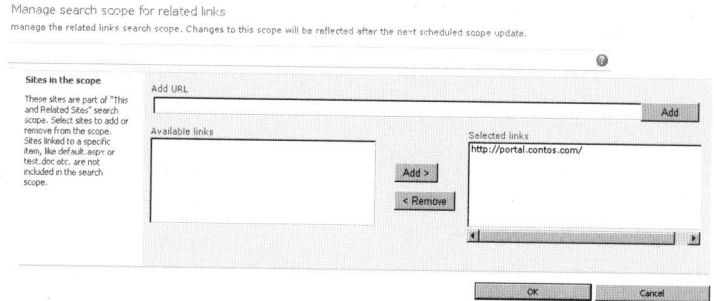

FIGURE 9-76 Manage Search Scope For Related Links page.

Type the full URL of the site in the Add URL box, including the protocol and with a slash "/" at the end. Click Add to add the link to the Selected Links list. Highlighting the URL and selecting Remove will move the link to the Available Links list. As you can see from Figure 9-76, the page will accept invalid URLs, which will simply not be added to the collection of contextual scopes when it is built.

After it is built, the scope will be available in the scope picker for searches only if the drop-down configuration includes contextual scopes. It will be available only for the single site where it was configured. This tool permits site owners a limited capability for building one additional scope for the users of the site.

CHAPTER 10

Enterprise Content Types and Metadata

■ Understanding Enterprise Content Management **329**

■ Configuring the Managed Metadata Service **331**

■ Managed Taxonomies, Folksonomies, and Term Sets **342**

■ Enterprise Content Types **349**

■ Consuming Metadata **351**

Today, enterprise content management (ECM) for many large organizations means managing document storage well into the multi-gigabyte range. Tomorrow, it could mean managing documents and metadata well into the petabytes and, eventually, exabytes. So how do we file away all those mountains of files and still be able to retrieve them in a meaningful manner? The simple answer is to use managed taxonomies via enterprise metadata and enterprise content types. The purpose of this chapter is to help you understand enterprise content types and metadata and how to implement them in Microsoft SharePoint Server 2010.

Understanding Enterprise Content Management

Enterprise content types and metadata are the backbone of data classification, retention, retrieval, and consumption. Many corporations today are committed to understanding the data they own. The ability to strategically or tactically leverage the intellectual property within an enterprise is paramount. For an organization to more efficiently consume the data that it owns, it is critical to establish a taxonomy structure for the classification and organization of this information. *Taxonomy* is described as the science or technique of classifying information. Furthermore, organizations are allowing for the classification of content created by users, who tag information with freely chosen keywords, and for the cooperation among groups of users to create such classifications. This community-based contributed metadata is known as *folksonomy*.

Less than a decade ago, organizations were approaching information retention and classification much differently than today. There were four basic approaches to file retention, as outlined in Table 10-1.

TABLE 10-1 File Retention Types

RETENTION TYPE*	DEFINITION
Structured	Files and other data organized into folders, databases, and offline tapes, disks, or physical files in many locations.
Unstructured	Files stored in user profile spaces, detached drives, USB thumb drives, e-mail .pst files, tapes in personal file cabinets, physical files in personal cabinets, and so forth in many disparate locations.
File share	Network or local file storage locations bound by domain constraints, which are usually established for physical locations in larger corporations. There could be an innumerable amount of file shares for a large corporation. Files shares can be either structured or unstructured, and they are often used to store data that would not need the functionality of SharePoint to maintain.
SharePoint	A central location without domain constraints, either structured or unstructured, that provides the ability to add custom searchable metadata and tagging.

* Each of these approaches has its advantages and disadvantages.

Structured retention follows the basics of taxonomy by classification—files, databases, other offline storage media, and physical files are organized into folders, or libraries with meaningful references. The caveat is that structured retention doesn't take into account the potential need for multiple classifications. Files can be given only one physical location. To overcome this, organizations have resorted to using referential pointers or placeholders. These symbolic links are placed in alternate file locations that are pertinent. However, removal of the files, databases, or original physical media and files can result in the residual effect of bad references not being removed.

Unstructured retention follows the basics of a stack of unfiled papers in the inbox on your desk. Essentially, it's just a stack of data placed in a single location for easy access. Often, a heavy reliance on naming conventions is used to provide some aspect of taxonomy. The limitation here is that only so much data can be captured in the names of files, databases, and folders.

File shares can take on aspects of either structured or unstructured retention. The deviation is that file shares tend to be accessed by multiple people; therefore, organization is the key to creating effective file shares. Using this approach, files are often organized into multiple shares, using the shares themselves as one form of classification and then using the file structure as a second classification. File shares also provide a sense of security and help prevent inadvertent loss of data due to failures on individual machines.

SharePoint incorporates all the aspects of file shares, with several added bonuses. With file shares, the limitation on access is at a physical level. A user needs direct network access or virtual private network (VPN) access to use the files in a share. With SharePoint, that is no longer a constraint. File access is based intrinsically on the rights and permissions of the authenticated user and is constrained only by the ability to connect to the SharePoint Server 2010 site itself. In addition to this, SharePoint has enabled the expanded classification of data. Data repositories are organized into types of data at a high level, but cross classification or links can be created to other pieces of data. This directly correlates to the way relational data is managed in enterprise databases.

In SharePoint 2007, content types were managed at the site-collection level. As a result, a global taxonomy methodology could not be applied to all site collections for an organization by editing one term store[1]. SharePoint Server 2010 introduces expanded use of term sets that are managed at the service-application level. The result is that you have the ability to define universally applicable managed term fields that can be used as attributes to augment navigation, search, sort and filter, policy, and workflow operations. These syndicated[2] metadata[3] lists or classifications can then be applied to any of the aforementioned.

Configuring the Managed Metadata Service

Managed Metadata Services, also known as the *term store*, allows for the organization of terms, lists, and classifications to be leveraged across multiple SharePoint Web applications or site collections. Managed Metadata Services can be published to, or subscribed to, from another SharePoint farm or multiple SharePoint farms. Managed Metadata Services are accessible through Central Administration, Application Management, Manage Service Applications, Managed Metadata Service.

The Managed Metadata Services Content Type Syndication Hub should be created as its own site collection. It can exist in any Web application, but it should be isolated in a dedicated Web application if your hardware is sufficient. Multiple Content Type Syndication Hubs can be used to serve up different subsets of content types, allowing for a great degree of applied customization so that they

---

[1] A central repository for hierarchical term definitions.

[2] Is able to be subscribed to.

[3] Data that describes or otherwise classifies the context of its object.

fit the needs of any organization. Only one syndication hub can be enabled per site collection. In addition to providing the Content Type Syndication Hub, each Managed Metadata Services Application provides a dedicated term store. The term store is capable of servicing one or many term set groups, and each group is able to host one or many term sets.

Creating the Content Type Syndication Hub Web Application

In this section, you will create a dedicated Web application and site collection to serve as the Content Type Syndication Hub. In this example, the Team Site template is used. Perform the following steps:

1. Click the New button on the far left side of the Ribbon. The Create New Web Application dialog box appears. Fill in the appropriate information for the new Managed Metadata Services Internet Information Services (IIS) Web site.

2. Set the appropriate authentication provider and other security configurations.

3. Set the public URL. This should already reflect the Host Header entry that was previously entered in the IIS Web site information.

4. Set the appropriate application pool name, and select its service account, as seen in Figure 10-1.

5. Set the database server, database name, and authentication information.

6. Click OK to create the Web application. After a few moments, the confirmation dialog box appears.

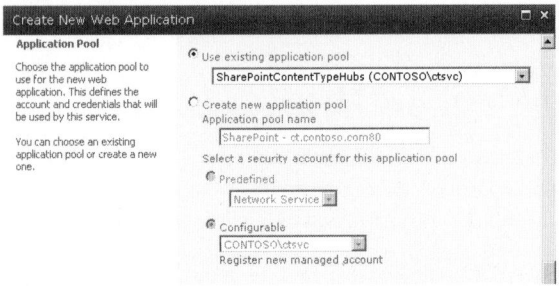

FIGURE 10-1 Setting the application pool for Managed Metadata Services and the Content Type Syndication Hub.

BEST PRACTICES The Content Type Syndication Hub should be isolated in its own application pool within IIS under separate service credentials. The service account must first be configured by clicking the Register New Managed Account link.

Creating the Content Type Syndication Hub Site Collection

The Content Type Syndication Hub is used to manage the content types to be published via the Managed Metadata Service. Site collections within other Web applications subscribe to the central repositories for managed metadata and content types published by the Managed Metadata Service Application. There is a one-to-one relationship between a Managed Metadata Service Application and a Content Type Syndication Hub. However, there can be as many Content Type Syndication Hubs and Managed Metadata Service Applications as needed to fulfill the data management policy needs of an organization. (See Figure 10-2.)

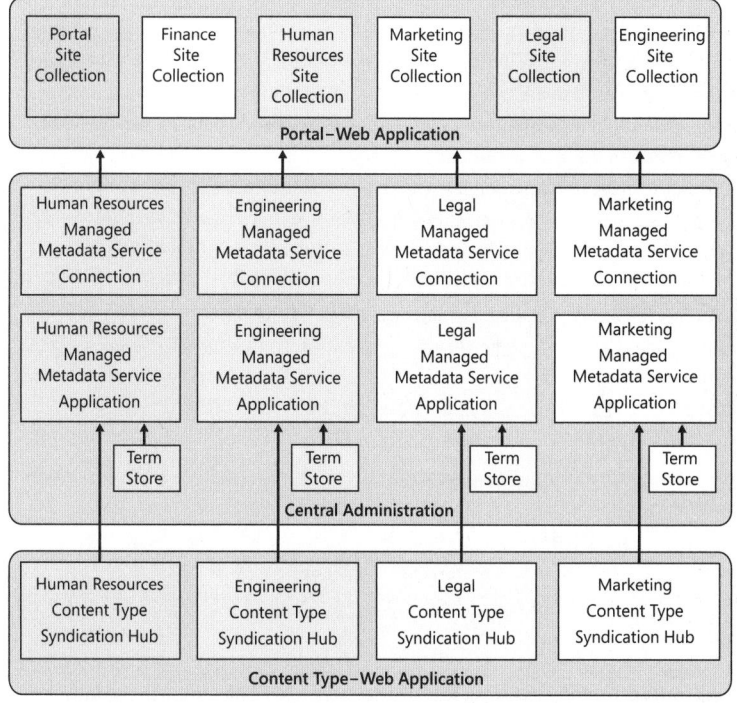

FIGURE 10-2 Example of multiple Content Type Syndication Hubs and Managed Metadata Service Applications.

Managed paths can be created to correlate the management policies of an organization. If an organization has no need for multiple Content Type Syndication Hubs, using an explicit inclusion path to host the Content Type Syndication Hub is acceptable. However, if an organization wants to employ multiple Content Type Syndication Hubs, it would be more appropriate to use a wildcard-inclusion managed path.

Data-retention policies and document templates are prime examples of why an organization might implement multiple Content Type Syndication Hubs. There are many regulatory reasons why organizations might have different data management policies that apply to independent bodies in the organization. The human resources department might need to retain application, resume, and employee records data for seven years; the Sarbanes-Oxley Act (in the USA) requires that financial data be retained for ten years; and for liability reasons, the retention of patent and contracts data might need to extend for up to 20 years.

Marketing or business development departments in an organization might have templates that differ significantly from those used by the legal department; human resources or benefits administrators might have a significant number of specialized document templates to handle the specialized and sometimes sensitive work that they handle. Setting up independent Content Type Syndication Hubs can provide the ability to incorporate specialized document-retention policies, auto-expiration policies that provide significant space reduction without the excessive work of manual purging, and customized and secured document types and templates. These are examples of why you might create multiple Content Type Syndication Hubs. However, keep in mind that although the service is very flexible, you should keep it as simple as possible.

To begin creating this pairing of service application to Content Type Syndication Hub, you should create a site collection in the Content Type Syndication Hub Web application previously created. Site collections can be created from three different locations within Central Administration:

- From the confirmation dialog box that displays immediately after you create the Web application, by clicking the Create Site Collections link
- From the Central Administration main page, by clicking the Create Site Collections link in the Application Management block
- From the Application Management page, by clicking the Create Site Collections link in the Site Collections block

The following steps should be performed to create the Managed Metadata Services site collection:

1. Using one of the methods just listed, open the Create Site Collection page.
2. Select the Web application by clicking the Web application drop-down arrow and selecting the Change Web Application menu item. Choose the appropriate Web application from the list of available Web applications.

3. Type the title and description for the Managed Metadata Services site.

4. Type the name of the primary site collection administrator.

5. Click OK to create the site collection.

Depending on the data management policies and processes within an organization, the complexity of the Content Type Syndication Hubs can be left to the whimsical imagination of the business systems analysts and legal department. Figure 10-3 shows an example of a top-level, data management policy configuration applied to the Content Type Syndication Hubs. Verify that the Content Type Syndication Hub site collection feature has been activated, as shown in Figure 10-4.

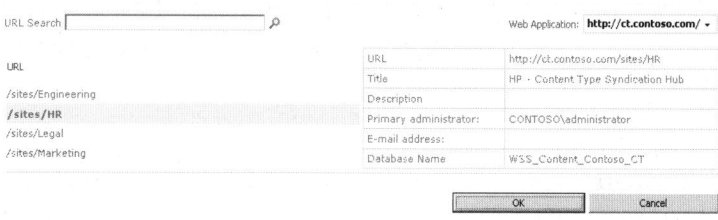

FIGURE 10-3 Example of a complex Content Type Syndication Hub taxonomy.

Activating the Content Type Syndication Hub

Before the new site collection will function as the management engine for content types, you need to activate the site collection feature for the Content Type Syndication Hub.

NOTE The feature should be activated automatically during service application creation. However, it is always wise to verify this feature has been activated.

To do this, open the site collection in a new window and go to the Site Settings page. Within the Site Collection Administration section of the Site Settings page, click the Site Collection Features link. On the Features page, click Active to activate the Content Type Syndication Hub feature, as shown in Figure 10-4.

FIGURE 10-4 Activating the Content Type Syndication Hub on a site collection.

IMPORTANT Activate the Content Type Syndication Hub within the newly created site collection before trying to link it to the service application for Managed Metadata Services. The Managed Metadata Services Application can be created before attaching it to a Content Type Syndication Hub.

Creating the Managed Metadata Service Application

To enable the Content Type Syndication Hub so that the content type data it contains can be consumed by other sites within SharePoint, you need to provision the Managed Metadata Service Application and link it to the Content Type Syndication Hub. The Managed Metadata Service Application can be accessed through Central Administration, Application Management, Manage Services Application.

The Managed Metadata Service Application functions as the publisher for term stores and, optionally, content types created within the Content Type Syndication Hub. Additionally, Managed Metadata Connections consume the data being published from the Managed Metadata Service Application. Both the Content Type Syndication Hub's data and the term stores' data are published by the service application.

Perform the following steps to create a Managed Metadata Service Application:

1. Click the New button on the far left side of the Ribbon, and select Managed Metadata Service. The Create New Managed Metadata Service dialog box appears.

2. Fill in the appropriate name. It is a good practice to intelligently name the Content Type Syndication Hub that will be linked to this Managed Metadata Service. Generally, this is done by filling in the name, title, and description of the Content Type Hub site collection.

3. Fill in the database information. Always name the database to reflect the metadata being stored within this service.

4. Select or create an application pool to handle the publishing of content types and metadata to the Managed Metadata Connections. Specify an appropriate user to obtain the necessary IIS service isolation.

   NOTE Application pools isolate the memory space that a specific service uses; therefore, you might consider evaluating the available memory on the Web front-end servers before configuring these services in isolated application pools.

5. Type the URL for the site collection that contains the Content Type Syndication Hub that is to be published by this Managed Metadata Service Application, as shown in Figure 10-5.

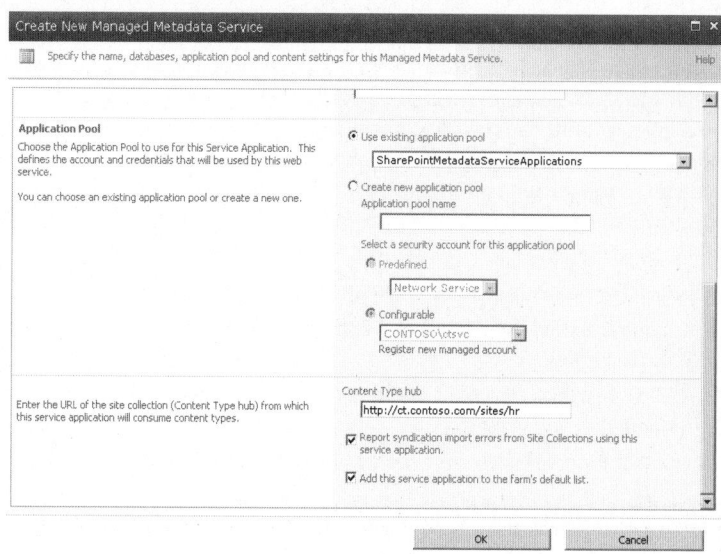

FIGURE 10-5 Managed Metadata Service Application Pool settings with an optional hub link configuration.

The completed creation of Managed Metadata Service Applications should look like Figure 10-6 with respect to the site collections created and displayed in Figure 10-3. Each service application functions as a publisher of the metadata and content types contained within each Content Type Syndication Hub site collection. The Content Type Syndication Hub link in each Managed Metadata Service Application is what ties the site collection's Content Type Syndication Hub to the service application.

Contoso Search Service Application	Search Service Application	Started
Contoso Search Service Application	Search Service Application Proxy	Started
Contoso User Profile and People Services	User Profile Service Application	Started
Contoso User Profile and People Services	User Profile Service Application Proxy	Started
Managed Metadata Service - Engineering	Managed Metadata Service	Started
Managed Metadata Service - Engineering	Managed Metadata Service Connection	Started
Managed Metadata Service - HP	Managed Metadata Service	Started
Managed Metadata Service - HR	Managed Metadata Service Connection	Started
Managed Metadata Service - Legal	Managed Metadata Service	Started
Managed Metadata Service - Legal	Managed Metadata Service Connection	Started
Managed Metadata Services - Marketing	Managed Metadata Service	Started
Managed Metadata Services - Marketing	Managed Metadata Service Connection	Started
Search Administration Web Service for Contoso Search Service Application	Search Administration Web Service Application	Started
Security Token Service Application	Security Token Service Application	Started

FIGURE 10-6 List of Managed Metadata Service Applications.

Modifying the Managed Metadata Service Connection

Along with the Managed Metadata Service Application, SharePoint 2010 establishes the Managed Metadata Service Connection to provide the conduit for Web applications to subscribe to both content types consumed from the Content Type Syndication Hub and also the term sets stored within its term store. The connection can be set as the default service application to handle both managed keywords as well as column-specific term sets. Figure 10-7 shows the management dialog box for the Managed Metadata Service Connection where these settings can be configured.

Perform the following steps to manage these connections:

1. Open Central Administration, Application Management, Manage Service Applications.

2. Click the row to the right of the Managed Metadata Service Connection name that you want to edit.

3. Select Properties from the management Ribbon.

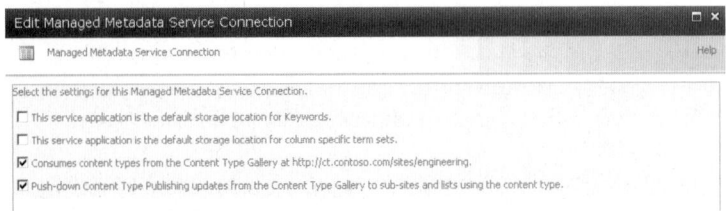

FIGURE 10-7 Editing the Managed Metadata Service Connection.

Associating Managed Metadata Service Applications

Web applications can be directly associated with any and all available Managed Metadata Service Connections. Alternatively, each metadata service application can be added to the default service connection associations' application proxy group.

> **NOTE** During the initial Managed Metadata Service configuration, you have the option of adding it to the default proxy group by selecting the check box that referenced the default service connections list (also known as the default proxy group).

The list of default service connections can be changed from Central Administration, Application Management, Configure Service Application Associations. If you select the default link, you are presented with the dialog box to modify the selected default associations.

CAUTION Be sure to exercise caution when changing associations! If you remove the association a Web application had to a service application that was in use, you are affecting all functionality in the given Web application. For example, if there were columns that depended on the associated service application, those columns will cease to function properly.

Figure 10-8 shows the associations enabled for a Web application. Custom connection selections can be made for each Web application. You can use the associations wholesale or create a custom set of associations by specifying a custom group of connections from the drop-down menu. There are two methods that can be used to get to the associations:

- You can manage service connections through the Manage Web Applications section of Central Administration. To accomplish this, do the following:
    1. Select a Web application by clicking it.
    2. Select Service Connections from the Ribbon.

- You can access the Configure Service Application Associations section through the Application Management page on the Service Applications section of Central Administration.
    1. Select Configure Service Application Associations from the Service Applications section.
    2. Select the application in which to manage the associations by clicking its name under the heading Web Application / Service Application.

The Configure Service Application Associations dialog box is displayed as seen in Figure 10-8. The only way to change selections is to specify a custom group of connections. You can create custom groups via Windows PowerShell, as seen in the Appendix, "Working with Windows PowerShell and SharePoint 2010."

FIGURE 10-8 The Configure Service Application Associations dialog box.

Publishing the Managed Metadata Service Application

The Managed Metadata Service Application must be published before the metadata can be consumed by interfarm Web applications. It is not required that the service application be consumed from a Web application within the same farm. Figure 10-9 displays the publishing dialog box used to extend this capability. To publish the service applications for interfarm consumption, perform the following steps:

1. Navigate to Manage Service Applications in Central Administration.

2. Select a Web application by clicking its row in the white space to the right of the application name.

3. Click Publish on the Ribbon.

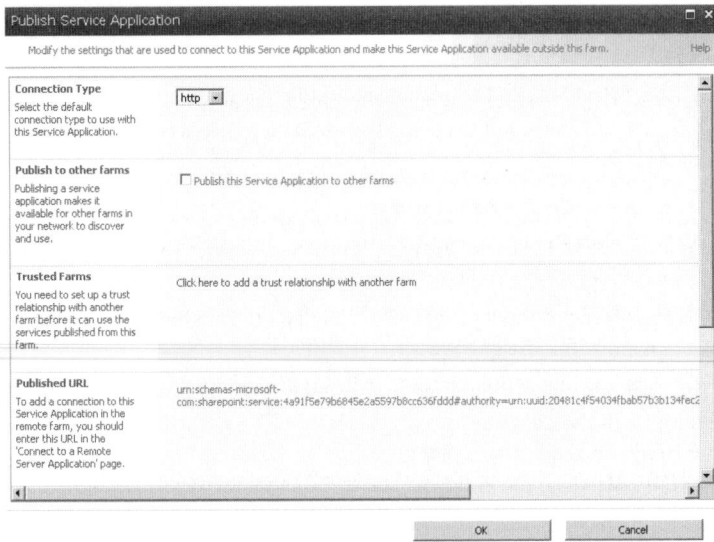

FIGURE 10-9 The Publish Service Application dialog box.

4. Enable the ability for metadata services for interfarm consumption by selecting the Publish This Service Application To Other Farms check box.

A trust relationship needs to be established with the remote farm. You can use the wizard to do this, or you can specify the Web application pool identify from the consuming Web application in the Service Application Permissions page. Note the difference between the Administrators and Permissions groups on the management Ribbon. Administrators administer the service application, while the Permissions section defines accounts that can consume the service application.

The remote farm uses a unique published URL similar to that shown in the following code sample to establish communication with the service application:

```
urn:schemas-microsoft-com:sharepoint:service:4a91f5e79b6845e2a5597b8cc
636fddd#authority=urn:uuid:2481c4f54034fbab57b3b134fec29d0&authority=
https://dc01.contoso.com:32844/Topology/topology.svc
```

Starting the Managed Metadata Web Service

After configuring the Managed Metadata Service Application, you must define what physical server will service the application within the farm. Creating the Managed Metadata Service Application makes the service application available throughout the farm, but you must next define where the processing will occur. If you do not perform this last step, the content types, managed keywords, and term sets will not be available to any Web applications within the farm.

IMPORTANT The Managed Metadata Services will not work on the SharePoint farm until the Managed Metadata Web Service has been started on at least one server within the farm.

To start these services, browse to Central Administration, System Settings, Manage Services On Server. The Services On Server page will be displayed where you can perform the following:

1. Select the server that you will be managing from the Servers drop-down menu at the top of the page.

2. Find the Managed Metadata Web Service reference, and click the Start link on the rightmost side of that page.

Administrators for Management Metadata Services

Administrators of the Managed Metadata Service can be specified, as shown in Figure 10-10, by clicking on the area to the right of the Managed Metadata Service Application name and then selecting Administrators from the Ribbon. *By default, users added as administrators for Management Metadata Services will have limited access to Central Administration.* Farm administrators already have rights to manage all service applications.

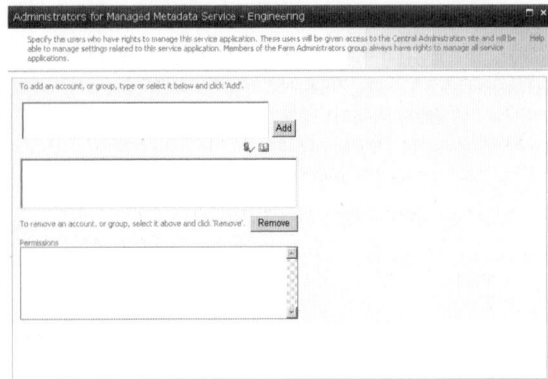

FIGURE 10-10 Adding administrators for Managed Metadata Services.

Managed Taxonomies, Folksonomies, and Term Sets

Managed taxonomies are collections of term sets, managed content types, and keywords that are provided through the Managed Metadata Services. *Global taxonomies* can employ the community for modification and maintenance of the terms within the term store. The result of this process is known as *folksonomies* because of the community involvement in the management of terms.

Term sets are used within taxonomies to organize the terms into meaningful categories. Term sets are maintained as members of groups within the term store. These groups allow for isolated security settings for each term group, and therefore provide for the flexible assignment of maintenance tasks and contributing parties.

Enterprise Metadata: The Term Store

The term store is the central repository for the hierarchical representation of terms that can be used through syndication to classify data stored within SharePoint Server 2010. The subscription of terms can be used for data classification, retention, retrieval, and consumption. The term store provides a vehicle for the management of these terms and their hierarchical structure, groups, and relationships.

Corporate taxonomies are often not maintained as a global policy but rather by the community haphazardly tagging content with whatever terms they can think of at the time. This approach provides a degree of separation and a potentially high degree of gaps in search results. To provide for more succinct management of terms and still provide for community involvement, the term store incorporates a mix of managed taxonomy and contributed folksonomy to the definition of the term sets.

Managed Metadata Roles

SharePoint 2010 has four distinct roles for managed metadata. These roles are defined specifically for the interaction with the term store. The purpose of role-based abstraction is to facilitate the granular permission sets that can exist in both taxonomy policy use as well as creation. Roles are the distinct barriers in the permission policy and provide the framework for security.

The benefit is the ability for corporate user communities to participate in both the consumption of these terms and in the creation and refinement of the term sets. Who better to know which categorical specifics are needed to organize the mountains of data than the corporate community itself? This logic parallels that of the contributor and consumer roles that have been in place for other content within SharePoint.

Table 10-2 identifies the specific roles available for the term store and the actions that each group of users can perform.

TABLE 10-2 Managed Metadata Roles and Capabilities

ROLE	CAPABILITIES
Contributor	■ Create, rename, copy, reuse, move, and delete term sets. ■ Modify a term set's properties. ■ Create, rename, copy, reuse, merge, deprecate, move, and delete terms. ■ Modify a term's properties.
Group manager	■ Perform all actions available to the contributor role. ■ Import term sets. ■ Assign users to or remove users from the contributor role. ■ Modify the term set's properties.
Term store administrator	■ Perform all actions available to the group manager role. ■ Create and delete term groups. ■ Assign users to or remove users from the group manager role. ■ Modify the term store properties.
Farm administrator	■ Create a new term store. ■ Connect to an existing term store. ■ Assign users to or remove users from the term store administrator role.

Assigning Term Store Administrators

You also have the flexibility of defining different administrators for each term store. Similar to the permissions associated with content owners or Content Type Syndication Hub site owners, Term Store Administrators (as seen in Figure 10-11) can create new term set groups, assign users to the group manager role, and import metadata terms. Users who have been assigned to the group manager role are able to add terms to the term store.

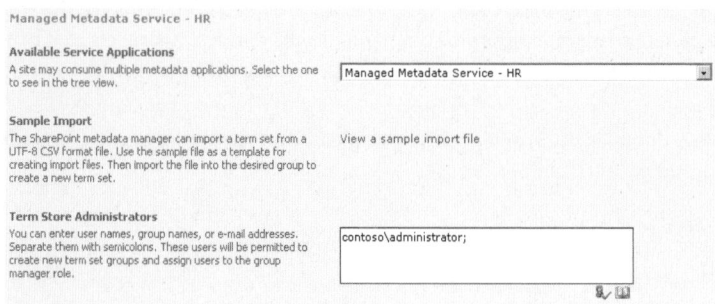

FIGURE 10-11 Assigning term store administrators.

The Term Store Management Tool

SharePoint 2010 includes the Term Store Management Tool. This tool is used to manage terms and term sets. There are few basic processes that should become second nature while working in the term store.

Metadata Groups

Term sets, also referred to as *metadata groups*, are organized into groups that define a hierarchy and serve as a permissions handler for the term sets that are contained within them. A folksonomy depends on the contributions of an organization's general community to keep it up to date. By using groups, you can compartmentalize the assignment of rights, and allow a greater degree of flexibility to the contributing agents. To create a new term set group, do the following:

1. Click the Managed Metadata Service link in the Service Applications list.

2. Highlight the Managed Metadata Service Name on the leftmost navigation pane of the Term Store Management Tool.

3. Select New Group from the drop-down menu. The cursor focuses automatically on the new unnamed group so that you can then type the new group's name.

   TIP If you do not see the drop-down arrow when selecting an object, be sure the Central Administration URL is included in your Local Intranet sites.

To delete a term set group, highlight the group name and select Delete Group from the drop-down menu. This is a permanent action, so use caution when deleting term store groups. All term sets and the included hierarchy will also be deleted.

Managed Term Set

Term sets are child elements under the term set groups. There can be one or many term sets assigned to a term set group. To create a managed term set, do the following:

1. Highlight the group name.
2. Select New Term Set from the drop-down menu.
3. To modify the term set properties, click the term set and modify the properties on the rightmost panel.
4. Define the stakeholders. Stakeholders are people who should be notified that changes are going to be made to a term set.
5. Finally, the submission policy can be used to prevent a term set from being edited, with the exception of term sets that are managed by the term store administrator role.

> **NOTE** The person defined as the term set contact does not have modification permissions. However, if a contact is specified for a term set, site users can make suggestions about the term set and the defined contact will be notified via e-mail about the suggestion. If you do not want to use the feedback feature, leave this field blank.

Managed Terms

Terms can be either the direct child of the top-level term set identifier or another term. The entire term's contextual hierarchy describes the meaning of the term. In the following example, the term *Red*, by itself, means nothing; however, when the term is put into context the meaning becomes clearer. Figure 10-12 shows an example of a contextual hierarchy that self-describes the term *Red*.

FIGURE 10-12 A term's contextual hierarchy.

As you can see in Figure 10-12, the term *Red* can have very different meanings! To create a new term from the user interface, do the following:

1. Highlight the term set or term that will be the parent, and select Create Term from the drop-down menu.

2. Press Enter, or click anywhere on the screen.

After you type text for the term's label, the Term Store Management Tool automatically begins to create another term as a sibling to the one just created. This automated action is intended to allow for the rapid creation of terms at the same level. If you do not need to create the next new term, you can click on any other term, term set, group, or property area to remove the partially created term.

> **NOTE** A term can be disabled within tagging tools. This capability can be useful if a term is being modified, is no longer needed, or is used only temporarily.

Arranging Managed Terms or Term Sets into a Hierarchy

Taxonomy is more than a way of organizing terms to classify and tag data. One of the most important aspects of managed terms with respect to taxonomy is the ability to arrange them into a cascading hierarchy. This arrangement provides a self-describing term set with which to associate navigation, search, sort and filter, policy, and workflow operations. The following options are available for arranging your hierarchy:

- To copy a term or term set, highlight the term or term set name and select the Copy Term [<Set>] from the drop-down menu. The term or term set is duplicated at the same level as its source. The name of the new term or term set is prepended with Copy of.

- To copy a term with all its child terms, highlight the term and select Copy Term With Children from the drop-down menu. This duplicates all child terms to the new term. Remember to rename the new term copy after duplication.

- To search and verify that terms are not being duplicated, you can use the Reuse Term Or Term Set functionality.

- To merge terms, highlight the term and select Merge Term from the drop-down menu. Doing this removes the term that is being merged, and all content that has been tagged with this term still references the legacy term. To account for this, the term being merged is added to the other labels of the destination term.

> **WARNING** After terms are merged, the other label cannot be deleted.

- To deprecate a term, highlight the term and select Deprecate Term from the drop-down menu. Doing this discontinues the use of the term and removes it from availability for tagging. This procedure does not remove all references to the term, and the term can still be used for search and backward compatibility.

- To move a term or term set, highlight the term or term set and select Move Term [<Set>] from the drop-down menu. Select the new parent for the term or term set for the term being moved, or select the new group for the term set being moved.

NOTE A term cannot be moved under the seventh-level terms in a term set. Only seven levels are allowed in the term set hierarchy.

Term Synonyms

The ability to refer to a term by another name provides the contributors the ability to tag content with terms comfortable to them. It gives you the ability to provide a grouping within the synonyms for navigation, search, sort and filter, policy, and workflow operations. Term synonyms can be defined by doing the following:

1. Select the term to modify, and open its properties.
2. Locate the Other Labels area of the properties, and enter synonyms for the term.
3. Save the term by clicking the Save button at the bottom of the dialog box.

NOTE Only one label can be entered per line. Press Enter to add a new line.

Keywords

Keywords are independent terms that have no hierarchical precedence. As a result, they are wholly independent of any term set and have no parents or child terms. They are meant to remain independent and can be added or maintained only by the term store administrator.

- To create a new keyword, highlight Keywords and select New Keyword from the drop-down menu.

- To delete a keyword, highlight the keyword and select Delete Keyword from the drop-down menu.

Converting Managed Keywords into Managed Terms

You can convert managed keywords into managed terms by moving them from the keywords set into a term set. Doing this removes the term from the keywords set and allows it to subsequently have child terms assigned to it. The term automatically inherits the permissions of the term set that it is assigned to. To move the keyword into a term set, do the following:

1. Highlight the keyword.
2. Select Move Keyword from the drop-down menu.
3. Select the new parent for the term for the keyword being moved.

Importing Managed Term Sets

Although terms sets can be created by using the Term Store Management Tool via the user interface, a large and complex hierarchy is very time consuming to create. For mature taxonomies, you should use the importing functionality.

The term store allows for only seven levels of hierarchy within a taxonomy set. Specific column information about an import file is located in Table 10-3 and an example is shown in the code block that follows the table.

TABLE 10-3 Import Term Set File Format*

COLUMN	ADDITIONAL INFORMATION
Term Set Name	The term set name.
Term Set Description	The term set description.
LICD	The locale identifier that represents the language of the term set. For example: 1033 – English.
Available for Tagging	Set to TRUE to allow users to use the term. Set to FALSE to prevent users from using the term.
Term Description	An optional description for the term.
Level 1–7 Terms	The seven columns of the term hierarchy. You must provide a value for all levels down to the level of the term that you are representing.

* The term set import file format is a .csv file that contains only 12 columns. Name and Description columns can be encapsulated in quotes as shown in the code sample that follows.

The code sample shown next is an example of a term set import file. Although there is no data represented down to the seventh level of abstraction, be aware that the commas are required to notate the hierarchy. All parent levels are required for proper classification within the term set. The LCID is the language code that the term set is written in. The *Available for Tagging* Boolean field designates whether the term is available for discovery during tagging for navigation, search, sort and filter, policy, and workflow operations.

```
"Term Set Name","Term Set Description","LCID","Available for Tagging","Term
Description","Level 1 Term","Level 2 Term","Level 3 Term","Level 4
erm","Level 5 Term","Level 6 Term","Level 7 Term"
"Sites","Locations where the organization has offices",,TRUE,,,,,,,,
"Locations",,1033,TRUE,,"North America",,,,,,
"Locations",,1033,TRUE,,"North America","Washington",,,,,
"Locations",,1033,TRUE,,"North America","Washington","Redmond",,,,
"Locations",,1033,TRUE,,"North America","Washington","Seattle",,,,
"Locations",,1033,TRUE,,"North America","Washington","Tacoma",,,,
"Locations",,1033,TRUE,,"North America","Massachusetts",,,,,
"Locations",,1033,TRUE,,"North America","Massachusetts","Boston",,,,
"Locations",,1033,TRUE,,"North America","Massachusetts","Cambridge",,,,
"Locations",,1033,TRUE,,"Europe","England","London",,,,
"Locations",,1033,TRUE,,"Europe","Germany","Berlin",,,,
"Locations",,1033,TRUE,,"Europe","Austria","Vienna",,,,
```

Enterprise Content Types

Content types allow you to separate the declaration of list metadata from the list itself so that you can reuse the same metadata in multiple columns. List metadata is the collection of fields associated with each column in the list. Content types consist of site columns, which in turn are bound to fields.

To understand content types in the context of document management, you might find it helpful to think of each document as an item in a list in which the list columns map to document properties. This is a fundamental concept—that document properties map directly to site column definitions. SharePoint Server 2010 uses the site column definitions to create document properties, to copy data to and from documents as they move into and out of SharePoint document libraries, to associate information management policies and templates with documents, and to manage the state of workflow instances that might be associated with a given document. This ability to capture workflow state extends the scope of content types to include document behavior as well as static properties.

Creating Content Types

Content types are site-collection scoped. In this chapter, we are referring to the Content Type Syndication Hub site collection. To create a new enterprise content type, complete the following steps:

1. Browse to the Content Type Syndication Hub—for example, *http://ct.contoso.com/.*

2. From Site Actions, select Site Settings.

3. Select Site Content Types in the Galleries grouping.

4. Click Create. You should now see the New Site Content Type page as shown in Figure 10-13.

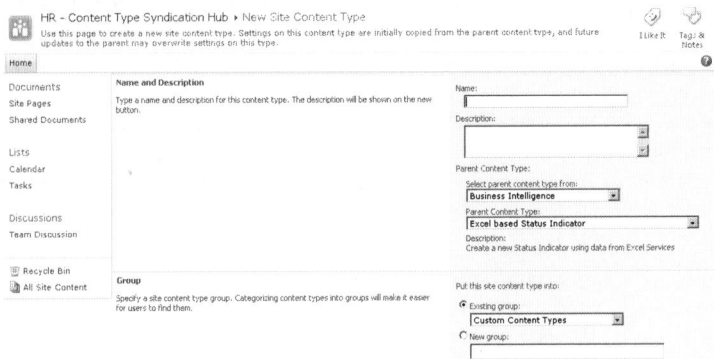

FIGURE 10-13 Creating a new site content type.

5. Type a name and description for the new content type into the appropriate fields.

6. Choose an existing content type as the parent by selecting it from the Select Parent Content Type From drop-down list. To locate the parent type and then filter the list by group, use the Parent Content Type drop-down menu. Every content type is derived either from the base system content type or from one of its child types. This built-in inheritance mechanism enables one content type to extend its functionality by incorporating all the columns declared in its parent.

NOTE If you'll use the content type in a document library, the Document content type must be in the prior lineage. Otherwise, you will not be able to use the content type in a library. For example, if you are inheriting from the HR content type for a policy template, HR must be inherited from Document.

7. To make it easier for users to find your new content type, select an existing group or type the name of a new group that best describes how your content type is to be used.

8. Click OK to return to the Site Content Type summary page.

NOTE After the content type has been created, you can add the columns that best describe the metadata you want to use in your documents. Use the Add From Existing Site Columns link to select from the existing site columns, or create a new column if the existing columns do not meet your needs.

Dealing with Content Type Dependencies

Content types can be based on other content types. When changes are made to a parent content type, those changes are not reflected automatically in child content types that derive from it unless those changes are explicitly pushed down to the derived content types. Pushing down the changes from a parent content type to its child types means that the schema associated with each child is overwritten with the new schema defined in the parent. Because the Document Information Panel (DIP) is stored as an embedded XML document within the content type schema, pushing down the schema also overwrites any custom DIP that might be associated with the child content type. You can prevent this overwriting by marking the child content type as sealed. Sealed content types are not affected by push-down operations. To mark content type as sealed, perform the following steps:

1. Open the Site Content Type page from Galleries within Site Settings.
2. Select the content type by clicking its name.
3. Click the Advanced Settings link.
4. From the Site Content Type Advanced Settings page, select the Yes option button in the Read Only section.
5. Click OK to save the changes.

Consuming Metadata

Metadata is of little use unless it can be consumed by SharePoint Server 2010 at the site-collection level. The most useful taxonomy would be without merit if not for the columns, navigation, search, sort and filter, policy, and workflow operations that make up the consumption of its data. Managed metadata as consumed by document libraries and lists is the embodiment of a successful taxonomy policy.

The majority of consumption circles around site columns because these provide the basis for filtering and navigation. Tagging is also pertinent to the consumption of metadata. Search, workflow, and policy operations are consumers of the columnar and tag information.

Working with Site Columns

SharePoint Server 2010 ships with a default collection of predefined site columns. These site columns are organized into groups that map loosely to the way each column is typically used. To see the available site columns, browse to the Site Columns gallery, which is found under Site Actions, Site Settings, Site Columns in the Galleries grouping.

From the Site Columns gallery, you can view or edit the definition of existing columns or create new columns for the site you are currently viewing. The name of the column appears as a hyperlink under the Site Column heading. If a column name does not appear as a hyperlink, it means that the column is declared in a parent site of the site you are viewing. To modify column definitions declared within a parent site, you must first go to the parent site and then to its Site Columns gallery. To modify an existing column definition, click its hyperlink.

NOTE Columns created in the Site Columns gallery are available only within the current site and subsites.

From the New Site Column page, you can specify the name, data type, and group affiliation for the new column. Although every column belongs to a group, the groups are used only to organize the columns. You can change the group affiliation at any time. In practice, you often need to use columns from many different groups when creating a new content type. Although the New Site Column page contains a Description text box that can hold informative text about how a given field should be used, the built-in site columns do not make use of this property. It is good practice, however, to include a brief description when creating new site columns to make it easier to match a given column to its intended use.

TIP When choosing an existing site column, you should be aware that this list includes both sealed and unsealed columns that have been added by various features that have been enabled on your site. Using sealed site columns might cause problems with your content type declarations because they cannot be removed through the user interface once they have been added to a content type. This problem is exacerbated when modifying an existing content type from which other content types have been derived. Table 10-4 lists some of the sealed columns that are added by the publishing feature. Use caution when adding them to custom content types.

TABLE 10-4 Sealed Site Columns Added by the Publishing Feature

COLUMN NAME	COLUMN GROUP
Article Date	Publishing Columns
Contact	Publishing Columns
Contact E-mail Address	Publishing Columns
Contact Name	Publishing Columns
Contact Picture	Publishing Columns
Scheduling Start Date	Publishing Columns
Scheduling End Date	Publishing Columns

COLUMN NAME	COLUMN GROUP
Target Audiences	Publishing Columns
Byline	Page Layout Columns
Image Caption	Page Layout Columns
Page Content	Page Layout Columns
Page Icon	Page Layout Columns
Page Image	Page Layout Columns
Rollup Image	Page Layout Columns
Summary Links	Page Layout Columns
Summary Links 2	Page Layout Columns

Managed Metadata Site Columns

In addition to having a collection of predefined site columns, custom site columns can be added to augment the tagging of list and document data. Custom columns can be added to any list within SharePoint. A custom site column can be enabled to consume managed metadata. Perform the following steps to begin creating a custom managed metadata site column:

1. Open the list or document library to which you want to add the column.
2. Click the Library Tab under Library Tools.
3. Click the Library Settings button on the far right on the management Ribbon, as shown in Figure 10-14.
4. Under the Columns section, click Create Column.

FIGURE 10-14 A document's Library tab on the management Ribbon.

5. The Create Column page opens, as shown in Figure 10-15.
6. Type the Column name.
7. Select the Managed Metadata option from the type of information list. This enables the managed term list selection area.

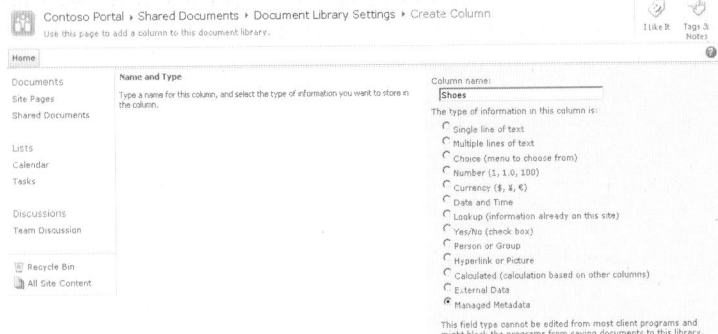

FIGURE 10-15 Creating the Managed Metadata site column.

8. Configure the additional properties, including Description, Require That This Column Contains Information, Enforce Unique Data, and Add To Default View.

NOTE If you select Yes for the Require That This Column Contains Information, the DIP as well as uploaded metadata information forms will require that the Metadata field be populated.

9. Make sure to select the Allow Multiple Values check box if you need to allow multiple value inputs in the metadata field.

10. Select the appropriate Display value. The Display value can be either the term label or the entire term hierarchical path.

11. Select a managed term set, as shown in Figure 10-16. The search field is provided to aid in this process by filtering the term sets listed by the search entry parameter, as shown in Figure 10-17. Only one term set can be selected. You can also edit a new term set in the term store management tool.

12. You can also type a default value for the column. The choice list is populated with the data retrieved from the term set.

It is important to understand the significance of selecting the managed term sets in the Managed Metadata column. The use of a managed term set provides a central location where changes can be made to the column selection or tagging data. Regardless of which list or document library uses the column for classification purposes, all data across the entire site will be synchronized. This is the fundamental change in global taxonomy policies that the term store has empowered within SharePoint Server 2010. Data isn't isolated within a single site collection; therefore, it does not need to be duplicated to exist symbiotically in another site collection or Web application. Data changes automatically flow across all consumer sites with minimal administrative effort. The only step you need to take to use this data is to select it for consumption by the Managed Metadata column, as shown in Figure 10-16.

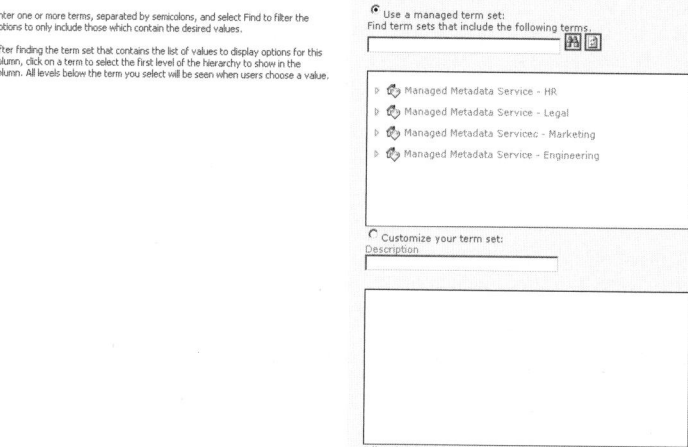

FIGURE 10-16 Using a managed term set.

To make this selection of data even easier, the ability to search the available term stores for the correct term reference filters out all the unmatched term sets, and it minimizes the potential for improper term set selection. Figure 10-17 shows a filtered term set result where *Red* was entered in the search field. *Red* matches both the Shoes term set and the Locations term set, although "Locations" is a partial word match.

NOTE Search filtering returns even partial label matches.

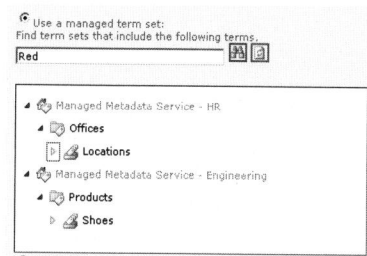

FIGURE 10-17 Filtered managed term set list for the selection of a term set.

Managed Metadata and the Document Information Panel

Gathering document metadata is an important part of an effective document management solution. However, most users focus on the document content and not the metadata. Consequently, important metadata is often captured inconsistently or not at all. Document Information Panels (DIPs) help avoid this problem by enabling users to enter metadata at any time during the editing process and also by enforcing the entry of data values for required fields.

Document Information Panels are displayed in Professional and Enterprise versions of the Microsoft Office System. These client applications support integrated enterprise content management features, and they automatically generate a default DIP for any document that is created or opened from within a Windows SharePoint Services document library. The data fields in the form are derived from the content type associated with the document. SharePoint Server adds the option of creating a custom DIP using Microsoft Office InfoPath 2007. Although you are limited to one custom DIP per content type, each DIP can contain multiple views.

Using the Default Document Information Panel

When you are saving a document to SharePoint, the managed metadata columns that require input are displayed in the upload form. These fields are also part of the DIP for all documents opened from SharePoint within the respective documents library. When a document is opened from SharePoint that is missing required fields within the DIP, a warning is displayed, as shown in Figure 10-18.

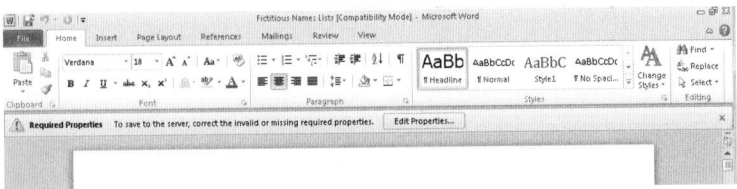

FIGURE 10-18 A Required Properties warning for the Document Information Panel.

At any time, the Edit Properties button can be clicked from the Required Properties warning and the full Document Information Panel will be displayed. Required fields are noted with a red asterisk. Figure 10-19 shows an example of a managed metadata column that has been added to the documents library in SharePoint. The button next to the column opens a selection dialog box where terms can be selected from the term set being consumed by the document library for tagging.

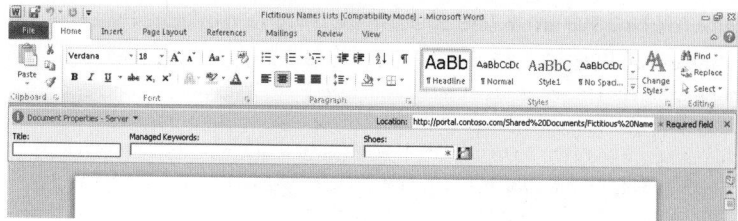

FIGURE 10-19 An example of the Document Information Panel.

Depending on the settings within the Managed Metadata column, the selection dialog box allows for either one selection or multiple-choice selections. The resulting metadata can be displayed as either the label or the entire label path. Perform the following steps to select the appropriate term labels for tagging:

1. Click the button next to the field name in the DIP. The dialog box shown in Figure 10-20 opens.
2. Click the name of the term label.
3. Click the Select button.

   NOTE If the column settings allow for multiple selections, steps 2 and 3 can be performed as many times as needed to appropriately tag the document.

4. Click OK when you are done.

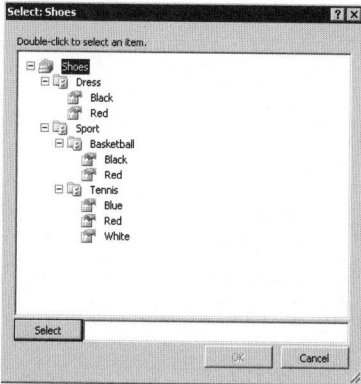

FIGURE 10-20 Term Label Selection dialog box.

The same columns that are displayed within the Document Information Panel are also displayed during the file upload into the document library, as shown in Figure 10-21. Required fields are highlighted with a red asterisk.

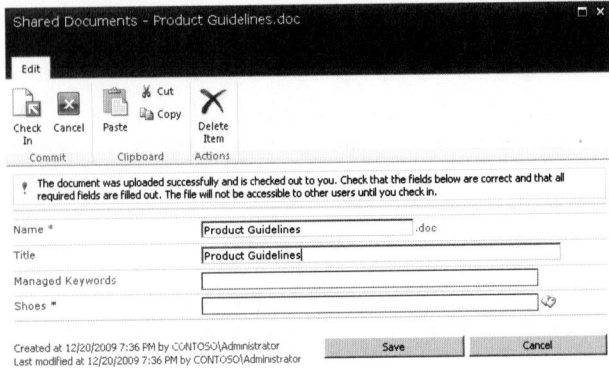

FIGURE 10-21 Document upload properties.

The document tagging operates similarly to that of the Document Information Panel. Depending on the column settings, either one value or many values can be selected to tag the document. Figure 10-22 is the dialog box displayed while selecting term labels to tag the document with.

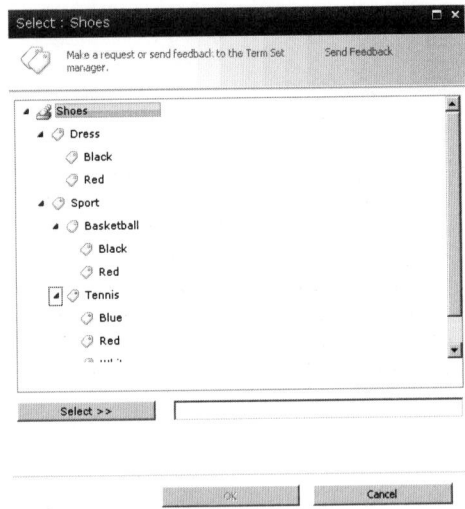

FIGURE 10-22 Term Label Selection dialog box during file upload.

Creating a Custom Document Information Panel

You can create a custom DIP either from the SharePoint user interface or from within the Microsoft Office InfoPath application. To create a DIP from the SharePoint user interface, perform the following steps:

1. Go to the Content Type Settings page for the document content type you want to edit. Click the Change Document Information Panel Settings link.

   TIP Only the Business Intelligence, Document, Publishing, and Page Layout content types have the Document Information Panel Settings link.

2. From the Document Information Panel Settings page (shown in Figure 10-23), link or upload the new InfoPath template.

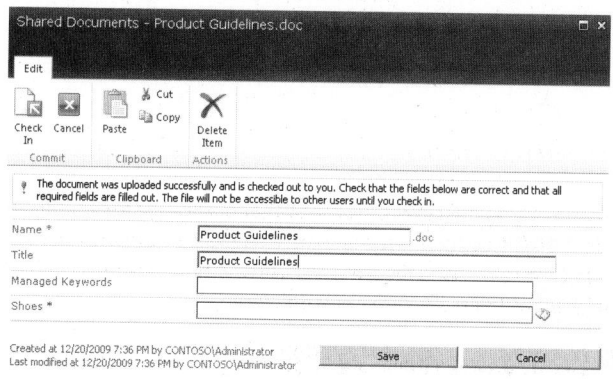

FIGURE 10-23 The Document Information Panel settings.

NOTE You have the option of uploading DIP templates directly or to publish them to a different location and then link them using the URL, UNC, or URN. SharePoint Server updates the content type to reference the location you choose. If you publish to a location other than the content type resource folder used by the Upload procedure, additional security restrictions might be applied to the form that cause it to open in Restricted mode. In that case, the data connections between the form and SharePoint Server might not work properly. To ensure that the form opens in Full Trust mode, either digitally sign the form or create a Windows Installer that registers the form on each client machine.

Metadata Navigation Settings

Metadata navigation can be enabled on any list in SharePoint. This provides linking to managed terms that are being referenced in Managed Metadata columns within the list. By default, content types and folders are available for a list. A Managed Metadata column must be enabled on a list for the metadata to be used as a navigational hierarchy. You can configure metadata navigation by browsing to Document Or List, Library Or List Tools, Library Or List, Library Or List Settings and selecting Metadata Navigation Settings under General Settings to display the page as shown in Figure 10-24. The Configure Key Filters area also enables the list to be filtered in views by the metadata noted in the Available Key Filter Fields area.

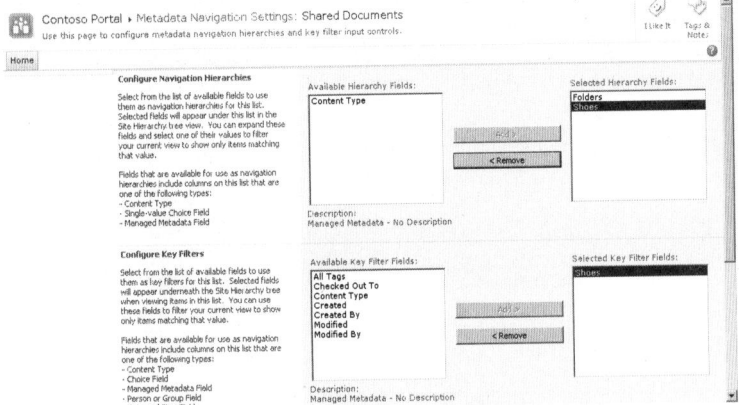

FIGURE 10-24 The page for configuring metadata navigation and key filters.

Managed keywords are consumed from all metadata connections that are subscribed to by the site collection. As Figure 10-25 shows, keywords are automatically suggested based on input. The label must match the data in a term store or an error will be presented.

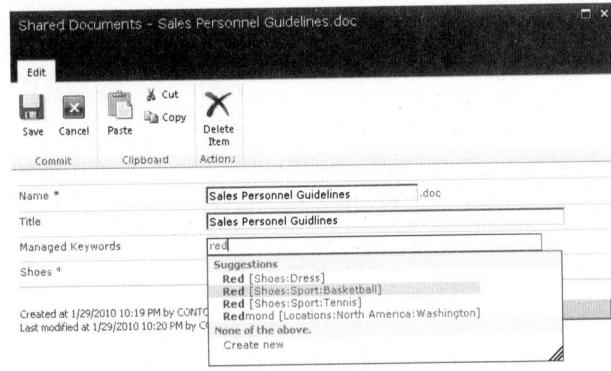

FIGURE 10-25 Tagging with managed terms.

CHAPTER 11

Document Management

- Managing Documents in SharePoint 2010   **361**

- Document IDs and Sets   **365**

- List and Library Relationships   **369**

- Document Version Control   **372**

- Workflows   **374**

- Inbound E-mail   **375**

- Offline Support   **377**

- The Document Center   **378**

Document management is one of the most important processes in any organization. As document workspaces grow while organizations shift to paperless processing, the mountains of electronic copies begin to grow exponentially. Beyond dealing with just the documents themselves, organizations also face a shift in the way they handle documents. Document versions, workflows, libraries, unique IDs, document sets, collaboration spaces, and offline availability must be considered when developing the document management policies for an organization. The purpose of this chapter is to provide you with an understanding of how Microsoft SharePoint Server 2010 provides the resources and tools to efficiently and effectively manage documents.

Managing Documents in SharePoint 2010

SharePoint Server 2010 greatly enhances the feature set available for collaboration with improvements in document management. These improvements stem from new features such as document sets and document IDs, as well as additional functionality to improve the content types and columns features.

Organizations planning to implement SharePoint 2010 need to consider these new features and evaluate how they will enhance their either existing or newly formulated collaboration models. SharePoint document management, managed metadata, and other features center on the intrinsic methodologies of collaboration and community contribution.

What Is Document Management?

Your organization might already have a document management plan. This plan might simply be a definition of document types, and it could be as involved as the entire process life cycle for managing document control and change management. Document management is the evolution of planning and design that encompasses the document life cycle for an organization. Ideally, the design and development of a document management plan is a management function.

This chapter focuses on how SharePoint 2010 can be used to implement a document management plan. The following are some key factors that should be included in a well-rounded document management plan:

- **Participant roles description**   Identifies key participants for the document management processes and what their responsibilities will be. This description breaks down the specific roles, and defines the relationships with other roles within the plan.

- **Catalog of document types**   An exhaustive list of categories that the organization must maintain, and the specific policies and requirements that govern each type of data.

- **Document organizational taxonomy**   An organized and logical schema for organizing, tagging, and otherwise identifying the documents that will be maintained within the document management plan. The more detailed and expanded this taxonomy is, the greater the degree is of cross-referencing capabilities available for tag-based identification. The fine line here is that the taxonomy should not be too complex or cumbersome to use.

- **Document movement plan**   Describes the policies and procedures for how documents should be transitioned between servers, people, storage media, and so forth.

- **Workflow plan**   Outlines the major steps necessary in a document life cycle and the relationships these steps have to their participant role. This plan establishes the flow of data from end to end and encapsulate any change-management procedures.

Document management can mean different things to different people. These subtle differences are directly related to how people understand its use. In general, *document management* is the process of applying organizational policies and rules to how documents are created, where and how they are stored, how long they are retained, and ultimately when and how they are destroyed.

The first fundamental step an organization needs to take before it can begin creating lists and libraries to store its documents is to understand how these documents will be created and managed. The lists and libraries are then built around these defining factors.

For example, a document library that will be used by the legal department needs to have standard templates for various legal documents. These templates can be depositions, contracts, disclosure and noncompetition agreements, and so on. The templates should be stored as content types within the library for ease of creation and also tagging. Documents that need to be kept should be sent to the retention library to be held for the specific length of time for the content type.

These specific document-management requirements determine how an organization approaches document management. Several attributes make up the framework of this document-management approach:

- Content types
- Metadata columns
- Lookup columns
- Records center Send To link
- Information management policy

Document Collaboration

There is often a great deal of confusion between document management and document collaboration. *Document collaboration* is the process of two or more people creating, editing, tagging, and interacting with the document and also communicating about it.

A document might not require any collaboration simply because a single person performs all tasks related to its creation and editing. Collaboration typically exists on a document when that document is either being created or revised and needs the input of two or more people. Document management might also be required as part of that collaboration, but sometimes there is no need for management, just collaboration. After the document is created, it can be processed through a workflow plan so that additional work can be done on it. At some point within the document life cycle, the document can be switched from a collaboration document to a managed document.

You should always consider the overhead of having document-management features turned on by default because these features can require additional resource investment in disk space for version and auditing information. If business needs and logic require these specific document-management capabilities, the resource requirements for disk space and performance should be analyzed.

Document Libraries

Document libraries are the premier container for storing and managing documents. They include all the elements required to enable collaboration and document management across documents that are stored within them. A document library can also be saved as a template so that other document libraries can be defined using the same predefined information—including content types, rights management policies, versioning requirements, workflows, and more—rather than just having a blank library. This method of organization reduces the amount of configuring that needs to be done to establish a new document library.

All the previous functionality from SharePoint 2007 has been included:

- Major and minor versioning
- Required checkout
- Content types
- Information management policies
- Built-in workflows
- Incoming e-mail support

New features that have been added in SharePoint 2010 include the following:

- Document IDs
- Document sets
- Metadata navigation
- Relational lists
- Multiple check-in
- Content organizer; rule-based submission
- Offline management

Settings for document libraries can be changed by browsing to Library Tools, Library, Library Settings in the Settings section, which displays the Library Settings administration page as shown in Figure 11-1.

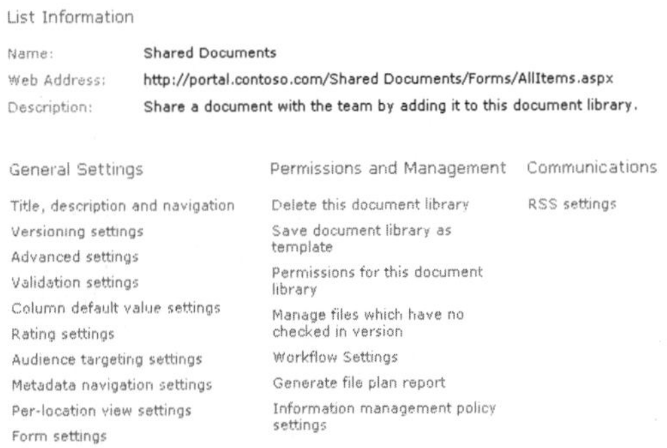

List Information

Name: Shared Documents
Web Address: http://portal.contoso.com/Shared Documents/Forms/AllItems.aspx
Description: Share a document with the team by adding it to this document library.

General Settings	Permissions and Management	Communications
Title, description and navigation	Delete this document library	RSS settings
Versioning settings	Save document library as template	
Advanced settings		
Validation settings	Permissions for this document library	
Column default value settings	Manage files which have no checked in version	
Rating settings		
Audience targeting settings	Workflow Settings	
Metadata navigation settings	Generate file plan report	
Per-location view settings	Information management policy settings	
Form settings		

FIGURE 11-1 Document library settings.

Library permissions can be accessed by browsing to Library Tools, Library, Library Permissions in the Settings section. Figure 11-2 shows that a library, by default, inherits permissions from its parent. However, this behavior can be disabled and independent permissions established instead. These unique permissions on the library or items control access and security trimming, which as a result control the ability to see the library or content within it. A person who does not have read access to the library cannot see the library because of the security trimming related to the user's view. The library will also not be displayed in any of the user's search results.

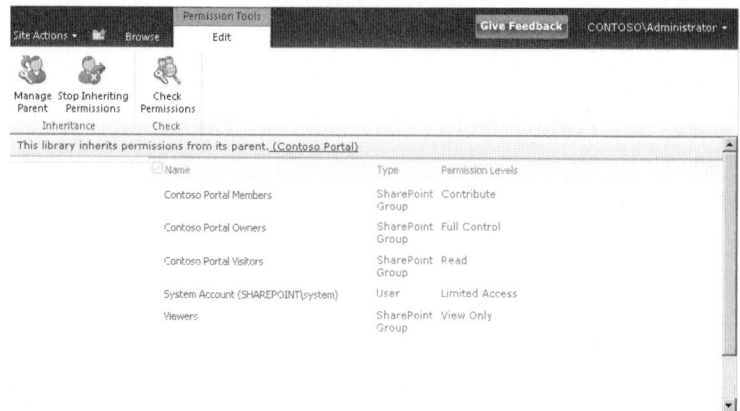

FIGURE 11-2 Document library Permission Tools tab.

NOTE Many tasks related to configuring and managing document libraries are left to the end user, not the SharePoint administrator.

Document IDs and Sets

Two new features within SharePoint 2010 are the use of document IDs and document sets. These two features are important tools for document management. *Document IDs* provide a unique identifier for each document within a site collection. *Document sets* enable documents to be grouped into a version-capable or distributable group. A version-capable or distributable group can be packaged (through the use of a .zip file) and distributed in its entirety. Previous versions of SharePoint provided document control at an individual document level only—that is, groups of documents folders were the only option.

Document IDs

Another new feature in SharePoint 2010 provides you with the ability to assign unique document IDs to an item. Here's a list of the key elements of a document ID:

- Unique metadata tagging
- Site-collection scoped

- Activated through a site collection feature
- Defined logical naming structure
- Consumed by enterprise components, lists, and libraries as well as the Records Center, Document Center, search, and workflow. The Document ID Service must be enabled before document IDs can be assigned to any documents within a site collection. To enable the Site Collection feature for the Document ID Service, perform the following steps:

1. Browse to Site Actions, Site Settings, Site Collection Features under Site Collection Administration.

2. Click the Activate button in the Document ID Service section, as shown in Figure 11-3.

Document ID Service
Assigns IDs to documents in the Site Collection, which can be used to retrieve items independent of their current location.

Activate

FIGURE 11-3 Activate the Document ID Service site collection feature.

NOTE You can also enable document IDs on a site collection within Windows PowerShell using the following command:

```
enable-spfeature -id [idcharacters] -url [site collection URL]
```

After the Site Collection feature has been enabled, you can configure the naming convention that will be used within the site collection, as shown in Figure 11-4. The naming convention entered prefixes all document IDs with the specified characters. A timer job is enabled that automatically processes the new document ID to implement it across your site collection. You can also reset all document IDs in the site collection to begin with the entered characters.

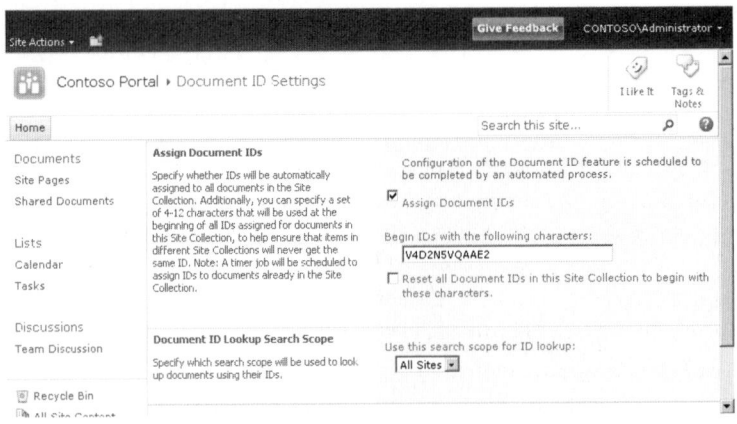

FIGURE 11-4 Document ID Settings page.

The Document ID field is not automatically enabled in a view, but it can be selected from Create View by completing the following steps:

1. Use Library Tools, Library, Create View to create a custom view.
2. Enter a name for the custom view.
3. Select the Document ID check box, as seen in Figure 11-5.

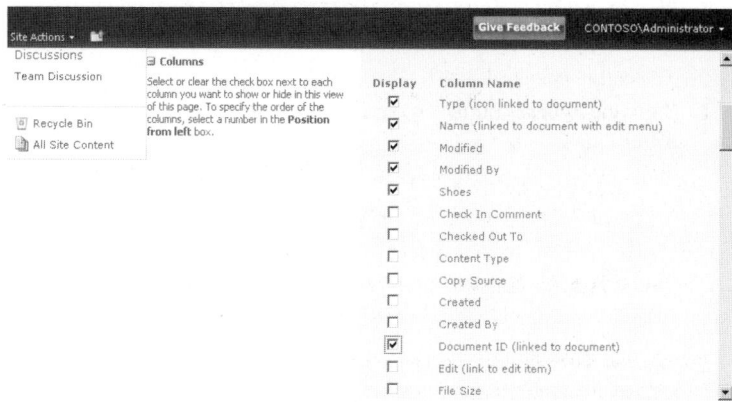

FIGURE 11-5 Select Document ID check box in Create View.

As documents are created, unique IDs will be associated with each and, as shown in Figure 11-6, the Document ID field is a value that can be used in columns and search.

Type	Name	Document ID	Shoes
	Shoe 2010 Sales Forecast	V4D2N5VQAAE2-1-1	Sport; Dress
	2010 Sales Revenue Streams	V4D2N5VQAAE2-1-2	Dress; Sport

Add new document

FIGURE 11-6 A custom document view that includes the Document ID field.

Document Sets

A document set is a content type that allows you to group documents that can then be managed as a set. The management of this set of documents can be based on a workflow or metadata, thus making the document set a perfect container within a document library for grouping key documents.

To enable document sets within a document library, you need to verify that the Document Sets site collection feature has been activated:

1. Click Site Actions, Site Settings.
2. Under Site Collection Administration, select Site Collection Features.
3. Click the Activate button in the Document Sets section if it is not already activated, as shown in Figure 11-7.

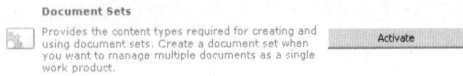

FIGURE 11-7 Activate the Document Sets site collection feature.

After the site collection feature has been activated, you can start to enable document sets within a document library. To do this, you need to allow for the management of content types on the document library by completing the following steps:

1. Navigate to the document library by clicking on its title.
2. When you're in the document library, select Library Tools, Library on the management Ribbon for the document library.
3. Select Library Settings in the Settings section.
4. Under General Settings, select Advanced Settings.
5. Ensure that the Content Types section shows the Yes option selected for Allow Management Of Content Types, as shown in Figure 11-8.

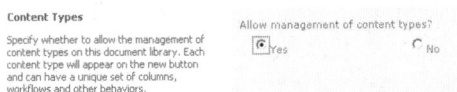

FIGURE 11-8 Allow Management Of Content Types option in the Content Types section.

After you have enabled the management of content types within the document library, a Document Sets content type can be added to the document library. This allows document sets to be created from the New Document menu on the Document Library management Ribbon. To add a Document Sets content type to the available New Document menu options, complete the following steps:

1. Navigate to the document library by clicking on its title.
2. When you're in the document library, select Library Tools, Library on the management Ribbon for the document library.
3. Select Library Settings in the Settings section.
4. Scroll down to the Content Types section, and select Add From Existing Site Content Types, as shown in Figure 11-9.

Content Types

This document library is configured to allow multiple content types. Use content types to specify the information you want to display about an item, in addition to its policies, workflows, or other behavior. following content types are currently available in this library:

Content Type	Visible on New Button	Default Content Type
Document	✔	✔

Add from existing site content types
Change new button order and default content type

FIGURE 11-9 Add document sets from existing site content types.

5. On the Add Content Types page, select Document Set from the Available Site Content Types list.
6. Click Add and then click OK to save your changes.

NOTE You can change the default document type and menu display order using the Change New Button Order And Default Content Type link in the Content Types section of the document libraries settings page.

List and Library Relationships

You will often need to link multiple libraries or lists together with common information. These relationships were possible with previous version of SharePoint; however, with SharePoint 2010 you have the added ability to enforce the relationship behavior. There are two options that provide an added measure of data integrity: one prevents referenced data from being removed from another list without the references being removed first, and the other option provides you with the ability to cascade that removal. Figure 11-10 shows the two options for restricting the action on deletes to one of the following:

- **Restrict Delete** If an attempt is made to delete an item from the list that is being referenced for a lookup column, SharePoint displays an error message informing the user that the row cannot be deleted because it is being referenced in another list.

- **Cascade Delete** If an attempt is made to delete an item from a list that is being referenced for a lookup column, SharePoint deletes that row from the list, as well as rows that reference it from any other list that used that value in a lookup column, as shown in Figure 11-10.

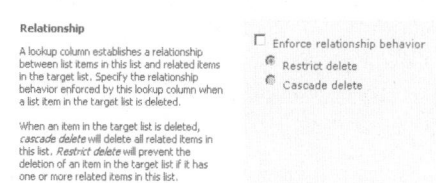

Relationship

A lookup column establishes a relationship between list items in this list and related items in the target list. Specify the relationship behavior enforced by this lookup column when a list item in the target list is deleted.

When an item in the target list is deleted, *cascade delete* will delete all related items in this list. *Restrict delete* will prevent the deletion of an item in the target list if it has one or more related items in this list.

☐ Enforce relationship behavior
◉ Restrict delete
○ Cascade delete

FIGURE 11-10 Enforcing relationship behavior on a lookup field.

Check In/Check Out

SharePoint provides the ability to handle the Check Out For Edit option within its document libraries. It is important for users to check out documents before they edit them. The newest feature is the ability to check in or check out multiple files at the same time.

There are several unique features that SharePoint provides as part of the Check Out functionality. These features provide for single-user locking, restricted visibility to those with the ability to check out a document, and an offline sandbox that retains the working copy on the user's computer while the user is editing the document and until it is checked back in. The Check In feature provides the ability to check in a document with comments, which provides the user the means to note what was changed within the document.

Administrators frequently encounter the situation where a document is checked out by an individual who is not available to check the document back in or who just forgot to check the file back in. SharePoint provides the ability to take ownership of an already checked-out file and either undo the check out or check in of the document. Of course, the other person's changes will not be saved, and that user will need to implement them at a later date.

SharePoint 2010 also adds the ability to check in or check out multiple documents at the same time. By selecting the check box next to the desired items, a user can check in or check out all the selected items at the same time, as shown in Figure 11-11.

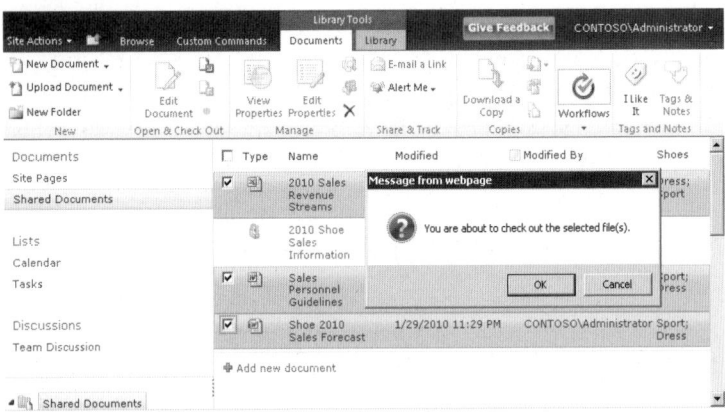

FIGURE 11-11 Check in or check out multiple documents at the same time.

Content Types

Document libraries store documents based on properties set up within the library's document type source template. Content types are a collection of settings, metadata, workflows, and policies that define the source template. There can be more than one source template document type set up for a document library. Document types can have a content type associated with them that provide consistent data management and workflow rules across multiple documents, libraries, and sites.

In SharePoint 2010, content types can be created at many levels in the farm, from enterprise-wide content types to site-level content types. This is fundamentally different from SharePoint 2007, where only site-level content types were available.

List and libraries can make use of content types by enabling them in the settings for the list or library. To enable content type management on a list, as shown in Figure 11-12, perform the following steps:

1. Navigate to the document library by clicking on its title.

2. In the document library, browse to Library Tools, Library on the management Ribbon for the document library.

3. Select Library Settings in the Settings section.

4. Under General Settings, select Advanced Settings.

5. In the Content Types section, under Allow Management Of Content Types, select Yes.

6. Click OK to apply change.

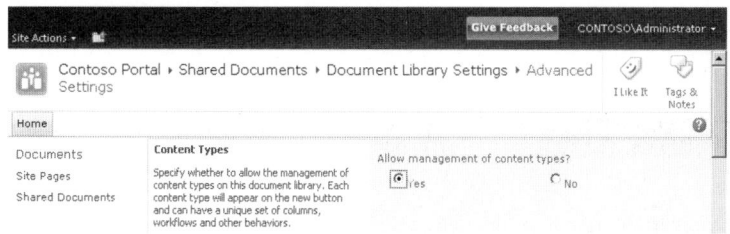

FIGURE 11-12 Allow Management Of Content Types section.

The default content type and the order in which the content types appear in the new document drop-down list are configurable from the list settings.

> **IMPORTANT** Any document type can be uploaded into any document library regardless of the configured content types. Content types dictate only types available in the new document selection list.

Each content type can have its own configuration settings, such as a unique file template, file type, workflow settings, document information panel (DIP), information management policy, and column metadata values. These content type settings can be inherited from enterprise content types, and metadata can be leveraged from the managed metadata services. More information on enterprise content types and metadata can be found Chapter 10, "Enterprise Content Types and Metadata," which covers enterprise content types and managed metadata.

Document Version Control

Document libraries support version control at several levels. By default, versioning is not enabled but is enabled in the document library settings. Versions are complete copies of the document, not deltas. To enable versioning, perform the following steps:

1. Navigate to the document library by clicking on its title.

2. In the document library, select Library Tools, Library on the management Ribbon for the document library.

3. Select Library Settings in the Settings section.

4. Under General Settings, select Versioning Settings.

5. Select the versioning options required, as shown in Figure 11-13, under Document Version History.

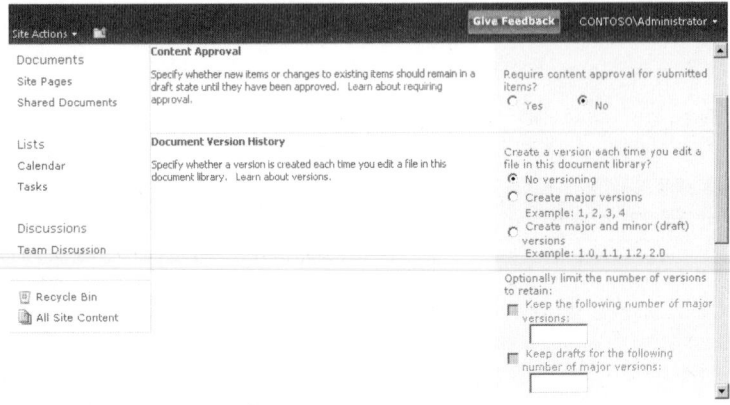

FIGURE 11-13 Document Version History settings.

Depending on the process flow and business requirements put in force by the document management plan within an organization, document versioning requirements might be succinctly different. Some document management plans might require approval for inclusion within the library. Retention policies might require the pruning of older versions and the removal of drafts or minor revisions upon the publication of a major version.

Content Approval

You can designate that a document or document set be approved before the version becomes available for consumption. This requirement might include changes to existing documents as well as the addition of new items. This can be used in conjunction with an approval workflow to streamline the approval process.

Major Versioning

All versions are considered to be "published" versions when major versioning is enabled in a document library. The option is provided to the user during check-in to identify which version the file or document set should be marked with. Only whole number versions are created and retained.

Major and Minor Versioning

Minor versions that are marked with the fractional number in the second octet are considered drafts. This option is designed to support the publishing model in which draft versions or working copies are used until a point in time when publishing will change the major version number. Major versions are marked as "published" in the versions list. When a document is checked in, users can choose to mark it as one of the following version types: Existing Minor, New Minor, or New Major. Users can also elect to keep the document checked out, with the exception of checking it in as Major version, as there could be a workflow attached to the Major version publishing.

Version Pruning

The choice of either versioning structure allows for limiting the number of versions retained by the document library. These limits can be established at both the Major and Minor version level. Pruning works on the first-in, first-out basis, with older versions being pruned. If a major version is removed, all minor versions related to that major version are also removed. Version pruning is a significant planning issue that affects the content database sizes, quotas, and disaster recovery. Because each version is a complete copy of the document, not a delta, decisions regarding pruning can significantly affect the infrastructure requirements, length of retention, and ability to recover.

Draft Item Security

Drafts are minor versions or items that have not been approved. The Draft Item Security feature specifies which users should be able to view drafts in the document library. There are three options that can be set in the Versioning settings for the document library, as shown in Figure 11-14:

- Any User Who Can Read Items
- Only Users Who Can Edit Items
- Only Users Who Can Approve Items (And The Author Of The Item)

IMPORTANT As an administrator, you need to understand that without pruning turned on, large numbers of document versions can be created, which can greatly increase the size of the SQL database.

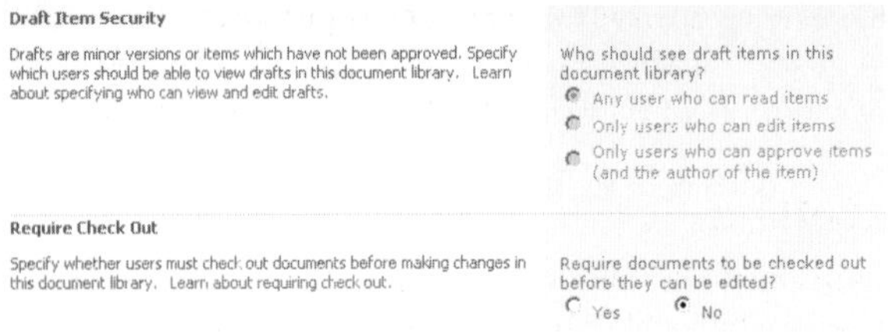

Draft Item Security

Drafts are minor versions or items which have not been approved. Specify which users should be able to view drafts in this document library. Learn about specifying who can view and edit drafts.

Who should see draft items in this document library?

- ○ Any user who can read items
- ○ Only users who can edit items
- ○ Only users who can approve items (and the author of the item)

Require Check Out

Specify whether users must check out documents before making changes in this document library. Learn about requiring check out.

Require documents to be checked out before they can be edited?

- ○ Yes   ● No

FIGURE 11-14 Draft Item Security and Require Check Out sections.

If you are using large file sizes (greater than 200 MB) and do not want to keep those items stored in the SQL Server database, you can use Remote binary large object (BLOB) Storage (RBS) outside of SQL on a file system.

Workflows

SharePoint provides several default workflows that can be used for controlling actions that happen to the document at a specific point in its life cycle. These default workflows include the following:

- **Approval**   Routes a document for approval. Users with the correct permissions can approve or reject the document, reassign the approval task, or request changes to the document.
- **Collect Feedback**   Routes a document for review. Reviewers can provide feedback, which is compiled and sent to the document owner when the workflow is completed.
- **Collect Signatures**   Gathers signatures needed to complete an Office document.
- **Disposition Approval**   Manages document expiration and retention by allowing participants to decide whether to retain or delete expired documents.
- **Three-State Workflow**   Can be activated at the site-collection level to provide a workflow for tracking the status of items.

Many organizations have needs that extend beyond the capabilities of the default workflows. The default workflows are not sufficient for the complete business solution models of some organizations; for that reason, the following additional tools are available that can be used to create much more complex workflow designs:

- **SharePoint Designer**   Designed for the power user, it provides the ability to create multistep workflows that have many more options than the default workflows.
- **Visual Studio**   Used by developers to create complex business logic workflows, such as state machine workflows.

There are also many third-party companies that have developed custom workflow tools to make the end user's life as easy as possible. These tools provide for the designing and deploying of workflows without the need for a developer.

Assigning Workflow Settings

Workflow settings can be assigned to a document library or list by enabling them in the settings for the list or library. To enable a workflow on a list or library, follow these steps:

1. Navigate to the document library by clicking on its title.
2. In the document library, select Library Tools, Library on the management Ribbon for the document library.
3. Select Library Settings in the Settings section.
4. Under Permissions And Management, select Workflow Settings.
5. Select the versioning options required, as shown in Figure 11-13, under Document Version History.

Custom workflow templates created through either SharePoint Designer, Microsoft Visual Studio, or a third-party tool will be available after they have been added to the site collection. Workflows are assigned by reference to the available workflow templates.

Inbound E-mail

Enabling inbound e-mail support in a document library provides the benefit of integrating SharePoint with e-mail. E-mail is the most common method of document collaboration used today. Perhaps the simplest and least intrusive way to introduce SharePoint sites to existing users is to e-mail–enable a document library and then add the address to an existing distribution list being used by a team. After this is done, all documents sent by team members are copied into the site for future reference and searching.

When you enable a document library for incoming e-mail, you need to ensure that the name you choose for the list e-mail address is unique in your SharePoint farm because only one address can be used with a specific name—for example, listName@contoso.com or listName@serverName.contoso.com. To mail-enable a document library or list, complete the following steps:

1. Navigate to the document library by clicking on its title.
2. In the document library, select Library Tools, Library on the management Ribbon for the document library.
3. Select Library Settings from the Settings section.
4. Under Communications, select Incoming E-mail Settings.
5. Configure the incoming e-mail settings for the document library.

IMPORTANT Inbound e-mail must be enabled from Central Administration to be able to enable inbound e-mail in the library or list. E-mail settings can be configured in Central Administration, Systems Settings, as shown in Figure 11-15.

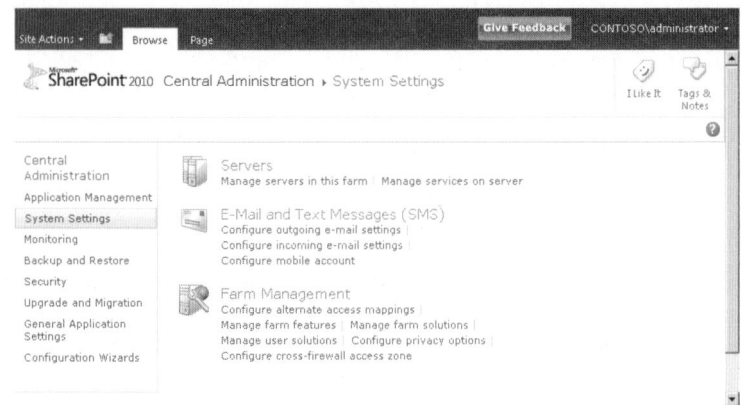

FIGURE 11-15 E-Mail And Text Messages options in the System Settings area in Central Administration.

Grouping Submissions

Submissions can be grouped by the subject line of the e-mail or by the sender. These options can help to preserve the original context of the file, even if you choose not to archive the original e-mail message. If Yes is selected for the Overwrite Files With The Same Name option, a random number is appended to the file name of any new documents with the same names that are e-mailed to the library, as shown in Figure 11-16.

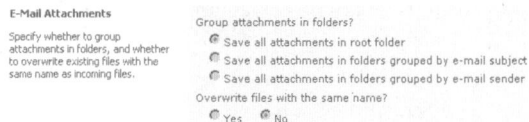

FIGURE 11-16 E-mail Attachments section.

Allowing Contributions from Outside the Organization

Mail-enabled libraries are an excellent way to allow users from outside the organization, who do not have access to the SharePoint site, to submit files for review internally. To support this feature, you must enable the Archive All E-mail Regardless Of Sender option. This is enabled in the E-mail Security section of the document library incoming e-mail settings by selecting the Accept E-mail Messages From Any Sender option, as shown in Figure 11-17.

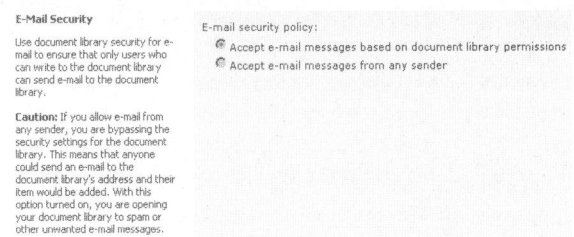

E-Mail Security

Use document library security for e-mail to ensure that only users who can write to the document library can send e-mail to the document library.

Caution: If you allow e-mail from any sender, you are bypassing the security settings for the document library. This means that anyone could send an e-mail to the document library's address and their item would be added. With this option turned on, you are opening your document library to spam or other unwanted e-mail messages.

E-mail security policy:
- ○ Accept e-mail messages based on document library permissions
- ○ Accept e-mail messages from any sender

FIGURE 11-17 Options for accepting e-mail from outside the organization.

Offline Support

Users often need to access collaboration spaces while not online. A primary example of this is when a user is traveling and online access is limited. SharePoint 2010 offers the following two methods by which users can take content offline:

- Outlook 2003 and later. (Outlook 2003 only provides read-only content. Outlook 2007 and 2010 allow two-way synchronization for documents.)
- Microsoft SharePoint Workspace 2010 (formerly known as Groove)

Many users who work remotely from the office will appreciate the offline capabilities in SharePoint 2010. The level of synchronization required determines which client should be used. Microsoft SharePoint Workspace is shown in Figure 11-18.

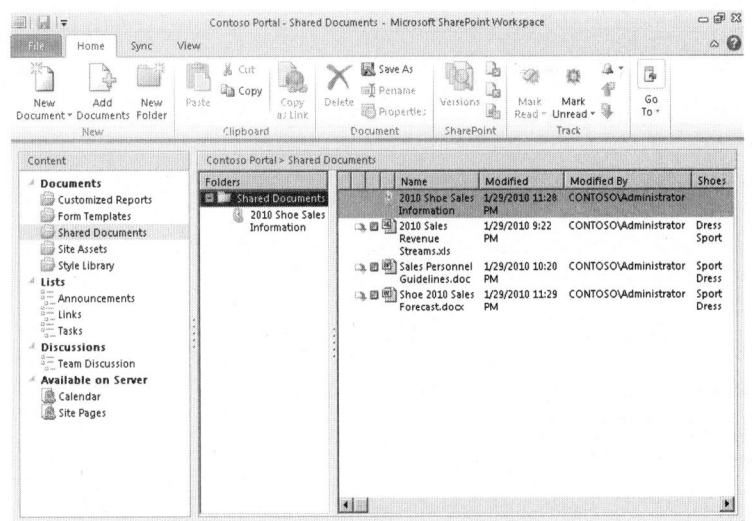

FIGURE 11-18 Microsoft SharePoint Workspace 2010.

The Document Center

The Document Center template, shown in Figure 11-19, is a tailored site template that has many of the document management settings enabled by default. It's a convenient mechanism for organizations to create a central repository for documents or other information that might no longer need to be in a collaborative workspace.

The document center template should not be confused with the Records Center template, which will be discussed in Chapter 13, "Portals and Collaboration." The records center is there to deal with official files within the business, such as compliance requirements. The document center, however, is aimed at creating a document repository. The document center is also a template that can accommodate editing of documents as well as uploading them, but these functions are controlled through permissions for key content managers.

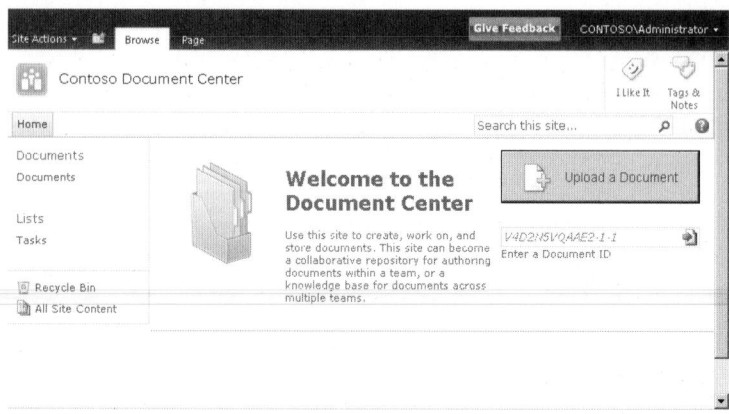

FIGURE 11-19 Document Center example.

After it is created, the document center has several functions turned on by default:

- Versioning: major and minor
- Metadata navigational settings
- Drop-off library (content organizer)
- Document ID Search Web part
- Document break-down Web parts (highest rated, newest, and modified by me)
- Upload Document button

There are several ways in which documents can be added to the document center. These include but are not limited to the following:

- By using the Upload A Document button
- By using the Send To Other Location function

- Via part of a workflow using the officialfile.asmx Web service
- By creating a new document directly in a library in the document center
- By being added through offline tools such as Outlook or SharePoint Workspace

A new feature in SharePoint 2010 is the ability to use the Send To function in combination with the content organizer feature, which allows the same automated routing mechanism to be used that's available in the Records Center template. To enable the content organizer feature, complete these steps:

1. Click on Site Actions, Site Settings.
2. Under Site Collection Administration, select Site Collection Features.
3. Click the Activate button in the Content Organizer section if it is not already activated, as shown in Figure 11-20.

Content Organizer
Create metadata based rules that move content submitted to this site to the correct library or folder.   Deactivate   Active

FIGURE 11-20 Content Organizer feature activation.

For example, a document library for a legal site is used for creating and updating legal documents, petitions, motions, and contracts. When a new document becomes a final version, it is sent to the document center to be stored in the correct library. In the document center, there are several libraries for storing these documents, and they are structured based on the regions and case number that the document is created for.

Content Organizer and Send To Functionality

The content organizer feature must first be enabled in the site where the documents are being sent to. After the content organizer site feature is enabled, a new document library, Drop Off Library, will be available in the document center. This library acts as a routing mechanism for incoming documents. It uses content organizer rules to match the content type and metadata with the correct document library and thereby routes them to their respective storage libraries. In the example we used earlier, the legal documents are sent to the drop-off library. The Send To function does not remove the original document from the source library; instead, it creates a full copy of the document in the drop-off library. The document was created using the various legal document content types. These content types have several metadata required fields, such as client name, case number, and region.

In the document center, a *content organizer rule* is created that defines the content type match and the condition of the match that determines which document library the document is routed to after it arrives in the drop-off library. To create content organizer rules, complete the following steps:

1. Click on Site Actions, Site Settings.
2. Under Site Collection Administration, select Content Organizer Rules.

3. Click the Add New Item link. The dialog box shown in Figure 11-21 will be displayed.

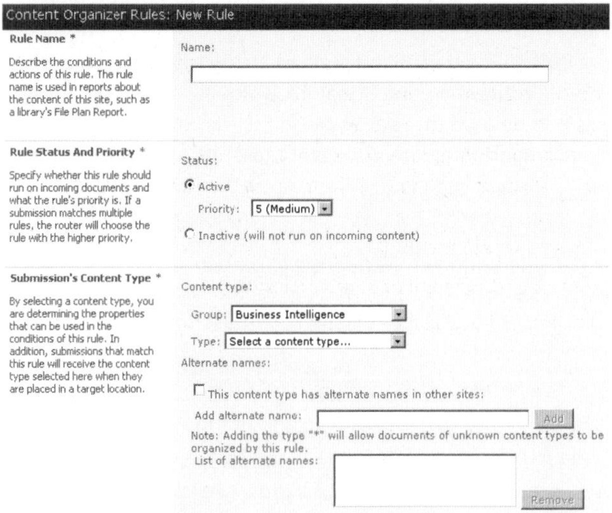

FIGURE 11-21 Content Organizer Rules: New Rules page, with the Rule Name, Rule Status And Priority, and Submission's Content Type sections.

When specifying a submission content type to be used, you must ensure that the type also exists at the target location library in the document center. (See Figure 11-22.) In the earlier example, the enterprise content types for various legal documents must also be assigned to the target location library in the document center.

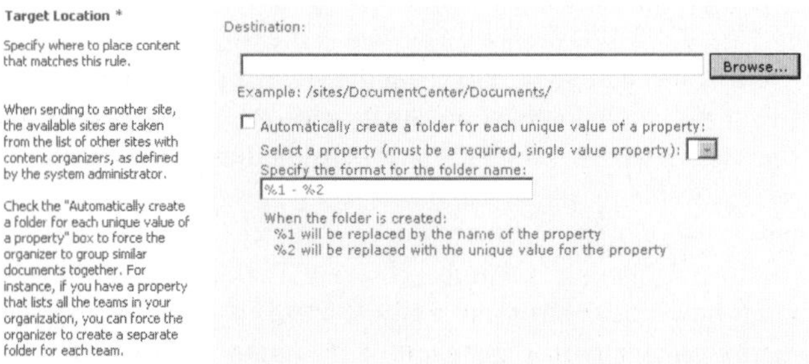

FIGURE 11-22 Content Organizer Rules page, Target Location section.

Multiple conditions can be added to the content organizer rule as well, such as *region=north* and *Report Status=Final*. To add more conditions, click the Add Another Condition link, as shown in Figure 11-23.

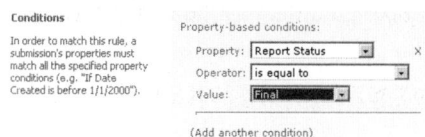

Conditions

In order to match this rule, a submission's properties must match all the specified property conditions (e.g. "If Date Created is before 1/1/2000").

Property-based conditions:

Property: Report Status   ✕

Operator: is equal to

Value: Final

(Add another condition)

FIGURE 11-23 Content Organizer Rules page, Conditions section.

On the site collaboration space where the actual documents are located, create a Custom Send To Destination link. This is done via the Advanced settings in the Library Settings menu accessed via Library Tools on the management Ribbon. Follow these steps to create the link:

1. Navigate to the document library by clicking on its title.

2. In the document library, select Library Tools, Library on the management Ribbon for the document library.

3. Select Library Settings in the Settings section.

4. Under General Settings, select Advanced Settings.

5. Configure the Custom Send To Destination for the document library, as shown in Figure 11-24.

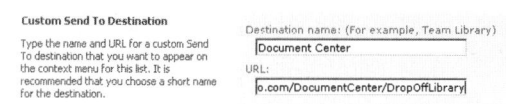

Custom Send To Destination

Type the name and URL for a custom Send To destination that you want to appear on the context menu for this list. It is recommended that you choose a short name for the destination.

Destination name: (For example, Team Library)
Document Center

URL:
o.com/DocumentCenter/DropOffLibrary

FIGURE 11-24 Custom Send To Destination section.

NOTE Only one custom Send To destination can be created per document library, although using workflow can aid in the creation of multiple send to locations based on business logic and status of the document.

When creating the custom Send To location, you should ensure that you specify the drop-off library as the final destination because it is the only library that has the content organizer associated with it. The URL should be something similar to the following:

```
http://portal.contoso.com/DocumentCenter/DropOffLibrary.
```

When a document is now uploaded or sent to the drop-off library, it will be routed correctly. A timer job definition is created for each Web application for processing the content organizer rules.

NOTE By default, the Content Organizer Processing timer job is set to Daily, so if you want the documents to be moved quicker from the drop-off library, change the timings for the definition rule in Central Administration.

After the timer job has successfully run, documents will be routed to the correct library location in the order specified by the active priority that was defined in the content organizer rules.

Metadata Navigation and Filtering

More and more, documents are stored in sites like the document center. The result is that when people need to find information, their search center results or views return far too many items for them to efficiently find what they need.

To counter this trend, SharePoint 2010 includes a new configuration option in the document library called Metadata Navigation Settings. These settings allow for the creation of custom metadata and for tag-based query Web parts to be placed on the Quick Launch toolbar. This allows the user to quickly sort and filter for documents based on attributes defined on the Metadata Navigation Settings page. To configure the Metadata Navigation Settings, complete the following steps:

1. Navigate to the document library by clicking on its title.

2. In the document library, select Library Tools, Library on the management Ribbon for the document library.

3. Select Library Settings from the Settings section.

4. Under General Settings, select Metadata Navigation Settings.

5. Configure the metadata navigation settings for the document library, as shown in Figure 11-25.

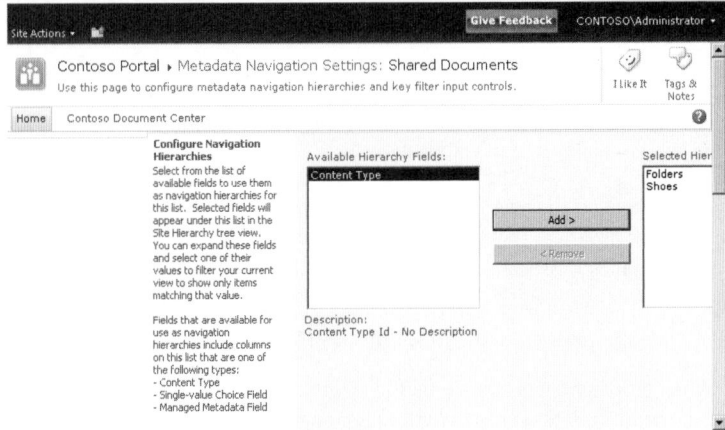

FIGURE 11-25 The Configure Navigation Hierarchies section for a document library.

After these settings are configured, the new query Web parts appear below the site navigation area and can be used to filter and sort for content in the document library. When using filter and sort, all documents in the library are returned that match the filter, even if the documents were in folders or document sets. All items matching the sort criteria are returned, as shown in Figure 11-26.

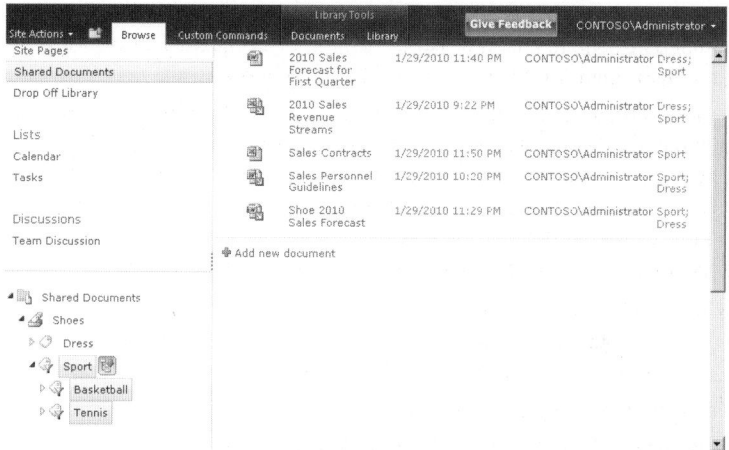

FIGURE 11-26 The documents with attributes specified in the Metadata Navigation Settings area.

CHAPTER 12

Records Management

- Information Management Policies **385**
- In Place Records Management **392**
- The Records Center **394**

Organizations will always be faced with the responsibility of handling and maintaining permanent records. When those records were physical files, the possibilities of management were rather limited and easy to document. Information management policies could be defined based on labeling rules for the physical files. Retrieval of those records was quite cumbersome and potentially required the manual handling of all records to search for a specific record.

With Microsoft SharePoint Server 2010, the handling and maintenance of records is far more flexible and can adhere to any level of complexity in information management policies. At the same time, records management is also wholly usable by the collaborative community. Data that would otherwise not be accessible after it was declared as a record becomes easily accessible with in-place records management.

With records grouped and linked through a records center, copies of all records are stored in a central repository where they can be easily queried when the need arises. The principle of automatic categorical filing of records is the same as using a document center; therefore, it provides you with a robust grouping of metadata with which to search and retrieve the records.

Information Management Policies

Information management policies are a set of rules applied to document libraries and content types. These policies enable administrators to control how document information is retained, audited, and disposed of. The task of defining and managing these policies typically is performed by a compliance officer, records manager, or other content specialist. There are three ways that information management policies are defined:

- On a document library, including folders
- On a content type
- At the site-collection level

Furthermore, there are four key areas that can be defined for a policy:

- Retention
- Auditing
- Barcodes
- Labels

Document libraries always enforce policies that are defined on the specific content types included within the library. However, additional policies can be chosen to define policies at the library level, which then affect all content types within the library, including folders.

One of the primary settings that can be configured at the document library–level is the source of retention. This setting configures where a library receives its retention schedule from. There are only two options: Content Types and Library And Folders. To change the Source Of Retention settings for a document library perform the following steps:

1. Navigate to the document library by clicking on its title.
2. After you have accessed the document library, select Library Tools, Library on the Ribbon for the document library.
3. Select Library Settings from the Settings section.
4. Under Permissions And Management, select Information Management Policy Settings.
5. On the Library Based Retention Schedule page, click the Change Source link.
6. Select either Content Types or Library And Folders, as shown in Figure 12-1.

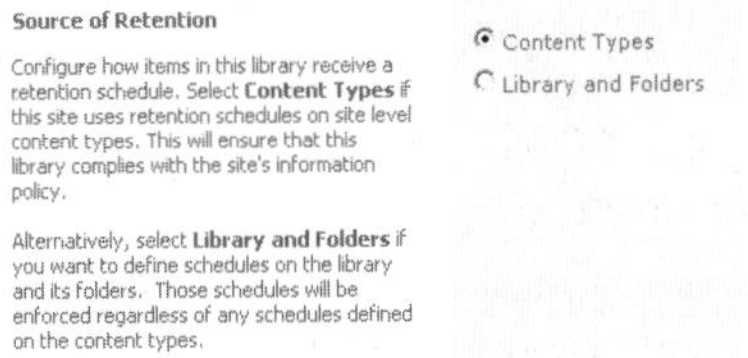

Source of Retention

Configure how items in this library receive a retention schedule. Select **Content Types** if this site uses retention schedules on site level content types. This will ensure that this library complies with the site's information policy.

Alternatively, select **Library and Folders** if you want to define schedules on the library and its folders. Those schedules will be enforced regardless of any schedules defined on the content types.

◉ Content Types
○ Library and Folders

FIGURE 12-1 Information Management Policy page, Source Of Retention settings.

SharePoint Server 2010 introduces the functionality of enterprise content types; therefore, it makes more sense to maintain control of policies via these content types. This approach allows you to have centralized control of both the templates and metadata defined on the content type and a centralized policy mechanism regarding how to manage documents of the associated type.

One reason to establish retention policies for the document library, however, might be that you want to enforce a standard approach to document retention in the library itself, regardless of the content types it contains. This policy might establish a rule for all documents older than 90 days within the library, which can be automatically moved to an external data source while a link is left in place.

An information management policy on a content type must be defined within the properties of the content type. If the content type is an enterprise content type, policies must be defined in the Content Type Store site. Permission-level requirements for defining policies are also a possible reason why users who are only site administrators might choose to enable and create policies at the library level rather than the content-type level.

Retention

Retention involves defining what to do with an item when a particular stage is reached, and it is usually triggered by a defined action of some sort. Some of the actions available can be coupled with custom-developed solutions, such as a workflow.

Two types of retention policies are available in SharePoint Server 2010: records and nonrecords. Both types of policies share the same configuration options. There are three configuration options for a retention policy. Table 12-1 lists these configuration event options and the applicable actions for each.

TABLE 12-1 Retention Policy Configuration Options

CONFIGURATION OPTIONS	ACCEPTABLE VALUES DEFINITIONS
Event	<ul><li>By time period</li><li>Created</li><li>Modified</li><li>Set by a custom formula installed on the server</li></ul>
Action	<ul><li>Move to Recycle Bin</li><li>Permanently delete</li><li>Transfer to another location (which works with farm Send To locations)</li><li>Start a workflow (which can also use custom-developed workflows)</li><li>Skip to next stage</li><li>Delete previous drafts</li><li>Delete all previous versions</li></ul>

CONFIGURATION OPTIONS	ACCEPTABLE VALUES DEFINITIONS
Recurrence	<ul><li>Only available for certain actions (such as delete previous drafts)</li><li>Defined by a period of time</li></ul>

You can have more than one retention policy action defined for a specific event, as shown in Figure 12-2.

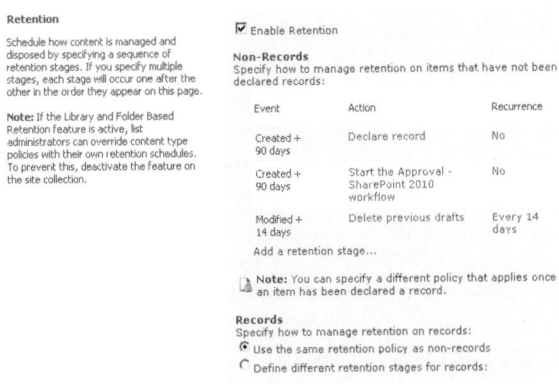

Retention

Schedule how content is managed and disposed by specifying a sequence of retention stages. If you specify multiple stages, each stage will occur one after the other in the order they appear on this page.

Note: If the Library and Folder Based Retention feature is active, list administrators can override content type policies with their own retention schedules. To prevent this, deactivate the feature on the site collection.

☑ Enable Retention

Non-Records
Specify how to manage retention on items that have not been declared records:

Event	Action	Recurrence
Created + 90 days	Declare record	No
Created + 90 days	Start the Approval - SharePoint 2010 workflow	No
Modified + 14 days	Delete previous drafts	Every 14 days

Add a retention stage...

Note: You can specify a different policy that applies once an item has been declared a record.

Records
Specify how to manage retention on records:
◉ Use the same retention policy as non-records
○ Define different retention stages for records:

FIGURE 12-2 Retention policy management settings.

NOTE You can choose to have one policy action defined for when the item is deleted, as well as a separate action for when the item is modified.

Nonrecords

A document or group of documents that have not been declared or that have no reason to be declared as an official file or document set can still have requirements for policy management. You might find it important to use retention policies in collaborative spaces, which is beneficial to both records managers and Information Technology (IT) departments. These retention policies can be used to automatically clean up inactive, nonrecord content as a part of resource conservation policies.

If permitted, a contributor can convert a document from a nonrecord into a record by *declaring* it a record. The ability to declare records is controlled by the site collection administrator. This ability effects information that is retained in lists and document libraries, and it determines how contributors can trigger records management on the items. To manage record declaration policies, perform the following steps:

1. Click Site Actions, Site Settings.
2. Under Site Collection Administration, select Record Declaration Settings.

3. Select the appropriate level of actions that can be performed by contributors and administrators within the site collection, as shown in Figure 12-3.

NOTE Record declaration location availability as well as delete restrictions can also be managed within the Record Declaration settings.

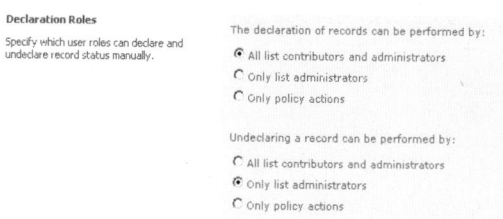

FIGURE 12-3 Declaration Roles section within the Record Declaration settings.

Records

Typically, after a document has been declared as a record it has reached a stage in its life cycle where it has a legal, compliance, or business process requirement. Records have two possible options when being configured:

1. Use the same retention policy as the nonrecords.
2. Define a different set of retention requirements after it becomes a record.

After a document becomes a record, it can be sent automatically as part of a workflow to the official corporate records center to become part of the audit and compliance requirement of the business. The declaration of the document as a record can require that the document be sent to the document center, as in the case of a final version of a company's employee benefits policy, which when completed must be available to all employees in the organization through the document center.

The determination of what becomes a record is at the discretion of the organization's compliance officer, records manager, or other content specialist, and the process is exercised in accordance with the information management policies of the organization.

Auditing

When auditing is enabled, it addresses and logs information related to the following actions, and that information can then be viewed as part of an audit trial policy (as shown in Figure 12-4):

1. Open or download documents, view items in lists, or view item properties.
2. Edit items.
3. Check out or check in items.

4. Move or copy items to another location in the site.

5. Delete or restore items.

Users can query SharePoint to assemble reports of audit event information as needed.

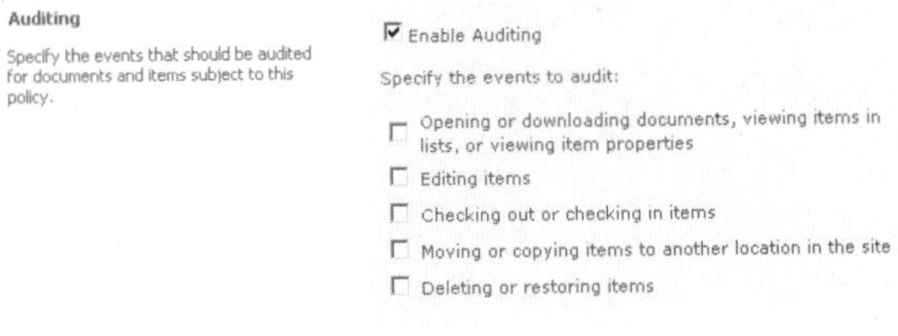

FIGURE 12-4 Settings for auditing policy information.

Document Bar Codes

Document bar codes are similar to document labels, but instead of text, they represent a unique identifier rendered in a machine-readable format. To view the generated bar code, click the View Properties command on the document drop-down list.

Document Labels

The document label feature is designed to assist in organizing documents for systematic storage and retrieval. Document labels are text labels that SharePoint can generate automatically based on a content type's metadata. Document labels can be printed and attached to a physical copy of the document or inserted as graphics into the file. Changes to a document label can be prevented after the label is attached to a document, as shown in Figure 12-5.

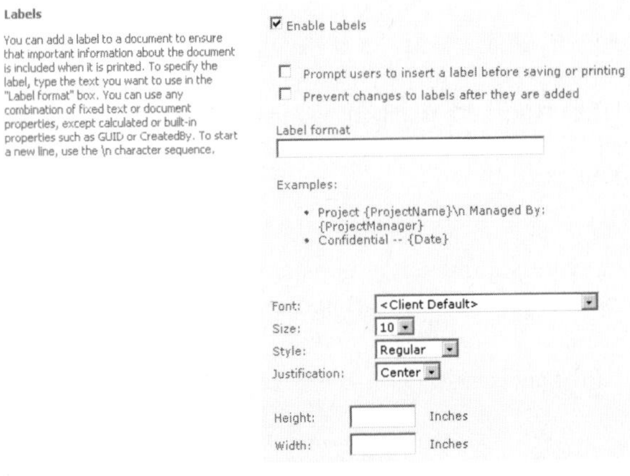

FIGURE 12-5 Document labels policy settings.

When the information management policy has been created or updated on a content type that has been created as an enterprise content type, the content types needs to be republished to force the changes down to the site collections that are consuming that content type. There is a timer job that runs on a periodic basis and synchronizes libraries and sites that use the content types with the enterprise content types.

NOTE The Content Types Subscriber timer job can be run manually to force changes down to the site collections.

After the policy has been applied, you can view the new details for the policy by looking at the compliance details for a document that used the content type changed with the policy or that exists in a library that has had a policy applied to it.

To see the compliance details, click the Compliance Details command on the document drop-down list, as shown in Figure 12-6.

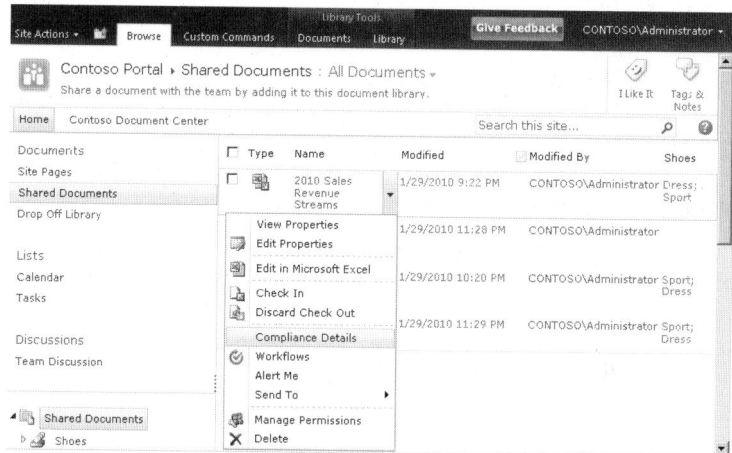

FIGURE 12-6 Compliance Details option in the document drop-down list.

The result displays the compliance details in the Compliance dialog box, and the new retention stages as configured in the information management policy should be visible, as shown in Figure 12-7.

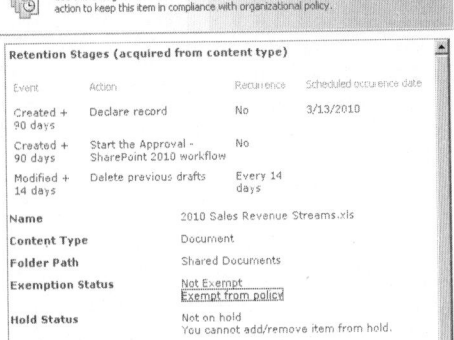

FIGURE 12-7 Compliance details dialog box.

In Place Records Management

Another new feature in SharePoint Server 2010 is in-place records management. Several new functions have been made available to help companies architect a compliance and record-declaration mechanism:

- Allowing record declaration at the list and library level
- Delegating user control for declaring records
- Declaring through a workflow

One of the common configuration problems that compliance architects were faced with in SharePoint 2007 was that the only place where document declaration could take place was within the records center. The obvious problem with this was that not all documents needed to live in a records center, and many existed in other sites, such as a document center or a policies site. If for some reason it was necessary to locate all the documents that were part of the compliance request, doing so was very difficult because they were not all in the records center.

To solve these problems, SharePoint Server 2010 no longer requires that a document reside in the records center. Instead, document declaration can be carried out in place in established sites such as the document center and alongside nonrecord documents. This arrangement allows for a more fluid manipulation of record and nonrecord documents, which can coexist within the same document space and therefore be consumed more freely.

To enable in-place record management, the Site Collection feature must first be turned on. You can do that by completing these steps:

1. Click Site Actions, Site Settings.
2. Under Site Collection Administration, click Site Collection Features.

3. Activate the In Place Records Management feature if it is not already active, as shown in Figure 12-8.

FIGURE 12-8 In Place Records Management feature for site collections.

Allowing Record Declaration at the List and Library Level

Official record declaration is governed by either a policy or a workflow that invokes the declaration. You can, however, allow records declaration at the list or library level. The following two choices are available when enabling this option, as shown in Figure 12-9:

- Manual Record Declaration Availability
- Automatic Declaration

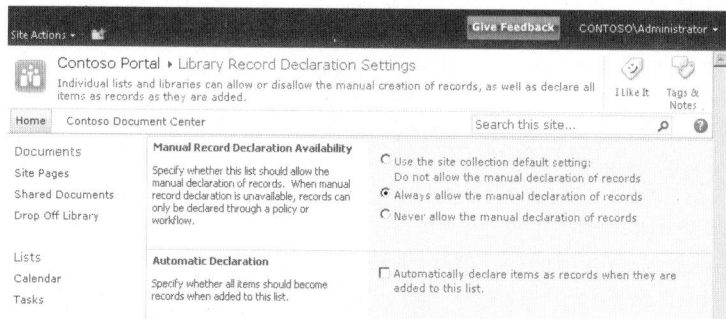

FIGURE 12-9 Library Record Declaration Settings page.

Manual Record Declaration

Users cannot manually declare a document as a record within a library without this option first being made available. This option is not enabled by default and takes the settings from the site collection. To allow the user to override these settings, enable Manual Record Declaration Availability on the library by following these steps:

1. Navigate to the document library by clicking on its title.
2. After you access the document library, select Library Tools, Library on the management Ribbon for the document library.
3. Select Library Settings in the Settings section.
4. Under Permissions And Management, click Library Record Declaration Settings.
5. Select Always Allow The Manual Declaration Of Records, and then click OK.

A new option named Declare Record is available in the Documents tab on the management Ribbon under Library Tools, as shown in Figure 12-10. Select the document that you want to declare, and then click the Declare Record button. There is also an Undeclare Record button you can click if the document no longer is needed as part of an official record storage and retrieval process.

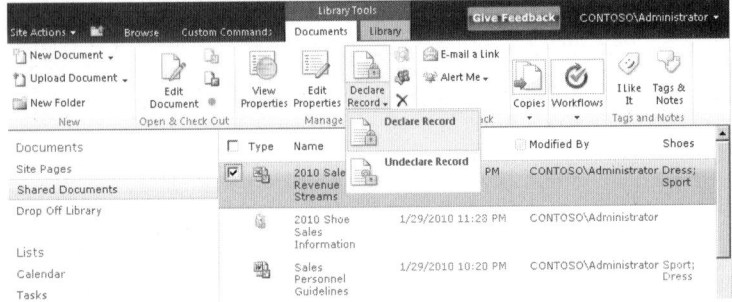

FIGURE 12-10 Options to manually declare or undeclare a record.

After the document has been declared, the document is locked, as indicated by a small padlock icon. As a locked document, it cannot be edited unless it is undeclared. Also, now that it is a record, it can form part of a hold process if a legal or compliancy request is put into place.

Automatic Declaration

Some lists or libraries need to have all documents become records, and although the list or library might exist in a standard collaboration site, it holds formal records. To initiate this process, simply go back to the Record Declaration setting in the library and choose Automatically Declare Items As Records When They Are Added To This List, as shown in Figure 12-9.

> **NOTE** For any existing items in the library, you need to check them out and then check them in for the lock to be put into place. For all new items, the process is automatic as you are requested to check the document in.

The Records Center

In SharePoint 2007, these functions were limited to only the templates, such as the records center for storing declared records. With SharePoint Server 2010, that limitation has been lifted. So the question now becomes why does the records center need to exist? With in-place record management, you can manage records independent of a central repository. The simple answer to this question is related to the work process.

Planning for the Records Center

Because it is possible to have both declared records and nondeclared records in the same list or library and use the document centers to control high-level repositories, much of the work that the old records center did has been taken care of in the collaboration environment. This is only partly true, however. Many organizations still need to create records centers for longer term compliance needs, because central storage and organization of these records is a requirement for simplifying various audit tasks. An additional benefit is the ability to group many types of records into a single location, such as documents, e-mail messages, list data, and pages that are all related to the same item.

For this model to be designed correctly, an organization needs to design an information management policy that matches the exact requirements of information that is stored in the records center. This information management plan includes a file plan as a matrix that lists all the information for each type of data that will be stored, how it is managed, for how long it is retained, and what happens to it in certain situations such as disposal. An example of a file plan matrix is shown in Table 12-2.

TABLE 12-2 Record Management Planning

RECORD TYPE	REQUIRED METADATA	EXPIRATION POLICY	AUDIT POLICY
Contracts	Contract date (date field)	Retain for 15 years after contract date.	Audit View events
	Assign Bar Code	Delete on expiration.	
Project Requirements and Deliverables	Delivery date (date field)	Retain for 7 years after delivery date.	None
	Label with delivery date (read only)	Review by project management for deletion.	
E-mail Correspondence	Subject (string property, single line of text)	Retain for 5 years from date created.	None
		Delete on expiration.	

The information management policy also defines who has access to what information after it is stored in the records center. This access list might contain read-access policy requirements for auditors and access requirements for information management policy managers. Rarely do normal users have access to the records center, although they can be set up to submit items as records.

To build the records center, you use many of the functions already discussed in various chapters of this book, specifically those in the following list:

- **Content Organizer**   To manage the routing of documents. (See Chapter 11, "Document Management.")
- **Metadata Navigation and Filtering**   To aid in the discovery process. (See Chapter 10, "Enterprise Content Types and Metadata.")
- **Information Management Policies**   To define how the item is held. (See the "Information Management Policies" section in this chapter.)

The routing mechanism within the records center works the same as automated routing processing does within the content organizer. When a records center is created, certain site features are automatically enabled or can be enabled to make it function within the information management policy requirements. These features include the following:

- Content Organizer
- E-Mail Integration with Content Organizer
- Hold and eDiscovery
- Metadata Navigation and Filtering
- Offline Synchronization for External Lists
- SharePoint Server Enterprise Site Features
- SharePoint Server Standard Site Features
- Team Collaboration Lists

Most site collections do not require all these features to be enabled. However, most corporations require strict security, processing, and isolation for these sites. Always consider giving the records center its own site collection or Web application. From a design and architectural perspective, it rarely makes sense to have a corporation's official records center be part of a collaboration model.

The greatest advantage of isolating the records center in its own Web application is that it will also have security isolation. It can, therefore, also have its own Microsoft Internet Information Services (IIS) Web site, which can have its own IIS application pool and independent security credentials. Adopting this approach prevents other application pools or Web sites from affecting what happens to this site. IIS or the server would need to have a problem before it could be affected.

A special group, called Records Center Web Service Submitters, is created in the records center site. This group allows you to define the other application pool IDs, which allow them to submit items using the *officialfile.asmx* Web service. When users or workflows submit items to the records center, the Web application's application pool, rather than the user, has the job of communicating and submitting the records.

After you create the records center site, a configuration page is available from the Site Actions menu that outlines the steps required to configure the site and get it up and running. The primary steps, which are shown in Figure 12-11, are as follows:

1. Create the required content types.
2. Create the record libraries.
3. Create content organizer rules.
4. Design the site welcome page.

Even though enterprise content types are configured in the farm, they still need to be subscribed to within the records center site collection before they can be added to the organizer rules.

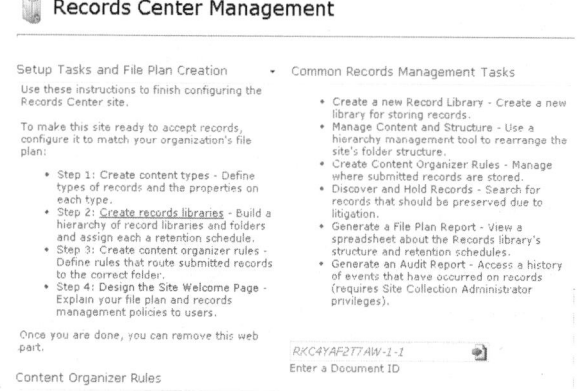

FIGURE 12-11 Records Center Management page.

As you did with other sites, such as the Document Center, you create document libraries with the specific information management policies assigned to them. After these document libraries are created, configure the content organizer rules to define which content types get routed to which library. You can customize the welcome page, and you can change Web parts just as you can with any other site.

After the primary configuration steps are completed, the next step is to define how information will get routed to the records center. There are several methods you can use to make this happen:

- By using the Send To function (which uses the officialfile.asmx Web service)
- Through an automated workflow (which uses the officialfile.asmx Web service)
- As part of e-mail journaling (which is configured with Microsoft Exchange Server)
- By manually submitting a record (which requires users to manually denote records)

Configuring the Farm Send To Action

The Send To function can be defined from either of two locations: from the advanced properties in a document library, or from the Farm option in SharePoint Central Administration.

An advantage of configuring Send To locations in Central Administration is that after you create them, they are available to users in every site collection in a Web application and farm. This approach makes it easy to deploy the central records store Send To location regardless of the collaboration model used.

Another advantage of using the Central Administration method is that you can configure multiple Send To locations, which is useful for an organization that has more than one records center. Previously, in SharePoint 2007, you could have only a single Send To location for the entire farm.

To configure the farm Send To locations, perform the following steps:

1. Open Central Administration, General Application Settings, External Service Connections, Configure Send To Connections.

2. Select the Web application from the drop-down list for which the Send To location will show up.

3. You can also choose to allow the sites in the Web application to send items outside the site subscription, perhaps to another farm where a global records management system is in place.

4. Make sure to specify a friendly name in the Display Name field. This is the name that users see when they select the document in the library. Naming conventions are important, especially if multiple Send To locations are available to the user in both farmwide and locally configured locations.

5. Specify the Send To URL. To create the connection, you must specify the URL of the records center site including the Web service file name, *officialfile.asmx.*—for example, http://server/site url/_vti_bin/officialfile.asmx.

6. You can also choose to allow users to manually submit files to the records center using the 'Send To' feature on the document menu.

   IMPORTANT If the planned approach for official files is to have the process automated by a workflow only, you need to clear the Allow Manual Submission From The Send To Menu check box.

7. Choose what to do with the item being sent to the records center. There are three options: Copy, Move, and Move And Leave A Link.

8. Click OK to create the Send To connection.

Configuring the Content Organizer Rules and Permissions

To automatically route documents to the correct library, you configure routing rules that are based on content types and metadata values. The same process applies when creating libraries as well as those for the document center. In Chapter 11, the "Content Organizer and 'Send To' Functionality" section outlines how to create content organizer rules. These consist of the following:

1. Create a document library in the Record Center site that will act as a drop-off library. (For details on creating a document library, see Chapter 11.)

2. Configure the drop-off library to allow content types, and then add the same content types as the source library. When specifying a submission content type to be used, the type must also exist at the target location library in the document center.

3. Add any custom metadata required on the library. The metadata fields must also match the source document library.

4. Create the content organizer rules, as shown in the "Content Organizer and 'Send To' Functionality" section of Chapter 11.

After the rule is created, grant submission rights to the application pool ID that will be used by the sending process, as shown in Figure 12-12. To grant submission, rights, perform the following steps:

1. Click Site Actions, Site Settings.

2. Under Users And Permissions, click Users And Groups.

3. Click on the Groups header in the left navigation pane.

4. Select the Record Center Web Service Submitters group from the list.

5. Grant permission by adding the application pool ID to the group. Click the New button to add the application pool ID.

FIGURE 12-12 Records Center Web Service Submitters page.

Now that the content organizer rule and required libraries are in place, the new library is ready to accept records submitted by users. The Allow Manual Submission setting must be enabled on the document library itself before the record center content organizer rule will be able to process documents submitted with the Send To feature. The Send To feature can be configured for the site collection or for an individual document library.

To enable Manual Submission on the site collection for all document libraries other than those that have custom record declaration settings, perform the following steps:

1. Click Site Actions, Site Settings.
2. Under Site Collection Administration, click Record Declaration Settings.
3. In the Record Declaration Availability area, select Available In All Locations By Default to enable the Send To menu item to be available in all document libraries.

> **IMPORTANT** Not all document libraries will need to allow for manual submission of records to the records center. Before enabling this at the site collection, you should ensure that the records management policy is adapted for this setting and content organizer rules have been put in place to support document libraries as they are created.

To enable Manual Submission on the document library, which turns on the Send To menu item in the document drop-down menu, perform the following steps:

1. Navigate to the document library by clicking on its title.
2. In the document library, select Library Tools, Library in the management ribbon for the document library.
3. Select Settings, Library Settings.
4. Under Permissions And Management, select Record Declaration settings.
5. Configure Manual Record Declaration Availability to Always Allow The Manual Declaration Of Records.

The records center content organizer rule can be verified by sending a document that has been created with a matching type from a document library.

Perform the following steps, as shown in Figure 12-13:

1. Inside a document library, click a check box to select a document
2. Click the document drop-down arrow, and select the Send To option.
3. Select the records center name that you configured in the farm's Send To settings.
4. The record will be sent to the drop-off library in the records center.

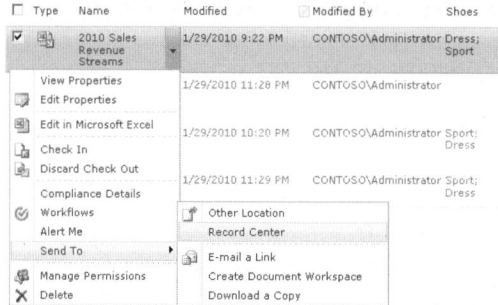

FIGURE 12-13 Manual submission of a document to the records center.

After the record has been submitted, an Operation Completed Successfully screen is displayed, as shown in Figure 12-14, unless additional metadata is required in the destination library in addition to the metadata already stored in the content type itself.

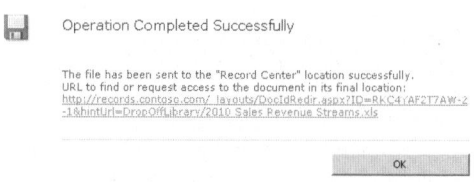

FIGURE 12-14 Submission to records center completed successfully.

If the submission was another item type, such as an e-mail message, a prompt appears as part of the journaling method to provide the metadata that was configured on the destination library. If the submission was part of a workflow, no manual process is required and the document is correctly routed at the time the call is made to submit the document.

Managing the Records

After the records center has been established for a period of time, certain compliance actions might need to be taken on the documents submitted to the records center and also on other documents in the system that had previously been declared as records. The records center carries certain unique compliance management functions to enable you to do this:

- Discover and hold records
- Generate a file plan report
- Generate an audit report

To access the three options, click Manage Records Center in Site actions in the Common Records Management Tasks area; you can also find the hold and eDiscovery management settings under the site settings.

Discover and Hold Records

At certain times, an organization might be required to produce all records pertaining to a specific set of criteria. This is true for audits or to meet certain legal requirements. As part of some legal requirements or audits, all records pertaining to a specific contract or some other criteria might be required. It is critical to be able to track down all items that match the requirements. With the Discover And Hold feature, you are able to issue a search query to discover the items in question and issue a hold on those found records.

To discover and hold records as available in Record Center Management Tasks, perform the following steps:

1. Select Site Actions, Manage Record Center.
2. Under Common Records Management Tasks, select Discover And Hold Records.
3. Enter relevant search criteria, and specify or create a relevant hold definition.
4. Click the Add Results To Hold' button to start the search.

There are three configuration options for discover and hold records. Both the search criteria and the relevant hold must be specified before starting the search:

- **Search Criteria**   Defines the URL and the search query context for discovery.
- **Local Hold Or Export**   If you select Local Hold, the items remain in their current location and cannot be deleted even if an information management policy was defined to delete them after a certain period of time. The items remain until the hold is lifted. If you select Export, you can choose another location to copy all the discovered items to. A hold is placed on the copied items.
- **Relevant Hold**   Specifies which hold to apply to the search results. The hold definition specifies the manager of the hold, and any additional documenta-tion about the hold can be attached to the hold definition. You can create multiple hold definitions. The records being placed on hold will have the relevant hold associated with them.

After the search has finished and the relevant hold has been defined, select Add Results To Hold and the items discovered will be placed on hold. You can specify that a record be held for more than one relevant hold at the same time. You might want to do this when you have more than one legal requirement or audit that pertains to a file. In these instances, an item still remains on hold even if one of the holds is lifted.

Generate a File Plan Report

You can create a Microsoft Office Excel file that outlines your file plan as it is currently figured in your records center, and you can export it. To create the file plan, you need to specify a location to store it in, as shown in Figure 12-15.

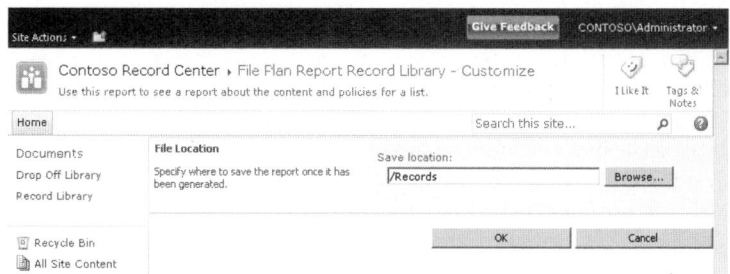

FIGURE 12-15 File Plan Report Record Library customization page.

To generate a file plan report perform the following steps:

1. Select Site Actions, Manage Record Center.
2. Under Common Records Management Tasks, select Generate A File Plan Report.
3. Specify the file location where the report will be stored when it is generated, as shown in Figure 12-15.
4. Click OK.

The file plan report is generated as an Excel document that contains detailed information about the configured records center file plan. The file plan report contains the following information:

- Site details, such as declaration settings and the number of items on hold
- Content types used in the policies
- Policy names associated with the content types
- Policy description details
- Retention details, which you can drill down into for more information on the secondary worksheet within the Excel report file
- Folder details, which you can drill down into for information on folders, such as item totals and security

Each new report is stored separately in the folder specified, as shown in Figure 12-16.

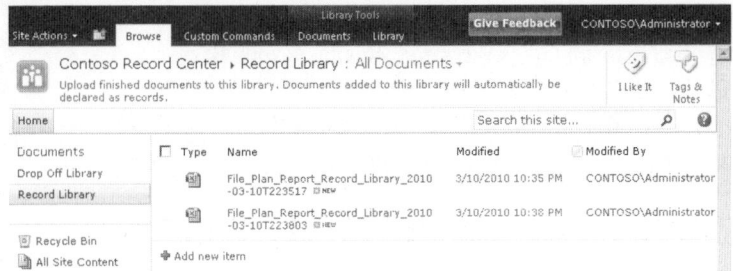

FIGURE 12-16 Record library showing the exported file plan summary.

Generate an Audit Report

Auditing reports provide the ability to drill down into specific areas of declared records activities. The reports are divided into four categories, with each category having specific reports available:

- Content Activity Reports
  - Content modifications
  - Content type and list modifications
  - Content viewing
  - Deletion
- Custom Reports
  - Run a custom report
- Information Management Policy Reports
  - Expiration and disposal
  - Policy modifications
- Security and Site Settings Reports
  - Auditing settings
  - Security settings

The longer the records center has been in place, the more information you will find available to generate the reports. This information will be vital to compliance officers or auditors and could be required as part of legal enquiries. Custom reports can be used to gain a more detailed picture of specific events.

CHAPTER 13

Portals and Collaboration

■ Publishing Infrastructure   **405**

One of the first things many administrators notice about SharePoint Server 2010 is the lack of a fully functioning portal. The lack of a portal is a result of the expansive feature set included in SharePoint Server 2010. There simply is no way to develop a portal that will work for every organization. Instead, you have been provided with a rich feature set to build your own, distinct portal. This chapter discusses the core features most administrators will use when building a portal.

Publishing Infrastructure

The publishing infrastructure of SharePoint Server 2010 contains many different features and a wide range of functionality. The major elements of this infrastructure are master pages, page layouts, and content types. Before continuing with the details of the publishing infrastructure, here is an overview of the major components.

■ **Master pages**   Microsoft Office SharePoint Server 2010 uses ASP.NET master pages to define the look and feel of the common page elements used in a site. The use of master pages reduces a site's design and development overhead by imparting changes made to a single file to the entire site. Master pages commonly include headers, footers, and navigation controls. SharePoint Server 2010 master pages also contain the Ribbon user interface, which was introduced in Microsoft Office 2007.

■ **Page layouts**   Page layouts are another key component of the SharePoint Server 2010 publishing infrastructure. Page layouts reference a SharePoint Server 2010 master page and control how the content is presented to the user. Page layouts depend on content types to provide instruction as to what information should be surfaced in the page layout. Page layouts are stored in the Master Page Gallery and can, like master pages, be applied throughout a site.

- **SharePoint Designer 2010**   SharePoint Designer 2010 is a tool that many administrators and designers will use when customizing master pages and page layouts on sites. SharePoint Designer 2010 is a free program; therefore, controlling access to this tool is critical to maintaining control of the content and layout of a SharePoint Server 2010 site. With SharePoint Server 2010, you now have the ability to easily control access to SharePoint Designer 2010 through both Central Administration and the Site Settings menu.
- **Themes**   SharePoint Server 2010 has brought about significant change with regard to customizing site themes. These changes make working with SharePoint Server 2010 themes easier for the end user. As with many aspects of SharePoint Server 2010, the amount of latitude given to the end user to customize a site's color scheme and fonts depends on the level of control that is allocated to the user.

Enabling the Publishing Infrastructure

Many SharePoint Server 2010 site templates do not have the publishing infrastructure enabled. To discover whether a site has the publishing infrastructure enabled, open the Site Actions menu. If you do not see the Manage Content And Structure option, as shown in Figure 13-1, you most likely do not have the publishing infrastructure enabled.

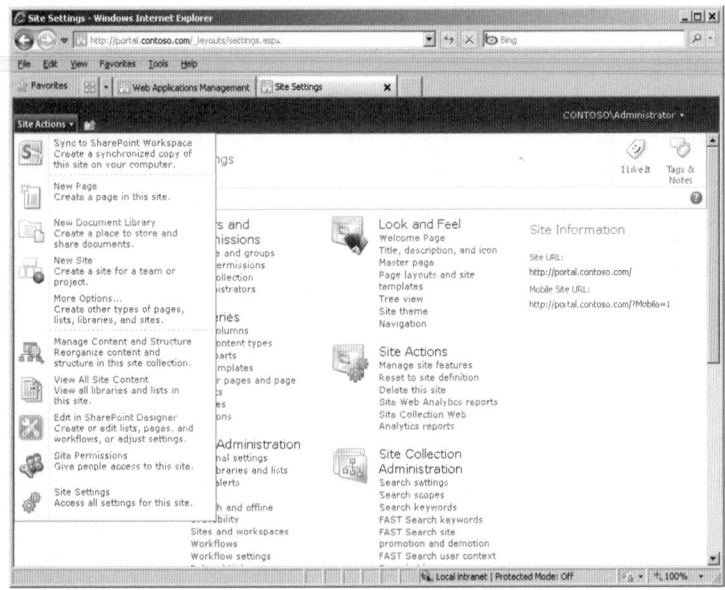

FIGURE 13-1 A publishing infrastructure Site Actions menu.

To enable the publishing infrastructure, you must first activate the feature at the site-collection level, and also for each site within the collection. To enable the publishing infrastructure for the top-level site, do the following:

1. From Site Actions menu, open Site Settings and select Site Collection Features in the Site Collection Administration grouping.

2. Click the Activate button to the right of the SharePoint Server Publishing Infrastructure feature, as seen in Figure 13-2.

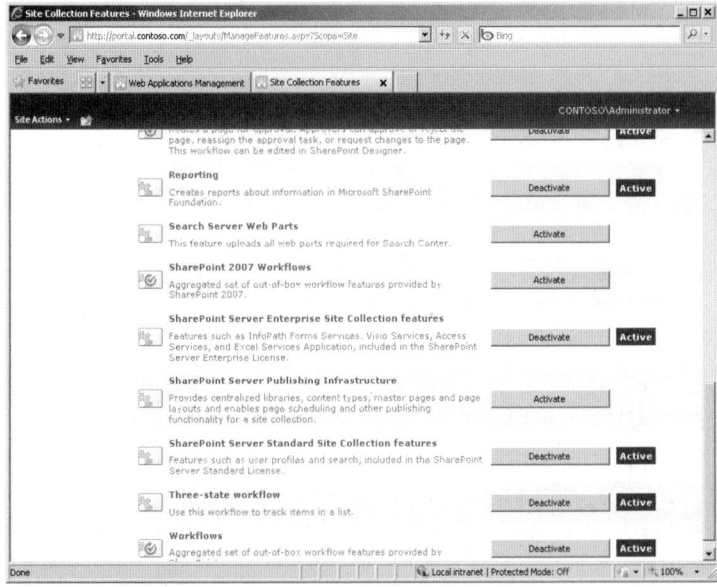

FIGURE 13-2 Click Activate to enable the feature.

3. From the Site Actions menu, open Site Settings and select Manage Site Features in the Site Actions grouping.

4. Click the Activate button for the SharePoint Server Publishing feature.

Master Pages

After enabling the publishing infrastructure, you can add and remove master pages, and select the availability of those master pages within your sites. In SharePoint Server 2010, you now have the flexibility of branding application master pages without modifying the files on the Web server. In previous versions of SharePoint Server, pages within a site were branded with the site master page, and pages on the hard disk of the Web server were branded differently. To enable application master pages to use the site master page, do the following:

1. Browse to Central Administration, Application Management, Manage Web Applications.

2. Select the Web application you want to modify, and select General Settings from the Web Applications tab on the management Ribbon.

3. Scroll down until you see the Master Page Setting For Application _Layouts Pages option, as shown in Figure 13-3.

4. Select Yes to reference site master pages.

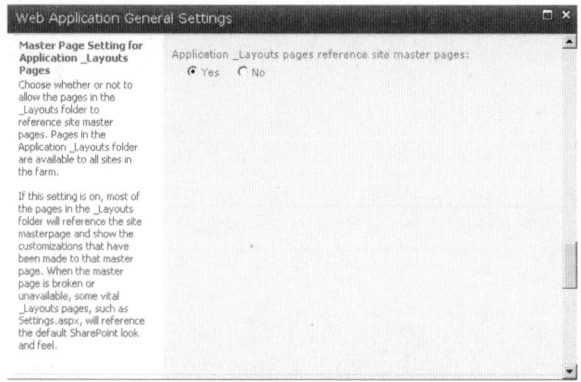

FIGURE 13-3 Select Yes to have application pages reference site master pages.

Master pages are applied in the Site Settings area. There are two options for master pages: Site Master Page and System Master Page. The site master page is used by all publishing pages, such as those in the /sitepages/ library. If you configured the _layout pages to use site master pages, those pages will adhere to this setting.

The system master page is the second option that you can configure. This master page is used for all forms and view pages throughout the site—essentially, all pages *except* those in publishing libraries. To change the site or system master page, do the following:

1. From the Site Actions menu, open Site Settings and select Master Page in the Look And Feel grouping.

2. In the drop-down menu for either the Site Master Page section or the System Master Page section, select a master page, as seen in Figure 13-4.

3. If desired, you can reset all subsites to inherit this master page.

4. Click OK.

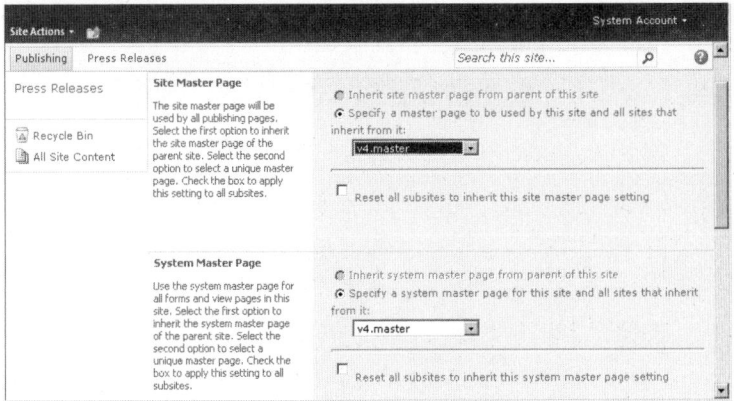

FIGURE 13-4 Change the master page via the drop down menu

TIP Subsites can inherit the system master page without activating the publishing infrastructure on those subsites. This reduces the page size and the complexity of managing those subsites.

You can also upload custom master pages that are created by your developers or designers. This allows for greater delegation of administration than with a nonpublishing site collection. Without the publishing infrastructure enabled, a site collection administrator cannot change or upload master pages without SharePoint Designer 2010. To upload a custom master page for use, do the following:

1. From the Site Actions menu, open Site Settings and select Master Pages And Page Layouts in the Galleries grouping to get to the page shown in Figure 13-5.

2. Select Documents on the Library Tools tab from the management Ribbon.

3. Select Upload Document.

4. Browse and select your custom master page.

5. Click OK.

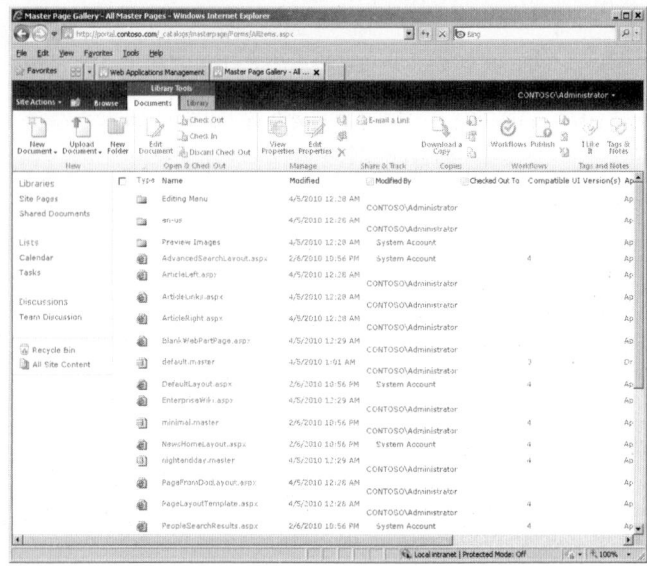

FIGURE 13-5 Select Upload Document to upload your custom master page.

Before master pages will work for nonadministrative users, they must first be published and approved in the Master Page And Page Layout Gallery. To publish a master page, Select Publish A Major Version, as seen in Figure 13-6.

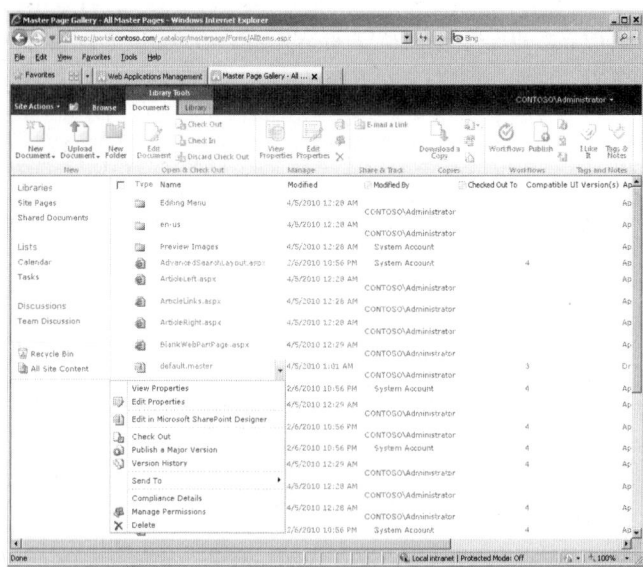

FIGURE 13-6 Select Publish A Major Version to make the master page available.

Page Layouts

Page layouts are the component of SharePoint Server 2010 that define the look and feel, as well as the placement, of your content in a site. These pages define content zones, including the placement of Web part zones and field controls, and they can also contain Web parts. The content type and associated page layout control the information collected for the page. This content type also defines what type of content, such as text or images, needs to be collected for the field. This collected information is stored in a list and is displayed on the page, according to the page layout. To upload a new page layout, do the following:

1. From the Site Actions menu, open Site Settings and select Master Pages And Page Layouts in the Galleries grouping.
2. Select Documents from the Library Tools tab on the management Ribbon.
3. Select Upload Document.
4. Browse and select your custom master page.
5. Select Publish A Major Version in the page layout drop-down menu.
6. Click OK.

You can control which page layouts are available to end users in a publishing site. To limit the page layouts available to users, do the following:

1. From the Site Actions menu, open Site Settings and select Master Pages And Site Templates from the Look And Feel grouping.
2. Highlight the allowed page layouts, and click Add, as seen in Figure 13-7.

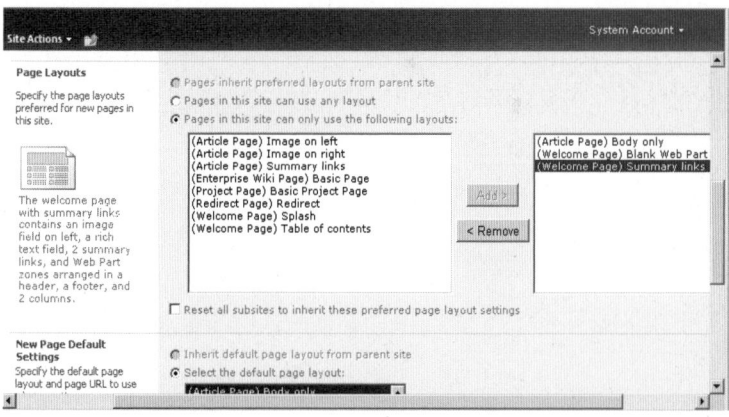

FIGURE 13-7 Click Add or double-click to allow specific page layouts.

3. Click OK.

SharePoint Designer 2010 Access

SharePoint Designer 2010 is available to create and modify both page layouts and master pages. However, SharePoint Designer 2010 is a powerful tool and can quickly break your site if an untrained user has access. To prevent SharePoint Designer 2010 editing of master pages and page layouts, you can disable SharePoint Designer 2010 access. A farm administrator can limit the use of SharePoint Designer 2010 in a Web application, and site collection administrators can limit the use of SharePoint Designer 2010 in a site, assuming it is allowed for the Web application it is contained in.

To limit SharePoint Designer 2010 access for a Web application, do the following:

1. Browse to Central Administration, Application Management, Manage Web Applications.

2. Select the Web application you want to modify.

3. From the General Settings drop-down menu, on the Web Applications tab, select SharePoint Designer.

4. Deselect the type of access you want to deny in SharePoint Designer 2010, as seen in Figure 13-8.

5. Click OK.

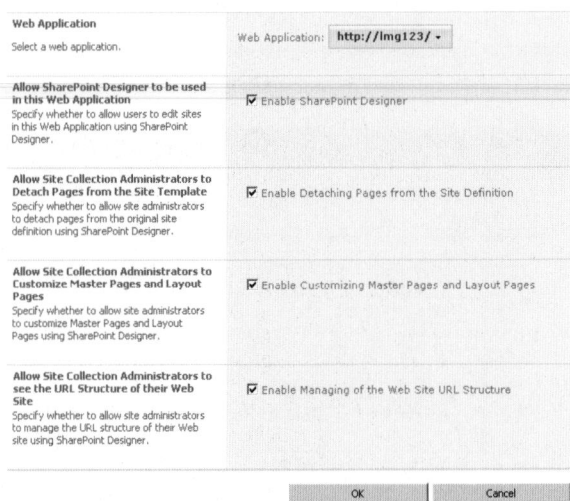

FIGURE 13-8 Deselect options you do not want to have in your site.

Only SharePoint Designer 2010 features that are enabled for the Web application are available to manipulate in Site Collection Administration. To limit SharePoint Designer 2010 functionality within a site collection, do the following:

1. From the Site Actions menu, open Site Settings.

2. From the Site Collection Administration grouping, select SharePoint Designer Settings.

3. Select or deselect SharePoint Designer 2010 settings, as seen in Figure 13-9.

4. Click OK.

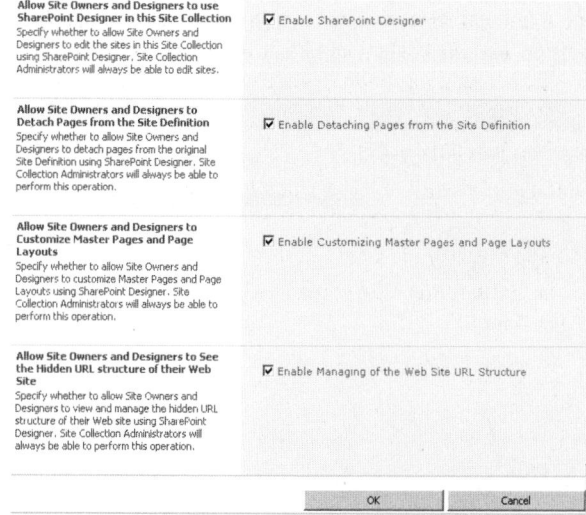

FIGURE 13-9 Deselect settings to make them unavailable.

Table 13-1 shows the restrictions and their corresponding results when modifying SharePoint Designer 2010 settings in Site Collection Administration.

TABLE 13-1 SharePoint Designer 2010 Setting Restriction Descriptions

SETTING	RESULT FOR HEADINGS
Enable SharePoint Designer	Gives either all access or no access to the site from SharePoint Designer 2010
Enable Detaching Pages from the Site Definition	Allows or disallows editing a page with content on it in SharePoint Designer 2010 to customize it
Enable Customizing Master Pages and Page Layouts	Allows or disallows editing and customizing master pages and page layouts in SharePoint Designer 2010
Enable Managing of the Web Site URL Structure	Allows or Disallows editing and managing the URL structure of a site from SharePoint Designer 2010

Themes

SharePoint Server 2010 has undergone a drastic change when it comes to the theme engine for customizing the look and feel of sites. The changes to the SharePoint Server 2010 theme engine have made it easier for users to customize the color scheme and fonts used within the site. To browse available themes and change the theme for a site, browse to Site Actions, Site Settings, Site Theme in the Look And Feel grouping. You'll be presented with a page similar to Figure 13-10.

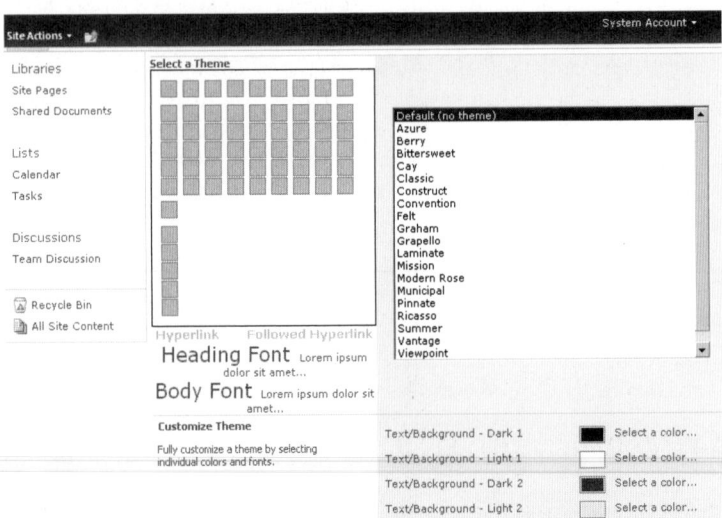

FIGURE 13-10 You can easily change the theme and colors in SharePoint Server 2010.

In previous versions of SharePoint Products and Technologies, themes were created by a developer and loaded on the file system of the Web server. In SharePoint Server 2010, you can create theme files (.thmx) in Office applications such as Microsoft Office PowerPoint 2010. Many companies may already have existing .thmx files that they would like to use to customize the branding of their site. These theme files are now stored in a theme gallery, much like master pages and page layouts. To upload files to this gallery, the user must have either administrator or designer privileges.

There are also some other changes to the theme engine that make changes to themes easier to perform. You can now preview the theme as it will appear on the site from Site Settings when applying the theme to the sites. You can also select to have them push the changes down to any existing child site or page when themes are applied through the browser UI in Site Settings.

Large Pages Library

New in SharePoint Server 2010 is the ability to use folders in publishing site libraries. In SharePoint Server 2007, folders were not supported in publishing libraries and management of large libraries was limited to a single level. With this new ability to use folders, you can organize the pages created for your site instead of having them all in a single library. With this enhancement comes the ability to structure pages for a site in a nested folder structure.

The ability to create a nested folder structure allows designers to logically connect the global navigation and current navigation menus. When new pages are created and a site has been configured to use auto-navigation, the new page is added to the root of the pages library and is automatically added to the Global Navigation and Current Navigation menus. If new pages are not added to the root of the pages library, the auto-navigation setting will not work. To resolve this, you will need to explicitly add each item to the Global Navigation and Current Navigation Menus.

Navigation

When you activate the publishing infrastructure for a site, the navigational options are greatly enhanced. You have the ability to use both headings and links to Active Directory groups through the Title and URL text boxes, as shown in Figure 13-11.

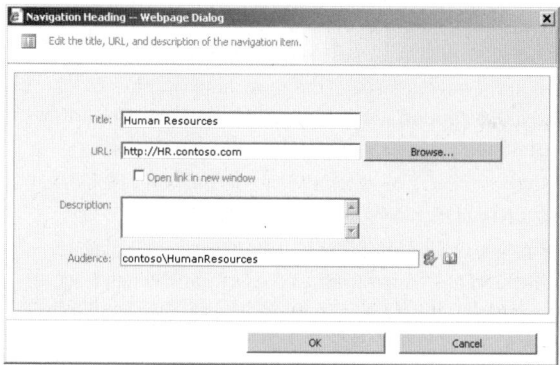

FIGURE 13-11 Use the Audience text box to select the Active Directory group to target a navigational item.

You can also granularly control headings and links. To add an item to the Navigation menu, do the following:

1. Browse to Site Actions, Site Settings.
2. In the Look And Feel grouping, click Navigation.
3. For the Global Navigation area, also referred to as the Top Link Bar, select whether to display the same navigation items as the parent site. If you are in the top-level site settings, this option will be grayed out.

4. Next, select whether to display subsites in the current navigation. The current navigation is also referred to as the *quick launch area*, as shown in Figure 13-12.

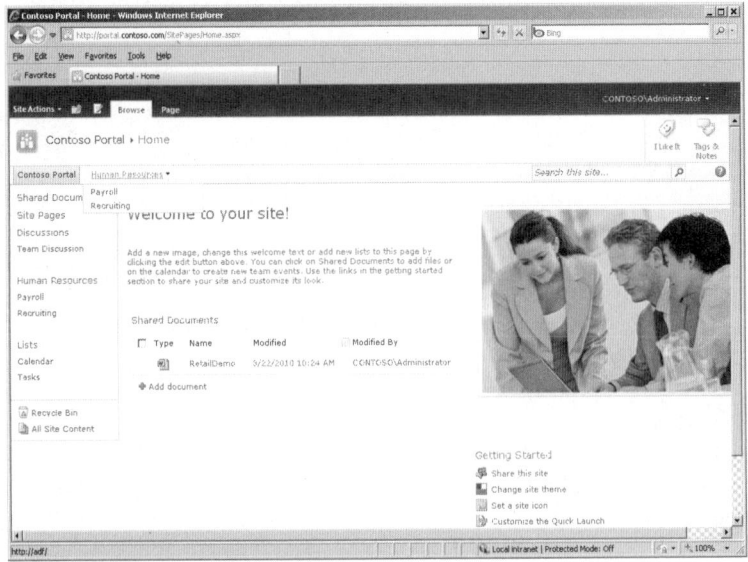

FIGURE 13-12 Current navigation includes libraries and lists by default.

5. For both global and current navigation, set the maximum number of dynamic items to show. Use caution when raising this setting beyond the default of 20. Always test the navigation with a load testing tool when you increase this number.

6. Decide whether to sort pages manually or automatically.

7. You can edit, add, or delete headings and links. Headings are displayed on the navigation page, and links appear as *fly-outs* under the heading. In Figure 13-13, Payroll and Recruiting are *links* under the Human Resources *heading*.

> **TIP** If you do not see your headings and links in the Global Navigation area, verify they were created under Global Navigation and not under Current Navigation. This is a common mistake made by both new and seasoned administrators.

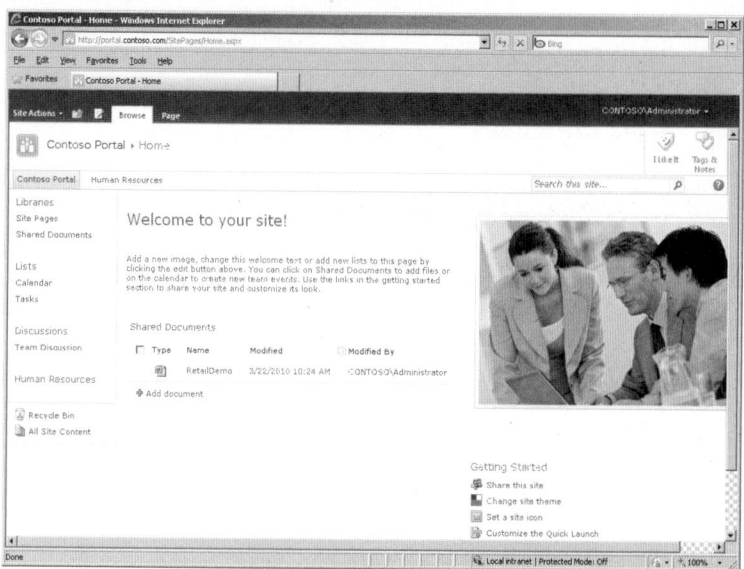

FIGURE 13-13 The selection of links under the Human Resources heading.

8. Decide whether to make the Show Ribbon and Hide Ribbon commands available.

CHAPTER 14

User Profiles and My Sites

- Creation and Maintenance Tasks in the User Profile Service
- Service Administration
- Profile Property Administration
- Profile Synchronization
- Enabling Social Features for Users and Groups
- Social Tags and Note Boards
- My Site Settings

The User Profile Service in Microsoft SharePoint Server 2010 is a shared service that provides a central location to create and manage various features and capabilities related to information about users in the farm. The features and capabilities managed by the User Profile Service are as follows:

- User profile properties
- Audiences
- Profile synchronization
- Settings specific to My Site

The information contained within a user profile is used as the basis for all social and personal functions. Administration of user profiles within Microsoft SharePoint Server 2010 can now be delegated to a service application administrator rather than to the farm administrator.

SEE ALSO For detailed information about the User Profile Service, see *http://technet.microsoft.com/en-us/library/ee721050(office.14).aspx.*

Creation and Maintenance Tasks in the User Profile Service

Before performing any of the creation or maintenance steps within the User Profile Service, make sure the site collection was created from the My Site host template. Also, an individual must be a service administrator to perform these steps.

To create a User Profile Service application, do the following:

1. Browse to Central Administration, Application Management, Manage Service Applications. The Manage Service Application page appears, as seen in Figure 14-1.

FIGURE 14-1 Manage Service Application page.

2. On the management Ribbon, in the Create group, click New. The list of service applications appears, as shown in Figure 14-2.

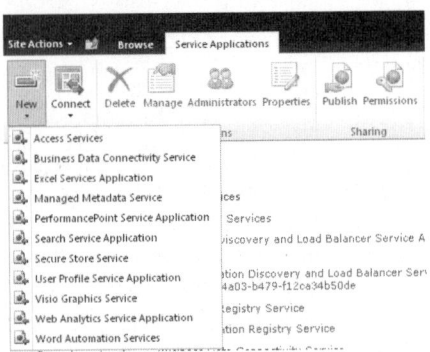

FIGURE 14-2 The Service applications list on the New menu.

3. Click User Profile Service Application. The Create New User Profile Service Application dialog box appears, as shown in Figure 14-3.

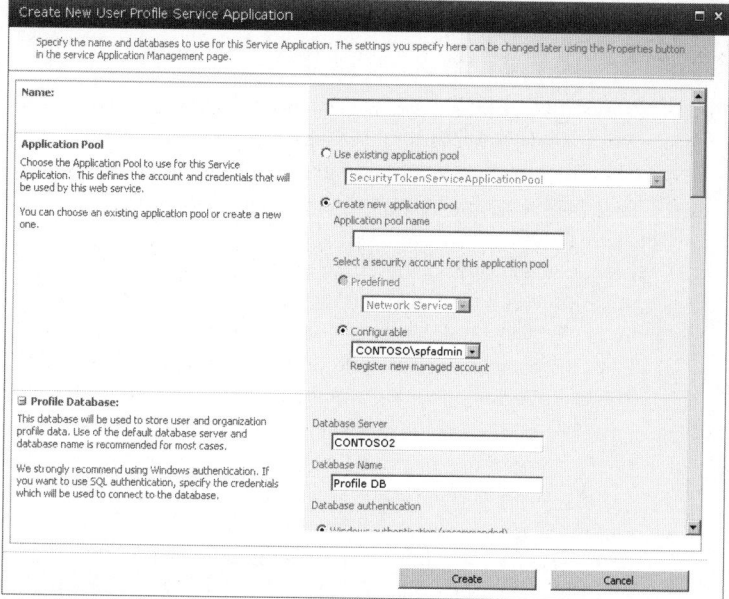

FIGURE 14-3 Create New User Profile Service Application dialog box.

4. In the Create New User Profile Service Application dialog box enter a unique name in the Name text box.

5. A service application requires the use of an application pool. This pool identifies the account and credentials that will be used by this service. In the Application Pool section, do the following:

    a. Select the Use Existing Application Pool option, and choose an existing application pool from the drop-down list. Or select the Create New Application Pool option to create a new one.

    b. For the Select A Security Account For This Application Pool option, select the Predefined option, and choose an existing predefined security account from the drop-down list. Or select the Configurable option, and choose an existing managed account from the drop-down list.

    You can register a new managed account by clicking the Register New Managed Account link, which displays the Register Managed Account dialog box.

6. The profile database is used to retain the user and organization profile information. In the Profile Database section, do the following:

    a. In the Database Server text box, enter the name of the database server on which the profile database will be located.

    b. In the Database Name text box, enter the name of the database that will be created in the server you specified in the preceding step.

c. Select the Windows Authentication (Recommended) option as the authentication method for the database when you want to use Integrated Windows authentication. Or select the SQL Authentication option, and enter the relevant credentials in the Account and Password text boxes that will be used to connect to the database.

If you want to specify a failover server (used in database mirroring) for the profile database, enter the server name in the Failover Database Server text box in the Failover Server section.

7. The profile synchronization database is used to retain configuration and staging information for synchronization of profile information from external sources. In the Synchronization Database section, do the following:

   a. Enter the name of the database server in the Database Server text box. This is the server where the synchronization database will be located.

   b. Enter the name of the database in the Database Name text box. This will be the name of the database that will be created in the server specified in the preceding bullet point.

   c. Select the Windows Authentication (Recommended) option as the authentication method for the database when you want to use Integrated Windows authentication. Or select the SQL Authentication option, and enter the relevant credentials in the Account and Password text boxes that will be used to connect to the database.

8. If you want to specify a failover server (used in database mirroring) for the synchronization database, enter the server name in the Failover Database Server text box in the Failover Server section.

9. The social tagging database is used to store social tags and notes created by users. In the Social Tagging Database section, do the following:

   a. In the Database Server text box, enter the name of the server on which the social tagging database will be located.

   b. In the Database Name text box, enter the name of the database that will be created in the server specified in the preceding step.

   c. Select the Windows Authentication (Recommended) option as the authentication method for the database when you want to use Integrated Windows authentication. Or select the SQL Authentication option, and enter the relevant credentials in the Account and Password text boxes that will be used to connect to the database.

10. If you want to specify a failover server (used in database mirroring) for the social tagging database, enter the server name in the Failover Database Server text box in the Failover Server section.

11. From the drop-down list in the Profile Synchronization Instance section, select the machine in the farm on which you would like to run the Profile Synchronization service.

12. In the text box in the My Site Host section, enter the URL of the site collection where you would like to provision the My Site host. Make sure the site collection you have provisioned is based on the My Site Host template.

13. In the My Site Managed Path section, enter the managed path where all the personal sites will be created. This, combined with the My Site Host URL, will form the URLs for My Sites—for example, *http://<My Site Host Web Application Path>/<My Site Managed Path>/<Site Naming Format>* will be the URL for the personal site for a user.

Three formats are available to name new My Sites:

- User name (does not resolve conflicts)—for example, *http://<My Site Host Web Application Path>/<My Site Managed Path>/username*

- User name (resolves conflicts by using *domain_username*)—for example, *http://<My Site Host Web Application Path>/<My Site Managed Path>/ username or .../domain_username*

- Domain and user name (will not have conflicts)—for example, *http://<My Site Host Web Application Path>/<My Site Managed Path>/ domain_username*

Select Yes or No from the drop-down list in the Default Proxy Group section if you want the proxy of this service to be part of the default proxy on this farm.

14. Click Create. You can also click Cancel to cancel out of the operation.

To edit a User Profile Service application, do the following:

1. Browse to Central Administration, Application Management, Manage Service Applications. The Manage Service Application page appears.

2. Scroll down, and in the Type column, click the User Profile Service Application link to select the row. (See Figure 14-4.)

Usage and Health data collection	Usage and Health Data Collection Service Application	Started
Usage and Health data collection	Usage and Health Data Collection Proxy	Started
User Profile Service Application	User Profile Service Application	Started

FIGURE 14-4 User Profile Service Application link.

3. On the management Ribbon, click Properties. The Edit User Profile Service Application dialog box appears.

4. Modify the relevant information.

5. Click OK to save the changes, or click Cancel to cancel out of the operation.

To delete a User Profile Service application, do the following:

1. Browse to Central Administration, Application Management, Manage Service Applications. The Manage Service Application page appears.

2. Scroll down, and in the Type column, click the User Profile Service Application link to select the row.

3. On the management Ribbon, click Delete. The Delete Service Application dialog box appears, as shown in Figure 14-5.

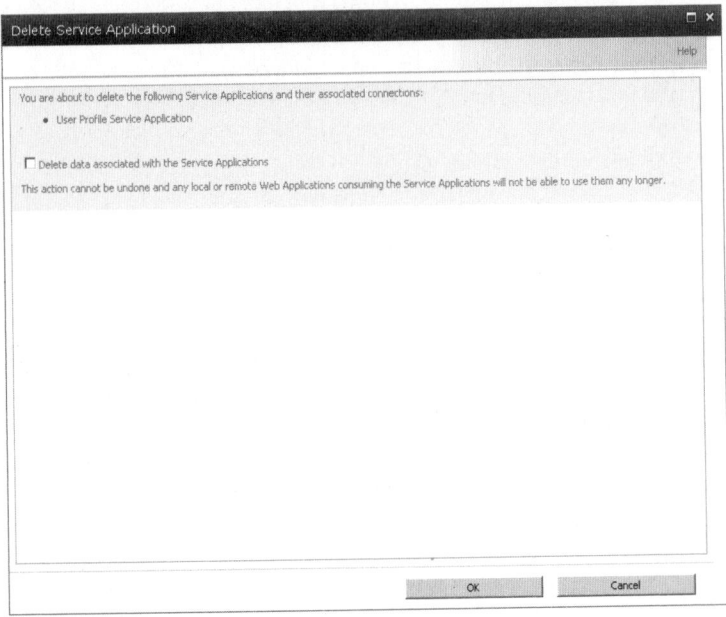

FIGURE 14-5 Delete Service Application dialog box.

4. In the Delete Service Application dialog box, confirm that you selected the correct service.

5. Select the Delete Data Associated With The Service Applications check box if you want to delete all the data associated with the selected service. Leave it unselected if you do not.

6. Click OK to delete the service application, or click Cancel to cancel out of the operation.

Service Administration

Administration of the User Profile Service can be done by the farm administrator or by someone the farm administrator delegates the appropriate permissions to. This service application administrator can administer only the services that she has been given the permission for. This delegation capability allows the farm administrator to assign others the administrative responsibilities for specific services, thereby freeing up the farm administrator's time to focus on standard farm administration tasks.

To delegate the administration of a User Profile Service from within Central Administration, do the following:

1. Browse to Central Administration, Application Management, Manage Service Applications. The Manage Service Application page appears.

2. Scroll down, and in the Type column, click the User Profile Service Application link to select the row.

3. On the management Ribbon, click Administrators. The Administrators For User Profile Service Application dialog box appears, as shown in Figure 14-6.

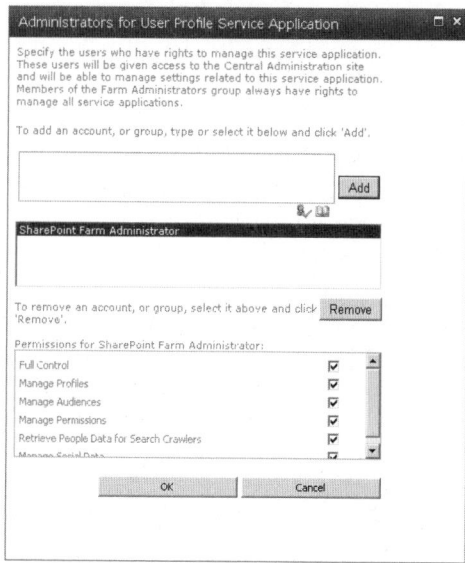

FIGURE 14-6 Administrators For User Profile Service Application dialog box.

4. In the provided fields, enter the group or account and click the Add button to add them to the list.

5. Make sure any newly added account is highlighted in the list.

6. In the Permissions For Account list, select the Full Control check box.

7. Click OK.

NOTE Delegating service administration privileges can also be done via Windows PowerShell by using the Get-SPServiceApplication, Get-SPServiceApplicationSecurity, New-SPClaimsPrincipal, Grant-SPObjectSecurity, and Set-SPServiceApplicationSecurity cmdlets. Details of the relevant script can be found at *http://technet.microsoft.com/en-us/library/ee721057(office.14).aspx#section2*.

Profile Property Administration

The Manage Profile Service page of the User Profile Service application is the central page to manage all currently available properties and where you create new user profile properties. Custom profile properties can be created to complement the out-of-the-box user profile properties to retain additional information related to personal or business attributes. For example, custom profile properties can be used to help associate users with additional business information based on those properties, thereby allowing for the creation of specific audiences. Having this additional information facilitates the organization of users from multiple business perspectives.

> **NOTE** Detailed information about user profile properties is available at *http://msdn.microsoft.com/en-us/library/ms543640.aspx*.

To create a new user profile property, do the following:

1. Browse to Central Administration, Application Management, Manage Service Applications. The Manage Service Application page appears.

2. Scroll down, and in the Type column, click the User Profile Service Application link to select the row.

3. On the management Ribbon, click Manage. The Manage Profile Service: User Profile Service Application page appears, as shown in Figure 14-7.

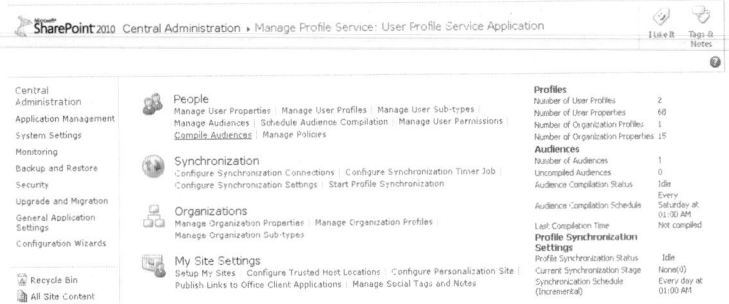

FIGURE 14-7 User Profile Service Application page.

4. Within the Manage Profile Service page, in the People section, click Manage User Properties. The Manage User Properties page appears, as shown in Figure 14-8.

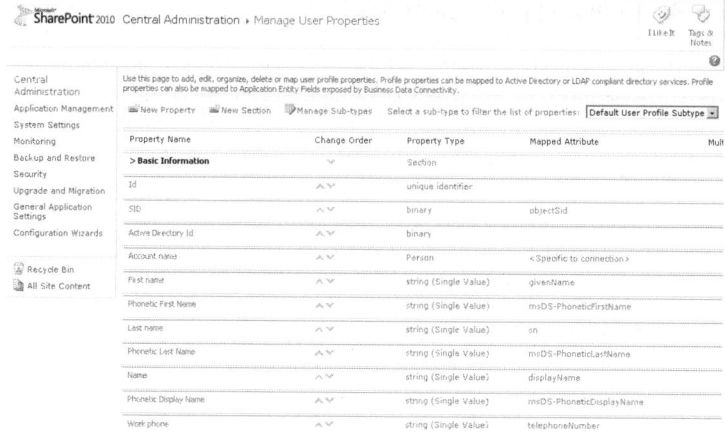

FIGURE 14-8 Manage User Properties page.

5. At the top of the properties list, click New Property. The Add User Profile Property page appears, as shown in Figure 14-9.

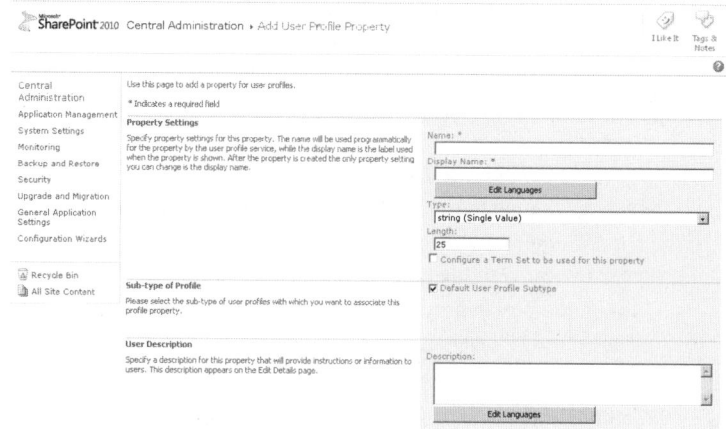

FIGURE 14-9 Add User Profile Property page.

6. In the Property Settings section, do the following:

a. Enter the internal name of the property in the Name text box.

b. Enter the display name of the property in the Display Name text box.

c. Select the data type of the property from the Type drop-down list. Note that clicking the Edit Languages button allows you to designate alternate display names in different languages for properties.

d. Enter the maximum amount of characters allowed for this property in the Length text box.

e. Selecting the Configure A Term Set To Be Used For This Property check box allows you to associate this profile property with a managed metadata term set and select a term set from the drop-down list that appears.

7. Select the Default User Profile Subtype check box in the Sub-Type Of Profile section to associate the default user profile subtype with this property.

8. Enter the description of the property in the Description text box in the User Description section. Note that clicking the Edit Languages button allows you to designate alternate descriptions in different languages for properties.

9. In the Policy Settings section, do the following:

   a. Select one of the following options from the Policy Setting drop-down list: Required, Optional, or Disabled.

   b. Select one of the following options from the Default Privacy Setting drop-down list: Only Me, My Manager, My Team, My Colleagues, or Everyone.

   c. Select the User Can Override check box to allow the user to override these settings.

10. The Edit Settings section allows you to designate whether or not the user can change the values for this property in his user profile. Choose one of the following options:

    - Allow Users To Edit Values For This Property, to allow users to change the value
    - Do Not Allow Users To Edit Values For This Property, to deny users the ability to change the value

11. The check boxes in the Display Settings section allow you to designate the property to do any of the following:

    - Show in the profile properties section of the user's profile page
    - Show on the Edit Details page
    - Show updates to the property in newsfeeds

12. The settings in the Search Settings section associate different behaviors with the property depending on the searches executed:

    - Select the Alias check box to designate the property as aliased.
    - Select the Indexed check box to designate the property as indexed.

13. In the Property Mapping For Synchronization section, click Remove to delete or change an existing mapping.

14. The settings in the Add New Mapping section allow you to set up mappings for the property when synchronizing user profile data. To correctly use the following settings, profile synchronization must be configured:

    - Specify the Source Data Connection by selecting it from the drop-down list.
    - Specify the Attribute by selecting it from the drop-down list.
    - Specify the Direction by selecting it from the drop-down list.

15. Click OK to create the property, or click Cancel to cancel the operation.

To edit an existing user profile property, do the following:

1. On the Manage Profile Service page, scroll down the list of properties to find the one you want to edit.

2. Hover the cursor over the desired property, click the down arrow to display the context menu, and select Edit. (See Figure 14-10.)

FIGURE 14-10 Profile Property context menu.

3. The Edit User Profile Property page appears. Modify the information desired, and then click OK to save the change or Cancel to cancel the operation.

To delete an existing user profile property, do the following:

1. From the Manage Profile Service page, scroll down the list of properties to find the one you want to delete.

2. Hover the cursor over the desired property, click the down arrow to display the context menu, and select Delete.

3. A confirmation dialog box appears. Click OK to delete the property or Cancel to cancel the operation.

Profile Synchronization

Profile synchronization allows you to bring together user and group information between the external data stores and the user profile store in SharePoint Server 2010. Profile synchronization within SharePoint Server 2010 facilitates the bulk import of information from that external store into SharePoint Server 2010. It also facilitates the export of information modified within SharePoint Server 2010 back to the external store. Profile synchronization facilitates maintaining the consistency of the user profile within SharePoint Server 2010 with multiple external data sources. The external sources supported by SharePoint Server 2010 are Active Directory Domain Services (AD DS), Business Data Connectivity (BDC) Services, Novell eDirectory v. 8.7.3 LDAP, and SunOne v. 5.2 LDAP.

To create a new profile synchronization connection, do the following:

1. Browse to Central Administration, Application Management, Manage Service Applications. The Manage Service Application page appears.

2. Scroll down, and in the Type column, click the User Profile Service Application link to select the row.

3. On the management Ribbon, click Manage. The Manage Profile Service: User Profile Service Application page appears.

4. In the Synchronization section, click the Configure Synchronization Connections link. The Synchronization Connections page appears. (See Figure 14-11.)

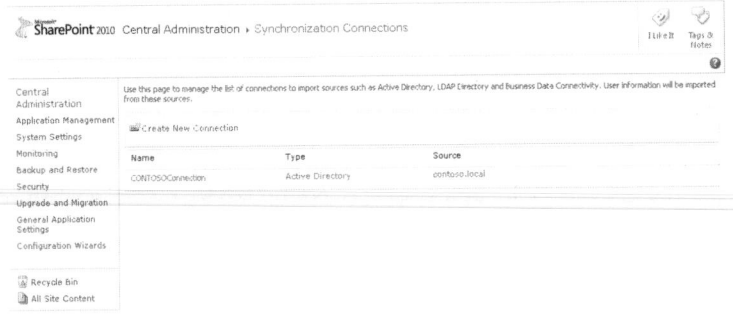

FIGURE 14-11 Synchronization Connections page.

5. At the top of the page, click the Create New Connection link. The Add New Synchronization Connection page appears, as shown in Figure 14-12.

6. Enter a name for the connection in the Connection Name text box.

7. Select the type of the connection from the drop-down list.

8. In the Connection Settings section, do the following:

   a. In the Forest Name text box, enter the name of the forest that you want to connect to.

   b. Select either the Auto Discover Domain Controller option or the Specify A Domain Controller option. If the latter is selected, enter the name of the domain controller into the Domain Controller Name text box.

   c. Select the Authentication Provider Type from the drop-down list.

   d. Enter the account credentials of the account to connect to the domain controller in the Account Name and Password fields.

   e. Enter the desired port in the Port text box.

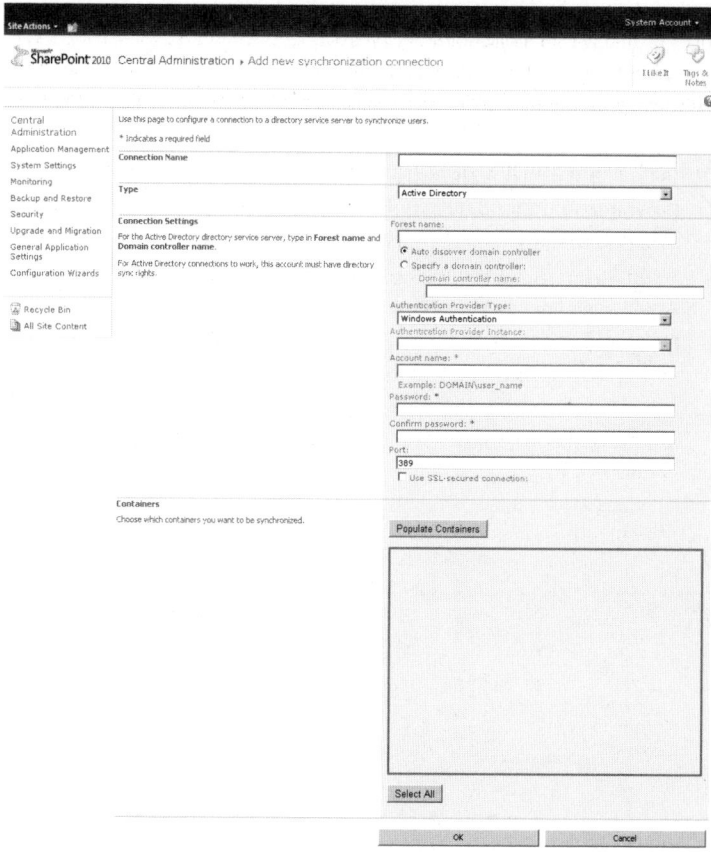

FIGURE 14-12 Add New Synchronization Connection page.

9. In the Containers section, click the Populate Containers button to display the directory service containers in the list, and then select the desired containers. You can also click the Select All button to select all the containers.

10. Click OK to execute the operation, or click Cancel to cancel the operation.

To edit an existing profile synchronization connection's connection filters, do the following:

1. Browse to Central Administration, Application Management, Manage Service Applications. The Manage Service Application page appears.

2. Scroll down, and in the Type column, click the User Profile Service Application link to select the row.

3. On the management Ribbon, click Manage. The Manage Profile Service: User Profile Service Application page appears.

4. In the Synchronization section, click the Configure Synchronization Connections link. The Synchronization Connections page appears.

5. Hover the cursor over the relevant connection, and click the down arrow to expose its context menu (as shown in Figure 14-13).

FIGURE 14-13 Connection Context menu.

6. Select Edit Connection Filters. The Edit Connection Filters page appears (as shown in Figure 14-14).

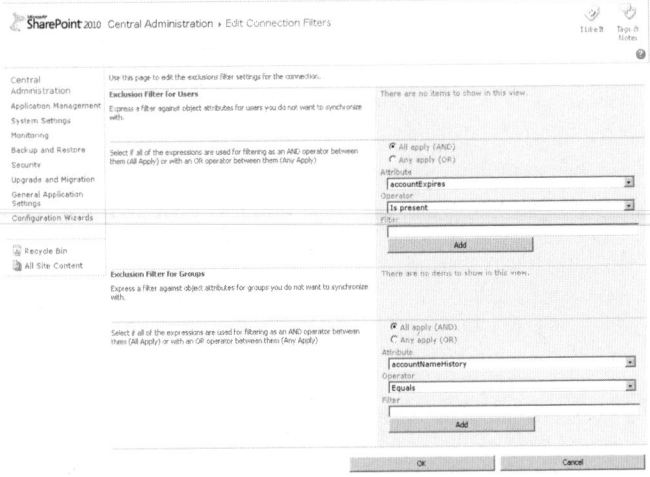

FIGURE 14-14 Edit Connections Filters page.

7. In the Exclusion Filters For Users section, in the Attribute drop-down list, select the user profile property for which you want to apply a filter, configure the filter parameters (Operator and Filter) for that property, and then click the Add button.

8. In the Exclusion Filter For Groups section, in the Attribute drop-down list, select the group profile property for which you want to apply a filter, configure the filter parameters (Operator and Filter) for that property, and then click the Add button.

9. Click OK to execute the operation, or click Cancel to cancel the operation.

To delete an existing profile synchronization connection, do the following:

1. Browse to Central Administration, Application Management, Manage Service Applications. The Manage Service Application page appears.

2. Scroll down, and in the Type column, click the User Profile Service Application link to select the row.

3. On the management Ribbon, click Manage. The Manage Profile Service: User Profile Service Application page appears.

4. In the Synchronization section, click the Configure Synchronization Connections link. The Synchronization Connections page appears.

5. Hover the cursor over the relevant connection, click the down arrow to expose its context menu, and select Delete.

The Mapping Profile Properties section allows you to assign mappings between the profile properties and the directory source properties. To map profile properties, follow these steps:

1. Browse to Central Administration, Application Management, Manage Service Applications. The Manage Service Application page appears.

2. Scroll down, and in the Type column, click the User Profile Service Application link to select the row.

3. On the management Ribbon, click Manage. The Manage Profile Service: User Profile Service Application page appears.

4. In the People section, click the Manage User Properties link. The Manage User Properties page appears. (See Figure 14-15.)

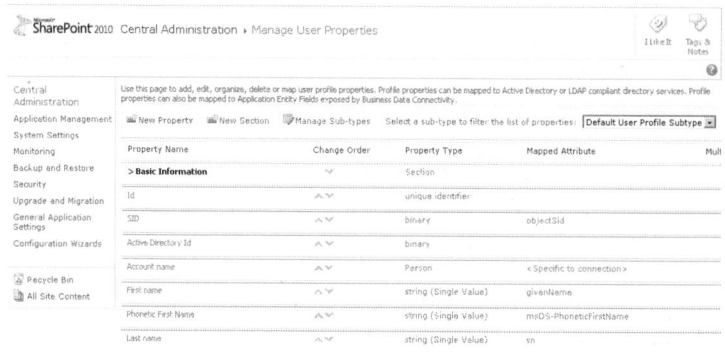

FIGURE 14-15 Manage User Properties page.

5. Hover the cursor over the property you want to map, click the down arrow to display the menu, and click Edit. The Edit User Profile Property page appears. (See Figure 14-16.)

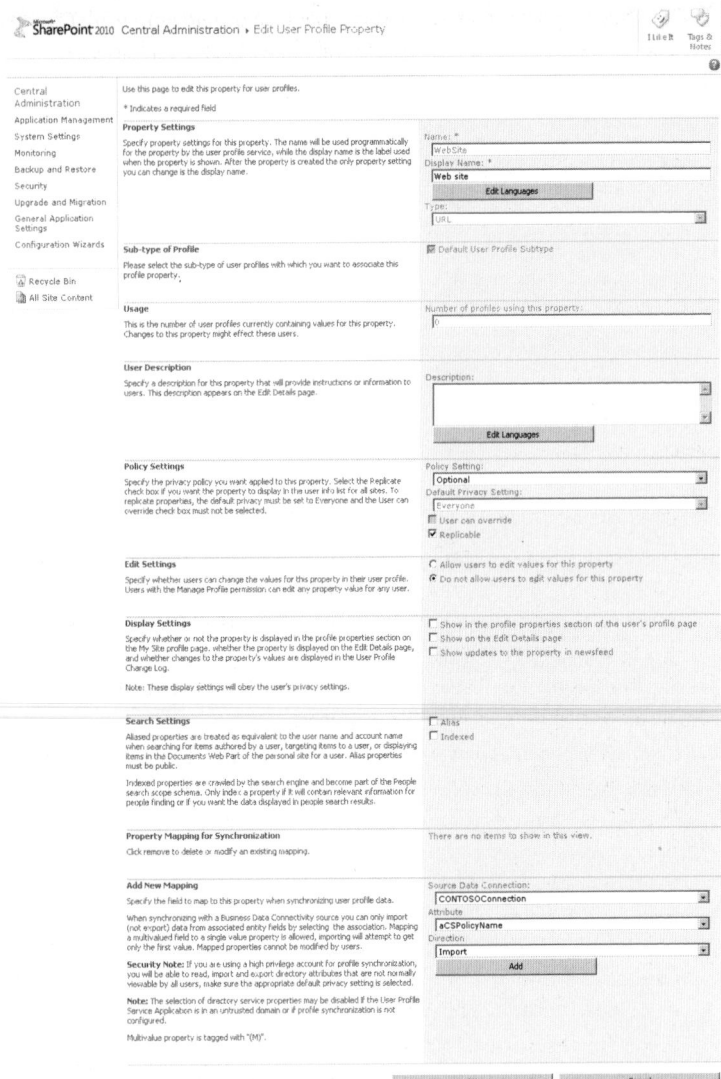

FIGURE 14-16 Edit User Profile Property page.

6. In the Add New Mapping section, select the Source Data Connection from the drop-down list, select the Attribute from the drop-down list, and then select the Direction of the mapping (Import or Export).

7. Click OK to save the mapping, or click Cancel to cancel the operation.

The Configure Synchronization Settings page (shown in Figure 14-17) allows you to manage the settings for profile synchronization of users and groups.

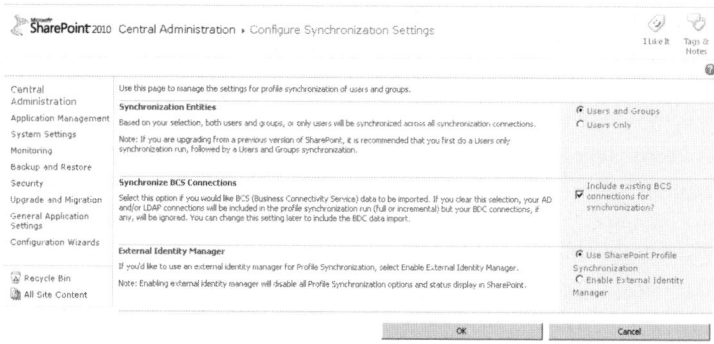

FIGURE 14-17 Configure Synchronization Settings page.

To configure the synchronization settings, complete the following steps:

1. Browse to Central Administration, Application Management, Manage Service Applications. The Manage Service Application page appears.

2. Scroll down, and in the Type column, click the User Profile Service Application link to select the row.

3. On the management Ribbon, click Manage. The Manage Profile Service: User Profile Service Application page appears.

4. In the Synchronization section, click the Configure Synchronization Settings link. The Configure Synchronization Settings page appears.

5. In the Synchronization Entities section, select the Users And Groups option to synchronize users and groups across all connections, or select the Users Only option to synchronize just users.

6. In the Synchronize BCS Connections section, select the Include Existing BCS Connections For Synchronization? check box to import your Business Connectivity Service (BCS) data during synchronization. Clear this check box if you do not want to include your BCS data during synchronization.

7. In the External Identity Manager section, select the Enable External Identity Manager option to use an external entity management system for profile synchronization. Select the Use SharePoint Profile Synchronization option to use SharePoint profile synchronization.

Enabling Social Features for Users and Groups

One of the many abilities a farm administrator controls is who has access to the social features within SharePoint Server 2010. These social features allow a user to bring into play the additional collaborative aspects of social networking within SharePoint Server 2010. The social features of the User Profile Service in SharePoint Server 2010 consist of the following:

- **User Personal Features**
  - **Memberships** SharePoint sites and distribution lists that the individual is a member of
  - **Colleagues** Information from the My Colleagues list and colleague recommendations made through SharePoint
  - **My Links** Links that a user tracks in her site
  - **My Personalization Links** Links to sites that are displayed in the user's personal site, whose visibility is governed by the personalization policy set for Personalization Site Pinning
  - **User Profile Properties** The profile properties that make up the user's profile, exposed by the service administrator
- **Create Personal Site** is a feature that allows a user to create his own My Site Web site that includes a personal area, a private page (My Home), and a publically available page (My Profile). Technically, a My Site is a site collection, and all rules governing site collections apply.
- **Social Features**
  - **Tagging** Provides the user with the ability to tag an object—such as a page, document, or site—to help the user remember or share it
  - **Notes** Provides the user with the ability to comment on an object (page, document, or site), and share those notes publically with others for viewing

Service administrators can also prevent specific users or groups from using the activated social features. Service administrators can give access to certain business groups or users so that they can contribute to the enterprise taxonomy, and they can restrict that function from being accessed by others. Users and groups who do not have this feature available to them will not see the I Like It and Tags & Notes buttons on the management Ribbon.

These social features are enabled through either Central Administration or via Windows PowerShell scripts.

To enable the social features for usage by users and groups, do the following:

1. Browse to Central Administration, Application Management, Manage Service Applications. The Manage Service Application page appears.

2. Scroll down, and in the Type column, click the User Profile Service Application link to select the row.

3. On the management Ribbon, click Manage. The Manage Profile Service: User Profile Service Application page appears.

4. In the People section, click the Manage User Permissions link. The Permissions For User Profile Service Application dialog box appears, as shown in Figure 14-18.

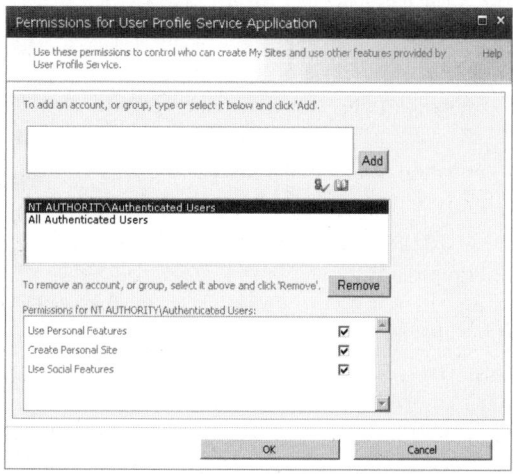

FIGURE 14-18 Permissions For User Profile Service Application dialog box.

5. Type or select a user or group account in the people picker, and then click the Add button.

6. In the Permissions For Users box, select all the relevant social features you want to enable for the given user.

7. Click OK to save, or click Cancel to cancel the operation.

Social Tags and Note Boards

Social features such as tagging and notes allow users to track and remember information, as well as state what information they'd like to share with others. These social features are enabled by default.

To activate or deactivate the tagging and notes social features via Central Administration, perform the following:

1. Browse to Central Administration, System Settings, Manage Farm Features. The Manage Farm Features page appears, as seen in Figure 14-19.

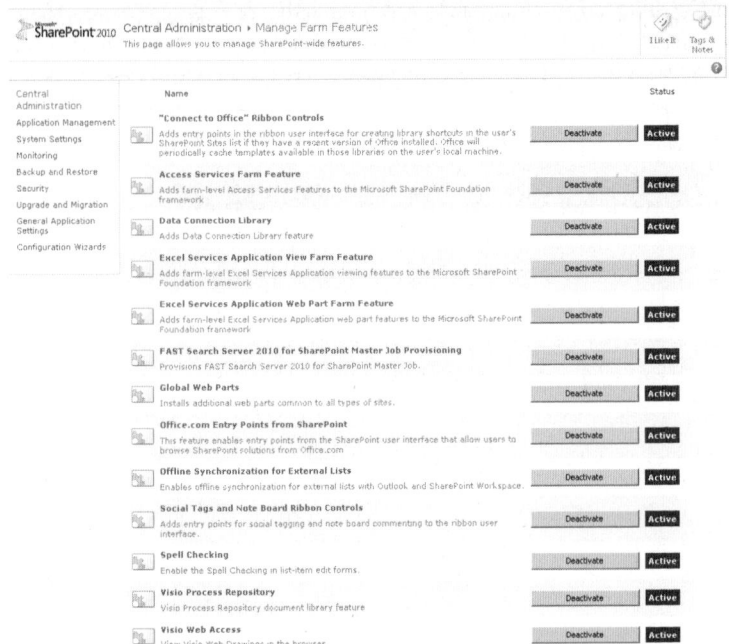

FIGURE 14-19 Manage Farm Features page.

2. If the Social Tags And Note Board Ribbon Controls feature has an Activate button, click it to activate the feature.

3. If the Social Tags And Note Board Ribbon Controls feature has a Deactivate button, click it, and the Deactivate Feature Warning page appears, as shown in Figure 14-20.

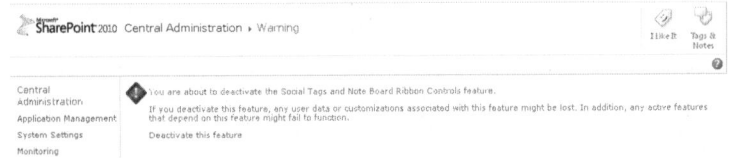

FIGURE 14-20 Deactivate Feature Warning page.

4. Click the Deactivate This Feature link to confirm the action.

NOTE Deactivation of this feature can also be accomplished via Windows PowerShell using the Get-SPFeature cmdlet. See *http://technet.microsoft.com/en-us/library/ee721062(office.14).aspx#section2*.

In addition to controlling the social features at a farm level, the service administrator can also manage the tags and notes directly. Tags and notes can be deleted for a specific link or user, within a date range, or at the even more granular level of the specific tag or note. Functions like this can be particularly useful for multiple scenarios, such as when an employee adds a tag that you might not want to be retained or used within the enterprise.

To delete all tags or notes for a specific user from within Central Administration, perform the following steps:

1. Browse to Central Administration, Application Management, Manage Service Applications. The Manage Service Application page appears.

2. Scroll down, and in the Type column, click the User Profile Service Application link to select the row.

3. On the management Ribbon, click Manage. The Manage Profile Service: User Profile Service Application page appears.

4. In the My Site Settings section, click the Manage Social Tags And Notes link. The Manage Social Tags And Note page appears, as shown in Figure 14-21.

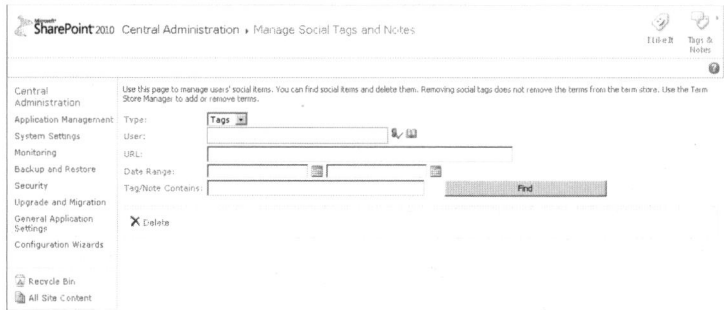

FIGURE 14-21 Manage Social Tags And Notes page.

5. From the Type drop-down list, specify either Tags or Notes as the type to search for.

6. Enter a user or group to search for in the User field.

7. Enter a URL to search for in the URL field.

8. Enter a date range to search for in the provided Date Range fields.

9. In the Tag/Note Contains field, enter information about a tag or note that you want to search for.

10. Click the Find button. The results are displayed in the grid below the search criteria, as shown in Figure 14-22.

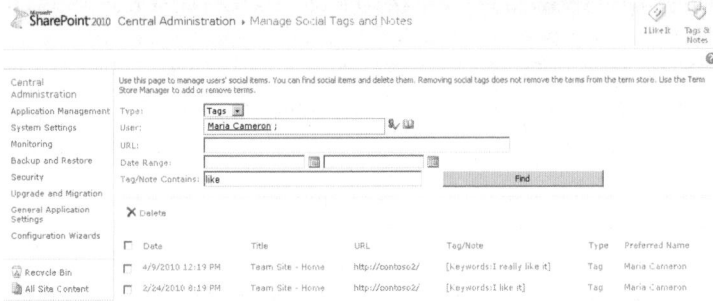

FIGURE 14-22 Social Tags And Notes search results.

11. Select the check box of the line item that you want to delete, and then click the Delete link.

12. A confirmation dialog box appears to confirm the deletion operation. Click OK to delete the item, or click Cancel to cancel the operation.

My Site Settings

My Site Web sites are personal Web sites that allow users to take advantage of the many social networking features of SharePoint Server 2010 within their enterprise. A My Site Web site consists of the following:

- **My Newsfeed** A collection of activities related to the following items:
  - **My Colleagues** Individuals a user can add to follow their profile updates, tags, notes, and the like
  - **My Interests** Keywords that describe both business and personal interests and are used to surface information that is tagged with them
  - **Settings** Configurable settings that allow users to dictate what information they want to see and follow
- **My Content** A page that organizes and facilitates the management of documents, lists, pictures, blog posts, and other types of content
- **My Profile** A page that organizes and facilitates the management of user profile properties, tags, and notes

The service administrator of the User Profile Service application manages the following settings of a My Site Web site:

- The setup of My Sites Web sites
- The creation and management of Trusted My Site host locations
- Personalization site links
- Links to Microsoft Office 2010 client applications

An individual's My Newsfeed page of a My Site Web site is shown in Figure 14-23.

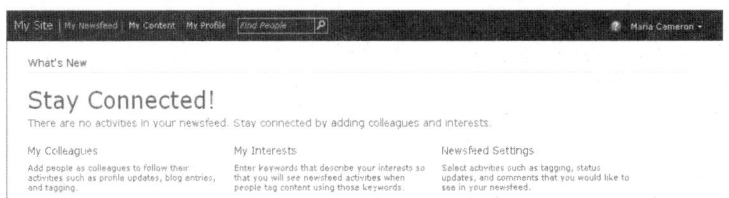

FIGURE 14-23 Example of a new My Site Web site My Newsfeed page.

Setup of My Sites Web Sites

Configuration of the My Sites Web sites is accomplished in the My Site host location. To configure the settings of My Sites Web sites, complete the following steps:

1. Browse to Central Administration, Application Management, Manage Service Applications. The Manage Service Application page appears.

2. Scroll down, and in the Type column, click the User Profile Service Application link to select the row.

3. On the management Ribbon, click Manage. The Manage Profile Service: User Profile Service Application page appears.

4. In the My Site Settings section, click the Setup My Sites link. The My Site Settings page appears, as shown in Figure 14-24.

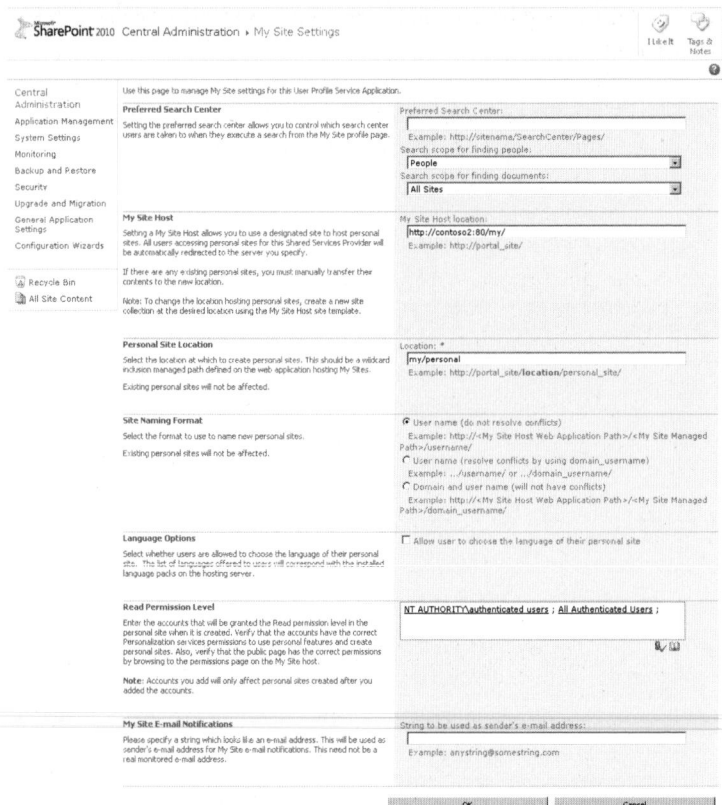

FIGURE 14-24 My Site Settings page.

5. The settings in the Preferred Search Center section allow you to dictate what search center is used when a user executes a search from within a My Site page:

- Enter the URL of the search center into the Preferred Search Center text box.

- Select the relevant scope in the Search Scope For Finding People drop-down list.

- Select the relevant scope in the Search Scope For Finding Documents drop-down list.

6. The My Site Host Location box allows you to specify a particular site to host all the My Site Web sites. Enter the specific URL into the text box.

7. The Personal Site Location section allows you to specify a particular location in which to create My Site Web sites. Enter the path into the text box.

8. The Site Naming Format section determines the format of a user's My Site Web site:

   - Select the User Name (Do Not Resolve Conflicts) option to use the individual's user name—for example, *http://<My Site Host Web Application>/<My Site Managed Path>/username/.*

   - Select the User Name (Resolve Conflicts By Using domain_username) option to use the individual's user name. Or, when there's a conflict, use the *domain_username* format.

   - Select the Domain And User Name (Will Not Have Conflicts) option to use the *domain_username* format at all times—for example, *http://<My Site Host Web Application>/<My Site Managed Path> /domain_username.*

9. The Allow User To Choose The Language Of Their Personal Site check box in the Language Options section determines whether users can choose the language of their My Site Web site. The list of available languages is determined by the language packs installed.

10. Accounts added in the Read Permission Level section are given read-level access to My Site Web sites when they are created. Enter the desired accounts here.

11. The text box in the My Site E-mail Notifications section contains the From e-mail address for all My Site notification e-mail messages. Enter a value here.

12. Click OK to save the settings, or click Cancel to cancel the operation.

Adding or Deleting a Trusted My Site Host Location

Trusted My Site host locations are typically used when users require access across multiple service applications, and they give users access to multiple My Sites across those applications.

To add a Trusted My Site host location, do the following:

1. Browse to Central Administration, Application Management, Manage Service Applications. The Manage Service Application page appears.

2. Scroll down, and in the Type column, click the User Profile Service Application link to select the row.

3. On the management Ribbon, click Manage. The Manage Profile Service: User Profile Service Application page appears.

4. In the My Site Settings section, click the Configure Trusted Host Locations link. The Trusted My Site Host Locations page appears, as shown in Figure 14-25.

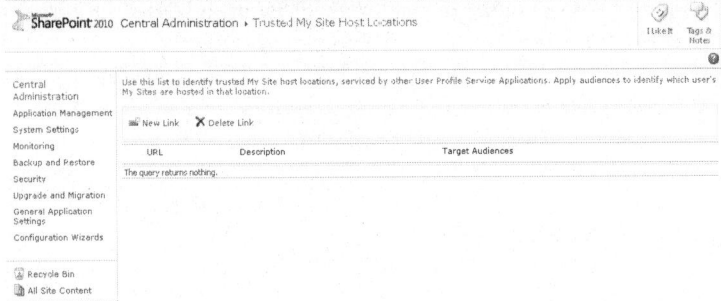

FIGURE 14-25 Trusted My Site Host Locations page.

5. Click New Link to bring up the Add Trusted Host Location page. (See Figure 14-26.)

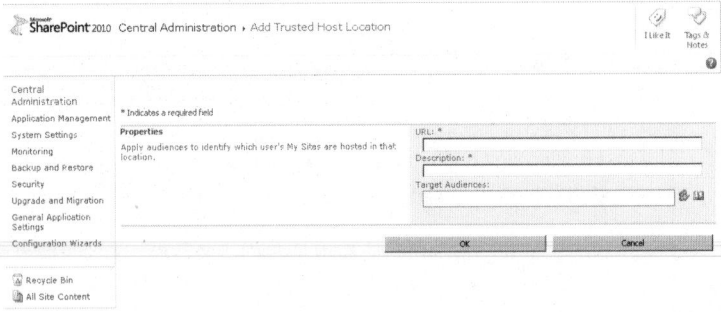

FIGURE 14-26 Add Trusted Host Location page.

6. In the Properties section, do the following:

   a. Enter the URL of a trusted location into the text box.

   b. Enter the description of the trusted location into the Description text box.

   c. Enter any target audiences for this location (optional).

7. Click OK to save the location, or click Cancel to cancel the operation.

To delete a trusted My Site host location, do the following:

1. Browse to Central Administration, Application Management, Manage Service Applications. The Manage Service Application page appears.

2. Scroll down, and in the Type column, click the User Profile Service Application link to select the row.

3. On the management Ribbon, click Manage. The Manage Profile Service: User Profile Service Application page appears.

4. In the My Site Settings section, click the Configure Trusted Host Locations link. The Trusted My Site Host Locations page appears.

5. In the list of trusted host locations that appears, select the check boxes of the locations you want to delete.

6. Click Delete Link and a confirmation dialog box appears.

7. Click OK to confirm the deletion, or click Cancel to cancel the operation.

Personalization Site Links

Personalization site links are links that are added to the Personal Link area at the top of the My Site page. These links that are added appear throughout all the My Site pages, allowing for a consistent look and feel.

To add a personalization site link, do the following:

1. Browse to Central Administration, Application Management, Manage Service Applications. The Manage Service Application page appears.

2. Scroll down, and in the Type column, click the User Profile Service Application link to select the row.

3. On the management Ribbon, click Manage. The Manage Profile Service: User Profile Service Application page appears.

4. In the My Site Settings section, click the Configure Personalization Site link. The Personalization Site Links page appears, as shown in Figure 14-27.

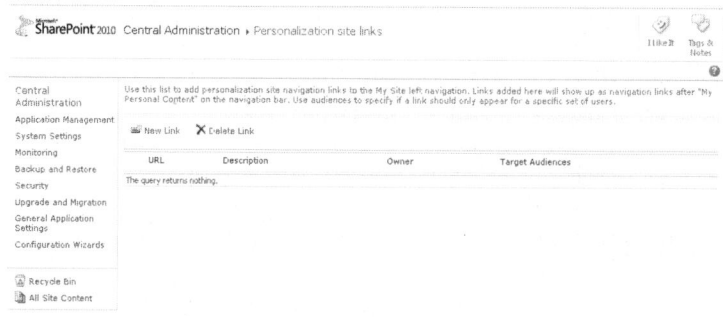

FIGURE 14-27 Personalization Site Links page.

5. Click New Link. The Add Personalization Site Link page appears, as shown in Figure 14-28.

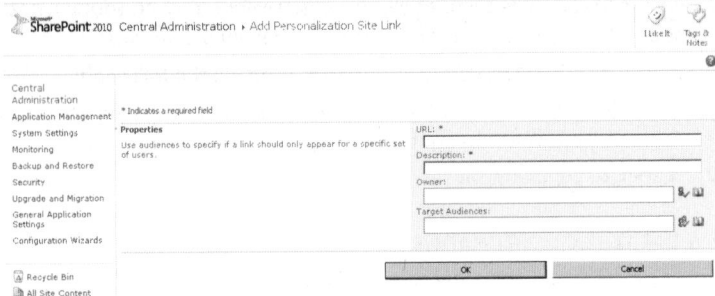

FIGURE 14-28 Add Personalization Site Link page.

6. In the Properties section, do the following:
   a. Enter the address of the link into the URL text box.
   b. Enter a description in the Description text box.
   c. Enter a user as the owner of this link. (This is optional.)
   d. Enter a target audience for this link. (This is optional.)
7. Click OK to save this link, or click Cancel to cancel the operation.

To delete a personalization site link, complete the following steps:

1. Browse to Central Administration, Application Management, Manage Service Applications. The Manage Service Application page appears.
2. Scroll down, and in the Type column, click the User Profile Service Application link to select the row.
3. On the management Ribbon, click Manage. The Manage Profile Service: User Profile Service Application page appears.
4. In the My Site Settings section, click the Configure Personalization Site link. The Configure Personalization Site Links page appears.
5. In the list of personalization site links that appears, select the check boxes of the site links you want to delete.
6. Click Delete Link and a confirmation dialog box appears.
7. Click OK to confirm the deletion, or click Cancel to cancel the operation.

Links to the Microsoft Office 2010 Client Applications

SharePoint Server 2010 and Office 2010 bring a deeper level of integration between the server and client tools than the previous versions. One of those additional integration points is the ability to publish links to SharePoint libraries and lists down to the client application. These links are exposed under the Favorite Links section in the

Save As dialog box of the client application. These links offer an additional level of integration when adding or saving items to SharePoint Server 2010.

To add a link to an Office 2010 client application, do the following:

1. Browse to Central Administration, Application Management, Manage Service Applications. The Manage Service Application page appears.

2. Scroll down, and in the Type column, click the User Profile Service Application link to select the row.

3. On the management Ribbon, click Manage. The Manage Profile Service: User Profile Service Application page appears.

4. In the My Site Settings section, click the Publish Links To Office Client Applications link. The Published Links To Office Client Applications page appears, as shown in Figure 14-29.

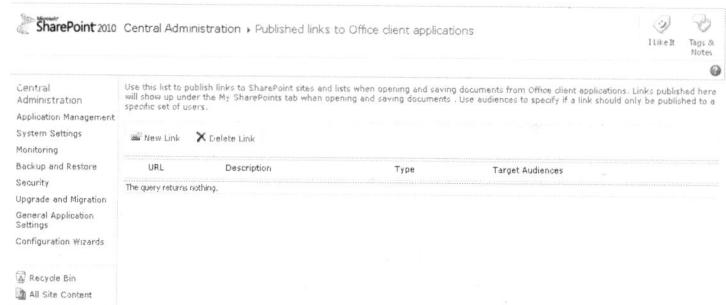

FIGURE 14-29 Published Links To Office Client Applications page.

5. Click New Link. The Add Published Link page appears, as shown in Figure 14-30.

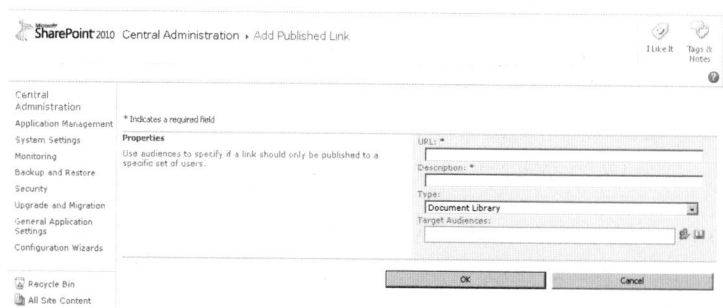

FIGURE 14-30 Add Published Link page.

6. In the Properties section, complete the following steps:
   a. In the URL text box, enter the address of the location to publish to.
   b. In the Description text box, enter a description.
   c. Select the type from the drop-down list.
   d. Enter a target audience for this link.
7. Click OK to save this link, or click Cancel to cancel the operation.

To delete a link to an Office 2010 client application, do the following:

1. Browse to Central Administration, Application Management, Manage Service Applications. The Manage Service Application page appears.
2. Scroll down, and in the Type column, click the User Profile Service Application link to select the row.
3. On the management Ribbon, click Manage. The Manage Profile Service: User Profile Service Application page appears.
4. In the My Site Settings section, click the Publish Links To Office Client Applications link. The Published Links To Office Client Applications page appears.
5. Select the check boxes of the links you want to delete, click Delete Link in the action bar, and click OK to confirm the deletion or Cancel to cancel the operation.

PART III

Operating SharePoint Server 2010

CHAPTER 15   Configuring Policies and Security   **451**

CHAPTER 16   Monitoring, Logging, and Availability   **489**

CHAPTER 17   Upgrading to SharePoint Server 2010   **517**

CHAPTER 18   Backup and Restore   **539**

Configuring Policies and Security

- Server Farm Security **451**
- Web Application Security **464**
- Web Application Policies **481**

Implementing security for Microsoft SharePoint Server 2010 is a multifaceted exercise. Although it is impossible to completely secure any system connected to a network, you can implement controls to mitigate the most common risks. The controls discussed here are a basic set of practices to use as you begin your secure design and implementation; they do not guarantee security. Your environment might require greater security than discussed here, or practices described in this chapter could possibly break your current implementation. For these reasons, you should always test new access, authentication, and authorization controls in a test environment before implementing these controls in your production installation.

MORE INFO For in-depth information on securing your Microsoft servers and applications, see *http://technet.microsoft.com/security*.

Server Farm Security

At the heart of your SharePoint Server 2010 security plan should be your server farm. For this chapter, the server farm refers to all the configuration data (configuration database) and physical servers consuming that data. Before moving directly into a SharePoint Server 2010 security configuration, be sure to consider all the dependent infrastructure supporting your implementation and how it affects your overall security posture.

To see an example of dependent infrastructure, consider both the hardware and software components of a three-tiered, small server farm, as seen in Figure 1-4:

- *Microsoft Windows Server 2008* is the foundation of both SharePoint Server 2010 and Microsoft SQL Server. If a hacker gains access to any of your server farm operating systems, he is a very short distance from all of your valuable SharePoint Server 2010 content.

- *Active Directory* is required for multiserver SharePoint Server 2010 farms and is often used for authorization to SharePoint Server 2010 content. If you use Active Directory, be aware that any domain administrator can quickly and easily escalate her privileges to gain administrator access to SharePoint Server 2010 configuration and content. Be sure to audit changes made to your SharePoint Server 2010 users and groups in Active Directory.

- *SQL Server 2005 or 2008* will host the majority of your SharePoint Server 2010 content. The content databases that hold site collections and sites can be copied and associated to almost any SharePoint Server 2010 Web application. You should control and audit users who have access to the physical databases.

- *Networking infrastructure* plays a vital role in SharePoint Server 2010 availability. Be sure to monitor your hubs, switches, and routers to ensure SharePoint Server 2010 availability.

- *Firewalls* often secure part or all of a SharePoint Server 2010 installation. Be sure to plan and test connectivity before deploying a production solution. Either an over-controlled firewall or under-controlled firewall can cause SharePoint Server 2010 outages.

- *Storage* is rapidly moving toward storage area networks (SANs) for manageability and availability. If the storage becomes unavailable (either through compromised security or a failure), for SharePoint Server 2010 servers or SQL Server servers, you will incur a complete SharePoint Server 2010 outage.

- *Server antivirus* is important to secure the operating system upon which SharePoint Server 2010 is installed. Compromised integrity of the file system or applications can result in a SharePoint Server 2010 security breach.

TIP Be sure to exclude the index file location from your server-based, antivirus scanning. Failing to do so can dramatically reduce the performance of the indexer.

Although this chapter is focused on SharePoint Server 2010 security, remember that your SharePoint Server 2010 security is only as secure as the underlying foundation of your physical servers, Active Directory, network infrastructure, and database servers.

Farm Administrators

Farm administrators have access to all parts of the SharePoint Server 2010 farm. Although the product is security trimmed and, by default, farm administrators don't have access to all site collections and service applications, they can always escalate privileges. Essentially, farm administrators have read/write access to all SharePoint Server 2010 databases. The most critical of these databases is the configuration database. When you add a person as a farm administrator, you are giving them access to configure your farm. Be very careful who you put into this group. To update the Farm Administrators group, browse to Central Administration, Security, Users, Manage The Farm Administrators group. It will look like most other SharePoint Server 2010 groups, but users in this group have more privileges than just the Central Administration site collection administrative role. For example, users in this group can create Web application policies that provide full control access to all site collections in the given Web application. To add a user, select New, Add Users.

> **NOTE** Active Directory groups are added using the same method as you do for adding users. Select New, Add Users, and enter the Active Directory group you want to make farm administrators. One downside to using Active Directory groups is that domain administrators can easily escalate their privileges by adding themselves to the Farm Administrators Active Directory group.

By default, the local server administrators are part of the Farm Administrators group. Local administrators include the Domain Administrators group. The problem with this is that all your domain administrators are also SharePoint Server 2010 farm administrators. This is likely undesired in most SharePoint Server 2010 installations that have critical or specialized security requirements. If this is the case, you'll probably want to ensure SharePoint Server 2010 administrators have basic training before granting them access to Central Administration.

> **TIP** If your SharePoint Server 2010 farm administrators and domain administrators are the same people, don't remove BUILTIN\administrators from the Farm Administrators group. This will ease system administration.

Password and Account Management

In SharePoint Server 2007, the ability to manage service account passwords across a farm was a nice addition to the password management found in SharePoint Portal Server 2003. It provided an interface to update the farm configuration of service accounts and their passwords. These changes were then propagated to the relevant locations, such as Internet Information Services (IIS) and Document Conversions services. This reduced the administrative effort of changing passwords on multiple servers and in multiple applications. There were still limitations, however. First, you had to change the password in Active Directory before changing it within SharePoint Server 2007. Second, the server Farm Account's password had to be managed from the command line. Third, the process in a multiserver farm was complex and prone to administrator user error. SharePoint Server 2010 introduces the concept and application of *managed accounts* in addition to service accounts. SharePoint Server 2010 also includes the automatic update of passwords, including the ability to set long, cryptographic passwords.

Managed Accounts

Managed accounts are used for all Web and service application accounts in the farm. Wherever these accounts are provisioned, such as in IIS and Windows Server services, you should not modify the instance of the accounts. If you want to modify either the account name or password, you should *always* use Central Administration or Windows PowerShell to update the farm configuration via Managed Accounts administration.

> **IMPORTANT** The first managed account is created automatically during farm creation. This account is referred to as the *managed farm account*. This account should not be used for Web applications or service applications other than Central Administration.

To create a new managed account, do the following:

1. Browse to Central Administration, Security, General Security, Configure Managed Accounts, as seen in Figure 15-1.

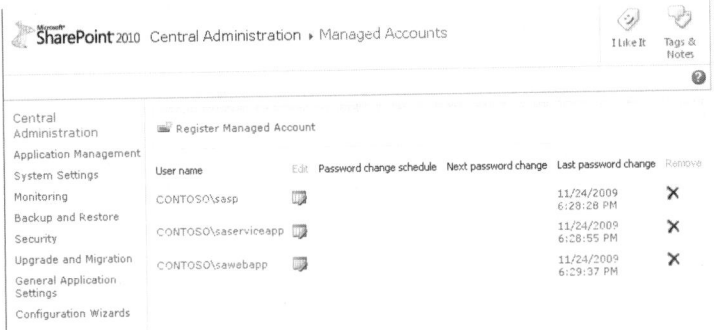

FIGURE 15-1 All managed accounts are shown in the User Name list.

2. Click Register Managed Account.
3. Type the service account credentials in the form DOMAIN\USERNAME.
4. If you want, you can enable Automatic Password Change.
   - Enter the number of days before the automatic change occurs.

- Decide whether you want to receive e-mail alerts about password change events. This e-mail address is set on the Password Management Settings page, seen in Figure 15-4.

5. Click OK.

TIP Most Web application and service application creation screens provide the ability to create managed accounts. Any account created using these configuration screens also appear in Central Administration, Managed Accounts. If you want to be better prepared for farm installation and configuration, you should create all necessary managed accounts prior to creating Web and service applications.

You can also configure existing accounts by selecting the Edit icon, as seen in Figure 15-1. The following options are available when editing a managed account:

- **Account Selection** Use this section to select the account you want to configure. Always verify you are modifying the correct account!
- **Credential Management** You can choose to immediately change a managed account's password, generate a new password automatically by the system, manually configure a password, or use the existing password. Note that you must know the existing password to choose the Use Existing Password option. These options are seen in Figure 15-2.

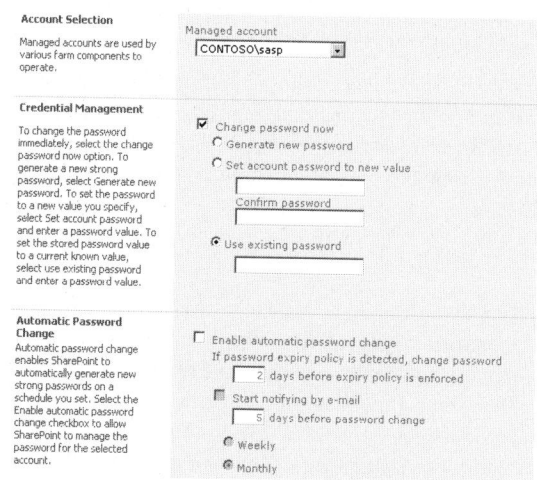

FIGURE 15-2 Select the managed account you want to modify.

- **Account Information** You can see the current status of a managed account, including the last password change, the next scheduled password change, and the Web and service applications using the account. If the Next Password Change value is shown as N/A, you do not have automated password changes enabled.

Removing a managed account should be performed with planning, testing, and forethought. You cannot remove a managed account that is currently bound to any farm component, such as a Web application or service application. To remove an account, do the following:

1. Change the managed account binding in each location it is used. The bindings can be seen by navigating to Central Administration, Security, General Security, Configure Managed Accounts and editing the managed account. At the bottom of the configuration screen, the current bindings are listed, as seen in Figure 15-3.

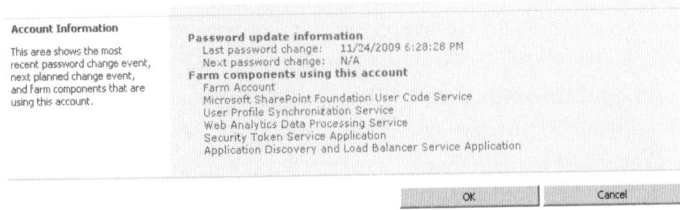

FIGURE 15-3 Current farm component bindings must be changed before managed account removal.

2. From Central Administration, Security, General Security, Configure Managed Accounts, click the Remove icon.

3. If you leveraged automatic password changes with this account and you need to know the account's password, you must change the password before removing the managed account from the farm. Note that SharePoint Server 2010 was previously managing the password, and it is most likely a long, cryptographic password.

4. Click OK.

Password Management

SharePoint Server 2010 password management dovetails nicely into managed accounts. Password management allows you to change a service account's password throughout the entire farm without the need to visit every server and location where it was used. Password management also allows for automatic password changes to meet your organization's *password roll* policies.

> **NOTE** *Password roll* refers to security requirements that mandate a password be changed on a regular basis, such as 90 days. The password changes, or rolls, are based on an organization's security policy.

GLOBAL PASSWORD MANAGEMENT SETTINGS

Before delving into the details of password management, you should first set the global password management settings, found in Central Administration, Security, General Security, Configure Password Change Settings, as seen in Figure 15-4.

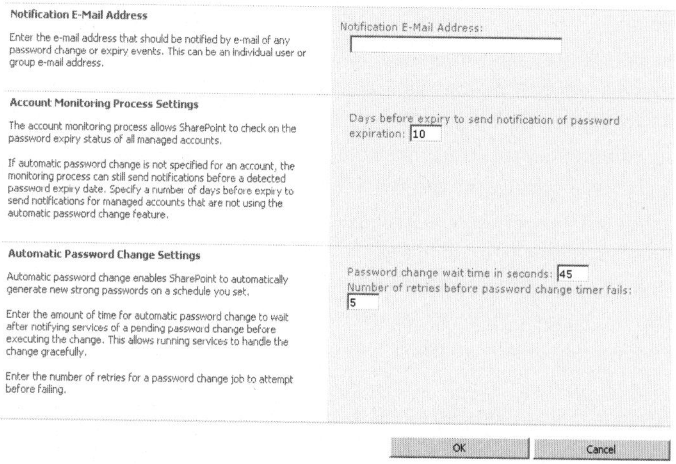

Notification E-Mail Address

Enter the e-mail address that should be notified by e-mail of any password change or expiry events. This can be an individual user or group e-mail address.

Notification E-Mail Address:

Account Monitoring Process Settings

The account monitoring process allows SharePoint to check on the password expiry status of all managed accounts.

If automatic password change is not specified for an account, the monitoring process can still send notifications before a detected password expiry date. Specify a number of days before expiry to send notifications for managed accounts that are not using the automatic password change feature.

Days before expiry to send notification of password expiration: 10

Automatic Password Change Settings

Automatic password change enables SharePoint to automatically generate new strong passwords on a schedule you set.

Enter the amount of time for automatic password change to wait after notifying services of a pending password change before executing the change. This allows running services to handle the change gracefully.

Enter the number of retries for a password change job to attempt before failing.

Password change wait time in seconds: 45
Number of retries before password change timer fails: 5

OK   Cancel

FIGURE 15-4 Use this page to configure global password settings.

There are three options when configuring the global password management settings:

- **Notification E-Mail Address**   The e-mail address should be an active, monitored account. This account is used for notifications of managed accounts whose passwords will expire or are schedule for an automatic reset.
- **Account Monitoring Process Settings**   These settings allow you to set the default advance notification for accounts that are *not* using automatic password management.
- **Automatic Password Change Settings**   Unless a change is needed, leave the default settings in this section. Depending on the size and quantity of Web and service applications using a managed account, you might need to increase the wait time between the systemwide notification of a password change and the actual password change action.

CONFIGURING AUTOMATIC PASSWORD CHANGES

Automatic password changes can be configured either when you create a managed account or by editing an existing managed account, as seen in Figure 15-2.

To configure automatic password changes on an account, browse to Central Administration, Security, General Security, Configure Managed Accounts. On the

Manage Account screen, verify you have selected the correct account. You are presented with several options:

- **Change Password Now** This option allows you to immediately change a password. This is commonly done when an account is suspected of being compromised or when a SharePoint Server 2010 administrator leaves the organization.
  - If you want SharePoint Server 2010 to automatically generate a new password and synchronize SharePoint Server 2010 with the new Active Directory password, select Generate New Password.
  - If you want to manually set a password, as is required by some organizational security policies, type the new password and confirm it.
  - If a password has gotten out of synchronization within the farm, select Use Existing Password, type the existing password, and click OK.
- **Automatic Password Change** Use this option to define a schedule to automatically change passwords for the managed account. Upon enabling the option, you are presented with three options for configuration:
  - The expiration policy can detect your Active Directory password policy and change n days before expiration, as defined by here. This is seen in Figure 15-4.
  - Receive notification by e-mail that the password is schedule for change. Enter the number of days in advance that you'd like to be notified.
  - Select the frequency of password changes. Note that the options change depending on the scope selected—weekly or monthly. You have the ability to set password changes on a monthly basis *by* a given day, or you can define the specific day it should change.

IMPORTANT There are several facts you should know about automatic password changes:

- Password changes occur in the configuration database and affect every service using that managed account.
- Password change management does not work between server farms.
- Built-in machine accounts cannot be managed using automatic password changes.
- The password will meet your Active Directory policy for minimum password complexity and usually exceed it.
- The managed farm account can also be configured to use automatic password changes.
- Managed accounts using automatic password changes are first controlled by your Active Directory group policy, and then by the configuration in Central Administration.

Service Account Management

Service accounts are accounts being used for Web and service applications. Service accounts are essentially the association of a managed account used for startup with authentication for Web and service applications, such as a Web application's application pool identity. In SharePoint Server 2010, configuration and association of these service accounts is known as *credential management*. You can modify the association of service accounts and applications from Central Administration, Security, General Security, Configure Service Accounts. To view the current dependencies of a service account, select it from the drop-down menu, as seen in Figure 15-5. The dependencies are shown in the dependencies window.

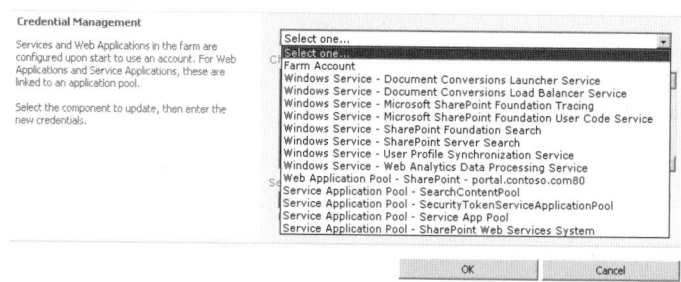

FIGURE 15-5 Select the service account you want to manage.

All service accounts must be managed accounts. Unlike SharePoint Server 2007, you cannot create an isolated service account. If you decide to change the association between a service account and managed account, be sure to test prior to making the change. Any custom code or third-party application dependent on that association will most likely fail until it is modified to use the new managed account.

Farm Passphrase

In SharePoint Server 2007, the farm account's password was used to generate the farm encryption key (FEK) and the FEK was stored in the registry of the Central Administration server and the configuration database. Each server that was added to the farm had the FEK written to its own registry. It was common for SharePoint Server 2007 administrators to inadvertently overwrite or orphan this FEK during the password reset process.

> **NOTE** The farm encryption key is used to encrypt secure traffic between servers of the farm and is not user configurable.

To address this problem in SharePoint Server 2010, the concept of a farm passphrase was introduced. The farm passphrase is defined when installing SharePoint Server 2010 and is used when joining additional servers to the farm. The farm passphrase is also now used to generate the FEK that is stored in the configuration database and in the server's registry.

NOTE The FEK registry location is encrypted and is accessible only by the server farm account.

This design, using a farm passphrase, solves three major problems with SharePoint Server 2007 farm account management. First, the farm passphrase, and in turn the FEK, can be reset using native tools. SharePoint Server 2007 requires a call to Customer Support Services to resolve a lost or orphaned FEK. Second, failed synchronization between servers, such as happens when a server is offline during farm updates, is now less difficult to resolve. Third, administrators no longer need to know the farm account and password to join servers to the farm; they need know only the passphrase.

There is not a graphical user interface to modify the farm passphrase. To change the farm passphrase using Windows PowerShell, do the following:

1. Open SharePoint 2010 Management Shell from Start, All Programs, Microsoft SharePoint 2010 Products.

2. Execute the following cmdlet:

   `Set-SPPassPhrase`

3. Type the new farm passphrase.

4. Confirm the passphrase.

Information Policies

Information policies in SharePoint Server 2010 refer to two different areas of functionality: Information Rights Management (IRM) and Information Management (IM) Policies. Although they sound similar in name, they are very different in practice.

Information Rights Management

IRM is a technology that allows users to protect information, regardless of where the content is stored. Based on a defined user and associated certificate, the creator of a document can limit forwarding, copying, modifying, printing, faxing, cutting, pasting, and using Print Screen, regardless of where a document is stored. The service is a function of Active Directory Rights Management Services (Active Directory RMS) and must be configured and functional outside of SharePoint Server 2010 before you can configure it in Central Administration. Although it's not extremely difficult to implement, it does take planning and also requires Enterprise Administrator rights in Active Directory. It also is limited to your Active Directory implementation, as you need to add external users to your Active Directory for them to leverage your RMS. However, you can federate with another Active Directory RMS implementation. This is useful when sharing and securing SharePoint Server 2010 information with trusted partners.

MORE INFO You can see more about how to implement Active Directory RMS at *http://technet.microsoft.com/en-us/library/cc771234.aspx*. A step-by-step setup guide is available at *http://technet.microsoft.com/en-us/library/cc753531.aspx*.

SharePoint Server 2010 integrates well with IRM and requires very little configuration within Central Administration. After it is configured, your users can protect documents at the user, document, group, and SharePoint Server 2010 library levels. SharePoint Server 2010 automatically converts IRM permissions on an object when uploaded to a library. Table 15-1 displays the IRM permissions and the SharePoint Server 2010 permissions that result upon upload.

TABLE 15-1 SharePoint Server 2010 Permissions and IRM Permission

SHAREPOINT SERVER 2010 PERMISSIONS	IRM PERMISSIONS
Manage permissions, Manage Web	Full control
Edit list items, manage list, add and customize pages	Edit, copy, and save permissions
View list item	Read permissions; cannot copy or delete

To configure IRM in SharePoint Server 2010, do the following:

1. Configure Active Directory RMS.
2. Browse to Central Administration, Security, Information Policy, Configure Information Rights Management.
3. Either use the default Active Directory RMS server (which will search in the Active Directory the physical machine belongs to) or define a new server.
4. Click OK.

After you configure IRM in Central Administration, your list and library settings are extended with RMS functionality. Figure 15-6 shows the IRM configuration settings in a document library.

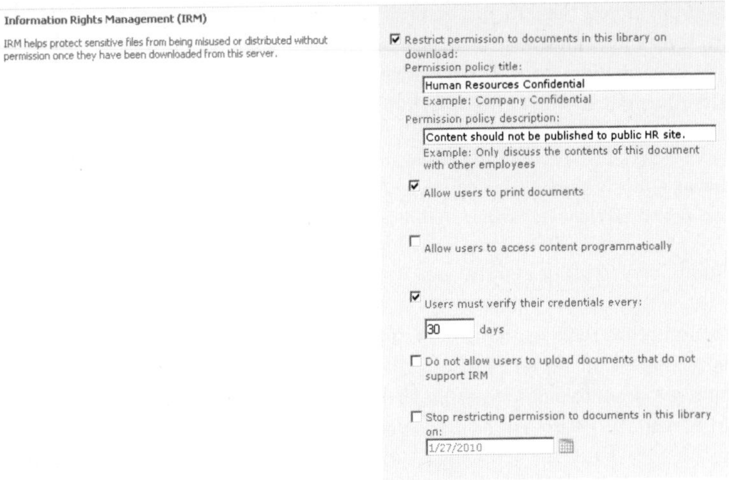

IRM helps protect sensitive files from being misused or distributed without
permission once they have been downloaded from this server.

☑ Restrict permission to documents in this library on
download:

Permission policy title:

Human Resources Confidential

Example: Company Confidential

Permission policy description:

Content should not be published to public HR site.

Example: Only discuss the contents of this document
with other employees

☑ Allow users to print documents

☐ Allow users to access content programmatically

☑ Users must verify their credentials every:

30   days

☐ Do not allow users to upload documents that do not
support IRM

☐ Stop restricting permission to documents in this library
on:

1/27/2010

FIGURE 15-6 IRM protects a document based on the library container.

To configure a list or library to use IRM, do the following:

1. Complete IRM configuration in Central Administration.

2. Go to the List Or Library settings, within a site collection, that you want to
   enable.

3. In the Permissions And Management column, select Information Rights
   Management. If you do not see this option, IRM has not been correctly
   configured in Central Administration.

4. Select the relevant options and click OK.

Information Management Policies

Information Management (IM) Policies are one of the strengths in SharePoint Server
2010 that was not available in SharePoint Foundation 2007. IM Policies allow you
to define labels, bar codes, and retention and auditing policies within site collections. The creation and application of policies is at the site-collection level, but farm
administrators can control the availability and functionality of policies for the farm.
Figure 15-7 shows the IM Policy Configuration page in Central Administration.

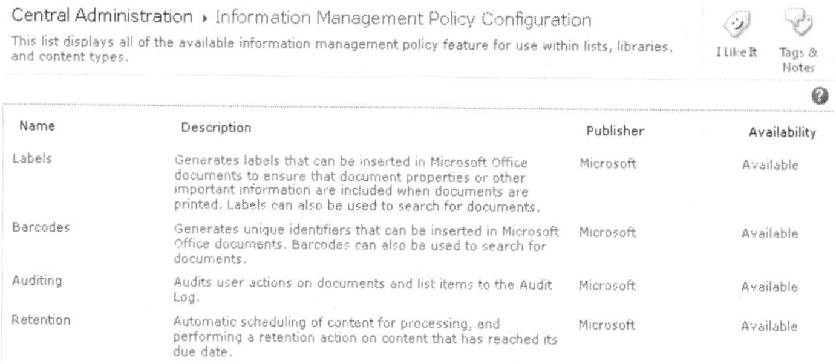

This list displays all of the available information management policy feature for use within lists, libraries, and content types.

I Like It   Tags & Notes

Name	Description	Publisher	Availability
Labels	Generates labels that can be inserted in Microsoft Office documents to ensure that document properties or other important information are included when documents are printed. Labels can also be used to search for documents.	Microsoft	Available
Barcodes	Generates unique identifiers that can be inserted in Microsoft Office documents. Barcodes can also be used to search for documents.	Microsoft	Available
Auditing	Audits user actions on documents and list items to the Audit Log.	Microsoft	Available
Retention	Automatic scheduling of content for processing, and performing a retention action on content that has reached its due date.	Microsoft	Available

FIGURE 15-7 The current status of IM policies are shown in Central Administration.

As you can see in Figure 15-7, the main configuration screen for IM policies shows the status and currently configured availability of policies. To enable or disable a policy, click on the name of the policy to be configured. When you decommission an IM policy at the farm level, it is no longer available in site collections. Figure 15-8 shows the configuration of a content type's IM policy with the default settings. Figure 15-9 shows an example of the same content type IM Policy settings when labels and bar codes have been deselected in Central Administration.

Retention

Schedule how content is managed and disposed by specifying a sequence of retention stages. If you specify multiple stages, each stage will occur one after the other in the order they appear on this page.

Note: If the Library and Folder Based Retention feature is active, list administrators can override content type policies with their own retention schedules. To prevent this, deactivate the feature on the site collection.

☐ Enable Retention

Auditing

Specify the events that should be audited for documents and items subject to this policy.

☐ Enable Auditing

Barcodes

Assigns a barcode to each document or item. Optionally, Microsoft Office applications can require users to insert these barcodes into documents.

☐ Enable Barcodes

Labels

You can add a label to a document to ensure that important information about the document is included when it is printed. To specify the label, type the text you want to use in the "Label format" box. You can use any combination of fixed text or document properties, except calculated or built-in properties such as GUID or CreatedBy. To start a new line, use the \n character sequence.

☐ Enable Labels

[OK]   [Cancel]

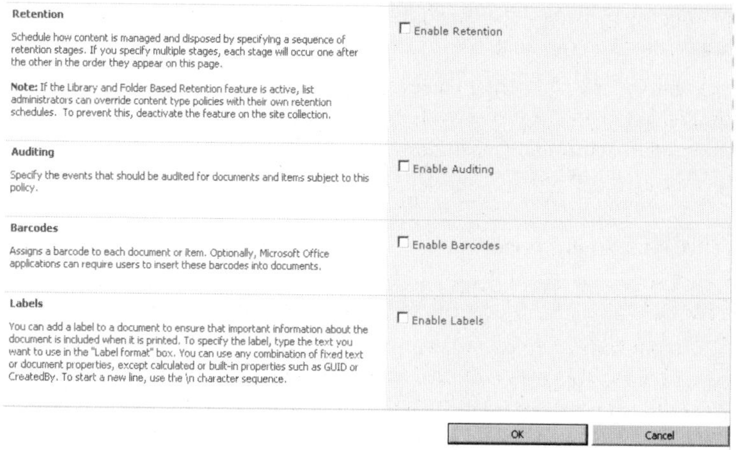

FIGURE 15-8 The content type IM policies available by default.

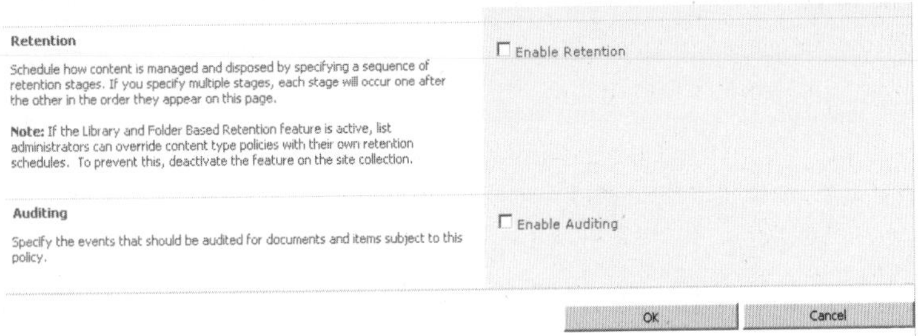

FIGURE 15-9 When deselected, policies are no longer available to content types.

The following options are available for configuring policies:

- **Configure Labels**   You can enable IM labels for use within the farm. You can decommission IM labels, but you cannot disable labels that are in use.

- **Barcodes**   You can enable bar code labels for use within the farm. You can decommission bar code labels, but you cannot disable bar codes that are in use. You have the additional options of selecting installed bar code styles and encoding options based on the style.

- **Auditing**   You can enable IM auditing for use within the farm. You can deselect IM auditing, but you cannot disable auditing policies that are in use.

- **Retention**   You can enable IM retention for use within the farm. You can decommission IM retention, but you cannot disable retention policies that are in use.

IMPORTANT   If the Microsoft SharePoint Foundation Workflow Timer service is not functioning correctly, SharePoint Server 2010 will not update expiration dates and policy processing.

MORE INFO   See Chapter 12, "Records Management", for detailed instructions on how to configure IM policies.

Web Application Security

Web applications contain all of your valuable user content and also provide the bedrock for the security of your site collections. There are several areas of Web Application security you need to take into consideration:

- Encryption
- Traceability
- Authentication

- Authorization
- Credential Management
- Malicious Software Prevention

The following section on Web application security covers each of these areas. A solid security plan for SharePoint Server 2010 requires some or all the topics covered here. What level of security you require completely depends on your organization's security policies, what information you are sharing, with whom you are sharing the information, and what level of trust you have in the connecting networks.

SSL and Assigned IP Addresses

Secure Sockets Layer (SSL) is the most common form of protecting HTTP traffic. SSL sites can be recognized by the *https://* prefix, contrasted with non-SSL sites that are prefixed with *http://*. SharePoint Server 2010 does not provide SSL services and does not store the certificate used to authenticate the Web application. To implement SSL, you must manage each Web application individually on every Web server in the farm. Although SharePoint Server 2010 doesn't manage SSL, it must be configured to recognize the URL change after enabling SSL. Last, most administrators will want to assign IP addresses when using SSL to avoid wildcard SSL certificates. Wildcard SSL certificates allow you to secure multiple subdomains under a single parent domain name.

> **NOTE** You can use host headers with a wildcard SSL certificate. The certificate should be assigned to a subnet, such as *.contoso.com. You can then use the certificate on any server ending with .contoso.com. Although this approach reduces the expense of obtaining SSL certificates, it should generally be avoided because the client cannot verify the Web application identity. Using wildcard certificates can also make it more difficult to trace network traffic using intrusion detection and firewalls.

Configuring SSL

Configuring SSL in Internet Information Services 7.0 is performed differently than in Internet Information Services 6.0. The process will vary slightly depending on whether you create your own SSL certificates internally or use an external certificate authority. To create a certificate using an external certificate authority, do the following:

1. Open Internet Information Services (IIS) Manager from Start Menu, All Programs, Administrative Tools.
2. Select the server name.
3. Double-click Server Certificates, as seen in Figure 15-10.

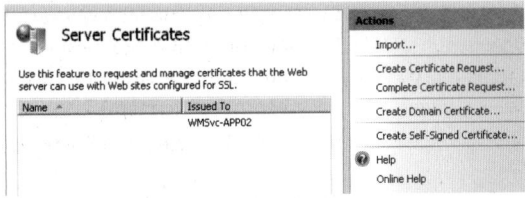

FIGURE 15-10 Click Server Certificates after changing the context to the server name.

4. From the Actions menu, as seen in Figure 15-11, select Create Certificate Request.

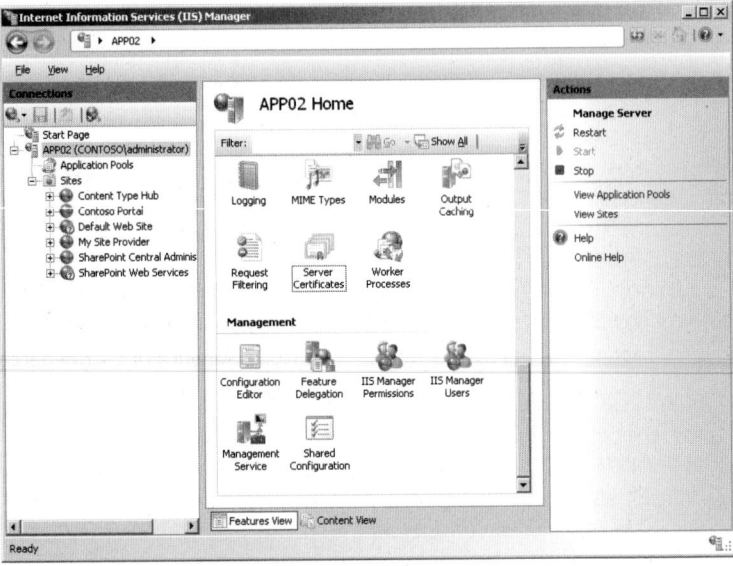

FIGURE 15-11 Select Create Certificate Request.

5. Type the common name, using the fully qualified domain name (FQDN)—for example, portal.contoso.com.

6. Type the organization name. This is usually your company name.

7. Type the organizational unit, such as North America or E-Commerce.

8. Type the city and state you want to associate to this certificate.

9. Type the country, and then click Next.

10. Select the cryptographic provider you want to use.

11. Select the bit length, and then click Next.

12. Select the file location where you'll store the certificate request, such as C:\ContosoPortalCertRequest.txt.

13. Click Finish.

14. Depending on your external certificate authority, this step will vary. Most likely, you'll copy the contents of C:\ContosoPortalCertRequest.txt into a form provided by your external certificate authority. After the certificate authority provides you with a certificate, proceed to step 15.

15. From the Actions menu (shown in Figure 15-11), select Complete Certificate Request.

16. Click the ellipses, and browse to the certificate you received from your provider.

17. Click OK.

If you'll be using this SSL-secured Web application internally and already have an internal certificate authority, follow these steps to create an internal, domain certificate:

1. Open Internet Information Services (IIS) Manager from Start menu, All Programs, Administrative Tools.

2. Select the server name.

3. Double-click Server Certificates, as shown earlier in Figure 15-10.

4. From the Actions menu, shown earlier in Figure 15-11, select Create Domain Certificate.

5. Type the common name, using the FQDN—for example, portal.contoso.com.

6. Type the organization name. This is usually your company name.

7. Type the organizational unit, such as North America or E-Commerce.

8. Type the city and state you want to associate to this certificate.

9. Type the country, and then click Next.

10. Select the online certificate authority for your organization.

11. Type a friendly name that associates this certificate logically, such as Portal Web Application Certificate.

12. Click Finish.

> **TIP** Be sure you select the Windows Server name in Internet Information Services Manager, not the Web application name, when creating a certificate. Certificates are stored in the Windows Server certificate store, not in Internet Information Services.

Binding the Certificate to the Internet Information Services Site

After you successfully install the certificate, you must then bind the certificate to the Web application to be SSL-secured. To bind a certificate to a Web application in Internet Information Services, do the following:

1. Open Internet Information Services (IIS) Manager from Start Menu, All Programs, Administrative Tools.

2. Select the Web application you want to modify under the Sites list, as seen in Figure 15-12.

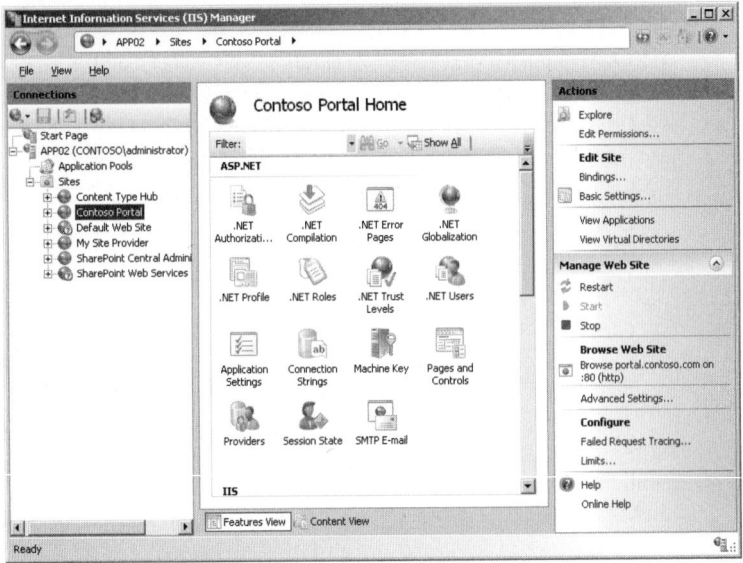

FIGURE 15-12 Select the site you want to modify and then select Bindings.

3. Select Bindings from the Actions menu, under Edit Site.
4. Click the Add button.
5. Change Type to https.
6. Select the IP address for this Web application.

   TIP If you previously assigned an IP address, it will always be cached in the list, even if the IP address is later removed from the network interface card. Always verify the IP address exists in Windows Server networking before selecting the IP address in Internet Information Services Manager.

7. Select the port number. This is almost always 443.
8. Select the certificate, as seen in Figure 15-13.

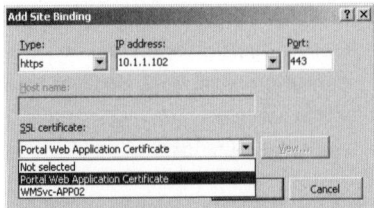

FIGURE 15-13 Select the previously installed certificate.

9. Optionally, remove the http binding if you'll no longer access the Web application via HTTP.

10. Click OK, and then click Close.

IMPORTANT Assigning IP addresses allows you to use non-wildcard SSL on multiple SharePoint Server 2010 Web applications in the same farm, and also to configure network load balancing for high availability and performance. You cannot assign IP addresses from within Central Administration because each server must have a unique IP address. In fact, you have to assign a unique IP address to every IIS Web site to be secured on every Web server in the farm.

Modifying Alternate Access Mappings

Before you can test your SSL-enabled Web application, you must first configure SharePoint Server 2010 to be aware of the URL change. The Web application was previously configured as *http://portal.contoso.com*. It now needs to be configured to include the *s* to designate the change to SSL. URL changes are made as Alternate Access Mapping changes. To modify the http://*portal.contoso.com* alternate access mapping, do the following:

1. Open Central Administration, System Settings. Under the Farm Management grouping, select Configure Alternate Access Mappings.

2. Select the Web application you want to modify.

3. Change the internal URL to the *https://* protocol scheme, as seen in Figure 15-14.

4. Click OK.

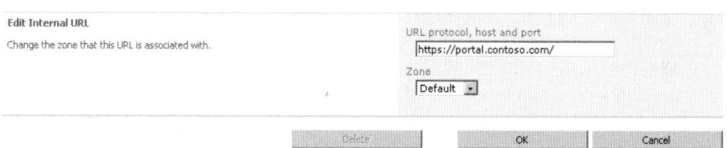

FIGURE 15-14 Change the protocol from http to https.

TIP Do not select a zone other than Default at this point. You will not be able to modify the zone until you define a new default internal URL for the zone.

If you want to access the Web application via both HTTPS and HTTP, you can add another public URL mapping. Be aware that the default internal URL is used for embedded e-mail URLs such as workflows and system messages. Therefore, you'll most likely want the default internal URL to be the SSL-enabled URL so that hyperlinks in e-mail always function, regardless of where the user is viewing e-mail. To add a second zone for the Web application, do the following:

1. Open Central Administration, System Settings. Under the Farm Management grouping, select Configure Alternate Access Mappings.
2. Select Edit Public URLs in the menu.
3. Select the Web application you want to modify, as seen in Figure 15-15.

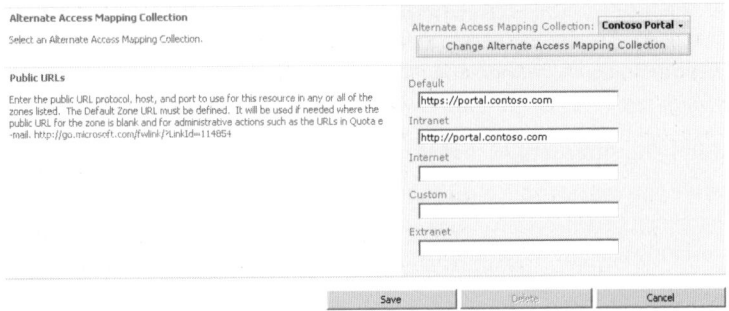

FIGURE 15-15 Select Change Alternate Access Mapping Collection from the drop-down menu.

4. Change the default URL to *https*, and type a new URL using *http*, as seen in Figure 15-15.
5. Click Save.

TIP If your users were previously using Windows Integrated authentication and also using Internet Explorer's automatic logon with the current user name and password, they might now be prompted for credentials. This is because you must add the new URL to the Internet Explorer security zone to include the *s*, as in *https://portal.contoso.com*.

Authentication

One of the foundations of Web application security is authentication. SharePoint Server 2010 authentication is usually provided by IIS via Windows Integrated authentication, but it can be provided by any number of sources through Forms-Based authentication and Claims-Based authentication. Because Forms-Based authentication and Claims-Based authentication are developer-oriented topics, only Windows Integrated authentication is discussed in this chapter.

Windows Integrated Authentication

Windows Integrated authentication provides a transparent authentication mechanism for intranet applications and some extranet SharePoint Web applications. This process increases the transparency to the user because no input is required to visit SharePoint servers when used in conjunction with Internet Explorer's automatic logon functionality. There are two types of Integrated authentication: Kerberos and NTLM.

KERBEROS

Kerberos is the preferred authentication mechanism for internal SharePoint Web applications. Because both the client and IIS server must see the Key Distribution Center (KDC), Kerberos does not work with most Internet-facing SharePoint Server 2010 installations. To enable Kerberos, simply choose the option during Web application creation. Remember that to use Kerberos you must have previously configured a service principal name (SPN) for the Web application pool identity. To configure an SPN, follow these steps:

1. Verify the application pool for the Web application you want to configure. In Internet Information Services Manager, select the Web application and select Advanced Settings from the Actions menu. Figure 15-16 shows an example of finding an application pool in Internet Information Services Manager.

FIGURE 15-16 Note the application pool for the Web application.

2. On the application pool noted in step 1, select Advanced Settings and note the application pool identity, as seen in Figure 15-17.

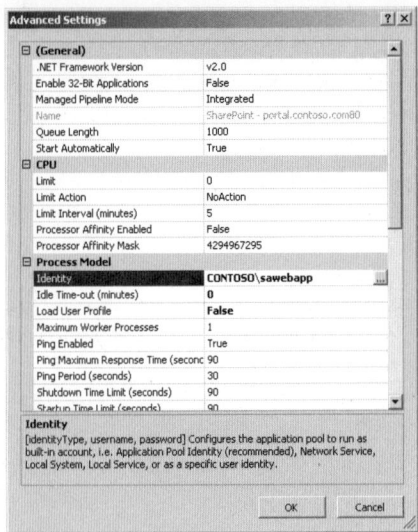

FIGURE 15-17 Note the identity of the application pool.

3. Go to the command prompt on the Windows server that will host the Web application to use Kerberos.

4. Create the SPN in the form of *setspn -a HTTP/<WebApplicationURL DOMAIN/AppPoolIdentity*. Using the examples in Figures 15-16 and 15-17, the command would be *setspn -a HTTP/portal.contoso.com CONTOSO\ SAWEBAPP*.

After you configure the SPNs, proceed to enabling SharePoint Server 2010 for Kerberos. Don't forget to enable SPNs for every Web application you need Kerberos for and on every server that will service those Web applications. To enable Kerberos for a Web application, do the following:

1. Browse to Central Administration, Application Management, Manage Web Applications, and select the Web application you want to configure.

2. On the management Ribbon, click Authentication Providers, as seen in Figure 15-18.

FIGURE 15-18 Highlight the Web application and then click Authentication Providers.

3. Select the zone for which you want to set Kerberos authentication.

4. In the IIS Authentication Settings section, select Integrated Windows Authentication and select the Negotiate (Kerberos) radio button.

5. Click Save.

6 Close the configuration window.

7. Perform an IISRESET from the command line.

NTLM

NTLM is the easiest of the negotiated protocols to implement because it requires no additional configuration outside of SharePoint Server 2010. If possible, you should enable both Kerberos *and* NTLM. Doing this ensures user authentication if Kerberos fails. Unfortunately, this dual enabling cannot be done from Central Administration. This action must be performed from the command line on each server that will serve content via the Kerberos-secured Web application. Note that IIS negotiates from the most-secure protocol to the least-secure protocol. Therefore, your users will authenticate with Kerberos first if both protocols are enabled. Run the following command to enable Kerberos and NTLM:

```
appcmd.exe set config /section:windowsAuthentication /-
providers.[value='Negotiate']
```

NTLM works with most SharePoint Server 2010 installations without further configuration. However, NTLM isn't as secure as Kerberos and should be considered insecure unless password lengths are longer than 14 characters. NTLM can also fail when traversing proxy servers, because it is connection-based and proxies don't always sustain connections. Additionally, not all browsers support NTLM and Kerberos and therefore will require Basic authentication support on the servers.

Basic Authentication

For remote users, for users behind proxy servers, for non-Windows clients, or to accommodate a custom program, you can implement Basic authentication. Basic authentication supports most browsers and works from almost anywhere on the Internet. Its downside is that the user name and password are sent as Base64 clear text. This information is easily compromised unless it is secured using encryption such as SSL. Therefore, *always* use Basic authentication in conjunction with an SSL-secured Web application. This sufficiently protects the user name and password from being compromised. To enable Basic authentication, do the following:

1. Browse to Central Administration, Application Management, Manage Web Applications, and select the Web application you want to configure.

2. On the management Ribbon, click Authentication Providers, as seen in Figure 15-18.

3. Select the zone for which you want to set Basic authentication.

4. In the IIS Authentication Settings section, choose Basic Authentication. If you select Integrated Windows Authentication and Basic Authentication, clients should attempt authentication in the order of Kerberos, NTLM, Basic authentication.

5. Click Save.

6. Close the configuration window.

7. Perform an IISRESET from the command line.

Anonymous Access

Care should be taken when enabling anonymous access. Although security is always important in a site collection when creating users and groups, it is particularly important when anonymous access is enabled in the Web application and site collection or collections. Although enabling anonymous access on a Web application doesn't enable any content to anonymous users, it does give the ability for site collection administrators to enable the feature. If a site collection is primarily used for collaboration, you should strongly consider limiting anonymous access when possible.

> **TIP** Always perform authentication provider changes from Central Administration, not from Internet Information Services Manager. Using this approach writes the changes to the configuration database for propagation to existing Web servers and to new servers added to the farm.

To enable anonymous access, you must do so on the Web application and the site collection. To enable anonymous access for a Web application, do the following:

1. Browse to Central Administration, Application Management, Manage Web Application, and select the Web application you want to configure.

2. On the management Ribbon, click Authentication Providers, as seen in Figure 15-18.

3. Select the zone for which you want to set Basic authentication.

4. In the Anonymous Access section, choose Enable Anonymous Access.

5. Click Save.

6. Close the configuration window.

7. Perform an IISRESET from the command line.

After enabling anonymous access for the Web application, you must then enable anonymous access for a site collection using these steps:

1. Browse to the site collection that you want to be accessed anonymously.

2. Select Site Actions, Site Settings.

3. In the Users And Permissions grouping, select Site Permissions.

4. On the management Ribbon, as shown in Figure 15-19, click Anonymous Access.

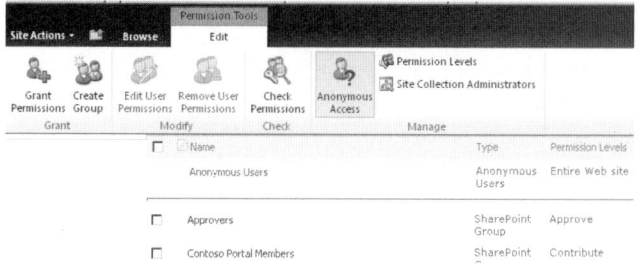

FIGURE 15-19 Click Anonymous Access on the management Ribbon.

5. Select the scope for which you'll allow anonymous access: Entire Web Site, Lists And Libraries, or Nothing.

Note that anonymous users have limited access to site collection content. From the native user interface, it is not possible to escalate anonymous permissions beyond limited read access.

Web Application User Permissions

SharePoint Server 2010 provides the ability to restrict permissions available to users within Web applications. Adding or removing a permission from a Web application defines whether that permission is available in site collections within that Web application. When modifying user permissions for Web applications in Central Administration, be aware that changes are applied immediately and can cause immediate problems. For example, if you remove the Manage List permission from *http://portal.contoso.com*, an administrator in the site collection *http://portal.contoso.com/sites/HR* would no longer be able to manage lists and libraries. Re-enabling a permission level for a Web application in Central Administration allows the level to be used once again in all site collections contained in the selected Web application.

IMPORTANT User permissions for Web applications affects *all zones*.

User permissions are managed on an individual Web application basis, so you might have a unique configuration for each Web application. Always verify that you are modifying the correct Web application before modifying permissions. Many an administrator has accidentally modified the wrong Web application. To change user permissions for a Web application, perform the following steps:

1. Browse to Central Administration, Application Management, Manage Web Applications, and select the Web application you want to configure.

2. On the management Ribbon, click User Permissions as seen in Figure 15-20.

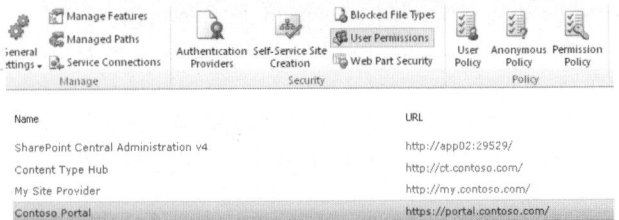

Name	URL
SharePoint Central Administration v4	http://app02:29529/
Content Type Hub	http://ct.contoso.com/
My Site Provider	http://my.contoso.com/
Contoso Portal	https://portal.contoso.com/

FIGURE 15-20 Click User Permissions on the management Ribbon.

3. Select or deselect permissions for a Web application.

4. Click Save.

Secure Store Service

The SharePoint Server 2010 Secure Store Service is roughly equivalent to SharePoint Server 2007 single sign-on (SSO). It is greatly enhanced, however, and provides improvements in the areas of management, extranet scenario usage, security trimming, and role provider support. The Secure Store Service is leveraged by many SharePoint Server 2010 service applications, such as Business Connectivity Services, PeformancePoint, Visio Services, Excel Services, and Project Server. Developers and designers will often use the Secure Store Service whenever they are connecting to systems where the SharePoint Server 2010 user has a different user name or uses a different account for the connecting system. Using the Secure Store Service in these instances overcomes the "double hop" problem for users authenticating with NTLM or Basic authentication. Although the Secure Store Service can resolve the double-hop issue, Kerberos is a more secure solution because it doesn't rely on middleware for authentication. For current information about the Secure Store Service, browse to *http://technet.microsoft.com/en-us/library/ee806889(office.14).aspx*.

> **NOTE** The Secure Store Service application can be published and consumed between farms. This functionality is both helpful and problematic. It is useful because credentials can be shared across an enterprise. It's problematic because a failure of a single Secure Store could break applications across multiple server farms. For enterprise credential management, you should consider Identity Lifecycle Manager or an equivalent application.

> **TIP** Remember to start the Secure Store Service in Central Administration, Systems Settings, Services on the physical processing server.

To create a Secure Store Service application, do the following:

1. Browse to Central Administration, Application Management, Manage Service Applications.
2. On the management Ribbon, select New, Secure Store Service.
3. Define the service application name, such as Contoso Secure Store.
4. Choose a database server. For highly secure implementations, this should be a SQL Server instance other than the instance used to host content databases.
5. Type a database name.
6. Select Windows authentication.
7. Optionally, define a failover database server.
8. Create a new application pool. Define the managed account for the application pool identity. This should be an isolated account in a secure environment.
9. Enable auditing, and define how long to retain audit logs for the Secure Store Service application.
10. Select OK.

After you create the Secure Store Service application, you still need to define on what physical server the processing will occur. You must also create an encryption key and configure permissions. To manage the Secure Store Service, you created, follow these steps:

1. Browse to Central Administration, System Settings, Manage Services On Server.
2. Locate the Secure Store Service in the list, and click Start, as seen in Figure 15-21.

Microsoft SharePoint Foundation User Code Service	Started	Stop
Microsoft SharePoint Foundation Web Application	Started	Stop
Microsoft SharePoint Foundation Workflow Timer Service	Started	Stop
PerformancePoint Service	Stopped	Start
Search Query and Site Settings Service	Started	Stop
Secure Store Service	Stopped	Start

FIGURE 15-21 Click Start in the options list.

3. Browse to Central Administration, Application Management, Manage Service Applications.
4. Highlight the Secure Store Service application, and on the management Ribbon, click Manage.
5. Click Generate New Key, as seen in Figure 15-22.

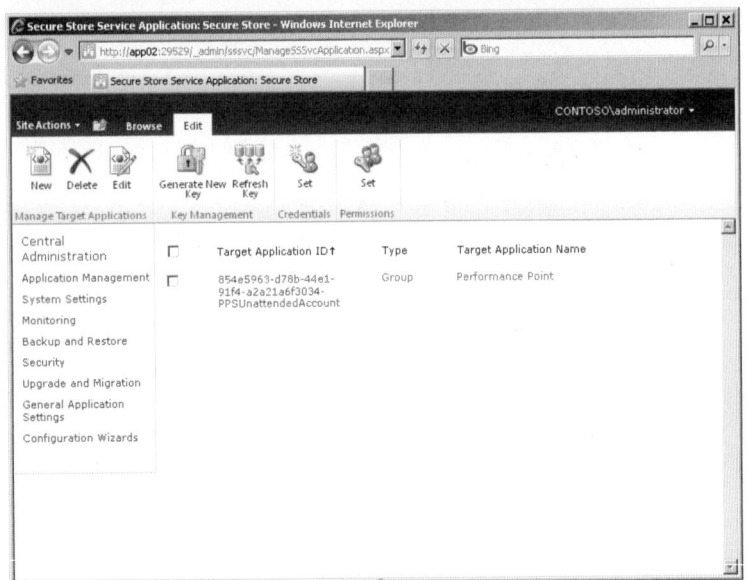

FIGURE 15-22 Click Generate New Key before using the Secure Store Service application.

6. Type a passphrase for key generation.

7. Click OK.

8. Optionally, create a new target application by clicking New on the management Ribbon, which is shown in Figure 15-22. You can execute `Get-SPIISWebServiceApplicationPool | select ID, Name` from the SharePoint 2010 Management Shell to find the ID of an application pool.

> **TIP** The Secure Store Service can service multiple back-end systems for authentication, or you can have multiple Secure Store Service applications for further performance and isolation. Remember to start the Secure Store Service in Central Administration, Systems Settings, Manage Services On Server on the physical processing server.

Blocked File Types

SharePoint Server 2010 provides basic functionality for blocking certain types of files from being uploaded into a Web application. The default list is too large to list here, but a few default blocked file types warrant mentioning:

- **.cer** These files are usually certificate files and can pose a minor threat if allowed to be served from your SharePoint installation. The downside to blocking .cer files is the inability to post root certificate authority certificates for users to install in their local browser.

- **.com, .dll, and .exe** These file name extensions should *never* be allowed on your SharePoint installation. Allowing .com or .exe files can cause catastrophic security consequences if a hacker finds and executes code, such as a cross-domain (site) scripting attack, on your server.
- **.pst** It is unwise to allow users to upload .pst files to any site collection. Doing so can take significant amounts of storage. In addition, users cannot use a .pst over HTTP in Microsoft Outlook.
- **.mp3, .wmv, .mpg** It's a good idea to block media files when they are not being used in your Web applications. But be sure to unblock them if you need to upload and manage these files.

Although users cannot upload a file and then change the extension to circumvent your settings, they can change the name of a file and upload it for storage. As an example, you can rename a blocked .exe file to .txt and upload it to a document library even if you have blocked it on a Web application. Consider Microsoft Forefront for SharePoint Server if you want to block a file based on the binary type, and not just the file extension. To block a file type, perform the following steps for each Web application you want to configure:

1. Browse to Central Administration, Security, General Security, Define Blocked File Types.
2. Select the Web application to configure.
3. Enter a carriage return after the last letter of an existing file extension, and type the extension to block.
4. Click OK.

Self-Service Site Creation

For highly collaborative and loosely governed Web applications, you can delegate authority to users for the purpose of site-collection creation. Just as it is for the Central Administration interface, the term *site* actually refers to a *site collection*. Self-service, site-collection creation is enabled on a per-Web-application basis to allow for greater control over your server farm. To enable self-service site creation, perform the following steps:

1. Browse to Central Administration, Security, General Security, Configure Self-Service Site Creation.
2. Select the Web application to configure.
3. Choose the On radio button.
4. Optionally, select the option to require a secondary contact.

By default, SharePoint Server 2010 places a new announcement in the Announcements list in the top-level site of the root site collection—for example, *http://portal.contoso.com/lists/announcements*. However, because the sign-up (creation) page exists in *_layouts*, you can create a new site collection from anywhere in the farm by appending **scsignup.aspx** to a list or site. As an example, *http://collab.contoso.com/_layouts/scsignup.aspx* would render the sign-up page in the Collab Web application.

Antivirus Settings

The installation of a correctly configured antivirus program is essential to protecting content in your SharePoint environment. To configure antivirus settings, you must have a SharePoint-aware antivirus program. Windows Server antivirus applications do not scan items in SharePoint databases. You must install a SharePoint Server 2010–aware antivirus program that runs at the Web-service level to intercept and scan files.

When installing the SharePoint antivirus program, the program must exist on all Web front-end (WFE) servers before you continue with the configuration. To configure antivirus settings for SharePoint products, perform these actions:

1. Browse to Central Administration, Security, General Security, Manage Antivirus Settings.

2. Under Antivirus Settings, you have four options:

   - **Scan Documents On Upload**   Many organizations choose to scan documents *either* when uploading or when downloading. Scanning documents both ways can increase processor utilization. Be sure to monitor server performance after installing antivirus software.

   - **Scan Documents On Download**   Scanning documents when downloading is usually the best choice if you must choose between upload scanning and download scanning. This ensures the latest virus definitions are available before downloads occur.

   - **Allow Users To Download Infected Documents**   Except in extreme circumstances, such as when configuring a mission-critical application, you should not allow users to download infected documents.

   - **Attempt To Clean Infected Documents**   Once again, cleaning infected documents is a processor-intensive function. If you do not have a highly collaborative environment—or if you have large, multiprocessor servers— you can consider cleaning infected documents.

3. Select the antivirus time out. The default of 300 seconds works well for most installations.

4. Optionally, you can change the number of antivirus threads. Most likely, the antivirus software you install will configure this for you. If you decide to change the number of threads, be sure to monitor the processor performance on Web application servers.

Web Application Policies

Web application policies provide both security and governance. They provide security by limiting access to content based on the user identity. They provide governance by limiting access based on rules. By levering zones and policies, you can restrict access based on the URL plus the user identity to enforce a robust policy. The type of restrictions provided at the Web-application level are as follows:

- SharePoint Designer Usage
- Read, Write, Modify, Delete
- View and Delete Versions
- Manage Lists
- Customize Web parts
- Leverage Web services

Before you can fully understand Web application policies, you must first understand the architecture of zones. Policies are applied to zones.

Zones

Zones are IIS Web sites that refer to a Web application. When you create a Web application, you create it in the *default* zone. There is a single IIS Web site that services the Web application. SharePoint Server 2010 provides the functionality to create up to five IIS Web sites that service a single Web application. Zones should *always* be manipulated through Central Administration, and they should never be created in Internet Information Services Manager. Zones will share an application pool and content database or databases because they are associated with the same Web application. Do not change the application pool associated with a zone. To create a new zone, perform the following steps:

1. Browse to Central Administration, Application Management, Manage Web Applications.

2. Select the Web application to configure, and click Extend on the management Ribbon, as shown in Figure 15-23.

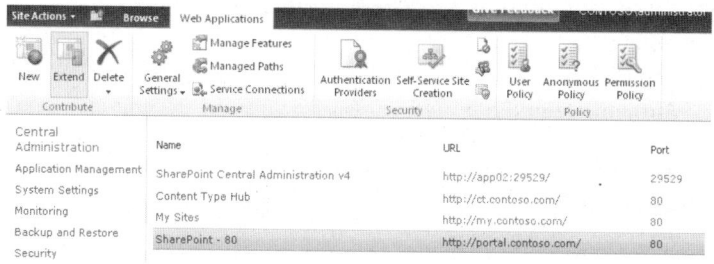

FIGURE 15-23 Click Extend on the management Ribbon.

3. Select Create A New IIS Web Site, and give it a name relevant to its purpose.

4. Define the port. This will most likely be 80 or 443.

5. Define the host header using the fully qualified domain name, such as http://portalext.contoso.com.

6. Select the authentication provider, remembering to register SPNs first if you are using Kerberos.

7. Enable anonymous access and SSL if desired. You can always enable anonymous access later on by clicking Authentication Providers on the management Ribbon.

8. Type the public URL.

> **IMPORTANT** The interface does *not* change the port to 443 when you select SSL. Be sure to either change the port or remove the :80 altogether.

9. Select the zone for the public URL, such as Extranet in this example.

10. Click OK.

> **TIP** After you create another zone, you will have multiple IIS Web sites associated with the same content database or databases. You can see this in Internet Information Services Manager.

You can modify security parameters on the new zone by browsing to Central Administration, Application Management, Manage Web Applications and selecting the Web application you want to modify. Click Authentication Providers on the management Ribbon, you are now presented with two zones to configure, as seen in Figure 15-24.

FIGURE 15-24 Select the Extranet zone to configure a different authentication.

After you select the zone, you are presented with six configuration options:

- **Authentication Type** You can select a different authentication type, such as Forms-Based authentication.
- **Anonymous Access** Specify whether to allow anonymous access on this zone.
- **Client Object Model Permission Requirement** This check box is cleared in a secure extranet implementation.

- **Integrated Windows Authentication**   Choose whether or not to use Windows authentication, and what protocol to use.

- **Basic Authentication**   If you are serving extranet users over SSL, Basic authentication is a reasonable approach.

- **Client Integration**   If you want users to have a fully functional Microsoft Office experience, you should enable client integration. Additionally, you'll need to also enable anonymous access if using Forms-Based authentication to the library hosting the logon page.

NOTE   Although the zone names in SharePoint Server 2010 look similar to Internet Explorer security zones, they are not related or connected. SharePoint Server 2010 zones are for the logical association of URLs within the farm. For example, if *https://portalextranet.contoso.com* was an extended zone of *http://portal.contoso.com* on the Extranet zone, you would see only *Extranet* when applying policies. Therefore, you should always document your zone-to-URL association.

Zones are important to your security posture because they allow any security settings an additional IIS Web site would provide. Examples of these settings are as follows:

- Dedicated IP Address per server, per zone for auditing and load-balancing
- SSL on a per-server, per-zone basis
- Choice of NTLM, Kerberos, or Basic authentication
- Custom authentication, such as Forms-Based, Claims-Based, or third-party two-factor
- Client integration
- Developer-oriented settings on a per-zone basis
- Performance throttling, IIS logging, and error tracing
- Client Object Model permissions

NOTE   Although the creation of zones should not be performed in Internet Information Services Manager, some settings (such as SSL and dedicated IP addresses) must be set in IIS. Be sure to document these server-based changes.

Web Application Permission Policies

Web application policies are essentially a wrapper, on a specific zone, that over-rides the default security of site collections in that Web application. If the Web application does not specify either an explicit grant or deny right, the default permissions of the site collection are in force. Don't confuse permission policies with permission levels in Central Administration. Permission levels remove the permission from all zones, for all users. Permission policies override those permission levels through the policy for a specific zone and specific users. The default Web application policies are shown in Figure 15-25.

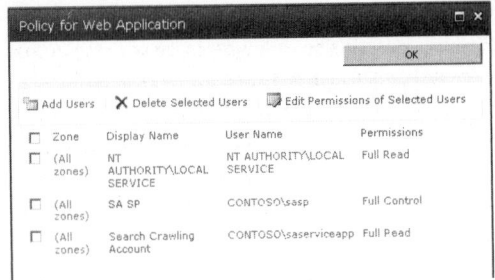

FIGURE 15-25 Do not change the default permission policies.

> **TIP** The default permissions allow for object and page caching as well as providing Full Read authentication for the search crawler. If you modify these, you could be limiting the functionality of your SharePoint Server 2010 farm.

Creating and applying a new Web application policy is a two-step process. You must first create the Web application permission policy. Then you must apply the new Web application permission policy to users or a group for a given zone. The three moving parts to a successfully deployed policy are

- Zone or zones where the policy will be applied
- Creation of the Web application policy
- Application of the policy to users or groups

Creating Policies

Web application policies you create are not used until you apply the policy to users or groups. This allows you to manage policies for a Web application separately from the zones where they are applied. You can have multiple policies per Web application, each applied independently for different users and zones. To create a new Web application policy, do the following:

1. Browse to Central Administration, Application Management, Manage Web Applications.
2. Select the Web application you want to manage.
3. Click Permission Policy on the management Ribbon, as seen in Figure 15-26.

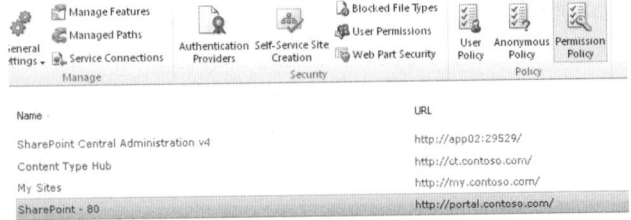

FIGURE 15-26 Click Permission Policy on the management Ribbon.

4. Select Add Permission Policy Level.

5. Give the policy a name, and type a description. It is wise to be verbose in the description and list all granted and denied permissions for the policy. This information is extremely useful when adding this policy in the future.

6. Optionally, define site collection permissions. Caution should be exercised when granting either Site Collection Administrator or Site Collection Auditor permissions. These permission levels give full access to all content in a Web application for specified users when the policy is applied.

7. Define the permissions for the policy. Note that a Deny will override a Grant defined in another policy and the existing privileges within a site collection.

8. Click OK. If your efforts are successful, your policy appears in the Manage Permissions Policy Levels screen, similar to Figure 15-27.

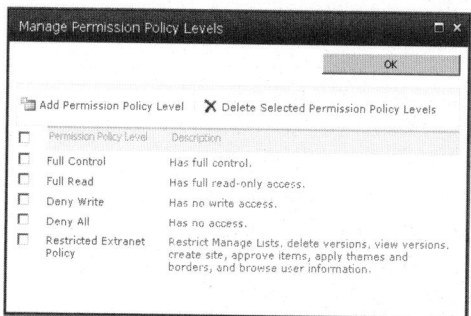

FIGURE 15-27 Screen that shows you were successful in creating your new policy and description.

Applying Policies

After you create a policy, it is available for application to a zone. The default policies of Full Control, Full Read, Deny Write, and Deny All are generally not useful. To apply a custom permission policy level you previously created, do the following:

1. Browse to Central Administration, Application Management, Manage Web Applications.

2. Select the Web application you want to manage.

3. Click User Policy on the management Ribbon.

4. Select Add Users.

5. Select the zone or zones where you will apply the policy, and then click Next.

6. Enter the users or groups, separated by semi-colons, that you want to govern with the policy. Figure 15-28 shows how to add users to a policy.

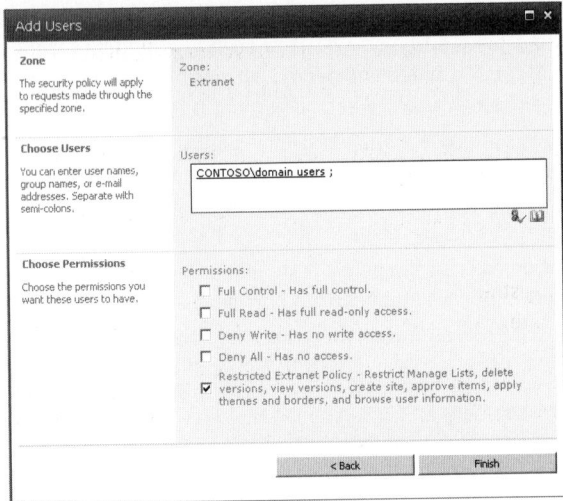

FIGURE 15-28 To affect all users in a zone, add DOMAIN\DOMAIN USERS.

7. Click Finish.

The application of a policy is immediate. If you are performing this on a production system, you should do so after hours and perform testing beforehand on a test server farm. by taking this approach, you can immediately unapply and then modify the policy if needed.

SharePoint Designer 2010 Governance

New in SharePoint Server 2010 is the ability to govern SharePoint Designer 2010 users. To manage SharePoint Designer 2010 policies, browse to Central Administration, Application Management, Manage Web Applications, and select the Web application to configure. Select SharePoint Designer from the General Settings drop-down menu on the management Ribbon, as seen in Figure 15-29.

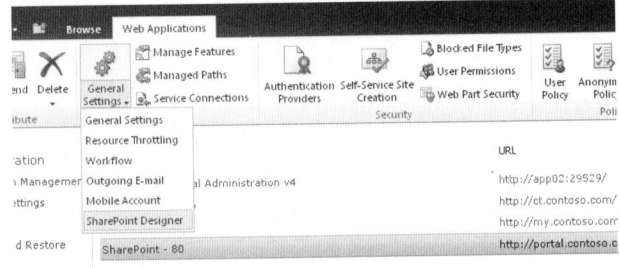

FIGURE 15-29 Select SharePoint Designer from the General Settings menu.

The following options are available to control SharePoint Designer 2010 users:

- Allow SharePoint Designer To Be Used In This Web Application
- Allow Site Collection Administrators To Detach Pages From The Site Template
- Allow Site Collection Administrators To Customize Master Pages And Layout Pages
- Allow Site Collection Administrators To See The URL Structure Of Their Web Site

Site collection administrators, if allowed from within Central Administration, can then further delegate permission to site owners. To delegate permissions to site owners, browse to a site collection. From Site Actions, Site Settings, select SharePoint Designer Settings in the Site Collection Administration grouping. Site collection administrators can then exercise control using the same options seen in Central Administration.

CHAPTER 16

Monitoring, Logging, and Availability

- Windows Server 2008 **489**
- SharePoint Server 2010 **495**
- Sequel 2008 Server **515**

C entral to the daily life of a SharePoint administrator is the ability to maintain the integrity, reliability, and availability of the Microsoft SharePoint Server 2010 environment. Therefore, knowing what the servers that make up the SharePoint farm are doing at any given time, and how they are doing it, is really important. This chapter describes how to use the SharePoint Server 2010 out-of-the-box diagnostic capabilities and details several Microsoft Windows Server tools that can be used to monitor the health of the server or servers and the farm.

Windows Server 2008

At the foundation of any SharePoint Server 2010 environment is the Windows operating system, which everything else relies on. Coupled with the server's hardware, the operating system is an integral part of keeping SharePoint Server 2010 up and running effectively. Whether issues that arise are related to memory, processor utilization, or the hard disk, each component has an impact on how the Windows operating system performs. There is a host of underlying server components that have a direct impact on the reliability and performance of SharePoint Server 2010—such as the Windows Identity Foundation (WIF), Microsoft Internet Information Services (IIS), the .NET Framework, the Transmission Control Protocol/Internet Protocol (TCP/IP) stack, and others. Making sure that the servers are sized appropriately increases the likelihood that the Windows operating system will have the necessary resources to turn over to SharePoint Server 2010.

If the base operating system is performing poorly, there will be a ripple effect and SharePoint Server 2010 will suffer. In turn, your users will ultimately feel the pain as well. Windows Server 2008 provides various diagnostic tools that are built in to the core operating system to help administrators manage the server or servers in the SharePoint Server 2010 farm. They include, but are not limited to, Event Viewer, Performance Monitor, Device Manager, and Task Manager. These are fundamental tools that any SharePoint administrator should become familiar with and understand.

Event Viewer

Windows Event Viewer has been a staple monitoring tool since Windows NT and has been revamped in Windows Server 2008 to be part of the Server Manager Diagnostics console (shown in Figure 16-1). Event Viewer is designed to provide information about what is taking place on the server. Depending on the role the server plays, other logs might also be kept, but information about the primary three repositories for event data are contained in the following logs:

- **Application Log** Provides detailed information for applications that are running on the server
- **Security Log** Provides security-related event details for activities that are occurring on the server
- **System Log** Provides details for Windows system events that are taking place on the server

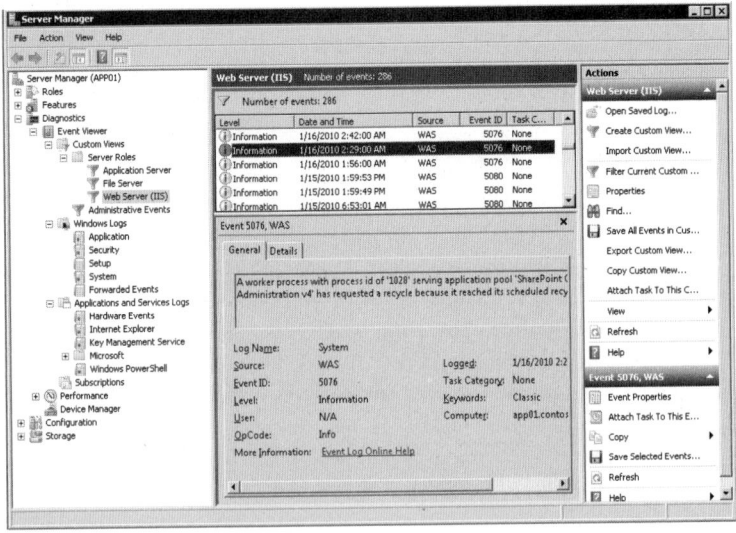

FIGURE 16-1 Windows Event Viewer.

A feature of the event logs in Windows Server 2008, known as Subscriptions, provides the ability to store event data from multiple servers onto one designated server. Depending on the scenario, you might find it useful to configure Subscriptions to aggregate SharePoint Server 2010 data into one centralized point. For Subscriptions to work, the Windows Event Collector and Windows Remote Management services must be running with a local firewall rule exception in place. Depending on which Windows Server 2008 server roles are installed, you can use Event Viewer's custom views to filter the role-specific events that are taking place on the server. For additional information about Windows Event Viewer, review the content found at *http://technet.microsoft.com/en-us/library/cc771823.aspx*.

Monitoring Tools

Along with Event Viewer, under the Diagnostics console tree, the Performance folder provides access to the Performance and Reliability monitors. These tools measure and report on the health and reliability of the server. As seen in Figure 16-2, the Performance Monitor tool can be used to track what is happening in real time and can also be used to collect valuable data over a period of time.

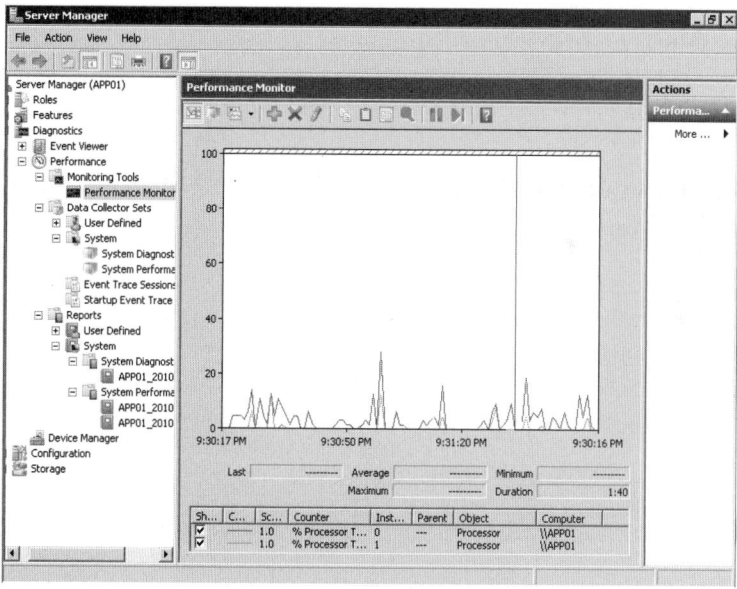

FIGURE 16-2 Monitoring server health with Performance Monitor.

Windows Server 2008 provides rich reporting tools based on data collection functionality that is built in. After the data gathering has taken place, reports can be generated for review as seen in Figure 16-3. The reports provide a wealth of information that can be useful for trend analysis and for determining anomalies in the configuration of the SharePoint Server 2010 environment.

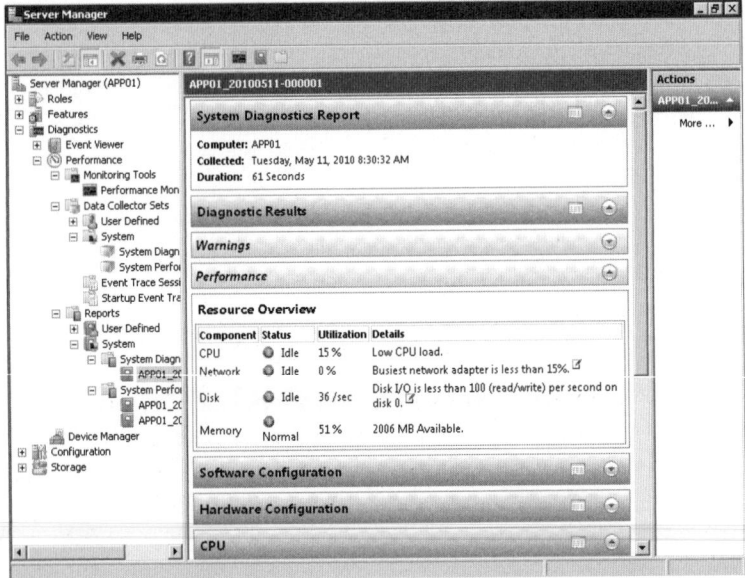

FIGURE 16-3 System diagnostic reports.

Windows Task Manager

An invaluable tool that has been in Windows since Windows NT 4 is Windows Task Manager. The utility has been upgraded, as seen in Figure 16-4, to provide an easy and immediate way to visualize what is happening on a local server. Using the various Task Manager tabs (Applications, Processes, Services, Performance, Networking, and Users), an administrator can quickly get a real-time picture of the activities that are occurring on the server.

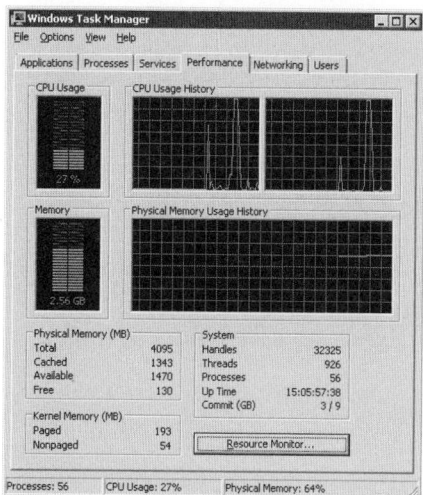

FIGURE 16-4 Windows Task Manager Performance tab.

By clicking the Resource Monitor button, which is located in the lower right corner of the Performance tab, an administrator can quickly drill into the specifics of what is going on. For example, as seen in Figure 16-5, the administrator can use Resource Monitor to selectively monitor and pinpoint which applications or processes are having an impact on the processor or processors, on the hard disk, and on network utilization or memory consumption.

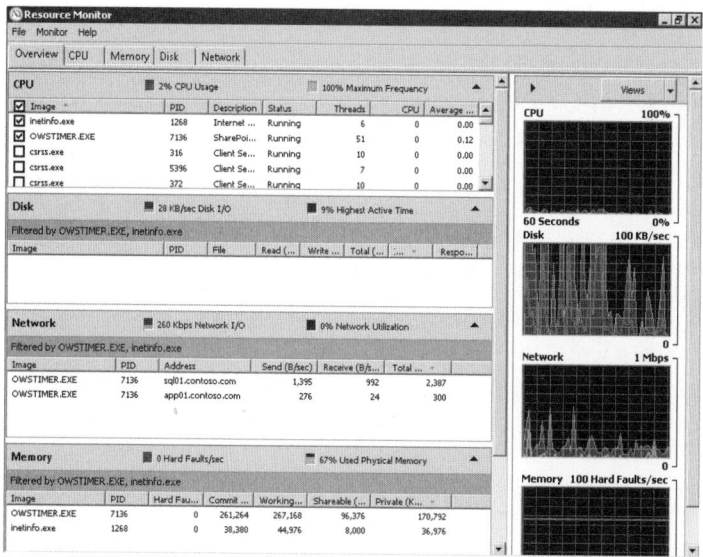

FIGURE 16-5 Resource Monitor in action.

As part of an ongoing effort to monitor a SharePoint Server 2010 farm environment, a system administrator should make it a priority to ensure that the configuration is consistently well documented. Using the System Information tool, an administrator can capture a local or remote system's hardware and software configuration to simplify this ongoing administrative effort. The tool is accessible by running Msinfo32.exe. It produces an exportable, printable, and searchable file as seen in Figure 16-6.

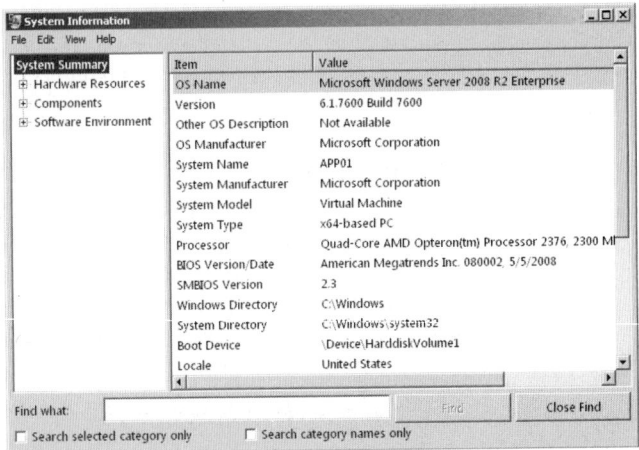

FIGURE 16-6 Using System Information to review the system configuration.

Internet Information Services

The SharePoint Server 2010 application sits neatly on top of Internet Information Services (IIS) version 7. To maximize Web server performance, several characteristics should be studied to identify how they are being used and then adjusted to aid in tuning or troubleshooting. IIS 7 provides several out-of-the-box health and diagnostic capabilities necessary for monitoring and optimizing your system. These features include Failed Request Tracing Rules, Logging, and Worker Processes.

- **Failed Request Tracing Rules** Allows an administrator the flexibility to collect XML-formatted log data for interpretation without having to re-create the problem prior to troubleshooting. More detailed information can be found at *http://technet.microsoft.com/en-us/library/cc731798.aspx*.

- **Logging** By configuring logging in IIS, an administrator can provide a wealth of information, including details such as the number of sites. The information can be collected on a per-site basis and at various timed intervals. More detailed information can be found at *http://technet.microsoft.com/en-us/library/cc732079(WS.10).aspx*.

- **Worker Processes** This feature provides a view into the worker processes that are running on the Web server, including an aggregated status of sites, application pools, and server worker processes that indicates service state, memory, and processor utilization. More detailed information can be found at *http://technet.microsoft.com/en-us/library/cc725918(WS.10).aspx*.

SharePoint Server 2010

SharePoint Server 2010 provides a variety of monitoring and diagnostic capabilities that have been enhanced since the last version. At a macro level, Central Administration provides the IT administrator with the ability to review problems and solutions, check the status of various timer-based jobs, and to use Web analytics to report on the health and utilization of the content on the servers.

SharePoint Server 2010 Health Analyzer

SharePoint 2010 Health Analyzer, also known as SharePoint 2010 Best Practices Analyzer, provides a detailed list of items that need to be analyzed. The Health Analyzer Rules Definition page in Central Administration provides a great deal of flexibility for the IT administrator to understand the health of a SharePoint Server 2010 environment. A red bar across the Central Administration screen indicates that there are critical issues that need to be addressed, as seen in Figure 16-7.

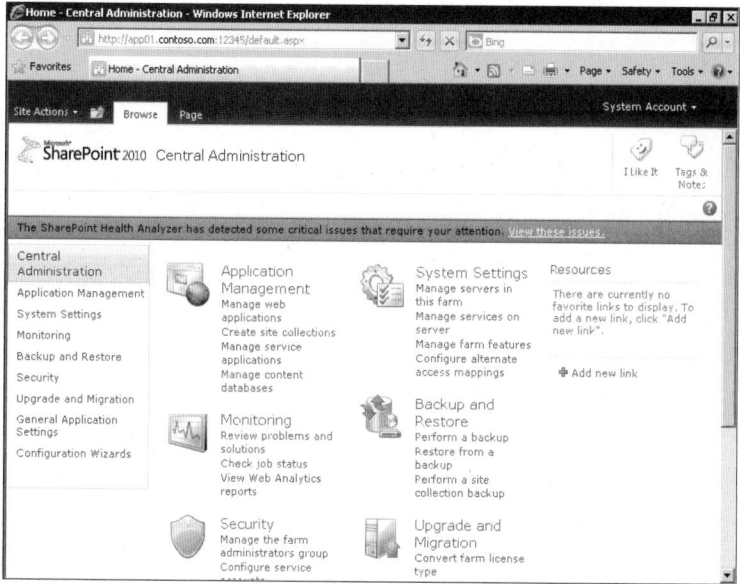

FIGURE 16-7 The red bar of the SharePoint Health Analyzer indicates there are issues for consideration.

Monitoring

SharePoint Server 2010 periodically reviews the status of all the servers in the farm to ensure that they are accessible and performing based on certain minimum preset thresholds. From Central Administration, click the Monitoring link to access details about the health of the SharePoint Server 2010 environment. Monitoring has been divided into three primary categories:

- Health Analyzer
- Timer Jobs
- Reporting

Health Analyzer

The Health Analyzer page has two options. The first option is for reviewing problems and determining if the issues can be corrected, while the second option is for reviewing the rule definitions.

Review Problems and Solutions

As seen in Figure 16-8, the Review Problems And Solutions screen is divided into three categories by SharePoint Server 2010, with rules designed to run at various intervals ranging from hourly to daily to weekly.

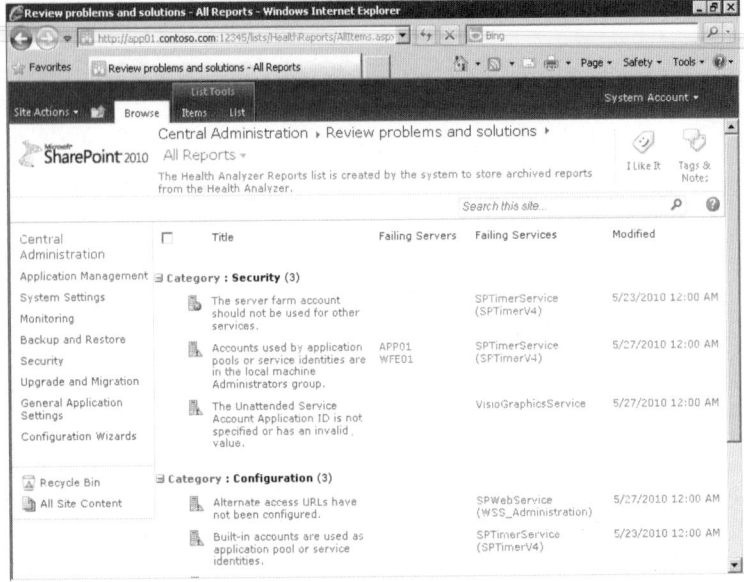

FIGURE 16-8 Problems And Solutions categories.

The problems are grouped into the following categories:

- Security
- Performance
- Configuration

Each of the categorized problems indicates which server or servers are being affected, which service is failing, and the date and time when the service was last modified. When a problem has been identified, you can examine the issue to determine how it should be addressed. As seen in Figure 16-9, the dialog box provides a severity level, and a more thorough description of the issue that has surfaced is provided. A potential remedy is displayed, and Knowledge Base articles from Microsoft are provided for additional reference material. The dialog box again highlights the service that is failing and which server or servers are being affected. Depending on the problem, some issues might provide the option to fix the problem automatically. After the problem has been fixed automatically or manually, you can click the Reanalyze Now button to rescan the issue to determine whether it has been fixed.

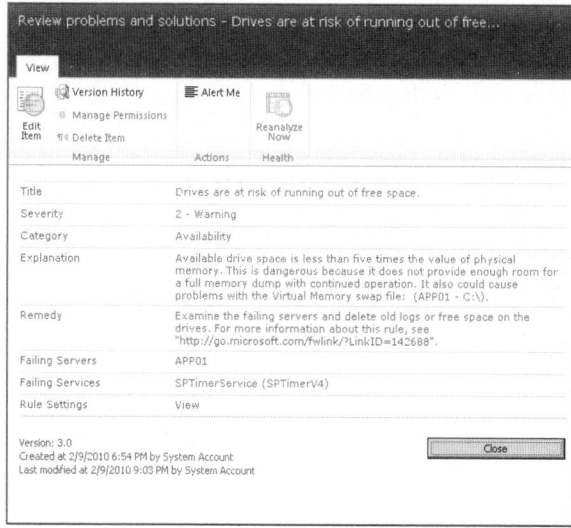

FIGURE 16-9 Details about the specifics of the problems and a potential remedy.

Review Rule Definition

On the Health Analyzer Rule Definitions page, a list of all active rule definitions is presented. On this page, each rule is presented in one of the aforementioned categories, and the option exists to edit, delete, or select the rule and run it manually. Each rule has four primary configuration options, including the scope or the servers where the rule will run, the scheduled frequency, whether or not the rule is enabled, and whether the fix should be performed automatically. (See Figure 16-10.) Click the rule and then click the Edit Item button.

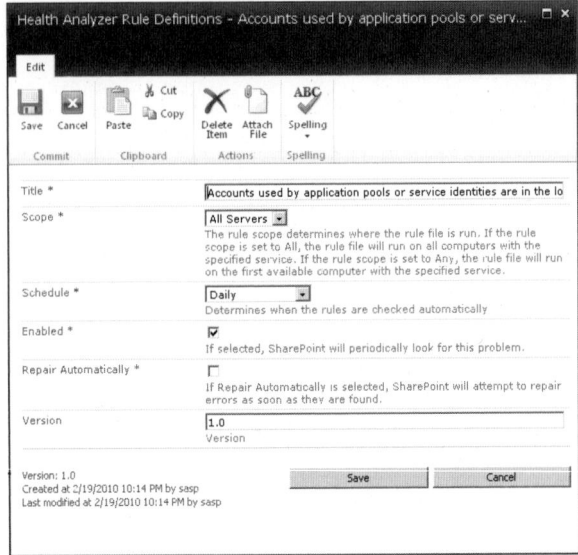

FIGURE 16-10 Health Analyzer Rule Definitions configuration.

There is also an option to include the version number, which can be helpful for Change Control purposes.

Timer Jobs

Just as the name suggests, timer jobs are triggers that are used to start a specific process at a scheduled time or interval. Timer jobs are created when services, Web applications, and features are enabled. Timer job management is divided into two tasks:

- Review job definitions
- Check job status

Review Job Definitions

The Job Definitions page allows the SharePoint administrator to see which of the various timer job definitions have been configured. As seen in Figure 16-11, the jobs are classified by title, the particular Web application that it is specified to run against, and the scheduled frequency.

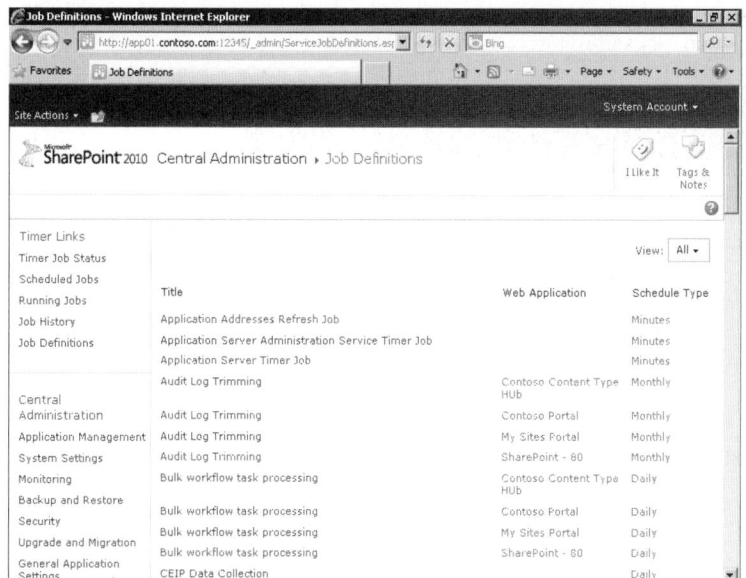

FIGURE 16-11 Job Definitions page.

You might also notice that some jobs appear only once, while others occur multiple times. Some jobs are system defined and apply to the farm, while other job definitions are associated with a particular application service. For the purpose of filtering, you can also use the View filter in the upper right corner of the page to modify the display to show everything, a particular service, or just a Web application.

In Figure 16-12, you can see the configuration settings of a particular timer job. This page can be used to modify, run, or disable a timer job.

Check Job Status

The Check Job Status page shows the status of various timer jobs. The page subdivides the jobs classifications into Scheduled, Running, and History. Each category shows the job title, the server where the job is being run, the Web application, and the time the job will run or when it has been run. As seen in Figure 16-13, a handful of jobs are scheduled to run, and in the Running section several jobs are currently running. In the History section, a tally of jobs that have succeeded as well as those that failed are listed. At the bottom of each section is a "1–10" label followed by a tiny arrow. If you click on the arrow, the next set of timer job status details will be displayed in that category.

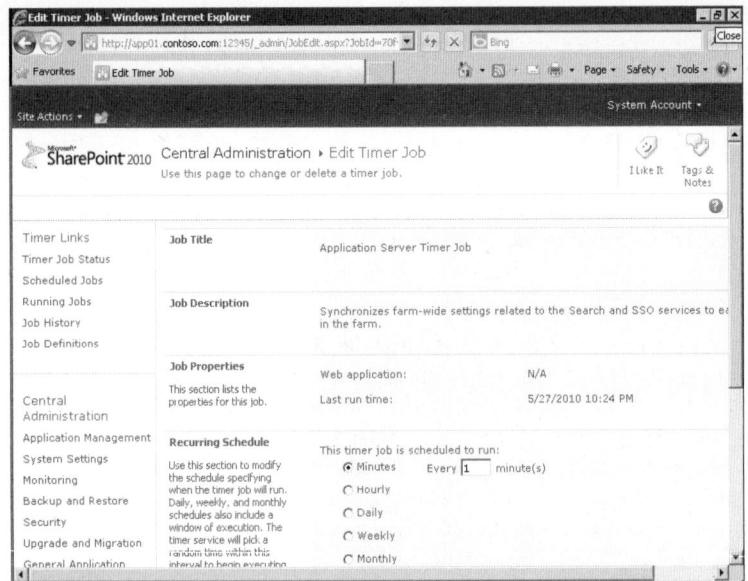

FIGURE 16-12 Edit timer jobs.

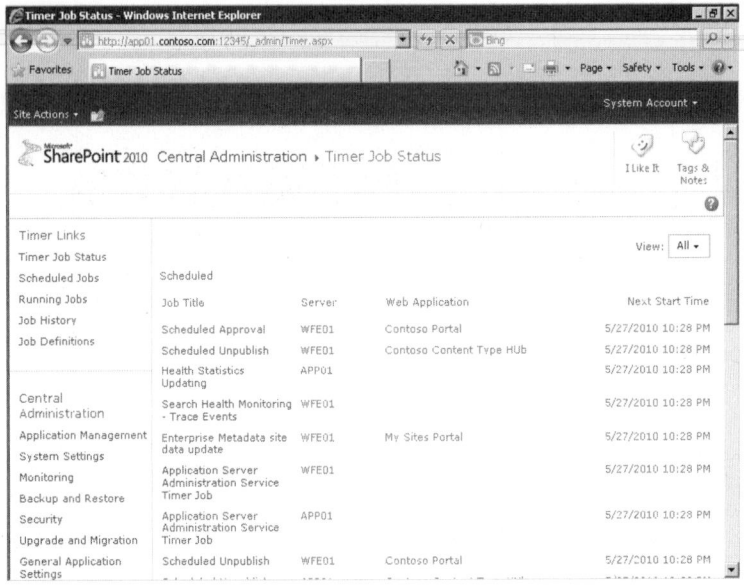

FIGURE 16-13 Timer job status details.

Along the upper left side of the page, there are a number of hyperlinks under the Timer Links navigation header. These hyperlinks provide quick access to each of the timer job management pages.

Reporting

The six categories in the Reporting section of Monitoring can be subdivided into two primary groups. The first is the creation of logs files, and the second is the viewing of the reports from the logging data.

CREATING THE LOGS

Diagnostic logging settings are accessed from the Reporting heading by clicking Configure Diagnostic Logging, which displays the Diagnostic Logging page shown in Figure 16-14. The Unified Logging Service (ULS) is responsible for managing the various systemwide aspects of logging. By default, the logs are stored at C:\Program Files\Common Files\Microsoft Shared\Web Server Extensions\14\LOGS. The SharePoint administrator has the ability to control what is being logged, where the files are being stored, and how much space will be taken up by the log files. There are three categories of configuration: Event Throttling, Event Log Flood Protection, and Trace Log. For troubleshooting purposes, you might find it helpful to use a utility called ULS Viewer for seeing real-time information or when reviewing historic events. Although the tool is not officially supported by Microsoft, it provides a wealth of information and useful insight into what is going on with SharePoint. The utility can be found at *http://code.msdn.microsoft.com/ULSViewer*.

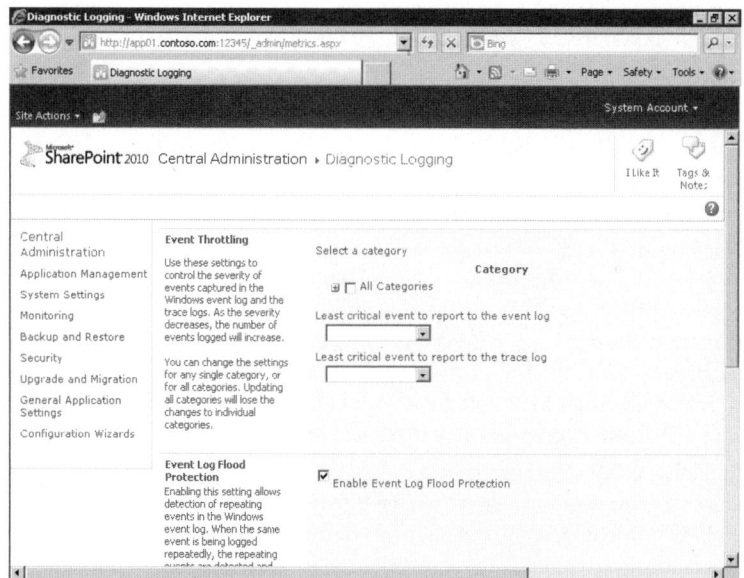

FIGURE 16-14 Configure Diagnostic Logging settings.

In Figure 16-15, you can see the myriad categories that can be used to control how much information is being captured. To set up event throttling, choose the category or categories by selecting the respective category check box. Then select the appropriate criteria for the *least critical event to report* to either the Event Log or the Trace Logs. Use the drop-down list to specify the level that must be triggered for the event to be recorded in the event log.

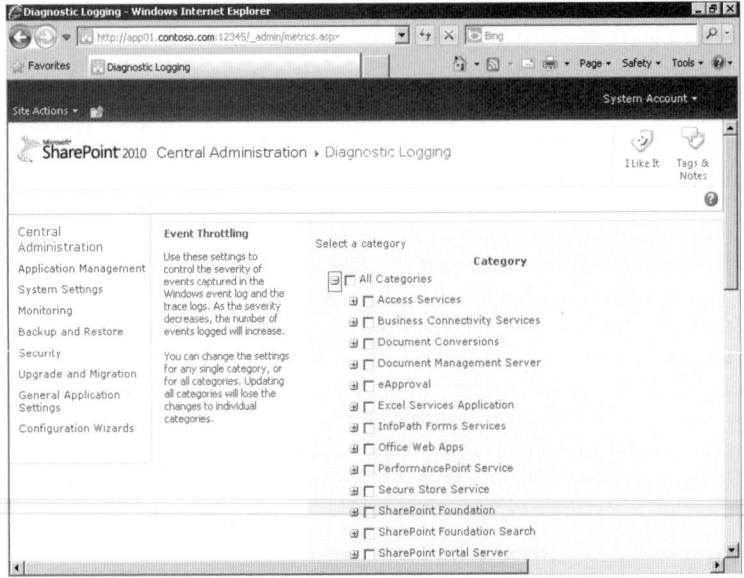

FIGURE 16-15 Configuring event throttling on the Diagnostics Logging page.

Event Log Flood Protection can be set to an enabled or disabled status. The purpose of this setting is to ensure that the server is not overwhelmed by recurring events being written to the Windows Event logs. The repeating events are suppressed until the condition has been returned to normal.

The Trace Log setting gives the administrator the option to specify where the trace logs are stored. For performance or fault tolerance, it might be advantageous to move the location of where the trace logs are stored to another hard disk drive. However, be sure to keep in mind that this location must be consistent on all servers in the farm. From the Trace Log section, you can also specify the number of days that the log files should be stored and restrict the amount of disk space that is consumed by the trace logs by setting a maximum limit.

The Configure Usage And Health Data Collection page is designed to create a log whenever specific events occur in the SharePoint Server 2010 environment. The goal of analyzing the collected usage data is to better understand how the various aspects are being used. Figure 16-16 shows the configuration options.

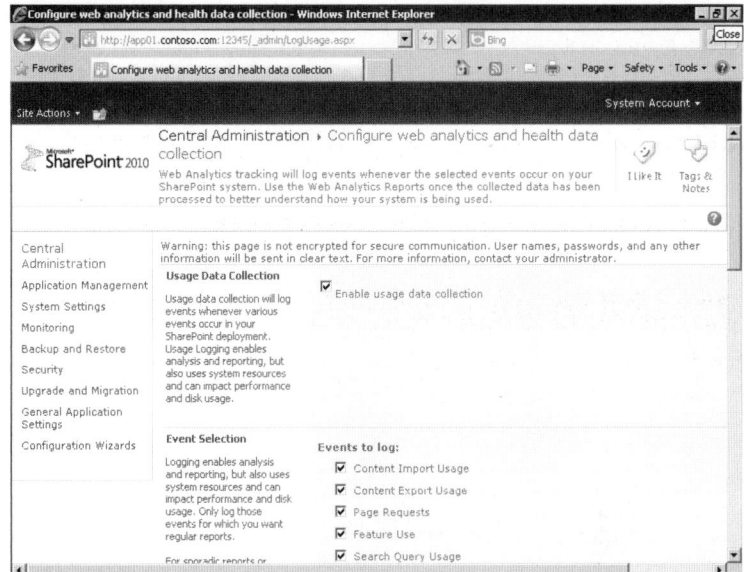

FIGURE 16-16 Configure usage and health data collection.

Be sure to consider the settings carefully when you enable the collection of usage data, because the number of events being logged can have an impact on system performance and disk usage.

The areas that can be selected are as follows:

- Content Usage (Import And Export)
- Page Requests
- Feature Use
- Search Query Usage
- Site Inventory Usage
- Timer Jobs
- Rating Usage

The other options include the ability to specify the size and location of the usage log files. Here, again, note that the location must exist consistently throughout the SharePoint Server 2010 server environment. Enabling health data collection can also be configured, as well as the scheduled frequency.

VIEWING THE LOGS

After you have enabled usage logging and it is running at some scheduled frequency, you can begin to view the reports it generates. By default, there are two types of reports that are viewable: farm-level and site-level reports.

The View Information Management Policy Usage Reports page can be configured on a Web-application basis, as seen in Figure 16-17. The generation of policy usage reports can be enabled, and you can specify that they be published in recurring fashion on a daily, weekly, or monthly basis.

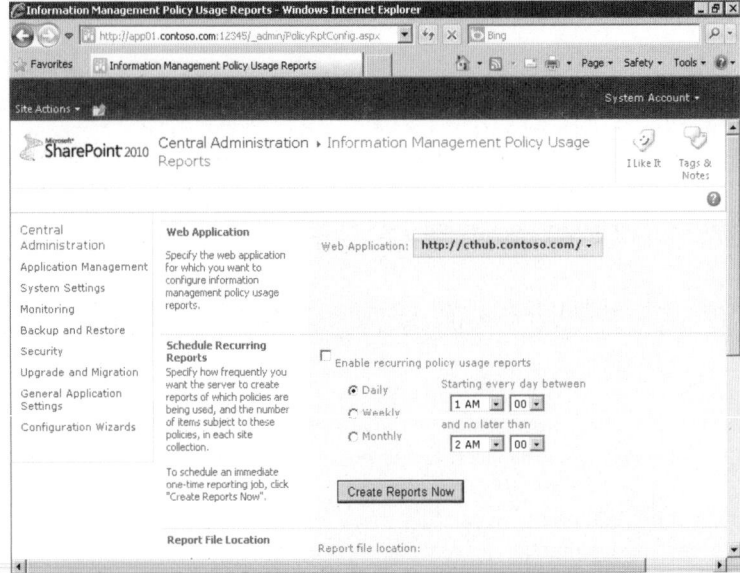

FIGURE 16-17 Select the Web application for information-management policy usage reports.

Web Analytics

Understanding how SharePoint Server 2010 is being used is essential to deriving the maximum benefit from it in terms of IT investment. Out of the box, the product has been improved dramatically from previous versions. It provides useful utilization and historical trend data to allow the SharePoint Administrator and the IT department to better understand and manage the existing environment. This data can be used to prepare for future growth, as well as provide the statistical ammunition necessary for business justification. The raw data should be used as a guide to practitioners and management alike and shine a spotlight on the way SharePoint Server 2010 is being used.

The three-tiered architecture of the Web analytics provides several collection points throughout the SharePoint Server 2010 environment. Usage data is aggregated at the farm, site-collection, and site levels. Meanwhile, the log data is actively collected through the server's event logs and through the SharePoint Server 2010 Trace and Service Application log files. A single staging database is used as the initial repository for the Logging Web Service data. The Analytics component then processes this data in preparation for storage in the Reporting database. At this point, the information can be distributed through the rich set of reporting capabilities available to the SharePoint administrator. From the Central Administration Monitoring section, as well as at the site-collection level, administrators have access to the Web Analytics report data. Reports can be generated on an as-needed basis or at scheduled intervals.

Configuring Web Analytics

To configure Web Analytics, from Central Administration select Manage Service Applications under Application Management. As shown in Figure 16-18, click New, and then select Web Analytics Service Application from the drop-down menu.

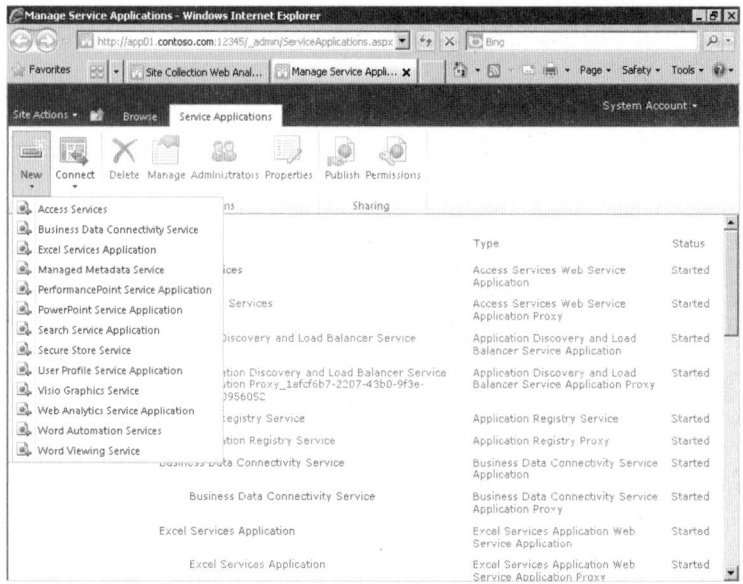

FIGURE 16-18 Adding a Web Analytics service application.

Figure 16-19 displays the various options that can be set. During the configuration process, a default name will be provided for the Web Analytics service application, or you can choose to use a different name. At this point, you can use an existing application pool or create a new one, as well as specify the account that will be used for this Web service. The database server needs to be specified, as well as the specific names for the Reporting and Staging database files. Finally, you can specify the length of time that the data will be retained. By default, the setting for the Reporting database is 25 months, while the Staging database will retain the data for 30 days.

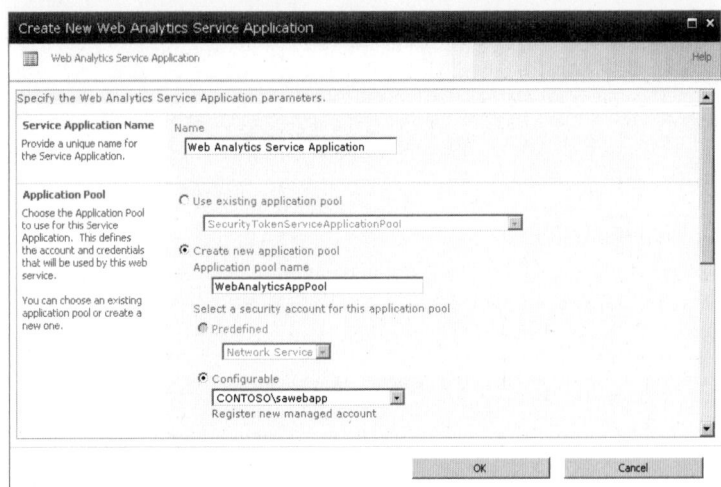

FIGURE 16-19 Parameters for the Web Analytics service application.

After the service application has been created, a message is displayed, as shown in Figure 16-20. As the message points out, you need to remember that the Web Analytics service application effectively has two parts. Make sure that both have been started. In a multiserver farm, make sure that the services have been started on the application server on which the service is intended to run.

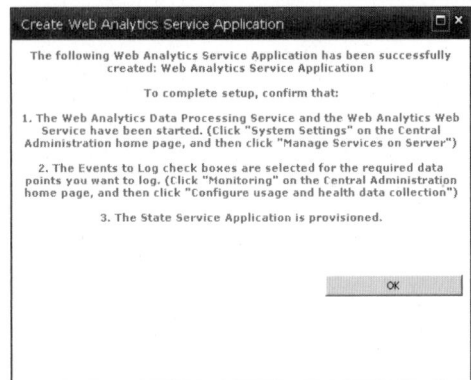

FIGURE 16-20 Web Analytics service-creation confirmation message.

If Web Analytics has already been configured—perhaps through the initial Configuration Wizard—several of the configurations settings can be modified to meet your needs. By selecting Manage Service Applications from the Application Management section of Central Administration, you can adjust the configuration, as seen in Figure 16-21.

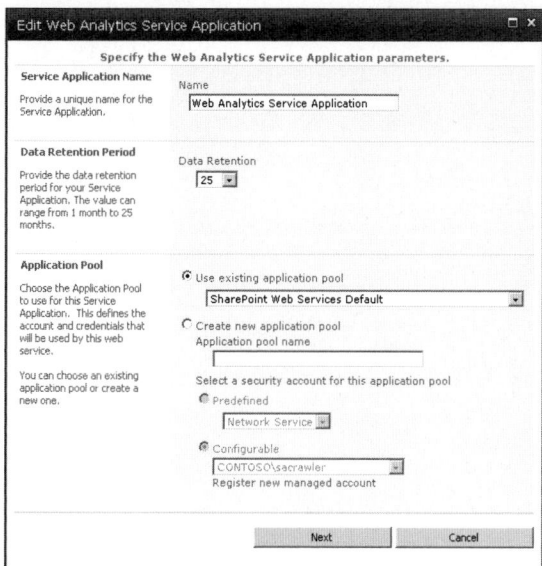

FIGURE 16-21 Specify the Web Analytics application parameters.

View Web Analytics Reports

From Central Administration, select Monitoring and then choose View Web Analytics Reports to bring up the Web Analytics Reports - Summary page as seen in Figure 16-22.

On the Summary page, each Web applications is shown with its corresponding URL displayed. Each site gives statistics for Total Number Of Page Views, Total Number Of Daily Unique Visitors, and Total Number Of Search Queries. Each Web application is depicted as a hyperlink, and you can follow this link to drill down into the specific data for a particular Web application. In Figure 16-23, a sample Summary page for the Contoso Portal is shown.

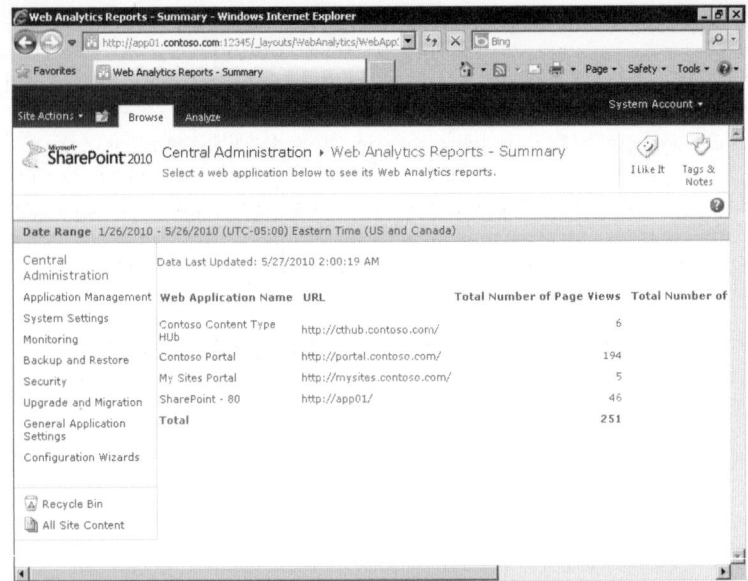

FIGURE 16-22 Summary display of the Web Analytics reports arranged by Web application name.

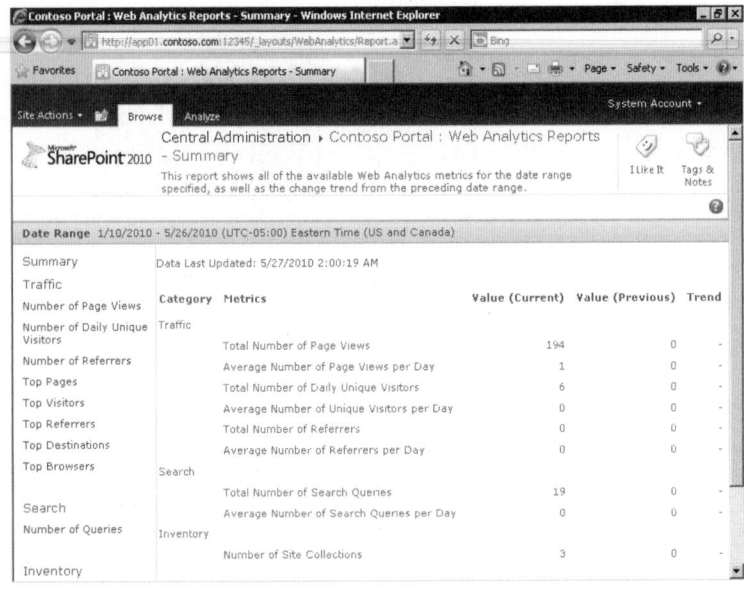

FIGURE 16-23 Web analytics summary page.

The Summary page is divided into three categories, with a variety of metrics displayed for each. The statistics show the current value, the previous value, and what the trend is. In the left navigation pane, there are Summary Traffic, Search, and Inventory links from which an administrator can find additional details. For example, in Figure 16-24 a report has been generated depicting the different types of Web browsers being used in the SharePoint environment. This might be useful in providing inventories of the specific types of browsers that are being used in the enterprise as compared to the corporate standard. This type of report might also be useful for showing what the various constituent browser types are to determine if broader browser or development support is needed to improve the end-user experience.

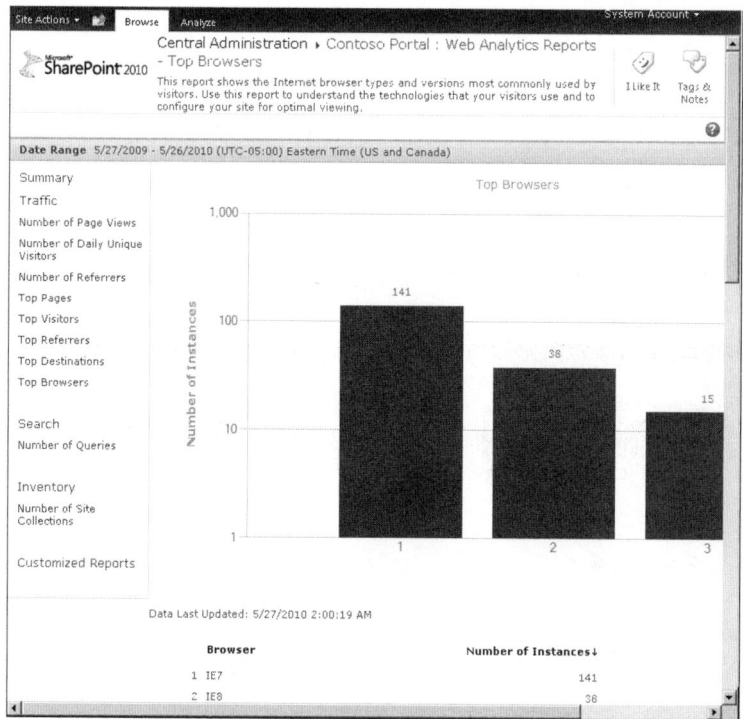

FIGURE 16-24 A report based on the variety of Web browsers being used.

In a SharePoint Server 2010 environment, each time a page is requested or a Web Part is rendered, this information is tracked through the Logging database. What makes this information particularly useful is that traffic patterns can be seen throughout the farm. In Figure 16-25, the graphic shows what URLs are being used for referral purposes.

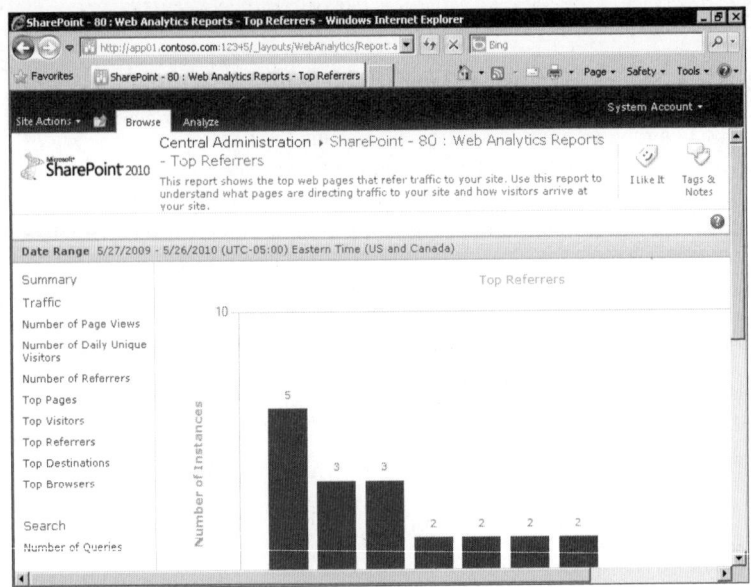

FIGURE 16-25 A report showing the URLs that are the top referrers.

Along with pages such as Top Referrers and Top Pages, these reports also indicate which portions of the SharePoint Server 2010 sites are being accessed. An administrator can easily use the logging and reporting capabilities to do trend analysis. If a new Web site has been implemented, an administrator can see the amount of traffic that is being generated based on a wide range of characteristics. In Figure 16-26, you can see that by selecting the Analyze tab, the UI displays a set of preconfigured, date-range queries that help to simplify the output of summary data. The date ranges start with the preceding day, the past 365 days, or a custom date you can specify.

Furthermore, this report data can be exported into a comma-separated value (CSV) file for further manipulation via a spreadsheet or a database. In the lower portion of left navigation menu, a Customized Reports link exists. By selecting this link, a SharePoint administrator is taken to a document library containing a number of diagnostic reports. In Figure 16-27, a listing of the general and advanced, out-of-the-box search administration reports is shown.

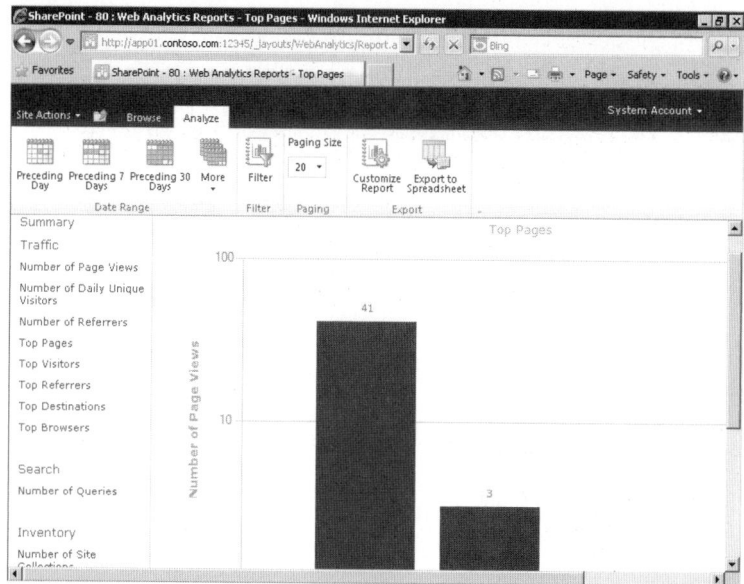

FIGURE 16-26 Custom analysis can be done by selecting various date ranges.

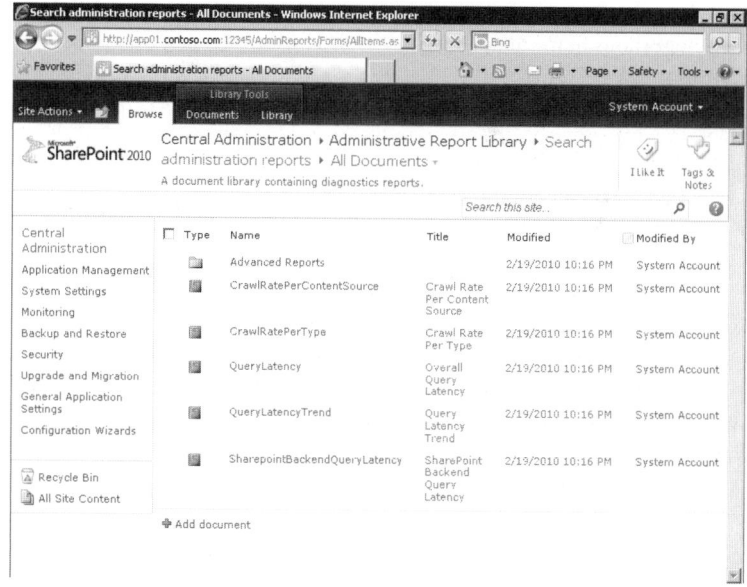

FIGURE 16-27 The administrative report library.

An administrator can run reports similar to the one found in Figure 16-28. These reports can include some or all application and content sources to build customized reports based on certain date ranges.

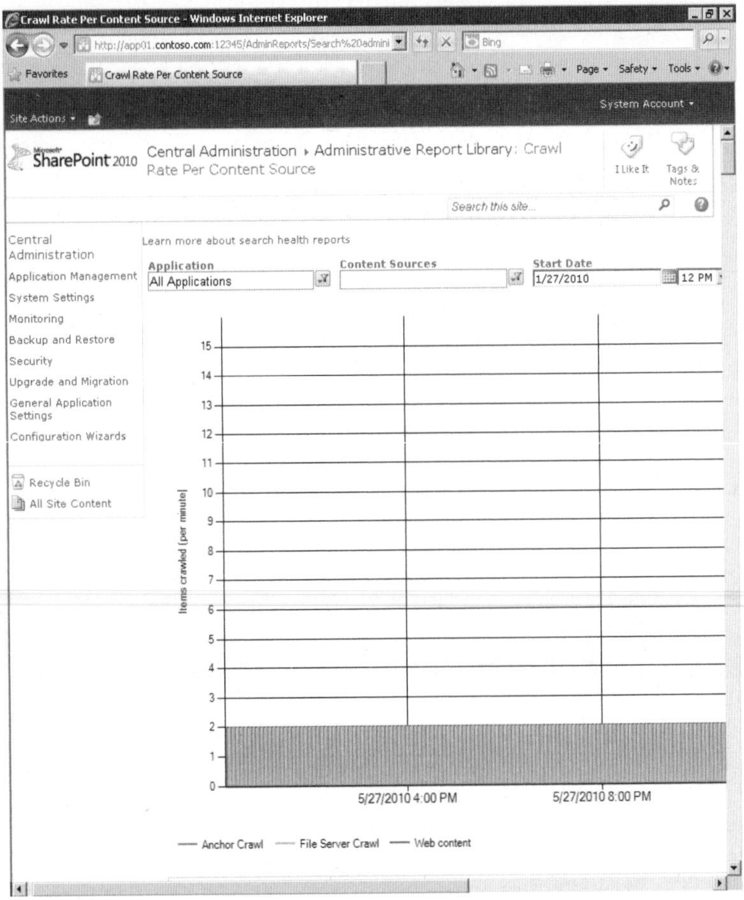

FIGURE 16-28 Reports based on crawl rate per content source.

Web Analytics reports can be generated at the site and site-collection levels as well. From the site, select Site Actions, Site Settings to access the menu seen in Figure 16-29.

Site Actions
Manage site features
Reset to site definition
Delete this site
Site Web Analytics reports
Site Collection Web Analytics reports

FIGURE 16-29 Accessing Web Analytics reports at the site and site-collection levels.

Here again at the site level, an administrator can use the Web Analytic reporting to understand how the site is being used. An administrator can easily determine important site benchmarks, such as the number of pages viewed, unique visitors, top visitors, referrers, and destinations, to name a few. Additionally, the administrator can use the customized reports shown in the left navigation menu of Figure 16-30 to access a document library to create and store additional diagnostic reports.

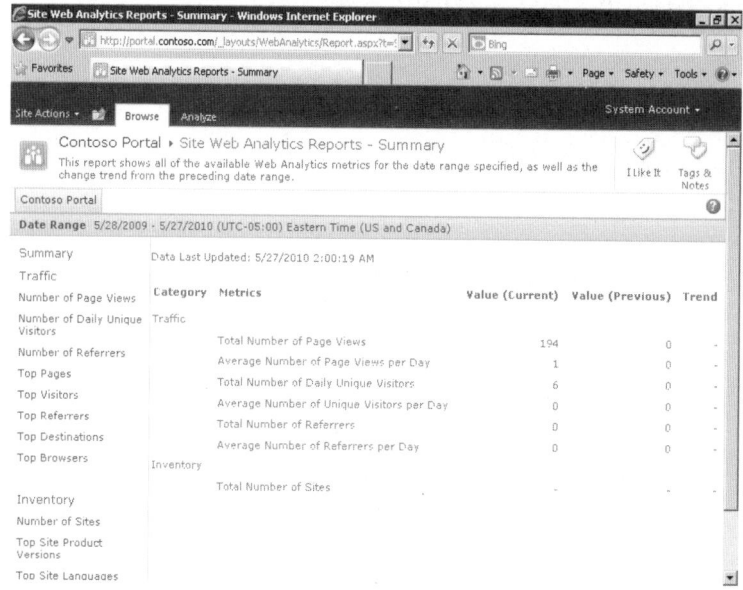

FIGURE 16-30 Site-level Web Analytics reports summary.

The site-collection Web Analytics reports include even more statistical data about utilization at the site-collection level. Consistent with the previous summary navigation categories (Traffic, Search, and Inventory), at the site-collection level each of the categories includes even more information that an administrator can use. As seen in Figure 16-31, under the Search section of the left navigation pane, there are reports on query-specific data, such as frequency, top queries, and failed queries. There are additional reports to help an administrator understand how site-specific searches are performing. This might be useful in shaping search results and increasing the effectiveness and, ultimately, accuracy and meaningfulness of the search results. In the Inventory section, there are reports to help the administrator visualize details about the site, such as storage usage, top site product versions, and languages.

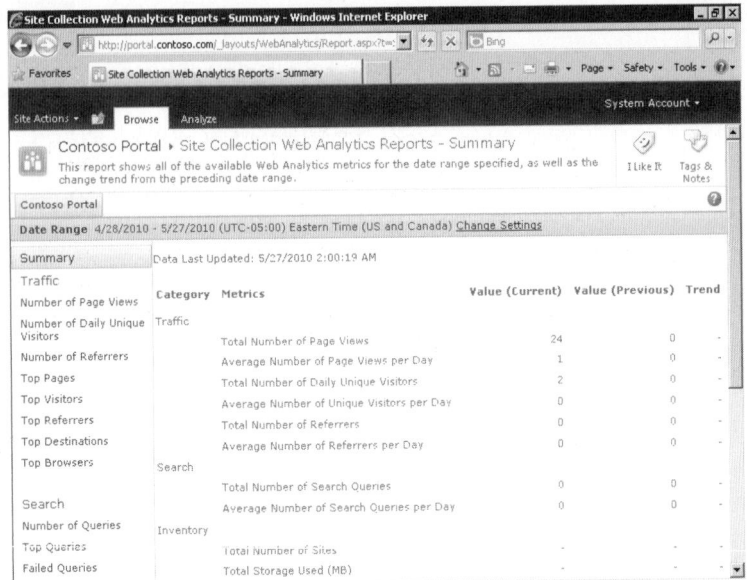

FIGURE 16-31 Site Collection Web Analytics Reports Summary view.

Finally, there are the customized reports that can be created to give the SharePoint administrator additional levels of granularity and control to better monitor and manage the sites.

Diagnostic Logging

To help you keep track of what is going on with the servers, SharePoint Server 2010 has diagnostic-logging capabilities that are set by default from the installation. There are several guidelines that should be considered when implementing this tracking mechanism. Use caution whenever making a configuration change and setting the logging levels to Verbose. Although this setting might be necessary and useful when troubleshooting, because of the resource constraints that it can place on a server, you should use it sparingly.

By default, diagnostic logging is configured to write to the partition where SharePoint Server 2010 was installed. For performance and fault-tolerance reasons, you should consider moving the location of where these files are stored to another physical disk to reduce the possibility of I/O contention. However, if the location is adjusted, the setting needs to be consistently mirrored throughout the rest of the SharePoint Server 2010 environment.

SQL 2008 Server

Because the vast majority of the SharePoint Server 2010 farm resides on servers using SQL Server, it is important to monitor SQL Server and the databases to make sure that they are working well. Whether SharePoint Server 2010 has been configured in a small, medium, or large farm configuration, understanding each of the essential components of the primary repository will help to make the lives of a SharePoint administrator more enjoyable. Where possible, begin by building SharePoint Server 2010 in a test environment. This approach allows you to optimize the configuration and simulate the load that is to be expected. From there, take a baseline measurement and watch to see how the server performs. From the baseline, you will be able to monitor and track the production environment to get trend data and compare it to the original test data.

As with any solution, understanding what the performance should be like is vital. Coordination with the database administrator (DBA) teams will help to ensure that the farm is performing reliably and at the level expected. Carefully consider the physical and logical placement of the database files and the logs to ensure that there will not be resource contention. The underlying anatomy of the SQL environment will have an impact on SharePoint performance.

Within the SQL Server instance, a number of performance counters should be monitored. Table 19-1 is not an exhaustive list, but at a minimum, the components that should be considered are CPU, disk, and memory.

TABLE19-1 SQL Performance Counters

PERFORMANCE COUNTERS	DESCRIPTION
Physical Disk: % Disk Time	Captures the percentage of time that the disk is busy with read/write activities.
Physical Disk: Average Disk Queue Length	Provides an average count of the number of system requests that are waiting for disk access. A consistent value greater than 2 likely indicates a disk bottleneck.
Logical Disk: Free Megabytes	Describes the amount of disk space that is free on a given drive.
Memory: Available Bytes	Specifies how many bytes of memory are currently available for use by system processes. A low value indicates there is an overall lack of memory or that an application is not releasing memory consistently.

PERFORMANCE COUNTERS	DESCRIPTION
Memory: Pages/Sec	Refers to the number of pages that have been retrieved from disk due to page faults. A high number of these could indicate an excessive amount of paging.
Processor: % Processer Time	Provides a percentage tally of the amount of time that the processor is being used to execute a thread. A consistent value of greater than 80 percent might indicate the need for additional processors or an upgrade.
System: Processor Queue Length	Indicates the number of threads that are in a server's processor queue that are waiting to be executed.

For additional information on the Monitoring Resource Usage tool, review the content found at *http://msdn.microsoft.com/en-us/library/ms191246.aspx*.

CHAPTER 17

Upgrading to SharePoint Server 2010

- Planning Tools **518**
- In-Place Upgrade **526**
- Database Attach Upgrade **533**
- Upgrading Sites and Site Collections **537**

Depending on the level of complexity and customization of your current system, there are many variables to take into consideration when upgrading to Microsoft SharePoint Server 2010. If your current system isn't highly customized or complex, the upgrade process will be fairly painless. However, if you have deployed custom code and made system modifications, your implementation will require significant planning and testing. The following steps should be followed when upgrading from SharePoint Server 2007:

- Study and understand the upgrade options available to you.
- Thoroughly document your current system to include databases, features, solutions, Shared Services, Internet Information Services, SQL Server, hardware, and farm-level customizations such as alternate access mappings and host headers.
- Communicate to users and stakeholders about potential system outages and changes.
- Plan your upgrade, and verify it aligns with a supported upgrade scenario. The support upgrade paths can be found at *http://technet.microsoft.com/ en-us/library/cc303420(office.14).aspx*.
- Test your upgrade in a nonproduction environment with a copy of production data.
- Create and test your rollback plan in the event of upgrade failure.

- Upgrade your server farm or farms, deploy custom code, and execute a test plan.
- Validate a successful upgrade by testing all components detailed in your system documentation. Be sure to test any customizations in features and solutions as well as new features (such as visual upgrades), and get plenty of user feedback.

It's possible your first attempt will not be 100 percent successful. Always prepare for the worst and hope for the best by having multiple, reliable backups of all systems and databases. Good planning and testing performed in advance will greatly reduce the chance of a failed upgrade.

> **SEE ALSO** For detailed information on planning and documenting your current environment for the purposes of upgrading, see *http://technet.microsoft.com/sharepoint*.

Planning Tools

The most common upgrade scenario is an upgrade from SharePoint Server 2007 to SharePoint Server 2010. There are two basic options available—in-place and database attach—and almost unlimited variations of those options. Many planning and execution variables affect both the in-place and database attach options. For example, many administrators will ask "How long will it take?". This depends on both your current software configuration and target hardware configuration. The current number of site collections, subsites, document libraries, lists, custom lists with numerous columns, number of documents, document size, version history, and site collection size will significantly alter both the time and complexity of an upgrade.

Likewise, the hardware that you perform the actual upgrade on will affect the time for upgrading. Items affected include the processor speed and disk speeds of your SQL Server hardware, the SharePoint Server 2010 Web server memory and processor, the application server memory and processor, and the speed and complexity of your network environment.

> **IMPORTANT** Always back up your current system and test system restores before attempting an upgrade. The latter, an adequate system restoration plan, is a key requirement before attempting an upgrade. Many administrators fail to test the ability to completely restore a server farm in the event of a disaster. See *http://technet.microsoft.com/en-us/office/sharepointserver/bb736212.aspx* for information on creating a SharePoint Server 2007 disaster recovery plan.

For testing and troubleshooting, the following steps are performed by the upgrade process during an in-place upgrade, but they might not be apparent to the administrator:

1. Begin the upgrade via PSConfig.exe or PSConfigui.exe.
2. Lock the configuration database, and upgrade to SharePoint Server 2010.

3. Upgrade the Central Administration Web service.
4. Upgrade the Central Administration content database.
5. Upgrade content databases.
6. Upgrade site collections.
7. Upgrade SharePoint Server 2007 Shared Services to SharePoint Server 2010 Service Applications.
8. Upgrade Web templates.
9. Upgrade relevant features.

NOTE The system upgrade steps are performed in serial. Therefore, the more objects you have to upgrade, the longer the upgrade will take. This is especially important if you are upgrading hundreds or thousands of sites. The upgrade process will process each site in turn and not in parallel. The single exception to the rule is that you can attach multiple databases simultaneously, depending on your hardware. Many SQL Server instances will not perform well on simultaneous database upgrades.

Farm Planning

If you have more than a small server installation or many customizations, you need to do planning that is beyond the scope of this book. Only the basics of upgrade farm planning are covered in this section.

TIP Before you begin the upgrade planning and testing process, remove all unnecessary content, such as unused sites and customizations, such as Web parts and workflows, from your current server farm. Doing so will speed up the migration of the content and lessen the impact of customizations during the upgrade process.

Before beginning your upgrade, you must first meet the prerequisites for installing SharePoint Server 2010. It's possible you currently meet the prerequisites for SharePoint Server 2007 but that same hardware—either the SQL Server build or the Windows Server version—is not compatible with the new version. Refer to Chapter 1, "Deploying SharePoint Server 2010," for details on requirements.

Note that you must have Windows Server 2008 or Windows Server 2008 R2 to install SharePoint Server 2010. The 64 bit version of Windows Server 2003 is not sufficient to install SharePoint Server 2010. Additionally, remember you need, at a minimum, SQL Server 2005 with Service Pack 3 and Cumulative Update 3 or SQL Server 2008 with Service Pack 1 and Cumulative Update 2 to upgrade from SharePoint Server 2007. Generally, if you are choosing an in-place upgrade, it is best to upgrade all components of your SharePoint Server 2007 farm first. The prerequisites for SharePoint Server 2010 will work fine for SharePoint Server 2007 as well. Having the requirements running in your current environment will greatly simplify an in-place upgrade.

If you select the database attach option, you can build a new SharePoint Server 2010 farm and leave your SharePoint Server 2007 farm intact. This provides a failover platform in case the upgrade fails. Regardless of your upgrade path, verify you have the following software installed in your SharePoint Server 2010 environment:

- SharePoint Server 2007 Service Pack 2. This requirement is for either upgrade option.
- Windows Server 2008 or Windows Server 2008 R2.
- SQL Server 2005 or SQL Server 2008 with current minimum updates. See *http://technet.microsoft.com/en-us/library/cc262485.aspx* for the most recent requirements.
- Language Packs for Windows Server, SharePoint Foundation 2010, and SharePoint Server 2010. Verify they are consistent with your SharePoint Server 2007 production environment.
- All required hotfixes, as listed at *http://technet.microsoft.com/en-us/library/cc262485.aspx*.

Pre-upgrade Checker

SharePoint Server 2007 Service Pack 2 includes a new Stsadm.exe operation *preupgradecheck*. Pre-upgrade check can scan your existing SharePoint Server 2007 environment for problems that prevent a successful SharePoint Server 2010 upgrade. It is not a best practices analyzer, but it does provide a wealth of information about your server farm. The pre-upgrade checker does not write to your databases. It only processes rules and scans your current environment, outputting results to %CommonProgramFiles%\Microsoft Shared\Web Server Extensions\12\Config\Preupgradecheck. When possible, it will also include a hyperlink to the relevant Knowledge Base (KB) article at *http://support.microsoft.com*. To run the pre-upgrade checker, do the following:

1. Install Service Pack 2 for your SharePoint Server 2007 installation.
2. Install the October 2009 Cumulative Update for SharePoint Server 2007.
3. Execute *stsadm.exe –o preupgradecheck* from a server in the farm. Stsadm.exe is located in %CommonProgramFiles%\Microsoft Shared\Web Server Extensions\12\Bin.
4. Verify preupgradecheck is running. The output should be similar to Figure 17-1. If it fails, double-check the spelling and rules file, if applicable.

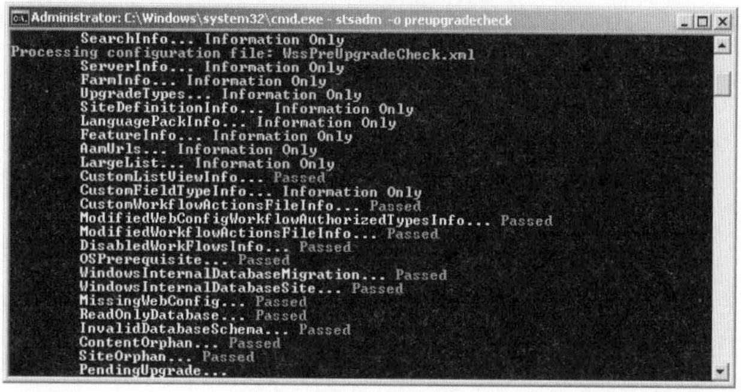

FIGURE 17-1 If it's accurately entered, preupgradecheck will display the status.

5. When the action completes, an Internet Explorer window should automatically open displaying the Pre-Upgrade Check report.

The output of the tool is useful for gathering information about your SharePoint Server 2007 farm. Many required planning and discovery requirements are automatically gathered and aggregated in a single file. Notable information reported with the tool includes the following:

- Shared Services providers and related database size
- Search topology and database size
- All servers in the farm
- Content database sizes
- Total number of site collections
- Supported upgrade types
- Site definitions installed.

IMPORTANT Custom site definitions need to be updated by a developer before the sites are migrated to SharePoint Server 2010.

- Language packs installed
- Installed features
- Alternate access mappings
- List and Libraries URI and item count
- Custom Field types that cannot be upgraded.

IMPORTANT Custom field types might be critical for custom applications. Be sure to verify every nonupgradeable field type with your development team.

As you can see from the previous list, many of the planning issues are addressed using the Pre-Upgrade Check tool. Many times, potential issues that might otherwise be missed, such as custom field types, are reported by the tool. Unlike the process of upgrading to SharePoint Server 2007, upgrading to

SharePoint Server 2010 does not require the tool to be run. However, you should always run the Pre-Upgrade Check tool before upgrading.

There are advanced options for running the Pre-Upgrade Check tool in addition to the default behavior. Note that you can execute the command only for the server where you are running Stsadm.exe. You can create custom rules that define what will be checked and the level of verbosity in the report. The following are the object names that are provided for use in the tool:

- **ServerInfo** Displays all farm servers referenced in the configuration database. For an upgrade to complete successfully, all members of the farm must be online. If you have a crashed server, you must remove it from the farm before completing the upgrade process.

- **FarmInfo** Displays all farm components. This includes servers, Web applications, content databases, sizes, and the number of site collections.

- **UpgradeType** Provides supported upgrade types (in-place and database attach).

- **SiteTemplates** Displays all site definitions installed. Be sure to install any new site definitions needed in SharePoint Server 2010.

- **Features** Displays all features installed in the farm.

- **LanguagePacks** All languages installed in SharePoint Server 2007 must be installed for SharePoint Server 2010 as well.

- **AAMURLs** Displays alternate access mappings and zones.

- **OSType** Displays only unsupported operating systems unless this setting is modified by a custom rule.

- **DatabaseSchema** Checks to see if the schema has been modified by the user. If so, it is blocked from upgrade. The tool might eventually block other types of schema changes, such as beta versions of products.

- **DataOrphan** Reports when the tool finds content orphans in the content database. (Orphans are objects with no parent relationship.)

- **SiteOrphan** Displays all sites that are not referenced in the configuration database or are without a parent.

- **UnfinishedGradualUpgrade** Indicates when a SharePoint Server 2007 gradual upgrade is in process on a database.

- **MissingWebConfig** Checks the local server for proper *Web.config* files for each SharePoint Server 2007 Web application in the farm.

- **InvalidHostNames** Checks the validity of all host names on the local server.

- **InvalidServiceAccount** Verifies all service accounts are available.

- **DatabaseReadOnly** Checks whether content database are set to read-only in SQL Server. Databases must be read/write before upgrading.

- **WYukonLargeDatabase** Checks Windows Internal Database (WID) databases for size. This is not applicable to SharePoint Server 2007, only to Windows SharePoint Services 3.0.

- **WYukonLargeSiteCollection** Checks WID site collections for sizes greater than 4 GB. This is not applicable to SharePoint Server 2007, only to Windows SharePoint Services 3.0.

- **SearchContentSourceInfo** Displays all content sources for SharePoint Server 2007 Search and all start addresses. If you are performing a database attach upgrade, you'll have to manually rebuild your content sources. This output is useful in rebuilding that information.

- **SearchInfo** Lists all search servers in the farm and their role (for example, Index and Query).

Local Only

Executing *stsadm.exe –o preupgradecheck –localonly* will limit the output of the command to rules relevant to the server where Stsadm.exe is entered. If you want to check only for the single farm server issues, such as features or a missing *Web.config* file, using –localonly will save both time and disk space. Be aware that many rules are not processed in this mode, such as custom field types, read-only databases, content database information, and orphaned objects. Be sure to also run the Pre-Upgrade Check tool without –localonly before performing the upgrade.

Local-only rules are marked as such in the *rule file*. Rule files can be found in the %CommonProgramFiles%\Microsoft Shared\Web Server Extensions\12\Config\ PreUpgradeCheck directory.

Rule Files

SharePoint Server 2007 SP2 ships with two rules files: OssPreUpgradeCheck.xml and WssPreUpgradeCheck.xml. The first is relevant to SharePoint Server 2007 rules and the latter to Windows SharePoint Services 3.0. Although it's possible to modify these files, you should always make a copy and edit the copy instead of the original. This preserves the original file in case you need to reference it later.

Last, never ignore the Pre-Upgrade Checker tool warnings. In fact, you should have a *clean* server farm. A clean server farm has no errors or warnings in the event logs, trace logs, or Pre-Upgrade Checker tool. It is also recommended that you have no errors on Windows Server for any member of the farm, including Active Directory and SQL Server. Be sure you have a clean farm before attempting an upgrade. If you have database issues, such as orphaned objects, you can use the stsadm.exe command to clean your databases:

```
Stsadm.exe -o databaserepair -url <URL> -databasename <database name> [-
deletecorruption]
```

For example, a site collection at *http://portal.contoso.com/* that is in a content database named *wss_content_portal* can be repaired using the following command:

```
Stsadm.exe -o databaserepair -url http://portal.contoso.com/ -databasename
wss_content_portal
```

If the corruption cannot be repaired, you have a final option of deleting the corruption. Be sure you have a solid backup of the content database before proceeding. Using the previous example, you would run the following command:

```
Stsadm.exe -o databaserepair -url http://portal.contoso.com/ -databasename
wss_content_portal -deletecorruption
```

Although this usually resolves the database errors and allows for an upgrade, you probably will lose some content. The output of the command should list the content that was removed. If you need the deleted content, you need to access the content via either backup tools or the Web interface and move it to the SharePoint Server 2010 farm after the upgrade is complete.

Test-SPContentDatabase

If you are attaching a SharePoint Server 2007 database to a SharePoint Server 2010 server farm for upgrade, you have the option of using the Windows PowerShell cmdlet *Test-SPContentDatabase*. This Windows PowerShell cmdlet checks to see whether all the server infrastructure customizations are present for the site collections in a SharePoint Server 2007 content database.

> **TIP** You can also execute the Test-SPContentDatabase cmdlet against a *SharePoint Server 2010* content database. It will verify that all server-side customizations are present for site collections contained in the database.

You should run this cmdlet *before* attaching the content database to a SharePoint Server 2010 Web application. It should not be associated with a SharePoint Server 2007 Web application, and you should not attempt an upgrade before running this cmdlet. Although you certainly can upgrade without running the Test-SPContentDatabase cmdlet, you cannot run the cmdlet *after* attempting a database attached upgrade. The cmdlet provides the following information about site collections in a given content database:

- Reports server-side customizations that are missing and required by site collections
- Compares the site collections contained in a content database against a specific Web application
- Identifies current or potential data orphans
- Identifies missing site definitions
- Identifies missing features
- Identifies missing assemblies
- Shows table sizing metrics

The following is an example of executing Test-SPContentDatabase with a SharePoint Server 2007 database named WSS_Content_Commodity2 and a SharePoint Server 2010 Web application named http://portal.contoso.com:

```
Test-SPContentDatabase -name WSS_Content_Commodity2 -WebApplication
http://portal.contoso.com
```

The following example is a content database that hosts a team site collection using Excel Services. The target SharePoint Server 2010 Web application does not have Excel Services available. Notice the error will not prevent (block) an upgrade. However, you should configure Excel Services in your SharePoint Server 2010 server farm before a production deployment.

```
Category         : MissingSetupFile
Error            : True
UpgradeBlocking  : False
Message          : File
[Features\ExcelServerSite\Microsoft.Office.Excel.WebUI.dwp] is referenced
[1] times in the database [WSS_Content_Commodity2], but is not installed on
the current farm. Please install any feature/solution which contains this
file.
Remedy           : One or more setup files are referenced in the database
[WSS_Content_Commodity2], but are not installed on the current farm. Please
install any feature or solution which contains these files.
```

The following options are available for the Test-SPContentDatabase cmdlet:

- **Name** The name of a content database. It must be online in SQL Server Management Studio before you attempt a test.

- **WebApplication** The Web application to test the content database with, which is a process also known as *pairing*. Pay close attention to the Web application you are testing against. For example, if the Web application you are using to test does not have an Excel Services service application associated with it, you'll get errors in the test.

- **DatabaseCredentials** If you are using SQL Server authentication, you should include the user name and password. Most administrators will not require this option. However, you need to verify the SharePoint Server 2010 farm account has sufficient access to the content database when using Windows authentication.

- **ServerInstance** The SQL server and instance name. If you are using the default instance, this will be the SQL server name.

- **ShowRowCounts** Displays the total row count in the database.

Web Enumeration

There is one additional command that is useful when planning an upgrade: Stsadm.exe -o enumallwebs. Although it isn't an upgrade command specifically, it provides information that is useful for planning an upgrade. *Stsadm.exe -o enumallwebs* can provide a list of all site collections and sites in a content database in addition to site definitions in use. Remember that in the object model the term *sites* is equivalent to *site collections* and the term *webs* is equivalent to *sites*. For example, running *stsadm.exe -o enumallwebs -databasename WSS_Content_Portal_Root* might produce the following output for a content database with a single publishing site:

```
<Sites Count="1">
  <Site Id="cb88eb37-395d-4bb2-9941-fff291a1eb34"
OwnerLogin="CONTOSO\administrator" InSiteMap="True">
    <Webs Count="1">
      <Web Id="f4d0c333-c883-4888-9f34-2b1eefdb75a5" Url="/"
LanguageId="1033" TemplateName="STS#0" TemplateId="1" />
    </Webs>
  </Site>
```

In-Place Upgrade

Whether they are upgrading a large or small farm, many administrators will need to perform an in-place upgrade. An in-place upgrade takes place on your existing hardware and operating systems. Be sure your current hardware will support SharePoint Server 2010 before performing an in-place upgrade. Likewise, verify your operating systems are all Windows Server 2008 or greater. Windows Server 2003 is not supported for SharePoint Server 2010. You should first upgrade your servers to Windows Server 2008, verify your version of SQL Server is a supported revision, and have SharePoint Server 2007 Service Pack 2 applied to all servers in the farm.

> **TIP** The operating system hosting SQL Server can use Windows Server 2003 or Windows Server 2008. It is recommended that you use a 64-bit operating system for SQL Server. You must be running the minimum versions of SQL Server 2005 or SQL Server 2008. For the latest minimum specification for SQL Server and SharePoint Server 2010, see *http://technet.microsoft.com/en-us/library/cc262485.aspx*.

Installing the Prerequisites and Binaries

For more detailed information about minimum permissions, hardware requirements, software requirements, installing the prerequisites, and installing the SharePoint Server 2010 binaries, see Chapter 1.

To begin the upgrade process, you should always have multiple, tested backups of your SharePoint Server 2007 server farm. It is *always* a good idea to make backups of your content databases via SQL Server in addition to SharePoint Server 2007 before performing a backup. If the upgrade completely fails, you can always get your valuable user content from the SQL Server backups. To upgrade the first server in the farm to SharePoint Server 2010, do the following:

1. Begin the SharePoint Server 2010 setup using the installation media. This will vary depending on your software purchase agreement.

2. After beginning the setup program, you should see the installation tool, as shown in Figure 17-2.

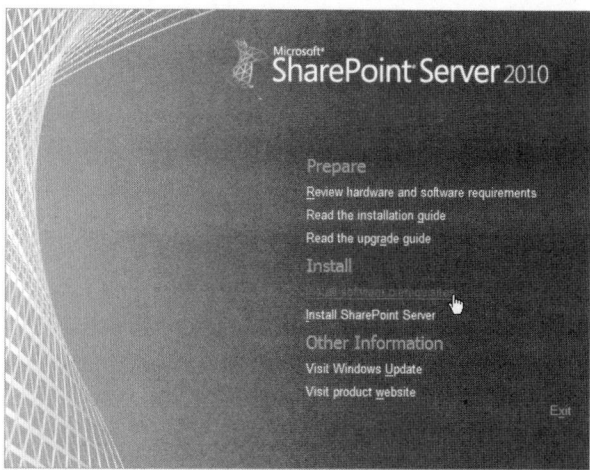

FIGURE 17-2 Install the software prerequisites.

3. Click Install Software Prerequisites, view the prerequisites, and click Next.
4. Accept the terms of the license agreements, and click Next.
5. IIS should be automatically configured, and any required prerequisites should be installed. When these tasks are complete, click Finish.
6. Click Install SharePoint Server.
7. Enter the product key. If you have SharePoint Server 2007 Enterprise, be sure to use a SharePoint Server 2010 Enterprise key. Otherwise, you will be stopped and presented with an error, such as the one shown in Figure 17-3.

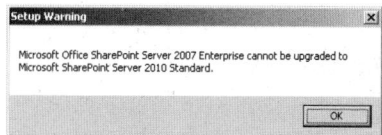

8. After entering the product key, and then click Continue.
9. Accept the license terms, and click Continue.
10. You should be presented with a screen detecting a previous version of SharePoint Server, as seen in Figure 17-4. If you are not, you should stop the installation and troubleshoot the problem. Otherwise, click Install Now to continue.

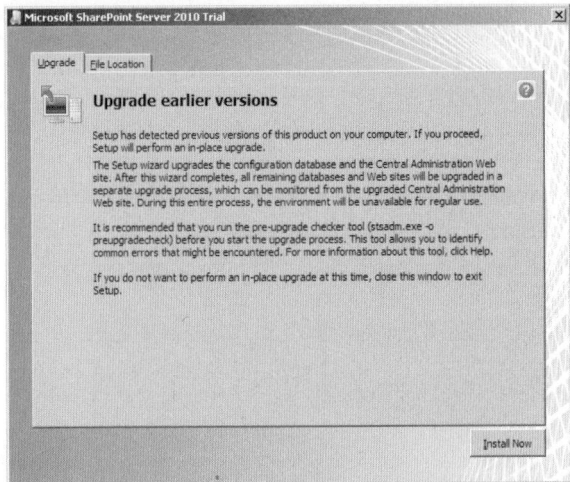

FIGURE 17-4 Click Install Now to continue.

11. If you have a single server in the farm, verify that Run The SharePoint Products Configuration Wizard Now is selected, and then click Close. If you have a multiserver farm, proceed to step 12.

12. Clear the Run The SharePoint Products Configuration Wizard Now check box, as seen in Figure 17-5. You need to install the prerequisites and SharePoint Server 2010 binaries on all servers in the farm before running the wizard.

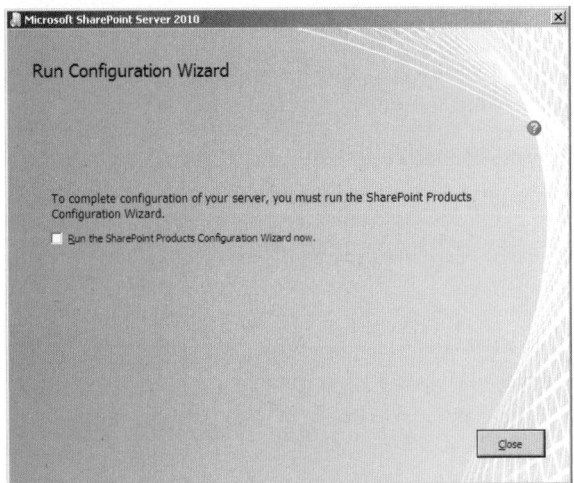

FIGURE 17-5 Deselect the Run The SharePoint Products Configuration Wizard Now check box.

13. After you have followed steps 1 through 11 on all servers in the farm, run the SharePoint Product 2010 Configuration Wizard on the first server in the farm. Although it is not mandatory, you might find it easier to run it on the Central Administration server. The SharePoint Products 2010 Configuration Wizard can be found in the Start, All Programs, Microsoft SharePoint 2010 Products programs group.

14. Click Next on the SharePoint Products Configuration Wizard.

15. Select Yes to restart IIS and related timer jobs.

16. Enter the server farm passphrase, and document the passphrase for future use. You will need this when adding servers to the farm.

17. Decide whether to offer Visual Upgrade or upgrade all sites now. Refer to the final section in this chapter for detailed information about this decision. Do not proceed until you fully understand the impact of the decision. An incorrect decision might require you to restore SharePoint Server 2007 and perform another upgrade attempt.

18. Click Next to continue.

19. If you have a single-server farm, you can click OK to continue. If you have a multiserver farm, you should pause at the screen shown in Figure 17-6. Do not click OK if you have multiple servers in the farm. You must run the same configuration wizard on every other server in the farm *first*. You will receive the same prompt on all servers in the farm. You should click OK on all servers in the farm. After you've completed this task on all other servers, you can proceed.

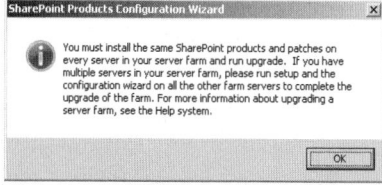

FIGURE 17-6 Warning that displays for multiserver farms.

20. After all servers in the farm have successfully had the binaries updated, you can click OK to continue.

21. When the upgrade completes, the final screen will detail the log file location for further inspection. Note that a timer job has been created and it might be several minutes to several hours before pages will correctly render, based on the scope of your initial SharePoint Server 2007 deployment.

Post In-Place Upgrade Tasks

After the upgrade wizard has finished, you should be taken to the Upgrade Status screen in Central Administration, as seen in Figure 17-7. The Upgrade Status screen shows each server in the farm and any relevant errors. To view errors specific to a farm member, click Succeeded to the left of the server name, as seen in Figure 17-7.

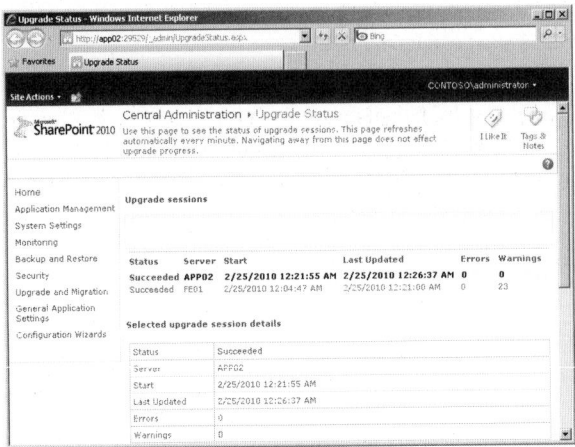

FIGURE 17-7 Server upgrade status and errors.

When the status shows Succeeded for all members in the farm, proceed to testing Web pages and basic functionality. After your server farm is upgraded, there are several possible tasks left to complete.

> **IMPORTANT** Always perform an IISReset on every server in the farm after an upgrade. Otherwise, items such as Visual Upgrade might not work correctly. Before troubleshooting an upgrade issue, always perform IISReset first.

Upgraded Shared Services

One of the most obvious upgrade changes is related to your Shared Services Provider (SSP). In SharePoint Server 2010, each shared service is now an independent service application. There is no longer an SSP. The upgrade process has performed a best-effort upgrade of the single SSP, but some upgraded shared services might not meet your permanent requirements. Even if you think you might change the configuration of your service application architecture later, generally you should begin with the standard upgrade. Be sure to change any required permissions on the service applications after upgrading. You might need to explicitly add administrative privileges to service applications before you can manage them.

The following service applications will be present after a SharePoint Server 2007 Enterprise upgrade to SharePoint Server Enterprise 2010. In this example, there was a Shared Services Provider named *Contoso Shared Services*.

- Application Discovery and Load Balancer Service Application
- Application Discovery and Load Balancer Service Application Proxy
- Contoso Shared Services - Search Service
- Contoso Shared Services - Search Service Proxy
- Contoso Shared Services_ApplicationRegistry
- Contoso Shared Services_ApplicationRegistry Proxy
- Contoso Shared Services_BusinessDataConnectivity
- Contoso Shared Services_BusinessDataConnectivity Proxy
- Contoso Shared Services_ExcelCalculationServices
- Contoso Shared Services_ExcelCalculationServices Proxy
- Contoso Shared Services_StateServiceApp
- Contoso Shared Services_StateServiceAppProxy
- Contoso Shared Services_Taxonomy
- Contoso Shared Services_TaxonomyProxy
- Contoso Shared Services_UserProfile
- Contoso Shared Services_UserProfileProxy
- Search Administration Web Service for Contoso Shared Services - Search Service
- Security Token Service Application
- SharePoint Server ASP.NET Session State Service
- WSS_UsageApplication
- WSS_UsageApplication Proxy

After the upgrade is complete, you can change your service application architecture as needed. With the advancement in search and user profile service applications, you will likely want to move components in a multiserver farm. Reference the chapters relevant to the service application in question.

You'll also notice that all shared services that belonged to a SharePoint Server 2007 SSP are now part of the same proxy group. This makes it easy to associate service applications with Web applications. If you want to customize the association of service applications and Web applications, you can do so after verification that the new service applications perform as desired.

New Service Applications

There are some changes you need to be aware of immediately. First, you will now have a managed metadata service application. It will be suffixed with _*Taxonomy* and will be named the same as your SharePoint Server 2007 SSP. Once again, if permissions cannot be migrated during the upgrade process, you need to manually add administrative privileges after the upgrade completes. To add an administrator to the Managed Metadata Service Application, do the following:

1. Open Central Administration, and browse to Application Management, Manage Service Applications.

2. Select the service application you want to modify, being careful not to click on the URL itself, as seen in Figure 17-8.

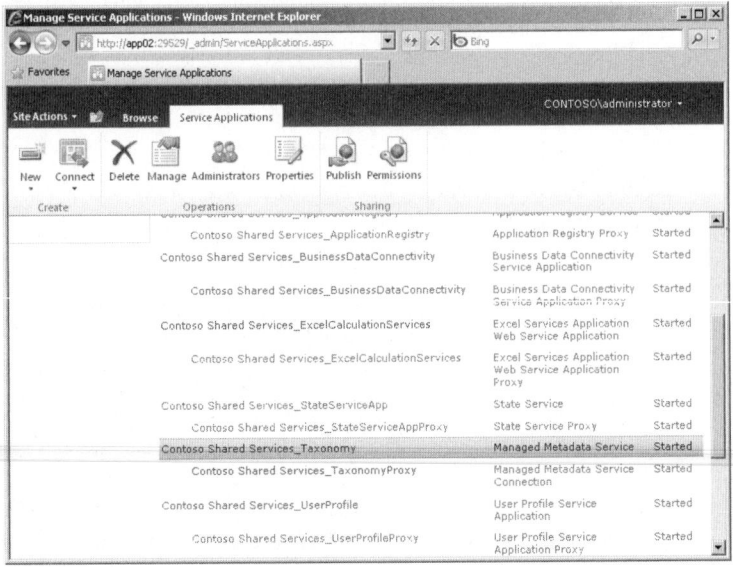

FIGURE 17-8 Select the service application you want to modify.

3. From the management Ribbon, click Administrators.

4. Type the name of the user who will administer the service application, and click Add.

5. Select the required permissions for the user.

6. Click OK.

Next, you'll notice you have a new Search Service Application. Because the classic role of an index server is gone in SharePoint Server 2010, you'll probably want to review the search architecture. Review Chapter 2, "Scaling to a Multiserver Farm," and Chapter 8, "Configuring the Search Service Application," for more information on modifying the search architecture.

You now have a Secure Store Service Application. If you had a single sign-on configuration in SharePoint Server 2007, it has been upgraded to the Secure Store. Otherwise, the service application will be created with the default settings.

In SharePoint Server 2007, all the shared services were served by a single SSP. Therefore, they all used the same application pool. To successfully perform an upgrade, SharePoint Server 2010 uses the same application pool for all service applications that were upgraded. If this doesn't suit your security and isolation requirements, you can modify the application pools anytime, but be sure to test before doing it in a production deployment.

TIP If you simplify your search topology before you perform the upgrade, it can greatly decrease both the time and complexity of the upgrade. During the writing of this book, the search topology was reduced to a single search server that hosted both the query and index roles. After the upgrade is complete, you can then scale your search topology exactly as you want.

Database Attach Upgrade

The database attach upgrade method allows you to build a new, pristine SharePoint Server 2010 server farm. There are many items, such as Excel Services, that cannot be upgraded with the database attach method. If you need to upgrade a service such as Excel Services, you need to perform the following steps:

1. Restore your production SharePoint Server 2007 environment to a temporary location.
2. Verify the service is correctly functioning.
3. Perform an in-place upgrade in the temporary environment.
4. When you have completed the in-place upgrade and the service has been verified, use the SharePoint Server 2010 backup tools to back up the service application.
5. Restore the service application to your new SharePoint Server 2010 environment.

If you need the bulk of your SharePoint Server 2007 SSP content, an in-place upgrade might be a better approach. Be sure you have tested the upgrade process and understand what information cannot be upgraded by attaching the relevant database. Manually upgrading each application can be difficult and time consuming.

IMPORTANT Before you begin a SharePoint Server 2010 database attach upgrade, you must first have your SharePoint Server 2010 server farm configured. You must also have the databases you want to upgrade available on a SQL Server instance that is both accessible from the SharePoint Server 2010 server farm and that will be the permanent host.

Content databases contain most of your valuable user data in the form of site collections. When upgrading a content database, you must attach it to a SharePoint Server 2010 Web application. To test a SharePoint Server 2007 content database before attaching it to a Web application, you can first run the Windows PowerShell cmdlet, Test-SPContentDatabase. This was detailed earlier in the chapter, and it's similar to the following:

```
Test-SPContentDatabase -name WSS_Content_Commodity2 -WebApplication
http://portal.contoso.com
```

This command tests the WSS_Content_Commodity2 SharePoint Server 2007 content database against the http://portal.contoso.com SharePoint Server 2010 Web application. Be sure to resolve any errors that would cause a blocked upgrade before attaching a content database to the Web application. Upon attaching the database to a Web application, it will automatically upgrade.

You can use either Windows PowerShell or Stadm.exe to attach a content database to a SharePoint Server 2010 server farm. Windows PowerShell provides the most robust tool set and is the recommended option. To attach a content database using Windows PowerShell, you use the Mount-SPContentDatabase cmdlet. The following options are available for the cmdlet:

- **Name** Specifies the SharePoint Server 2007 content database to be attached to SharePoint Server 2010.
- **WebApplication** Specifies the SharePoint Server 2010 Web application where the site collection will be attached. This is often referred to as *associating* a content database with a Web application.
- **AssignNewDatabaseId** Creates a new database ID when the database is attached. This is usually not required.
- **Confirm** Requires you to confirm the command before executing.
- **ClearChangeLog** Clears the change log when the database is attached. If you have not trimmed the change log in SharePoint Server 2007, you should consider doing so to reduce the size of the content database.
- **DatabaseCredentials** If using SQL authentication, you must enter the database credentials.
- **DatabaseServer** Specifies the database server if it is not the default atabase server specified in Central Administration.
- **MaxSiteCount** Specifies the maximum number of site collections the database can contain. It must be at least the current number of site collections.
- **UpdateUserExperience** Decide whether to offer Visual Upgrade or upgrade all sites contained in the database now. Refer to the final section in this chapter for detailed information about this decision. Do not proceed until you fully understand the impact of the decision. An incorrect decision might require you to restore the SharePoint Server 2007 database and perform another upgrade attempt.

- **WarningSiteCount** Specifies the number of site collections created before a warning is generated. A value of 0 turns the warning off.
- **WhatIf** Shows what the effect of the command will be before modifying any content.

An example of running the Mount-SPContentDatabase cmdlet for a Web application named *http://portal.contoso.com*, a content database named *WSS_Content_Portal*, a warning site count of 0, and a maximum site count of 1 is as follows:

```
Mount-SPContentDatabase -name WSS_Content_Portal -WebApplication
http://portal.contoso.com -MaxSiteCount 1 -WarningSiteCount 0
```

The output of the command should look similar to the following with a single site collection:

```
Id                : ad9ddb61-867b-47db-93c5-be61691fe21a
Name              : WSS_Content_Portal
WebApplication    : SPWebApplication Name=Contoso Portal
Server            : app01
CurrentSiteCount : 1
```

You can also attach a content database for the purpose of upgrading using stsadm.exe -o. The following options are available:

- **url** Specifies the SharePoint Server 2010 Web application where the content database will be attached.
- **databasename** Specifies the SharePoint Server 2007 database name you want to attach.
- **databaseserver** The default SQL Server instance defined in Central Administration is used unless you specify otherwise with the *databasename* parameter.
- **databaseuser** If using SQL authentication, you must specify the user name.
- **databasepassword** If using SQL authentication, you must specify the user password.
- **sitewarning** Specifies the number of site collections created before a warning is generated. A value of 0 turns the warning off.
- **sitemax** Specifies the maximum number of site collections the database can contain. It must be at least the current number of site collections.
- **assignnewdatabaseid** Creates a new database ID when the database is attached. This is usually not required.
- **clearchangelog** Clears the change log when the database is attached. If you have not trimmed the change log in SharePoint Server 2007, you should consider doing so to reduce the size of the content database.
- **forcedeletelock** Forces the deletion of all locks on the database before the upgrade starts.

- **preserveolduserexperience** Decide whether to offer Visual Upgrade or upgrade all sites contained in the database now. Refer to the final section in this chapter for detailed information about this decision. Do not proceed until you fully understand the impact of the decision. An incorrect decision might require you to restore the SharePoint Server 2007 database and perform another upgrade attempt.

To attach a content database using Stsadm.exe using the previous example, use the following command:

```
stsadm.exe -o addcontentdb -url http://portal.contoso.com -databasename
WSS_Content_Portal -sitewarning 0 -sitemax 1
```

During either a Windows PowerShell or Stsadm.exe content database attach procedure for upgrading, you can see the status of the database in Central Administration. Figure 17-9 shows an example of the status screen.

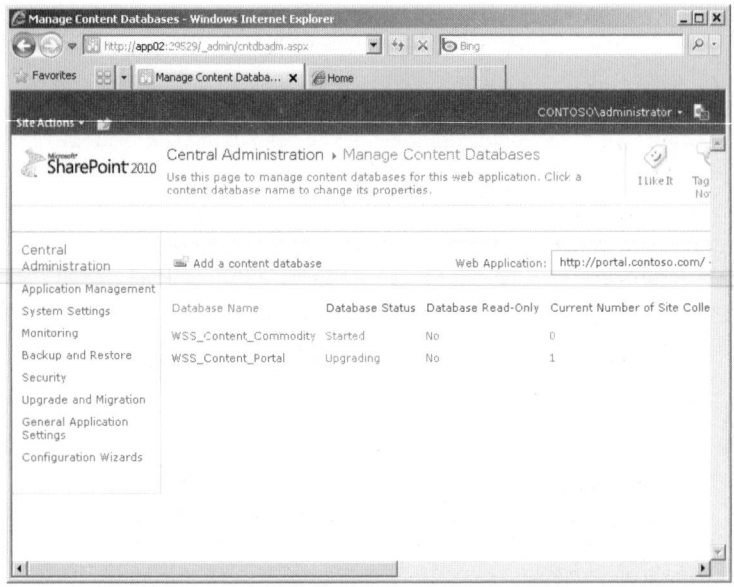

FIGURE 17-9 The content database upgrade status can be seen in Central Administration.

If the upgrade process does not upgrade the site collection, you can manually restart the upgrade process using the Windows PowerShell cmdlet Upgrade-SPContentDatabase. The unique option for this command is -*ForceDeleteLock*. This forces the deletion of all locks on the database before the upgrade starts.

Upgrading Sites and Site Collections

Upgrading the server farm to SharePoint Server 2010 is the first step to the upgrade process, regardless of the method used. However, that is only the first step. After you have configured the server farm and service applications, you must still upgrade the sites unless you upgraded them during the in-place upgrade process. Because many customizations change and break during the upgrade process, most administrators use the new functionality of *Visual Upgrade*. In fact, administrators will manage only the Visual Upgrade feature. Site Web designers will be responsible for making the sites function correctly in SharePoint Server 2010.

Visual Upgrade is the foundation for upgrading sites and site collections. Be aware that much custom code might not function correctly in SharePoint Server 2010, regardless of whether you use Visual Upgrade or not. Be sure you have tested all custom Web parts and code in a SharePoint Server 2010 test server farm before a conducting an upgrade in a production environment.

To begin, open the legacy URL in a browser window. For this example, the site collection is located at *http://portal.contoso.com*. Upon opening the site collection, it should look almost identical to how it appeared before the upgrade. The first change you'll notice is that the Site Actions menu has changed. There will still be some SharePoint Server 2007 items in the menu, but you should now also see Visual Upgrade in the menu, as seen in Figure 17-10.

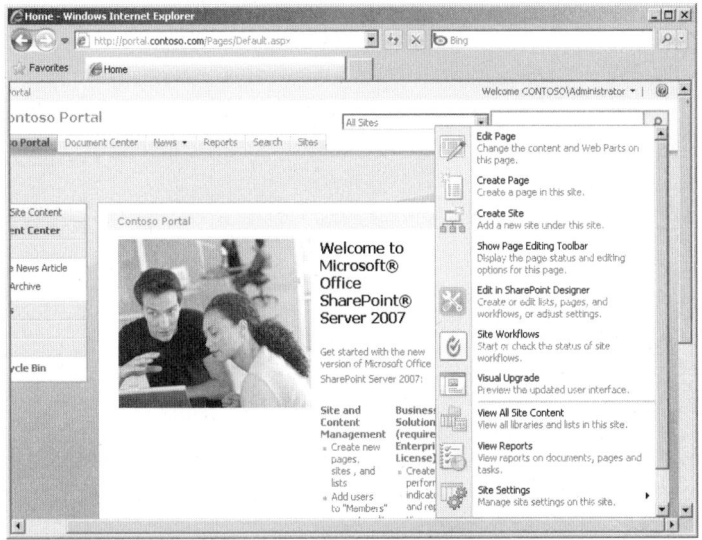

FIGURE 17-10 The menu is upgraded to include SharePoint Server 2010 functionality.

Selecting Visual Upgrade takes you to a configuration screen where you have three options relevant to Visual Upgrade:

- Use The Previous User Interface (Default)
- Preview The Updated User Interface
- Update The User Interface

Until you are sure that a permanent upgrade is desired, it is safer to use the Preview The Updated User Interface option. Using the Preview The Updated User Interface option allows you and your designers to modify the site, make changes, and prepare the site for users. After all testing and design is complete, you can use the previous configuration screen to update the user interface.

As a site collection administrator, you can control the Visual Upgrade settings for site owners. A site owner cannot override the site collection settings for Visual Upgrade unless they are granted the role of site collection administrator. To restrict the Visual Upgrade options, do the following:

1. From Site Actions, Site Settings,, select Visual Upgrade in the Site Collection Administration grouping. If you do not see this grouping, you are not a site collection administrator. You'll need to add yourself as a site collection administrator from Central Administration, Application Management, Change Site Collection Administrators.

2. To hide Visual Upgrade options, click Hide Visual Upgrade, as seen in Figure 17-11.

3. To apply the new user interface to all sites, click Update All Sites.

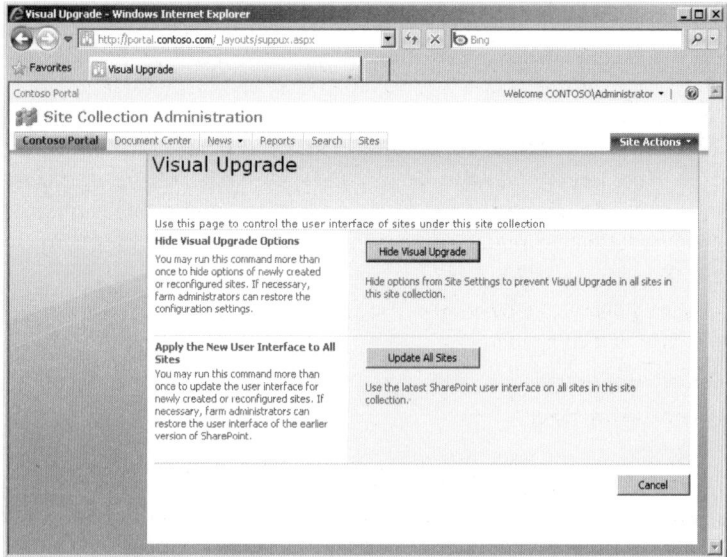

FIGURE 17-11 Select a Visual Upgrade option, or click Cancel.

CHAPTER 18

Backup and Restore

- Server Farm Backup and Recovery   **540**
- Service and Web Application Backup and Restore   **553**
- Granular Backup and Restore   **555**

Microsoft SharePoint Server 2010 provides robust tools to back up and restore your content and configuration. These tools have been improved from SharePoint Server 2007 and are tailored for the scope of the task. Although the core backup and restore methodology hasn't changed from SharePoint Server 2007, the available options and tools have changed substantially. Some of the tool changes, such as the Windows PowerShell backup and restore cmdlets, have been made to address the future of SharePoint Server 2010 management. Most other changes were made to support the new functionality in the Web and service application architecture.

As you read through this chapter, be sure to notice that your ability to restore at a specific scope, such as a site collection, depends on what tool is selected to perform the backup. For example, if you back up a farm using full farm backups, you won't be able to restore a site collection in a single step from a database hosting multiple site collections. Likewise, an export of a site hierarchy does not allow the restoration of an entire site collection. Always test your backup and restore plan to ensure you can retrieve the content and configuration dictated by your requirements.

SharePoint Server 2010 provides the following tools to back up and restore your server farm and components:

- Central Administration
- Windows PowerShell
- Stsadm.exe

Many organizations have strict Business Continuity Plans (BCPs) and require a combination of these backup methods to ensure a fully restored and functional server farm in the event of data loss. When determining your recovery plan, be sure to refer to your organization's BCPs and its Recovery Time Objective (RTO) and Recovery Point Objective (RPO). This chapter discusses the SharePoint Server 2010 backup and restore process—specifically, items stored outside of SharePoint Server 2010, such as Microsoft Windows Server 2008 and Microsoft SQL Server, are not covered in this book. Be sure to keep in mind that all the dependencies of SharePoint Server 2010 must be anticipated and the recovery plan must be tested.

Server Farm Backup and Recovery

Before performing your first server farm backup, you need to decide where you will store the backup files. SharePoint Server 2010 does not provide a way to back up directly to tape. SharePoint Server 2010 backs up to a Universal Naming Convention (UNC) file share.

A common backup strategy is backing up all content and configuration data to a file share and then using classic backup software and media to create offline backups. A good starting place for implementing this strategy is to create weekly full backups and daily differential backups. This approach allows you to quickly and easily restore content in the event of data loss. Unless another backup program is used to manage your data recovery, you should leave the last full backup and all differential backups from that full backup on disk. After you have successfully performed a subsequent full backup, you can then safely archive the last backup sent to tape or other media storage. Figure 18-1 shows an example of a basic SharePoint Server 2010 farm backup plan.

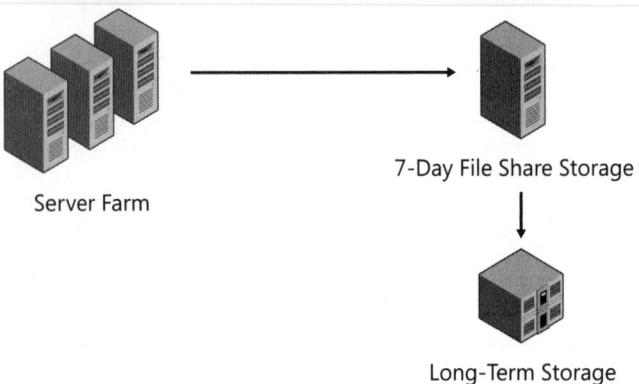

7-Day File Share Storage

Server Farm

Long-Term Storage

FIGURE 18-1 Multistage Backup Storage.

Preparing for Server Farm Backups

When backing up server farm data to file shares, care should be taken to minimize the access to storage locations. You should give the least amount of access possible for both the NTFS-level and share-level permissions. For the examples in this chapter, the file server is named *APP02* and the file share name is *Backups*. The following accounts need Full Control permissions to the backup location whether you are using Central Administration or command-line farm tools:

- SQL Server service account
- SharePoint 2010 Timer Log On Account (which can be verified in Windows Server 2008 Services Console)
- User account that is executing the command

Although this file share can technically exist anywhere that can be reached from the server farm member servers, it is best to have it on the same local area network. Testing has shown that farms in the tens and hundreds of gigabytes (GBs) will require gigabit Ethernet connections to avoid backups taking many hours or possibly days to complete. The following should be considered when planning the physical storage of your backup locations:

- **Capacity**   Verify that you have enough capacity for the planned backups. For example, if you'll keep one full backup and six differential backups on disk, you need the aggregate size of those backups plus up to 10 percent for logs and indexes.

- **Disk Speed**   Be sure the volume you are writing for backups supports adequate write speeds so that backups can be completed within the required maintenance window. Keep in mind that this disk volume will be very high during backups and will affect any users consuming the disks for file sharing.

- **Network Speed**   For all but the smallest server farms, you need gigabit Ethernet connections or better between all server farm members and the backup destination.

- **SQL Server**   All database backups and configuration data are written directly from SQL Server to the backup destination. Be sure the required network ports are open between the source and destination. If you have backups that are failing, first suspect permissions and network connectivity to SQL Server.

- **Long-Term Storage**   Unless you'll be backing up directly to a long-term storage system, you need to plan for backing up the file share to tape or other media. Be sure you verify the process for restoring data from tape to the file share is available for SharePoint Server 2010.

After you have prepared the target file share for backups, you need to decide what tool to use to perform farm backups. The following tools are available for performing farm backups:

- **Central Administration**   You cannot schedule a backup via Central Administration. Therefore, the primary use of Central Administration backups is to verify the configuration of the target backup location and to back up server farms before major operations.

- **Windows PowerShell**   The preferred way to schedule backups in SharePoint Server 2010 is by using Windows PowerShell. This method gives you the most options and will be fully supported in the future.

- **Stsadm.exe** Many of the Stsadm.exe commands implemented in SharePoint Server 2010 existed in SharePoint Server 2007. If you are looking to reduce the initial time to operation for SharePoint Server 2010, Stsadm. exe is a good choice. It is easier to configure command-line backups using Stsadm.exe than to use Windows PowerShell, but it is limited to basic farm backup functionality.

Farm Backup and Restores Using Central Administration

Central Administration provides the easiest way to begin backing up and restoring SharePoint Server 2010. Regardless of the method or software you use, always verifying you can perform a backup from Central Administration is a good idea. Doing so confirms all components in your farm can be successfully backed up and that your target device is properly prepared for backups. After a successful installation and configuration of SharePoint Server 2010, you should always perform a full farm backup.

Content and Configuration Backup

To access the Farm Backup And Restore section of Central Administration, either click Backup And Restore from the quick launch navigation bar or click Perform A Backup from the main screen (in the Backup And Restore area), as seen in Figure 18-2.

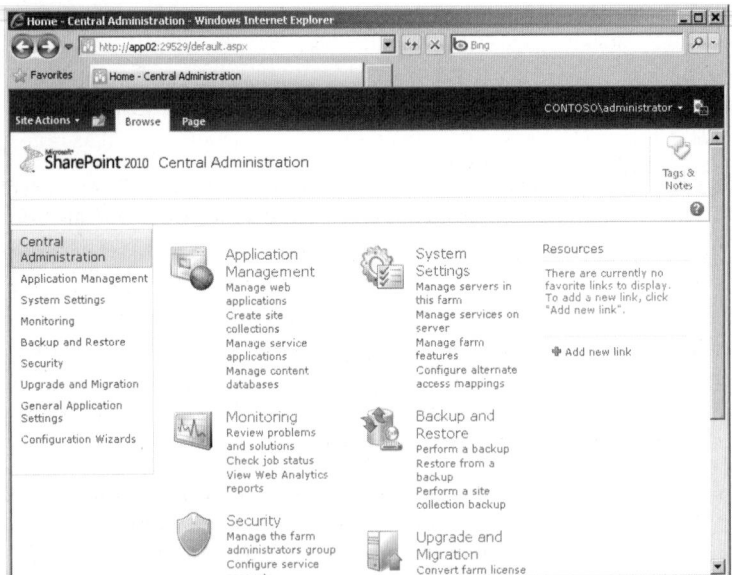

FIGURE 18-2 Click Perform A Backup to begin a full farm backup.

The first backup screen allows you to define what components of the farm you want to back up. You can select items individually or select the check box next to the Farm component, as seen in Figure 18-3.

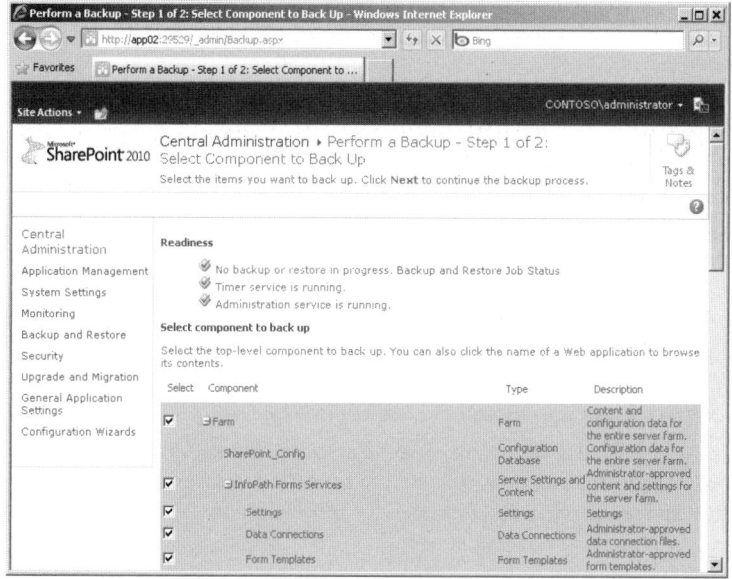

FIGURE 18-3 Select the Farm check box to select all components.

By selecting the Farm check box, you select all components in your farm. Your options will vary depending on the components you have installed, such as Excel Services and PerformancePoint.

After selecting all components, click Next. You will be presented with the second step in farm backups. You have two options when backing up the entire farm:

- **Back Up Content And Configuration Settings** The default option is to back up content and configuration settings. This option backs up all content databases, service applications, and configuration data.

- **Back Up Only Configuration Settings** New in SharePoint Server 2010 is the ability to back up only the configuration settings, as seen in Figure 18-4. This allows you to restore configuration to a different farm, which might be necessary when building a development server farm.

TIP A configuration-only backup can be used for development environments where the content isn't important or constantly changing. This option allows you to quickly recover the configuration content without restoring the content. In the event of custom code crashing the development farm because of modifications on the farm configuration, you can perform a configuration-only restore using the same database names.

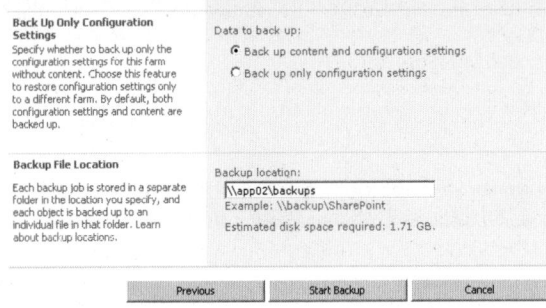

Back Up Only Configuration Settings
Specify whether to back up only the configuration settings for this farm without content. Choose this feature to restore configuration settings only to a different farm. By default, both configuration settings and content are backed up.

Data to back up:
- ☉ Back up content and configuration settings
- ○ Back up only configuration settings

Backup File Location
Each backup job is stored in a separate folder in the location you specify, and each object is backed up to an individual file in that folder. Learn about backup locations.

Backup location:
`\\app02\backups`
Example: \\backup\SharePoint
Estimated disk space required: 1.71 GB.

[Previous] [Start Backup] [Cancel]

FIGURE 18-4 The default back up setting is selected. Select Back Up Only Configuration Settings when restoring to a different farm.

Last, enter the backup location that you have prepared. An estimated disk space will be shown, but note that it can be off by as much as 100 percent. It is best to have plenty of disk space available and not rely on the estimator in this screen. After you have entered your backup location, click Start Backup.

If you receive errors during your backup, refer to the Windows Event Logs and your SharePoint Server 2010 trace logs. Be sure to verify permissions on the file share in the event of an error. The vast majority of backup errors are caused by insufficient permissions or network access.

You can use multiple file shares for backups, but only a single file share *per* backup. In the root of the backup file share is an XML file named *spbrtoc.xml*. The file name is short for "SharePoint Backup and Restore Table of Contents." It is essentially the catalog for all backups contained in the folder. Because it is unique, you should not have two SharePoint Server 2010 server farms using the same backup file location. You should always use a dedicated file share per server farm. The following is a sample Spbrtoc.xml file:

```
<?xml version="1.0" encoding="utf-8"?>
<SPBackupRestoreHistory>
    <SPHistoryObject>
        <SPId>4379e377-a6f1-4614-a17f-a5cb81dd2ad0</SPId>
        <SPRequestedBy>CONTOSO\administrator</SPRequestedBy>
        <SPBackupMethod>Full</SPBackupMethod>
        <SPRestoreMethod>None</SPRestoreMethod>
        <SPStartTime>02/22/2010 20:36:48</SPStartTime>
        <SPFinishTime>02/22/2010 20:50:53</SPFinishTime>
        <SPIsBackup>True</SPIsBackup>
        <SPConfigurationOnly>False</SPConfigurationOnly>
        <SPBackupDirectory>\\app02\backups\spbr0004\</SPBackupDirectory>
        <SPDirectoryName>spbr0004</SPDirectoryName>
        <SPDirectoryNumber>4</SPDirectoryNumber>
        <SPTopComponent>Farm</SPTopComponent>
```

```
        <SPTopComponentId>cc9a169c-9ae3-414c-a45b1378045
28661</SPTopComponentId>
        <SPWarningCount>0</SPWarningCount>
        <SPErrorCount>0</SPErrorCount>
    </SPHistoryObject>
  </SPBackupRestoreHistory>
```

This file can quickly show an administrator what was included in the backup and details about the process itself, such as errors and warnings. There is not a way to trim backup history from the Spbrtoc.xml file. Although you can edit the file and remove content, doing so is unsupported. If you need to create a new Spbrtoc.xml file, you should un-share the directory, rename it, and create a new folder for backups. Then share the new folder with the original name, and SharePoint Server 2010 will successfully back up to it. Remember to apply any required permissions.

To further troubleshoot backups, you can open the directory of the backup in question, such as *Spbr0004*, as we will do in the following example. Inside of a backup folder, you see many .bak files, a log file, and an Spbackup.xml file. Useful for troubleshooting is the *Spbackup.log* file. Upon opening the log file, you'll see all components that were backed up and the corresponding .bak files they are stored in. This list can assist you if you have backup or restore problems.

Of particular interest are the lines that define the content database backup files. Using the earlier example, the following line is in the Spbackup.log file:

```
@db_name=WSS_Content_CT_Hub, @db_loc=\\app02\backups\spbr0004\000000C5.bak
```

From this line, you can see which .bak file contains the Content Type Hub used for your farm. In a worst-case scenario, you can use SQL Server tools to restore the content database and the site collections contained therein. Always use the Central Administration or command-line tools first. But if the Spbrtoc.xml and Spbr0004.xml files are missing or corrupt, the content databases can still be recovered. If you are unsure about restoring this content, contact Microsoft Support Services.

Content and Configuration Restore

Remember, you can restore only what you've backed up. If you select specific components when backing up SharePoint Server 2010, only those components will be available during restore. To begin a server farm restore, browse to Backup And Restore in Central Administration and click Backup And Restore, and then click Restore From A Backup, as seen in Figure 18-5.

> **NOTE** Central Administration does not provide a way to back up directly to tape. You must first back up to a file share, and then back up the file share to tape. Additionally, you should always use a UNC path, such as shown in Figure 18-4, and not a file system path, such as C:\.

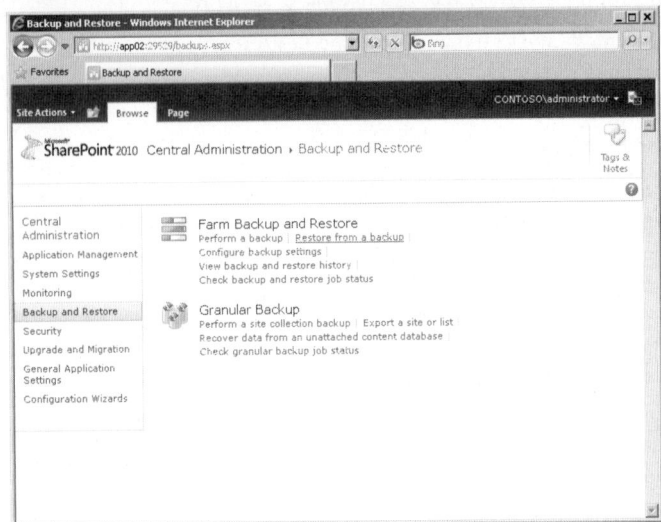

FIGURE 18-5 Click Restore From A Backup to restore content.

On the first of three Restore From Backup screens, you should see all of the available backups in the defined Backup Directory Location. In the example shown in Figure 18-6, backups are stored in *app02\backups*. You can expand the backup to see further details, such as the user that began the backup and the error count.

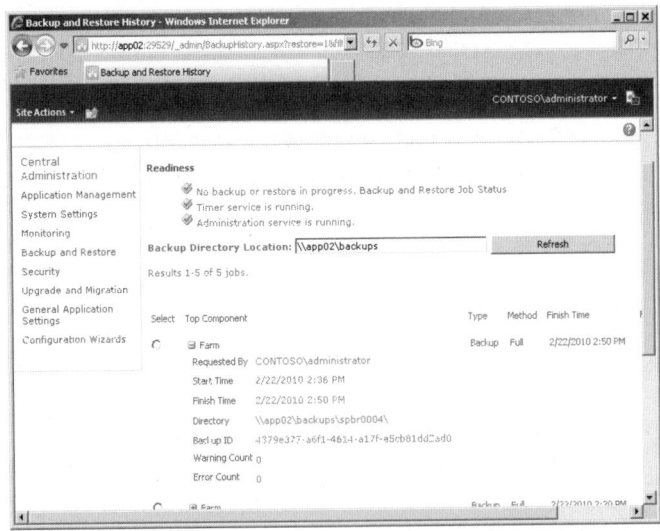

FIGURE 18-6 Expand Top Component to see details about the backup.

To restore from a previous backup, perform the following steps:

1. Browse to Central Administration, Backup And Restore.
2. Click Restore From A Backup.
3. Enter the backup directory location, and click Refresh.
3. Select the backup to restore from.
4. Click Next.
5. Select the farm component.
6. Click Next.
7. Choose the Restore Content And Configuration Settings option.
8. Optionally, select New Configuration to restore to a different database server or use different database names.
9. Select Same Configuration to overwrite existing content.
10. Enter the password for every application shown, as seen in Figure 18-7. It is not recommended to change the user name on this configuration screen.

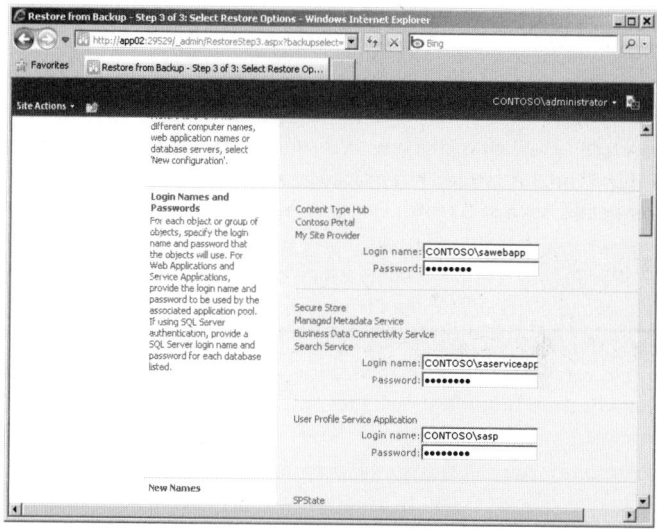

FIGURE 18-7 Enter the password for each application you are prompted about.

11. Click Start Restore.

Farm Backup and Restore Using Windows PowerShell

Using Windows PowerShell you can create custom scripts to back up your SharePoint Server 2010 server farm. This allows you to schedule backups during maintenance windows. Before performing the steps in this section, be sure you have prepared the backup location and performed at least one full backup using Central Administration.

To begin testing backup and restores using Windows PowerShell, open the SharePoint 2010 Management Shell from Start, All Programs, Microsoft SharePoint 2010 Products. Enter **Get-Help Backup-SPFarm** to see all farm backup options. You can use *get-help* in front of any cmdlet to see the available options. To see detailed help options for any cmdlet you can add the –detailed switch—for example, **Get-Help Backup-SPFarm –detailed**.

Back Up a Server Farm

To back up a server farm using Windows PowerShell, enter the following command:

```
Backup-SPFarm -directory \\app02\backups -BackupMethod Full
```

There are several options available when backing up the farm using Windows PowerShell:

- *Directory*   Defines the backup location previously prepared.
- *BackupThreads*   A definite advantage to using command-line tools for backing up SharePoint Server 2010 is the ability to increase the backup threads for processing. The default thread count is 3. Be sure to test increases in the thread count before implementing the change in a production environment. You can adversely affect the performance of both the SharePoint Server 2010 server farm and the destination storage location.
- *ShowTree*   Displays the objects in the farm that are available to be backed up. If you use this setting in conjunction with *Item*, it is scoped to the object underneath *Item*.
- *ConfigurationOnly*   Identical to the Central Administration option. This will back up only the farm configuration data. No content will be backed up when you select *ConfigurationOnly*.
- *Item*   You can back up a farm component—such as a Web application, content database, or service application—using the *Item* parameter. You cannot back up site collections, sites, list, libraries, or list items using the *Item* parameter.
- *Percentage*   You can specify the progress increments on the screen. If scripting, you do not need to use the *Percentage* option.
- *Force*   Using *force* will bypass the default behavior of halting the backup if the estimator calculates there is insufficient disk space.
- *Verbose*   If you want to see the progress of the backup, include the *Verbose* option. Otherwise, you won't be presented with current progress information, as was the default in SharePoint Server 2007 using stsadm.exe.
- *WhatIf*   You can display the output of running the backup without actually performing the backup.

Restore a Server Farm

Because of their ability to schedule backups, most administrators choose to use command-line tools to back up servers. However, the backups created by command-line tools can be restored using Central Administration. If you choose to restore from the command line, such as when performing a remote installation, you can do so with Windows PowerShell. The command options look similar to the backup commands, but you must know the *BackupId* you want to restore. To find the *BackupId*, you run the following command:

```
Get-SPBackupHistory -Directory <Backup folder> -ShowBackup [-Verbose]
```

If you have console access, you can also do the following to get the *BackupId* with additional information if needed:

1. Open the Spbrtoc.xml in the directory containing your backups. Using the previous example, it would be \\app02\backups\spbrtoc.xml.
2. Search for the relevant backup date, as can be seen in the following example.
3. Copy the SPId file. It is 8556232b-4985-470a-bfbe-aec1b3435349 in the example.

```
<SPHistoryObject>
        <SPId>8556232b-4985-470a-bfbe-aec1b3435349</SPId>
        <SPRequestedBy>CONTOSO\administrator</SPRequestedBy>
        <SPBackupMethod>Full</SPBackupMethod>
        <SPRestoreMethod>None</SPRestoreMethod>
        <SPStartTime>02/23/2010 03:04:17</SPStartTime>
        <SPFinishTime>02/23/2010 03:20:50</SPFinishTime>
        <SPIsBackup>True</SPIsBackup>
        <SPConfigurationOnly>False</SPConfigurationOnly>
        <SPBackupDirectory>\\app02\backups\spbr0005\</
SPBackupDirectory>
        <SPDirectoryName>spbr0005</SPDirectoryName>
        <SPDirectoryNumber>5</SPDirectoryNumber>
        <SPTopComponent>Farm</SPTopComponent>
        <SPTopComponentId>cc9a169c-9ae3-414c-a45b
137804528661</SPTopComponentId>
        <SPWarningCount>0</SPWarningCount>
        <SPErrorCount>0</SPErrorCount>
    </SPHistoryObject>
```

Using the example of *APP02* as the backup file server, *backups* as the share name, and the previously found *BackupId*, execute the following command for a full farm restore:

```
Restore-SPFarm -Directory \\app02\backups -BackupId 123456
```

There are several options when executing the Restore-SPFarm cmdlet:

- **Directory** Specifies the path to the SharePoint Server 2010 backup location you want to restore from. There must be a valid spbrtoc.xml file in the root of the backup directory.

- **RestoreMethod** You must choose either New or Overwrite. The New option restores the selected backup components and configuration using either new database names, a new SQL Server instance, or both. Overwrite is the same option displayed in Central Administration as Same. Using the Overwrite option restores your content and configuration to the same names.

- **BackupId** The unique backup ID you want to restore from.

- **ConfigurationOnly** Restores only the farm configuration data, and no content.

- **Confirm** Requires you to confirm the backup by typing **Y**.

- **FarmCredentials** You must supply the farm credentials when restoring content and configuration data.

- **Force** If you change content, as is the case when using *overwrite*, using *force* will suppress the prompt for confirmation. This is common when using remote command-line tools for restoring content.

- **Item** Indicates the part of the backup you want to restore. For example, if you have performed a full farm backup, you might choose to only restore a Web application or content database. An item name can be seen in the backup log files or by using the –showtree option.

- **NewDatabaseServer** If you want to restore to an alternate database server, you can specify that during the restore process.

- **Percentage** You can specify the progress increments on the screen. Percentage complete is seen only when using the *Verbose* option.

- **RestoreThreads** The default number of process threads is 3. This can be increased to 10 or decreased to 1.

- **WhatIf** Displays the effect of a command without running an actual restore process.

- **Verbose** Displays the output of a command.

Be sure to monitor the restore process. When restoring Web applications and some service applications, you might be prompted for the application pool password. The restore process will pause until you enter credentials. Although you can change the user names of these during the restore, doing so is not recommended unless there is no other option.

> **TIP** You can run Stsadm.exe and Psconfig.exe from the SharePoint 2010 Management Shell. You do not need to navigate to the file location at C:\Program Files\Common Files\Microsoft Shared\Web Server Extensions\14\BIN.

Farm Backup and Restore Using Stsadm.exe

You can also back up your entire farm by using *Stsadm.exe –o backup –directory*, also known as STSADM Catastrophic Mode. Using the *–directory* command-line option invokes additional options that you can use to back up the entire farm or individual items, such as Web applications or content databases. However, you cannot restore object-level items such as documents. Because you might already be familiar with Stadm.exe, using the command might be the best way to reliably schedule backup jobs on your server farm. Stsadm.exe should be executed from the SharePoint 2010 Management Shell. The following is an example of backing up an entire server farm using Stsadm.exe in Catastrophic Mode:

```
stsadm.exe -o backup -directory \\backupservername\backups\
-backupmethod full
```

This example is the simplest form of backing up your entire server using the Full option. There are several optional parameters you can define when backing up, such as *–backupthreads,* that you might find useful.

The parameters available using *stsadm.exe –o backup –directory* are as follows:

- **-item** The *–item* parameter is generally used in conjunction with the *–showtree* option. An item from the list generated by *showtree* must be specified and the command run again omitting the *showtree* parameter.

- **-percentage** The *–percentage* parameter shows the progress increments on screen. For example, 10 would show the progress in 10 percent increments.

- **-backupthreads** This value should be between 1 and 10. Be careful not to use high thread counts during content indexing or other system maintenance.

- **-showtree** The *–showtree* parameter shows all items that can be backed up. This information can also be found in Central Administration Backup And Restore.

- **-quiet** This option suppresses output and is used when scripting backups.

For example, the following command backs up a Web application named Portal and uses five CPU threads for the backup process:

```
stsadm -o backup -directory \\backupservername\backups -backupmethod full
-item "Portal" -backupthreads 5 -quiet
```

Restoring a Server Farm from a Farm-Level Backup

Follow these steps to restore a server farm from a farm-level backup:

1. Find the backup ID either by running

   ```
   stsadm.exe -o backuphistory -directory \\backupserver\sharename
   restore
   ```

or by viewing the history in Central Administration, Backup And Restore, Backup And Restore History. Every backup or restore job is assigned a unique identifier.

2. From the SharePoint 2010 Management Shell, execute

```
stsadm.exe -o restore -directory \\backupservername\sharename
-restoremethod [ new | overwrite ]
-item <item>
```

If you do not select the item, such as a Web application or content database, the entire farm is restored.

3. If prompted, you must enter the Web application pool identity and associated password for each component restored. Alternately, you can define these in the script using the –*username* and –*password* command-line options.

4. After restoring components to a server farm, it is always a good idea to perform an *IISReset* on every server in the farm.

From the command line, you also have the option to select a new database server. For example, you execute the following command to restore databases to a new SQL Server instance named DEV:

```
stsadm.exe -o restore -directory \\backupservername\sharename
-restoremethod new -backupid <id> -newdatabaserver DEV
```

Automating SharePoint Products and Technologies Backups

SharePoint Server 2010 does not provide an automated method to back up your content and configuration. You can schedule backups using a combination of Windows Server 2008 task scheduling and command-line tools. Using either Windows PowerShell or Stsadm.exe, do the following:

1. Create a batch file containing a tested command-line backup string, as shown previously.

2. Open Task Scheduler from the Administrative Tools program group.

3. From the Action menu, click Create Task.

4. Click New on the Actions tab and browse to choose the batch file you created in step 1.

5. Name the Task; *SharePoint Server backup*, for example, on the General tab.

6. Click New on the Triggers tab to configure the frequency, usually Daily.

7. Select the start time. Be careful not to set this to overlap with content indexing or other scheduled system maintenance.

8. Configure the credentials required to execute the scheduled task on the General tab. This user must have write access to the backup share destination and be a farm administrator.

9. Click OK.

Service and Web Application Backup and Restore

If you need to back up service and Web applications independently of the entire farm, you can do so using Windows PowerShell. You can also restore individual items, such as a service application, from a full farm backup without restoring the entire backup. This is useful in restoring functionality such as Search or the Secure Store.

CAUTION You must back up the Secure Store whenever you change or refresh the master key. The database is encrypted using the master key, and thus older Secure Store backups will not successfully restore.

To back up a service or Web application, you use the –*item* option of the Restore-SPFarm Windows PowerShell cmdlet. To get the exact name of the item you want to back up, use the *Backup-SPFarm –showtree* command. The following is an example of the output of the –*showtree* command:

```
Farm\
    [SharePoint_Config]\
    InfoPath Forms Services\
        Settings\
        Data Connections\
        Form Templates\
    SharePoint Server State Service\
        [SPState]\
            [SPState]\
    Microsoft SharePoint Foundation Web Application\
        Content Type Hub\
            WSS_Content_CT_Hub\
            [Timer Jobs Group]\
        Contoso Portal\
            WSS_Content_Portal_Root\
            WSS_Content_Commodity\
            [Timer Jobs Group]\
        My Site Provider\
            WSS_Content_My1\
            [Timer Jobs Group]\
    [WSS_Administration]\
        [SharePoint Central Administration v4]\
            SharePoint_AdminContent_f47411b9-a953-4135-9f36-
31db84421716\
        SharePoint Server State Service Proxy\
            [SPStateService_Proxy]\
        [Microsoft SharePoint Server Diagnostics Service]\
        Global Search Settings\
        Application Registry Service\
        Shared Services\
            Shared Services Applications\
                Secure Store\
                    [Service Application Endpoint Group]\
```

```
                    [Secure_Store_Service_DB]\
                PerformancePoint\
                    [Service Application Endpoint Group]\
                    [PerformancePoint_f44fae1fba514c538e043f542721a064]\
                Managed Metadata Service\
                    [Service Application Endpoint Group]\
                    [Term_Store]\
                SecurityTokenServiceApplication\
                    ClaimEncodingManager\
                    SecurityTokenServiceManager\
                    ClaimProviderManager\
                User Profile Service Application\
                    [Service Application Endpoint Group]\
                    [User Profile Service Application_ProfileDB_4a428abd987
345aa859b568e2b026811]\
                    [User Profile Service Application_SyncDB_75aeacf4d6b449
caa5cf5c51c83f16a6]\
                    [User Profile Service Application_SocialDB_925f69af7743
40c695f7bfee9ff80819]\
                    [Timer Jobs Group]\
                Business Data Connectivity Service\
                    [Service Application Endpoint Group]\
                    [BDCS_Service_DB]\
                Search Service\
                    [Service Application Endpoint Group]\
                    Search_Service_DB_a675c41b428e41a89cd093487a6d386d\
                        [Admin (C: on APP02)]\
                    [Search_Service_CrawlStoreDB_
d5c74208f4cf4452aa696b0df1f1fc14]\
                        [Crawl-0 (C: on APP02)]\
                    [Search_Service_PropertyStoreDB_788bde71b62f4e4890cefa6
b143c81b7]\
                    [Index Partition 0]\
                        [Query-0 (C: on APP02)]\
            Shared Services Proxies\
                Business Data Connectivity Service\
                Managed Metadata Service\
                PerformancePoint\
                Secure Store\
                Search Service\
                User Profile Service Application\

    [ ] - item cannot be selected.
     *   - not selected to be backed up.
```

From the output, you can see items such as Secure Store and Search Service. When backing up individual applications, you'll generally back up the entire service, and not a subcomponent such as a database. But if you are *restoring* a subcomponent, such as a Secure Store database, you might only restore what is required. Restoring the minimal set of content reduces the possibility that you are overwriting new content that has been added since the last backup. Using the previous example's server names and *BackupId*, the following command restores the Secure Store. Note that the Secure Store is named *Secure Store*:

```
Restore-SPFarm -directory \\app02\backups
-backupid 8556232b-4985-470a-bfbe-aec1b3435349
-item "Farm\Shared Services\Shared Services Applications\Secure Store"
```

If you also need to restore the Secure Store Proxy, run the following command next:

```
Restore-SPFarm -directory \\app02\backups
-backupid 8556232b-4985-470a-bfbe-aec1b3435349
-item "Farm\Shared Services\Shared Services Proxies\Secure Store"
```

Note that you can restore individual components from a full farm backup. You do not need to back up each component individually to restore a single component.

Granular Backup and Restore

There are many times when administering SharePoint Server 2010 servers that you need to back up and restore only site collections, sites, and lists. SharePoint Server 2010 has extended the functionality provided in SharePoint Server 2007 and surfaced some of the Stsadm.exe commands in Central Administration. In addition to restoring from granular backups, you also have the option of restoring site collections, sites, and lists from unattached content databases. The following granular backup and restore options are available in SharePoint Server 2010:

- Site Collection Backup and Restore
- Site Export and Import
- List Export

Site Collection Backup and Restore

If you need to back up a single site collection, you can use Central Administration, Windows PowerShell, or Stsadm.exe. But you can only restore using Windows PowerShell and Stsadm.exe. The basic functionality hasn't changed much since SharePoint Server 2007, with the notable exception that there are now cmdlets for Windows PowerShell.

Site collection backups are full fidelity. The backup will contain all content, workflows, alerts, settings, and the Recycle Bin. Be aware that restoring a site collection to a farm in a different Active Directory domain might produce suboptimal results with regard to permissions. The Active Directory security ID (SID) for objects will be orphaned. If you restore to another Active Directory domain, be prepared to associate users in the new domain with accounts referenced in the old domain.

Central Administration

To back up a site collection using Central Administration, perform the following steps:

1. Open Central Administration.
2. Browse to the Backup And Restore page.
3. From the Granular Backup grouping, click Perform A Site Collection Backup.
4. Select a site collection from the drop-down menu. Note that it might appear to be a Web application listed, but it is actually the root site collection in the Web application. Always verify you are working with the correct site collection.
5. Click Start Backup
6. Monitor the backup progress, as seen in Figure 18-8.

NOTE There is not a Central Administration interface to restore site collections.

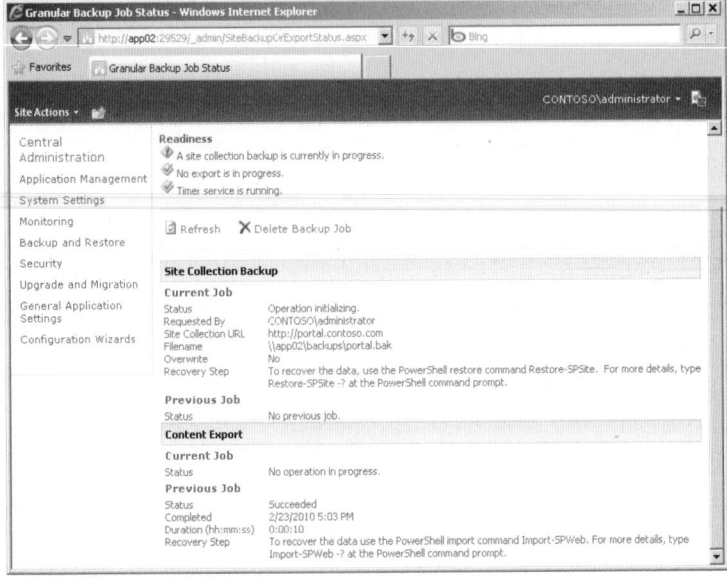

FIGURE 18-8 Backup status can be seen after beginning the backup.

Windows PowerShell

If you are remotely managing a server or building backup scripts for site collections, you can use Windows PowerShell. Many administrators prefer command-line tools after working with the product for a while. Additionally, Windows PowerShell will automatically lock the site collection during backup to reduce the risk of SQL blocking and locking errors. If you need to perform site collection backups during business hours, consider using a SQL snapshot to back up the data. Enter **Get-Help Backup-SPSite** to see all site backup options. You can use *get-help* in front of any cmdlet to see the available options. To see detailed help options for any cmdlet, you can add the –detailed switch—for example, **Get-Help Backup-SPSite –detailed**. The following options are available when backing up a site collection via Windows PowerShell:

- *Identity* Specifies the URL or GUID of the site collection to back up—for example, *http://portal.contoso.com/sites/HR*.
- *Path* The full backup path, including the file name. An example is *\\app02\ backups\portal.bak*.
- *Confirm* Requires you to confirm the backup by typing **Y**.
- *Force* If you want to overwrite an existing file, use the *Force* option.
- *NoSiteLock* If you want to back up the site collection without making it read-only, use the *NoSiteLock* option. Be aware that large site collection backups often fail without a site lock.
- *UseSqlSnapshot* If you need to back up site collections during the day and require users to continue full read/write operations, you'll need to create a SQL snapshot to back up from. Using this option creates a temporary SQL Server database snapshot. After the snapshot is created, the backup will be from the snapshot, not the live database. This is the best method to get a full fidelity site collection backup.
- *WhatIf* Shows the effects of a command without performing the actual backup.

To back up a site collection via Windows PowerShell, do the following:

1. Open the SharePoint 2010 Management Shell from Start, All Programs, Microsoft SharePoint 2010 Products.
2. Decide what options you'll use for the backup, such as SQL Snapshots.
3. Enter *Backup-SPSite -identity http://WebApp/sites/SiteCollection -path \\app02\backups\SiteCollection.bak*. Be sure to include any options you require from the previous list.

CAUTION During a Windows PowerShell site collection backup, the site collection is changed to read-only. This reduces the risk of SQL locking and blocking. Be aware that users will not have full collaborative functionality during the backup. Therefore, it is best to perform backups after normal business hours or use the SQL Snapshot option.

When you restore a site collection with Windows PowerShell, using the Restore-SPSite cmdlet, you have several options:

- *Identity* Specifies the URL where the site collection will be restored.
- *Path* Specifies the full location of the backup file, such as *\\app02\backups\portal.bak*.
- *Confirm* Requires confirmation before continuing the procedure.

- **ContentDatabase**   Specifies the content database the site collection will be restored to. If None is selected, the content database with the greatest remaining capacity will be used.
- **Force**   If there is a site collection at the location specified by *identity*, you must use the *Force* option to overwrite.
- **GradualDelete**   If overwriting an existing site collection, you can perform a gradual delete that will be executed by a timer job. This will reduce the impact to the server farm during restoration. Figure 18-9 shows how the timer job will appear in Central Administration, Running Jobs.

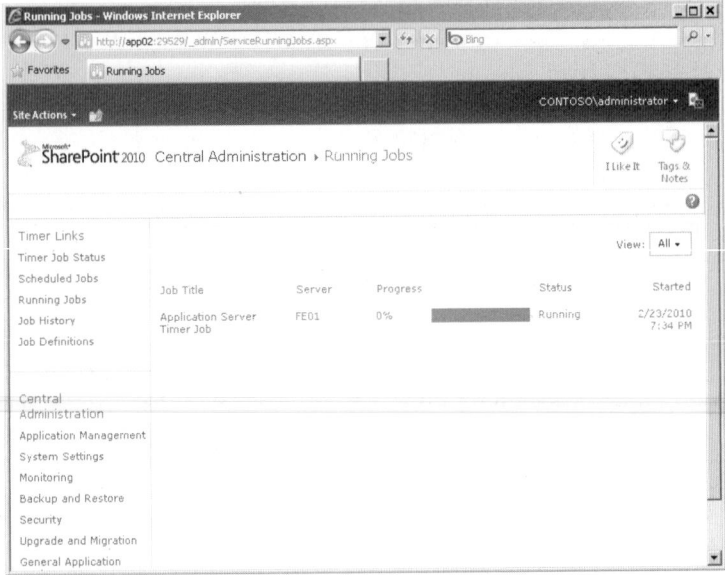

FIGURE 18-9 During the gradual delete, you will see an Application Server Timer Job option.

- **WhatIf**   Shows the effects of a command without performing the actual backup.

To restore a site collection using Windows PowerShell, perform the following steps:

1. Open the SharePoint 2010 Management Shell from Start, All Programs, Microsoft SharePoint 2010 Products.

2. Enter **Restore-SPSite -identity http://portal.contoso.com/ -path \\app02\backups\portal.bak**, inserting your URL and backup file location. Be sure to include any options, such as force and gradual delete.

3. Verify the site collection has restored. If you are using gradual delete, you need to wait until the timer job completes before verifying a successful restore.

Stsadm.exe

If you used the previous versions of SharePoint Products, you might be familiar with the *stsadm.exe -o [backup | restore]* commands. Without the *–directory* option, Stsadm.exe backs up and restores site collections instead of farm-level components. Although using Stsadm.exe to back up and restore site collections does indeed do a complete backup of these site collections, it does not back up any configuration database information, content indexes, or search databases. Stsadm.exe site collection back up has the following options:

- **URL**   Specifies the URL or GUID of the site collection to back up—for example, *http://portal.contoso.com/sites/HR*.

- **Filename**   The full backup path, including the file name. An example is *\\app02\backups\portal.bak*.

- **Overwrite**   If there is a site collection at the location specified by *identity*, you must use the *overwrite* option.

- **NoSiteLock**   If you want to back up the site collection without making it read-only, use the *NoSiteLock* option. Be aware that large site collection backups often fail without a site lock.

- **UseSqlSnapshot**   If you need to back up site collections during the day and require users to continue full read/write operations, you need to create a SQL snapshot to back up from.

To back up a site collection using Stsadm.exe, execute the following from the SharePoint 2010 Management Shell:

```
stsadm.exe -o backup -url <Site Collection URL>
-filename <backup file name>
```

Restoring a site collection from Stsadm.exe is also done from the SharePoint 2010 Management Shell. The URL should include the site collection name—for example, *http://portal.contoso.msft/sites/accounting*—if *accounting* is a site collection. To restore a site collection using Stsadm.exe, execute the following from the SharePoint 2010 Management Shell:

```
stsadm.exe -o restore -url <Site Collection URL>
-filename <backup file name>
```

Although you can restore this site collection with a different URL, thus creating a cloned site collection in the original Web application, doing so introduces the possibility of a site collection ID conflict. When a site collection is created, it is assigned a unique ID in the server farm. You should remove or overwrite the original site collection if you need to restore the backup to the same Web application.

Recovering from an Unattached Content Database

In previous versions of SharePoint Server, there were several steps involved in recovering site collections from farm backups. You had to restore the content database that hosted the site collection, attach the restored content database to a new

Web application or different server farm, and then perform a command-line backup of the site collection. New in SharePoint Server 2010 is the ability to restore directly from an unattached content database.

Unattached does not mean unattached in SQL Server. An unattached database in Central Administration refers to a database that isn't associated with a Web application. This allows for the restoration of site collections directly from SQL Server. To restore from an unattached content database, perform the following steps:

1. Restore the content database that hosts the site collection to be restored.

2. From Central Administration, Backup And Restore, click Recover Data From An Unattached Content Database, as seen in Figure 18-10.

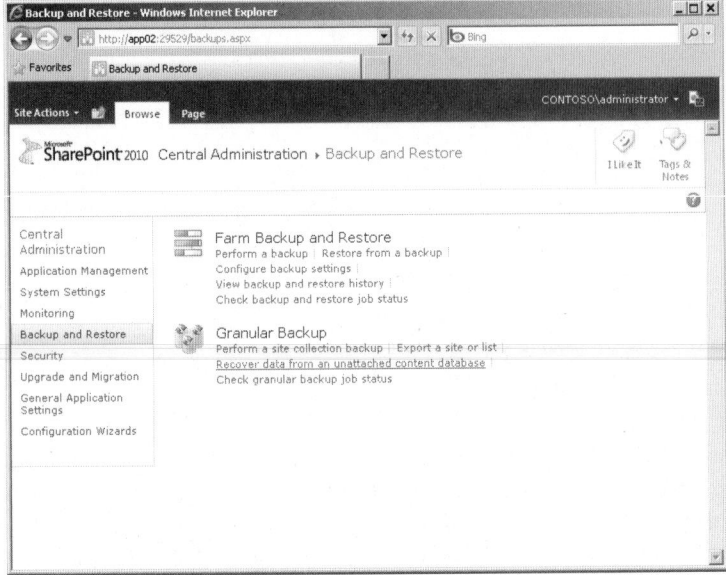

FIGURE 18-10 Click Recover Data From An Unattached Content Database.

3. Enter the database server and database name.

4. Select Backup Site Collection.

5. Click Next.

6. Select the site collection you want to back up.

7. Click Next.

8. Enter the full backup location, including the file name.

9. Click Start Backup.

The interface can be confusing because site collections appear to be under Central Administration. They are not. They should appear in the same relative URL as before, prefixed by the Central Administration URL. This is normal.

Working with Windows PowerShell and SharePoint 2010

MOST OF THE DAY-TO-DAY configuration and maintenance of Microsoft SharePoint Foundation Server 2010 and SharePoint Server 2010 is handled via the Central Administration pages. Only a few actions require administrators to access command-line tools. The most common use of a SharePoint command-line tool is to script repeatable actions against SharePoint—for example, batch creation of users or sites. Coverage of command-line tools in previous versions of SharePoint focused on STSADM. With the release of SharePoint Foundation Server 2010 and SharePoint Server 2010, Windows PowerShell is the default command-line and scripting tool. STSADM is still available to use, but it has limited coverage of administration actions compared to the SharePoint commands available using Windows PowerShell.

SharePoint 2010 Management Shell

Windows PowerShell is an extensible executable that can process scripts and interactive commands. Windows PowerShell has many standard scripting constructs—including variables, loops, and conditional logic—allowing administrators to create, save, and execute powerful scripts.

The SharePoint 2010 Management Shell is the new command-line, scripting tool for SharePoint 2010. The Management Shell is a Windows PowerShell host that loads the *Microsoft.SharePoint.PowerShell* module and makes available all of the SharePoint commands. Because SharePoint 2010 Management Shell is a Windows PowerShell host, all the Windows PowerShell features and functionality are part of the shell. This means that to create more robust scripts and commands administrators need to learn, at a minimum, some Windows PowerShell scripting. The management console (shown in Figure A-1) is available after a SharePoint installation from the Microsoft SharePoint 2010 Products program group. This is the command-line interface that is configured to work with SharePoint 2010. It is not the only Windows PowerShell host that administrators will use. Administrators can choose to configure other Windows PowerShell hosts to include all the SharePoint commands.

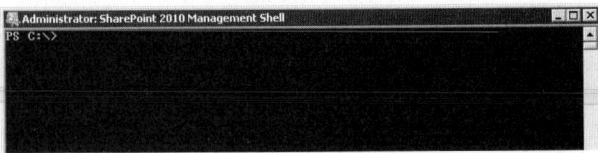

FIGURE A-1 The SharePoint 2010 Management Console.

Working with Commands

Windows PowerShell executes commands to get work done. Windows PowerShell uses many types of commands, including cmdlets (pronounced *command-lets*), functions, and scripts.

Working with Cmdlets

Cmdlets are common command types that are compiled code that can be executed using the Windows PowerShell host. Windows PowerShell installs and registers many cmdlets to use in the host. Examples of these cmdlets include Get-Process, Where-Object, Set-Location, and Get-Item. Cmdlets allow the administrator to work with many objects, including local drives, registry settings, and Windows Management Instrumentation (WMI) objects. Cmdlets also exist to allow administrators to work on objects, including filtering, sorting, and formatting. With these cmdlets, administrators can use a Windows PowerShell host to execute single-line commands or more complex commands and scripts. Examples of single-line commands for SharePoint 2010 include Get-SPSite, New-SPContentDataBase, and Enable-SPFeature.

Windows PowerShell has no SharePoint commands. SharePoint 2010 installs the SharePoint-specific commands along with the SharePoint 2010 Management Shell. At the time of this writing, there are over 500 cmdlets installed with SharePoint, allowing administrators to manage nearly every aspect of SharePoint in SharePoint 2010 Management Shell. All known cmdlets at the time of this writing are listed at the end of this chapter.

Executing an Command

To execute a command in the SharePoint 2010 Management Shell, open the Management Shell on a SharePoint 2010 server. The SharePoint commands included with SharePoint 2010 must be run on a SharePoint 2010 server. To execute a command in interactive mode, type the command at the command prompt.

Figure A-2 displays the shell after executing the Get-SPSite cmdlet.

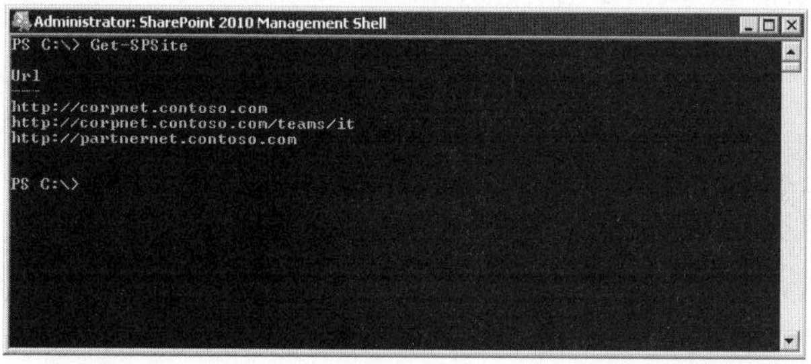

FIGURE A-2 Running the Get-SPSite cmdlet.

TIP Clear the console using the Clear-Host cmdlet, or use CLS. CLS is an alias of Clear-Host.

Applying Parameters to a Cmdlet

Most cmdlets have parameters that can be set to provide more information about the command. Parameters are placed after the command and are denoted using a dash (–). For example, the *Limit* parameter is a common parameter in many SharePoint *Get* commands. A command uses the *Limit* parameter to determine how many objects to return. Performance reasons limit the number of objects returned from a *Get* command to 20 items. The *Limit* parameter can be used to specify the number of items to return, or it can be used to return all items regardless of the number. To return all *SPSite* objects, use the following command:

```
Get-SPSite –Limit All
```

TIP The up and down cursor keys cycle the command history. The left and right cursor keys move the cursor left or right in the command. The Tab key provides tab completion or command completion.

Most parameters use the –name [argument] syntax. In the preceding example, *Limit* is the parameter name and *All* is the argument. Switch parameters do not require an argument. Switch parameters either exist or don't exist. The *WhatIf* parameter is a switch. It is a parameter that is used within many commands that will make a change to an object or data. If the *WhatIf* parameter is present, the command will not actually perform the action; instead, it will notify what actions the command would have taken. This is a great parameter to test potentially destructive commands. The "Removing Webs" section of this chapter demonstrates the *WhatIf* parameter.

Setting Privileges for Working with SharePoint

Running SharePoint commands requires the user to have the correct privileges to the SharePoint object model as well as to the SharePoint databases. When you are working with SharePoint objects, the connections to the database are generally created with the permissions of the current user. This user must have access to the databases. The *SPShellAdmin* commands are used to configure a user's privileges and security:

To list Shell administrators

```
Get-SPShellAdmin
```

To add a user as a Shell administrator

```
Add-SPShellAdmin –UserName <user name> –Database<database name>
```

For example, to allow user Jeff Hay to execute commands against the PartnerNet site, use the following command:

```
Add-SPShellAdmin –UserName Contoso\Jeff Hay –Database (Get-
SPContentDatabase –Identity PartnerNet_ContentDatabase)
```

Notice that the preceding example uses the Get-SPContentDatabase cmdlet and the PartnerNet content database name to retrieve the SPContentDatabase object .

To remove a user from Shell Admin

```
Remove-SPShellAdmin –UserName Contoso\Jeff Hay –Database (Get-
SPContentDatabase –Identity PartnerNet_ContentDatabase)
```

Using the Get-Help Cmdlet

Get-Help is a Windows PowerShell cmdlet that can be used to discover commands and command syntax. For example, to view the command syntax for Get-SPSite execute the following cmdlet in the shell:

```
Get-Help -name Get-SPSite
```

Figure A-3 displays the help text for Get-SPSite.

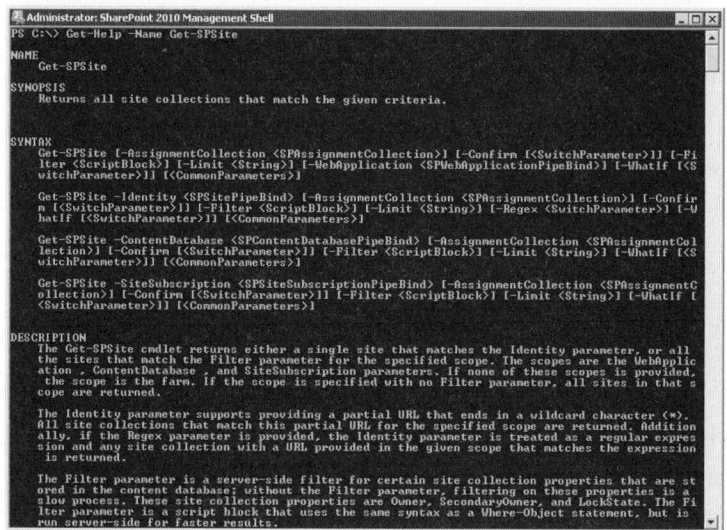

FIGURE A-3 Help text.

The *Name* parameter accepts many different values for the argument allowing a user to discover commands. Figure A-4 displays the results when the *Name* parameter is set to *site*.

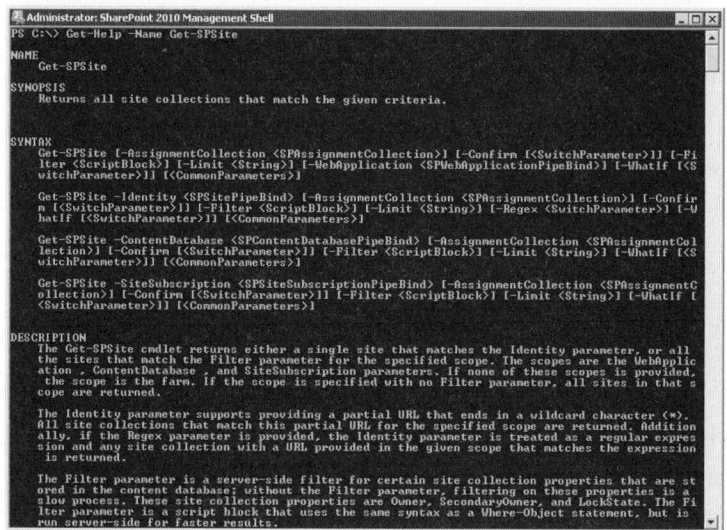

FIGURE A-4 Help text results.

Get-Help supports *Detailed* and *Examples* switch parameters to view more detailed information or examples of the command, respectively. To see detailed help options for any cmdlet, you can add the –detailed switch—for example, Get-Help GetSPSite –detailed.

Using the Pipeline

Windows PowerShell provides a pipeline to move objects from one command to the next. The pipeline is a powerful mechanism that allows administrators to chain together simpler commands to accomplish a larger task or a task that might not have a dedicated command. For example, there is no single command to find all Webs that have RequestAccessEnabled set to *false*.

Finding all Webs where *RequestAccessEnabled* is set to *false* is a multiple-step process:

1. Get all site collections (SPSite).
2. For each site collection, get all Webs (SPWeb).
3. Filter each Webs, keeping only those with a *RequestAccessEnabled* property set to *false*:

```
Get-SPSite -Limit All | Get-SPWeb –Limit All | Where-Object
$_.RequestAccessEnabled -eq $False}
```

NOTE The preceding command does not retrieve the Central Administration site or Webs. To include Central Administration use the –IncludeCentralAdministration switch parameter with the Get-SPWebApplication cmdlet.

The Get-SPSite cmdlet passes each site object(SPSite), one at a time, to the Get-SPWeb cmdlet. Get-SPWeb passes each Web (SPWeb) object within the current site collection, one at a time, to the Where-Object cmdlet. Where-Object checks the current object's (represented by $_) *RequestAccessEnabled* property to determine whether it is false. If a match occurs, it is passed out of the pipeline and formatted for display. This set of commands can easily be modified to set *RequestAccessEnabled* to *true* if that was the needed action.

The pipeline is not exclusive to commands. Another common method is to capture results in a variable and then pass the variable to a set of commands connected using the pipeline. In the next example, all Webs on the farm will be captured into a *$webs* variable. The *$webs* variable will be passed into the pipeline for processing:

```
Start-SPAssignment -Global
$webs = Get-SPSite | Get-SPWeb
$webs | Where-Object {$_. RequestAccessEnabled -eq $False}
 Stop-SPAssignment -Global
```

Start-SPAssignment and Stop-SPAssignment are resource commands that are needed. These commands are discussed in the "Assigning Resources" section.

Filtering and Sorting Objects

A common scenario is to filter or limit the objects passing through the pipeline. For example, an administrator might need to locate all Webs where the owner is a certain person or deactivate a feature on all team sites located under a specific Web application. Filtering limits the objects that are used or passed on in a command. Filtering is used to target the objects that a command or commands will work on.

USING THE WHERE-OBJECT CMDLET

The Where-Object cmdlet is commonly used to filter objects passing though the pipeline. Many of the SharePoint commands also have a *Filter* parameter and a *Limit* parameter that can be used to filter or limit objects

Where-Object is a Windows PowerShell cmdlet, and it is not specific to SharePoint. This command uses a script block parameter denoted by braces that determines which objects will be passed onward in the pipeline. Where-Object looks at each object passing though the cmdlet and determines whether the object should or should not be passed on based on the supplied script block.

The example code used in the "Using the Pipeline" section uses Where-Object to filter out SPWeb objects that have *RequestAccessEnabled* set to *true*:

```
Get-SPSite -Limit All | Get-SPWeb -Limit All | Where-Object
{$_.RequestAccessEnabled -q $False}
```

The script block, contained within braces, is used by Where-Object to determine whether the current object in the pipeline is allowed to continue. In this example, if the current pipeline object represented by *$_* has a *RequestAccessEnabled* property and is equal to *false*, Where-Object lets the object continue in the pipeline. If the object does not contain the *RequestAccessEnabled* property or is set to *true*, it is not passed on in the pipeline. It is effectively thrown out.

> **NOTE** Windows PowerShell has its own set of comparison operators and Boolean values. Use Get-Help with a Name parameter of about_comparison_operators.

USING THE LIMIT PARAMETER

SharePoint Get cmdlets such as Get-SPWeb and Get-SPSite limit the number of objects processed to 20 for performance reasons. The *Limit* parameter can be used to control the number of objects processed. When the command reaches the *Limit* value, it issues a warning to the shell. Figure A-5 shows the warning generated when attempting to get all SPWeb objects.

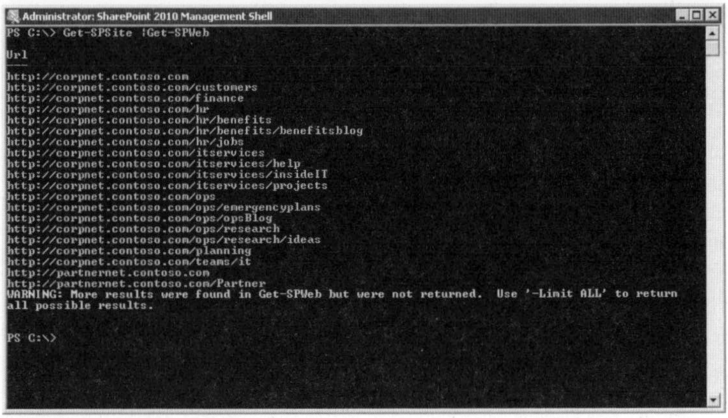

FIGURE A-5 A Warning message.

Setting the *Limit* parameter to All allows all SPWeb objects to process without a warning being generated, but doing this can lead to performance issues.

USING THE FILTER PARAMETER

SharePoint Get cmdlets also contain a *Filter* parameter. The *Filter* parameter with a script block limits the number of objects that are retrieved by Get-Parameter. In some ways, the *Filter* parameter functions like a Where-Object cmdlet. The major difference is the *Filter* parameter retrieves only the subset of objects where Where-Object is processing each object to determine whether the object passes on in the pipeline. Effectively, the *Filter* parameter should limit the amount of objects to be processed, while Where-Object needs to look at all of them.

The *Filter* parameter works only on the following properties of the object:

- Get-SPSite: Owner, Secondary Owner, LockState
- Get-SPWeb: Title, Template

Filters are less resource intensive because the processing is done up front on the server. The first example demonstrates how to get all Webs based on the Blog template using Where-Object:

```
Get-SPSite –Limit All | Get-SPWeb –Limit All |Where-Object{$_.WebTemplate
-eq "Blog"}
```

The cmdlet retrieves all SPWeb objects regardless of the template used to create the Web, and then Where-Object compares each object to the script block and determines which objects should continue on.

The next example uses the *Filter* parameter and script block to find all the Webs based on the Blog template.

To find all Webs based on the Blog template, use the *Filter* parameter:

```
Get-SPSite | Get-SPWeb -Filter{ $_.Template -eq "Blog"}
```

The same results are returned, but Get-SPWeb retrieves only the SPWeb objects that were based on the Blog template.

USING THE SORT-OBJECT COMMAND

The Sort-Object cmdlet sorts objects in either ascending or descending order by object property or a calculated value. The sort object accepts a comma-separated list of properties to sort on. Sort-Object can also be used to limit the results to unique values using the –Unique switch. To sort a set of SPWeb objects by title, pipe all SPWeb objects to Sort-Object –property Title, as shown here:

```
Get-SPSite |Get-SPWeb | Sort-Object -property WebTemplateId, Title |
Format-Table -Property WebTemplateId, Title, Url
```

Adding the *Unique* switch parameter to Sort-Object displays a single Web object for each unique *WebTemplateId*.

Formatting Objects

Under the covers, Windows PowerShell and SharePoint 2010 Management Shell works with .NET objects. To display these objects as text output to a file or console screen, Windows PowerShell uses various formatting commands. The most common time to use a formatting command is when an object reaches the end of the pipeline. If the object has not been captured in a variable or set to *Void* (a form of null), the shell formats the object as text. Formatting commands control the layout and contents of the data.

Common formatting commands are listed here:

- **Format-List** Formats object properties in a list, with each property appearing as a line of information
- **Format-Table** Formats object properties as a table, with each property aligned across the display
- **Format-Custom** Formats objects using an alternate view of the information
- **Format-Wide** Formats a single object property in columns across the display

For well-known objects, the default format for a particular layout is controlled by definition in a formatting file. Objects that are not defined in the formatting files are still displayed, with the host determining the displayed properties. Users can control the format layout by sending the object through the pipeline to a format command.

The default display for an SPFarm object is a table with Name and Status columns. Figure A-6 displays the output of the Get-SPFarm cmdlet.

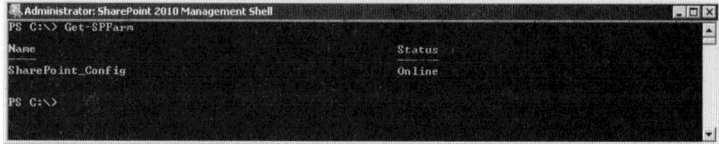

FIGURE A-6 The Get-SPFarm cmdlet output.

This output is controlled by a formatting file installed with SharePoint 2010 Management Shell. To format the SPFarm object in a list view, pipe the SPFarm object to Format-List. Figure A-7 displays the command and text results of Format-List.

FIGURE A-7 The command and the results.

The output has changed to display a list view of the SPFarm object's properties. To format a list to display in a table mode, send the SPSite objects to Format-Table. The output should match Figure A-8, which displays the default formatting. Use the *Property* parameter to provide a comma-separated list of property names to display. Figure A-8 displays the SPFarm object formatted in table view displaying the Name, BuildVersion, and Status columns.

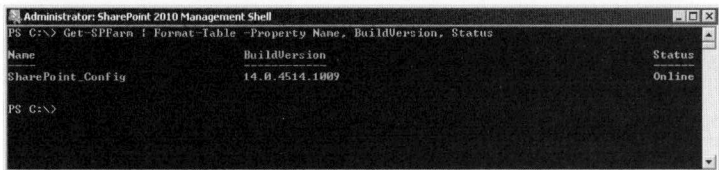

FIGURE A-8 Table view.

Discovering Commands

There are more than 500 SharePoint commands and nearly 400 commands that ship with Windows PowerShell. Command discovery is the process used to determine what command is available for a particular task. Windows PowerShell provides a number of methods that help with the discovery of available commands.

Common Naming Rules

There are many methods to determine which command to use. Cmdlets have a standard naming rule of Verb-Noun. Windows PowerShell verbs are standardized to a known list of acceptable verbs for various categories of actions. Nouns are not constrained to a finite list and can be any noun that provides a solid understanding of what object the action is working on. The cmdlet naming rules allow administrators familiar with Windows PowerShell and SharePoint to have a good chance of guessing the command name. For example, to back up a SharePoint site the command to use is Backup-SPSite. To delete a user, the command to use is Remove-SPUser. STSADM users might find the new commands confusing because of the Windows PowerShell cmdlet naming rules. Delete does not appear in the list of acceptable verbs. Clear and Remove are used depending on the context. To view the naming rules for verbs, see *http://msdn.microsoft.com/en-us/library/ ms714428(VS.85).aspx.*

> **NOTE** Windows PowerShell makes the transition between shells easy with the use of aliases. Aliases allow a user to create a new name for an existing command. To create a new alias named DeleteUser, execute the following statement in Windows PowerShell:
>
> ```
> New-Alias -Name DeleteUser -Value Remove-SPUser
> ```

Tab Completion

Windows PowerShell provides a tab or command completion function in the shell. Tab completion allows a user to start to type a command and then tab through a list of possible commands. Tab completion can also be used to complete a path to a file. To use tab completion, start to type a command—for example, **Get-S**—and then press the Tab key. The shell rotates though the various matching commands.

Get-Help

Get-Help is a Windows PowerShell cmdlet that can be used to discover commands and command syntax. For example, to view the command syntax for New-SPContentDatabase, execute the following:

```
Get-Help -Name New-SPContentDatabase
```

Figure A-9 displays the results of executing the command.

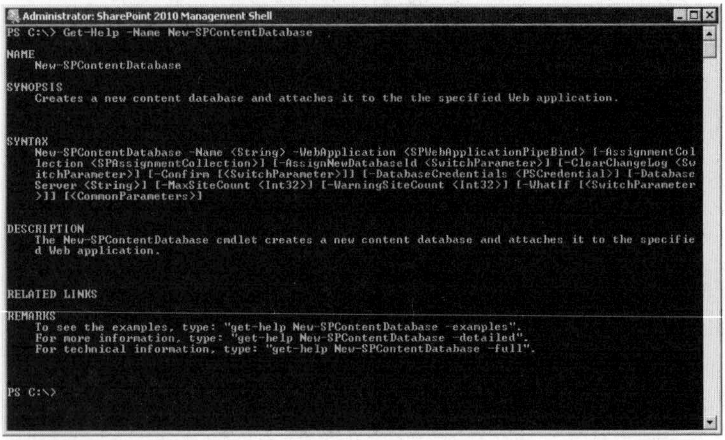

FIGURE A-9 A results window.

To get all the commands containing the word *ContentDatabase*, set the *Name* parameter's argument to *ContentDatabase*:

```
Get-Help -Name ContentDatabase
```

Get-Command

The final discovery method covered in this chapter is Get-Command. Get-Command is a Windows PowerShell cmdlet that displays information about commands. Get-Command with no parameters will list all known commands. To list only commands that are in the *Microsoft.SharePoint.PowerShell* module, use the optional *Module* parameter with an argument value of *Microsoft.SharePoint.PowerShell*. Figure A-10 displays the output of the following command:

```
Get-Command -Module Microsoft.SharePoint.PowerShell
```

FIGURE A-10 Output from Get-Command.

The screen should scroll by quickly, displaying a listing of all the commands located in the *Microsoft.SharePoint.PowerShell* module. To display one screen at a time, pipe the commands to *More*:

```
Get-Command | More
```

> **TIP** To cancel a running command or to get back to the prompt, use the keyboard combination Ctrl+C.

The output can be sent to a file using the Windows PowerShell pipeline. To send the output to a file, pipe the results of Get-Command to the Out-File cmdlet using the pipe character (|):

```
Get-Command –module Microsoft.SharePoint.PowerShell | Out-File –FilePath
<path here>
```

You can also use the Export-CSV cmdlet to export to a comma-separated file. The full command to export to a CSV file format is the following:

```
Get-Command –module Microsoft.SharePoint.PowerShell | Export-CSV –path
<path>
```

Working with Functions

Functions are another type of Windows PowerShell command. The following is a simple function declaration example that is used to retrieve Webs based on regions:

```
function ProvisionNewProductWeb($ProductNumber, $ProductName, $Region)
{
 if($Region -eq  "US") {
    $Site = Get-SPSite http://us.marketing.contoso.com
}elseif($Region -eq "Canada")
{
    $Site = Get-SPSite http://ca.marketing.contoso.com
}
}else
{
    Write-Host "Region is not our territory."
}
New-SPWeb -site "$site/$ProductNumber" -Name "$ProductName Marketing Site"
-Template STS#1 -Description "$ProductName Marketing Materials"
}
```

A function is a defined piece of code that can contain many commands to do a particular task. Functions are defined and run only when they are called. The host—in this case, SharePoint 2010 Management Shell—receives the function declaration and validates it. After the function is parsed, it is available to be called until the user exits the shell. Functions can be defined in a profile, where they are made available whenever the shell starts.

Functions can have input parameters and can return results. Function arguments can be passed to the function using the *$args* variable, but more commonly they are passed in as formal parameters. In the following function, *x* and *y* are formal parameters.

Working with SharePoint Cmdlets

There are over 500 commands for SharePoint in the release version. Demonstrating all the commands is impossible in a single appendix. In this section, we will work with some of the cmdlets to provide an introduction to using the SharePoint cmdlets.

Farms

The farm (SPFarm) object is the top-most object in SharePoint 2010. To access the farm, use the following cmdlet:

```
Get-SPFarm
```

Other farm-level settings are accessed using Get-SPFarmConfig:

```
Get-SPFarmConfig
```

To back up a farm, use the following cmdlet:

```
Backup-SPFarm –BackupMethod <Full | Differential> –Directory <Path to
Folder>
```

To restore a farm, use the following cmdlet:

```
Restore-SPFarm –Directory <Path> -RestoreMethod <Overwrite | New>
```

The *ShowTree* switch parameter of the Backup-SPFarm and Restore-SPFarm
methods displays a tree view of items to be backed up or restored. Figure A-11
displays the results of Backup-SPFarm with the optional –ShowTree parameter using
a tree view.

FIGURE A-11 Tree view.

Servers

Farms have one server or more (SPServer) associated with the farm. Common
properties on SPServer are *Address*, *Role*, *DisplayName*, and *Version*. To access and
list the servers, use the following cmdlet:

```
Get-SPServer
```

To access a specific server, use the *Identity* parameter. The *Identity* parameter can be the name of the server or the GUID ID value of the server:

```
Get-SPServer -Identity SP2010
```

To list all servers of a specific role—in this example, the Application role—use the following cmdlet:

```
Get-SPServer | Where-Object {$_.Role -eq "Application"}
```

> **TIP** Windows PowerShell has a robust parameter parsing process. For parameters such as Identity, only the argument is required, not the parameter name. It is common to see the previous example displayed as Get-SPServer SP2010.

Web Applications

Web applications (SPWebApplications) represent an Internet Information Services (IIS) load-balanced Web servers to host SharePoint Sites. Web applications can be created, listed, and removed. Commands also are available to manage Web-application throttling.

To create a Web application

```
New-SPWebApplication  -Name <Name> -Port <Port> -HostHeader  <Host Header>
-URL <Url>  -ApplicationPool <Application Pool>  -ApplicationPoolAccount
(Get-SPManagedAccount  <managed account name>)
```

Here is an example:

```
New-SPWebApplication  -Name SPPartnerNet -Port 80 -HostHeader
partnerNet.contoso.com -URL partnerNet.contoso.com  -ApplicationPool
SharePoint - partnerNet.contoso.com80 -ApplicationPoolAccount
(Get-SPManagedAccount  "Contoso\SP_ContentAppPool"
```

The managed account name must exist to use Get-SPManagedAccount. Notice in Figure A-12 that the result of the New-SPWebApplication cmdlet is that the newly created Web application is returned. It is common for a creation command to return the object created to allow for further processing. The returned SPWebApplication object can be ignored or placed into a variable. Figure A-12 displays the results of creating a new SPWebApplication object.

FIGURE A-12 A new SPWebApplication object.

To list Web applications

```
Get-SPWebApplication
```

Get-SPWebApplication does not return the Central Administration Web application unless the *IncludeCentralAdministration* switch parameter is present.

To return a specific Web application, use the *Identity* parameter, which can be the URL property or ID:

```
Get-SPWebApplication -Identity http://corpNet.contoso.com
```

Get-SPWebApplication returns only 20 items. This limit is placed on the command for performance reasons. To change the limit value, use the *Limit* parameter. Setting the argument for the *Limit* parameter to ALL returns all SPWebApplication objects.

The management shell prompts the user to confirm the removal of a Web application:

To remove Web applications

```
Remove-SPWebApplication -Identity <Url or Id>

Remove-SPWebApplication -Identity http://partnerNet.contoso.com
```

To remove the associated IIS site, use the *DeletelisSite* switch.

To remove the associated content databases, use the *RemoveContentDatabases* switch.

Figure A-13 displays the expected Confirm prompt when using Remove-SPWebApplication.

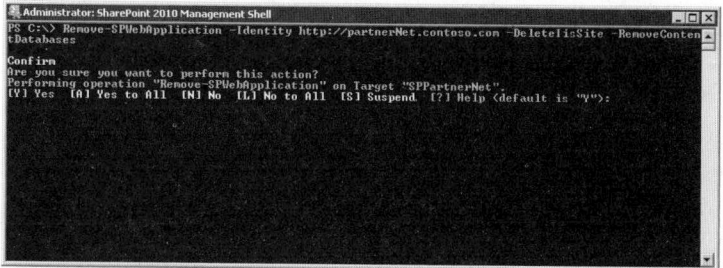

FIGURE A-13 The Confirm prompt.

TIP To bypass the confirmation message, use the Confirm parameter with a false value: –Confirm:$False. Use this with caution. The shell performs the deletion without any prompt.

Managing Sites

Sites (SPSite) can be managed with commands that work on SPSite or SPSiteAdministration objects. SPSite limits administrators who do not have general access to work with and view only a few properties. The SPSiteAdministration object allows an administrator access to many more properties and settings when the administrator does not have access to the site.

Create New Sites

A new site can be created using the New-SPSite cmdlet. There are many options on this command. The *Template* parameter determines the type of site created. To view the installed templates and find the proper template name for this parameter, use the Get-SPWebTemplate cmdlet:

```
New-SPSite -Url http://partnerNet.contoto.com/  -OwnerAlias
Contoso\administrator  -Name PartnerNet –Template STS#1
```

List Sites

To list all sites on the farm, use Get-SPSite or Get-SPSiteAdministration:

```
Get-SPSiteAdministration
```

To get a single site, use the *Identity* parameter.

```
Get-SPSiteAdministration –Identity http://partnerNet.contoso.com
```

Get-SPSite and Get-SPSiteAdministration return only 20 items. This limit is placed on the command for performance reasons. To change the limit value, use the *Limit* parameter. Setting the argument for the *Limit* parameter to All returns all SPSite or SPSiteAdministration objects.

Back Up Sites

Backup-SPSite backs up a site collection to a file location. Use the *Identity* parameter, and provide a path and file name for the backup file:

```
Backup-SPSite –Identity http://partnerNet.contoso.com –path <filename>
```

Remove Sites

Remove-SPSite deletes the site. The *Identity* parameter determines which site to delete. The command will not execute without a valid *Identity* parameter, which can be the site ID, a URL, or an SPSite object:

```
Remove-SPSite –Identity http://partnerNet.contoso.com
```

Remove-SPSite prompts the user to confirm that the site should be deleted, as shown in Figure A-14.

FIGURE A-14 Confirm the site deletion.

Multiple sites can be deleted by selecting the sites and passing each site to the Remove-SPSite cmdlet using the pipeline.

Managing Webs

Webs are represented as SPWeb objects. Many of the commands for working with SPWebs are similar to the commands for working with sites.

Creating Webs

To create new Webs, use the following command:

```
New-SPWeb -Url http://partnerNet.contoso.com/partner1 -Language 1033
-Template STS#1 -Name "Partner 1" -Description "Partner 1 Team Site"
-UniquePermission
```

Similar to many of the creation commands, the command returns the newly created object.

Listing Webs

To list available Webs, use the Get-SPWeb cmdlet. Unlike Get-SPSite, running the Get-SPWeb command without any input parameters or an object passed in through the pipeline will result in an error. To list all Webs on a farm, including Central Administration, use the Get-SPSite cmdlet and pass each site object to Get-SPWeb:

```
Get-WebApplication -IncludeCentralAdministration | Get-SPSite
-Limit All  | Get-SPWeb -Limit All
```

Get-SPWeb has a *Filter* parameter that accepts a script block. This filters the objects based on the criteria in the script block:

```
Get-SPSite | Get-SPWeb -Filter {$_.Title  -eq "Partner 1"}
```

Removing Webs

The Remove-SPWeb cmdlet deletes the identified Web:

```
Remove-SPWeb -Identity http://partnerNet.contoso.com/partner1
```

SPWeb objects can be passed to Remove-Web via the pipeline:

```
Get-SPSite | Get-SPWeb -Filter {$_.Name -Like  "Partner*"} |Remove-SPWeb
```

> **IMPORTANT** The confirm prompt is there for a reason. Be cautious when working with numerous objects. It is not uncommon to accidentally allow an object through the pipeline. Consider using the WhatIf parameter to verify exactly what actions will be taken. Here is the previous example with the WhatIf parameter:

```
Get-SPSite | Get-SPWeb -Filter {$_.Name  -Like  "Partner*"}
|Remove-SPWeb  -WhatIf
```

Each SPWeb object passed to Remove-SPWeb prompts the user for a confirmation. To avoid the confirmation prompt, set the *Confirm* parameter to *$False*:

```
Get-SPSite | Get-SPWeb -Filter {$_.Name  -Like "Partner*"} |Remove-SPWeb
-Confirm:$False
```

Assigning Resources

Certain SharePoint objects require the use of the disposal pattern to release resources allocated to the object. Common SPSite and SPWeb objects require the proper use of disposal to insure the SharePoint server continues to function efficiently. Failure to reclaim resources can affect server performance.

Single-line commands release their resources correctly at the end of the pipeline. This means simple commands and commands that are chained together will be automatically disposed of correctly. SharePoint objects that are captured and referenced in variables will not be disposed of correctly, leading to memory leaks.

The SharePoint commands Start-SPAssignment and Stop-SPAssignment are used to track objects and properly dispose of SharePoint objects. The simplest use of the Start-SPAssignment and Stop-SPAssignment commands is when they are used with the *Global* switch parameter. The example from the "Changing a Property" section used Start-SPAssignment and Stop-SPAssignment cmdlets with the *Global* switch parameter:

```
Start-SPAssignment -Global

$webs = Get-SPSite | Get-SPWeb

$webs | Where-Object {$_.WebTemplateId -eq "#BLOG1#)

Stop-SPAssignment -Global
```

Start-SPAssignment is called with the *Global* switch parameter before resources are used. Stop- SPAssignment is called when the resources will no longer be used. Objects created between the start and stop actions will be tracked and released correctly.

Modifying Properties.

One of the reasons that an administrator would want access to various SharePoint objects is to modify a setting or property. Many SharePoint commands do exactly that. Administrators should look for a command that will provide the action needed.

For example, by using Get-SPWebApplication, Get-SPSite, and Get-SPWeb cmdlets, an administrator has access to the *Feature* collection, which lists the SharePoint features activated for the associated scope. The SharePoint commands contain a number of feature-related cmdlets (Get-SPFeature, Enable-SPFeature, Install-SPFeature, and Uninstall-SPFeature) that are simpler to use than to script against the SPWebApplication, SPSite, and SPWeb objects.

Not all of the actions an administrator needs to perform are available via a dedicated command. For example, there is no command to change a Web's title. To change a Web site's title property, an administrator must retrieve an SPWeb object and change the *Title* property.

Changing a Property

To change the *Title* property of a Web with a title of Partner1 to Contoso Partner 1, use the following command:

```
Start-SPAssignment –Global

$web = Get-SPSite | Get-SPWeb –Filter {$_.Name  –eq "Partner 1"}

$web.Title = "Contoso Partner 1"

$web.Update()

Stop-SPAssignment –Global
```

Many objects in SharePoint require the *Update* method to be called to persist the changes.

Discovering Object Properties and Methods

Get-Member lists the properties of a given object. To use Get-Member, send the object to the command using the pipeline:

```
Get-SPSite -Identity http://partnerNet.contoso.com | Get-Member
```

To limit the display of Get-Member, use the *MemberType* parameter. To view only properties, set the argument for the *MemberType* parameter to *Properties*:

```
Get-SPSite -Identity http://partnerNet.contoso.com | Get-Member –MemberType
Properties
```

SharePoint Cmdlet Listing

As we stated before, there are over 500 cmdlets for Microsoft SharePoint Server 2010. This section lists the known cmdlets available in the Microsoft SharePoint 2010 Management Shell. To learn more about each cmdlet, view the "Discovering Commands" section in this appendix.

Add-SPClaimTypeMapping

Add-SPDiagnosticsPerformanceCounter

Add-SPInfoPathUserAgent

Add-SPPluggableSecurityTrimmer

Add-SPServiceApplicationProxyGroupMember

Add-SPShellAdmin

Add-SPSiteSubscriptionFeaturePackMember

Add-SPSiteSubscriptionProfileConfig

Add-SPSolution

Add-SPUserSolution

Backup-SPConfigurationDatabase

Backup-SPFarm

Backup-SPSite

Clear-SPLogLevel

Clear-SPMetadataWebServicePartitionData

Clear-SPPerformancePointServiceApplicationTrustedLocation

Clear-SPSecureStoreCredentialMapping

Clear-SPSecureStoreDefaultProvider

Clear-SPSiteSubscriptionBusinessDataCatalogConfig

Connect-SPConfigurationDatabase

Copy-SPBusinessDataCatalogAclToChildren

Disable-SPBusinessDataCatalogEntity

Disable-SPFeature

Disable-SPInfoPathFormTemplate

Disable-SPSessionStateService

Disable-SPSingleSignOn

Disable-SPTimerJob

Disable-SPWebApplicationHttpThrottling

Disconnect-SPConfigurationDatabase

Dismount-SPContentDatabase

Dismount-SPStateServiceDatabase

Enable-SPBusinessDataCatalogEntity

Enable-SPFeature

Enable-SPInfoPathFormTemplate

Enable-SPSessionStateService

Enable-SPTimerJob

Enable-SPWebApplicationHttpThrottling

Export-SPBusinessDataCatalogModel

Export-SPEnterpriseSearchTopology

Export-SPInfoPathAdministrationFiles

Export-SPMetadataWebServicePartitionData

Export-SPSiteSubscriptionBusinessDataCatalogConfig

Export-SPSiteSubscriptionSettings

Export-SPWeb

Get-SPAccessServiceApplication

Get-SPAlternateURL

Get-SPAuthenticationProvider

Get-SPBackupHistory

Get-SPBrowserCustomerExperienceImprovementProgram

Get-SPBusinessDataCatalogMetadataObject

Get-SPBusinessDataCatalogThrottleConfig

Get-SPCertificateAuthority

Get-SPClaimProvider

Get-SPClaimProviderManager

Get-SPContentDatabase

Get-SPContentDeploymentJob

Get-SPContentDeploymentPath

Get-SPCustomLayoutsPage

Get-SPDatabase

Get-SPDataConnectionFile

Get-SPDataConnectionFileDependent

Get-SPDesignerSettings

Get-SPDiagnosticConfig

Get-SPDiagnosticsPerformanceCounter

Get-SPDiagnosticsProvider

Get-SPEnterpriseSearchAdministrationComponent

Get-SPEnterpriseSearchCrawlComponent

Get-SPEnterpriseSearchCrawlContentSource

Get-SPEnterpriseSearchCrawlCustomConnector

Get-SPEnterpriseSearchCrawlDatabase

Get-SPEnterpriseSearchCrawlExtension

Get-SPEnterpriseSearchCrawlMapping

Get-SPEnterpriseSearchCrawlRule

Get-SPEnterpriseSearchCrawlTopology

Get-SPEnterpriseSearchExtendedClickThroughExtractorJobDefinition

Get-SPEnterpriseSearchExtendedConnectorProperty

Get-SPEnterpriseSearchExtendedQueryProperty

Get-SPEnterpriseSearchIndexPartition

Get-SPEnterpriseSearchLanguageResourcePhrase

Get-SPEnterpriseSearchMetadataCategory

Get-SPEnterpriseSearchMetadataCrawledProperty

Get-SPEnterpriseSearchMetadataManagedProperty

Get-SPEnterpriseSearchMetadataMapping

Get-SPEnterpriseSearchPropertyDatabase

Get-SPEnterpriseSearchQueryAndSiteSettingsService

Get-SPEnterpriseSearchQueryAndSiteSettingsServiceInstance

Get-SPEnterpriseSearchQueryAndSiteSettingsServiceProxy

Get-SPEnterpriseSearchQueryAuthority

Get-SPEnterpriseSearchQueryComponent

Get-SPEnterpriseSearchQueryDemoted

Get-SPEnterpriseSearchQueryKeyword

Get-SPEnterpriseSearchQueryScope

Get-SPEnterpriseSearchQueryScopeRule

Get-SPEnterpriseSearchQuerySuggestionCandidates

Get-SPEnterpriseSearchQueryTopology

Get-SPEnterpriseSearchRankingModel

Get-SPEnterpriseSearchSecurityTrimmer

Get-SPEnterpriseSearchService

Get-SPEnterpriseSearchServiceApplication

Get-SPEnterpriseSearchServiceApplicationProxy

Get-SPEnterpriseSearchServiceInstance

Get-SPEnterpriseSearchSiteHitRule

Get-SPExcelBlockedFileType

Get-SPExcelDataConnectionLibrary

Get-SPExcelDataProvider

Get-SPExcelFileLocation

Get-SPExcelServiceApplication

Get-SPExcelUserDefinedFunction

Get-SPFarm

Get-SPFarmConfig

Get-SPFeature

Get-SPHelpCollection

Get-SPInfoPathFormsService

Get-SPInfoPathFormTemplate

Get-SPInfoPathUserAgent

Get-SPInfoPathWebServiceProxy

Get-SPLogEvent

Get-SPLogLevel

Get-SPManagedAccount

Get-SPManagedPath

Get-SPMetadataServiceApplication

Get-SPMetadataServiceApplicationProxy

Get-SPMobileMessagingAccount

Get-SPPerformancePointSecureDataValues

Get-SPPerformancePointServiceApplication

Get-SPPerformancePointServiceApplicationTrustedLocation

Get-SPPluggableSecurityTrimmer

Get-SPProcessAccount

Get-SPProduct

Get-SPProfileServiceApplicationSecurity

Get-SPSearchService

Get-SPSearchServiceInstance

Get-SPSecureStoreApplication

Get-SPSecurityTokenServiceConfig

Get-SPServer

Get-SPServiceApplication

Get-SPServiceApplicationEndpoint

Get-SPServiceApplicationPool

Get-SPServiceApplicationProxy

Get-SPServiceApplicationProxyGroup

Get-SPServiceApplicationSecurity

Get-SPServiceContext

Get-SPServiceHostConfig

Get-SPServiceInstance

Get-SPSessionStateService

Get-SPShellAdmin

Get-SPSite

Get-SPSiteAdministration

Get-SPSiteSubscription

Get-SPSiteSubscriptionConfig

Get-SPSiteSubscriptionEdiscoveryHub

Get-SPSiteSubscriptionEdiscoverySearchScope

Get-SPSiteSubscriptionFeaturePack

Get-SPSiteSubscriptionMetadataConfig

Get-SPSolution

Get-SPStateServiceApplication

Get-SPStateServiceApplicationProxy

Get-SPStateServiceDatabase

Get-SPTaxonomySession

Get-SPTimerJob

Get-SPTopologyServiceApplication

Get-SPTopologyServiceApplicationProxy

Get-SPTrustedIdentityTokenIssuer

Get-SPTrustedRootAuthority

Get-SPTrustedServiceTokenIssuer

Get-SPUsageApplication

Get-SPUsageDefinition

Get-SPUsageService

Get-SPUser

Get-SPUserSolution

Get-SPVisioExternalData

Get-SPVisioPerformance

Get-SPVisioSafeDataProvider

Get-SPVisioServiceApplication

Get-SPVisioServiceApplicationProxy

Get-SPWeb

Get-SPWebAnalyticsServiceApplication

Get-SPWebAnalyticsServiceApplicationProxy

Get-SPWebApplication

Get-SPWebApplicationHttpThrottlingMonitor

Get-SPWebPartPack

Get-SPWebTemplate

Get-SPWorkflowConfig

Grant-SPBusinessDataCatalogMetadataObject

Grant-SPObjectSecurity

Import-SPBusinessDataCatalogDotNetAssembly

Import-SPBusinessDataCatalogModel

Import-SPEnterpriseSearchTopology

Import-SPInfoPathAdministrationFiles

Import-SPMetadataWebServicePartitionData

Import-SPSiteSubscriptionBusinessDataCatalogConfig

Import-SPSiteSubscriptionSettings

Import-SPWeb

Initialize-SPResourceSecurity

Initialize-SPStateServiceDatabase

Install-SPApplicationContent

Install-SPDataConnectionFile

Install-SPFeature

Install-SPHelpCollection

Install-SPInfoPathFormTemplate

Install-SPService

Install-SPSolution

Install-SPUserSolution

Install-SPWebPartPack

Install-SPWebTemplate

Merge-SPLogFile

Mount-SPContentDatabase

Mount-SPStateServiceDatabase

Move-SPBlobStorageLocation

Move-SPProfileManagedMetadataProperty

Move-SPSite

Move-SPUser

New-SPAccessServiceApplication

New-SPAlternateURL

New-SPAuthenticationProvider

New-SPBusinessDataCatalogServiceApplication

New-SPBusinessDataCatalogServiceApplicationProxy

New-SPCentralAdministration

New-SPClaimProvider

New-SPClaimsPrincipal

New-SPClaimTypeMapping

New-SPConfigurationDatabase

New-SPContentDatabase

New-SPContentDeploymentJob

New-SPContentDeploymentPath

New-SPEnterpriseSearchCrawlComponent

New-SPEnterpriseSearchCrawlContentSource

New-SPEnterpriseSearchCrawlCustomConnector

New-SPEnterpriseSearchCrawlDatabase

New-SPEnterpriseSearchCrawlExtension

New-SPEnterpriseSearchCrawlMapping

New-SPEnterpriseSearchCrawlRule

New-SPEnterpriseSearchCrawlTopology

New-SPEnterpriseSearchExtendedConnectorProperty

New-SPEnterpriseSearchLanguageResourcePhrase

New-SPEnterpriseSearchMetadataCategory

New-SPEnterpriseSearchMetadataCrawledProperty

New-SPEnterpriseSearchMetadataManagedProperty

New-SPEnterpriseSearchMetadataMapping

New-SPEnterpriseSearchPropertyDatabase

New-SPEnterpriseSearchQueryAuthority

New-SPEnterpriseSearchQueryComponent

New-SPEnterpriseSearchQueryDemoted

New-SPEnterpriseSearchQueryKeyword

New-SPEnterpriseSearchQueryScope

New-SPEnterpriseSearchQueryScopeRule

New-SPEnterpriseSearchQueryTopology

New-SPEnterpriseSearchRankingModel

New-SPEnterpriseSearchSecurityTrimmer

New-SPEnterpriseSearchServiceApplication

New-SPEnterpriseSearchServiceApplicationProxy

New-SPEnterpriseSearchSiteHitRule

New-SPExcelBlockedFileType

New-SPExcelDataConnectionLibrary

New-SPExcelDataProvider

New-SPExcelFileLocation

New-SPExcelServiceApplication

New-SPExcelUserDefinedFunction

New-SPLogFile

New-SPManagedAccount

New-SPManagedPath

New-SPMetadataServiceApplication

New-SPMetadataServiceApplicationProxy

New-SPPerformancePointServiceApplication

New-SPPerformancePointServiceApplicationProxy

New-SPPerformancePointServiceApplicationTrustedLocation

New-SPProfileServiceApplication

New-SPProfileServiceApplicationProxy

New-SPSecureStoreApplication

New-SPSecureStoreApplicationField

New-SPSecureStoreServiceApplication

New-SPSecureStoreServiceApplicationProxy

New-SPSecureStoreTargetApplication

New-SPServiceApplicationPool

New-SPServiceApplicationProxyGroup

New-SPSite

New-SPSiteSubscription

New-SPSiteSubscriptionFeaturePack

New-SPStateServiceApplication

New-SPStateServiceApplicationProxy

New-SPStateServiceDatabase

New-SPSubscriptionSettingsServiceApplication

New-SPSubscriptionSettingsServiceApplicationProxy

New-SPTrustedIdentityTokenIssuer

New-SPTrustedRootAuthority

New-SPTrustedServiceTokenIssuer

New-SPUsageApplication

New-SPUsageLogFile

New-SPUser

New-SPVisioSafeDataProvider

New-SPVisioServiceApplication

New-SPVisioServiceApplicationProxy

New-SPWeb

New-SPWebAnalyticsServiceApplication

New-SPWebAnalyticsServiceApplicationProxy

New-SPWebApplication

New-SPWebApplicationExtension

New-SPWordConversionServiceApplication

Ping-SPEnterpriseSearchContentService

Publish-SPServiceApplication

Receive-SPServiceApplicationConnectionInfo

Remove-SPAlternateURL

Remove-SPBusinessDataCatalogModel

Remove-SPClaimProvider

Remove-SPClaimTypeMapping

Remove-SPConfigurationDatabase

Remove-SPContentDatabase

Remove-SPContentDeploymentJob

Remove-SPContentDeploymentPath

Remove-SPDiagnosticsPerformanceCounter

Remove-SPEnterpriseSearchCrawlComponent

Remove-SPEnterpriseSearchCrawlContentSource

Remove-SPEnterpriseSearchCrawlCustomConnector

Remove-SPEnterpriseSearchCrawlDatabase

Remove-SPEnterpriseSearchCrawlExtension

Remove-SPEnterpriseSearchCrawlMapping

Remove-SPEnterpriseSearchCrawlRule

Remove-SPEnterpriseSearchCrawlTopology

Remove-SPEnterpriseSearchExtendedConnectorProperty

Remove-SPEnterpriseSearchLanguageResourcePhrase

Remove-SPEnterpriseSearchMetadataCategory

Remove-SPEnterpriseSearchMetadataManagedProperty

Remove-SPEnterpriseSearchMetadataMapping

Remove-SPEnterpriseSearchPropertyDatabase

Remove-SPEnterpriseSearchQueryAuthority

Remove-SPEnterpriseSearchQueryComponent

Remove-SPEnterpriseSearchQueryDemoted

Remove-SPEnterpriseSearchQueryKeyword

Remove-SPEnterpriseSearchQueryScope

Remove-SPEnterpriseSearchQueryScopeRule

Remove-SPEnterpriseSearchQueryTopology

Remove-SPEnterpriseSearchRankingModel

Remove-SPEnterpriseSearchSecurityTrimmer

Remove-SPEnterpriseSearchServiceApplication

Remove-SPEnterpriseSearchServiceApplicationProxy

Remove-SPEnterpriseSearchSiteHitRule

Remove-SPExcelBlockedFileType

Remove-SPExcelDataConnectionLibrary

Remove-SPExcelDataProvider

Remove-SPExcelFileLocation

Remove-SPExcelUserDefinedFunction

Remove-SPInfoPathUserAgent

Remove-SPManagedAccount

Remove-SPManagedPath

Remove-SPPerformancePointServiceApplication

Remove-SPPerformancePointServiceApplicationProxy

Remove-SPPerformancePointServiceApplicationTrustedLocation

Remove-SPPluggableSecurityTrimmer

Remove-SPSecureStoreApplication

Remove-SPServiceApplication

Remove-SPServiceApplicationPool

Remove-SPServiceApplicationProxy

Remove-SPServiceApplicationProxyGroup

Remove-SPServiceApplicationProxyGroupMember

Remove-SPShellAdmin

Remove-SPSite

Remove-SPSiteSubscription

Remove-SPSiteSubscriptionBusinessDataCatalogConfig

Remove-SPSiteSubscriptionFeaturePack

Remove-SPSiteSubscriptionFeaturePackMember

Remove-SPSiteSubscriptionMetadataConfig

Remove-SPSiteSubscriptionProfileConfig

Remove-SPSiteSubscriptionSettings

Remove-SPSocialItemByDate

Remove-SPSolution

Remove-SPSolutionDeploymentLock

Remove-SPStateServiceDatabase

Remove-SPTrustedIdentityTokenIssuer

Remove-SPTrustedRootAuthority

Remove-SPTrustedServiceTokenIssuer

Remove-SPUsageApplication

Remove-SPUser

Remove-SPUserSolution

Remove-SPVisioSafeDataProvider

Remove-SPWeb

Remove-SPWebApplication

Remove-SPWordConversionServiceJobHistory

Rename-SPServer

Repair-SPManagedAccountDeployment

Restart-SPEnterpriseSearchQueryComponent

Restore-SPEnterpriseSearchServiceApplication

Restore-SPFarm

Restore-SPSite

Resume-SPEnterpriseSearchServiceApplication

Resume-SPStateServiceDatabase

Revoke-SPBusinessDataCatalogMetadataObject

Revoke-SPObjectSecurity

Set-SPAccessServiceApplication

Set-SPAlternateURL

Set-SPBrowserCustomerExperienceImprovementProgram

Set-SPBusinessDataCatalogMetadataObject

Set-SPBusinessDataCatalogServiceApplication

Set-SPBusinessDataCatalogThrottleConfig

Set-SPCentralAdministration

Set-SPClaimProvider

Set-SPContentDatabase

Set-SPContentDeploymentJob

Set-SPContentDeploymentPath

Set-SPCustomLayoutsPage

Set-SPDataConnectionFile

Set-SPDesignerSettings

Set-SPDiagnosticConfig

Set-SPDiagnosticsProvider

Set-SPEnterpriseSearchAdministrationComponent

Set-SPEnterpriseSearchCrawlContentSource

Set-SPEnterpriseSearchCrawlDatabase

Set-SPEnterpriseSearchCrawlRule

Set-SPEnterpriseSearchCrawlTopology

Set-SPEnterpriseSearchExtendedConnectorProperty

Set-SPEnterpriseSearchExtendedQueryProperty

Set-SPEnterpriseSearchIndexPartition

Set-SPEnterpriseSearchMetadataCategory

Set-SPEnterpriseSearchMetadataCrawledProperty

Set-SPEnterpriseSearchMetadataManagedProperty

Set-SPEnterpriseSearchMetadataMapping

Set-SPEnterpriseSearchPropertyDatabase

Set-SPEnterpriseSearchQueryAuthority

Set-SPEnterpriseSearchQueryComponent

Set-SPEnterpriseSearchQueryKeyword

Set-SPEnterpriseSearchQueryScope

Set-SPEnterpriseSearchQueryScopeRule

Set-SPEnterpriseSearchQueryTopology

Set-SPEnterpriseSearchRankingModel

Set-SPEnterpriseSearchService

Set-SPEnterpriseSearchServiceApplication

Set-SPEnterpriseSearchServiceApplicationProxy

Set-SPEnterpriseSearchServiceInstance

Set-SPExcelDataConnectionLibrary

Set-SPExcelDataProvider

Set-SPExcelFileLocation

Set-SPExcelServiceApplication

Set-SPExcelUserDefinedFunction

Set-SPFarmConfig

Set-SPInfoPathFormsService

Set-SPInfoPathFormTemplate

Set-SPInfoPathWebServiceProxy

Set-SPLogLevel

Set-SPManagedAccount

Set-SPMetadataServiceApplication

Set-SPMetadataServiceApplicationProxy

Set-SPMobileMessagingAccount

Set-SPPassPhrase

Set-SPPerformancePointSecureDataValues

Set-SPPerformancePointServiceApplication

Set-SPProfileServiceApplication

Set-SPProfileServiceApplicationProxy

Set-SPProfileServiceApplicationSecurity

Set-SPSearchService

Set-SPSearchServiceInstance

Set-SPSecureStoreApplication

Set-SPSecureStoreDefaultProvider

Set-SPSecureStoreServiceApplication

Set-SPSecurityTokenServiceConfig

Set-SPServiceApplication

Set-SPServiceApplicationEndpoint

Set-SPServiceApplicationPool

Set-SPServiceApplicationSecurity

Set-SPServiceHostConfig

Set-SPSessionStateService

Set-SPSite

Set-SPSiteAdministration

Set-SPSiteSubscriptionConfig

Set-SPSiteSubscriptionEdiscoveryHub

Set-SPSiteSubscriptionMetadataConfig

Set-SPSiteSubscriptionProfileConfig

Set-SPStateServiceApplication

Set-SPStateServiceApplicationProxy

Set-SPStateServiceDatabase

Set-SPSubscriptionSettingsServiceApplication

Set-SPTimerJob

Set-SPTopologyServiceApplication

Set-SPTopologyServiceApplicationProxy

Set-SPTrustedIdentityTokenIssuer

Set-SPTrustedRootAuthority

Set-SPTrustedServiceTokenIssuer

Set-SPUsageApplication

Set-SPUsageDefinition

Set-SPUsageService

Set-SPUser

Set-SPVisioExternalData

Set-SPVisioPerformance

Set-SPVisioSafeDataProvider

Set-SPVisioServiceApplication

Set-SPWeb

Set-SPWebAnalyticsServiceApplication

Set-SPWebAnalyticsServiceApplicationProxy

Set-SPWebApplication

Set-SPWebApplicationHttpThrottlingMonitor

Set-SPWebTemplate

Set-SPWordConversionServiceApplication

Set-SPWorkflowConfig

Start-SPAdminJob

Start-SPAssignment

Start-SPContentDeploymentJob

Start-SPEnterpriseSearchQueryAndSiteSettingsServiceInstance

Start-SPEnterpriseSearchServiceInstance

Start-SPInfoPathFormTemplate

Start-SPServiceInstance

Start-SPTimerJob

Stop-SPAssignment

Stop-SPEnterpriseSearchQueryAndSiteSettingsServiceInstance

Stop-SPEnterpriseSearchServiceInstance

Stop-SPInfoPathFormTemplate

Stop-SPServiceInstance

Suspend-SPEnterpriseSearchServiceApplication

Suspend-SPStateServiceDatabase

Test-SPContentDatabase

Test-SPInfoPathFormTemplate

Uninstall-SPDataConnectionFile

Uninstall-SPFeature

Uninstall-SPHelpCollection

Uninstall-SPInfoPathFormTemplate

Uninstall-SPSolution

Uninstall-SPUserSolution

Uninstall-SPWebPartPack

Uninstall-SPWebTemplate

Unpublish-SPServiceApplication

Update-SPFarmEncryptionKey

Update-SPInfoPathAdminFileUrl

Update-SPInfoPathFormTemplate

Update-SPInfoPathUserFileUrl

Update-SPProfilePhotoStore

Update-SPSecureStoreApplicationServerKey

Update-SPSecureStoreCredentialMapping

Update-SPSecureStoreGroupCredentialMapping

Update-SPSecureStoreMasterKey

Update-SPSolution

Update-SPUserSolution

Upgrade-SPContentDatabase

Upgrade-SPEnterpriseSearchServiceApplication

Upgrade-SPSingleSignOnDatabase

Index

A

AAMs (alternate access mappings), 128, 137–139, 469–470
access control, 171
Access Database Services, 70
Access Server Settings page, 188
Access Services, 187–189
  software requirements for, 7
account management, 453–460
Active Directory
  account creation, 21
  configuring for incoming e-mail, 89–90
  groups, 174, 453
  organizational units, delegating permissions to, 89–90
  schema, extending, 90
Active Directory Domain Services (AD DS), 430
Active Directory Rights Management Services (Active Directory RMS) IRM, 460
Add and Customize Pages permissions, 176
Add Content Source page, 196, 247
Add Content Types page, 153
Add Crawl Component page, 255–256
Add Crawl Database dialog box, 254–255
Add Crawl Rule page, 248
Add Federated Location page, 271
Add File Type page, 251
Add Host Rule page, 259–260
Add Items permissions, 175
Add Keyword page, 294
Add New Synchronization Connection page, 431
Add Personalization Site Link page, 445–446
Add Property Database dialog box, 256–257
Add Published Link page, 447
Add Query Component dialog box, 258
Add/Remove Personal Web Parts permissions, 178
AD DS (Active Directory Domain Services), 430

Add Scope Rule page, 286
Add Server Name Mapping page, 250
Add Trusted Data Connection Library page, 193
Add Trusted File Location page, 191
Add Trusted Host Location page, 444
Add User-Defined Assembly page, 193
Add User Profile Property page, 427–428
administration interface of service applications, 182
administrative tasks
  farm account for, 4
  Windows PowerShell for, 24–26
administrative tools
  Central Administration. *See* Central Administration; Central Administration Web site
  stsadm.exe, 82
  Windows PowerShell, 82
administrators
  assigning, 4
  of Managed Metadata Service, 341–342, 532
  secondary site collection administrators, 146
  of service applications, 185
  site collection administrators, 146, 147, 171–172
  site creation, 142
  term store administrators, 344
Administrators dialog box, 185
Administrators For User Profile Service Application dialog box, 425–426
Advanced Search pages, 305–310
Advanced Search Web part, 278, 306
  languages, 308
  Miscellaneous section, 309
  Properties section, 307
  Property Definition section, 308–309
  Scopes section, 307
  search queries, passing, 310
alerts
  configuring for, 37
  creating, 160–161
  for mobile accounts, 134–135
  Mobile Alert feature, 93
  throttling, 93, 134

alerts (*continued*)
    for Web applications, 130–131
    for workflows, 133
All Content scope rules, 287
AllowCASPolicies, 231
AllowGACDeployment, 231
All Site Content page, 209
alternate access mappings (AAMs)
    accessing, 137–138
    changes, 469–470
    configuring, 139
    managing, 128
Alternate Access Mappings area (Farm Management), 96
Alternate Access Mappings page, 138
analytics information service, 201. *See also* Web Analytics
Announcements list, 146
anonymous access, 118
    site collections, enabling for, 474–475
    Web applications, enabling for, 474
anonymous messages, allowing, 37
antivirus protection, 480–481
application bits, 182
application connection groups, editing, 184–185
Application Logs, 490
Application Management section (Central Administration), 83, 97, 188
application.master pages, 131
application pool accounts, 9
application pools, 111–112
    configuring, 120
    creating, 39
    extended sites and, 125
    finding, 471
    for Managed Metadata Services and Content Type Syndication Hub, 332
    isolating, 4
    for publishing content types and metadata, 336
    for search service, 244–245
    for service applications, 182, 421
    sharing, 112
    for upgraded shared services, 533
application proxy groups, 184
Application Registry Service, 70
Application Registry Service database, 36
application servers, 51
    RBS, installing on, 45–46
    for service application redundancy, 182
    service applications on, 181
    services, placing on, 70–73

application services, finding and viewing, 86
Apply Style Sheets permissions, 177
Apply Themes and Borders permissions, 176
Approval workflow, 374
Approve Items permissions, 176
artifacts
    deploying, 222. *See also* full-trust solutions
    retracting, 228–230
ASP.NET, membership and role provider settings, 119
assemblies
    Safe Control entries, 206
    for Web parts, 206
assigned IP addresses, 124
    use of, 65
associations, changing, 339
audiences, 200
audience targeting, 151
auditing, 389–390
    Information Management, 464
auditing policy features, 167
auditing reports, 404
audit trial policies, 389–390
authentication
    Basic authentication, 473–474
    for crawl rules, 249–250
    double-hop issue, 476
    for federated locations, 276–277
    for Web applications, 470–475
    Windows Integrated authentication, 470–472
authentication providers, 118
authentication types
    for databases, 122
    for Web applications, 115, 125
authoritative pages, defining, 268–270
authored search scopes, 284
Authoritative Web Pages input boxes, 268–269
Auto Host Distribution page, 260–261
Automatically Declare Items As Records When They Are Added To This List option, 394
Automatic password changes, 457–458
auto-navigation, 415
availability, Search Service, 79–80

B

backup
before upgrading, 526
capacity for, 541, 544
with Central Administration, 542–547, 556
disk write speeds and, 541
errors during, 544
granular, 555–560
long-term storage and, 541
network speed and, 541
restoring from, 547
scheduling, 552
of server farms, 540–552
of service applications, 553–555
of site collections, 555–559
strategy for, 540
with Stsadm.exe, 551–552, 559
tools for, 539. *See also* Central Administration; Stsadm.exe; Windows PowerShell
troubleshooting, 545
of Web applications, 553–555
with Windows PowerShell, 547–550, 556–558
Backup And Restore area (Central Administration), 84
backup files, storage of, 540–541
Backup-SPFarm cmdlet, 548
Backup-SPSite cmdlet, 557
bar code labels, 464
barcode policy features, 167
bar codes, document, 390
Basic authentication, 116, 119, 473–474
for crawl rules, 249
Basic Search Centers
search pages, 298
site template, 297
BCPs (Business Continuity Plans), 539–540
BCS (Business Connectivity Services), 189
BDC (Business Data Catalog), 189
BDC (Business Data Connectivity) Services, 24, 70, 430
Bdc_Service_DB_<GUID>, 26
Best Bet management dialog box, 295–296
Best Bets, 293–296
display of, 296
managing, 295
Best Bets Web part, 295, 319–320
binaries
installing, 528
SharePoint Foundation 2010, 15–16
SharePoint Server 2010, 28–30, 49–50

binary large objects (BLOBs), storage of, 43–46
blocked file types, for Web applications, 478–479
Blocked File Types list, 151
Blog API, 130
blog settings, 130
Body Only page layout, 208
Boolean Ignore SSL Warnings choice, 241
breadcrumb links to portal sites, 166
Browse Directories permissions, 177
browser file handling settings, 130
Browse User Information permissions, 177
Business Connectivity Service DB, 26, 35
Business Connectivity Services (BCS), 189
Business Continuity Plans (BCPs), 539–540
Business Data Catalog (BDC), 189
Business Data Connectivity (BDC) Services, 24, 70, 430

C

cabinet (.CAB) files, 222
calendar settings, 148
CAS (Code Access Security) policies, 225
CEIP (Customer Experience Improvement Program), 97, 123, 132
Central Administration, 81–86
Application Management section, 97, 188
architecture of, 82–84
areas of, 83–84
Backup And Restore section, 545
changes made from, 65
Configure Alternate Access Mappings, 63, 128
Configure Password Change Settings, 457
Configure Send To Connections, 106
Configure Service Application Associations section, 338, 339
Configure The Data Retrieval Service, 104
content database, 83
content database upgrade status, 536
Crawler Impact Rules management page, 241
deploying to other servers, 84
Farm Backup And Restore section, 542
features management from, 217–218
full-trust solutions, deleting with, 230
full-trust solutions, deploying with, 226–227

Central Administration (*continued*)
General Application Settings section, 196
Health Analyzer Rules Definition page, 495
IM Policy Configuration page, 462
IRM management in, 461
Manage Content Databases, 113
for managed accounts configuration, 454
Manage Farm Solutions link, 226
Manage Service Applications page, 183, 420
Manage Services On Server, 67
Manage Web Applications page, 110–111, 339
Monitoring link, 496
permission levels, 483
provisioning, 84–85
Recycle Bin management from, 165
repairing, 86
Review Problems And Solutions page, 200
Ribbon interface, 128–129
Search Administration page, 73
security of, 83
Send To function configuration, 398
for server farm backup and restore, 541–547
service application management from, 66
Services On Server page, 69, 341
SharePoint 2010 Timer, 93
SharePoint Designer 2010 policy management, 486–487
site collection backups with, 556
site collection creation with, 334
site creation in, 145–147
social features, enabling with, 436–437
solutions, retracting with, 229
System Settings area, 86–97
unattached databases in, 560
unprovisioning, 86
Upgrade Status screen, 530
Web application creation in, 110
Web application management with, 110–111
working with Web applications in, 84–86
zone management with, 481
Central Administration content database, 26, 35

Central Administration service, 70
Central Administration Web application, server host for, 51
Central Administration Web site
Configuration Wizards page, 23
Configure Alternate Access Mappings, 47
configuring, 20
hosts for, 61
installation of, 36
Manage The Farm Administrators Group tab, 36
Manage Web Applications, 37
Monitoring page, 40
centralized search environments, 297
.cer files, 478
certificate authorities, 465–467
check in/check out, 149–150, 370
Check Permissions dialog box, 180
Claims-Based authentication, 115, 119, 199
security configuration, 118–119
Classic Mode Authentication, 115
security configuration, 117–119
classification of content, 329–330
click distance, 268
client applications, adding links to, 447–448
client certificates, 249
Closed Web Parts gallery, 210
Code Access Security (CAS) policies, 225
collaboration on documents, 363
collaboration spaces, and offline access, 377
Colleagues feature, 436
Collect Feedback workflow, 374
Collect Signatures workflow, 374
.com files, 479
Compliance Details command, 391
Compliance dialog box, 391–392
compliance management functions, 401–404
compliance officers, 385
config DB, 26
Config directory, 266
configuration
post-installation, 36–49
problems, viewing, 497
settings, backing up, 543
configuration databases, 81, 109
administrative access to, 453
connecting to, 58
provisioning, 19

configuration databases (*continued*)
    servers, removing from, 87
    specifying settings, 59
    SQL Server cluster for, 57
Configuration Wizards area (Central Administration), 84
Configure Cross-Firewall Access Zone area (Farm Management), 97
Configure Incoming E-mail Settings (System Settings), 90–91
Configure Privacy Options area (Farm Management), 97
Configure Service Accounts page, 243
Configure Service Application Associations dialog box, 184, 339
Configure Synchronization Settings page, 435
Confirm parameter (features), 217
Confirm Site Use And Deletion link, 143
connection filters, editing, 431
connections
    default service connections list, 338
    Managed Metadata Service Connection, 338
    profile synchronization, 430–433
    Web part connections, 211–212
connection strings of Web parts, 214
Connect To A Remote Service Application dialog box, 186
contacts
    creating, 90
    storing, 89
content
    approval for documents and document sets, 372–373
    backing up, 543
    classification of, 329–330
    content metadata, 156
    content pages, adding Web parts to, 208–209
    offline access to, 377
Content Access account, 9
content crawling, 79
content databases, 26, 35, 112–115
    attaching to Web applications, 524–525, 534–536
    backing up, 526
    Central Administration, 83
    configuration options, 98
    Database Capacity settings, 114
    database information, 113
    Database Versioning and Upgrade property, 114
    deleting, 126

content databases (*continued*)
    Failover Server setting, 114
    isolation of, 112
    management of, 98–104, 113–115, 128
    naming, 39
    Preferred Server For Timer Jobs setting, 114
    properties of, 113–114
    read-only, 100
    recovering, 545
    Remove Content Database setting, 114
    removing, 114
    Search Server setting, 114
    site collections, number of, 99–100
    sizes of, 98–99
    state of, viewing, 101
    status of, 100
    unattached, restoring, 559–560
    upgrading, 533–534
    for Web applications, 109
    Web applications and site collections and, 110
content database servers, default, 104
content locations
    adding, 196–197
    trusted, 195
content organizer
    enabling, 379
    Send To function and, 379
Content Organizer feature, enabling, 106
Content Organizer Processing timer jobs, 381
content organizer rules, 379–380, 397
    creating, 399–400
    verifying, 400
content sources
    adding, 196–197
    crawling, 198
    creating, 246–247
    types of, 247
Content Source scope rules, 287
Content Sources link, 247
content types, 156–158, 349
    configuration settings, 371
    creating, 349–350
    dependencies of, 351
    in document libraries, 153, 370–371
    document management and, 349–351
    document sets, 367–368
    enterprise level, 329–331, 386

content types (*continued*)
information management policies, associating with, 168
information management policy on, 387
levels of, 371
management of, enabling, 368
management of, in lists, 371
management settings, 150
for page layouts, 411
republishing, 391
scope of, 156
sealed, 351
submission content types, 380
Content Types Subscriber timer jobs, 391
Content Type Syndication Hub, 331–332
activating, 335
isolation of, 332
multiple, 333–334
naming, 336
site collection, creating, 333–334
Web application, creating, 332
content zones, 411
contextual search scopes, 284
Contribute permissions, 175
Contributor role, 343
cookie-based authentication, for crawl rules, 250
core operations, 81
Core Search Results, 312–317
corruptions, repairing, 524
crawl components, adding, 255–256
crawl databases, 36, 254–255
host distribution rules, 258–259
redundancy and availability of, 80
crawled properties, 278–284
bulk actions on, 283–284
categories of, 282–283
editing, 281–282
grouping, 278
mapping, 278–279, 282
Crawled Properties page, 281
crawler impact rules, 241–242
Crawler Impact Rules management page, 241
crawlers, 239
crawl rate, 242
crawl times, 242
farm-wide search settings, 240–241
functionality of, 240
redundancy and availability of, 80
requests, number of, 242
Crawl History page, 259

crawling
after adding keywords, 296
content sources, 198
full crawls, 282
recrawls, 289
crawl logs, 259–263
Crawl History view, 262–263
Error Message view, 263
URL page, 261–262
Crawl Logs page, 259–261
crawl rule paths, 249–250
crawl rules
adding, 197–198
application of, 248
authentication, 249–250
exclude/include options, 249
file type management, 250–252
for lists and libraries, 326–327
managing, 247–250
site-level rules, 326–327
crawl times, improving, 78
Create Alerts permissions, 176
Create A New Server Farm option, 18
Create Column page, 353
Create Group page, 172
Create Groups permissions, 177
Create New Managed Metadata Service dialog box, 336
Create New User Profile Service Application dialog box, 420–421
Create New Web Application dialog box, 332
Create Personal Site feature, 436
Create, Read, Update, and Delete (CRUD) functions, 158–160
Create Site Collection page, 145–146
Create Site Collections link, 145
Create Subsites permissions, 176
credential management, 459
Cross-Web Part Query ID picker, 316–317
Cross-Web Part Query ID property, 311
Current Navigation menu, 415–418
custom code, 221
installing in server farms, 64
upgrading and, 537
Customer Experience Improvement Program (CEIP), 97, 123, 132
custom locations, installing SharePoint to, 29
custom site groups, creating, 171–172

D

database attach upgrades, 518, 533–536
  planning for, 519–520
database errors, resolving, 524
database maintenance, 26
database management, 97–105
database mirroring, 40, 114, 122
database names, configuring, 121
databases
  authentication type, configuring, 122
  cleaning, 523–524
  created during installation, 26, 35
  dedicated SQL Server installation
    for, 3
  location, configuring, 103
  securing access to, 452
  for service applications, 182
  size of, 98
  Web application logical structure in,
    109
database servers
  default, 104
  number of, 55
  RBS, installing on, 45
  specifying, 121
data files, separating from transaction log
  files, 102
data integrity, 369
data repositories, 350
  organization of, 331
Data Retrieval Service, configuring,
  104–105
datasheet mode, 151
Deactivate Feature Warning page, 438
Declare Record button, 394
dedicated servers
  grouping services and databases
    on, 56
  for sandboxed solutions, 233
Default Content Access Account, 246
default content database servers, 104
default permissions, 484
default service connections list, 338
default URLs
  choosing, 123
  editing, 140
default workflows, 374
default zone, 481
deleted documents, preservation in
  Recycle Bin, 164
Delete Items permissions, 175
deletes, restricting, 369

Delete Service Application dialog box,
  424–425
Delete Versions permissions, 176
dependencies of content types, 351
Deployed element (solutions), 224
deployment locations, 222
  for full-trust solutions, 225
Deploy Solution hyperlink, 227
Design permissions, 174
destination sites, enabling Content
  Organizer feature for, 106
developer artifacts. *See also* full-trust
  solutions; sandboxed solutions
  managing, 221
diagnostic logging, 514
  configuring, 42–43
Diagnostic Logging page, 501–502
diagnostics. *See* logging; monitoring
DIPs (Document Information Panels), 351,
  356–360
Directory Management Service, 89–90
discover and hold records, 402–403
discussion lists, 162–163
discussion topics
  creating, 163
  replies, posting, 163
  views of, 162–163
disk usage, logging and, 503
Display Groups page, 292
Disposition Approval workflow, 374
distribution groups, creating, 90
distribution lists
  creating, 91
  creating automatically, 90
  storing, 89
.dll files, 479
DNS configuration for incoming e-mail,
  92
DNS entries for Web servers, 63
document bar codes, 390
document centers, 378–383
  adding documents, 378–379
  content organizer feature, 379–382
  default functionality, 378
document collaboration, 363
Document content type, 153, 350
Document Conversions Launcher service,
  51, 70
Document Conversions Load Balancer
  service, 70
document declaration, 392–394
  locked documents and, 394
document IDs, 365–367

Document ID Service, enabling, 366
Document Information Panels (DIPs), 356–359
  custom, 359–360
  default, 356
  overwriting of, 351
  Required Properties warning, 356
  templates, uploading or publishing, 359
Document Information Panel Settings link, 359–360
document labels, 390–392
document libraries, 363–365, 386
  Advanced Settings page, 150
  Allow Manual Submission setting, 400
  audience targeting, 151
  Blocked File Types list, 151
  check in/check out, 370
  column values settings, 151
  configuring, 364
  content organizer rules, 397
  content types and, 153–154, 370–371
  creating and managing, 148–154
  custom Send To destination links, 381
  datasheet mode, 151
  document sets, enabling, 367–368
  draft item security, 373–374
  filtering and sorting content in, 383
  inbound e-mail, enabling for, 375–377
  information management policies, associating with, 168
  information management policies for, 397
  IRM settings, 461–462
  manual submission, 400–401
  metadata navigation, 151, 382–383
  offline client availability settings, 151
  permissions for, 364–365
  retention settings, 386–388
  source template document types, 371
  templates of, 364
  validation settings, 151
  version control in, 372–374
  view management, 151
Document Library Settings page, 153, 168
document life cycles, 362. See also document management
document management, 361–383. See also managed metadata; metadata; taxonomies
  content types and, 349–351
  vs. document collaboration, 363
  document libraries, 363–365

document management (continued)
  inbound e-mail, enabling, 375–377
  metadata, gathering for, 356
  overhead of, 363
  version control, 149–150, 372–374
  workflows, 374–375
document management plans, 362–363
  catalog of document types, 362
  document movement plans, 362
  document versioning requirements, 372
  organizational taxonomy, 362
  participant roles descriptions, 362
  workflow plans, 362
document repositories, 378. See also document centers
documents. See also document management; records
  check in/check out, 149–150, 370
  compliance details, 391
  content approval, 372–373
  conversion into Microsoft Office Word formats, 201
  dialog box settings, 151
  document center, sending to, 389
  folder settings, 151
  major and minor versioning, 373
  nonrecords, 388–389
  opening settings, 150
  ownership of, 370
  ratings for, 151
  restoring from Recycle Bin, 165
  search settings, 151
  send to options, 150
  size limitations on, 152
  tagging, 357–358
Document Set content types, 368–369
document sets, 365, 367–369
  content approval, 372–373
document submission, journaling methods, 401
document templates, 149, 150
domain administrators, 453
double-hop issue, 476
draft item security, 373–374
drop-off libraries, 379, 381

E

ECM (enterprise content management), 329–331
Edit Connection Filters page, 432
Edit Crawled Property page, 282
Edit Items permissions, 175

Edit Permissions page, 179
Edit Personal User Information permissions, 177
Edit Policy page, 167
Edit Scope Display Group page, 292–293
Edit Trusted Content Location dialog box, 196
Edit User Profile Property page, 434
Edit User Profile Service Application dialog box, 423
element files, 215
e-mail. *See also* inbound e-mail; outgoing e-mail
 integrating SharePoint with, 375
E-mail and Text Messages section (System Settings), 88–93
e-mail drop folders, 91
end user Recycle Bin, 164
enterprise content management (ECM), 329–331
enterprise content types, 329–331
Enterprise Search Centers, 297–298
 results page, 310
 search pages, 298
 site template, 297
Enumerate Permissions permissions, 177
EnumSolutions, 224–225
errors, in upgrading, 530
event logs, 490–491, 504
 disk space usage, 43
 flood protection, 43
 storage of, 43
 tracing, 43
events, logging, 40
event throttling, configuring, 42, 502–503
Excel Calculation services, 70
Excel Services, 189–194
 configuring, 190–191
 trusted data connection libraries, 192–193
 trusted file locations, 191–192
 user-defined function assemblies, registering, 193–194
Excel Services Application Settings page, 190
.exe files, 479
expansion sets for search thesaurus, 267–268
expiration policy features, 167
exporting information, 429
extended zones, deleting, 127
external certificate authorities, 465–466
external data sources, 430
external entity management systems, 435

F

Failed Request Tracing Rules, 494
failover database servers, 40
 defining, 122
failover servers
 for social tagging database, 422
 for synchronization database, 422
farm account, for administrative tasks, 4
farm administrators, 343
 access privileges, 453
 configuring, 36
 delegation capability, 424
 User Profile Service administration, 424–425
Farm Administrators group, 36
 service application management, 184–186
 updating, 453
farm backups. *See also* backup
 before deletions, 126
 content and configuration settings, backing up, 543
Farm Configuration Wizard, 23–24, 32–33
 Configure Your SharePoint Farm page, 23, 24
 running, 32–33
 for service application deployment, 183
 for State Service configuration, 199–200
 Web application creation with, 110
farm encryption keys (FEKs), 459
Farm Management area (System Settings), 96–97
farm operations, core operations, 81–107
farm passphrases, 459–460
farm planning for upgrades, 519–526
farm security. *See also* security
 Completing the SharePoint Products Configuration Wizard page, 21
farm topologies, 9–13
Farm-Wide Search Administration page, 243
farm-wide search settings, 240–241
Farm-Wide Search Settings page, 241
FAST indexes, 274
FAST Search Center site template, 297
fault tolerance, 52
Favorite Links section, 446
FBA (Forms-Based authentication), 116, 119, 250
feature header files, 215
feature receivers, 216

features, 205, 215
    activating and deactivating, 217–220
    architecture of, 215–216
    Central Adminsitration management of, 217–218
    dependencies of, 216
    element files, 215
    feature header files, 215
    installing, 216–217
    life cycle of, 216–217
    managing, 136–137
    scopes of, 215
    uninstalling, 220–221
    uses of, 215
Feature.xml files, 215, 217
Federated Claims authentication, 119
Federated Location Definition (FLD) files, 271
federated locations
    adding, 271
    authentication for, 276–277
    author information, 272
    copying, 277
    deleting, 277
    description, 271–272
    display information, 275–276
    editing, 271
    exporting, 277
    location information, 274–275
    managing, 270–277
    name of, 271
    prefix trigger, 273
    restrictions, 276
    trigger configuration, 272
    version information, 272
federated queries, 270–277
Federated Results Web part, 275, 318–319
feeds, subscribing to, 164
FEKs (farm encryption keys), 459
field controls, placement of, 411
file access, 331
Filename parameter (features), 219, 221
file plan matrix, 395
file plan reports, 403–404
file retention, approaches to, 330
file shares, 330–331
    backing up to, 540–541, 544, 545
FILESTREAM, enabling, 43
file types, blocking, 479
file upload properties, 358–359
firewalls, 452
FLD (Federated Location Definition) files, 271
flood protection, for event logs, 43

folders, in publishing site libraries, 415
folksonomies, 330, 342, 344
Force parameter (features), 220, 221
Forms-Based authentication (FBA), 116, 119
    for crawl rules, 250
forms, custom, 156
Form Settings page, 158
Full Control permissions, 142, 174
full crawls, 282. *See also* crawling
full-trust solutions, 221–232
    adding, 223–224
    contents, inspecting, 222
    deleting, 230–231
    deploying, 222, 225–228
    ID of, 224
    life cycle of, 222–223
    managing, 223–225
    Manifest.xml file, 225
    retracting, 228–230
    upgrading, 231–232

G

GAC (global assembly cache), 225
General Application Settings area (Central Administration), 84
Get-SPFeature cmdlet, 438
Get-SPServiceApplication cmdlets, 425
global assembly cache (GAC), solutions deployed to, 225
Global Navigation menu, 415–418
global password management settings, 457–458
global taxonomies, 342
Go To Top Level Site Settings hyperlink, 218
governance, with Web application policies, 481–487
grant sets, 27
granular backup and restore, 555–560
Groove, 377
Group manager role, 343
group permissions
    custom levels, 175–177
    default levels, 174
    viewing, 172–173
groups
    nesting Active Directory groups in, 174
    security groups, 171

H

hardware requirements, 5–6
Header-Footer-4-Columns page, 209
Health Analyzer, 200, 496–498
  Review Problems And Solutions
    screen, 496–497
  Rule Definitions page, 497–498
Health Analyzer Reports list, 200
health-related timer jobs, 41
Health Reports list, 200
health status data collection service, 199
Hierarchy Manager permissions, 142
high availability
  increasing, 53
  scaling out for, 51
host distribution rules, managing,
  258–259
Host Distribution Rules management
  page, 259
host headers, 3, 63
  defining, 117, 124
  with wildcard SSL certificates, 465
hosts, for My Site Web sites, 442
hotfix KB963676, 27
HTTP, accessing Web applications with,
  469–470
HTTPS, accessing Web applications with,
  469–470

I

identity management services, 199
Identity parameter (features), 220, 221
identity providers, 118–119
Identity Provider Security Token Service
  (IP-STS), 118
ID parameter (features), 219–220, 221
iFilters, 240, 251–252
IIS (Internet Information Services), 37, 65,
  111–112, 494–495
IISReset, 530
IIS Web sites
  creating, 116
  deleting, 126, 127
  path for, 117
  port numbers for, 117
  removing SharePoint from, 127
I Like It button, 436
import files, for term sets, 348–349
importing information, 429
inbound e-mail
  configuring, 89–93
  contributions from outside the
    organization, allowing, 376–377

inbound e-mail (continued)
  DNS configuration, 92
  enabling in document libraries,
    375–377
  list e-mail address, 375
  lists and libraries for, 92
  Safe E-Mail Servers setting, 92
  server display address, 92
  submissions, grouping, 376
incoming traffic, zones, 120
indexer, functionality of, 240
indexes, 74, 239
  freshness, improving, 78
  removing information from, 289
index partitions, 74, 257, 258
  redundancy and availability of, 79
index servers, placing services on, 70
Information Management (IM) Policies,
  167–169, 385–392, 462–464
  auditing, 389–390
  creating, 167
  defining, 386
  document bar codes, 390
  document labels, 390–392
  document libraries, associating with,
    168
  in-place records management,
    392–394
  nonrecords, 388–389
  policy features, 167
  record center design and, 395–396
  records, 389
  retention, 387–388
information policies, 460–464
Information Rights Management (IRM),
  249, 460–462
in-place records management, 385,
  392–394
in-place upgrades, 526–533
  upgrade process tasks, 518–519
installation
  considerations for, 7
  databases created during, 26, 35
  of first SharePoint Foundation 2010
    server, 13
  of first SharePoint Server 2010 server,
    26–36
  hardware and software requirements,
    5–6
  preparing for, 4–9
  prerequisites, 7–8
  service accounts, planning, 8–9
  of SharePoint Foundation 2010, 4

installation (*continued*)
    of SharePoint Foundation 2010
      binaries, 15–17
    SharePoint Products and
      Technologies Preparation Tool,
      14–15
installation media, 526
Install Or Uninstall Display Languages
    dialog box, 48
internal certificate authorities, 467–468
internal URLs, editing, 140
Internet Information Services (IIS), 37
    application pools, 111–112
    health and diagnostic tools, 494–495
    for server farm management, 65
Internet Information Services (IIS)
    Manager, configuring SSL in, 465–466
IP addresses
    assigned, 3
    assigning, 469
    assigning to Web applications, 46–47
IP-STS (Identity Provider Security Token
    Service), 118
IRM (Information Rights Management),
    249, 460–462

J

journaling methods, 401

K

Kerberos, 471–473
    for user authentication, 118
    service principal name, 125
Kerberos Distribution Center (KDC), 118
key filters, configuring, 360
keyword search tool, 294
keywords, managed, 347, 359–360
keywords, search, 293–296
    adding, 294–295
    display of, 296
    filter views of, 294
    keyword definitions, 295

L

labeling policy features, 167
labels, Information Management, 464
language packs
    installing, 47–49
    as SharePoint prerequisite, 520

languages
    for My Site Web sites, 443
    for sites, 145
large farms, 12–13, 56
layout of Web parts pages, 208
layout pages, customizing, 169
_layouts pages, 131
least-privileged accounts, 8
Left-Column-Header-Footer pages, 209
libraries. *See also* document libraries
    crawl rules for, 326–327
    Manual Record Declaration
      Availability option, 393
    permissions on, 364–365
    relationships to other libraries,
      369–371
    security for, 179–180
Library Based Retention Schedule page,
    386
Library Record Declaration Settings page,
    393
Library Settings administration page, 364
library types, 154
links to Office client applications, 447–448
list content types, 156
list forms, 158–160
list metadata, 349
lists
    content type management, enabling,
      371
    crawl rules for, 326–327
    Create, Read, Update, and Delete
      functions, 158–160
    creating, 154
    discussion lists, 162–163
    mail enabling, 375–376
    managed terms, linking with, 359
    managing, 154–159
    metadata naviagtion, 359–360
    relationships to other lists, 369–371
    RSS settings for, 164
    security for, 179–180
    shared list columns in, 154–155
    site columns, adding to, 156
List Settings page, 158, 164
load balancing, 53
    readying servers for, 63
    sandboxed solutions, 238
Locale settings, 148
local-only rules, 523
local server administrators, 453
locked documents, 394

log files
- creating, 501–503
- location of, 41, 503
- maximum size, 41
- for setup, 17
- size of, 503
- for upgrades, 529
- viewing, 503–504

logging
- event logs, 490–491
- events, 40
- event throttling, configuring, 502–503
- flood protection, 502
- IIS feature, 494
- Trace and Service Application log files, 504
- trace logs, 502
- usage and health data, 502–503

Logging database, 509
Logging Web Service data, 504
Lotus Notes Connector service, 70

M

major versioning, 373
Manage Alerts permissions, 177
Manage Content Sources page, 196
managed accounts, 454–456
- creating, 454–455
- editing, 455
- registering, 421
- removing, 456–457
- selecting, 121
- service accounts, 459–460

managed farm accounts, 454
managed keywords
- consumption of, 360
- converting to managed terms, 347

managed metadata, 194. *See also* metadata
- Document Information Panels and, 356–359
- roles and capabilities, 343

Managed Metadata database, 36
Managed Metadata Service, adding administrators, 532
Managed Metadata Service Applications, 531
- accessing, 336
- application pool settings, 337
- multiple, 333
- provisioning, 336–338
- publishing, 340–341
- server for, 341

Managed Metadata Service Applications (*continued*)
- settings for, 337–338
- starting, 341

Managed Metadata Service Connections
- associating with Web applications, 338–339
- managing, 338

Managed Metadata Services
- administrators of, 341–342
- configuring, 331–342
- managed taxonomies, 342

Managed Metadata Services Content Type Syndication Hub, 331–332
managed metadata site columns, 353–355
Managed Metadata Web service, 71
managed paths, 136, 145
- creating, 334
- for personal sites, 423–424
- wildcard, 147

managed properties, 278–284
- automatically generated, 284
- properties of, 279–281

managed taxonomies, 342
managed terms, 345–346
- converting from managed keywords, 347
- linking with lists, 359
- taxonomy of, 346–347

managed term sets. *See also* term sets
- creating, 345
- selecting, 354–355

Manage Excel Services Application page, 191, 192
Manage Farm Features area (Farm Management), 96, 437–438
Manage Farm Solutions area (Farm Management), 96
Manage Farm Solutions link, 226, 227
Manage Features option, 136–137
Manage Federated Locations page, 271
Manage File Types page, 250–251
Manage Keywords page, 294
Manage Lists permissions, 175
Manage Paths option, 136
Manage PerformancePoint Services Application page, 195, 196
Manage Permissions permissions, 176
Manage Personal Views permissions, 178
Manage Profile Service page, 426
Manage Profile Service: User Profile Service Application page, 426
Manage Search Application Topology page, 253

Manage Search Scope For Related Links page, 327

Manage Servers In This Farm link (Servers section), 86–87

Manage Service Applications page, 183, 243–245, 420

  Access Services link, 188

Manage Services On Server page (Servers section), 87–88

Manage Site Features hyperlink, 219

Manage User Properties page, 426, 433–434

Manage User Solutions area (Farm Management), 96

Manage Web Site permissions, 176

Manifest.xml files, 222, 225

Manual Record Declaration Availability option, 393

manual submissions for Send To connections, 107

mapping

  crawled properties, 278–279, 282

  user profile properties, 433–436

master key, changing, 553

Master Page And Page Layout Gallery, 410

master pages, 131, 405, 407–410

  branding, 407

  custom, 409

  customizing, 169

  publishing, 410

  site master page, 408

  system master page, 408

Master Page Setting For Application _Layouts Pages option, 408

Maximum Number Of Sites That Can Be Created In This Database setting, 98

Maximum Upload Size setting, 153

medium farms, 12, 55

Memberships feature, 436

Members security group, 171

memory, application pools and, 4, 112

Message content types, 162

metadata. *See also* managed metadata

  consuming, 351–360

  custom, 382

  enterprise metadata, 329

  gathering, 356

  list metadata, 349

  navigation, 359–360

  tagging, 351

metadata groups, 344–345

metadata navigation, 151, 382–383

Metadata Property Mappings page, 279

Microsoft Access services, 187–189

Microsoft InfoPath Designer 2010, 158

Microsoft Office

  Microsoft Office 2010, integration with SharePoint 2010, 446–448

  themes files, creating, 414

Microsoft Office Outlook 2003 and later, offline content access with, 377

Microsoft.Office.Server.Search. Administration.ManagedProperty class, 280

Microsoft Office Visio, 4

Microsoft Office Word, conversion of documents into, 201

Microsoft Server Speech Platform, 7

Microsoft SharePoint Foundation Incoming E-mail service, 71

Microsoft SharePoint Foundation Sandboxed Code service, 51

Microsoft SharePoint Foundation Subscription Settings service, 71

Microsoft SharePoint Foundation Timer service, 93–96

Microsoft SharePoint Foundation User Code service, 71

Microsoft SharePoint Foundation Web Application service, 72

Microsoft SharePoint Foundation Workflow Timer service, 72

Microsoft SharePoint Products and Technologies Preparation Tool, 5

Microsoft SharePoint Workspace 2010, 377

Microsoft software licenses, 28

minor versioning, 373

mobile alert feature, 93, 134–135

Modify Topology link, 243

monitoring

  Performance and Reliability monitors, 491–492

  SharePoint tools for, 496–505

  SQL Server, 515–516

  Windows Event Viewer, 490–491

Monitoring area (Central Administration), 84

Monitoring Resource Usage tool, 516

Mount-SPContentDatabase cmdlet, 534–535

.mp3 files, 479

.mpg files, 479

ms-Exch-mail-Nickname attributes, 90

ms-Exch-RequireAuthToSendTo attribute, 90

Msinfo32.exe, 494

multitenancy, 106

My Alerts page, 162
My Colleagues, 440
My Content, 440
My Interests, 440
My Links feature, 436
My Newsfeed, 440–441
My Personalization Links feature, 436
My Profile, 440
My Site hosts, provisioing, 423
My Site host template, 420
My Sites, 200
My Site Settings page, 441–442
My Site Web sites, 440–448
    configuring, 441–443
    personalization site links, 445–446
    site naming format, 443
    Trusted My Site host locations,
      443–445

N

Name parameter (features), 217, 219, 221
naming conventions for document IDs,
  366
navigation, 415–417
    metadata navigation, 359–360
nested folder structures, 415
network infrastructure, planning, 51–52
Network Interface Card (NIC) teaming, 52
Network Load Balancing (NLB) service, 53
New Alert page, 161
New Search Service Application page, 243
New Site Collection page, 144, 147
New Site Column page, 352
New Site Content Type page, 157, 350
New Web Parts page, 206
NIC (Network Interface Card) teaming, 52
NLB (Network Load Balancing) service, 53
noise word files, configuring, 266–267
noise words, ignoring, 316
nonrecords, 388–389
    retention policies for, 387–388
notes, 200
    deleting, 439
Notes feature, 436–440
notification e-mail address for password
  management, 457
notifications about sites, 143
Novell eDirectory v. 8.7.3 LDAP, 430
NTLM, 473
    for authentication, 118

O

object names for Pre-Upgrade Check tool,
  522–523
objects, controlling access to, 171
Office Communicator Server (OCS), 129
OfficeServer.exe, 33
officialfile.asmx, 105, 396
offline backups, 540
offline client availability, 151
offline support, 377
Open Items permissions, 176
Open permissions, 177
OpenSearch 1.0/1.1, 274
Operation Completed Successfully screen,
  401–402
organization profiles, 200
OssPreUpgradeCheck.xml file, 523–524
outbound HTTP, 97
outgoing e-mail
    alerts and, 161
    configuring settings for, 37, 133–134
    settings for, 88–89
Override Check Out permissions, 175
Owners security group, 171

P

page content area, editing, 208
page layouts, 405–406, 411
pages, 207. *See also* Web part pages
    Body Only page layout, 208
    detaching, 169
    Web parts and, 207–210
passphrases
    for farm security, 19, 31
    for server farms, 60
password management, 453–460
    automatic password changes,
      457–458
    farm passphrases, 459–460
    global password settings, 457–458
password roll policies, 456
Path parameter (features), 217
paths, managed, 136
pattern queries, 273
People and All Sites scopes, 285
People And Groups page, 178
People Picker, 147
People Search Results page, 310–311
Perform A Backup option, 542
performance
    BLOB storage and, 43
    logging and, 503
    problems, viewing, 497

performance (*continued*)
of SharePoint 2010 Search, 78–79
scaling out and, 51
SQL Server environment and, 515
Performance and Reliability monitors,
491–492
performance counters for SQL Server
monitoring, 515–516
PerformancePoint Services, 72, 194–196
PerformancePoint Services Application
Settings page, 195
permission inheritance, breaking, 179
permission levels, 483
permission policies, 483–485
permissions. *See also* user permissions
assigning to users, 174
available permissions, 175–177
checking, 180
Contribute permissions, 175
Create Alerts permissions, 176
Create Groups permissions, 177
Create Subsites permissions, 176
custom permission levels, creating,
175–177
default permissions, 484
delegating to site owners, 487
Delete Items permissions, 175
Delete Versions permissions, 176
Design permissions, 174
Edit Items permissions, 175
Edit Personal User Information
permissions, 177
Enumerate Permissions permissions,
177
Full Control permissions, 142, 174
group permissions, 172–174
Hierarchy Manager, 142
levels of, 142, 174
for libraries, 179–180
for lists, 179–180
Manage Alerts permissions, 177
Manage Lists permissions, 175
Manage Permissions permissions, 176
Manage Personal Views permissions,
178
Manage Web Site permissions, 176
modifying, 176, 178
for objects, 171
Open Items permissions, 176
Open permissions, 177
Override Check Out permissions, 175
Read permissions, 175
for search administrators, 245–246
for SharePoint Designer, 135

permissions (*continued*)
Site Collection Administrator
permissions, 485
Site Collection Auditor permissions,
485
for site collections and subsites, 142
specifying, 171
Update Personal Web Parts
permissions, 178
Use Client Integration Features
permissions, 177
Use Remote Interfaces permissions,
177
user permissions, for Web
applications, 475–476
Use Self-Service Site Creation
permissions, 177
View Application Pages permissions,
176
viewing, 172–173
View Items permissions, 176
View Pages permissions, 177
View Versions permissions,
176
View Web Analytics Data permissions,
176
on Web applications, 475–476
Permissions For User Profile Service
Application dialog box, 437–438
personalization of Web part pages,
213–214
personalization site links, 445–446
Personalization Site Links page, 445
Personalize This Page option, 213–214
phonetic name-matching functionality, 7
policy features, 167
portals, 166
lack of, 405
portal site connections, 166–167
port numbers for IIS Web sites, 117
prerequisites, 519
installing, 7–8, 527
Prerequisites installer, 7–8
presence settings for Web applications,
129
Pre-Upgrade Checker, 520–521
tool warnings, 523–524
preupgradecheck (Stsadm.exe), 520–521
local only option, 523
process security, 4
product keys, entering, 28
profile databases, 421–422

profile properties
    custom, 426
    mapping, 433–436
profile synchronization, 429–435
profile synchronization connections, 430–433
profile synchronization databases, 36, 422
properties of Search schema, 278–284
property databases, 256–257
    redundancy and availability of, 80
Property Query scope rules, 287
proxy groups, 122
proxy server error messages, 63
proxy servers
    local addresses and, 31
    for search service applications, 246
pruning, 373
PSCDiagnostics files, 22, 31
.pst files, 479
public URLs
    defining, 126
    editing, 139
    for Web applications, 120
    for Web servers, 63
Publish A Major Version option, 410
Published Links To Office Client Applications page, 447
publishing infrastructure, 405–417
    enabling, 406–407
    master pages, 405, 407–410
    navigational options, 415–417
    page layouts, 405–406, 411
    service applications, 185–186
    SharePoint Designer 2010, disabling, 412
    themes, 406, 414
publishing site libraries, folders in, 415
Publish Service Application dialog box, 185, 340

Q

queries. *See also* search queries
    duplicate results, removing, 316
    federated queries, 270–277
    keywords in, 293
    pattern queries, 273
    query pages, 301–302
    query reports, 325
    query terms, modifying, 267
    restrictions on, 274
    thesaurus and noise word file usage, 266
query availability, improving, 79

query components, 257
    failover-only, 258
    mirroring, 77–78
    moving to another server, 74–76
    multiple, 258
    redundancy and availability of, 80
Query Language picker, 316
query logging, 246
Query Manager, 311–312
query pages, 301–302
query reporting, 325
query response times
    improving, 79
query role, hosting, 74
query servers, 74
    redundancy of, 74
query templates, 274
Quick Launch area
    Content Sources link, 247
    Crawl Rules link, 248
    File Types link, 251
    links to search management pages, 245
quota templates for Web applications, 129

R

rapid application development (RAD), 187
RBS (Remote BLOB Storage), 43–47
read-only content databses, 100
Read permissions, 175
Really Simple Syndication (RSS), 163
    Web application settings, 130
Record Declaration settings, 389
records, 389
    declaring, 388–389, 393–394
    discovering and holding, 402–403
    list- and library-level, 393–394
    manual submission to document library, 400–401
    retention policies for, 387–388, 389
Records Center connection, 105
Records Center Management page, 397
records centers, 385, 394–404
    access to, 395
    auditing reports, 404
    compliance management functions, 401–404
    file plan reports, 403–404
    isolating, 396
    planning for, 395–397
    records management, 401–404
    routing information to, 397–401

records centers (*continued*)
routing mechanism, 396
site configuration, 396–397
site features, 396
submitting items to, 396
Records Center template, 378
Records Center Web Service Submitters
group, 396
Records Center Web Service Submitters
page, 399
records management, 385
file plan matrix, 395
in-place, 392–394
record declaration, 393–394
records centers, 385, 394–404
records managers, 385
record submission Operation Completed
Successfully screen, 401–402
recoverability, 165
recovery. *See also* restore
of server farms, 540–552
Recovery Point Objectives (RPOs), 540
Recovery Time Objectives (RTOs),
539–540
Recycle Bin, 164–165
configuring use of, 131
redundancy
of query servers, 74
of Search Service, 79–80
of service applications, 182–183
Refinement Panel Web part, 323–324
regional site settings, 148
Register Managed Account dialog box,
421
Related Queries Web part, 311, 322
relationship behavior, enforcing, 369
relevance settings for search, 270
Remote BLOB Storage (RBS)
configuring, 46–47
enabling, 45
installing, 43–44, 44–45
testing, 46
remote farms
service applications, connecting to,
186–187
trust relationships with, 340
Remove SharePoint From IIS Web Site
option, 127
Remove URLs From Search Results page,
289
replacement sets for search thesaurus,
268

reporting, 501–504
on system diagnostics, 492–493
resource measures, 237
resource points, 236–237
resources per point values, 237
resource throttling, enabling, 132–133
restore
with Central Administration, 542–547
granular, 555–560
scope of, 539
of server farm, 545–547, 549–550,
551–552
of single components, 555
of site collections, 555–559
with Stsadm.exe, 551–552, 559
tools for, 539
of unattached content databases,
559–560
of Web applications, 553–555
with Windows PowerShell, 547–550,
556–558
Restore-SPFarm cmdlet, 549–550
-*item* option, 553
Restore-SPSite cmdlet, 557–558
results pages, 310–312
retention, 387–388
Information Management, 464
source of, setting, 386
Retract Solution hyperlink, 229
Ribbon interface, 128–129
Administrators and Permissions
groups, 340
Authentication Providers, 472
Delete button, 126, 127
Extend button, 123, 481
focus of, 128
Format Text tab, 208
i Like It button, 436
Insert tab, 208
Library tab, 149, 153, 353, 386
Library Tools tab, 409
Manage button, 245
Manage Features button, 136,
136–137
Manage Paths option, 136
Manage section, 152
New button, 115
Permission Policy, 484
Resource Throttling option, 132
Security section, 142
Share and Track section, 163
Site Permissions page, 171
Solutions tab, 234

Ribbon interface (continued)
Tags & Notes button, 436
User Permissions, 475–476
Web Applications tab, 218, 408
Web Part Tools tab, 210
Right-Column-Header-Footer pages, 209
roles, managed metsdata, 343
routing mechanism
for incoming documents, 379
records center, 396
RPOs (Recovery Point Objectives), 540
RSS (Really Simple Syndication), 130, 163
RTOs (Recovery Time Objectives),
539–540
rule files, 523

S

Safe Control entries, 206–207
safe controls, 207
Safe E-Mail Servers setting, 92
Sandboxed Code service, 234
sandboxed solutions, 160–161, 221,
232–238
allowed and disallowed functions,
233–234
architecture of, 233
blocking, 238
downloading, 234–235
life cycle of, 234
load balancing, 238
monitoring, 235–238
resource points, 236
security of, 232
uploading, 234
usage quotas, 235–237
Sandboxed Solutions Resource Quota
value, 236
Save As dialog box, Favorite Links section,
446
scaling out
account for performing, 57
high availability and, 51
performance and, 51
preparing for, 51–56
Search Service application, 74–80
service applications, 65–80
setup and, 3
SharePoint Server 2010 Search, 74–80
system services, 65–80
Web servers, adding, 57–64
Web servers per SQL Server cluster,
57

Scope Properties And Rules page,
287–288
scopes, of features, 215
scripted deployment, Windows
PowerShell for, 24–26, 33–35
search. *See also* search service; SharePoint
Server 2010 Search
best bets, 293–296
centralized search environments, 297
compilation process, 288
configuration options, 325–327
contextual scopes, 327
custom pages, 300
FAST indexes, 274
federated queries, 270–277
keywords, 293–296
local indexes, 274
managed properties, 278–284
noise word files, configuring, 266
OpenSearch 1.0/1.1, 274
optimized, 54
query reports, 325
relevance settings, 270
results pages functionality, 311–312
searchable columns, 325–326
search pages, customizing, 300–324
Search Web parts configuration,
312–318
site-level crawl rules, 326–327
term stemming, 316
thesaurus, configuring, 267–268
Search Administration component,
redundancy and availability of, 80
Search administration database, 35
redundancy and availability of, 80
Search Administration page, 196, 245–246
search administrators permissions,
245–246
Search And Offline Availability page, 326
search application topology, managing,
252–258
Search Application Topology dashboard,
245–246, 253–254
Search Box Web part, 301–305
advanced search link, 305
Display Submitted Search check box,
305
links management, 305
Miscellaneous section, 304
Query Suggestions section, 303–304
Query Text Box section of, 303
scope display group, 305
Scopes Dropdown section of,
302–303

Search Box Web part (*continued*)
  Search button images, 305
  Target Search Results Page URL
    setting, 305
search centers, 297–300
  Advanced Search pages, 305–310
  custom scopes with, 291
  designating, 442
  Enterprise Search Center, 297–298
  local, 297
  new tabs, creating, 299–300
  query pages, 301–302, 301–325
  Related Queries Web part, 311
  results pages, 310–312
  search pages, 298
  site templates, 297
  Summary Web part, 311
search connectors, downloading, 277
Search Connectors Gallery, 277
search databases, hardware for, 54
search pages
  accessing, 300
  Advanced Search pages, 305–310
  creating, 298
  customizing, 300–324
  Preferences link, 301
  results pages, 310–312
  Search Box Web part, 301–305
  tabs, adding, 299–300
Search Paging Web part, 320–321
Search Property Database, 35
search queries, 265. *See also* queries
  noise word files, 266–267
  viewing, 325
Search Query And Site Settings Web
  Service, 72, 244
search query box, configuring, 290–291
Search Query Web parts, 290
search results
  displaying, 275
  relevance settings, 268–270
  removing, 289
search results pages, custom pages, 290
search scopes, 284–288
  adding rules, 286
  compilation process, 288
  contextual scopes, 327
  creating, 285–286
  excluding specific content, 287
  People and All Sites scopes, 285
  scope display groups, 293
  scope rules, 287
  shared scopes, 291
  site-level management, 291–293

search servers, defining, 122
search service, 73, 196–198. *See also*
  search
  content sources, 196–197
  crawler, 239
  crawling, starting, 198
  crawl rules, 197–198, 247–250
  farm-wide search settings, 240–241
  index partitions, 257–258
  multiple instances of, 240
  starting, 240
search service accounts, 9, 243
Search Service Application page,
  Federated Locations, 270–271
search service applications, 532
  Contact E-mail Address setting, 246
  creating, 243–245
  Query Logging option, 246
  scaling out, 74–80
  Scopes Update Schedule option, 246
  Search Alerts Status setting, 246
  topology of, 243
Search Settings page, 290
Search Statistics Web part, 321–322
Search Summary Web part, 322
search topology, simplifying, 533
Search Web Analytics reports, 325
Search Web parts, 301
  Best Bets Web part, 319–320
  configuration, 312–318
  display properties, 313–316
  Federated Result Web part, 318–319
  location properties, 312–313
  miscellaneous conguration options,
    317–318
  Refinement Panel Web part, 323–324
  Related Queries Web part, 322
  results query options, 316–317
  Search Paging Web part, 320–321
  Search Statistics Web part, 321–322
  Search Summary Web part, 322
  Top Federated Result Web part, 319
secondary contacts, 143
secondary site collection administrators,
  146
Secure Sockets Layer (SSL), 116, 465–470
  Alternate Access Mapping changes,
    469
  certificates, binding to Web
    applications, 467–468
  configuring, 465–466
  enabling, 118
  server certificates, configuring,
    465–467

Secure Store Service, 72, 199, 476–478
  backing up, 553
  managing, 477–478
Secure Store Service applications, 532
  creating, 477–478
  multiple, 478
Secure Store Service DB, 35
security
  account management, 453–460
  application pools and, 112
  assigned IP addresses and, 3
  of Central Administration, 83
  example configuration, 452
  farm security passphrase, 19, 31
  of incoming e-mail, 92
  information policies, 460–464
  least-privileged accounts, 8
  password management, 453–460
  process security, 4
  sandboxed solutions and, 232
  of server farms, 451–464
  for site collections, 171–180
  for term groups, 342
  Web application policies, 481–487
  for Web applications, 117–119,
    464–480
  Web page security validation, 130
  workflow settings and, 133
Security area (Central Administration), 84
security groups, default, 171
security logs, 490
security problems, viewing, 497
Security Token Service (STS), 119, 199
security trimming, 171
self-service site-collection creation, 479
Self-Service Site Collection Management
  dialog box, 143
self-service site creation, 142–143
Self-Service Site Creation button, 142
self-service URL for site creation, 146–147
Send To connections
  configuring, 105–107
  manual submissions, 107
  multiple, 106
Send To destination links, custom, 381
Send To function
  content organizer and, 379
  defining, 398–399
Send To locations, multiple, 398
Send User Name And Password In E-mail
  option, 130

server certificates
  creating, 465–466
  Web applications, binding to,
    467–468
server farms, 28
  account/database access account, 9
  administrator account name, 30
  backup and recovery of, 540–552
  configuration databases, 81
  configuration failures, 63
  configuring, 23–24, 32–33
  connecting to, 58
  custom code, installing, 64
  definition of, 17
  farm passphrases, 459–460
  IIS management, 65
  information processing, location of,
    88
  large farms, 56
  medium farms, 55
  passphrase for, 60
  provisioning, 17–22, 30–31
  scaling, 3, 51–80
  securing, 451–464
  server management, 86–87
  single-server farms, 52
  three-tier small farms, 53–54
  traffic patterns, viewing, 509–510
  two-tier farms, 52–53
  Web parts, installing, 64
  Web servers, adding, 57–64
server groups, 10, 78
server hardware planning, 51
Server Manager Diagnostics console, 490
Server Name Mapping management
  page, 250
server name mappings, 250
servers
  configuration, performance, and
    security problems, viewing, 497
  health and reliability of, 491–492
  IISReset on, 530
  managing, 86–87
  removing from configuration
    database, 87
  security of, 452
  sizing properly, 489
  SKU information, 86
  status of, viewing, 87
  for timer jobs, 95
  upgrading to SharePoint Server 2010,
    526–529
server services, managing, 87–88

Servers section (System Settings), 86–88
  Manage Servers In This Farm link,
    86–87
service account management, 459–460
service account password management,
  453
service accounts
  for services configuration, 23
  specifying, 8–9
service administrators, 424
  My Site Web site management,
    441–442
  social features administration,
    438–439
  user profile administration, 419
service application connection groups,
  184
service application instances, system
  services as, 68
service application proxies, 182
service applications, 181
  Access services, 187
  administration interface, 182
  administrators, managing, 185
  after upgrading, 531
  application bits, 182
  application pools, 182, 421
  architecture of, 66–73, 181–183
  backup and recovery of, 553–555
  Business Connectivity Services, 189
  Central Administration management
    of, 66
  connections configuration, 122
  consumption of, 69
  creating and configuring, 32
  databases, 182
  deleting, 185
  Excel Services, 189–194
  PerformancePoint Services, 194–196
  publishing, 68–69, 185–186
  redundancy of, 182–183
  remote, connecting to, 186–187
  scaling, 65–80
  search applications, 243–245
  Search service, 196–198
  Secure Store Service, 199
  security token service, 199
  and services interaction, 67
  in SharePoint Server, 187–202
  versus SharePoint services, 88
  State Service, 199–200
  topologies, 182–183
  Usage And Health Data Collection
    Service, 199

service applications (continued)
  User Profile Service, 200–201
  Visio Graphics Service, 199
  Web Analytics Service, 201
  Web applications, associated with, 67
  Word Automation Service, 201–202
Service Applications Associations page,
  184
service application service instances, 66
Service Applications model, 9
service connections list, default, 338
service instances, 182
  multiple, 183
Service Job Definitions page, 94
service principal names (SPNs),
  configuring, 471–472
services
  grouping on servers, 10
  installing, 33
  services infrastructure, 65
  upgrading, 533
Services On Server page, 341
Set-SPPassPhrase cmdlet, 60, 460
setup, failure of, 17
Setup.exe, 14
Set Up Groups For This Site page, 147
setup program, starting, 526
Setup user account, 8
setup wizard, options in, 3–4
shared scopes, 285, 291
  versus local scopes, 292
shared service providers (SSPs), 122, 181,
  530
shared services, 66
  upgrades and, 530–531
Shared Services Provider model, 9
SharePoint 2010
  for file retention, 330–331
  Office 2010, integration with,
    446–448
  offline support, 377
SharePoint 2010 Best Practices Analyzer,
  495
SharePoint 2010 Health Analyzer,
  495–496
SharePoint 2010 Products Configuration
  Wizard
  Central Administration, repairing
    with, 86
  Completing The SharePoint Products
    Configuration Wizard page, 31,
    60–61
  Configuration Successful page, 62

SharePoint 2010 Products Configuration Wizard (*continued*)

Configure SharePoint Central Administration Web Application page, 20, 31

Connect To A Server Farm page, 18, 30, 58

for provisioning servers, 58

running, 84

running after language pack installation, 48

Specify Configuration Database Settings page, 19, 30, 59

Specify Farm Security Settings page, 19, 31

starting, 30

for upgrading to SharePoint Server, 49

Welcome To SharePoint Products page, 17, 30, 58

SharePoint 2010 Timer service server, 114

SharePoint_AdminContent_<GUID> database, 82

SharePoint configuration database, 26, 35

SharePoint Designer

access to, 406, 412–413

blocking of, 170–171

enabling, 169

governance, 486–487

setting restrictions, 413–414

settings, 169–171

Settings page, 169

users, governance of, 135–137

workflow creation with, 374

SharePoint.exe, 14

SharePoint Foundation

binaries, installing, 15–17

configuration failures, 22

default service applications, 24

hardware and software requirements, 5–6

installing, 4, 13

installing first server, 13–26

service applications in, 187

services infrastructure, 65–66

system services, 66

upgrading to SharePoint Server, 49–50

SharePoint Foundation 2010 Farm Configuration Wizard, 23–24

SharePoint Foundation 2010 Start page, 14

SharePoint Foundation Logging database, 26

SharePoint Foundation Sandboxed Code service, 233

SharePoint Foundation Search service, 72

SharePoint Foundation User Code service starting, 233

SharePoint Foundation Workflow Timer service, malfunctioning of, 464

SharePoint Health Analyzer, 200

SharePoint Product 2010 Configuration Wizard, 529

SharePoint Products and Technologies Preparation Tool

Installation Complete page, 15

License Terms For Software Products page, 14

running, 14–15, 27

SharePoint Foundation 2010 Start page, 14

Welcome To The Microsoft SharePoint Products And Technologies Preparation Tool page, 14

SharePoint Products Configuration Wizard

Completing the SharePoint Products Configuration Wizard page, 22

Configuration Successful page, 22

running, 17–22, 30–31, 49

SharePoint Search 2010, phonetic name-matching functionality, 7

SharePoint Server

custom location, installing to, 29

service applications in, 187–202

upgrading from SharePoint Foundation, 49–50

SharePoint Server 2007, upgrading from, 517–538

SharePoint Server 2010

binaries, installing, 28–30, 49–50

configuration failures, 31

default services in, 33

diagnostic-logging capabilities, 514

document management in, 361–365

feature set, 405

hardware and software requirements, 5–6

mirroring awareness, 114

monitoring and diagnostic capabilities, 495–514

monitoring functionality of, 496–505

prerequisites for, 519

servers, installing first server, 26–36

SharePoint 2010 Health Analyzer, 495–496

upgrading to, 517–538

Web Analytics, 504–514

SharePoint Server 2010 Search, 73. *See also* search; search service
performance, improving, 78–79
role configuration, 74
scaling out, 74–80
SharePoint Server Logging database, 35
SharePoint services versus service applications, 88
Show Shared View option, 214
Simple Mail Transport Protocol (SMTP) service, configuring, 37
single-server farms, 10, 52
single-server topology for service applications, 182
Single Sign-on service, 199
Site Actions menu, 144
Manage Content And Structure option, 406
New Page option, 208
Site Assets Library, 151
Site Collection Administrator permissions, 485
site collection administrators, 147, 170–172
record declaration control, 388
Site Collection Auditor permissions, 485
Site Collection feature, enabling, 392–393
Site Collection Features hyperlink, 218
site collection galleries, sandboxed solutions in, 232
Site Collection Policies page, 167
site collection quotas, 98
site collection Recycle Bin, 165–166
site collections
anonymous access, enabling for, 474–475
backing up and restoring, 555–559
content databases for, 112
creating, 33, 110, 144–147, 334, 479
creating in Central Administration, 334
document IDs, enabling, 366
features management for, 218–219
Information Management policies, 462
isolating, 100, 106
listing, 525–526
managing, 147
number of, 99–100, 114
sandboxed solutions for, 160–161
security for, 171–180
SharePoint Designer, limiting functionality in, 412–413

site collections (*continued*)
SharePoint Designer settings for, 169–170
upgrading, 537–538
URL structure, 169
usage quotas, 235
Web application for hosting, 37–40
Web applications and content databases and, 110
Web part gallery, 206
site collection search management, 290
search scopes, 291–293
Site Collection Search Settings page, 290
site columns, 154–155
custom, 353–355
definitions, document property mappings to, 349
modifying, 352
predefined, 351–352
sealed and unsealed, 352–353
Site Columns gallery, 351
Site Columns page, 155
Site Content Types page, 157
Site Content Type summary page, 350
site creation
administratively-controlled, 142–143
modes of, 141–144
secondary contacts, 143
self-service mode, 142–143, 146–147
site definitions, listing, 526
site groups, 171
custom, creating, 171–172
Site Master Page master pages, 408
site owners, 147
delegating permissions to, 487
Site Permissions page, 171
site quotas, 114
configuring, 99
sites
adding users to, 147, 178
Announcements list, 146
contextual search scopes, 327
crawl rules for, 326–327
deleting, 143–144
diagnostic reports on, 513
features managements, 219
listing, 525–526
managed paths for, 145
navigation options, 415–417
notifications about, 143
regional settings, 148
settings, 147–170
upgrading, 537–538

Site Settings page, 147, 169
  Regional Settings link, 148
site subscription, 106
site templates, 145. *See also* templates
  Document Center, 378–383
  for Web application root, 4
site use confirmation and deletion,
  143–144
Site Use Confirmation And Deletion page,
  144
SMTP servers
  adding, 89
  relaying, allowing, 89
  third-party, 90
SMTP (Simple Mail Transport Protocol)
  service, 37
social features
  access to, 436
  enabling, 436–437
  tags and notes, 200, 437–440
social tagging databases, 36, 422
social tags, 200, 437–440
Social Tags And Note Board Ribbon
  Controls feature, 438
software requirements for SharePoint,
  5–6
Solution Management interface, 226
solution packages, 206, 216
  feature files, removing, 220
solutions, 205
  full-trust solutions, 221–232
  managing, 221–238
  sandboxed, 160–161, 232–238
  Web application–specific, 224–225
Solutions hyperlink, 234
solution stores contents, displaying, 224
Sort Order settings, 148
Spbrtoc.xml file, 544–545
Specify Update Schedule dialog box, 288
speech recognition, registry changes
  and, 7
*SPEnterpriseSearchMetadata-
  ManagedProperty*, 280
SPNs (service principal names), 471–472
SPUCWorkerProcess process, 235
SQL authentication, 122
SQLIO.exe tool, 104
SQL Server
  backing up, 526
  backing up from, 541
  clustered back end, 51
  clustering or mirroring, 53
  databases created during installation,
    26, 35

SQL Server (*continued*)
  default content server, 104
  host for, 526
  maintenance plans and system
    configuration, 102
  monitoring, 515–516
  planning installation, 52
  SQL Server 2005/SQL Server 2008 as
    SharePoint prerequisite, 520
  SQL Server 2008 R2 Reporting
    Services Add-in for SharePoint
    Technologies, 7
  updating for use with SharePoint, 7
SQL Server clusters
  adding, 57
  for configuration database, 57
  ratio to Web servers, 57
SQL Server Express, installing, 3
SQL Server Management Studio, 44
SQL Server service account, 8
SQL Server type, choosing, 3
SSL (Secure Sockets Layer), 116, 118,
  465–470
SSL certificates, 125
SSP database, 35
SSPs (shared service providers), 122, 181,
  530
Stage Properties dialog box, 168
stakeholders, 345
start addresses, 247
State database, 36
State Service, 199–200
storage, securing, 452
structured file retention, 330
STS (Security Token Service), 119, 199
Stsadm.exe, 82, 109
  Catastrophic Mode, 551
  content databases, attaching with,
    535–536
  EnumSolutions, 224–225
  features, activating and deactivating
    with, 219–220
  features, installing with, 217
  features, uninstalling with, 221
  full-trust solutions, managing with,
    223
  -o enumallwebs, 525–526
  preupgradecheck, 520–521
  preupgradecheck, local only, 523
  for server farm backup and restore,
    542, 551–552
  site collection backups with, 559
  solutions, deleting with, 230
  solutions, deploying with, 225–226

Stsadm.exe (*continued*)
    solutions, retracting with, 229–230
    solutions, upgrading with, 231
submission content types, specifying, 380
submissions, grouping, 376
Subscriptions, 491–492
subsites, creation of, 142, 144
Success dialog box, 187
Summary Web part, 311
SunOne v. 5.2 LDAP, 430
support upgrade paths, 517
synchronization connections, 430–433
Synchronization Connections page, 430
synchronization databases for user
    profiles, 422
synchronization settings, configuring, 435
synonyms, term, 347
system alerts, 88–89. *See also* alerts
system-generated e-mail messages, 123
System Information tool, 494
system logs, 490. *See also* logging
System Master Page master pages, 408
system services, 66
    placement of, 69
    scaling, 65–80
    as service application instances, 68
System Settings area (Central
    Administration), 83, 86–97
        E-mail and Text Messages section,
        88–93
        Farm Management area, 96–97
        Servers section, 86–88
System Status dashboard, 246
system upgrades, 519. *See also* upgrading

T

Tabs In Search Pages list page, 299
tagging, 200, 357–358, 436, 437–440
    deleting tags, 439
    metadata and, 351
Tags & Notes button, 436
task forms, modifying, 158–160
taxonomies, 329–330
    of managed terms, 346–347
    term sets in, 342
_Taxonomy suffix, 531
TEMPLATE\FEATURES directory, 215
templates. *See also* site templates
    of document libraries, 364
    document templates, 149, 150
    for sites, 145
template.xls, 153
Term Label Selection dialog box, 358

terms
    copying, 346–347
    creating, 345–346
    deprecating, 347
    disabling, 346
    keywords, 347
    management of, 342
    merging, 346
    moving, 347
    reuse of, 346
    siblings of, 346
    subscription of, 342
    synonyms for, 347
term set contacts, 345
term set groups
    creating, 344
    deleting, 345
term sets, 331, 342. *See also* managed
  term sets
    copying, 346–347
    importing, 348–349
    managed, 345
    moving, 347
    organization of, 344
    taxonomies of, 346–347
term stemming, 316
term store administrators, 343
    assigning, 344
Term Store Management Tool, 194,
  344–349
term stores, 331, 342–343
    administrators of, 343, 344
    managed metadata roles and, 343
    searching, 355
term synonyms, 347
Test-SPContentDatabase cmdlet, 524–525
Text Message (SMS) service, configuring,
  93, 134–135
theme gallery, 414
themes, 406, 414
    Office applications, creating in, 414
thesaurus, configuring, 267–268
Thread content types, 162
Three-State workflow, 374
three-tiered server farm, 11, 53
    security for, 452
throttling, 132–133
    alerts, 93, 134
time format settings, 148
timer jobs, 498–501
    configuration settings, 499–500
    creating and deleting, 93
    definitions of, 498–499
    server for, 95

timer jobs (continued)
status of, 96, 499–500
Timer service and, 93
for upgrades, 529
viewing, 94
Timer Job Status page, 96
time zones settings, 148
for Web applications, 129
Top Federated Result Web part, 319
topology
changes in, 73
design of, 9–13
Trace and Service Application log files, 504
trace logs, configuring, 502
tracing, for event logs, 43
traffic patterns, viewing, 509–510
transaction log files, separating from data files, 102
Trusted Content Locations page, 195
trusted data connection libraries
adding, 192–193
trusted file locations, adding, 191–192
Trusted File Locations page, 191
Trusted My Site host locations, 443–445
deleting, 444–445
trust relationships, with remote farms, 340
Tsenu.xml file, 267
two-server farms, 10
two-tier farms, 11, 52–53

U

ULS Viewer, 501
unattached content databases, restoring, 559–560
unattended installations, 26, 35
Undeclare Record button, 394
unghosting, 169
Unified Logging Service (ULS), 501
Universal Naming Convention (UNC) file share, backing up to, 540
unstructured file retention, 330
Update Personal Web Parts permissions, 178
Upgrade And Migration area (Central Administration), 84
Upgrade Status screen, 530
upgrading
backing up and testing restores before, 518
custom code and, 537
database attach upgrade method, 533–536
errors, viewing, 530

upgrading (continued)
IISReset after, 530
in-place upgrades, 526–533
manually restarting, 536
planning for, 519–520
planning tools for, 518–526
services, 533
sites and site collections, 537–538
steps for, 517–518
support upgrade paths, 517
time for, 518
visual upgrades, 529, 537–538
uploads
file properties, 358–359
Maximum Upload Size setting, 153
size settings, 132–133
URLs. See also public URLs
alternate access mapping for, 138
on authoritative pages, 268–269
changes in, 469–470
for connecting to service applications, 341
for crawl rule paths, 249–250
mapping, 140
Send To URL, 398
for service applications, 186
URL templates, 274
Usage And Health Data collections, 24
configuring, 40–42
Usage And Health Data Collection Service, 199
usage data
collecting, 504
enabling collection, 40
usage quotas, for site collections, 235
Use Client Integration Features permissions, 177
user alerts. See alerts
user authentication, Kerberos for, 118
user content, storage of, 109
user-defined function assemblies, registering, 193–194
User-Defined Functions page, 193
user-defined workflows, 133
Use Remote Interfaces permissions, 177
User Information page, 161
user permissions, for Web applications, 475–476. See also permissions
User Personal Features, 436
User Profile Database, 36
user profile properties
creating new, 426–428
deleting, 429–430
editing, 429

User Profile Properties feature, 436
user profiles, 200
    admninistration of, 419
    external data sources and, 430
    policy settings, 428
    profile synchronization, 429–435
    property mapping for
      synchronization, 429
    property settings, 427
    search settings, 428
User Profile Service, 68, 73, 200–201
    administration of, 424–425
    creation or maintenance tasks,
      420–424
    features and capabilities managed
      by, 419
    Manage Profile Service page, 426
    My Site Web sites, 440–448
    profile synchronization, 429–435
    properties management, 426–429
    social features, enabling, 436
    tags and notes, 437–440
User Profile Service applications, 68
    creating, 420–422
    deleting, 423–424
    editing, 423
User Profile Synchronization service, 73
users
    Active Directory accounts for, 21
    adding to sites, 177, 178
    alerts management, 162
    My Sites, 200
    permissions, modifying, 178
    properties, modifying, 178
    site creation by, 142–144
    Web part pages, personalizing,
      213–214
    Web parts modification, 205
user solutions, 160
Use Self-Service Site Creation permissions,
    177

V

validation, for site columns, 156
version control, 372–374
    content approval, 372–373
    draft item security, 373–374
    major versioning, 373
    minor versioning, 373
    version pruning, 373
versioning, 149–150
Versioning Settings page, 150
version pruning, 373

View Application Pages permissions, 176
View Items permissions, 176
View Pages permissions, 177
View Scopes page, 285, 286, 292
View Versions permissions, 176
View Web Analytics Data permissions, 176
Visio Graphics Service, 73, 199
Visitors security group, 171
Visitors To This Site section, 147
Visual Studio, workflow creation with, 374
visual upgrades, 529, 537–538
volatile functions, 192

W

Web Address scope rules, 287
Web Analytics, 201, 504–514
    administration reports, 510–511
    configuring, 505–507
    report data, exporting, 510
    reports, viewing, 507–515
    site-collection reports, 513–514
    Summary page, 509
    traffic patterns, viewing, 509–510
Web Analytics Data Processing service, 73
Web Analytics Reporting Database, 36
Web Analytics Reports - Summary page,
    507–508
Web Analytics service applications
    adding, 505
    starting, 506
Web Analytics Staging Database, 36
Web Analytics Web service, 73
Web Application General Settings page,
    152
Web application policies, 481–487
    applying, 485
    creating, 484–485
Web application root, site template for, 4
Web applications
    accessing with HTTPS and HTTP,
      469–470
    alerts, 130
    analytics on, 507–514
    anonymous access, enabling for, 474
    antivirus protection, 480–481
    application pools, 111–112
    architecture of, 110–114
    assigning IP addresses to, 46–47
    associations of, 339–340
    authetication type, 115
    backing up and restoring, 553–555
    blocked file types, 478–479
    blog settings, 130

Web applications (*continued*)
  browser file handling settings, 130
  configuration databases for, 109
  configuring, 32, 128–135
  content databases, attaching to,
    524–525, 534–536
  content databases for, 26, 112–115
  creating, 32, 110, 115–123
  deleting, 126
  enabling for Kerberos, 472–473
  extending, 123–126
  general settings, 129–133
  host headers for, 117
  for hosting site collections, 37–40
  installing on servers, 64
  IP addresses, assigning, 3
  logical structure of, 109
  managing, 110–111, 128–137
  master page settings, 131
  multiple, 95
  permission policies, 483–485
  presence settings, 129
  quota template settings, 129
  Recycle Bin settings, 131
  resource throttling, 132–133
  RSS settings, 130
  scaling, 57–65
  securing, 464–480
  security configuration of, 117–119
  security validation, 130
  Send User Name And Password In
    E-mail option, 130
  server certificates, binding to,
    467–468
  service applications associated with,
    67
  serving, 63–64
  site-collection creation, 479
  site collections and content databases
    and, 110
  timer jobs of, 94
  time zone settings, 129
  upload settings, 132
  user content, 109
  user permissions, 475–476
  Web sites for, 110
  worker processes, 111
  workflows, configuring, 133
Web front end (WFE), service application
  proxy on, 182
Web front-end (WFE) servers, 51, 124
Web page security validation, 130
Web part gallery, 206

Web part pages
  adding Web parts, 210
  creating, 208–210
  Header-Footer-4-Columns page, 209
  Left-Column-Header-Footer pages,
    209
  Right-Column-Header-Footer pages,
    209
  shared view of, 214
Web parts, 205. *See also* Search Web parts
  adding to page, 301
  adding to Web part pages, 210
  architecture of, 206–207
  assemblies, 206
  closed, viewing, 211
  Closed Web Parts gallery, 210
  closing, 210–211
  connection strings and, 214
  connectivity model, 211–212
  Cross-Web Part Query ID property,
    311
  custom, 206
  deleting, 210
  installing in server farms, 64
  pages and, 207–210
  placing on page, 207–208
  private, 214
  properties of, 212–214
  properties, states of, 213–214
  Safe Control entries, 206–207
  on search pages, 301–305
  XML files for, 206–207
Web Parts Maintenance page, 211
Web part zones, 207, 411
  empty, 208–209
Web servers
  adding to server farm, 57–64
  for Central Administration Web
    application, 51
  DNS entries for, 63
  language packs, installing, 47
  public URL for, 63
  query role, hosting, 74
  ratio to SQL Server clusters, 57
  RBS, installing on, 45
  server tiers, 66
  services, placing on, 71–73
Web single sign-on (SSO) authentication,
  116
Web sites. *See also* IIS Web sites
  for Web applications, 110
Welcome User control, 213
WFE (Web front end), 51, 124, 182
WIF (Windows Identity Foundation), 116

wildcard SSL certificates, 465
Windows authentication, 39, 42
   use of, 104
Windows Event Viewer, 490–491
Windows Identity Foundation (WIF), 116
Windows Integrated authentication,
   470–472
Windows PowerShell
   content databases, attaching with,
     534–536
   deactivation of features with, 438
   for farm configuration, 82
   farm passphrase management with,
     460
   features, activating and deactivating
     with, 220
   features, installing with, 217
   features, uninstalling with, 221
   full-trust solutions, deleting with,
     231–232
   full-trust solutions, deploying with,
     227–228
   full-trust solutions, managing with,
     223–225
   for managed accounts configuration,
     454
   sandboxed solutions metrics,
     displaying, 236
   for scripted deployment, 24–26,
     33–35
   for server farm backup and restore,
     541, 547–550
   service administration privileges,
     delegating with, 425
   service and Web applications,
     backing up and restoring with,
     553–555
   Set-SPPassPhrase cmdlet, 60
   site collection backups with, 556–558
   solutions, retracting with, 230–231
   solutions, upgrading with, 232–233
   for State Service configuration,
     199–200
   version compatibility, 7
Windows Server 2008
   Event Viewer, 490–491
   monitoring tools, 489–495

Windows Server 2008 (*continued*)
   Performance and Reliability monitors,
     491–492
   Server Manager Diagnostics console,
     490
   updating to work with SharePoint, 7
   Windows Server 2008/Windows
     Server 2008 R2 as SharePoint
     prerequisite, 519
   Windows Task Manager, 492–494
Windows Task Manager, 492–494
   Performance tab, 493
   Resource Monitor button, 493
.wmv files, 479
Word Automation Services, 73, 201–202
Word Automation Services database, 36
Word Automation Services page, 201
worker processes, 111
   IIS view into, 494
workflows, 156
   configuring, 133
   for documents, 374–375
   execution of, 95
   participants in, 133
   settings, assigning, 375
work week settings, 148
WPCATALOG folder, 206
.wsp file extension, 224
WSS_Logging, 26, 35
WssPreUpgradeCheck.xml file, 523–524

X

XML files for Web parts, 206–207

Z

zones, 120, 123, 481–484
   adding, 470
   configuration options, 482
   creating, 481
   deleting, 127
   security settings and, 483

About the Author

Ben Curry (CISSP, MVP, MCP, MCT) is an author and enterprise network architect specializing in knowledge management and collaboration technologies. Ben is a Managing Partner at Summit 7 Systems, a company focused on the next generation of Microsoft products. Ben's philosophy is that the best solutions are inspired by the best ideas, and he encourages his team to generate and share ideas on a continuous basis. His philosophy is also exemplified in his numerous published books, and in his willingness to share his ideas as an instructor, both in the IT world and in the under-world—Ben is a certified scuba instructor with a passion for diving. Other passions for life include riding his Harley Davidson through his hometown of Huntsville, Alabama, coaching his daughter's softball team, and of course, being a husband to his wife, Kimberly, and a proud father of his children, Madison and Bryce.

These industry experts contributed to this volume as well:

James R. W. Curry is the Lead Developer with Summit 7 Systems where he has worked with companies in the finance, entertainment, health, manufacturing, utilities and education sectors as well as numerous government organizations. James has been developing for so long it is starting to make him feel old telling people how long. James is an alumnus of Marshall Space Flight Center and resides in Madison, Alabama with his wife, the love of his life, Joy.

Josh Meyer (MCSD,MCTS) is a Developer/Architect with 8 years of experience developing in .NET, with the past 5 years spent primarily on SharePoint architecture and development. He has contributed to multiple books, including *Developer's Guide to Windows SharePoint Services 3.0* and *SharePoint Products and Technologies Administrator's Pocket Consultant*. He currently serves as the president of the Rocket City SharePoint User Group.

Phil Greninger (MCSE, MCSA, PMP, CSM, CGEIT) is a solutions architect and project manager with more than 15 years of experience designing and implementing Microsoft enterprise infrastructure solutions. He recently completed a Master of Project Management degree and resides in the northern suburbs of Atlanta with his wife and four kids. He spends his free time coaching youth soccer and volunteering as a Boy Scout leader.

Daniel Webster is a SharePoint Enterprise Architect and has worked with all versions of SharePoint technology. His clients include industries such as international energy, interstate health providers, international law, global professional organizations, international financial institutions, federal agencies and all branches of the US military. As an author, speaker and educator, Daniel has specialized on SharePoint technologies since 2003. He was coauthor, *Microsoft Office SharePoint Server 2007*

Administrator's Companion and Technical Editor, *Microsoft Office SharePoint Server 2007 Best Practices*. Daniel began as a technical trainer teaching Windows 3.1 in 1994 and has been certified as a MCT since 1995.

Fred Devoir is an author and Senior Systems Analyst focusing on Microsoft SharePoint Technologies. Fred is the principal partner and lead analyst for Aspire Interactive Technologies, LLC, a Midwest-based Microsoft Partner focused on cloud technologies to deliver SharePoint, Exchange, Communication Server, and other business process and collaboration tools. Fred has worked with NASA and other Government Services to implement SharePoint portals and collaboration, as well as business process management systems. Fred has worked with SharePoint Technologies since the release of SharePoint Portal Server 2003. You can contact Fred via e-mail at fred.devoir@aspireforit.com or twitter (devoirf).

Darrin Bishop is a speaker, author and developer focusing on Microsoft SharePoint Technologies. Darrin is the president and lead developer for Darrin Bishop Group, Inc., a Midwest-based Microsoft Partner focusing on SharePoint Technologies, portals and collaboration. Darrin is an international speaker and speaks at many SharePoint conferences, SharePoint Saturdays, MOSS Camps and User Groups. Darrin has been working with SharePoint Technologies since the release of SharePoint Portal Server 2001. You can contact Darrin via his blog (*www.darrinbishop.com/blog*) or twitter (bishopd).

Michael Mukalian is a 2010 Microsoft SharePoint Services MVP, Director and Architect for LiquidHub, Inc. (*www.liquidhub.com*) an information technology consultancy based in the Philadelphia area serving clients worldwide. With over 20 years of IT experience and certifications in VB.NET and Microsoft Office SharePoint Server 2007 and involvement with the Tri-State SharePoint User Group (*www.tristatesharepoint.com*), Michael has architected and developed solutions for companies of all sizes. Check out Michael's blog, the SharePoint Coffee House, at *http://www.mukalian.com/blog*.

What do you think of this book?

We want to hear from you!

Do you have a few minutes to participate in a brief online survey?

Microsoft is interested in hearing your feedback so we can continually improve our books and learning resources for you.

To participate in our survey, please visit:

www.microsoft.com/learning/booksurvey/

...and enter this book's ISBN-10 number (appears above barcode on back cover*). As a thank-you to survey participants in the United States and Canada, each month we'll randomly select five respondents to win one of five $100 gift certificates from a leading online merchant. At the conclusion of the survey, you can enter the drawing by providing your e-mail address, which will be used for prize notification only.

Thanks in advance for your input. Your opinion counts!

*Where to find the ISBN-10 on back cover

ISBN-13: 000-0-0000-0000-0
ISBN-10: 0-0000-0000-0

0 0 0 0 0

R.C.L.

SEP. 2010

G

0 000000 000000

Example only. Each book has unique ISBN.

No purchase necessary. Void where prohibited. Open only to resi... ...cludes District of Columbia) and Canada (void in Quebec). For of...

www.microsoft.com/learning/booksurvey/